# A Contemporary History of the U.S. Army Nurse Corps

# A Contemporary History of the U.S. Army Nurse Corps

Mary T. Sarnecky

DNSc, RN, FNP

Colonel, USA (Retired)

**Borden Institute**
Martha K. Lenhart, MD, PhD, FAAOS
Colonel, MC, US Army
Director and Editor in Chief

**Editorial Staff:** Marcia A. Metzgar
*Volume Editor*

Douglas Wise
*Layout Editor*

The opinions or assertions contained herein are the personal views of the authors and are not to be construed as doctrine of the Department of the Army or the Department of Defense.

CERTAIN PARTS OF THIS PUBLICATION PERTAIN TO COPYRIGHT RESTRICTIONS. ALL RIGHTS RESERVED.

NO COPYRIGHTED PARTS OF THIS PUBLICATION MAY BE REPRODUCED OR TRANSMITTED IN ANY FORM OR BY ANY MEANS, ELECTRONIC OR MECHANICAL (INCLUDING PHOTOCOPY, RECORDING, OR ANY INFORMATION STORAGE AND RETRIEVAL SYSTEM), WITHOUT PERMISSION IN WRITING FROM THE PUBLISHER OR COPYRIGHT OWNER.

Published by the Office of The Surgeon General
Borden Institute
Walter Reed Army Medical Center
Washington, DC 20307-5001

**Library of Congress Cataloging-in-Publication Data**
Sarnecky, Mary T.
 A contemporary history of the U.S. Army Nurse Corps / Mary T. Sarnecky.
  p. cm.
 Includes bibliographical references and index.
 1. United States. Army Nurse Corps--History. 2. Military nursing--United States--History. I. Title.
 UH493.S269 2010
 355.3'45--dc22
                              2010000862

For sale by the Superintendent of the Documents, U.S. Government Printing Office
Internet: bookstore.gpo.gov   Phone: toll free (866) 512-1800;  DC area (202) 512-1800
Fax: (202) 512-2104 Mail: Stop IDCC, Washington, DC 20402-0001

ISBN 978-0-16-085125-4

*To the long line of Army nurses, serving yesterday, today, and tomorrow, heroines and heroes all.*

*Luck is what happens when preparation meets opportunity.*

Seneca
Roman dramatist, philosopher, and politician
5 BC - 65 AD

# Contents

| | |
|---|---|
| Foreword by Gale S. Pollock | xi |
| Preface | xiii |

**PART ONE**
The Decade After the Vietnam War ... 1

    Chapter One
        Evolution and Reorganization ... 3

    Chapter Two
        Gender and Minority Issues ... 25

    Chapter Three
        Educational Concerns and Career Advancement ... 41

    Chapter Four
        Readiness Challenges ... 59

    Chapter Five
        Administrative Questions ... 79

    Chapter Six
        Innovative Roles ... 103

    Chapter Seven
        Humanitarian Relief and Assistance Missions in the 1970s ... 141

**PART TWO**
A Decade of Change ... 165

    Chapter Eight
        New Leadership and Expanding Horizons ... 167

Chapter Nine
 Refining Quality of Care Strategies ... 189

Chapter Ten
 The Shortage Intensifies ... 219

Chapter Eleven
 Preparing for Action ... 255

Chapter Twelve
 Refugee and Humanitarian Operations during the 1980s ... 287

Chapter Thirteen
 Additional Deployments in the 1980s ... 305

PART THREE
The Concluding Decade of a Century of Service ... 331

Chapter Fourteen
 The Post Cold War Period ... 333

Chapter Fifteen
 Revamping the Medical Department and Army Nursing ... 363

Chapter Sixteen
 New Frontiers for Army Nurse Corps Officers ... 389

Chapter Seventeen
 The Army and the Army Medical Department in Operation Desert Shield/Operation Desert Storm ... 413

Chapter Eighteen
 Army Nurse Corps Leadership in Operation Desert Shield/Operation Desert Storm ... 425

Chapter Nineteen
 Army Nurse Corps Activities in Combat Hospitals in Operation Desert Shield/Operation Desert Storm ... 435

Chapter Twenty
 Army Nurse Corps Activities in Europe and the Continental United States in Operation Desert Shield/Operation Desert Storm and in the Aftermath ... 467

Chapter Twenty-one
 Operation Restore Hope in Somalia ... 483

Chapter Twenty-two
    Operations in the Former Republic of Yugoslavia    503

Chapter Twenty-three
    Operation Uphold Democracy in Haiti    541

Chapter Twenty-four
    The Final Word: Epilogue    553

Acronyms and Abbreviations    xix

Index    xxiii

# Foreword

The U.S. Army Nurse Corps has a long and extraordinary history. Mary T. Sarnecky's recounting of our history in her 1999 volume, *A History of the U.S. Army Nurse Corps,* was superb. Now, we are delighted to release her exciting next analysis documenting the Army Nurse Corps history from the end of the Vietnam War to the year 2000.

Here Sarnecky addresses a remarkable episode in the organization's evolution, a period characterized by a series of progressive steps empowering our officers to assume key command and leadership positions in the Army Medical Department. Once this momentum was established, it challenged the limitations of the proverbial "glass ceiling" so prevalent during this period.

Sarnecky's new publication also explores the vital roles of the Army Nurse Corps in supporting and sustaining high-level military operations that began with Operation Desert Storm. Professionalism, clinical competency, adaptability, and flexibility remain the hallmark of the Army Nurse Corps, clearly illustrated in this long-awaited volume. In tandem with her previous work, Sarnecky offers us a wealth of scholarly research narrated in her unique, straightforward style imparting a rich institutional history of which all professional nurses should be exceptionally proud.

It is imperative that we review the "lessons learned" from this period in our nursing history and utilize the experiences, knowledge, and leadership of these extremely talented and dedicated professional nurses. The foundation that previous Army nursing leaders had built allowed this new period to be fruitful and exciting. I am confident that because of these nursing leaders, professional nursing will continue to flourish in America and around the world.

GALE S. POLLOCK
Major General (Ret), CRNA, FACHE, FAAN
22nd Chief, U.S. Army Nurse Corps

# Preface

This book focuses on an organization, the U.S. Army Nurse Corps, which I have been privileged to be affiliated with—in one way or another—for the greatest part of my adult life. As an active duty officer, I had first-hand knowledge about the Army Nurse Corps inner workings and spent the last years of my Army career (from 1992) researching and writing the Corps history. In 1998 I completed the first volume of the history, subsequently published by the University of Pennsylvania Press in 1999. Several years after my 1996 retirement from active service, I agreed to extend the written history of the Corps beyond the conclusion of volume one. This insider/outsider perspective, albeit with a heavier emphasis on the internal point of view, gave me a unique advantage in tackling a historical examination of the organization's recent past. The resultant volume two focuses on the time frame from the early 1970s to the turn of the 21st century.

My objectives in publishing this history remain unchanged from those articulated in the preface of volume one. The passage of time has not altered their essence. Ten years ago I wrote:

> The intent of this volume is to outline the historical framework of [the] seemingly perpetual issues related to nursing, particularly in the Army of the United States of America. It describes how those who have gone before have faced and occasionally resolved familiar challenges. Hopefully, this story will enrich the U.S. Army Nurse Corps sense of pride, identity, and continuity while highlighting threads common to the fabric of Army nursing across the ages. This work also aspires to offer affirmation and encouragement to those who have experienced comparable dilemmas in the past and those who presently face similar concerns. Additionally, the book functions as a resource for those negotiating the minefields of today and offers a historical background for those responsible for future decisions and actions. Finally, the history of the Army Nurse Corps should remind us of the importance of the past, which has determined the present and will continue to affect the future. In summary, this work documents the history of the Army Nurse Corps while simultaneously providing a wealth of pragmatic information.[1]

Another goal in researching and writing this history was to intrigue and provide a sense of gratification for the reader. It certainly has fulfilled this promise for me. I have found the exploits of Army nurses endlessly amazing, fascinating, poignant, and personally rewarding. It is my wish that all who read this book be similarly captivated and entertained!

However, this volume is not intended to stand in place as an apologia for war. Some civilians—be they nurses or not—erroneously equate service as an Army nurse with advocacy for war. In truth, very few if any Army nurses have ever espoused the resolution of political differences through the means of combat. Instead, their higher aspirations have been to provide care to the sick or injured soldiers serving on the battlefield. No one who has witnessed the carnage of war can reasonably champion it.

At the time I began this work in 2000, I had significant misgivings in accepting what seemed both an honor and an extreme challenge, particularly the problematic issues associated with the practice of contemporary historical research.

I realized that recent history frequently represents fodder for revisionist historians in the days to come. Occupying the center of the bull's eye comes with the territory for a historian working on current issues without the perspective of time over the long term. Yet the act of blazing a new trail can yield constructive outcomes. It can also provide tomorrow's historians with a starting point and a foundation upon which forthcoming scholarship is based. It is my hope that this volume will also serve that function.

Another limitation to the practice of contemporary history that impacted the conduct of this study was mysteriously missing data. Like Voltaire's Pangloss, I optimistically believed that for some good cause (my research), there surely would be masses of valid and reliable evidence easily accessible to analyze and serve as the basis for this investigation. How erroneous that assumption proved to be! Although the Army has abundant regulations governing the storage and retirement of records, often the grassroots imperative to follow these directives yields to other higher priorities. I believe many of the never discovered records I could have utilized were either destroyed or are residing in dusty bottom file drawers in the back of remote offices. Then too, it has been my experience in the instances when records were properly retired to the National Archives and Records Administration, they typically languished there and remained inaccessible for decades, waiting in the queue to be "processed." Although there was a fairly broad sampling of available documentary evidence preserved in the Army Nurse Corps collection in the Army Office of Medical History in the Skyline complex in Falls Church, Virginia, I vigorously searched in vain for more specific answers to questions that arose from the available evidence. Fortunately, most of the lacunae in the recorded data were filled when I interviewed the actual participants—the key players who still live, are coherent, and are willing to tell their tales. Nonetheless, in the final analysis, the evidence I was able to gather and use sufficed, although it remains a mere glimpse in time and space.

As I advanced in this endeavor, a final drawback to researching contemporary history emerged. That handicap had to do with the limited hindsight that a researcher possesses while working in the abbreviated temporal period that separates the issues and occurrences being examined and the actual writing of a history. I fully expect that with the greater perspective of time, future historians will have much more to say about this exciting period as an ever expanding and dynamic pool of evidence emerges. I eagerly anticipate and welcome their forthcoming scholarship.

As with my previous volume, I regret that I could not study in any great depth and accurately include each and every example of patriotic service, heroism, dedication, leadership, readiness, and creative practice that dominated the Army Nurse Corps landscape. Neither could I include every instance of impropriety and each unfortunate misstep, dubious decision, or embarrassing controversy that transpired. However, I made every attempt to balance the predominant acts of diligent, morally upright service against the less frequent occurrences that reflected poorly on the Corps. The constraints of time, the limitations of other resources, and the hindrances of unavailable data have all left their mark on this book and rendered it something less than all-inclusive. I regret that reality.

I am the sole author of this book and I alone assume all responsibility for any inadvertent yet inevitable error that exists in these pages. Although I doubt anyone—myself included—has knowingly propagated any falsehood or misrepresentation, many have shared information as well as encouragement and sustenance.

I received considerable assistance along the way from a host of colleagues whose benevolent influence and support extend back in time. Retrospective to the mid-1980s, the then chief of the Army Nurse Corps, Brigadier General Connie L. Slewitzke, perceived the need to educate a nurse historian at the doctoral level to research and document the heritage of the Army Nurse Corps. Although it remains an arguable point whether I was the right person for the job, the school selection board did entrust me with that undertaking. Subsequently, when I was consumed with doctoral education from 1987 to 1990, Dr. Irene S. Palmer, another staunch advocate, graciously took me under her wing and over those three arduous years produced a fledgling nurse historian. After my education at the University of San Diego was complete, Brigadier General Nancy R. Adams and Colonel Terris E. Kennedy took the risk of freeing me of most of my earlier responsibilities and provided me with the wherewithal to concentrate exclusively on historical research in 1992. Their confidence in my ability was echoed by the chief nurses of Walter Reed Army Medical Center at that time, Colonels Mary L. Messerschmidt and Janet R. Southby and by the chiefs of the Nursing Research Service at Walter Reed, Colonels Valerie E. Biskey, Jean M. Reeder, and Cynthia A. Gurney. They all tolerated my altered focus and my presence, not at Walter Reed, but at the Department of Medical History at the Uniformed Services University of the Health Sciences in Bethesda, Maryland. Essentially they allowed me to occupy one of their valuable personnel slots in absentia. When detailed to the university for over four years, I spent my days in a tranquil little office off the third floor of the school library where I was surrounded by a superlative collection of military medical history tomes. There I researched and wrote under the aegis of two consummate mentors, Colonel (Dr.) Robert J.T. Joy and Dr. Dale C. Smith. Just prior to and after my retirement in 1996, Brigadier General Bettye J. Simmons and her assistant, Colonel Susan C. McCall, also added their sponsorship to my efforts and arranged a contract to put the finishing touches on volume one.

Throughout the years that I have been engaged in studying the history of the Army Nurse Corps, I have enjoyed extraordinarily close and fruitful associations with a number of keen, enthusiastic Army Nurse Corps historians including Majors Cynthia A. Gurney and Winona M. Bice-Stephens, Lieutenant Colonels Patricia Wise, Iris J. West, and Cheryl Capers, and Majors Constance J. Moore, Debora R. Cox, Jennifer L. Petersen, Charlotte W. Scott, and Richard M. Prior. To this day, simply evoking the rapport we shared and their many acts of kindness gladdens my heart.

I began work on volume two in 2000 at the behest of Dr. John T. Greenwood and Colonel William T. (Tom) Gray of the Army Surgeon General's Office of Medical History. They continued to serve as benefactors as my efforts progressed. During that same period I also enjoyed the patronage of Brigadier General William T. Bester and Major General Gale S. Pollock and their respective assistant/deputy chiefs of the Corps, Colonels Deborah A. Gutske and Barbara Bruno.

As I began this manuscript, slowly advanced paragraph by paragraph, and brought the volume to its conclusion, many Army Nurse Corps officers played crucial roles, disclosing a diversity of facts that upon occasion corroborated existing documents and in other instances represented new information. Without exception, these contributors responded to my questions in good cheer and with extraordinary candor. Because there were so many of these individuals who generously revealed their insights, it is impossible to provide a litany of all their names here. However, their voices will resonate forever from the leaves of this book.

A collection of other individuals also facilitated this enterprise and contributed to the in-process and the final reviews. They included Major General Nancy R. Adams, Brigadier General Clara L. Adams-Ender, Brigadier General William T. Bester, Dr. Carol Byerly, Lieutenant Colonel Debora R. Cox, Dr. Edward Drea, Colonel Eily P. Gorman, Dr. John T. Greenwood, Colonel John M. Hudock, Colonel (Dr.) Bonnie M. Jennings, Colonel (Dr.) Robert J.T. Joy, Colonel (Dr.)

Terris E. Kennedy, Colonel Constance J. Moore, Dr. Sanders Marble, Colonel Susan C. McCall, Colonel Nickey McCasland, Dr. Elizabeth M. Norman, Major Jennifer L. Petersen, Major General Gale S. Pollock, Brigadier General Bettye J. Simmons, Brigadier General Connie L. Slewitzke, Dr. Dale C. Smith, Mrs. Lisa Wagner, and Colonel Iris J. West. Their very important critiques, suggestions, and commentaries all improved the accuracy of the manuscript and enhanced the overall quality of the finished product.

Others assisted in sundry other ways. Over the years, Office of Medical History archivist Lisa Wagner and her assistant, William Edmondson, also helped me to navigate various archives and locate elusive documents and photographs to illustrate this text. Annita Ferencz, the Office of Medical History's director of operations, provided much appreciated administrative support as well. Reference librarian, Emily Court, and technical information specialist, Yevetta White, of the Armed Forces Medical Library performed virtual miracles on my behalf—unearthing articles, scanning them, and forwarding them to me electronically within minutes. Marcia A. Metzgar, the volume editor, and Colonel (Dr.) Martha K. Lenhart, the director of the Borden Institute at Walter Reed, also played essential roles in the publication of this work. I owe an enormous debt of gratitude to each and every one of these various supportive allies!

Finally, I especially express my deep appreciation to my family whose advice, abettance, and affection are constant companions. I happily acknowledge my parents, the late William and Leona Weber, whose love and encouragement have sustained me all the days of my life. Requiescant in pace! Lastly, I am greatly obliged to my husband and three sons for their inspiration and sympathetic understanding. Throughout this lengthy process, they patiently listened to my thoughts, time and again ventured their opinions, and good-naturedly put up with one ordeal after another. Mere words cannot express my thanks to all four—George, Joe, Jim, and Bill!

Mary T. Sarnecky
San Diego, California
Autumn 2008

---

1. Mary T. Sarnecky, *A History of the U.S. Army Nurse Corps* (Philadelphia: University of Pennsylvania Press, 1999), xi-xii.

*Part One*

The Decade After the Vietnam War

*Chapter One*
# Evolution and Reorganization

The Vietnam War (1961–1975) was a watershed event for the United States. It had a significant impact on the Army Nurse Corps, the Army Medical Department (AMEDD), the Army, and the nation. The protracted war drained the Army, cost it a decade of modernization, alienated the military from society, and left a "hollow force" to rebuild and reinvigorate. In effect, the infrastructure of the Army languished to pay for the war.

After the conclusion of the Vietnam War, several wide-ranging and significant changes exerted myriad effects on the Army Nurse Corps. The most influential of these phenomena included the dismantling of the Selective Service System, the reorganization of the Army, the launch of Health Services Command (HSC), the opening of the Academy of Health Sciences, the transformation of the Office of the Army Surgeon General, the inauguration of improvements in the Army Reserve and National Guard, and the revolution in the roles and status of women.

Between 1968 and 1974 the United States dismantled its Selective Service System and ended the draft. The Army became an all-volunteer force, a movement whose genesis lay in the nation's "historic . . . antimilitary tradition" coupled with "its aversion to compulsion."[1] An equally significant explanation for the end to the draft was President Richard Nixon's need to have support for the 1972 election and to produce a peace dividend. The country's widespread antipathy to the Vietnam War doubtlessly also tipped the scales. All of these realities resulted in the end of conscription. Critics predicted that the new volunteer army would not meet its quotas for both reserve and active officers. Because women had never been drafted, however, and the Army Nurse Corps had relied successfully on volunteers to fill its ranks in the past, most Army Nurse Corps officers anticipated only minor problems, if any, in recruiting sufficient nurses.[2] Simultaneously, critical shortages were expected to surface among physicians in the Army Medical Corps. Pundits articulated the curtailment of the draft and the suspension of the Berry plan as causes for the shortages. The Berry plan was a program that allowed physicians temporary deferment from the draft so that they might complete their medical specialty training. Following their completion of individual training programs, physicians subsequently were obliged to serve the usual two years in the military. Without the coercion of conscription, the AMEDD leaders expected significant shortfalls among Army physicians. To circumvent this eventuality, the Army implemented several countermeasures—among them, creating the Health Professions Scholarship Program; establishing the F. Edward Hébert Medical School at the Uniformed Services University of the Health Sciences in 1972[3]; encouraging the enactment of the Uniformed Services Variable Incentive Pay Act for Physicians of 1974; modernizing the Army Medical Treatment Facilities (MTFs), which, it was hoped, would enhance physician efficiency[4]; launching a course to train physician assistants in 1971; and, in 1972, commencing and later elaborating on the advanced practice roles,[5] as defined by the Army Nurse Corps Contemporary Practice Program or, as it was subsequently referred to, the Army Nurse Corps Clinician Program or Army Nurse Clinician Program. Planners conceived and implemented these last two initiatives to relieve available physicians of certain responsibilities, a trend emerging within the civilian health care community.[6]

As certain incentive programs to enhance AMEDD procurement evolved, others were terminated. On balance, the Army Medical Corps gain in funded initiatives such as the Health Professions Scholarship Program, Uniformed Services University of the Health Sciences, and special pay programs ultimately was offset to some degree by the Army Nurse Corps loss of educational subsidies such as the Army Student Nurse Program and Army Registered Nurse Program. To pay for these programs to support physician recruitment, the Army leadership shifted assets and eliminated Army Nurse Corps educational procurement incentives. Each participant in an Army Nurse Corps student program was commissioned in the last six months of his or her training program, thereby occupying one active duty personnel slot. To tie up hundreds of billets with no immediate return over a period of up to six months was no longer possible. Another consideration was economic, an unavoidable consequence in the postwar context of strict financial retrenchment, leading to the truncation or elimination of long-standing Army Nurse Corps programs. Because the Army Nurse Corps was managing, albeit with difficulty, to maintain its authorized strength in the immediate post–Vietnam War era, the Corps ended the Army Registered Nurse Program and the Army Student Nurse Program in 1975 and closed the Walter Reed Army Institute of Nursing in 1978.[7] Meantime, the Army Nurse Corps continued its successful recruiting, which some believed was the seeds of its undoing.[8] The AMEDD justified its decisions to cut educational subsidy programs by explaining that any future Army Nurse Corps recruiting deficits could be easily remedied. One recommendation was to suspend the basic educational standard for entry into the active component of the Corps (set by a 1974 regulation at the baccalaureate degree level) and accept non-baccalaureate nurses, that is, diploma graduates or associate degree nurses.[9] However, Army Nurse Corps leaders did not resort to such a strategy. Following the unsuccessful warrant officer/associate degree nurse program of the Vietnam War era, the only nurses accessed to active duty were those with baccalaureate degrees. College Reserve Officers' Training Corps (ROTC) programs with or without scholarships for prospective Army Nurse Corps officers seemed a promising source for future Army nurses. Army ROTC first accepted women as cadets in 1972 and, as hoped, this program has provided more and more Army nurses with the passage of time.[10]

The Army also restructured its forces as part of the modernization and reform of the post–Vietnam institution. Organizational changes began in January 1973 and were virtually completed by December 1975, but planning had been ongoing since 1967, particularly within the AMEDD through the Worldwide Organizational Structure for Army Medical Support Study Group.[11] Several factors precipitated the massive organizational makeover of the Army. These factors included the urgent necessity for more efficient use of people and money, the increased reliance on the reserves, the need for greater levels of readiness, and the commitment to enhance esprit de corps and service members' morale, which—it was thought—would render the Army a more attractive career choice in the context of the modern volunteer army.[12] The reorganization also reflected the prevailing opinion that the Army should assume a lower profile and decentralize its operations and command functions away from Washington, D.C. In the immediate post–Vietnam War period, both the wearing of uniforms and the massive military presence in Military District of Washington arguably were projecting an unpalatable image of the nation's capital as an "armed fortress."[13] Key among the organizational changes for the Army was the elimination of the Continental Army Command and the creation of the Forces Command, Training and Doctrine Command, and HSC.[14]

On 1 April 1973, HSC evolved at Fort Sam Houston, Texas; it was completely functional by 1 July 1973. Major General Spurgeon H. Neel, a Medical Corps officer, was HSC's first commander.[15] He functioned under the direct supervision of the chief of staff of the U.S. Army.[16] From the outset, HSC assumed command of almost all Medical Centers, General Hospitals, and Medical Department Activities, the Academy of Health Sciences, and certain other installations and activities, predominantly within the continental United States.[17] Formerly, the command of most of these facilities was vested in the local post commander and ultimately resided under the jurisdiction of the commander, Continental Army Command.[18] Frequently this command and control structure created financial issues. Installation commanders often favored funding of other higher priority on-post programs over the needs of the local MTFs. Thus, HSC evolved into a Major Command not only to consolidate the continental U.S. health care system but also to foster equitable resource distribution.[19]

As a Major Command, HSC's mission generally encompassed health care delivery, medical combat doctrine development, and provider education. First, the command furnished health care services for the Army within the continental United States, Alaska, Hawaii, and Panama, using a "single-manager approach." The professional services encompassed "hospitalization, outpatient care, environmental hygiene, dental care, veterinary services, nursing care, physical and occupational therapy, and dietetic services."[20]

Gradually, the responsibility for some Army Nurse Corps operations that previously had resided in the Office of The Surgeon General, Continental Army Command, and the various Army area headquarters moved to HSC.[21] Colonel Virginia L. Brown was the senior officer among the 12 Army nurses first assigned to HSC, and she served as the first chief of the Nursing Division and chief nurse of HSC. Brigadier General Lillian Dunlap, the chief of the Army Nurse Corps at that time, appointed Brown to this newly created position because it required "someone who was knowledgeable and a good staff officer." Other criteria that Dunlap deemed crucial for this post included abilities to deal with complex organizational relationships, garner respect among colleagues, and demonstrate loyalty in personal relations. Dunlap recalled that Brown "was one of the best choices I ever made."[22]

Among the 12 original Army Nurse Corps officers assigned to HSC were a nurse consultant, a nurse staff officer, an ambulatory care nurse administrator, and an Army health nurse consultant.[23] Another Army Nurse Corps officer served in the Troop Basis Branch.[24]

Four of the 12 Army nurses functioned on the HSC Manpower Team.[25] This unit developed policies for management of manpower resources; conducted on-site surveys at installations to evaluate manpower requirements; and programmed, controlled, and allocated command military and civilian manpower resources.[26] They usually surveyed all HSC facilities such as hospitals, clinics, garrisons, dental labs, and schools onsite on a biennial basis. Thus, the four Army nurses, approximately 12 Medical Service Corps officers, and six civilian employees of the Manpower Survey Branch were grouped into three teams, which were in travel status for 50 percent of their duty time. The primary mission of the branch was to determine staffing needs. However, because the Army Nurse Corps officers were "the only clinical professionals in the branch," they had an additional charge while on temporary duty to the various HSC installations, serving as consultants on matters of nursing as well as surveyors of manpower conditions.[27]

Two Army Nurse Corps officers served as the first Army nurses on the HSC Inspector General team.[28] The team's primary areas of concern were monitoring nursing mission performance and quality of care issues in nursing departments in the various MTFs of HSC.[29] Dunlap disclosed that it was a challenge to achieve the integration of Army nurses in the various HSC missions. She recalled that the Army Nurse Corps "had to fight for spaces every time." Other branches challenged their presence, asking, "Why do you need nurse spaces?" Dunlap relied on her administrative background and working relationships cemented in past assignments to counter the opposition. She recalled that

". . . fortunately, one of the officers who was the IG [inspector general] officer had been the IG up in The Surgeon General's Office and had been a student of mine when I was teaching in [the] hospital admin[istration course]. . . . he appreciated and wanted a nurse on the IG team. We really worked hard in establishing and trying to work within the formal organizational structure, but recognized that we had to work in an informal structure also, to be kept fully informed."[30]

Pictured is Colonel Virginia L. Brown, first chief of the Nursing Division and first chief nurse of the Health Services Command (1973).
Photo courtesy of Army Nurse Corps Archives, Office of Medical History, Falls Church, VA.

Although the shape of the Army organization changed, the ceaseless bureaucratic struggle remained constant. Also, the pervasive organizational culture did not change. The need to justify the existence of nursing, the necessity to explain its role, and the prodigious effort to gain and retain resources remained the same.

After existing approximately one year, HSC underwent an evaluation. During the year, a report noted that the Nursing Division inspected 43 installations to evaluate the quality of patient care and suggest methods for improvement. The assessment also showed that the division was developing guidelines of care for the new nurse clinicians, as the original nurse practitioners were called. The division had also achieved official recognition through manpower surveys for selected nurse clinician slots. The report also recognized and authorized a number of ward clerk spaces. Additionally, HSC promoted the formation of audit committees in various treatment facilities to develop criteria to bring facilities into compliance with the requirements of the civilian accrediting body, the Joint Commission for the Accreditation of Hospitals.[31] The division also set up a mechanism for chief nurses to request temporary replacement staff from HSC during times of acute personnel shortages.[32] The report had no negative findings.

Another major mission of HSC was to provide education for AMEDD personnel. It was thought that better-educated health providers would enhance the quality of health care that would, in turn, improve the quality of life for service members and their families. This then would promote recruitment and retention in the all-volunteer army.[33] HSC launched the Academy of Health Sciences at Fort Sam Houston, Texas, to support this arm of the mission.[34] The Academy of Health Sciences assumed the functions of both the Medical Field Service School and the Medical Training Center. Both of these latter organizations, whose emphases were officer and enlisted training, respectively, ceased to exist as such.

The massive reorganization also shuffled positions in the Office of The Surgeon General, which evolved into an Army staff agency with proponency for the worldwide AMEDD program. It placed The Surgeon General (TSG) in a staff position subordinate to the Army chief of staff.[35] TSG retained the traditional medical and administrative duties and functioned as chief of the AMEDD worldwide. TSG's global responsibilities, to name but a few, were the formulation of health policy, the exercise of accountability for AMEDD personnel management, the planning and directing of medical training, the setting of Army health standards, and the overseeing of research and development activities. In this latest organizational matrix, the chief of the Army Nurse Corps enjoyed direct access to TSG. She exercised special staff supervision over all Army Nurse Corps officers; directed nursing doctrine, practice, standards, and education; approved supplies and equipment used by Army nurses; proposed and reviewed legislation affecting Army nurses; and served as liaison for nursing matters with civilian nursing organizations, other agencies, and governments.[36] The Corps chief also had responsibility for nursing policy within the Army Reserve and National Guard.[37] In 1975, Army staff elements of the Surgeon General's Office moved from the Forrestal Building on Independence Avenue in Washington, D.C., across the Potomac River to the

Pentagon. The move's purpose was to improve collaboration and efficiency, to enhance access by the chief of staff, and "to consolidate all staff agencies" under a single roof.[38]

In this decade of turbulent change, still another reorganization occurred in the Surgeon General's Office. TSG formed four internal directorates: (1) Resources Management, (2) Health Care Operations, (3) Personnel, and (4) Professional Services.[39] The AMEDD assigned a number of Army nurses, including the nurse consultant, to the Directorate of Health Care Operations.[40] Additionally, in 1972, planners realigned the Army Nurse Corps Branch, situating it under the Directorate of Personnel, Army Medical Department Personnel Support Agency. At that time, the branch adopted a new identity as the Career Activities Office with two functional subunits: (1) Career Planning and (2) Assignments.[41]

Another major change in the post–Vietnam era was the political decision to assign an earlier, more active and inclusive role for the Army Reserve and National Guard components. During the Vietnam War, only a handful of reserve units served on active duty. In contrast, after the Vietnam War, the Army Reserve and National Guard were given a larger part to play in future conflicts. The Total Army Concept, the existing doctrine, specified that in the event of war, the active Army would assume the immediate taskings, while the reserve components would serve as a follow-up force. New doctrine specified that the reserve unit might augment and concurrently contribute to the active component's mission. Thus, reserve units had to assume their assignments promptly and efficiently as a result of the training and planning relationships they established during implementation of mutual support activities, variously referred to as Affiliation, Roundout, and Capstone concepts.[42] However, the Total Army Doctrine brought its own set of issues.

One major challenge faced by the Army Reserve and National Guard components was the age-old question of adequacy of numbers. Army-wide attrition rates in the reserve components were exceedingly high in the 1970s, a reaction to the end of the coercive effect of the draft and the wide-ranging antimilitary sentiment of the time. The mobilization requirement (the number required to go to war) of the Army National Guard overall was short 70,000 soldiers. U.S. Army Reserve strength was less than half of its mobilization requirement.[43] Difficulty in filling reserve authorizations involved not only finding applicants but also finding those who met the established standards. As discussed later in this volume, maintaining an adequate reserve force of nurses similarly proved problematic.

A final factor that profoundly shaped the Army Nurse Corps of the 1970s was the national feminist movement that struggled to obtain equality for women in all aspects of American life. Earlier in the century, the women's suffrage movement left its mark on the Army Nurse Corps trajectory to officer status, albeit only relative rank, and to other benefits such as retirement for service and/or disability for Army nurses. Likewise, the women's liberation crusade of the 1960s and 1970s had a powerful effect on the status of military women.

However, a unique group, predating the recent women's liberation movement, coalesced and began to serve as an advocate in support of women in the military.

General George C. Marshall, then secretary of defense, created The Defense Advisory Committee on Women in the Services in 1951. Composed of selected, usually influential, civilians, the committee members were appointed by the secretary of defense and served a three-year term. The committee directed itself to such objectives as providing consultation on women's concerns to the secretary of defense and serving as a conduit between the civilian and the military worlds as spokespersons on behalf of military women. Defense Advisory Committee on Women in the Services membership rolls occasionally included prominent civilian nurse leaders. Its contributions to military nursing included such achievements as promoting equal housing and equitable treatment in the service and publicizing to support recruiting efforts, particularly in times of nursing shortages.[44]

The women's movement also had significant consequences in the personal and professional lives of military women. A very determined women's liberation movement achieved a number of incremental victories in the struggle against sexism. In the early 1960s, President John F. Kennedy appointed former First Lady Eleanor Roosevelt to the helm of a Presidential Commission on the Status of Women. This commission sought to assess "women's place in the economy, the family, and the legal system." Its final report, submitted in 1963, brought to light women's issues such as "discrimination in employment, unequal pay, lack of social services such as child care, and continuing legal inequality." The commission's efforts resulted in new legislation, including a presidential order mandating gender-free hiring for federal jobs and the passage of the Equal Pay Act of 1963 that promulgated equal pay for equal work in both the federal and private workforce. The mid-1960s brought the passage of the Civil Rights Act, the creation of the Equal Employment Opportunity Commission, and the birth of the National Organization for Women, a private organization whose articulated objective was to "take action to bring women into full participation" so that they might assume a totality of "privileges and responsibilities . . . in truly equal partnership with men." By 1972, Congress had endorsed the Equal Rights Amendment.[45] However, only 35 states subsequently ratified the proposed amendment.[46] Nonetheless, the ever-increasing tide of women's activism ultimately resulted in "changing patterns of societal expectations," and its outcomes were felt in "the military organization itself."[47] Social change with the overwhelming magnitude of the women's movement could not fail to create a variety of aftershocks that reverberated through the foundations of the military world.

Change that could be attributed at least in part to the women's movement was evident in the education of potential female officers. In 1972 the Army began a pilot program, admitting women to ROTC at 10 civilian colleges and universities. The experiment succeeded beyond all expectations. By 1979, 25 percent of all Army ROTC cadets were women.[48]

Having achieved entrance into ROTC, women visionaries and their advocates turned their attention to having women appointed to the service academies. However, certain congressmen and Department of Defense (DoD) officials vehemently opposed the idea. The Army as a whole, including Brigadier General Mildred

Bailey, director of the Women's Army Corps, opposed the notion. Bailey argued that the Army could attract as many women as it needed "at no expense to the government" and questioned, "Why should we spend money to train them?" She concluded that the military should devote more time to issues of "national defense" and less attention to "items like this that we don't need and that would not really serve a useful purpose."[49] Lawsuits, congressional hearings, and challenges to the precedent banning women from the service academies soon followed. In spite of all efforts to the contrary, a bill authorizing the admission of women to the military academies passed Congress and was signed into law on 7 October 1975. In 1976 West Point admitted its first female cadets for the class of 1980.[50]

Another element of inequity affected significantly by the women's movement was spousal rights. Before 1973, married military women were forced to prove that they contributed more than half of the total family financial support for their civilian husband before the spouse was eligible for certain entitlements. These benefits included medical care, on-post housing or an off-post housing allowance, and commissary and exchange shopping privileges. In contrast, these stringent restrictions were not levied on families in which the husband was the military member. The 1973 Supreme Court ruling in the case of *Frontiero v. Richardson* rendered the requirement to prove the degree of family support unconstitutional.[51] Additionally, the Court directed the comptroller general of the Army to pay women retroactively for any Basic Allowance for Quarters, Family Separation Allowance, Station Housing Allowance, Cost of Living Allowance, Temporary Lodging Allowance, Dislocation Allowance, and Dependent Travel Allowance to which they were entitled.[52]

The long-standing policy barring women in the military from maintaining custody of minor children (those under 18 years of age) also came under scrutiny in the 1970s. To provide care in the home for children, whether adopted, stepchildren, or biological children, a military woman had to seek a waiver. Such a stipulation was never imposed on male officers who had sole custody of their minor children. Regardless, women had to obtain a formal approval to override the prohibition. The waiver process was arduous and time-consuming, and a positive response to the application was never a matter of certainty. However, after a number of protracted challenges and battles waged by concerned women throughout the military services, DoD lifted the requirement for waivers in 1975. Thereafter, military women were not prohibited by tradition, policy, regulation, or law from being the primary caretakers of their minor children.[53]

The next hurdle involved the contentious and emotion-laden subject of servicewomen's pregnancies. The campaign for pregnancy rights also entailed a progression of challenges and litigation.[54] Up to this time, DoD-wide policy mandated the immediate discharge of pregnant women irrespective of the wishes of the servicemember. But by the early 1970s, radical change was on the horizon. After several years of impassioned and volatile dialogue, DoD finally directed all services in October 1970 to allow pregnant servicewomen the right to submit a waiver to remain on active duty. The pregnant service member was to send the waiver to the

Department of the Army, where it was to be reviewed on a case-by-case basis. It might or might not be approved.[55] By April 1971 the Army complied with the directive but followed a policy allowing only pregnant soldiers who were married to remain on active duty. In December 1973 the Army amended the policy to allow all pregnant service members, "regardless of marital status, to request retention on active duty." By 1974 more than 3,000 pregnant service members, representing 6 percent of all enlisted women, were leaving the services annually. Thus, DoD concluded that "the involuntary separation with waiver policy [was] no longer 'viable'." Consequently, DoD eliminated the requirement to seek a waiver and discontinued involuntary separations because of pregnancy. After September 1974 all pregnant officers were allowed to elect to remain on active duty. DoD granted enlisted women the same right in April 1975.[56]

Among all the services, the Army was most unyielding and reluctant to accept the DoD directive, to change their system, and to accommodate all pregnant women, perhaps because of the positions taken by some of its leaders. For instance, Brigadier General Elizabeth Hoisington, Women's Army Corps director from 1966 to 1971, strongly opposed allowing married women and mothers to serve.[57] Army senior leaders routinely used a number of delaying tactics, requesting impact statements, suggesting modifications of policy, and announcing postponements of policy implementation. Still largely dissatisfied with the policy as late as 1978, the Army continued to try to reverse the directive but failed in one final attempt when the director of the Women's Army Corps and strong advocate for women's rights in the military, Brigadier General Mary E. Clarke, sided with the pregnant women's advocates and refused to support the Army's resistance any longer. Overwhelming forces compelled the Army to fully comply with the DoD edict in the long run and forced the institution to give the pregnant soldier her choice to leave or remain in the service. Although other attempts to regress to the old involuntary discharge for pregnancy policy followed in subsequent years, each one failed.[58] In the final analysis, the tidal wave of societal change overcame long-standing military tradition.

All of these national influences and military issues spurred a building momentum of change and created a vast ripple effect that coursed through the world of Army nursing. Although external forces imposed some of the realities, others evolved from within the Army and the Army Nurse Corps. The Corps managed some issues with painstaking wisdom and foresight. It confronted others in a spontaneous fashion. It viewed some challenges with distrust and resistance, while it welcomed and embraced others with enthusiasm. The post–Vietnam Army Nurse Corps evolved into a new chapter defined by golden opportunities, puzzling questions, unprecedented changes, and uncertain trends.

In the late- and post–Vietnam era, recurring change also occurred in the senior leadership ranks of the Army Nurse Corps. Three distinguished Army Nurse Corps officers served in that time frame as successive chiefs of the Army Nurse Corps and left their imprint for decades to come. Their organizational skills, acumen, extensive experience, and practical wisdom greatly enhanced the day-to-day

Pictured is Brigadier General Lillian Dunlap, 14th chief of the Army Nurse Corps from 1971 to 1975.
Photo courtesy of Army Nurse Corps Archives, Office of Medical History, Falls Church, VA.

function of the Corps.

Dunlap, previously chief nurse of Walter Reed Army Medical Center, assumed the responsibilities of the chief of the Army Nurse Corps and simultaneously was promoted to brigadier general on 1 September 1971. Dunlap followed her predecessor, Brigadier General Anna Mae V. Hays. Colonel Louise C. Rosasco was the first in a series of assistant chiefs of the Corps under Dunlap until she retired in December 1971, after which, Colonels Edith J. Bonnet, Rose V. Straley, and Edith M. Nuttall subsequently served.

Dunlap's initial tenure as chief of the Corps coincided with the drawdown of the Vietnam War. She presided over the final Army Nurse Corps presence in Southeast Asia and guided the Corps through the tumultuous transition to a period of national peace and phenomenal change. Dunlap adeptly managed the introduction of the expanded practice movement that augmented the Army Nurse Corps expertise, aptitudes, and abilities to make an even greater contribution to the health of the Army. Additionally, she continued the efforts of prior chiefs of the Corps in promoting improved levels of education for Army nurses.

After 33 years of active duty, Dunlap retired from the Army in September 1975, but never relinquished her sense of commitment to the Army and the Army Nurse Corps. Her retirement years continued to be equally prolific. She enthusiastically supported the Retired Army Nurse Corps Association and the Army Medical Department Museum, and she served on many charitable boards and nonprofit foundations. Dunlap died on 3 April 2003 in her hometown, San Antonio, Texas.

On 1 September 1975, Colonel Madelyn N. Parks, formerly chief of the Department of Nursing at Walter Reed Army Medical Center and earlier chief nurse of the Forces Command, assumed her responsibilities as the 15th chief of the Army Nurse Corps, replacing Dunlap. Parks was the third Army Nurse Corps officer to be promoted to the rank of brigadier general. Colonels Edith M. Nuttall and Virginia L. Brown served in turn as Parks' assistant chiefs of the Army Nurse Corps.

Park's four-year assignment at the helm of the Army Nurse Corps happened in exceedingly turbulent times. In four brief years, she confronted many complex issues, such as a major transformation of the organization, a persistent shortage of nurses, shifting personnel policies, and seismic doctrinal and role changes against the backdrop of a rapidly changing larger U.S. society. With a steady hand, Parks led the Army Nurse Corps through the troubled post–Vietnam era across the threshold of a new day. Her tenure continued until 31 August 1979, when she retired from active Army service. Following her retirement, Parks resided in San Antonio, Texas. This veteran of World War II, Korea, and Vietnam passed away on 24 November 2002.

In 1979 Colonel Hazel W. Johnson, a former director of the Walter Reed Army Institute of Nursing and chief nurse of the 18th Medical Command in Korea, became the 16th chief of the Army Nurse Corps. She was Park's successor. Johnson was the first nurse with a doctorate to serve as the chief of the Army Nurse Corps and the first African-American female general officer in DoD. During the

Pictured is Brigadier General Madelyn N. Parks, 15th chief of the Army Nurse Corps from 1975 to 1979. Photo courtesy of Army Nurse Corps Archives, Office of Medical History, Falls Church, VA.

Pictured is Brigadier General Hazel W. Johnson, 16th chief of the Army Nurse Corps from 1979 to 1983. Photo courtesy of Army Nurse Corps Archives, Office of Medical History, Falls Church, VA.

first months of Johnson's tenure, Colonel Virginia L. Brown served as her deputy. Following Brown's retirement, Colonel Connie L. Slewitzke became the assistant chief of the Corps.

Like her predecessor, Johnson dealt with many unparalleled changes and challenges that exerted a significant impact on the careers and practice lives of Army nurses. Additionally, she refined, strengthened, and professionalized many facets of Army Nurse Corps life. Both Johnson and Slewitzke served as incumbents in these two most senior positions until 31 August 1983.

Following her retirement, Johnson remained extremely active in professional nursing. She served for several years as the director of governmental affairs for the American Nurses Association. At the same time she was an assistant professor in nursing administration at Georgetown University in Washington, D.C. Johnson also accepted a full professorship in the School of Nursing at George Mason University in Fairfax, Virginia.

The Army Nurse Corps was fortunate to have such exceptionally inspired leaders in the tough times that followed the Vietnam War. As a result of its caring diligence, the Army Nurse Corps survived and for the most part thrived in this difficult era.

# Notes

1. Robert K. Griffith, Jr., *The U.S. Army's Transition to the All-Volunteer Force, 1968–1974* (Washington, DC: Center of Military History, U.S. Army, 1996), Howard H. Callaway to Lillian Dunlap, Typewritten Letter (TL), 11 October 1973, Army Nurse Corps Collection (ANCC), Office of Medical History (OMH).

2. Robert K. Griffith, Jr., *The U.S. Army's Transition to the All-Volunteer Force, 1968–1974* (Washington, DC: Center of Military History, U.S. Army, 1996), 255, 259. Mary E. Viehdorfer Frank and Robert V. Piemonte, "The Army Nurse Corps: A Decade of Change," *American Journal of Nursing* 85 (September 1985): 985–88.

3. Public Law 92-426, the Uniformed Services Health Professions Revitalization Act, 21 September 1972. Richard R. Taylor, "Team Work Needed for Army Medicine," *U.S. Medicine* 10 (15 January 1974): 60.

4. From 1969 to 1971, the Department of Defense commissioned two large studies using systems theory as a conceptual framework to design a "health care system for domestic military bases." Harry B. Wissman, *Systems Analysis for a "New Generation" of Military Hospitals, Summary, Final Report* (Cambridge, MA: Arthur D. Little, 1971), 1.1. The studies arose from a request by Secretary of Defense Melvin Laird for a program "that would involve medicine, be humanitarian, be a spin-off to the civilian community, and [not explicit] make the Nixon administration, then in trouble in Vietnam, look good." Robert J.T. Joy to Author, TL, 18 October 2002, ANCC, OMH. The goals of the dual-pronged venture were "to improve operating efficiency" of military MTFs to include all staff, facility construction, outpatient design, computer support, etc., while simultaneously "maintaining or improving the quality of patient care." Another objective of the studies was "to reduce costs." C.A. Sadlow, *Systems Analysis Study Towards a "New Generation" of Military Hospitals, Volume I: Executive Summary* (Pittsburgh, PA: Westinghouse Electric Corporation, 1970), iii. The Little (Wissman) contract was for $712,065, while the cost of the Westinghouse (Sadlow) version totaled $892,000. Only one military MTF was built on these models, the David Grant USAF Medical Center at Travis Air Force Base, California. Robert J. T. Joy, Conversation with Author. Robert A. Patterson, "AF Meets Demand of Volunteer Force," *U.S. Medicine* 10 (15 January 1974): 51. The studies recommended "unit dose pharmacies; . . . introduction of convenience foods; physicians' assistant programs; . . . and providing a suite of a private office with two adjoining examining rooms for each physician." Richard S. Wilbur, "Department of Defense," *Military Medicine* 137 (September 1972): 340.

5. "Advanced practice" is a term that came into common usage in the 1990s. As defined by the National Council of State Boards of Nursing in 1993, it is "practice based on the knowledge and skills acquired in a basic nursing education, through licensure as a registered nurse, and in graduate education and experience, including advanced nursing theory, physical and psycho-social assessment, and treatment of illness." Frances K. Porcher, "Licensure, Certification, and Credentialing," in *Advanced Practice Nursing: Changing Roles and Clinical Applications*, ed. Joanne V. Hickey, Ruth M. Ouimette, and Sandra L. Venegoni (Philadelphia: Lippincott, 1996), 180.

6. Robert K. Griffith, Jr., *The U.S. Army's Transition to the All-Volunteer Force, 1968–1974* (Washington, DC: Center of Military History, U.S. Army, 1996), 256–58. *Annual Report, The Surgeon General, United States Army Fiscal Year 1974* (Washington, DC: Office of the Surgeon General, U.S. Army, 1974), 2–4, 20–23. Richard S. Wilbur, "Department of Defense," *Military Medicine* 137 (September 1972): 337–38. Diane O. McGivern, "The Evolution to Advanced Nursing Practice," in *Nurses, Nurse Practitioners; Evolution to Advanced Practice*, ed. Mathy D. Mezey and Diane O. McGivern (New York: Springer Publishing Company, 1993), 4.

7. The Navy curtailed its student subsidies for potential Navy nurses in 1975 as well. Willard P. Arentzen, "Advances Logged by Navy Medicine," *U.S. Medicine* 13 (15 January 1977): 34.

8. Just as Army nurses were losing educational subsidies, the civilian world of nursing also was facing the loss of federal government support of nursing education. In 1978, President Jimmy Carter vetoed the Nurse Training Act. Letitia Cunningham, "Nursing Shortage? Yes!" *American Journal of Nursing* 79 (March 1979): 469–80.

9. *Annual Report, The Surgeon General, United States Army Fiscal Year 1975* (Washington, DC: Office of the Surgeon General, U.S. Army, 1975), 1–2, 15. *Report of the Surgeon General United States Army Fiscal Years 1976–1980* (Washington, DC: Office of the Surgeon General, Department of the Army, 1988), 242. Gerald D. Allgood, signed for Lewis H. Huggins, "Nursing Education Subsidization Programs," TL, 4 April 1975, ANCC, OMH. Department of the Army, AR 601-100, paragraph 2-61, October 1974. Department of the Army, "Army Nurse Corps Active Duty Program Fiscal Year 1977 through 15 January 1978," DA Circular 01-68, 13 October 1977.

10. The Air Force allowed women to participate in ROTC in 1969. The Army followed three years later. Rosemarie Skaine, *Women at War: Gender Issues of Americans in Combat* (Jefferson, NC: McFarland & Company, Inc., 1999), 58–59. Robert K. Griffith, Jr., *The U.S. Army's Transition to the All-Volunteer Force, 1968–1974* (Washington, DC: Center of Military History, U.S. Army, 1996), 259. Jeanne Holm, *Women in the Military: An Unfinished Revolution* (Novato, CA: Presidio, 1992), 270. Lieutenant Colonel Holley, "Information Paper, Subject: Women in ROTC," 4 April 1977, ANCC, OMH.

11. The 1967 report of the DA Board of Inquiry on the Army Logistics System (Brown Report) "recommended that a study be made to determine if the Surgeon General should be given worldwide medical support responsibility and command of the general hospital level." Worldwide Organizational Structure for Army Medical Support rejected the notion of a "single world-wide Health Service Command" but instead advised that the Army establish a "single CONUS-wide Health Services Command." Department of the Army, Office of the Surgeon General, *World-Wide Organizational Structure for Army Medical Support*, Volume I (Executive Brief), 20 August 1970, 1, 26–28.

12. Francis T. Julia, *Army Staff Reorganization, 1903–1985* (Washington, DC: Analysis Branch, U.S. Army Center of Military History), 35. "10th Anniversary, US Army Health Services Command," *HSC Mercury* 10 (April 1983): A1. U.S. Army Health Services Command,

"Activation, Evolution of a New Command," Program, 2, April 1973; and "The 196th Year," News Release No. 135-FO, 1 July 1971, Office of the Surgeon General, U.S. Army Technical Liaison Office (both in ANCC, OMH). "Army Reorganization, '74, Moving, Realignment at the Top; Pruning and Heavy Cutting Below," *Army* 24 (April 1974): 8–9. Manley G. Morrison, "The Modern Volunteer Army: Implications for Health Care Organization and Administration," Speech presented to Current Trends in Health Care Administration Professional Short Course on 29 March 1971, ANCC, OMH.

   13. Lillian Dunlap, *33 Years of Army Nursing* (Washington, DC: U.S. Army Nurse Corps, 2001), 266.

   14. Francis T. Julia, *Army Staff Reorganization, 1903–1985* (Washington, DC: Analysis Branch, U.S. Army Center of Military History), 35.

   15. J. Meidl, "Appointment of Commander," 16 July 1973, OTSG Collection, OMH.

   16. Headquarters, Department of the Army, "Organization and Functions, United States Army Health Services Command," AR 10-43, 2, 27 June 1973.

   17. Department of the Army, Headquarters, "United States Health Services Command," HSC Reg 10-1, 2-1, 30 May 1973.

   18. *Annual Report, The Surgeon General, United States Army Fiscal Year 1974* (Washington, DC: Office of the Surgeon General, U.S. Army, 1974), 89. *U.S. Army Health Service Command, Annual Historical Review, 1 July 1975 to 30 September 1977* (Fort Sam Houston, TX: Historical Office, HSC, 1979), 3.

   19. "Analysis of Alternatives," 12 March 1991, Draft Enclosure 2, in "Army Medical Department Realignment Study," n.d., ANCC, OMH.

   20. *Annual Report, The Surgeon General, United States Army Fiscal Year 1974* (Washington, DC: Office of the Surgeon General, U.S. Army, 1974), 88. U.S. Army Health Services Command, "Activation, Evolution of a New Command," Program, 2 April 1973, ANCC, OMH.

   21. Lillian Dunlap, "From the Chief," *U.S. Army Medical Department Newsletter* 4 (Summer 1973): 19, ANCC, OMH.

   22. Lillian Dunlap, *33 Years of Army Nursing* (Washington, DC: U.S. Army Nurse Corps, 2001), 267.

   23. Lieutenant Colonel Barbara R. Costello served as nurse consultant; Lieutenant Colonel Elizabeth A. Labbe was the nurse staff officer; Major Mary Lou Spine served as the ambulatory care nurse administrator; and Lieutenant Colonel Patricia A. Greene was assigned as Army health nurse consultant. "Army Nurse Corps Key Officer Assignments," Typewritten Document (TD), 5–6, 13 August 1973, ANCC, OMH.

   24. This officer was Lieutenant Colonel Essie M. Wilson. "Army Nurse Corps Key Officer Assignments," TD, 6, 13 August 1973, ANCC, OMH.

   25. The four were Lieutenant Colonel Mary A. Foley, Lieutenant Colonel Jeanne Hoppe, Major (P) Francis M. Rausch, and Major Nickey J. McCasland. "Army Nurse Corps Key Officer Assignments," TD, 6, 13 August 1973, ANCC, OMH.

   26. Department of the Army, Headquarters, "United States Health Services Command," HSC Reg 10-1, 5-4, 30 May 1973.

   27. Nickey J. McCasland to Author, E-mail Correspondence, 27 February 2002, ANCC, OMH.

   28. The two were Colonel Patricia A. Silvestre and Major Claire M. McQuail. "Army Nurse Corps Key Officer Assignments," TD, 6, 13 August 1973, ANCC, OMH.

   29. Edith Nuttall, "Presentation to First HSC's Chief Nurses' Conference, Gunter Hotel, San Antonio, Texas, 19 April 1974," Typewritten Text of Speech; and "Army Nurse Corps Key Officer Assignments," TD, 6, 13 August 1973 (both in ANCC, OMH). Carolyn M.

Feller and Debora R. Cox, eds., *Highlights in the History of the Army Nurse Corps* (Washington, DC: U.S. Army Center of Military History, 2000), 45–46.

30. Lillian Dunlap, *33 Years of Army Nursing* (Washington, DC: U.S. Army Nurse Corps, 2001), 270.

31. The function of the Joint Commission on Accreditation of Hospitals, a private, nonprofit group founded in 1951, was to evaluate and accredit hospitals. Carole H. Paterson, "Joint Commission on Accreditation of Healthcare Organizations," *Infection Control and Hospital Epidemiology* 16 (January 1995): 36–42.

32. "US Army Health Services Command, Command Evaluation, 1 April 1973, 30 June 1974, Detailed Evaluation, 15 November 1974," E-15, ANCC, OMH.

33. *Annual Report, The Surgeon General, United States Army Fiscal Year 1974* (Washington, DC: Office of the Surgeon General, U.S. Army, 1974), 36.

34. *Annual Report, The Surgeon General, United States Army Fiscal Year 1974* (Washington, DC: Office of the Surgeon General, U.S. Army, 1974), 89. "United States Army Medical Field Service School, Dedication Ceremonies, 10 December 1972," Program, ANCC, OMH. "MFSS Dedication at Brooke," *San Antonio Light* (10 December 1972), 1L–7L.

35. Richard R. Taylor, "Team Work Needed for Army Medicine," *U.S. Medicine* 10 (15 January 1974): 60. Richard R. Taylor, "Army Changes Its Ideas, Structure," *U.S. Medicine* 11 (15 January 1975): 55.

36. Francis T. Julia, *Army Staff Reorganization, 1903–1985* (Washington, DC: Analysis Branch, U.S. Army Center of Military History), 34–40. Edith Nuttall, "Presentation to First HSC's Chief Nurses' Conference, Gunter Hotel, San Antonio, Texas, 19 April 1974," Typewritten Text of Speech, 2; "Office of the Surgeon General," Washington, DC, n.d., appendixes A and H; and U.S. Army Health Services Command, "Activation, Evolution of a New Command," Program, 2 April 1973 (all in ANCC, OMH).

37. Connie L. Slewitzke to Author, E-mail Correspondence, 22 November 2002, ANCC, OMH.

38. *Annual Report, The Surgeon General, United States Army Fiscal Year 1975* (Washington, DC: Office of the Surgeon General, U.S. Army, 1975), 77. Richard R. Taylor, "Landmarks Point to Army's Future," *U.S. Medicine* 12 (15 January 1975): 39. Lillian Dunlap, *33 Years of Army Nursing* (Washington, DC: U.S. Army Nurse Corps, 2001), 297.

39. *Report of the Surgeon General United States Army Fiscal Years 1976–1980* (Washington, DC: Office of the Surgeon General, Department of the Army, 1988), 255. Charles C. Pixley, "Army Eyes Doctor Pay, Entitlements," *U.S. Medicine* 16 (15 January 1980): 49.

40. Lillian Dunlap, "Changes in Assignments," *U.S. Army Medical Department Newsletter* 4 (Summer 1973): 20, ANCC, OMH.

41. Lieutenant Colonel Edith Nuttall assumed responsibilities as chief of the branch, with Colonel Iladine Filer in charge of the career planning subunit and Lieutenant Colonel Elsie Nickel overseeing the assignments subunit. Lillian Dunlap, "Changes in ANC Branch," *U.S. Army Medical Department Newsletter* 3 (Winter 1972): 29; and Madelyn N. Parks, "Information for All ANC Officers," Memorandum 6-76, 2, 19 August 1976 (both in ANCC, OMH).

42. Richard B. Crossland and James T. Curie, *Twice the Citizen: A History of the United States Army Reserve, 1908–1983* (Washington, DC: Office of the Chief, Army Reserve, 1984), 211–70. The concept of mutual support described a jointly beneficial relationship between active and reserve components, wherein the active component unit provided tangible support during annual training or weekend field training in return for the provision of advantageous specialized services by reservists. The Roundout program involved replace-

ment of an active Army unit by a particular reserve unit. With the Affiliation program, the reserve unit augmented the capabilities of an active unit in a period of mobilization. Margaret B. Regan, "A Plan to Develop an Army Nurse Corps Reserve Component (ANCRC) Organizational Structure to Coordinate and Control ANCRC Nursing Activities, August 1976," TD, 3, ANCC, OMH. James H. Carter, "Mutual Support and Mobilization Preparedness: The Method of an Army Reserve Hospital," *Military Medicine* 155 (August 1990): 379–81.

43. Vincent Demma, "The Army in the 1970s," Information Paper, 2–3, ANCC, OMH.

44. "History of the Defense Advisory Committee on Women in the Services," Unpublished Manuscript, n.d.; "Defense Advisory Committee on Women in the Services (DACOWITS), April 1981," TD; and Lillian Dunlap, "DACOWITS Meets," *U.S. Army Medical Department Newsletter* 3 (Summer 1972): 21 (all in ANCC, OMH). Judith Youngman, "Defense Advisory Committee on Women in the Services (DACOWITS)," in Francine D'Amico and Laurie Weinstein, *Gender Camouflage: Women and the U.S. Military* (New York: New York University Press, 1999), 169–75.

45. Sara M. Evans, *Born for Liberty: A History of Women in America* (New York: Free Press, 1989), 274–77, 291.

46. In order for passage of the ERA as the 28th Amendment to the Constitution, 38 states were required to ratify the ERA. It has yet to be ratified. http://www.equalrightsamendment.org/ (accessed 4 June 2005).

47. M.C. Devilbiss, *Women and Military Service, A History, Analysis, and Overview of Key Issues* (Maxwell Air Force Base, AL: Air University Press, 1990), xi.

48. Jeanne Holm, *Women in the Military: An Unfinished Revolution* (Novato, CA: Presidio, 1992), 270.

49. Jeanne Holm, *Women in the Military: An Unfinished Revolution* (Novato, CA: Presidio, 1992), 306.

50. Ibid., 305–12. M.C. Devilbiss, *Women and Military Service, A History, Analysis, and Overview of Key Issues* (Maxwell Air Force Base, AL: Air University Press, 1990), 20.

51. *Frontiero v. Richardson*, 411 U.S. 677 (1973). "If You're Pregnant (a Predicament in Army-ese) You May Not Have to Leave the Corps," *American Journal of Nursing* 71 (July 1971): 1311. "Army Nurse Asks 'Benefits' for Mate," *San Francisco Sunday Examiner & Chronicle* (6 December 1970), Section A, 15. Jeanne Holm, *Women in the Military: An Unfinished Revolution* (Novato, CA: Presidio, 1992), 290–91. M.C. Devilbiss, *Women and Military Service, A History, Analysis, and Overview of Key Issues* (Maxwell Air Force Base, AL: Air University Press, 1990), 14. Office of the Surgeon General, U.S. Army Technical Liaison Office, "Recent Regulation Changes Affecting ANC Officers," News Release No. 76JD, 27 April 1971, ANCC, OMH.

52. C.W. Currier, "Retroactive Entitlements for Members with Civilian Husbands, While on Active Duty," TL, 12 December 1973, ANCC, OMH.

53. Jeanne Holm, *Women in the Military: An Unfinished Revolution* (Novato, CA: Presidio, 1992), 291–98. M.C. Devilbiss, *Women and Military Service, A History, Analysis, and Overview of Key Issues* (Maxwell Air Force Base, AL: Air University Press, 1990), 14. Supreme Court Decision Number 71-1694, dated 14 May 1973.

54. "Mothers in Army," *Washington Post* (7 October 1970): n.p.; and "Air Force Nurse Is Resisting Discharge over Her Pregnancy," *New York Times* (18 October 1970): n.p. (both Newspaper Clippings, ANCC, OMH). "If You're Pregnant (a Predicament in Army-ese) You May Not Have to Leave the Corps," *American Journal of Nursing* 71 (July 1971): 1311.

55. If the pregnant service member was an Army nurse, a board at Army Nurse Corps

Assignment Branch reviewed the request for waiver and made a recommendation to the chief of the Corps. Lillian Dunlap, *33 Years of Army Nursing* (Washington, DC: U.S. Army Nurse Corps, 2001), 277.

56. M.C. Devilbiss, *Women and Military Service, A History, Analysis, and Overview of Key Issues* (Maxwell Air Force Base, AL: Air University Press, 1990), 14. Deputy Chief of Staff, Personnel, "Retention of Pregnant Enlisted Women," in Department of the Army, Headquarters, U.S. Army Health Services Command, *Commander's Notes*, CG HSC Bulletin No. 8-74 (August 1974): 4, Record Group 112, Entry 452, National Archives. Edith Nuttall, "Current Department of Defense (DOD) Pregnancy Policy," Information Paper, 9 September 1976, ANCC, OMH.

57. Bettie J. Morden, *The Women's Army Corps, 1945–1978* (Washington, DC: Center of Military History, United States Army, 1992), 235–38.

58. Jeanne Holm, *Women in the Military: An Unfinished Revolution* (Novato, CA: Presidio, 1992), 298–303. M.C. Devilbiss, *Women and Military Service, A History, Analysis, and Overview of Key Issues* (Maxwell Air Force Base, AL: Air University Press, 1990), 14–15. Mildred C. Bailey, "Maternity, Mobility, and Mission (WAC)," Memorandum, 22 August 1974; John L. Naler, "Involuntary Separation of Women for Pregnancy and Parenthood (Misc 1425)," Memorandum, 30 June 1976; H.G. Moore, "Involuntary Separation of Women for Pregnancy and Parenthood—Decision Memorandum," 20 July 1976; Albert W. Singletary, "Report of the Women in the Army Study Group," Disposition Form, 28 July 1976; and Major Russell, "Information Paper, Subject: Pregnancy Policy," 4 April 1977 (all in ANCC, OMH). Gene Famiglietti, "DOD Off Hook on Pregnancy Policy," *Army Times* (30 May 1977): 2. Bettie J. Morden, *The Women's Army Corps, 1945–1978* (Washington, DC: Center of Military History, United States Army, 1992), 393–94.

*Chapter Two*
# Gender and Minority Issues

Concerns related to the gender, marital, parental, racial, and ethnic status of the Army Nurse Corps officer became more manifest after the Vietnam War. Issues and challenges that may have existed in the past assumed greater significance, generated more attention, sparked heated discussion, and demanded fair resolution. Among these were details relating to male nurses, officers' marital status, spousal benefits, pregnancy, parenting, sexual harassment, racial and ethnic diversity, and discrimination.

In the post–Vietnam era, more and more male nurses filled the ranks of the Army Nurse Corps. In the early days of the Vietnam War, men comprised only 3 percent of the Army Nurse Corps, but between 1973 and 1984 the percentage of male Army nurses rose to 28.4 percent.[1] This development was somewhat surprising because the draft had disappeared and men were no longer compelled by law to serve in the nation's armed forces. Conjecture sought to explain the trend. Some believed male nurses were attracted to the Army Nurse Corps rather than civilian nursing because of the better promotion opportunities that led to improved pay and greater responsibility. Others thought that the prospect of global travel, a generous retirement, and comprehensive health benefits were drawing men away from comparable civilian positions into the ranks of the Army Nurse Corps. Still others believed that the availability of educational programs, both civilian and military, drew male nurses into the Corps.[2] Moreover, many of the men had families to support, and the service provided a comfortable living. The Army then was a traditionally male environment whose ethos undoubtedly appealed as a way of life to male nurses.

As numbers of male nurses grew significantly, several phenomena emerged. First, male officers seemed to gravitate naturally to a few areas of specialty, such as anesthesia, within the Army Nurse Corps. In 1971, 68 percent of all nurse anesthetists in the Army were men.[3] Second, men also opted for careers in health care administration. In 1976, General Madelyn Parks expressed some dismay over this trend, perhaps surmising that male Army nurses were engineering a takeover of the specialty. When discussing the Health Care Administration Course, the master's preparation for the administrative role offered at the Academy of Health Sciences in conjunction with Baylor University, she noted that there "were only six applications" for five slots in "the course this year." Parks emphasized that only "*one woman*" applied." The Corps chief explained that it was her "policy and the desire of the Course Director that the mix in the course of male and female be maintained at the same percentage as the Corps—male, 25%; female, 75%." Parks encouraged chief nurses to identify choice candidates, presumably female, for the course and encourage them to apply. She expressed her preference for 10 to 15 applicants to ensure the quality and proper distribution of the student population.[4] The obvious intent underlying the actual message to chief nurses was to promote more participation by female officers in the health care administration career field. Perhaps with more applicants, more latitude would be available to select the best-qualified applicants for the course in the preferred gender ratio. The evenhandedness and legality of such gender-based quota setting appear dubious and probably would be taboo in today's postmodern era.

A third issue involved discrimination against male nurses by their female counterparts. Male nurses encountered gender intolerance in the civilian side of professional nursing. Luther Christman, a male nurse whose lengthy career was highlighted with important accomplishments, experienced "more barriers than most nurses." Christman attributed the long-standing prejudice he encountered to issues of control and said "women in nursing have fought to retain their power."[5] Nonetheless, reports of workplace discrimination affecting male nurses in the Army were mostly inconclusive. Individual experiences differed. Some men claimed to be victims of bigotry, while others denied experiencing any prejudice. Lieutenant Colonel Carmen F. Riviello was one among many male nurses in the Army who disavowed being the target of minority discrimination. Reviewing his 20 years of Army service, Riviello declared that he "never really encountered any conflict with women Army nurses." Additionally, he added, "neither have any of the men nurses I've known." Riviello asserted that "rumors of conflict are just . . . myth."[6]

Others, however, stated that they definitely felt some degree of discrimination. Lieutenant Colonel Jim Sokoloski reflected:

> "I can honestly say that I never had a problem with a patient having me as a male take care of them. That was never a problem. But I can recall some incidents when I was certainly made to feel very uncomfortable by fellow nurses that just were not terribly excited about men being involved in the profession. . . . It wasn't always easy for us."[7]

Sokoloski's level of education exaggerated his minority status. Because he came into the Army when few Army nurses had a bachelor's degree and served when rancor often existed between the diploma graduates and those with an academic degree, Sokoloski received more than a few hostile comments. Diploma graduates would remark maliciously, "You have the degree, you should have all the answers, you're so well-educated. . . ."[8]

As the professional careers of the first male Army nurses progressed, they attained a number of important landmarks. On 15 June 1967, Captain Lawrence Washington raised his right hand and became the first male Army nurse to be sworn into the Regular Army.[9] Less than 10 years later, or some 20 years after the Army Nurse Corps first opened for men, the first male nurse achieved the rank of colonel. In April 1974, Colonel Lawrence W. Scheffner stood at attention and had colonel's eagles pinned on his shoulders at Fort Sam Houston, Texas.[10]

Although the introduction of greater numbers of male nurses into the Army Nurse Corps was largely a sign of progress, it also created some points of conflict. The same could be said regarding the innovation of allowing married nurses to serve on active duty in the organization. Both single and married Army Nurse Corps officers regularly levied either explicit or implicit accusations against their opposite numbers regarding favoritism in matters such as housing or assignments during the Vietnam War era, particularly when female officers first were allowed to marry and continue to serve in the Army Nurse Corps. The apparent schism between the married and single contingents did not disappear after the war's end. In 1975, Parks spoke about preferential treatment in relation to assignments. First, she publicly declared that the Army Nurse Corps did "not have two Corps—one for single officers and one for married officers." Parks added that she would allow "no cliques or favoritism." She intended that all officers' assignments would "be fair and equal" and that the sole criterion determining every assignment selection would be that the individual chosen would "be the best qualified for the job." Parks continued by affirming that homesteading—or lengthy—successive assignments in the same locale, would not be tolerated. She explained that joint domicile for married officers would be considered whenever possible but also said that there was "not now nor has there ever been a guarantee of *always* being assigned together."[11] The problem persisted and Parks reiterated her stand less than one year later.

In March 1976, the chief of the Corps revealed that she had received numerous requests from married officers asking to have their overseas tours postponed or orders revoked "because their husbands couldn't go or because of young children." Parks reminded all officers that the Corps strength had sunk to extraordinarily low levels and that "all members must take their turn" with hardship assignments. She advised the Corps that "ANC [Army Nurse Corps] officers who cannot or will not meet their service obligations should resign. . . . I cannot have ANC officers who are not deployable immediately." Parks again explained that she "did not want to seem harsh; however, the smaller the Corps gets—the more responsibility each member has to fill any requirement." She affirmed once again that the "single officers will not and cannot do all of the overseas duty."[12] Maintaining a fair and impartial assignment policy was never simple.

Concerns grew about fair-mindedness in the treatment of married and single Army nurses. For example, significant inequities existed overseas and in the continental United States in both on-post and off-post housing, an important facet of

The career of Major Lawrence W. Scheffner was distinguished by many achievements. Here he sits for a portrait as the first male Army nurse assigned to the Office of The Surgeon General on 21 January 1965.
Photo courtesy of Army Nurse Corps Archives, Office of Medical History, Falls Church, VA.

military living. In 1976, when approximately 60 percent of the Army Nurse Corps was single and 78 percent were company grade officers, regulations specified all bachelor lieutenants and captains to live on post whenever bachelor officer quarters were available. Often the quarters available were substandard in some manner because the Office of the Secretary of Defense cut the services' military construction budgets for a number of years to finance the Vietnam War. In Europe, for instance, only Bremerhaven and Berlin had "adequate bachelor quarters." Approximately 50 percent of the bachelor officers living in Germany resided on the local economy "at great personal expense," as rental costs were exorbitant and acquiring furnishings was problematic, since bachelors were not allowed to ship their own furniture overseas. In Korea, conditions in bachelor officer quarters were "deplorable." Typically, one officer was housed in a 9' x 7' room, and four to five officers shared one commode and shower. Fire hazards abounded and general maintenance and repair were substandard in the cramped Korean War era hooches.

In the continental United States, if no on-post bachelor quarters were available, the officer had to live off post, again at significant expense that often exceeded the quarters allowance. In some cases, when on-post quarters became available, the post billeting officer directed the bachelor officer to move into the bachelor officer quarters. Then a troublesome and expensive downsizing that involved the disposal of personal effects and furnishings became imperative.[13]

Inequities also existed in the prescribed length of overseas tours for bachelor and married officers in the Army Nurse Corps. Regulations specified disparate tour lengths for various categories of officers. Before 1 January 1976, single women served 24 months in a long-tour area (primarily Europe and Hawaii), while single men were obliged to remain overseas for 36 months. Parks argued that all bachelor officers regardless of gender should serve 24 months in long-tour overseas assignments.[14] However, her appeals fell on deaf ears. After 1 January 1976, the secretary of the Army ordered all bachelors to serve the same amount of time, usually 36 months, in an overseas assignment, the same tour length served by married officers who were accompanied by their dependents. Married officers who did not elect to have their families accompany them overseas, however, were allowed to serve a shorter tour. The Army Nurse Corps observed that the new policies governing overseas assignments were equally "discriminatory and obsolete" because it cost the government far more to move and maintain entire families overseas, and so married officers should serve for a longer term overseas. Furthermore, bachelor officers on an overseas tour were separated from their immediate families and had to endure other impositions such as limited weight allowances for hold baggage and inequitable housing benefits. As a result of the discriminatory practices, morale suffered and bachelor officers left the service.[15] Ultimately, the Department of Army set the usual assignment for all officers in long-term overseas areas at 36 months.

Another area of concern that generated considerable deliberation was service-member's pregnancies. The Army Nurse Corps had to make major adjustments when confronted with the Department of the Army's evolving pregnancy policy in the 1970s. Early in the decade, when a sweeping change in policy was imminent, the Army Nurse Corps required all individuals—both men and women—who applied for any procurement program to sign an affidavit that confirmed a "participant's or officer's understanding that his dependents [would] not interfere with the performance of duties expected of him." This written affirmation was predicated on the belief that with "a female officer who has infant or minor children, a conflict of responsibilities can almost inevitably occur."[16] When the Army allowed pregnant officers to submit waivers to remain on active duty, General Lillian Dunlap ensured that "there was no blanket approval."[17] Instead, each waiver request was reviewed on a case-by-case basis. The main criterion considered was whether—based on past performance—the pregnant Army nurse would be able "to manage her affairs after the baby was born." If the answer was yes, the Army Nurse Corps retained the nurse. If senior leaders judged that the pregnant nurse could not cope with both a military career and parental responsibilities, then the waiver was not approved.[18] In fiscal year 1972, 35 Army nurses requested a waiver for pregnancy. The Army Nurse Corps approved 16 for retention and disapproved the others.[19] As time passed, Army policy allowed all pregnant Army nurses to remain in service automatically, a decision that ignited a firestorm of controversy among military and civilian men and women. The decision begged the contentious question of maternity leave.

Intense debate within the Army Nurse Corps centered on how much maternity leave commanders should grant, whether morning sickness dictated relief from duty, and whether maternity leave should be deducted from the officer's quota of 30 days' annual, ordinary leave or whether it should be deemed convalescent leave and not subtracted from annual leave. Here Dunlap's perspicacity tempered with compassion prevailed. She took the flexible position that maternity leave should be granted on an individual, as-needed basis at the discretion of the physician and should be regarded as standard convalescent leave. To those who disagreed, Dunlap countered, "Why not make [the] husband take his annual leave and take care of the baby if the nurse's condition was such that she could return to active duty?"[20] By 1976, the Department of Defense (DoD) policy prescribed four weeks of convalescent leave before delivery and six weeks after the child's birth.[21] In 1977, the Department of the Army again revised the regulation to remove overly rigid guidelines mandating a specific time for pregnancy leave before delivery. Instead, the exact point at which a pregnant servicemember was to begin leave was to "be based on medical indications for work stoppage." After discharge from the postpartum ward, the convalescence period was not to exceed six weeks.[22]

The pregnancy policy change created a military force that included a variable percentage of pregnant members at any one time and thus potentially affected the ability of the Army Nurse Corps to achieve its mission of providing nursing care. In July 1976, for instance, a total of 71 Army Nurse Corps officers were at some stage of pregnancy, either antepartum or postpartum. Pregnancy leave for those 71 Army nurses totaled 623 working days. The significant number of lost workdays and other military contingencies had profound repercussions on the Army Medical Department's mission.

The new policy produced "innumerable complaints," including many describing a negative influence on unit readiness, deployability, and mission accomplishment. Commanders and chief nurses reported excessive absences resulting from morning sickness, hospital appointments, and other excuses. Furthermore, pregnant servicewomen physically could not fulfill many—if not most—of their job responsibilities, were considered nondeployable, and, because of their temporary medical conditions, the command could not obtain interim staffing replacements. Reports also cited repeated instances where the servicemember requested separation from the service after completing her six-week postpartum convalescent leave, during which time she had received her full pay and allowances. There was an overall effect on Army Nurse Corps morale. Colonel Edith Nuttall, the assistant chief of the Corps, said that "non-pregnant military members do not appreciate providing coverage for absences, assuming extra duties, or accepting overseas assignments generated by pregnant servicewomen."[23]

In response to the pregnancy/parenthood issues and arguable abuses, the Department of the Army issued guidance directing commanders to deal with relevant substandard performance on the part of pregnant servicewomen by applying "normal leadership methods." Ultimately, the directive advised, commanders should encourage members displaying recurring nonproductivity and/or inability to deploy for mission-related assignments to seek hardship discharges. It concluded:

> Each member must be able to carry his/her own weight, must have individual assignment mobility to meet the needs of the Army, and must make a meaningful contribution to unit readiness and mission accomplishment.[24]

A survey conducted by the Health Services Command Inspector General Team offered a slightly different picture of grassroots attitudes toward the Army pregnancy policy. Investigators drew their relatively small survey sample from five military treatment facilities in the continental United States. They distributed a total of 74 questionnaires, and 70 were returned. When queried, 69 percent of the small sample felt that their coworkers' pregnancies did not adversely affect morale. When asked about the policy's effect on patient care delivery, 57 percent replied that the pregnancies had no impact on mission accomplishment. Respondents were almost evenly split in their opinions about the need for policy change regarding pregnancy. Those who advocated a change in policy suggested a range of possibilities from "the commander should be more aggressive in eliminating abuses of quarters and convalescent leave" to "pregnant females should be discharged."[25]

In a related issue, some in the Army undoubtedly concluded that certain female soldiers or Army Nurse Corps officers used pregnancy to evade their service obligations for scholarships and other subsidies. These abuses may have existed because the Army subsequently issued regulations and changes effective 1 May 1978 mandating that pregnant female officers, usually Reserve Officers' Training

Corps (ROTC) scholarship graduates, could not be released from active duty before completion of their initial service obligations. Moreover, regulations required commanders to counsel all pregnant personnel in accordance with a specified Department of the Army circulated checklist. The list detailed the options available for the pregnant officer to continue on active duty, maternity care entitlements, and existing maternity leave and overseas deployment policies. Finally, the regulation required the pregnant soldier "to outline how she [would] physically and financially provide for the child's welfare."[26] Clearly, this was the genesis of what was later known as the "family care plan," a commonsense blueprint outlining plans for discharging familial responsibilities in the case of a deployment; updating it would eventually become an annual requirement for all servicemembers with dependent children.[27]

Like the complicated issues of pregnancy, standards regarding the identification and management of sexual harassment also had to be defined. Across the centuries, sexual harassment in the Army—indeed in American society—has been a constant major problem. With the women's liberation movement and the enlistment of many more women into the Army, however, consciousness about such transgressions was elevated, and DoD acknowledged that sexual harassment in its various forms was a serious issue. The Army defined sexual harassment as "unwelcome sexual advances, requests for sexual favors, or verbal or physical conduct of a sexual nature."[28] It characterized its outcomes as including adverse effects on readiness and the accomplishment of a unit's mission. It also affirmed that it lowered "unit cohesion, morale, and productivity, and [increased] attrition rates, lost time, unacceptable costs, and human misery."[29] To deal with harassment issues, the secretary of the Army announced his commitment on 4 January 1980 to uphold "the human dignity of all military and civilian personnel." The Army chief of staff simultaneously ordered the Army inspector general to investigate all alleged incidents of sexual harassment. By 1981, evidence suggested that sexual harassment contributed significantly to decisions by first-term Army women to leave the service.[30] Without doubt, such harassment also had been a problem for Army Nurse Corps officers.

A series of incidents surfaced in the early 1990s when female anesthesia students in the clinical phase of their training at William Beaumont Army Medical Center in El Paso, Texas, alleged that they were the victims of sexual harassment. They stated that male faculty and staff made reference to their "behavior being the result of having 'periods,' child care problems, and the performance of menial tasks as being womanly duties." These same students alleged that they were "treated unfairly by being reprimanded for actions which when committed by their male classmates do not result in retribution from faculty." Other students raised a related issue when they charged that faculty "screamed at women students" and threatened the women with academic probation. Consequently, they affirmed that an adversarial relationship between faculty and students evolved.[31] As a result of these allegations and a subsequent inspector general review, faculty added instruction to the Anesthesia Course Program of Instruction designed to raise consciousness about sexual harassment. Moreover, anesthesia students and faculty participated in Prevention of Sexual Harassment classes.[32] Sexual harassment of both female and male soldiers has always been a grave issue in the military; however, only in the recent past has it been treated as a serious offense detrimental to unit performance and morale.

As the injustice of sexual harassment ultimately had to be rectified, so too did the inequities accorded to racial minorities have to be eliminated. Additionally, the Army had to acknowledge the valuable contributions made by African-American Army Nurse Corps officers. Just as the women's movement and the curtailment of the draft opened doors in the military for women, it also offered greater prospects for minorities, particularly for African-American women. Minority women have made valuable contributions and great strides in the Army Nurse Corps. During the Corps first half-century, the Army allowed few African-American nurses to serve, and they found themselves scarcely welcomed. With the lowering of some barriers, the numbers of African-American women serving in the military expanded and correspondingly increased in the Army Nurse Corps. For all intents and purposes, however, the predominantly white Army begrudgingly allowed their integration only after African-American activists and supporters exerted extreme political pressure. African-American nurses in the segregated Army were merely tolerated during times of national emergency, that is, during the war years. In the second half of the 20th century, however, Truman's Executive Order No. 9981 partially resolved the deep-seated social injustice but, again, only gradually—at a snail's pace—and as a result of strenuous efforts expended by a number of courageous individuals with vested interests in securing social justice for all.

With the passage of time, the presence of African-Americans increased. There were only 131 African-Americans in the Army Nurse Corps in 1972, representing 3 percent of the Corps total strength.[33] By 1993, many more African-American nurses were Army Nurse Corps officers. Their strength, which included both male and female nurses, had grown to an impressive 16.4 percent.[34] In 1971, African-American women accounted for 3.3 percent of all female officers on active duty in all branches. By 1989, that figure had risen to 13.2 percent.[35]

Credit for the greater presence of minorities can be partially attributed to the Army's increased attention to its equal opportunity/race relations programs. Efforts in the early 1970s to sponsor measures "to ensure fairness, justice, and equity for all soldiers regardless of race, color, ethnicity, gender, or religion" incorporated elements such as "affirmative action, education and training" and a research component to evaluate the program's effectiveness.[36]

The ROCKS was an independent volunteer program that also worked to enhance professional advancement for African-Americans in the Army. Commemorating the Army service of General Roscoe (Rock) C. Cartwright, the group of senior African-American Army officers mentored and guided junior officers and ROTC cadets in historically black colleges and universities. A number of African-American Army nurses participated in this endeavor and supported and facilitated the careers of many potential and newly commissioned Army Nurse Corps lieutenants.[37]

While she served as chief nurse, European Medical Command and deputy commander for nursing, Landstuhl Regional Medical Center, Colonel Lucretia McClenney also was the first female president of the ROCKS European Chapter. McClenney, center, is pictured here in the fall of 1999 at a dining out with Brigadier General Michael Kussman, commanding general of European Medical Command, left, and Command Sergeant Major Paul Cervantes, right.
Photo courtesy of Colonel Lucretia McClenney, Alexandria, VA.

Brigadier General Clara Adams-Ender, chief of the Army Nurse Corps from 1987 to 1991, served as the first female president of ROCKS. Lieutenant Colonel Joyce Johnson-Bowles served a term as the first female vice president.[38] Colonel Lucretia McClenney worked with students at Morgan State University in Baltimore, Maryland. She served in various recruitment and retention activities, acted as a role model for Army ROTC cadets, and met with the professor of military science and his cadre and the university president to solicit support for Army ROTC cadets. Her work, combined with that of others on her team, resulted in the university's granting "free room and board to 4-year Army ROTC scholarship recipients" and awarding "academic credit for ROTC leadership and training courses." The ROCKS' European chapter elected McClenney as its first president. She guided the organization in mentoring company grade (captain and below) officers and in initiating a yearly scholarship for students in the DoD school system.[39]

Colonel Margaret Bailey was in the vanguard of the integration movement. In January 1970, she was the first African-American woman to be promoted to colonel.[40] Bailey was an exemplary professional officer, and her contributions to the Army Nurse Corps continued on after her retirement in 1972. In retirement, she was a consultant to the surgeon general and charged with promoting "increased

Gender and Minority Issues   35

Colonel Margaret Bailey was the first African-American Army nurse promoted to colonel (January 1970).
Photo courtesy of Army Nurse Corps Archives, Office of Medical History, Falls Church, VA.

participation by minority group members in the Army Nurse Corps recruitment programs."[41] Bailey joined then-major Clara Adams (now Adams-Ender), another African-American, and their endeavors on behalf of affirmative action involved traveling about the country to promote racial equality in the Corps. The women searched for qualified African-American students to matriculate in the Walter Reed Army Institute of Nursing at a time when that program was under fire from black activists such as United Blacks Against Discrimination for failing to maintain minority representation.[42]

Colonel Hazel W. Johnson was another trailblazer who overcame racial prejudice to excel in the Army Nurse Corps. In June 1979, Johnson was the first African-American woman in DoD to be promoted to brigadier general. Additionally, she was the first officer to hold a doctorate in nursing to serve as the chief of the Army Nurse Corps.[43] Clearly Johnson was an outstanding professional officer who overcame great obstacles to make enormous contributions to the Army and the nation.

African-Americans never easily achieved upward career mobility. Neither could they effortlessly rise to the levels of major professional achievements. More often than not, the minority nurse had to carefully negotiate what seemed to be an unending series of hurdles. Many opted not to fight the system, but those who did, did so with a rare combination of audacity and grace that added much to the Army Nurse Corps.

In 1979, before her selection as chief nurse of the 97th General Hospital in Frankfurt, Germany, the commander of that military treatment facility ordered a newly promoted Colonel Clara Adams (now Adams-Ender) in for an interview. The commander told Adams that he regarded her as doubly inferior because she was both an African-American and a nurse. He admonished her to always keep two dictums in mind. His first statement directed Adams to remember that "no matter how good you are, because you're black you'll never be as good as a white person." Secondly, he decreed, she must understand "that in any difference of opinion between nurses and physicians, the physician is always right." At this point in the interview, Adams took a calming breath and replied:

> "Sir, in terms of your first comment, I'm going to give you an opportunity to demonstrate your point whenever you see fit. And I will call upon you as our commander to support the department of nursing. But if you ever stumble, and let anyone else know that's the way you feel about me, I'll slap a class action suit on you so fast it'll make your head swim. And as for that thing about physicians always being right, I won't even grace that with a comment."[44]

Despite these belligerent beginnings, Adams recalled that their association developed into "a good working relationship." Whether or not the commander's perception of her personal qualities improved, "he never behaved otherwise." She said, "That's all I really cared about."[45] Adams continued to rise above the glass ceiling of racial suppression to achieve the rank of brigadier general and lead the Army Nurse Corps. Following her tenure as chief of the Army Nurse Corps, Adams-Ender remained on active duty and served as post commander of Fort Belvoir, Virginia.

# Notes

1. Constance J. Moore, "Demobilization of the Army Nurse Corps after World War II, Vietnam, and Operation Desert Storm," Unpublished Information Paper, 3, 30 January 1997, USA Center of Military History, Washington, D.C. Mary E. Viehdorfer Frank and Robert V. Piemonte, "The Army Nurse Corps: A Decade of Change," *American Journal of Nursing* 85 (September 1985): 985–88.

2. Office of the Surgeon General, U.S. Army, Technical Liaison Office, "Facts about the Male Army Nurse Corps Officers," News Release No. 330, J Day (12 November 1970): 3; Nancy R. Adams, "The Army Nurse Corps: A Corps in Transition 1939-1967," 7, 27 April 1986, USAWC Military Studies Program Paper; and Jim Sokoloski, Interview by Annie Okubo, 41, 23 September 1989, U.S. Army Center of Military History, Washington, D.C. (all in Army Nurse Corps Collection [ANCC], Office of Medical History [OMH]).

3. Hal B. Jennings, "Report from the United States Army Medical Department," *Military Medicine* 136 (October 1971): 774–75.

4. Madelyn N. Parks, "Information for Army Nurse Corps Officers," 27 January 1976, 2, ANCC, OMH.

5. Eleanor Sullivan, "In a Woman's World," *Reflections on Nursing Leadership* 28 (Third Quarter 2002): 10–16.

6. "Walson Nurse Tells Men's Story," *HSC Mercury* 3 (November–December 1975): 4.

7. Jim Sokoloski, Interview by Annie Okubo, 6–7, 23 September 1989, U.S. Army Center of Military History, Washington, D.C., Army Nurse Corps Oral History Collection, OMH.

8. Ibid., 7.

9. "Shown is Capt Lawrence C. Washington going R.A., the first male nurse to go R.A. at Walter Reed," 15 June 1967, Photograph; and Mildred I. Clark to Captain Lawrence C. Washington, Typewritten Letter (TL), n.d. (both in ANCC, OMH).

10. "Army Nurses Get First Male Colonel," *San Antonio Light* (22 April 1974): n.p., Newspaper Clipping, ANCC, OMH.

11. Madelyn N. Parks, "Information for Key ANC Officers," 2, 24 September 1975, ANCC, OMH.

12. Madelyn N. Parks, "Information for Key ANC Officers," 1–2, 16 March 1976, ANCC, OMH.

13. Don Hirst, "Nurses Protest Army Housing Rules," *Army Times* (8 November 1976): 10. Edith Nuttall, "Bachelor Officer Housing for Army Nurse Corps Officers," Information Paper, 27 September 1976, ANCC, OMH.

14. Madelyn N. Parks, "Oversea Tour of Female Bachelor Personnel," Disposition Form, 8 September 1975; and Rothrock, "Oversea Tour of Female Bachelor Personnel—Decision Paper," n.d. (both in ANCC, OMH).

15. Edith Nuttall, "Length of Oversea Tours—Army Nurse Corps," Information Paper, 27 September 1976; and Madelyn N. Parks, "Information for Army Nurse Corps Officers," 2, 27 January 1976 (both in ANCC, OMH).

16. Louise C. Rosasco, "Progress Report: The Army Nurse Corps and Army Nursing," 16 June 1971, with Inclosure, "Equalization of Benefits and Entitlements for All Military Members," ANCC, OMH.

17. Lillian Dunlap, *33 Years of Army Nursing* (Washington, DC: U.S. Army Nurse Corps, 2001), 277.

18. Ibid., 277–78.

19. Lillian Dunlap, "Briefing for Department of Defense Nursing Advisory Committee," Typewritten Document, 3, 6 July 1972, ANCC, OMH.

20. Lillian Dunlap, *33 Years of Army Nursing* (Washington, DC: U.S. Army Nurse Corps, 2001), 278–79.

21. Edith Nuttall, "Current Department of Defense (DOD) Pregnancy Policy," Information Paper, 9 September 1976, ANCC, OMH.

22. W. Brott, "Pregnancy and Abortion in Active Duty Personnel," Information Paper, 1-2, 13 June 1977, ANCC, OMH.

23. Edith Nuttall, "Current Department of Defense (DOD) Pregnancy Policy," Information Paper, 9 September 1976, ANCC, OMHN

24. Headquarters, Department of the Army, "Nonproductive/Nondeployable Pers due to Preg/Parenthood," TWX, June 1976, Inclosure 16, in Madelyn N. Parks, "Information for Army Nurse Corps Officers," 2, December 1976, ANCC, OMH. Deputy Chief of Staff, Personnel, "Pregnancy and Parenthood," in Department of the Army, Headquarters, U.S. Army Health Services Command, *Commander's Notes*, CG HSC Bulletin No. 8-76 (August 1976): 2, Record Group 112, Entry 452, National Archives.

25. Wayne L. Simpson, "Results of Maternity Policy Survey," Disposition Form, 21 March 1977, ANCC, OMH.

26. "Pregnant Officers Must Serve Out Obligations," *Pentagram News* (27 April 1978): 13, News Clipping and Inclosure 8, in Madelyn N. Parks, "Information for ANC Officers," Memorandum, 5 July 1978, ANCC, OMH. *Report of the Surgeon General United States Army Fiscal Years 1976-1980* (Washington, DC: Office of the Surgeon General, Department of the Army, 1988), 67. AR 635-10, Change 24-2. AR 635-120, Change 14-1. AR 635-100, Chapter 3.

27. Deputy Chief of Staff, Personnel, "Pregnancy and Dependent Care Counseling," in Department of the Army, Headquarters, U.S. Army Health Services Command, Commander's Notes, CG HSC Bulletin No. 3-79 (March 1979): 11, Record Group 112, Entry 452, National Archives.

28. Michael D. Mahler, "Guidelines on Sexual Harassment Issues," *Army* (February 1997): 10–12.

29. Nancy G. Wilds, "Sexual Harassment in the Military," *Minerva: Quarterly Report on Women and the Military* 8 (Winter 1990): 1–16.

30. "Women in the Army and Sexual Harassment, Historical Milestones," Typewritten Manuscript, 11–12, n.d., ANCC, OMH. Lois M. Beck, "Sexual Harassment in the Army:

Roots Examined," *Minerva: Quarterly Report on Women and the Military* 9 (Spring 1991): 29–40.

31. TL to Betty J. Horton, 26 May 1992; and Cecil B. Drain to Nancy R. Adams, TL with extensive attachments, 15 July 1993 (both in ANCC, OMH).

32. Clarise B. Golightly-Jenkins, "Inspector General Inquiry of the Phase II Anesthesia Nursing Program at William Beaumont Army Medical Center," Typewritten Memorandum, 16 October 1992; and Clarise B. Golightly-Jenkins, "Inspector General Inquiry of the Phase II Anesthesia Nursing Program at William Beaumont Army Medical Center," Typewritten Memorandum, 2 December 1992 (both in ANCC, OMH).

33. Lillian Dunlap, "Briefing for Department of Defense Nursing Advisory Committee," Typewritten Document, 1, 6 July 1972, ANCC, OMH.

34. "African American Nurses in the Army Nurse Corps," Unidentified Typewritten Manuscript, n.d., ANCC, OMH.

35. Brenda L. Moore, "African-American Women in the U.S. Military," *Armed Forces & Society* 17 (Spring 1991): 363–84.

36. "Affirmative Action in the Army," Unidentified Typewritten Manuscript, n.d., ANCC, OMH.

37. Terris E. Kennedy to Author, E-mail Correspondence, 21 November 2002; and Clara L. Adams-Ender to Author, E-mail Correspondence, 1 December 2002 (both in ANCC, OMH). National Board of Directors, ROCKS, Inc., http://www.rocksinc.org/ (accessed 22 June 2005).

38. Lucretia McClenney to Author, E-mail Correspondence, 4 March 2003, ANCC, OMH.

39. Lucretia McClenney to Author, E-mail Correspondence, 3 March 2003, ANCC, OMH.

40. Margaret E. Bailey, *The Challenge* (Lisle, IL: Tucker Publications, 1999), 144–45; Lillian Dunlap, "Thoughts upon Retirement of an Army Nurse," *U.S. Army Medical Department Newsletter* 2 (Fall 1971): 44–45.

41. Margaret E. Bailey, *The Challenge* (Lisle, IL: Tucker Publications, 1999), 149–50. "African American Nurses in the Army Nurse Corps," Unidentified Typewritten Manuscript, n.d., ANCC, OMH.

42. Clara L. Adams-Ender, *My Rise to the Stars, How a Sharecropper's Daughter Became an Army General* (Lake Ridge, VA: Cape Associates, 2001), 160–61.

43. "African American Nurses in the Army Nurse Corps," Unidentified Typewritten Manuscript, n.d., ANCC, OMH. Clara Adams-Ender, "The Future of Minorities in Military Nursing," *Journal of Military Nursing Research* 1 (Fall 1995): 40, 42–43.

44. Clara L. Adams-Ender, *My Rise to the Stars, How a Sharecropper's Daughter Became an Army General* (Lake Ridge, VA: Cape Associates, 2001), 200–01.

45. Ibid.

*Chapter Three*
# Educational Concerns and Career Advancement

The determination to upgrade skills and expand professional knowledge through formal education was a persistent theme in the Army Nurse Corps in the 1970s. Army Nurse Corps officers improved their knowledge and skills by working toward compliance with the 1974 mandate for baccalaureate preparation, participating in continuing education offerings, partaking in specified short nursing courses, attending graduate school, and focusing on advancement through military education.[1]

Dating back to post–World War II days, a number of previous chiefs of the Corps had battled to establish the baccalaureate degree as a minimum educational prerequisite for entry into the Army Nurse Corps. The Corps reached that goal in 1974. However, the movement toward an all-baccalaureate Corps entailed progressively implemented steps. In 1971, the Army Nurse Corps procurement efforts assigned priority for granting commissions to baccalaureate graduates. The accessions board selected those with the preferred, stipulated educational background first among potential applicants. As an added incentive, these applicants were commissioned as first lieutenants upon entry to active duty, which entitled them to extra pay, allowances, and status. All others initially served as second lieutenants. Non-baccalaureate Army nurses who wished to serve beyond their initial tour of duty had to show documented proof of working toward completion of a degree.[2]

An Army Nurse Corps task force met in 1973 to study the issue and develop specific justification for the anticipated change to an all-baccalaureate Corps. Task force members agreed that professional nurses educated at the baccalaureate level were indispensable in performing essential nursing responsibilities expected of an Army Nurse Corps officer, such as "administration, supervision, education, and research." The working group concluded "that the ANC [Army Nurse Corps] in peacetime must be comprised only of professional nurses prepared at the baccalaureate level . . . [who] would serve as a strong, viable 'hard core' from which to expand in the event of mobilization."[3]

At approximately the same time, the Navy and Air Force pondered the same perplexing educational entry-level questions. To facilitate joint resolution of the issues, representatives from all three nurse corps met as a Medical Task Force on Tri-Service Nursing Education. Like the Army, the Navy Nurse Corps preferred "an all baccalaureate Corps." Some had the erroneous perception that the Air Force Nurse Corps was not striving to achieve the same standard.[4] However, this was inaccurate. The Air Force surgeon general noted that in the final six months of 1976, the Air Force Nurse Corps (AFNC) raised their "accession of nurses with a baccalaureate degree to 50 percent of the total."[5] In 1978, the AFNC set this goal at 75 percent.[6] The Air Force surgeon general added that the Corps expected "to reach 100 percent" by 1980.[7] However the Air Force objective was not achieved as expected in 1980. It was not until December 1982 that AFNC first required a bachelor of science in nursing (BSN) for all new accessions. Exceptions were made for critical career fields such as anesthesia.[8] The actual educational composition of the three nurse corps in the mid-1970s verified that the Army was in the forefront at least in the area of educational credentials. The Army Nurse Corps counted 74 percent of its officers as prepared at the baccalaureate level, while the Navy had 64 percent with a BSN.[9] Only 32 percent of Air Force nurses claimed the BSN in the mid-1970s. In 1978, 41 percent completed a college education. By 1980, 67 percent of AFNC had earned a baccalaureate degree.[10]

At one point, a particular task force member, a non-Army lieutenant, discussed several possible strategies proposed by the Army to achieve the educational goal. This individual believed that using the Reserve Officers' Training Corps to foster baccalaureate accessions would fail—at least with the Navy—because "the 'line' part of the Navy was not too interested in using Reserve Officers' Training Corps programs." The lieutenant also discounted the notion of establishing a baccalaureate nursing program at the Uniformed Services University of the Health Sciences, stating "that university is now in troubled waters and cannot be counted on for anything. . . ."[11]

General Lillian Dunlap encountered powerful resistance from many quarters, questioning the wisdom of striving for an all-baccalaureate Army Nurse Corps. Opponents cited the grave, ever-present shortage of nurses that—they felt—adding a BSN requirement would only aggravate. Among those who fought against the all-baccalaureate standard were staff members at the Department of the Army, Department of Defense, and Office of the Secretary of Defense, Health Affairs— particularly reserve general officers. These individuals argued the obvious. A dearth of Army nurses existed and lowering or maintaining existing standards would facilitate entry into military service by associate degree nurses and diploma school graduates, thus reducing shortages. Their analysis concluded that the influx of diploma and associate degree nurses also would eliminate the need for such expensive programs as the Walter Reed Army Institute of Nursing and the Army Student Nurse Program.[12] Their shortsighted rationale ignored ominous, unintended outcomes that probably would accompany such a course of action. For example, with the quick fix would come a possible lowering in the quality of care provided and a degrading of professional leadership attributes. Moreover, Army Nurse Corps officers' ability to maintain parity with the rest of the Army's commissioned officer corps, which required officers to have a college degree, would suffer and professional respect and authority would be lost. Army Nurse Corps officers would find themselves consigned to subservient positions and unable to intervene in important realms such as patient advocacy. Similar challenges to the all-baccalaureate policy emerged on a regular basis in the years to follow.[13]

Although many fought against the educational requirement, others supported the move toward an all-baccalaureate Corps. Surgeon generals Lieutenant General Hal Jennings and Lieutenant General Richard Taylor, senior Army Nurse Corps leaders, and civilian professional nursing organizations were among the proponents.[14] In 1965, the American Nurses Association (ANA) position paper advocated the baccalaureate degree as the minimum educational entry level for all professional practice.[15] Thus, the ANA backed an Army Nurse Corps policy that closely reflected its own position. Both the ANA and the National League for Nursing provided valuable assistance in the form of "advice, support, letter writing, phone calling" and other "things that might be needed."[16] For instance, the National League for Nursing shared its brief in support of baccalaureate education for nurses with the Army Nurse Corps, noting that the professional degree developed nurses' "potential as individuals, as citizens, and as professional practitioners." It added that a baccalaureate education prepared nurses to deliver, explain, and demonstrate effectual nursing care; identify patient care needs and plan, direct, and evaluate care; adapt fundamental principles from other sciences to unique nursing situations; and led the nurse with a bachelor's degree to acknowledge "the need for continuing personal and professional development."[17]

In the years that followed the 1974 regulation, the Corps accepted only graduates of accredited collegiate nursing schools, and ever-increasing numbers of diploma-graduate Army nurses already on active duty had complied with the new policy. By 1978, over 90 percent of the Army Nurse Corps had bachelor's degrees. Failure to obtain a baccalaureate degree adversely affected Army nurses' military careers. After General Madelyn N. Parks took part in a promotion board in 1978, she reported that "any marginal or poor OER [officer efficiency report] was a deciding factor" that made promotion to the next grade unlikely. The first criterion that usually precluded promotion was obesity. The second most frequent criterion was the lack of a bachelor's degree. Parks disclosed that a rare few nondegree Army nurses were selected for promotion, but only after they had "demonstrated (*many* semester hours') effort towards a degree."[18] About this time, issues about educational qualifications, body weight, and lack of fitness became important as crucial and sensitive discriminators affecting future promotions and career progression.[19]

Many Army nurses were placed at a disadvantage and offended—both personally and professionally—by the Corps emphasis on the baccalaureate degree standard. Some simply did not have the ability or stamina to pursue additional education, especially when it involved additional hours attending classes during off-duty time after exceedingly demanding and arduous workdays. Some of the required classes were lackluster and probably seemed irrelevant to working professionals. Many officers who in the past had made significant contributions to the Corps saw the demands as—at best—extremely ungrateful, and at worst, a major rebuke to their professional self-image. In 1971, Colonel Louise Rosasco, the assistant chief of the Army Nurse Corps, addressed these perceptions, writing that the emphasis on collegiate education

> . . . does not reflect a dissatisfaction with those many highly capable Army nurses who did not attain these academic credentials in the past. It reflects a growing awareness and a conviction that the times in which we live demand this preparation for responsible, innovative leadership in the future.[20]

Before long, the beneficial effects of the Army Nurse Corps progressive education policy manifested themselves. In 1982, an *Army Times* exposé spotlighted the wounded but "on the mend" condition of Army health care.[21] Although the series brutally detailed a host of the Army Medical Department (AMEDD) failures, it highlighted Army nurses as invaluable assets of the system. The critique revealed that Army Nurse Corps officers were "distinguished by the quality of care they provide" and added that they "top all other Army medical personnel in surveys of patient preferences." The newspaper disclosed that one representative patient survey demonstrated that "Army nurses outranked all other medical personnel in courtesy and consideration." It attributed the high levels of patient satisfaction to "the superior credentials of Army nurses," noting that approximately 98 percent of all Army nurses were baccalaureate graduates, of whom 19 percent held the advanced preparation of a master's degree. The article also confirmed that more than 54 percent of Army nurses claimed at least six years of professional nursing experience.[22] Whether a scientifically proven causal relationship exists between levels of nurse education/experience and patient satisfaction is debatable. Nonetheless, many would ascribe empirically to the benefits of higher education and a modicum of professional experience. The implementation of advanced educational credentials and the introduction of more rigorous standards for Army nurses arguably enhanced performance, improved measures of patient satisfaction, and probably affected clinical outcomes. Army nurses led the AMEDD health care providers in several parameters of professional performance and also served as an exemplar for professional nursing. This suggests that the choice to mandate the baccalaureate degree as the educational entry level was a shrewd, well-reasoned decision.

During the 1970s, the nursing profession at large was coming to recognize another imperative, that is, the desirability of continuing education as a career-long commitment for professional nurses. The discipline saw education as one strategy to preserve quality of care. Selected states codified the requirement as state boards of nursing established directives requiring proof of continuing education activities as a prerequisite for nursing license renewals.[23] Different states required varying numbers of continuing education units or contact hours of education.[24] Army regulations obliged Army nurses to be licensed, but allowed nurses to hold a li-

Pictured is Colonel Louise C. Rosasco, assistant chief of the Army Nurse Corps from 1970 to 1971. Photo courtesy of Army Nurse Corps Archives, Office of Medical History, Falls Church, VA.

cense from any state. Since many maintained their license in jurisdictions that required continuing education, the Army Nurse Corps took responsibility for providing selected continuing education programs for Army nurses to supplement offerings available in the civilian community. On 14 November 1977, the ANA's North East Regional Accrediting Committee endorsed the Army Nurse Corps Continuing Health Education Program (ANC-CHEP) and granted it the authority to approve educational programs at military treatment facilities around the world for credit in the form of contact hours or continuing education units.[25] The ANA authorization, which covered a two-year period, was renewed regularly thereafter.[26]

Educators in the AMEDD facilities worldwide submitted proposed continuing education programs to the ANC-CHEP. A board of Army Nurse Corps officers evaluated the proposed program and either approved it or made suggestions for improvements before resubmission. Once educators in military treatment facilities received approval for the learning activity, they presented the program and awarded attendees credit for participation. In its first year of activity, the ANC-CHEP reviewed 177 planned programs and approved 155 for continuing education units. In all, 4,940 professional nurses in the continental United States, Europe, and Korea attended these approved programs and earned an impressive total of 36,854 contact hours.[27] Judging by the numbers alone, the ANC-CHEP was a successful, beneficial endeavor that also likely enhanced the quality of nursing care provided in Army installations.

Another educational venture that proved advantageous was the Army Nurse Corps panel of professional postgraduate short courses. Since the post–World War II period, the Army Nurse Corps had sponsored an increasing variety of short-term courses to improve professional nurse proficiencies. In most cases, these classes were classified as temporary duty courses, intended to last no longer than 179 days. In 1973, for instance, the Army Nurse Corps sent various officers to the AMEDD Officer Basic, the Army Nurse Corps Clinical Head Nurse, the Chief Nurses Orientation, and the Community Health Nursing courses and others such as the Basic Operating Room, Environmental Hygiene, and Army Installation Management courses and the Nurse Methods Analyst Short course.[28]

Affirming the never-ending importance of improving nurse provider skills and knowledge, the Army Nurse Corps had long recognized and authorized a nursing role to support educational endeavors in Army hospitals.[29] By the mid-1970s, this role was designated as chief, nursing education and training service, and in 1986 it became known as chief, nursing education and staff development service.[30] The change of name precipitated little if any change in the unit's structure or function. The size and scope of education and staff development in each military treatment facility were based on the learning needs of military, civilian, officer, and enlisted staff and also was influenced by quality-of-patient-care issues and hospitals' requirements.[31] The service managed continuing education programs focusing on such topics as "reading electrocardiograms, diagnosing ventricular fibrillation, and initiating medical action in emergencies." Other responsibilities involved "orienting new employees, training nurses' aides and technicians, and developing leadership qualities in nursing personnel."[32] The AMEDD considered these duties essential in the contemporary environment of stringent downsizing and personnel shortages that dictated every staff member be versatile, optimally productive, and competent. Nurse educators also oriented, trained, and counseled all department of nursing personnel. Furthermore, they apprised junior officers in particular "of the career options and alternatives available and of the expectations of professional performance and continued personal development which the AMEDD" required.[33] The Army nurse assigned to this educational role also assessed "educational needs and skill levels" and acted as a liaison with other local or distant civilian or military educators.[34]

The Army Nurse Corps, however, did not restrict its educational venues to the military setting. It also took advantage of courses offered in civilian institutions of higher learning. In the early 1970s when the Army Nurse Corps was promoting the goal of all-baccalaureate status, it channeled the bulk of its civilian education funds into the bachelor's degree completion or similar programs, thus providing support for nondegree nurses' academic endeavors. After only a few years, however, the percentage of Army nurses with a bachelor's degree steadily increased, and the Army Nurse Corps sought to promote and subsidize graduate education.[35] In 1973, the Army Education Review Board validated 571 Army Nurse Corps positions as requiring master's degrees and another 16 for doctoral degree preparation. One year later, the Surgeon General's Professional Education Review Board recommended that in fiscal year 1974, 908 Army Nurse Corps positions be validated for the master's level and 39 for the doctorate.[36] This paved the way for greater numbers of Army Nurse Corps officers to attend graduate school under the Army's Long Term Civilian Training sponsorship program every year. During fiscal year 1973, the Army Nurse Corps projected that a total of 42 Army nurses would complete their graduate education in civilian institutions and another 70 Army Nurse Corps officers would enter school full-time in programs leading to a degree in various civilian academic institutions.[37] By fiscal year 1984, 120 Army nurses' graduate and doctoral educations were either fully or partially funded by the Army. Following graduation, these advanced degree nurses returned to duty positions validated for their educational levels, such as clinical practice roles, administrative jobs, education assignments, or research responsibilities.[38]

Military education level was another component gaining in importance for career progression. Promotion boards expected field grade (major and above) officers Army-wide competing for promotion to have successfully completed Command and General Staff College, either in residence or by correspondence, and the expectation also quickly became applicable to rising Army Nurse Corps officers. Lieutenant colonels Doris S. Frazier and Connie L. Slewitzke opened the doors for women in the traditional Army schools. Frazier became the first Army nurse to attend the Command and General Staff College in 1967 as a resident student. In 1973, Frazier was again a pioneer when she graduated from the Army War College at Carlisle Barracks, Pennsylvania. Frazier later recalled that she "was thrilled and honored to be selected for each [school]. I learned much and met many outstanding and wonderful officers who went on and did great things for our country." That same year, Slewitzke became the first woman officer to serve as class president of the Command and General Staff College at Fort Leavenworth, Kansas.[39] Most of the student body, Slewitzke remembered, was supportive of her appointment with a few exceptions. Those few were anything but pleased. Medical Service Corps students wrote a letter of protest to Surgeon General Lieutenant General Charles Pixley. Slewitzke's appointment also riled a British officer, who commented that "women didn't belong in these kinds of schools and definitely should not be Class President." Slewitzke found the class director, a faculty member, "interesting." His remarks strengthened her resolve to accept the challenging assignment. He told Slewitzke, "Well, you know, you don't have the background, and you are going to have all of this work to do, and maybe you really don't want it." She responded, "Look, my Corps would never forgive me if I didn't accept the job." Slewitzke decided that if the commandant, "a very nice man," accepted her, she would serve as the class president. She recalled:

> So I went in to see the Commandant. . . . He made the decision to accept me. . . . I told him that I didn't know about a lot of command stuff. As you see, we didn't have the experience background as we weren't allowed to command. But I certainly had management background from my experiences and he said, "Don't worry about it. You are fine with me."[40]

Frazier and Slewitzke broke new ground for all women in the Army.

Captain Harriet H. Werley and later Lieutenant Colonel Ida Graham Price developed and then formalized the concept of career planning for Army Nurse Corps officers. Werley originated the system during her assignment in the Office of The Surgeon General's Career Guidance and Planning Office from 1951 to 1955.[41] Career planners typically operated in collaboration with the assignment officers in what then was referred to as the Army Nurse Corps Branch. Later in 1972, this umbrella agency became the Career Activities Office (CAO) with two components: (1) an Assignment Branch and (2) a Career Planning Branch. A senior Army nurse served as chief of the Army Nurse Corps branch and oversaw and coordinated all the branch's activities.[42] The intent of career planning was to identify and prepare the best-qualified person for the job at hand and to develop future Corps leaders. The process in part involved setting up a logical progression or a master plan for officers to follow throughout their careers. The blueprint was not rigid or firmly set but had flexibility based on individual differences and other contingencies. The individual Army Nurse Corps officer and the career planning officer ideally worked together to develop the blueprint, considering personal preferences, individual abilities, past assignments, and educational background. In short, career planning officers identified those Army nurses who demonstrated promise and nurtured their potential by carefully advising on assignments and encouraging these individuals in educational pursuits.[43] The career planners then made recommendations to the assignment officers for certain individuals who might best fill specific positions.

Around this time, other non-Army nurse AMEDD officers regularly asked why

Doris S. Frazier, right, was the first Army nurse to attend the Command and General Staff College in Fort Leavenworth, Kansas, in residence in 1967. Several years later, Frazier was the first Army Nurse Corps officer to graduate from the Army War College at Carlisle Barracks, PA. Here Frazier is pictured sometime after she was promoted to colonel, standing next to, left to right, General Lillian Dunlap, chief of the Army Nurse Corps and Colonel Edith J. Bonnet, the assistant chief of the Corps.
Photo courtesy of Colonel Doris Frazier and Colonel Barbara Davis, Evans, GA.

Major Ida Graham Price, portrayed here in 1958, followed Major Harriet H. Werley in the Office of The Surgeon General's Career Guidance and Planning Office. She helped to refine the Army Nurse Corps career planning process.
Photo courtesy of Army Nurse Corps Archives, Office of Medical History, Falls Church, VA.

Army nurses—who were in such short supply—should be assigned as staff to monitor career planning and assignments in CAO or, as it was formerly known, the Army Nurse Corps Branch. They recommended that Medical Service Corps officers fill these positions instead. However, most Army Nurse Corps officers wanted their assignments and careers guided by another Army nurse, one who could fully appreciate their unique wants and needs. When Dunlap served as chief of the Army Nurse Corps in the 1970s, she responded to these unsolicited and unwelcome proposals by asking, ". . . could someone other than a nurse do that [job]? Would that person have the understanding, the appreciation of that assignment?" Dunlap's answer to these questions was "I don't think so."[44] Over the years, virtually all have agreed that the best person to guide careers and make assignments for Army Nurse Corps officers also needed to be an Army nurse.

For a number of years, CAO was located in the Forrestal Building on Independence Avenue in southwest Washington, D.C. However, in the spring of 1978, CAO had to seek other accommodations when the newly formed Department of Energy took over the Forrestal office space. CAO subsequently moved to Buzzard's Point in southeast Washington, D.C. As sometimes happens during a move, two boxes of documents were lost in the hasty relocation. Those missing boxes became an Army Nurse Corps legend. A personnel management officer, Major Nickey McCasland, recalled that "from then on whenever anything couldn't be found, we were able to say that whatever it was, . . . [it] probably [was] in one of the two boxes that were lost in the move."[45] CAO faced another metamorphosis in 1985. At that time, its contingent of assignment officers began operating under the jurisdiction of the Military Personnel Center. Professional development officers became part of a field operating agency "incorporating the Education and Training Division of [Army Medical Department Personnel Support Agency] AMEDDPERSA."[46]

In that same timeframe, Congress enacted the Defense Officer Personnel Management Act (DOPMA) that generated a paradigm shift and resulted in considerable repercussions in the Army Nurse Corps. DOPMA was a career management tool that applied to all the military services.[47] Its concepts originated in the 1970s, and the law had a wide range of implications for Army Nurse Corps officers for decades. DOPMA legislation was first introduced into Congress in 1974, signed into law in 1980, and became effective in September 1981.[48] Its goals were threefold: (1) to create a management system common to all services; (2) to make available better career opportunities for the individual servicemember; and (3) to improve the services' flexibility of management.[49] Thus, DOPMA sought to "improve the Army's management of officers" and accordingly to "retain more highly educated and technically trained officers." DOPMA set the stage for a single promotion system that was applicable Army-wide. Before DOPMA, an officer initially received a temporary promotion to the next higher grade, and later on a permanent basis to that same grade.[50] With DOPMA, all officers were placed on only one "Active Duty List" for single promotions. DOPMA also set promotion guidelines. It directed that promotion boards select 80 percent of all captains who had served the requisite time in grade to be promoted to major. It mandated that 70 percent of all eligible majors be selected for promotion to lieutenant colonel and 50 percent of eligible lieutenant colonels be promoted to colonel.[51] Furthermore, DOPMA decreed that all officers were to be integrated into the Regular Army at the 11-year mark in service, ideally at the field grade level. DOPMA also mandated that all officers had to serve for three years in grade to be eligible for retirement in that grade. Moreover, the upper limit for involuntary separation (severance) pay increased from a lump sum of $15,000 to $30,000. DOPMA also set "uniform, general constructive credit rules for prior service, experience and education.[52]

DOPMA was based on the premise that all officers were due course officers, that is, all entered the Army as second lieutenants and their careers progressed in line with specified DOPMA guidelines.[53] This was not the case with many Army Nurse Corps officers. Before DOPMA, the Corps recruited and welcomed professional nurses with various and advanced "levels of experience, graduate education and specialty training" to maintain high patient care standards. The Army awarded these nurses, as well as Medical Corps, Dental Corps, Medical Service Corps scientists, and Judge Advocate General officers, all with advanced education or experience, constructive credit (increased rank) upon entering the Army. As a consequence, many joined the Army as captains or majors with several years in grade for promotion and pay purposes. DOPMA's career template frequently did not fit or adequately support the career progression of these non-due course Army nurses. Because the grade structure of the Army Nurse Corps did not allow direct commission officers "a reasonable career progression" for promotion to lieutenant colonel and colonel, these talented officers suffered, became disillusioned, and resigned their commissions.[54] DOPMA also imposed an ironclad year group strength management system that forced the Army Nurse Corps "to refuse voluntary indefinite (VI) status to highly qualified officers" who were on active duty for three to four years. At the same time, the Corps was "unable to get enough second lieutenants to replace them numerically, much less qualifications-wise." Such predicaments were the unintended outcomes of DOPMA, which imposed "a rigid, arbitrary grade structure designed for West Point graduates" on the entire Army officer corps.[55] In the 1980s the AMEDD initiated a major structure study to rectify these inequitable situations.[56] However, in the interim, a personnel management nightmare existed. The prevailing personnel system essentially rejected highly qualified officers.

Another DOPMA problem involved non-due course Army Nurse Corps officers who entered service as majors and were quickly promoted to lieutenant colonel and, when first eligible, to colonel. Thus, these officers serving as colonels had significantly less time in service than the due course officers, and many stayed in the service for 20 years (retirement). With their high rank, they monopolized senior positions and created a logjam in the upper echelons of the grade structure, slowing the rate of promotions for upcoming officers who were as well qualified and had longer active duty tenures.

An illustration of the consequences of the slow-moving promotion lists appeared in 1984 when those selected for promotion to colonel had to wait two years or longer for their actual promotion. LTC (P), Gus N. Alexander and Fredrick Phelps were each in key positions as chief nurse, Army Recruiting Command, and chief nurse, Training and Doctrine Command, respectively. Their relatively low rank put them at a disadvantage in conducting routine duties, particularly coordination with high-ranking officers at battalion and brigade levels and with the Reserve Officers' Training Corps Professors of Military Science. To circumvent the grade inequities and to facilitate professional interactions, the chief of the Army Nurse Corps requested approval for both of these Major Army Command chief nurses to be frocked and allowed to pin on the insignia of colonel.[57] Although the Department of Army approved both of these requests, only Alexander was frocked. The Training and Doctrine Command commanding general "did not believe in frocking" and the Training and Doctrine Command surgeon did not support the action. Consequently, Phelps did not pin on his eagles until his promotion sequence number moved to the top of the list.[58] Less than a decade later, these rank structure difficulties were partially rectified by several measures, such as the AMEDD Officer Structure Study and the controversial and draconian Selective Early Retirement Board, which undertook to force officers in the upper ranks to retire. As will be discussed later in this book, the Selective Early Retirement Board ultimately proved effective in its organizational aims but deleterious on a personal level.

A number of Army Nurse Corps leaders foresaw the serious difficulties that would ensue for the Army Nurse Corps with the implementation of DOPMA. Dunlap wrote:

> ... I didn't function under DOPMA, but as it was presented in briefings, we were led to believe that DOPMA was the savior coming. It was going to cure all of our ills. But some of us anticipated some problems for the Army Nurse Corps promotion-wise. Thank goodness, I wasn't there.[59]

# Notes

1. Department of the Army, AR 601-100, paragraph 2-61, October 1974. Department of the Army, DA Circular 601-68, "Army Nurse Corps Active Duty Program Fiscal Year 1977 through 15 January 1978," 13 October 1977, Army Nurse Corps Collection (ANCC), Office of Medical History (OMH).

2. Office of the Surgeon General, U.S. Army, Technical Liaison Office, "ANC Requirements Changed," News Release, 2 June 1971; and U.S. Department of the Army, "Army Nurse Corps and Army Medical Specialist Corps Active Duty Program, FY 1977," DA Circular 601-68, 1 October 1976 (both in ANCC, OMH). "Army Nurse Corps Raises Commissions for Applicants with Bachelor's Degrees," *HSC Mercury* 1 (18 February 1974): 8.

3. Billie Barcus "Report of Ad Hoc Committee Meeting on Educational Preparation of ANC," Memorandum for Record, 1 June 1973; Edith M. Nuttall, "DOD Study on Nursing Education," Memorandum for Record, 15 September 1975 (both in ANCC, OMH).

4. Edith M. Nuttall, "DOD Study on Nursing Education," Memorandum for Record, 15 September 1975, ANCC, OMH.

5. George E. Schafer, "Budget Constraints Occupy Air Force," *U.S. Medicine* 13 (15 January 1977): 38.

6. George E. Schafer, "Austerity Marks Air Force's Year," *U.S. Medicine* 14 (15 January 1978): 54.

7. George E. Schafer, "Budget Constraints Occupy Air Force," *U.S. Medicine* 13 (15 January 1977): 38.

8. "Plan Would Lower Nurse Education Standards," *Army Times* (10 July 1989): n.p., Newspaper Clipping; and Clara L. Adams-Ender, Interview by Virginia Ruth Cheney, 90, 1992, Project 92-3, U.S. Army Military History Institute, Senior Officer Oral History Program (both in ANCC, OMH). Mary C. Smolenski, Donald G. Smith, and James S. Nanney, *A Fit, Fighting Force, The Air Force Nursing Services* Chronology (Washington, DC: Office of the Air Force Surgeon General, 2005), 39.

9. In 1970, 48 percent of Navy nurses had a baccalaureate degree. Susan H. Godson, *Serving Proudly: A History of Women in the U.S. Navy* (Annapolis: Naval Institute Press, 2001), 240.

10. Edith M. Nuttall, "DOD Study on Nursing Education," Memorandum for Record, 15 September 1975, ANCC, OMH. Mary C. Smolenski, Donald G. Smith, and James S.

Nanney, *A Fit, Fighting Force, The Air Force Nursing Services Chronology* (Washington, DC: Office of the Air Force Surgeon General, 2005), 37.

11. Edith M. Nuttall, "DOD Study on Nursing Education," Memorandum for Record, 15 September 1975, ANCC, OMH.

12. Lillian Dunlap, *33 Years of Army Nursing* (Washington, DC: U.S. Army Nurse Corps, 2001), 229–38. Mary E. Viehdorfer Frank and Robert V. Piemonte, "The Army Nurse Corps: A Decade of Change," *American Journal of Nursing* 85 (September 1985): 986.

13. Responses to Lewis Letter titled "Best Nurses," Letters to the Editor by Connie L. Slewitzke, Julie M. Johnson, Charly L. Hough, and Catherine M. Olinik, *Army Times* (18 August 1986): 24.

14. Lillian Dunlap, *33 Years of Army Nursing* (Washington, DC: U.S. Army Nurse Corps, 2001), 230–34.

15. American Nurses Association, "Education for Nursing," American Journal of Nursing 65 (December 1965): 106–11. Rosemary Donley and Mary Jean Flaherty, "Revisiting the American Nurses Association's First Position on Education for Nurses," *Online Journal of Issues in Nursing* 7 (31 May 2002): 1–17. http://www.nursingworld.org/ojin/topic18/tpc18_1.htm (accessed 22 June 2005).

16. Lillian Dunlap, *33 Years of Army Nursing* (Washington, DC: U.S. Army Nurse Corps, 2001), 236.

17. National League for Nursing, "Characteristics of Baccalaureate Education in Nursing," Code Number 15-1319, 1968, attachment to Typewritten Letter, Dorothy McMullan to Lillian Dunlap, 24 November 1974, ANCC, OMH.

18. Madelyn N. Parks, "Information for All ANC Officers," Memorandum 3-78, 1, 5 July 1978, ANCC, OMH.

19. Clare Thomas "Army to Weigh HSC Soldiers," *HSC Mercury* 4 (January 1977): 1, 8. Ann M. Ritchie Hartwick, *The Army Medical Specialist Corps, The 45th Anniversary* (Washington, DC: Center of Military History, United States Army, 1993), 40.

20. Louise C. Rosasco, "Progress Report: The Army Nurse Corps and Army Nursing," 16 June 1971, with Inclosure, "Criteria for Appointment as ANC Officer in the US Army Reserve and Regular Army," 3, ANCC, OMH.

21. Another widely read, scathing article appeared in 1985 chronicling military medicine's "shocking malpractice, flagrant cover-ups and even corruption." It reported on the "slum conditions" in military hospitals. This depiction had little to say about military nurses except to characterize the shortage of nurses as "much worse" than that of physicians. Donald Robinson, "The Mess in Military Medicine," *Reader's Digest* 126 (February 1985): 49–53.

22. Neil Roland, "Army Nurses Rated Tops by Patients They Serve," *Army Times* (6 December 1982): 3, 10, 30, 39, 66.

23. For instance, California required 30 contact hours of continuing education within a two-year period to renew a professional nurse license.

24. Rosemary T. McCarthy, "ANC-CHE Update," Inclosure 3, in Madelyn N. Parks, "Memorandum 1-78, Information for All ANC Officers," 10 January 1978; and Marcie Lee Thomas, "CE Fact Sheet," Clipping from *California Nurse*, May 1978, Inclosure 3, in Madelyn N. Parks, "Memorandum 4-78, Information for All ANC Officers," 18 October 1978 (both in ANCC, OMH). By the summer of 1978, 10 states required continuing education for relicensure. They were California, Colorado, Florida, Iowa, Kansas, Kentucky, Massachusetts, Minnesota, New Mexico, and South Dakota. "ANC-CHEP Update," Inclosure 15, in Madelyn N. Parks, "Memorandum 4-78, Information for All ANC Officers," 18

October 1978, ANCC, OMH.

25. One continuing education unit equaled 10 contact hours.

26. Mary E. Viehdorfer Frank and Robert V. Piemonte, "The Army Nurse Corps since Vietnam, 1974–1984," Unpublished Manuscript, 4, n.d.; and "Nursing Continuing Education Update," October 1979, Inclosure 3, in Madelyn N. Parks, "Memorandum 4-79, Information for All ANC Officers," 16 November 1979 (both in ANCC, OMH).

27. Rosemary T. McCarthy, "ANC-CHE Update," 19 October 1978, Inclosure 6, in Madelyn N. Parks, "Memorandum 1-79, Information for All ANC Officers," 29 January 1979, ANCC, OMH.

28. Major Moore, "History of Professional Postgraduate Short Courses," Information Paper, 20 December 1996; Edith M. Nuttall, "Army Nurse Corps Short Courses Involving TDY," Disposition Form, 31 January 1973; and Katherine F. Galloway, "To Discuss Purpose and Educational Objectives for the Nurse Methods Analyst Short Course, 10–14 Sep 73," Disposition Form (all in ANCC, OMH).

29. Army Regulations first validated the unique role of "nursing instructor" in 1954 in AR 40-20. By 1969, the position title became "educational coordinator." Rosemary T. McCarthy, "Parallels and Paradoxes: Differentiated Nursing Practice," in *Differentiating Nursing Practice into the Twenty-first Century*, ed. I.E. Goertzen (Kansas City, MO: American Nurses Association, American Academy of Nursing, 1991), 361–81.

30. Academy of Health Sciences, U.S. Army, "Nursing in Army Hospitals," Study Guide 310, 29, November 1974; Connie L. Slewitzke, "Memorandum from the Chief, US Army Nurse Corps," 4, July 1986 (both in ANCC, OMH).

31. "Army Nurse Corps Goals, Requirements, and Programs," 3, Typewritten Document (TD), n.d., Box 9, Army Nurse Corps Papers, Archives, U.S. Army Military History Institute, Carlisle Barracks, PA.

32. "Nursing Forecast, Education & Training Forecast," TD intended to develop the position using a Delphi methodology, 5, July 1973, ANCC, OMH. This document predicted with great accuracy the technological changes and quality measures that would ensue in the 1980s. It prophesized that "nurses . . . would occupy line positions as a matter of course." It foretold the advent of unit dose medications and predicted that "sophisticated electronic sensors and recording devices which monitor vital patient signs will be adopted on a larger scale and computers may even be used to interpret data. . . " 12.

33. Doris Frazier, "Major Items of Interest, FY 1973," Disposition Form, 6 January 1972, ANCC, OMH.

34. Headquarters, Department of the Army, "AR 40-6, Army Nurse Corps," 6, 26 October 1977, ANCC, OMH.

35. Edith Nuttall, "Presentation to First HSC's Chief Nurses' Conference, Gunter Hotel, San Antonio, Texas, 19 April 1974," Typewritten Text of Speech, 13, ANCC, OMH.

36. "Army Nurse Corps Goals, Requirements, and Programs," TD, 5, n.d., Box 9, Army Nurse Corps Papers, Archives, U.S. Army Military History Institute, Carlisle Barracks, PA.

37. "Army Nurse Corps Goals, Requirements, and Programs," TD, 5, n.d., Box 9, Army Nurse Corps Papers, Archives, U.S. Army Military History Institute, Carlisle Barracks, PA. Edith Nuttall, "Presentation to First HSC's Chief Nurses' Conference, Gunter Hotel, San Antonio, Texas, 19 April 1974," Typewritten Text of Speech, 13, ANCC, OMH.

38. Mary E. Viehdorfer Frank and Robert V. Piemonte, "The Army Nurse Corps: A Decade of Change," *American Journal of Nursing* 85 (September 1985): 986–87.

39. Madelyn N. Parks, "Information for All ANC Officers," Memorandum 3-78, Inclosure 7, 4, 5 July 1978, ANCC, OMH. Lillian Dunlap, "Military Education Selectees," *U.S.*

*Army Medical Department Newsletter* 3 (Summer 1972): 22; and Doris Frazier to Author, E-mail Correspondence, 21 January 2002 (both in ANCC, OMH). Carolyn M. Feller and Debora R. Cox, *Highlights in the History of the Army Nurse Corps, 100th Anniversary Edition* (Washington, DC: U.S. Army Center of Military History, 2000), 41, 46. Clara L. Adams-Ender and Amelia J. Carson, "Capabilities of Army Nurse Corps Officer Graduates of the United States Army War College," *Medical Bulletin of the US Army*, Europe 43 (September/October 1986): 27–29.

40. Connie L. Slewitzke, Interview by Beverly Greenlee, 167–69, 1988, ANCC, OMH.

41. Harriet H. Werley, "Shared Responsibilities for Career Planning for Army Nurse Corps Officers," *Military Surgeon* 115 (December 1954): 436–41.

42. Among those who served in the ANC Branch or in CAO in the 1960s and 1970s were Colonel Edith Nuttall and lieutenant colonels Cassandra Smith, Lillian Dunlap, Katherine Galloway, Edith Knox, and Rose Straley. Lillian Dunlap, *33 Years of Army Nursing* (Washington, DC: U.S. Army Nurse Corps, 2001), 243, 247. Lillian Dunlap, "Changes in ANC Branch," *U.S. Army Medical Department Newsletter* 3 (Winter 1972): 29; and Edith Nuttall, "Presentation to First HSC's Chief Nurses' Conference, Gunter Hotel, San Antonio, Texas, 19 April 1974," Typewritten Text for Speech, 4 (both in ANCC, OMH).

43. Harriet H. Werley, "Harriet H. Werley," in *Making Choices, Taking Chances, Nurse Leaders Tell Their Stories*, ed. Thelma M. Schorr and Anne Zimmerman (St. Louis, MO: Mosby, 1988), 366. Lillian Dunlap, 33 Years of Army Nursing (Washington, DC: U.S. Army Nurse Corps, 2001), 242–43.

44. Lillian Dunlap, *33 Years of Army Nursing* (Washington, DC: U.S. Army Nurse Corps, 2001), 242–45, 248.

45. Nickey McCasland to Author, E-mail Correspondence, 16 July 2002, ANCC, OMH.

46. Connie L. Slewitzke, "Memorandum from the Chief US Army Nurse Corps," 1, December 1985, ANCC, OMH. "AMEDD Officers Join Army System," *HSC Mercury* 13 (January 1986): 12.

47. Senator Sam Nunn, Democrat of Georgia and chair of the Senate Armed Forces Committee, introduced S. 1918, the DOPMA bill, whose official title was "An original bill to amend title 10, United States Code, to revise and make uniform the provisions of law relating to appointment, promotion, separation, and retirement of regular commissioned officers of the Army, Navy, Air Force, and Marine Corps, to establish the grade of commodore admiral in the Navy, to equalize the treatment of male and female commissioned officers, and for other purposes." P.L. 96-513.

48. Senator Sam Nunn held up DOPMA for six years, objecting to its up-or-out promotion policy, which the committee felt forced out of the service too many knowledgeable officers who failed to be promoted. The committee also thought that DOPMA allowed for too many middle- and upper-range officers. The legislators and Department of Defense finally compromised, agreeing to more separation pay for departing officers and fewer officers than DoD preferred. The Senate finally passed DOPMA in 1980. http://www.defense-and-society.org/vandergriff/rha/sld040.htm (accessed 22 June 2005).

49. "Defense Officer Personnel Management Act," Information Paper, 24 November 1980; Hazel W. Johnson, "Information for all ANC Officers," Typewritten Memorandum, 9 February 1981 (both in ANCC, OMH).

50. The first, temporary promotion was referred to as an AUS (Army of the United States) promotion. It potentially could be reversed. When an AUS promotion occurred, the insignia of rank was pinned on and pay for the new rank was awarded. Several years later, the permanent promotion in the Regular Army (RA) or USAR took effect. Nickey McCa-

sland to Author, E-mail Correspondence, 30 July 2002, ANCC, OMH. Karl E. Cocke and others, *Department of the Army Historical Summary, Fiscal Year 1981* (Washington, DC: Center of Military History, United States Army, 1988), 92.

51. "Officer Personnel Management," Typewritten Document, 4, n.d.; and Lieutenant Colonel Harrington, "Defense Officer Personnel Management Act (DOPMA)," Information Paper, 1, 15 May 1981 (both in ANCC, OMH). Richard V.N. Ginn, *The History of the U.S. Army Medical Service Corps* (Washington, DC: Office of the Surgeon General and Center of Military History, United States Army 1997), 382–83.

52. "DOPMA Brings Major Changes," *HSC Mercury* 8 (February 1981): 3.

53. DOPMA excluded Medical and Dental Corps officers from grade limitations in all grades up to O-6 because "of the unique problems of obtaining and retaining physicians and dentists." Thus, these branches did not experience the difficulties that the Army Nurse Corps faced. DOPMA allowed physicians and dentists to be eligible for "accelerated promotion as a retention incentive." "Officer Personnel Management," TD, 2–4, n.d.; "Defense Officer Personnel Management Report on the Committee on Armed Services, to Accompany S. 1918," TD, 4, 13 November 1980; and Lieutenant Colonel Harrington, "Defense Officer Personnel Management Act (DOPMA)," Information Paper, 1, 15 May 1981 (all in ANCC, OMH).

54. Connie L. Slewitzke, "Nurse Corps Can Be Proud," *Army Times* (3 July 1989): n.p., Newspaper Clipping, ANCC, OMH.

55. Nickey McCasland to Author, E-mail Correspondence, 30 July 2002, ANCC, OMH.

56. Connie L. Slewitzke, "Nurse Corps Can Be Proud," *Army Times* (3 July 1989): n.p., Newspaper Clipping, ANCC, OMH.

57. Frocking was an Army-wide practice that required prior approval from DA level. It involved the wearing of rank insignia of a higher grade on the uniform after a promotion board had selected an officer for promotion to that grade but before that officer had actually been promoted. Frocked officers did not receive the pay and benefits of the higher grade until the actual promotion took place. Edward J. Juycke to Deputy Chief of Staff for Personnel, DA, "Frocking for Army Nurse Corps (ANC) Officers," Action Memorandum, 22 August 1984; Bobby B. Porter to The Acting Surgeon General, "Frocking for Army Nurse Corps (ANC) Officers," Memorandum, 17 September 1984 (both in ANCC, OMH).

58. Fredrick Phelps to Author, E-mail Correspondence, 27 March 2003, ANCC, OMH.

59. Lillian Dunlap, *33 Years of Army Nursing* (Washington, DC: U.S. Army Nurse Corps, 2001), 311.

## Chapter Four
# Readiness Challenges

After the catastrophic circumstances of the Vietnam War, the Army as a whole suffered from "low morale, popular distaste for military service, low self-esteem, and a tarnished public image." Additionally, severe budget and personnel reductions left the organization a hollow Army—that is, an institution with an intact shell but a significantly diminished core that was seriously deficient in facilities, funding, manpower, and materiel.[1] The Army, at low ebb, was compelled to recreate itself. A critical period of innovation, modernization, and reform materialized. Important components of the Army's renaissance were the upgrading of the Table of Organization and Equipment (TO&E) units and field equipment and the improving of individual and unit readiness, the ability to respond quickly and competently to achieve the mission.[2]

A major factor in field nursing and the state of readiness was the evolution of field units, including their staffing, physical facilities, and configurations. In 1975, the Army Medical Department (AMEDD) began a large-scale conversion of the Evacuation Hospitals (EVACs) and Mobile Army Surgical Hospitals (MASHs) from tentage into Medical Unit, Self-contained, Transportable (MUST) facilities and equipment.[3] The MUST concept entailed "inflatable shelters, together with a power package [to support] heat, light, air-conditioning, hot and cold water, and other utility requirements." The surgeon general directed that EVACs and MASHs be reconfigured into the modern Combat Support Hospitals (CSHs). A further change in doctrine dictated that divisions would be supported in future combat operations by a matrix of two CSHs that were 200-bed MUSTs and one EVAC. Previously, division medical assets included one surgical and two EVACs.[4] The doctrine changed once again in 1982 when the configuration of combat divisional support evolved into one MASH, one CSH, and one EVAC. This change raised combat division allocation from 800 to 1,060 beds and increased operating tables from 14 to 20. The AMEDD then terminated the MUST program and began preparations to develop the Deployable Medical System, which would enhance

AMEDD's capability "to provide the soldier with timely, state-of-the-art medical and surgical care in a combat environment."[5]

In the mid-1970s, the commander of Forces Command ordered all TO&E units to achieve and maintain a level of operational readiness so they might clearly meet their mission. He also directed that unit training be the highest priority. Before that, Army policy had restricted the full-time assignment of professional caregivers to Modified Table of Organization and Equipment (MTO&E) units, the deployable wartime hospital units. This limitation resulted from the extreme staff shortages in the Table of Distribution and Allowances (TDA) hospitals, referred to as the fixed facilities or the Army medical centers and Army Medical Department Activities (MEDDACs). Thus, stringent ceilings were set for Army Nurse Corps participation in MTO&E units, and the Corps assigned only a minimal number of such officers to ensure that training needs were met and operational readiness was maintained. The Army Nurse Corps assigned only six Army nurses full-time to the 18 existing MTO&E units. They served as staff officers and advised on training matters related to nursing and the other allied health fields.[6]

After the new policy mandating increased readiness levels went to the field, the Army Nurse Corps selected officers from its meager supply and placed them in all the MTO&E hospitals, by then 17 in number.[7] These nurses were responsible for improving readiness and assisting with a transition to CSH configuration and MUST equipment. They implemented the required changes in "SOPs, procedures, ward layouts, sterile loads, packing and loading plans, plus a total training program for all patient care personnel."[8] However, certain aspects of the utilization of Army nurses in MTO&E units remained problematic.

Generally speaking, the Army Nurse Corps considered the manner in which Medical Service Corps commanders used Army nurses in MTO&E units to be "very poor" in 1973. The commanders had the latitude to use their personnel as they saw fit, and many decided to send their Army Nurse Corps officers to the local military treatment facility, usually the nearby MEDDAC, because there was "nothing for a nurse to do in the unit." Male nurses assigned to MTO&E units frequently were given administrative, nonnursing responsibilities such as training officer or as supply officer, which required signing and being responsible for the entire unit's training or equipment. This allowed them little if any time to focus on nursing issues. Colonel Madelyn Parks, the Continental Army Command chief nurse, observed that the male nurses seemed to fall into this trap more readily, wanting "to be one of the fellows." Rarely did any "female ANC's find themselves in this situation." Support and consultation for these Army Nurse Corps officers— usually captains—from the local TDA or MEDDAC chief nurse often was not forthcoming. A few TDA chief nurses resented the MTO&E nurses, viewing their assignments as a foolish waste of personnel when nursing resources in the TDA hospital were so scarce. Others backed the MTO&E nurse "to the hilt" and consistently went "to bat for them when they [had] a problem." At times, however, the TDA chief nurse was hamstrung by insufficient command support and a lack of understanding. Many of the MEDDAC commanders were consumed by the daily demands of their TDA hospital and had neither the time nor interest to devote to the MTO&E unit assigned to them and usually co-located on their post.

To mitigate some of these difficulties, Parks recommended that all newly assigned MTO&E chief nurses undergo an orientation with an exemplary unit, such as the 41st CSH at Fort Sam Houston, with an outstanding chief nurse such as the 41st's Captain Grace Squires. She also suggested that all MTO&E nurses meet annually to exchange ideas, set standards, and acquire current information. Moreover, Parks asserted that Health Services Command should direct MEDDAC commanders to exercise active involvement in the ongoing activities of their MTO&E unit. Parks added some comments that reflected the state of MTO&E unit readiness in 1973:

> "The state of the readiness of the medical MTO[&]E units is terrible now. We know this. The ANC [Army Nurse Corps] effort has been tremendous in getting nurses in all of these units to try to upgrade their patient care capability. They can't do it alone."[9]

In another move to improve readiness, the Army developed guidelines for weapons training for female soldiers and distributed them to the field. In January 1976, Headquarters, Department of the Army established a policy that all female officers participate in individual weapons training on the same level as their male complement. The rationale was that all personnel, including female soldiers, should be capable of defending "themselves and their unit regardless of their location on the battlefield."[10] The existing unwillingness on the part of the rank and file of the Army to allow women to handle firearms was a reluctance rooted in tradition. In the past, the Army rarely authorized women or nurses to participate in weapons training or to carry or discharge arms even for their own personal protection.

By the mid-1990s, the bearing of arms such as the 9-mm pistol or the M16 rifle with ammunition while on deployments became mandatory for all Army nurses, regardless of gender. At a minimum, Army Nurse Corps officers attended weapons familiarization sessions annually but most were fully qualified on their weapon. When traveling off the hospital compound while deployed, the Army nurse carried the weapon that—upon return to the hospital—was secured in a weapons room or on a weapons rack on the hospital unit. Sometimes pepper spray also was issued as a less lethal option for self-defense. Lieutenant Colonel Charlotte Scott recalled that by the late 1990s, Army nurses carried a weapon at all times while on deployed status, on duty in hospital wards, at the mess hall, and even on trips to showers and latrines. When traveling, the weapons were loaded but kept on "safe." Scott added that a "clearing barrel" filled with sand sat at every hospital entrance. Both hospital personnel and visitors were "required to remove ammo, perform a safety check, and 'dry' fire their weapon . . . prior to entry into the hospital." This safety check helped to prevent an unintended weapon discharge within the hospital perimeter.[11]

Over the period of two decades, regulations and policy transitioned from almost totally banning weapons for Army nurses to fully mandating their use in the theater of combat. This transition mirrored the slightly slower assimilation of Army Nurse Corps officers from a segregated, separate status within the Army into nearly full integration as Army commissioned officers.

The more stringent adherence to weight control and physical fitness standards was an additional strategy used by the Army to enhance individual soldier readiness to go to war. The introduction of the new expedients affected Army nurses as it did virtually all members of the officer corps and the enlisted ranks. Headquarters, Department of the Army distributed the revised Army Regulation 600-9, "The Army Weight Control Program," to the field late in 1976. Its intent was to foster weight control awareness and thus improve physical fitness and individual readiness. The newly established weight standards contained within the regulation were much more stringent than previous parameters. The earlier guidelines based on civilian life insurance height and weight tables dated back to 1945.

The new program defined in the regulation also recommended physical fitness requirements for every soldier and directed commanders to conduct year-round fitness programs. Eventually, all soldiers younger than age 40 were to be weighed and tested annually according to the new physical fitness standards. The Health Services Command commander cautioned that "soldiers who consistently fail to comply may well earn poor ratings on efficiency reports, bars to re-enlistment and finally involuntary separations. In short, they must measure up."[12]

Before 1976, the Army as a whole virtually ignored the dictates of Army Regulation 600-9. However, over time, commanders paid increasing attention to this regulation. Army Nurse Corps officers who—for one reason or another—could not or would not meet the weight standards paid a penalty in the long run. They were not promoted, not selected to attend service or civilian schools, passed over for the choice assignments, and ultimately many were eliminated from the service. Their commanders and peers harassed many Army Nurse Corps officers about their inability to comply. Ironically, a significant number of these individuals who did not meet the fitness requirements were among the brightest, most diligent, and dedicated officers on the Army Nurse Corps rolls. Their elimination unquestionably represented a significant loss for the Army. Nonetheless, there was no question that soldiers had to be physically fit to survive in modern combat and contribute meaningfully to the mission. Colonel Carol Reineck shared her thoughts about the contradictions in the system:

"... certainly the military force needs to be strong and healthy and capable. But there is also ... a benefit from wisdom in whatever body size it comes in. That's what I saw lost was the wisdom, the experience, and the commitment. How could we have a value system that would actually place those qualities as less valuable than the stature of the individual physically. I couldn't imagine a system like that, but I accepted it, and figured that there may be something that I didn't know that drove it."[13]

The weight control program was a bitter pill to swallow, but an essential undertaking for the Army in its quest for improved fitness and readiness.

Although the weight and fitness standards were consistent across the width and breadth of the Army, one noteworthy discrepancy did exist between the AMEDD and the Army line. For instance, readiness to deploy carried radically different implications for the tactical units, the combat arms, and the AMEDD. In situations of rapid mobilization, the AMEDD and the Army Nurse Corps were at a distinct disadvantage. When committed to a deployment, the line units shifted into a higher gear, moving from training to operational status. Skeleton units performed garrison duties while the main force deployed. The AMEDD, conversely, had to support—simultaneously and fully—both garrison and field responsibilities because the population at the home base who needed health care simply did not disappear when units went to war. Thus, in times of mobilization, Army Nurse Corps officers were required to be in two places simultaneously, which affected the Army Nurse Corps response to such emergencies. Factors affecting this response included the available numbers of active duty, reserve, and National Guard Army Nurse Corps officers; the ability to retain officers on active duty and to activate the reserve component; the authority to draft nurses; the effectiveness of existing recruitment and training programs; and public opinion of the military by the profession of nursing at large.[14] To improve its state of readiness, the Army Nurse Corps recognized that it had to study and deal with these issues. It also had to increase its participation in field exercises.

In September 1978, 20 Army nurses participated in the Return of Forces to Germany exercises.[15] Their participation signified a recognition of the imperative for Army Nurse Corps involvement in such exercises to enhance overall readiness and improve deployment proficiency. Likewise, in January 1979, three Forces Command and 11 Health Services Command Army nurses deployed to this large-scale winter training exercise. That same year, Lieutenant Colonel Betty Brice, the obstetrics/gynecology nursing consultant, deployed with the 1st Infantry Division to evaluate health care needs of the division's women.[16]

Brice's assignment was a public acknowledgment by the Army that female soldiers had unique health care issues. Female soldiers by then carried out combat support and combat service support responsibilities in unprecedented numbers. Furthermore, there was a greater percentage of women in the active military as a whole. In 1970, 41,479 women, or 1.3 percent, were serving in the total active duty military force of 3,066,294. By 1980, the number of women in all the U.S. armed forces totaled 71,418, or 3.5 percent of the entire force of 2,050,627.[17]

This revolution represented a major change for women, the Army, and the Army Nurse Corps. In the 1980s, women's opportunities grew and the Army devoted extensive time and effort to developing policies to cope with the influx of women and their new military roles. The Army Nurse Corps correspondingly faced challenges such as caring for the distinctive needs of female patients in the field setting. As a predominantly female organization, it also benefited from the greater presence of women in the military, which forced the Army to augment facilities for women, treat women in an equitable manner, enhance women's medical support, and improve uniforms and equipment.

Although the state of individual and unit readiness for mobilization was still unsatisfactory by 1979, it had improved during the 1970s. Junior and senior Army

Nurse Corps officers worked alike to get the Army where it needed to be. A large portion of the readiness picture was the part played by the Reserve and National Guard components.

The Ready Reserve was composed of three elements in the early 1970s. The U.S. Army Reserve (USAR) Army Nurse Corps officers could potentially belong to one of the three elements. The first element, the Troop Program Units (TPUs), consisted of various hospitals and medical detachments in locations across the United States. Army nurses in TPUs drilled for one weekend per month at military or civilian hospitals or at Army Reserve Centers with their unit. They also served two weeks of active duty for training or annual training per year with their unit at selected active military installations. The second element, the USAR School members, had to participate in class for one evening per week for about nine months each year. They might also attend a USAR School for two weeks annually. The third element, the Annual Training Control Group, could be assigned to a TPU with a possibility of two weeks of active duty for training.[18]

The USAR and the Army National Guard (ARNG) faced a number of challenges in the post–Vietnam era. Few nurses were interested in joining or maintaining their status in the reserves. In 1971, only 10 percent of Army Nurse Corps billets in reserve units were filled.[19] In the summer and fall of 1976, a mere 25 percent and then 35 percent of requirements, respectively, were filled. By spring of 1977, only 36 percent of Army Nurse Corps authorizations in the reserves were occupied. To fill vacancies, the Office of The Surgeon General used various strategies, including some that potentially degraded the quality of the reserve component while improving personnel numbers. Among these new policies was a relaxation of standards to make reserve service more attractive, which included eliminating certain military education standards viewed as mandatory for promotion, allowing and sometimes funding attendance at professional conferences in place of annual training, and permitting Army Nurse Corps reservists and guard personnel to remain in service up to age 64. To augment procurement efforts, new policies permitted and even encouraged certain reserve units to recruit above and beyond their authorizations whenever possible to compensate for under-strength units, to use "proven marketing techniques" such as widespread advertising in a variety of media, and to accept registered nurses regardless of their educational level.[20] All of these strategies slightly improved the strength of the USAR and ARNG. Nonetheless, these components remained seriously shorthanded, and the USAR and ARNG situation would worsen before it improved significantly.

In early 1976, the Army Nurse Corps reserve component picture suddenly became more challenging and complex. The USAR increased authorizations in TPUs from about 1,900 Army Nurse Corps officers to more than 5,100 officers. This change happened because, as General Madelyn N. Parks wrote, the "readiness posture of the . . . Corps to meet its primary mission during a contingency is critical." By April 1977, there still were only 1,911 Army nurses in these units. Acknowledging that there were far too few Army nurses, the USAR leadership liberalized appointment criteria for Army Nurse Corps officers and thus gave a "broader and clearer interpretation" to the existing standards to boost numbers of reserve nurses.[21] At that time, the AMEDD Personnel Support Agency selected applicants with specific educational credentials or with a combination of educational background plus certain amounts of professional experience. For example, applicants with a bachelor's of science degree in nursing and six months' clinical practice within the preceding year or those with a hospital school diploma or an associate degree in nursing plus 24 months of experience were allowed to apply for a commission in the USAR.[22] Other criteria for a USAR or ARNG appointment included graduation from a nationally accredited nursing program and a license to practice as a registered nurse.[23] By January 1978 the Army Nurse Corps had procured more than 2,000 officers to fill the TPU vacancies.[24]

Nevertheless, attracting quality applicants into the USAR remained a challenge. USAR recruiters could not cast their nets "in the most obvious and fruitful sources—universities and schools of nursing." These sites represented the "preserves of the active Army recruiters," and there was neither coordination nor a "central organization" for USAR recruiting. Every activity was "strictly on its own."[25] Efforts to end this fragmentation and decentralization began in 1978 when the vice chief of staff of the Army directed that the responsibility for recruiting Active, Guard, Reserve officers would be combined outside of USAR command channels. The surgeon general subsequently ordered that all AMEDD recruiting occur under his aegis, with the exception of Army Nurse Corps recruiting. All Active, Guard, Reserve Army Nurse Corps officers' recruitment was vested—as it had been traditionally—in the U.S. Army Recruiting Command. This new system consolidating all AMEDD Active, Guard, Reserve recruitment was fully operational by July 1980.[26] With the dawning of the decade of the 1980s, the picture was somewhat brighter. By then, the Army Nurse Corps Reserve and National Guard reported filled authorizations at a much improved 59 percent level.[27]

Another important issue linked to the expanded reliance on the USAR and ARNG was the mandate to improve their state of readiness. In 1972, a private think tank, the Research Analysis Corporation, examined this question. Its final report noted that the intent of the USAR system was "to provide . . . units and individuals that can be made combat ready faster, on mobilization, than can newly organized units composed primarily of untrained personnel."[28] The investigators concluded that the USAR system "succeeded only marginally" in achieving this end "in the partial mobilizations" that occurred after World War II. They attributed the failures to flawed national policies that affected the USAR's and ARNG's recruitment and manpower practices; deficiencies in equipment, training locations, and amenities; and "improper organization of Reserve component units."[29]

By the end of the decade, the AMEDD had incorporated certain parts of the study's findings into its planning. The Office of The Surgeon General, like the rest of the Army, pre-positioned equipment overseas for use by mobilized reserve hospital units, in line with Army-wide policy. Additionally, it sought ways to improve supplies and equipment for deploying units. The Office of The Surgeon General also arranged for priority units designated for early deployment to be filled to

Before her retirement in 1981, Colonel Garnet I. Willow served as Mobilization Designee to the Chief of the Army Nurse Corps.
Photo courtesy of Army Nurse Corps Archives, Office of Medical History, Falls Church, VA.

the maximum or even to over strength manning levels.[30] Moreover, the AMEDD expanded opportunities for training both at the unit level and at the Academy of Health Sciences.[31]

Furthermore, the AMEDD adopted a comprehensive approach to promote overall readiness, inclusiveness, and cohesiveness. Lieutenant Colonel Garnet Willow of the 2290th U.S. Army Hospital in Rockville, Maryland, articulated the problematic, widely held opinion of reservists in regard to the Total Army Concept:

Under the "One Army" concept the USAR has been with us for years. Yet many reservists feel, not entirely without justification, that they have been left at home crouching in the ashes while their more favored stepsisters (and stepbrothers) of the active forces dance at the ball. We sympathize with their viewpoint.[32]

To bridge the gulf and unify the components, the AMEDD used several strategies. For example, the AMEDD expanded its Mobilization Designee program, included USAR and ARNG representation at the Department of the Army level whenever feasible, and reminded all involved in the process of policy making to keep in mind "What is the impact on the reserve components?"[33] Finally, the Army Nurse Corps assigned an officer full-time to U.S. Army Reserve Components Personnel and Administration in St. Louis, Missouri. In October 1977, the Corps selected Lieutenant Colonel Margie O. Burt, Army Nurse Corps-USAR, to assume responsibilities for the integration of the Officer Personnel Management System in the USAR. She also managed personnel activities such as Specialty Skill Identifier changes for Army Nurse Corps USAR officers.[34] After implementing these measures, the AMEDD was closer to achieving its goal of improved reliance on the USAR and ARNG components and was in better compliance with the expectations of the Total Army Concept.

The opening of the Reserve Officers' Training Corps (ROTC) program to future Army Nurse Corps officers was another milestone that produced several beneficial effects. One of those positive outcomes for Army nurses who participated in this program was greater readiness to function in the combat setting. Although the contemporary Army ROTC originated with the National Defense Act of 1916, women were first allowed to participate in the program in the 1972–1973 academic year.[35] Although it is true that not all potential Army Nurse Corps officers were women, nonetheless the elimination of the bar that limited ROTC participation to men opened the door for all baccalaureate nursing students—regardless of gender—to apply for this program.

At this time, ROTC became the preferred choice for future accessions to the Army Nurse Corps. As years passed, the Army customarily prized and valued—to an increasingly greater extent—professional military traits in Army Nurse Corps officers. Thus, the institution favored nurses who were ROTC graduates because this basic preparation developed leadership attributes and soldiers' skills. Additionally, it cultivated military proficiencies and promoted a professional demeanor and military bearing. The program also provided a comprehensive orientation to the Army as an organization, its goals, values, and mores. Finally, ROTC fostered a sense of esprit de corps among its members and other Army officers.[36]

New incentives also attracted collegiate nursing students to ROTC. Financial advantages included the potential to be awarded a two- or three-year scholarship with full payment of tuition, books, supplies, and specific fees along with a maximum $1,000 annual subsistence allowance. Cadets who did not qualify for the full scholarship benefit could still receive the $1,000 annual allowance in their junior and senior years of school. ROTC graduates also enjoyed expedited participation in advanced and/or specialized educational programs. Moreover, ROTC cadets could choose either the Cadet Troop Leadership Program or the six-week Alternative

Advanced Summer Camp specifically designed for nurse cadets during their summer. While attending these programs, cadets had transportation and room and board furnished; they also were paid about a $500 subsistence allowance.[37]

As early as 1978, ROTC chief nurses discussed forming an Army Nurse Corps summer camp for ROTC cadets to augment or replace the traditional Cadet Troop Leadership Program, an all-branch Army summer camp. Both advantages and disadvantages were implicit in the Army Nurse Corps branch-specific program. Although the nurse-specific option would undoubtedly hone the cadets' clinical skills and enhance their preparation for a future career as an Army nurse, it would not offer as much exposure to the rest of the Army world.[38] Texas Christian University cadet Teresa Parsons participated in the traditional ROTC summer camp and favored that option. She felt that it was "one of the few times that we . . . had the opportunity to . . . actually be a part of the main body of the military." Parsons recalled that while at the Cadet Troop Leadership Program, she "had to write operation orders, and place land mines, and conduct patrols, and all that lieutenants did in the rest of the Army all the time."[39] Outgoing chief of the Corps, Parks, opposed the Army Nurse Corps-specific plan on that very basis, reasoning that "the present structure" should not be disturbed, because it offered "some of our best Nurses with much better insights into the Army as a whole."[40] Nonetheless, by the summer of 1981, Brigadier General Hazel Johnson, the subsequent chief of the Army Nurse Corps, approved the concept and implementation of a special summer camp for ROTC nurse cadets.[41] A total of 24 cadets participated that first year at four sites, one in each ROTC region.[42] The overall objective of the camp was "to provide a realistic leadership experience in the clinical setting" and to furnish "firsthand knowledge of the duties, responsibilities and living conditions of the junior ANC [Army Nurse Corps] officer in the Army."[43] As prerequisites for attendance at the camp, cadets had to volunteer for the special camp, have completed three years of their nursing curriculum, and be eligible to graduate with a baccalaureate degree in nursing in the spring of 1982.[44] Cadet volunteers who attended the six-week summer program actually shadowed an Army Nurse Corps junior officer, who served as their preceptor. The students participated in other selected hands-on experiences and also spent some time in the field with a CSH.[45]

Each year the program evolved and improved. Based on 1981 camp participants' suggestions, ROTC leaders decided to incorporate common military proficiencies and skills into the summer 1982 camp program of instruction. Accordingly, exposure to subjects such as physical training; weapons qualification; nuclear, biological, and chemical protection; day and night land navigation skills; field first aid and sanitation; and individual tactical training was added to the experience in 1982.[46]

By the summer of 1983, the entire program had grown exponentially, testifying to the idea's success and value. A total of 121 cadets participated in the ROTC Nursing Advanced Camp (ROTCNAC). In addition, 61 more ROTC nursing cadets participated in Cadet Troop Leadership Training, the traditional Advanced Summer Camp that focused exclusively on military skills.

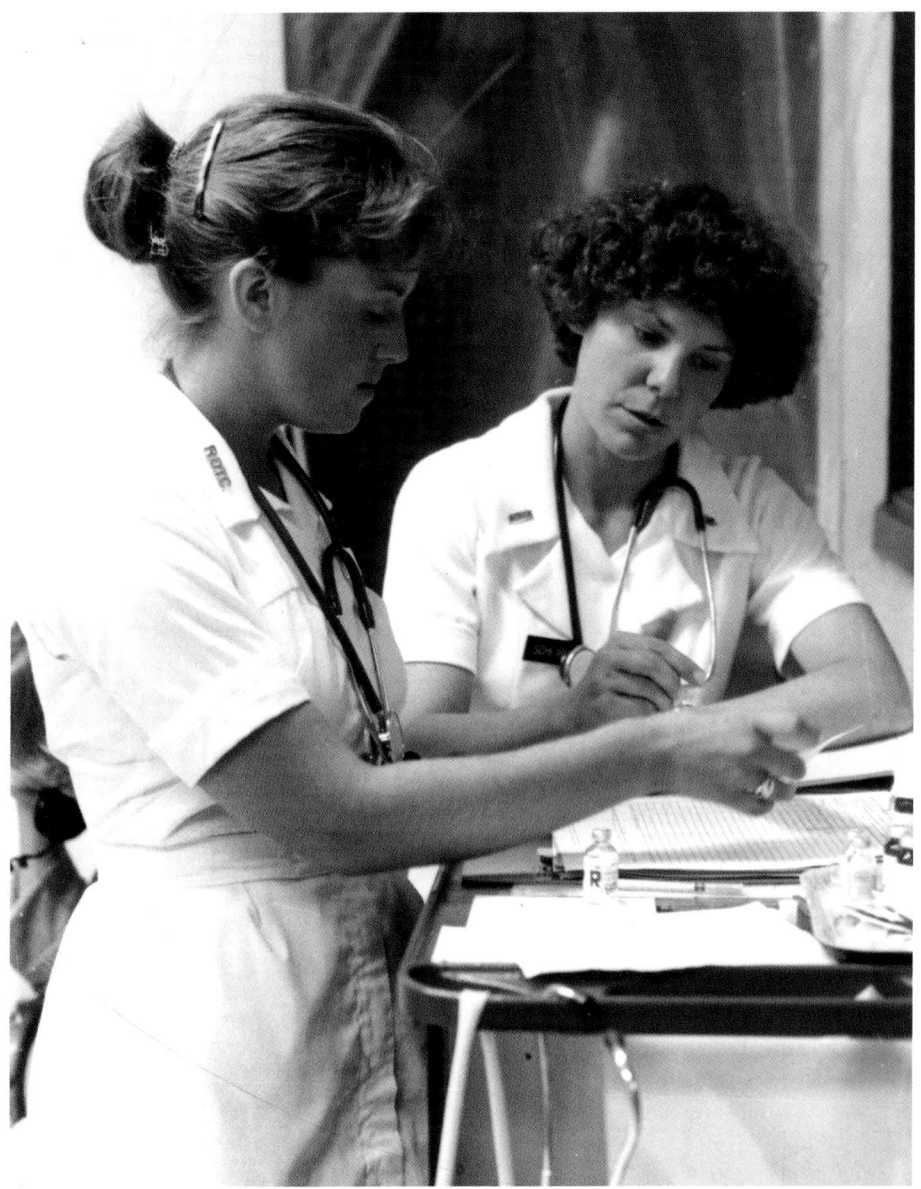

First Lieutenant Monica Scheibmeir of the U.S. Army Medical Department Activity, Fort Riley, Kansas, mentors ROTC Cadet Pam Olson from the University of Kansas, Kansas City, as she prepares a medication for a patient on 8 July 1987.
Photo courtesy of Army Nurse Corps Archives, Office of Medical History, Falls Church, VA.

In 1983, 82 deans of university schools of nursing visited the ROTCNAC sites.[47] In succeeding years, the deans' visits became an annual ritual. ROTC nurse leaders conceived and implemented the familiarization program to more fully convince the civilian academic administrators of the value of the ROTC experience. They hoped that the deans' exposure to the program would influence them to encourage further student participation. Such was the case in 1989 with Dr. Lea Acord, the director of the University of Maine School of Nursing. That summer, Acord accepted the invitation to visit the Fort Bragg ROTCNAC for two days. While there, she decided to attempt rappelling off a wall and also to participate in the slide of life. Her success with these two maneuvers and other experiences there led Acord to declare that "she was impressed by the organization and motivational techniques employed . . . and would encourage students . . . to try it." Acord added that she "always thought of the service as rigid." However, her ideas were transformed when she "found instead during her visit that positive reinforcement was widely used to encourage improvement."[48]

The ROTCNAC program continued to evolve. By 1983, 32 collegiate nursing programs had begun to award academic credit for ROTCNAC. Another 15 nursing schools were considering granting academic credit for ROTCNAC from their institutions.

Various problems needing additional attention surfaced and were resolved as ROTCNAC was regularly put into practice on an annual basis. These concerns revolved around issues such as standardization of field training, appropriate billeting, and adequacy of transportation.[49] By 1984, 27 Army hospitals were hosting ROTCNAC for a total of 162 cadets.[50] In 1985, the camp's title was changed to the Nurse Summer Training Program.[51]

The use of ROTC as a procurement source got underway very slowly. In fiscal year (FY) 1976, the first two nurses graduated from ROTC and entered the Army Nurse Corps.[52] In the following FYs 1977, 1978, and 1979, ROTC claimed two, 32, and 29 accessions, respectively, to active duty.[53] By FY 1980, the number of new accessions procured through ROTC recruiting channels had gradually increased to 35 new officers of a total of 425 accessions.[54] In FYs 1981, 1982, and 1983, ROTC produced 58, 46, and 50 new Army Nurse Corps officers annually.[55] The modest growth in ROTC accessions reflected the greater attention and increased assets channeled into ROTC as a recruiting tool.

To improve recruitment and coordination of ROTC cadets, the Army Nurse Corps undertook several measures. It selected and assigned ROTC chief nurses to the four ROTC regions in the early 1980s. These Army Nurse Corps officers met a variety of expectations. They served as the region commander's nursing staff officer and developed plans for accomplishment of the mission. They identified and visited promising sites of recruitment, implemented staff visits to summer camps and accredited colleges of nursing, and produced publicity information. They also interfaced with the U.S. Army Recruiting Command recruiters and shared information and leads.[56] Additionally, the ROTC chief nurses advocated for the cadets vis-à-vis professors of military science assigned to the universities. Nursing cadets carried heavy class loads between their traditional collegiate courses, nursing classes that involved many extra hours of clinical experience, and their ROTC classes. "The PMS [professor of military science] was not always willing to make allowance for [the intense demands made on the time of] nursing students." Also, on occasion, no ROTC programs existed on the nurse cadets' campuses, which necessitated time-consuming travel to another institution with a ROTC program.[57] Nonetheless, ROTC continued as a mainstay for recruitment and a key producer of high-quality Army Nurse Corps officers for the rest of the 20th century.

Airborne training was another option for certain nursing ROTC cadets as the 1970s ended, and it too served to improve readiness in those nurse paratroopers who achieved that mark of distinction. Cadet Teresa Parsons competed against all other ROTC cadets at Texas Christian University for one of two slots to attend jump school at Fort Benning, Georgia. The university's ROTC unit decided that the two cadets—regardless of gender—that earned the highest physical training test scores would attend. To make the competition among the Texas Christian University cadets fair, Parsons volunteered to compete using the men's more stringent parameters for the two-mile run and push-ups. She won the competition, was chosen to attend the course, and successfully achieved airborne status.[58]

Participation in airborne training was grueling but definitely worthwhile for those who qualified for jump wings. Cadet Jimmie Keenan participated in the training in 1983 right after her freshman year at Henderson State University in Arkansas. She explained:

> Jump school was a defining moment for me. . . . Airborne School really tested me and made me understand how a soldier really felt. I believe . . . having to buff the floors, clean the toilets, march everywhere, do more pull-ups, push-ups and side straddle hops than I thought possible, broke me down and built me up. . . . I knew that if I could make it through Airborne school I could do anything. I finally felt like a soldier. Now almost 20 years later, when I have on my BDUs [battle dress uniforms] or my class A's I always stand a little straighter because I went through Airborne school . . . it has also helped me to take care of my patients. They knew when they looked at my uniform that I understood what they had been through. It helped establish instant creditability with the line officers that I have worked with in Recruiting, AMEDD C&S, CAS3, Resident CGSC, and as the Chief Nurse in Kosovo, going head to head with the Line guys fighting for space to set up the combat support hospital.[59]

In the 1950s, a handful of Army Nurse Corps male nurses—many of whom were anesthetists—became jump-qualified. Some of these officers were attached to Special Forces units. Second Lieutenant Robert M. Stauffer and Captain Patrick J. Ferry were among the first Army Nurse Corps officers to qualify for this demanding role. The twosome, assigned to the 101st Airborne Division at Fort Campbell, Kentucky, attended Airborne School in 1956.[60]

Lieutenant Colonel Susan McCall was 43 years old when she attended jump school. Since she was directed to help design an airborne/airdroppable unit, she decided that she "needed to know what the capabilities were of the personnel" in the proposed unit. Hence, she went to "airborne school to see what was involved." Still later McCall chose to participate in jump master school with the 82nd Airborne Division at Fort Bragg, North Carolina. She was the only female

Lieutenant Colonel Susan McCall, sitting on the "Green Ramp" at Fort Bragg, North Carolina, was waiting to board the aircraft to jump in 1988. Her main parachute was on her back and her reserve parachute was on her front with the bag to stow her chute strapped under the reserve. After jumping she would gather her chute and stow it to carry it off the drop zone. To the left of Lieutenant Colonel McCall on the tarmac is her full Alice pack.
Photo courtesy of Susan McCall, Houston, TX.

in the class and one of the oldest of all the students. Faculty informed her "that the pass rate [was] about 40% but our class [ultimately] had about a 90% pass rate." McCall surmised that "those guys were not about to let some little old lady out do them."[61] Thus, possessing the elite Airborne School qualification proved to be an advantageous distinction not only for key Army Nurse Corps officers but also for a selected few ROTC cadets.

Another Army nurse, Captain Jose F. Rivera, pioneered the way for Army Nurse Corps participation in air assault training with the 101st Airborne Division in 1978. While assigned to Fort Campbell, Kentucky, Rivera was among 77 of a class of 136 to earn the coveted air assault badge by rappelling from a tower and later from a helicopter, completing a strenuous road march with full pack and weapon, and integrating various other air assault techniques and acumen into his armamentarium.[62] The acquisition of these advanced military proficiencies enhanced the quality of the contributions made by Army Nurse Corps officers to the Army mission.

# Notes

1. Edward Drea, "Historical Perspective on CSA Roles during Times of Budget or Personnel Austerity, 17 June 1991; Vincent Demma, "Indicators of a Hollow Army," 5 June 1996; and Vincent Demma, "The Army in the 1970s," 27 March 1997 (Information Papers all in Army Nurse Corps Collection [ANCC], Office of Medical History [OMH]). Robert H. Scales, *Certain Victory* (Washington, DC: Office of the Chief of Staff, United States Army, 1993), 15–16.

2. Quinn H. Becker, Interview by Gary Sadlon, 121–123, 129, 9, 10, and 11 February 2000, Research Collection, OMH.

3. Richard R. Taylor, "Team Work Needed for Army Medicine," *U.S. Medicine* 10 (15 January 1974): 60. MUST equipment had been used by *selected* units, particularly in Vietnam, since 1967. "New Field Equipment for Military," *Journal of the Nebraska Dental Association* 44 (September 1967): 7.

4. Hal B. Jennings, "Army Medical Department," *Military Medicine* 137 (September 1972): 345. "Conversion Schedule to Medical Unit Self-Contained, Transportable (MUST) and Combat Support Hospital Configuration," Typewritten Document originating from Headquarters, Continental Army Command, 12 January 1973, ANCC, OMH. Hal B. Jennings, "Report from the United States Army Medical Department," *Military Medicine* 136 (October 1971): 772. *Report of the Surgeon General United States Army Fiscal Years 1976–1980* (Washington, DC: Office of the Surgeon General, Department of the Army, 1988), 103–12.

5. Bernhard T. Mittemeyer, "Army Medical Department," *Military Medicine* 147 (November 1982): 918–28.

6. Madelyn N. Parks to Lillian Dunlap, Typewritten Letter (TL), 19 June 1973, ANCC, OMH. "Army Nurse Corps Goals, Requirements, and Programs," Typewritten Document (TD), 3, 4, n.d., Box 9, Army Nurse Corps Papers, Archives, U.S. Army Military History Institute, Carlisle Barracks, PA. John E. Haggerty, "MEDO LETTER Manning of Oversea TOE Units," TL, 30 January 1974, Record Group 112, Entry 63, Box 2, National Archives.

7. Madelyn N. Parks to Lillian Dunlap, TL, 19 June 1973, ANCC, OMH.

8. Ibid. "Army Nurse Corps Goals, Requirements, and Programs," TD, 3, 4, n.d., Box 9, Army Nurse Corps Papers, Archives, U.S. Army Military History Institute, Carlisle Barracks, PA.

9. Madelyn N. Parks to Lillian Dunlap, TL, 19 June 1973, ANCC, OMH.

10. Lieutenant Colonel Perry, "Weapons Training for Female Soldiers," Information Paper, 23 March 1977; and Larry L. Jones, "Weapons Training for Female Soldiers, Active Army, Army National Guard and Army Reserve," Joint Message Form, February 1976, Inclosure 1, in Connie L. Slewitzke for Marjorie J. Wilson, "Nursing Information Letter 1-76," 20 April 1976 (both in ANCC, OMH).

11. Charlotte Scott, Untitled Printed Document, 26 August 2005, ANCC, OMH.

12. Clare Thomas "Army to Weigh HSC Soldiers," *HSC Mercury* 4 (January 1977): 1, 8. Linden E. Schuyler, "Personnel-General, The Army Physical Fitness and Weight Control Program," MAMC Supplement 1 to AR 600-9, 2 February 1979; and "Standards of Conduct and Fitness, Weight Control Program," MAMC Memorandum Number 632-01, 11 February 1980 (both in Record Group 112, National Archives). Quinn H. Becker, Interview by Gary Sadlon, 237–38, 9, 10, and 11 February 2000, Research Collection, OMH.

13. Carol Reineck, Interview by Mary T. Sarnecky, 36, 25 April 2001, Army Nurse Corps Oral History Collection, OMH.

14. Mary Frank, "Historical Review of ANC Mobilization Efforts (M-M+180) 1898–1973," Typewritten Memorandum, 1 December 1984, ANCC, OMH.

15. Charles C. Pixley, "Army Medical Department," *Military Medicine* 144 (September 1979): 586.

16. Madelyn N. Parks, "Information for All ANC Officers," Memorandum 1-79, 1, 29 January 1979, ANCC, OMH.

17. M.C. Devilbiss, *Women and Military Service, A History, Analysis, and Overview of Key Issues* (Maxwell Air Force Base, AL: Air University Press, 1990), 17–18.

18. Garnet I. Willow, "Army Nurse Corps, Reserve," Fact Sheet, 30 August 1972, ANCC, OMH.

19. Garnet Willow, "One Army—Active and Reserve Forces—ANC," *U.S. Army Medical Department Newsletter* 2 (Fall 1971): 43–44, ANCC, OMH.

20. *Report of the Surgeon General United States Army Fiscal Years 1976–1980* (Washington, DC: Office of the Surgeon General, Department of the Army, 1988), 249–52.

21. Madelyn N. Parks, "Information for All ANC Officers," 3, 29 April 1977, ANCC, OMH.

22. Henry Mohr, "Appointment Criteria for ANC, USAR," TD, 22 February 1977; DA-TWX Message 171600Z, March 1977; and AR 135-01, 22 November 1976, C 1, 21 October 1977, "Appointment of Reserve Commissioned Officers for Assignment to Army Medical Department Branches" (all in ANCC, OMH).

23. "Requirement Criteria for Nurses," *The Officer* 53 (October 1977): 9, 36.

24. Charles C. Pixley, "Army Efforts Aim at Troop Support," *U.S. Medicine* 14 (15 January 1978): 26.

25. Garnet Willow, "One Army—Active and Reserve Forces—ANC," *U.S. Army Medical Department Newsletter* 2 (Fall 1971): 43–44, ANCC, OMH.

26. *Report of the Surgeon General United States Army Fiscal Years 1976–1980* (Washington, DC: Office of the Surgeon General, Department of the Army, 1988), 250–51. Charles C. Pixley, "Army Eyes Doctor Pay, Entitlements," *U.S. Medicine* 16 (15 January 1980): 49.

27. *Report of the Surgeon General United States Army Fiscal Years 1976–1980* (Washington, DC: Office of the Surgeon General, Department of the Army, 1988), 249–52.

28. Albert D. Tholen, "Foreword," in *Review and Analysis of Recent Mobilizations and Deployments of US Army Reserve Components*, I. Heymont and E.W. McGregor (McLean, VA: Research Analysis Corporation, 1972), iii.

29. I. Heymont and E.W. McGregor, *Review and Analysis of Recent Mobilizations and Deployments of US Army Reserve Components* (McLean, VA: Research Analysis Corporation, 1972), 1–10.

30. *Report of the Surgeon General United States Army Fiscal Years 1976–1980* (Washington, DC: Office of the Surgeon General, Department of the Army, 1988), 249–52. Richard B. Taylor, "Army's Programs Fitted to Mission," *U.S. Medicine* 13 (15 January 1977): 51–52.

31. "United States Army Health Services Command," Printed Brochure, n.d.; Amie Modigh, "Historical Background for Nursing Service 3274th Army Hospital (1,000 Bed)," 7 August 1976; and Major Jones, "Reserve Components—AMEDD," Information Paper, 12 November 1973 (all in ANCC, OMH). Richard R. Taylor, "Team Work Needed for Army Medicine," *U.S. Medicine* 10 (15 January 1974): 60.

32. Garnet Willow, "One Army—Active and Reserve Forces—ANC," *U.S. Army Medical Department Newsletter* 2 (Fall 1971): 43–44, ANCC, OMH.

33. A Mobilization Designee (MOB DES) was "any officer, warrant officer or enlisted person in a Ready Reserve status who [was] preselected, trained, and available to fill a key authorized augmentation position in a selected Active Army TDA unit as required during early mobilization." DA HQ USA HSC, HSC Regulation 140-1, "Army Reserve, Individual Reserve Training, Mobilization Designee Program," 2, 5 October 1977. Individual Mobilization Augmentees (IMAs) were USAR officers not assigned to a reserve unit but instead assigned to "an active Army organization or Staff Agency" in Individual Ready Reserve (IRR) status. The Army required the IMA to have "premobilization experience and training." A number of Army Nurse Corps positions, such as the assistant chief of the Army Nurse Corps, had IMAs assigned. U.S. Army Reserve Components Personnel and Administration Center, "Information Pamphlet for Officers of the United States Army Reserve," 1, January 1975. By 1983, there were 81 IRR Army nurses participating in this program. Charles J. Reddy, "Nursing Newsletter Number 83-2," 3, 1 November 1983, Office of Medical History, Army Nurse Corps Collection. Normally, IMAs trained in their active component assignment for at least 12 days a year. James H. Carter, "Mutual Support and Mobilization Preparedness: The Method of an Army Reserve Hospital," *Military Medicine* 155 (August 1990): 379–81. Major Jones, "Reserve Components—AMEDD," Information Paper, 12 November 1973, ANCC, OMH.

34. Madelyn N. Parks, "Information for All ANC Officers," 4–5, 10 January 1978, ANCC, OMH.

35. *225 Years of the Army* (Tampa, FL: Faircount, LLC, 2000), 79.

36. Copies of Untitled Presentation Slides, 6 October 1983, ANCC, OMH.

37. "Becoming an Army Nurse through ROTC," TD, n.d.; and "ROTC Cuts College Costs," *Pentagram News* (30 July 1981): n.p., Newspaper Clipping (both in ANCC, OMH).

38. B.J. Ulcak, "Army ROTC and the Army Nurse Corps," TD, 1, 1 June 1978; Eugenia A. Vineys, "Trip Report," Typewritten Memorandum, 1 August 1980; and Eily P. Gorman, "ROTC Summer Camp," Disposition Form, 14 November 1980 (all in ANCC, OMH).

39. Teresa Parsons, Interview by Mary T. Sarnecky, Transcript, 3, 11 January 2001, Army Nurse Corps Oral History Collection, OMH.

40. Unidentified Author to Colonel McCarthy, "ROTC for Nurses," Routing and Transmittal Slip, 26 June 1978, ANCC, OMH.

41. Brigadier General Parks retired in 1979 and by 1981 the new senior leadership supported the establishment of a nurse-specific summer camp.

42. These four sites were situated in Army hospitals at Fort Bragg, North Carolina, where

eight cadets were involved; Fort Knox, Kentucky, where seven cadets participated; Fort Riley, Kansas, where three cadets were assigned; and at Madigan Army Medical Center in Washington state, where six cadets took advantage of the program. Eugenia A. Vineys, "ROTC Alternative Advanced Camp," TD, 4, 17 February 1981, ANCC, OMH. Denise Boucher, "Experimental Advanced Camp," *The Cadet, Fort Bragg, North Carolina* 3 (2 July 1981): 1–2. Laura Elder, "Trial Nurse Program Conducted," *ROTC Leader, Ft. Knox, Kentucky* 7 (16 July 1981): 1. Jeff Behuniak, "Student Nurse Program in Full Swing," *Kaleidoscope, Ft. Riley, Kansas* 8 (8 July 1981): 1. Myrna Hall, "New ROTC Program Designed for Nurses," Unidentified Newspaper Clipping, n.d., ANCC, OMH.

43. Jeff Behuniak, "Student Nurse Program in Full Swing," *Kaleidoscope, Ft. Riley, Kansas* 8 (8 July 1981): 1. Eugenia A. Vineys, "ROTC Alternative Advanced Camp," TD, 1, 17 February 1981, ANCC, OMH.

44. Denise Boucher, "Experimental Advanced Camp," *The Cadet, Fort Bragg, North Carolina* 3 (2 July 1981): 1–2.

45. Laura Elder, "Trial Nurse Program Conducted," *ROTC Leader, Ft. Knox, Kentucky* 7 (16 July 1981): 1.

46. Sandi Pellicano, "Cadet Nurses, Madigan Training Takes Patience," *Western Warrior* 12 (2 July 1982): 1. Keith Birdsong, "Nurse Cadets Train at Womack, Dewitt Army Hospitals," *The Cadet* 3 (2 July 1982): 1–2.

47. Copies of Untitled Presentation Slides, 6 October 1983, ANCC, OMH.

48. Margaret Warner, "Nursing, ROTC Style, Is an Adventure," Maine Weekend, *Bangor Daily News* (17–18 July 1989): 11.

49. Copies of Untitled Presentation Slides, 6 October 1983, ANCC, OMH.

50. Deborah Shumate, "Fort Knox Hosts Nursing Advanced Camp," *Leader* 10 (5 July 1984): 1–2.

51. Lark A. Ford, "U.S. Army Cadet Command Nurse Program," TD, 5 October 1995, ANCC, OMH. Kim Thompson, "Program Trains Future Army Nurses," *Cadet* 7 (1 August 1986): 3.

52. James J. Arnold, "Nurse Cadets," *Soldiers* 39 (December 1984): 34–36. Richard B. Taylor, "Army's Programs Fitted to Mission," *U.S. Medicine* 13 (15 January 1977): 49.

53. Copies of Untitled Presentation Slides, 6 October 1983, ANCC, OMH.

54. *Report of the Surgeon General United States Army Fiscal Years 1976–1980* (Washington, DC: Office of the Surgeon General, Department of the Army, 1988), 242.

55. Copies of Untitled Presentation Slides, 6 October 1983, ANCC, OMH.

56. Copies of Untitled Presentation Slides, 6 October 1983, ANCC, OMH.

57. Connie L. Slewitzke to Author, E-mail Correspondence, 22 November 2002, ANCC, OMH.

58. Teresa Parsons, Interview by Mary T. Sarnecky, Transcript, 3–4, 11 January 2001, ANCC, OMH.

59. Jimmie O. Keenan to Author, E-mail Correspondence, 23 March 2002, ANCC, OMH.

60. "Army Selects First Nurse Corps Officer for Airborne Duty with 101st Division," 30 November 1956, News Release No. 1248-56, Department of Defense, Office of Public Information; and "Utilization of Male Army Nurse Corps Officers in AMEDS Activities," TD, 2, 23 September 1959 (both in ANCC, OMH). "Rewarding Career for Males in Army Nursing," *RN* (March 1957): 12–13.

61. Susan McCall to Author, E-mail Correspondence, 25 May 2002, ANCC, OMH. J.R. Moreland, "Jumpin' Susan McCall," *Soldiers* 43 (February 1988): 52.

62. "Army Nurse Earns AA Badge," *Fort Campbell Courier* (19 May 1978): 14.

## Chapter Five
# Administrative Questions

A number of administrative questions arose during the 1970s. Although some were unprecedented concerns, others were age-old dilemmas that had been addressed in the past and recurred later in a climate of new and changing circumstances. Foremost among the administrative challenges were concerns that dealt with the augmentation of the Army Nurses Corps personnel strength; the quest for quality in the provision of health care; and the search for appropriate, comfortable, and appealing uniforms for Army nurses.

Despite predictions that the Army Nurse Corps would have no trouble in maintaining an adequate nurse force during the 1970s, shortages of nurses remained a pressing concern. The grim deficits resulted from at least two conditions. At first, the primary causal factor was the classic postwar retrenchment in resources following the Vietnam War. As the size of the standing Army was cut, the Army Medical Department (AMEDD) also was on the wane, and Army Nurse Corps authorizations correspondingly regressed.[1] Often these cuts seemed exorbitant and inexplicable. Although the active duty troop strength declined, its decrease was more than offset by the ever-increasing number of other beneficiaries. This population included additional family members linked to the all-volunteer army and the rising numbers of retired military personnel and their dependents, all of whom required health care.[2] At the same time, in-hospital care needs had become increasingly complicated, with more acutely ill patients and new technological modalities, thus requiring a higher professional nurse-to-patient ratio to provide adequate, safe care.[3] Also, after several years passed and the surgeon general increased the authorized strength, the Corps faced formidable challenges in its efforts to recruit sufficient applicants amid a national nurse shortage. Clearly, the Army Nurse Corps was in a tight spot.

Authorizations in the post–Vietnam War Army Nurse Corps steadily declined for several years. The authorized year-end strength was 4,752 in the early days of fiscal year (FY) 1972 but quickly plunged. For FY 1972 and FY 1973, year-end strengths were 4,107 and 3,597, respectively.[4] The year-end quota was 3,830 for FY 1974.[5] The actual year-end strength for FY 1975 was 3,706.[6] For FY 1976, the Army Nurse Corps was allowed to fill only 3,510 authorizations. General Madelyn N. Parks reassured the Corps that she was "fighting" to obtain "some relief from this impossible ceiling."[7] But the steady decline continued and the actual FY 1976 year-end strength remained at 3,510 as projected.[8] The trend began reversing in 1977 when the surgeon general authorized 98 additional slots "directly related to support of the new Walter Reed Army Medical Center." This increase brought the Corps to a strength of 3,608, and Parks rightfully noted that year-end strength might be expanded further "as a result of making our manpower shortages widely known."[9] By April 1977, the FY 1977 year-end strength rose to 3,710. Parks also predicted that the intense, painful summertime nursing shortfall—so typical in the past when the Corps would cut desperately needed active duty nurses to bring actual numbers into compliance with fiscal year-end strength limits—would not be repeated in the summer of 1977. Congress had shifted the beginning of the FY from 1 July to 1 October, which meant more nurses could be carried on the books for three months longer.[10] Authorized year-end strengths for FY 1978 and FY 1979 were 3,886 and 3,727 each.[11] The latter figure reached 3,759 by November 1979.[12] By FY 1980, the authorized year-end strength had partially recovered to 3,801 slots.[13]

Although illogical and baffling, the painful cuts imposed on the Army Nurse Corps in a decade when it was launching a major new program, the Army Nurse Clinician Program, and assuming even greater responsibilities probably were a part of an overall military force reduction. When a task force met in 1977 to assess the program's past accomplishments and plan future directions, participants noted that between 1971 and 1977, the strength of the Army Nurse Corps had dropped from 4,495 to 3,608, a total loss of 887 slots. At the same time, the strength of the Medical Corps had "remained relatively constant." When no physicians could be found or recruited to fill the empty general medical officer authorizations, the Medical Corps converted these billets into medical specialty or physician assistant spaces. Simultaneously, the "Medical Service Corps also remained at a relatively stable strength."[14] This meant a shrinking Army Nurse Corps was assuming the responsibilities of other health care providers as well as its own when its own resources were steadily declining and the strengths of the other branches remained virtually unchanged. The inability of the Army Nurse Corps to defend against reductions in the face of power and politics probably played a large part in this conundrum.

The Army Nurse Corps implemented measures to bring actual numbers into compliance with the proposed drastic downsizing that occurred in the Army after the Vietnam War. One strategy was to curtail new accessions to the Corps.[15] By 1973, a "zero-procurement objective" was in effect. In other words, the Corps was recruiting almost no nurses, which produced an unwelcome consequence—"a 30% shortfall" in the Army Nurse Corps Contemporary Practice Program courses. Senior Army Nurse Corps leaders then predicted that under these conditions they would "be forced to place less prepared nurses on independent duty, and quality," consequently, would be jeopardized. This would cause "anger, frustration and apathy" among patients, nurses, and doctors. In the final analysis, patients, it was predicted, would become "the victims."[16] The chief of the Corps, General Lillian Dunlap, anticipated the crisis and formally briefed the Surgeon General (TSG), Lieutenant General Hal Jennings, on its implications. When faced with the critical state of affairs, TSG initiated measures designed to increase Army Nurse Corps authorizations by 300 spaces. These authorizations were to be subsequently distributed to the field. The Army Nurse Corps designated 260 of these nurse clinician slots for the continental United States, 25 for the U.S. Army, Europe, and approximately 15 for the U.S. Army, Pacific. However, the recommendations for distribution of the 300 nurse clinician spaces were not included with the Budget Manpower Guidance that went forward to the Health Services Command (HSC).[17] Later in 1977, Colonel Edith Nuttall, assistant chief of the Army Nurse Corps, reiterated that the "300 never appeared as . . . ANC [Army Nurse Corps] spaces on manpower documents in the field in 1972." Nuttall again attributed the failure to a "lack of specific guidance by OTSG [Office of The Surgeon General] in PBG [Program Budget Guidance]."[18] The entire episode probably was a slipup that inadvertently happened in a busy, complex time when many pressing concerns claimed the attention of Army Nurse Corps leaders. Subsequently, the phantom 300 slots were lost in the vast, confusing collection of manpower numbers and were dispersed elsewhere.[19]

In addition to curtailing new accessions, the Army Nurse Corps reluctantly implemented even more problematical measures to reduce numbers, knowing that these measures would be detrimental to esprit de corps. The Corps had no choice but to impose more stringent ceilings on all promotions.[20] As a result of the slower promotions and longer time in grade, the morale of many Army nurses suffered.

Furthermore, in FY 1972, the Army Nurse Corps released 579 officers from active service. In FY 1973, it forced another 404 officers to leave.[21] A change in Army policy dictated this reduction in forces. In November 1971, the Army, "in contrast to previous fiscal years," made "established year-end strengths . . . mandatory."[22] By FY 1976, the Department of the Army constrained the Army Nurse Corps to release "approximately 328 fine young officers."[23] Many Army nurses affected by the reduction in forces left embittered, resolving never to recommend a career in the Army Nurse Corps to friends or associates. Many vowed never to return to the Army, swearing never again to respond in time of national need.

Another solution regularly proposed to deal with the Army's inability to recruit new personnel for the Army Nurse Corps—albeit rarely implemented—involved converting additional existing military authorizations to civilian registered nurse billets. In FY 1974 and FY 1975, military installations were employing 2,447 and 2,221 civilian nurses, respectively.[24] On a recurring basis during the 1970s, civilian and military leaders and professionals suggested additional civilianization to increase numbers. The Army Nurse Corps regularly rejected the option because it hampered its flexibility to use nursing resources and hindered stabilizing

Colonel Edith Nuttall served as assistant chief of the Army Nurse Corps from 1974 to 1978. Photo courtesy of Army Nurse Corps Archives, Office of Medical History, Falls Church, VA.

assignment tours for Army nurses. Furthermore, the excessive employment of civilian nurses was thought to result in a chronic failure to fulfill teaching requirements and enforce discipline for enlisted corpsmen and patients.[25] Evidently, the leadership held the opinion that the authority vested in an Army Nurse Corps officer was a prerequisite for dealing with these responsibilities. It also was essentially impossible to convert the civilianized slots back to military billets when needs and circumstances changed in the future. Most recognized that civilianization was a flawed short-term fix with long-term ramifications.

In the immediate post–Vietnam period, Army Nurse Corps leaders were unwaveringly assured—albeit erroneously—that authorizations would not be reduced. Thus, with confidence in a stable future, the leaders focused on creative strategies to fill existing authorizations. One option posed was the Volunteer Army Student Nurse Program, a collegiate variation of the Army Student Nurse Program. Broached in 1971 but never implemented, the plan suggested offering three-year subsidies annually to 150 baccalaureate nursing students who had already completed one year in an approved university nursing program. The students would be reimbursed for tuition and certain expenses and receive the pay and allowances of an enlisted soldier. At the time, the Army Nurse Corps received more than 1,000 applications each year for the Walter Reed Army Institute of Nursing (WRAIN) program. Of these 1,000, only 170 potential WRAIN students were selected. Planners hypothesized that the balance of the remaining "outstanding applicants who could not be selected" for WRAIN would constitute a ready, motivated pool for the Volunteer Army Student Nurse Program.[26] The program demonstrated significant potential for not only supplementing Army Nurse Corps numbers but also for expanding the proportion of Army nurses with a baccalaureate degree. Sadly, it too fell victim to fiscal restraints.

A different perspective on the causes of the cyclically recurring shortages has affirmed that the deficits were not only supply shortages. The demands for nurses also burgeoned. In this regard, Joan E. Lynaugh reiterated the "lesson of the unintended outcome." Although the creation and blossoming of the innovative practice realms of critical care and primary care nursing were strategies at least partially used in this era to "conserve" personnel resources, they had unintended consequences.[27] The unprecedented successes of the advanced practice movement within the Army filled the primary care provider void but also created a demand for more nurse practitioners. A 1973 report verified that there existed an "increasing number of requests by Army medical facility commanders for nurse clinicians in every specialty area."[28] Additionally, the intensive care nurses "made it possible to deploy technology successfully and to try more vigorous treatments." Finally "more progressive therapy made nurses even more in demand as well as more expert."[29] Thus, the solutions generated a new demand and a new imbalance between requirements and resources. Regardless of whether a decreased supply or an increased demand or a combination was at fault, the reality was that there were too few nurses both in the civilian and the military workforces during the 1970s.[30]

As the decade progressed and the authorizations picture improved, a blend of both adverse and auspicious signs appeared. Finally, those who controlled manpower resources heard the persistent message of a critical need for more nurses. Attention shifted from a climate of tense, active conservation of personnel resources to a state of intense procurement. After several years spent dismissing those who wished to serve in the Army Nurse Corps, recruiters suddenly welcomed high-quality candidates and were pressed to find even more applicants who met its rigorous standards.

From a pessimistic vantage point, the Army had discontinued both the hugely successful Army Student Nurse Program and Registered Nurse Student Program in 1975, and WRAIN closed in 1978.[31] The Reserve Officers' Training Corps program for nurses and women, the only available subsidized program for attracting nurses to the Army, was in its infancy in the mid-1970s and not yet a significant source of new nurses. Therefore, the Army Nurse Corps had to refocus the burden for recruiting new accessions to finding and capturing the interest of graduate nurses with baccalaureate degrees, an onerous challenge.[32] In the main, direct commissions and—to a lesser extent—voluntary recalls of reservists filled the active duty rolls.[33] However, since not all reservists had a bachelor of science in nursing, a necessary requirement for active duty, the U.S. Army Reserve and Army National Guard did not represent a highly productive source for accessions.[34]

During the 1970s, yearly recruitment goals steadily declined from 325 in FY 1974, 100 in FY 1975, to a nadir of 80 in FY 1976. Only in 1976 was the recruiting goal achieved, with a 101 percent mission attainment. It also marked the beginning of a recovery period. In FY 1977, the recruiting mission was 414 and in FY 1978 through FY 1980 the mission goals were 920, 500, and 468, respectively.[35] To help meet the enormous FY 1978 mission of 920 accessions, the Corps decided to offer qualified reservists, those with a bachelor of science in nursing and at least 24 months of prior active duty, the option to return to active duty for a period of 12, 18, or 24 months.[36] Similar reserve recall opportunities surfaced in later years.[37] However, such recruiting strategies were tantamount to robbing Peter to pay Paul. The active component, U.S. Army Reserve, and Army National Guard numbers all were equally dismal. Appropriation of nurses from the reserve components to augment the active component profited the latter but seriously constrained the former. Recruitment of officers for the U.S. Army Reserve was an even greater challenge because, in FY 1976 for instance, there was a "shortfall of over 800 Army Nurse Corps officers in . . . Reserve Units."[38]

With limited recruiting prospects in 1975, the U.S. Army Recruiting Command (USAREC) proposed to transfer Army Nurse Corps recruiting responsibilities from USAREC to OTSG, which recruited most other branches of the AMEDD.[39] The Army Nurse Corps did not favor the move from the USAREC to OTSG because it never got its "fair share of [procurement] support from OTSG." Nor did the Army Nurse Corps think OTSG accorded it with equitable funding. At USAREC, the Army Nurse Corps concluded that it received a fair "share of dollars and resources."[40] Ultimately, the Army Medical Department Personnel Support

Agency rejected the USAREC proposal because of insufficient personnel, funds, and logistical elements for OTSG to assume the added task of procuring Army Nurse Corps officers.[41]

A number of factors ultimately combined to improve the overall numbers of the Army Nurse Corps. Among these was the retention of pregnant women on active duty after 1975.[42] This decision expanded the pool of nurses readily available. Furthermore, after 1975 no new accessions were accepted in the Army Student Nurse Program, and after 1978, WRAIN ceased operation. Although these two decisions were primarily based on fiscal considerations, they had secondary effects. The personnel slots previously occupied by those attending school in these programs became available to the Army Nurse Corps and thereafter were filled by nurses on duty in Army facilities.[43] A number of military treatment facilities also closed permanently, freeing more nurses for assignments elsewhere. For example, in 1974, the hospital at Fort Wolters, Texas, and the Valley Forge General Hospital in Phoenixville, Pennsylvania, ceased operations.[44] In 1977, the Army transferred responsibility for staffing the health care facilities in Okinawa to the U.S. Navy.[45] That same year HSC began the reduction of the U.S. Army Medical Department Activities (MEDDAC) at Carlisle Barracks, Pennsylvania, into a U.S. Army Health Clinic. It also modified the status of the MEDDACs at Aberdeen Proving Ground, Maryland; Fort Benjamin Harrison, Indiana; and Fort McPherson, Georgia, into U.S. Army Health Clinics.[46] These closures somewhat reduced the demands imposed on the overworked and understaffed Army Nurse Corps.

Meeting the recruitment mission during the 1970s was difficult. The requirement specifying that all active component Army Nurse Corps officers have earned a baccalaureate degree in nursing from a program accredited either by the National League for Nursing or the secretary of education was strictly enforced and effectively decreased the available applicants for commissioning. In 1972, 80.5 percent of all employed registered nurses had *less* than a baccalaureate degree in the United States. Only 12.1 percent of working nurses had a baccalaureate degree. Those with credentials higher than a baccalaureate degree represented 3.4 percent of the national nurse workforce. Thus, the Army Nurse Corps was able to recruit from only 15.5 percent of the marketplace.[47] By 1974, those numbers improved slightly. Approximately 15.2 percent of employed registered nurses held a bachelor's degree in nursing, while about 3.3 percent had earned a master's degree or higher.[48] The Army Nurse Corps then had a somewhat expanded recruiting pool, roughly 18.5 percent of the available population of employed registered nurses. From 1977 to 1978, 18.1 percent of the registered nurse population had a baccalaureate degree and 4.0 percent claimed a master's or a doctoral degree. At this point, the pool of eligible applicants for a commission in the Army Nurse Corps had risen to a significantly improved 22.1 percent of all employed registered nurses.[49] Civilian health care organizations faced similar challenges but were able to hire those registered nurses with less than a bachelor's degree and could offer a few enticements that the Army Nurse Corps could not match.[50] In 1976, a second lieutenant's salary was $839.70 and a first lieutenant's monthly base pay was $973.80. The Army also paid housing and subsistence allowances. Starting salaries in civilian institutions ranged from $800 to $1,075 monthly. Civilian hospitals also variously offered "fully paid comprehensive health insurance, 3 weeks vacation, . . . tuition reimbursement, . . . shift differentials, time and a half for overtime, ten paid holidays and/or travel and moving allowances."[51] The Army's benefits were almost comparable to those offered by civilian institutions. The major difference was the extra pay awarded by civilian hospitals for working undesirable shifts (usually evening and nights) and overtime. After the FY 1976 low was reached and long-standing educational subsidies were discontinued, the Army Nurse Corps faced a perplexing dilemma about how best to encourage future accessions. Soon thereafter, the Nursing Reserve Officers' Training Corps program emerged as the ideal answer.

Concerns about adequate numbers of nurses persisted throughout the 1970s. These worries about quantity soon were complicated by questions about the quality of nursing care.[52] After the Vietnam War, the AMEDD faced major personnel and budget cuts, rapidly escalating expenses, and a deteriorating reputation. Many beneficiaries perceived the AMEDD as an inept institution that was difficult to access, inadequately staffed, poorly equipped, and usually providing only minimally acceptable care.[53]

During this challenging time, Army Nurse Corps officers tested and implemented various strategies and nursing care delivery models to improve the quality of care. A task force initiated a preliminary study to identify what nurses were doing, what factors had an impact on "maximum utilization" of nurses, and what nurses ideally should be doing to meet patient care needs. This investigation examined 10 components: (1) staffing ratios, (2) workload distributions, (3) absentee rates, (4) nursing activities, (5) tasking time, (6) personnel trade-off time, (7) escort services, (8) personnel turbulence, (9) patient acuity, and (10) the ratio of nursing care hours to patient care requirements. Among their findings, investigators discovered that nurses "filled the gap between the patient or his environment and the centralized areas of resources." Study results also indicated that excessive non-nursing demands prevented "nursing personnel from accomplishing their primary mission of patient care." Administrative tasks, for example, consumed about 40 percent of nurses' time and detracted from quality service.

Although these studies were being conducted, nurses in U.S. Army Medical Centers and U.S. Army Medical Department Activities were planning and subsequently implementing additional efforts to monitor quality of care. These undertakings involved establishing requirements that directed caretakers involved in unusual occurrences such as patient falls or medication errors to complete a written report, initiate active and retrospective audits of nursing documentation, and carry out patient and staff satisfaction questionnaires. One outcome of all these efforts was the development of the Pri-Team concept.[54]

Previously, patient care services were delivered in the case, the functional, or the team method of staff assignment, or in a combination of several such nursing delivery models.[55] The intent of the newly conceived Pri-Team delivery model was to focus "authority, responsibility, and accountability at the operational level," to capitalize on available resources, and to create "a holistic and unified approach to patient care."[56] Pri-Team involved having one professional nurse responsible for the patient's care from admission to discharge. However, a team of caregivers provided the nursing care for the patient, which involved the nursing process of "assessing, planning, implementing, and evaluating the nursing care of a group of patients."[57] The Pri-Team consisted of a clinical coordinator accountable for quality, supervision, and coordination of patient care activities; a senior clinical nurse tasked with monitoring total nursing activities; the Pri-Team leader responsible for delivering nursing care for a specific group of patients; the clinical nurse who offered direct patient care and clinical support for paraprofessional nursing staff; the clinical specialist (91C), or licensed practical nurse; and the ward specialist (91B), or nursing assistant. An associate team cared for the patient when the patient's Pri-Team was off duty. Among all members of the team, the patients themselves were spotlighted as the most important component.[58] Planners pilot-tested the system at the Walter Reed Army Medical Center and the Dwight David Eisenhower Army Medical Center.[59] Those who initially evaluated Pri-Team reported that the various care providers and support personnel could "be made complementary to each other." In their opinion, Pri-Team had the potential to utilize staff more efficiently, better define roles and responsibilities, enhance personalization of patient care, and improve personnel performance.[60] As it moved into a new, more modern facility in 1978, the Walter Reed Army Medical Center concurrently implemented this delivery model.[61] Lieutenant Colonel Mary Messerschmidt served on a female medical ward at the new Walter Reed Army Medical Center when the Department of Nursing implemented Pri-Team. She noticed a "180° turn" for the better in the quality of care provided within the framework of this new model.[62]

The AMEDD implemented another innovation, the Hospital Unit Dose Drug Distribution System (HUDS), to improve quality of care. Both the civilian health care environment and Letterman Army Medical Center pilot tested HUDS with positive results. This led the Government Accountability Office and the U.S. Army Audit Agency to recommend it for implementation in virtually all Army hospitals. Before the 1970s, most nursing units maintained a bulk supply of medications on the ward in a locked medicine cabinet. When a physician ordered a drug, the nurse filled in a small medication card with details such as patient's name, bed number, drug, dosage, and route and times of administration. At the time specified on the card for the drug's administration, the nurse selected the preparation from the bulk supply, placed it in a medication cup, and administered it to the patient. With HUDS, the central hospital pharmacy prepared and delivered the medication in a "packaged, labeled and ready-to-administer form." Proponents thought that such a system would decrease medication errors, improve patient safety, and increase staff productivity. Advocates also predicted that the system would control theft and abuse of medications, an important consideration in an era when drug abuse was rampant.[63] HUDS grew to be the standard for medication administration in all health care facilities, both military and civilian.

For many years, the Army Nurse Corps worked on developing, publishing, and implementing its own distinctive, comprehensive Standards of Nursing Practice in another effort to improve quality. The intent of this credo was to establish basic guidelines for professional nursing practice in the Army in accordance with the nursing profession's responsibility "to assess, provide, evaluate, and improve nursing practice." The standards set the stage for the introduction of a quality assurance program for the Army Nurse Corps.[64] They also served as a "yardstick" by which the Corps evaluated its professional commitment in terms of safety and competence in areas such as "licensure, certification, accreditation, quality assurance, peer review, and . . . policy."[65] The Army Nurse Corps published the first draft of the standards in 1979, and then it evaluated, revised, and implemented the standards in every Army hospital and—in due course—published them in pamphlet form in 1981.[66]

The Physician-in-Charge (PIC) Program was an undertaking addressing quality of care. Colonel Robert J.T. Joy, an Army physician, originally conceived the idea at the request of Surgeon General Richard Taylor, who was concerned that "young MC [Medical Corps] officers had no training or practice in leadership or administration" and virtually no preparation for future command roles. Joy recommended that the PIC plan be cautiously pilot-tested on a limited, experimental basis at one Class I hospital such as the U.S. Army Medical Department Activities at Fort Benning, Georgia, or Fort Bragg, North Carolina.[67]

The PIC Program sought to return the Medical Corps officer to greater involvement with "ward administrative and property accountability activities" after a hiatus of some 30 years. There had been few or no Medical Corps officers implementing the ward officer role since the days of post–World War II Army medicine.[68] The model's intent was to strengthen "the authority and influence of Medical Corps officers . . . at the ward and clinic level." An additional aim was "to improve patient care and professional satisfaction, and to ensure that the ethical, moral and legal implications of the practice of medicine" were achieved to "the fullest extent."

In March 1974, TSG instructed the HSC commander, Major General Spurgeon Neel, to put PIC into practice.[69] Neel then delegated the responsibility for initiation of a six-month evaluation trial of PIC to the HSC chief of staff, Brigadier General Philip A. Deffer. In May 1974, Deffer handpicked six military treatment facilities to serve as sites for an initial evaluation phase of the PIC Program and directed these installations to develop comprehensive implementation plans.[70] The staff at Brooke Army Medical Center fleshed out a road map intended "to assist [the] PIC in asserting his leadership role." It detailed specific responsibilities for the PIC, some of which seemed reasonable and advantageous and others that appeared to intrude on the domains of independent nursing practice. Among these were meeting "daily with head nurse to discuss ward/clinic activities," reviewing "nursing care plans with head nurse once a week," acting "as control or regulator for limiting patient census when staffing requirements cannot be met," auditing the "medical record/nursing record on an ongoing basis," reviewing and approving "all work orders and supply requisitions pertaining to his ward/clinic," and "assisting in the orientation of all new staff members on ward/clinic. He [the PIC] will set the standards of care."[71] Another aspect of the program designated the PIC as the officer efficiency report rater of the head nurse with the endorsement section to be completed by nursing superiors. This changed the rating chain for the clinical head nurse's officer efficiency report, the duty performance appraisal.[72]

The introduction of the PIC proposal came when American women were increasingly rejecting sexism, subjugation, and paternalism. It also coincided with widespread attempts by American nurses to gain greater autonomy and control over their unique professional practice. The nation's professional nurses also were attempting to identify the exclusive domains of nursing.[73] For these reasons, the reaction of the majority of Army Nurse Corps officers to the PIC Program was overwhelmingly one of "indignation, frustration and betrayal." On the positive side of the ledger, a few agreed that the notion "of having a primary physician in each nursing unit . . . for health care planning and for . . . leadership [was] an appealing one," and they also acknowledged that "the PIC *could* produce very real improvement in the quality and depth of care." But, most Army nurses believed "that the PIC would . . . evaluate the performance of the head nurse against a single criterion—how well and how directly does the nurse respond to his medical orders and his wishes." Finally, a large segment of Army Nurse Corps officers

> . . . remarked that they truly believe . . . the motivation of today's physician. . . is solely toward medical care of his patient, accomplished in a disease-centered care orientation. These nurses believe the physician cannot and should not be burdened with ward management, logistic problems, personnel and training problems, coordination of support services and the myriad of other activities of the nursing unit. (The Army physician now complains of paperwork and the pressure of time—one has but to review. . . the declining quality of physicians' progress notes in clinical records to clearly perceive the pressures already placed on him resulting in his slighting even clinically—essential, administrative records.)[74]

One of the most promising senior leaders of the Corps of that era, Colonel Doris S. Frazier, collated the points summarized above. She wrote the preceding letter, observing that the PIC Program disregarded precepts of effective organizational leadership, would fragment professional and military authority, and would "hopelessly burden" the PIC "with despised, non-clinical paper work." Frazier predicted that PIC would "result in duplication of effort" and would cripple "the Department of Nursing as a viable force in AMEDD hospitals." Finally, she prophetically observed that PIC would "force out of the Army Nurse Corps its best administrators . . . [and] its most highly skilled and empathetic clinical practitioners as well." Frazier concluded that professional "nurses will not remain where they are not permitted to think or to control nursing practice and nursing personnel."[75]

Frazier shared the letter's contents with several Army Nurse Corps officers, who subsequently "leaked" it to the American Nurses Association at its convention in San Francisco, California, in June 1974. ANA members were outraged by the PIC concept and, in response, resolved to prevent its implementation. Accordingly, American Nurses Association members sent letters of protest to TSG and to Dunlap expressing their disapproval and displeasure concerning the notion of physicians encroaching on nursing's turf.[76]

The Army viewed this whole debacle as a violation of an unwritten but cardinal rule proscribing the airing of any internal AMEDD business outside the institution. Subsequently, Frazier saw her career truncated, regardless of her significant past contributions and seemingly exceptional potential.[77] Known for her perception and integrity, she courageously voiced her convictions and paid the penultimate price. Sadly, hers was the regrettable fate of rejection that commonly awaits those who take a brave stand on a sensitive public issue.

Although skeptical about the wisdom and viability of PIC, Dunlap was in the awkward and conflicted position of needing to demonstrate loyalty to the vision of her immediate superior, the surgeon general, and her allegiance to the Corps. Accordingly, she did not take a strong stand on the matter. Instead, Dunlap chose an approach marked by an openness to try and test the program and allow it to sink or swim on its own merits. The final word on PIC ultimately belonged to Dunlap. She wrote that "over a period of time, the whole project withered on the vine."[78]

The Army Nurse Corps has invested intense interest and copious time and attention on the subject of women's uniforms throughout its history.[79] This issue has numerous roots. Critics pointed to the Army Nurse Corps all-female past and the questionable notion that women display an inordinate focus on clothes. However, male uniforms also have changed. Others ascribe the fascination to the fact that women in the military had an ever-present need to be comfortable, project an attractive image, and appear professional. Another consideration was recruiting, that is, presenting an appealing role model for potential Army nurses. Whenever worries about nursing shortages were paramount, leaders in the Army Nurse Corps quickly recognized that the quality, styles, and colors of uniforms influenced the recruiting mission's success. Attractive uniforms were a major selling point. In the 1970s, with the pervasive and acute nursing shortage, uniform issues became even more important.

Many uniform changes—some subtle, some conspicuous—emerged in the 1970s and affected the Army Nurse Corps. In 1972, regulations authorized Army women to wear patent leather shoes with their Class A uniforms and to carry and use black umbrellas when in uniform.[80] That same year, the Army allowed women in the Army to wear a prescribed white shirt with a black tab centered under the rounded collar along with the Army green uniform as a replacement for the similarly styled tan shirt. Army Regulation 670-30 authorized the wearing of a white neck scarf year-round under the uniform topcoat. It also set the standard for uniform gloves, permitting the wearing of white gloves for summer and gray-beige gloves for other seasons. A regulation change phased out the gray-beige gloves by the end of 1975. By 1977, uniform regulations authorized a black raincoat of "London Fog" style for purchase by both men and women from commercial retailers. It was to be worn in place of the Army green raincoat or double-breasted Army green overcoat with a zip-out liner as an outer garment.[81]

By 1974, the Army added more refinements to the wearing of the uniform. The chief of the Army Nurse Corps directed that in most instances the handbag should be carried over the arm rather than the shoulder. Moreover, the Army Nurse Corps leadership cautioned women Army nurses to tailor their uniform skirts in accordance with standards of good taste and informed them that an acceptable skirt length was no shorter than two inches above or no longer than one inch below the middle of the knee. Regulations also authorized plain black civilian mid-calf boots for wear with the uniform in inclement weather.[82]

In 1974, the Department of the Army initiated a far-reaching study of Army women's uniforms. As a part of the study process, the Army Natick Research and Development Command asked the Women's Uniform Board to study the options and recommend uniforms for women. Members of this board included both the director of the Women's Army Corps and the chief of the Army Nurse Corps, two women with divergent needs and preferences. By December 1976, the study group had surveyed female troops, solicited ideas from civilian dress designers and manufacturers, and carried out a historical review of women's uniforms. They recommended adoption of a "year-round uniform . . . to make men and women look like soldiers of one Army, without sacrificing the femininity of the women; and to use . . . versatile components, such as shirts, slacks, and skirts."[83]

The black beret for Army women made its debut in the clothing line in 1973, several years before the completion of the large-scale study. Its appearance was accompanied by extensive controversy. The director of the Women's Army Corps, Brigadier General Inez Bailey, an acknowledged fashion plate, promoted the semi-rigid, formed black felt hat. Her Army Nurse Corps counterpart, Dunlap, however, found the beret to be "terrible." Dunlap recalled that it was "plopped every which way" on women's heads and in no way "was complimentary to the rest of the uniform." Dunlap found it politically expedient to accept the black beret because "when you have two people . . . representing two different views, you can't have women fighting women. That's what the men love." The laws for social interactions varied depending on gender. Although it seemingly was unladylike for women to actively disagree or strenuously air conflicting views, it was not unusual for men to differ passionately and insist on the primacy of their ideas. Dunlap ultimately agreed to the adoption of the black beret, but initially restricted its wear to the green cord or hospital white duty uniforms, not the green Class A uniform.[84] At that time, the latter was to be worn only with the traditional visor cap.[85] Bowing to pressure by 1975, the chief of the Corps approved the black beret for wear with the Army green uniform "on informal occasions," such as when traveling. Essentially, the Army perceived the black beret as a replacement for the garrison or overseas cap.[86] General, across-the-board discontent with the black beret led to the trial of another felt Class A hat in 1975. Efforts at testing soon were abandoned because, as Parks said, "We thought it looked like the 'Keystone Cops' hat—tall, domed crown and a narrow brim! It was awful!"[87]

Another ill-advised uniform item that had a short life was the mint green outfit, officially known as the "Women's Summer Uniform, Warp Knit." It replaced the green-and-white cord uniform—a summer-weight, short-sleeved, two-piece skirt and top set—that was comfortable and cool but easily wrinkled. The green-and-white cord's replacement uniform soon became known as the Jolly Green Giant outfit. Its mint green polyester fabric construction and various mix-and-match options such as a dress, jacket, skirt, long-sleeved and short-sleeved blouses, and a vest became available in the summer of 1977.[88]

Also during 1977, the Army wear tested a durable press fatigue (utility) uniform for women similar to the men's version.[89] It was intended to replace the Vietnam era women's fatigue uniform and was part of a larger movement toward a combined male/female uniform. However, the Army cancelled plans to authorize the women's adaptation in 1979 because of other far-reaching plans. Instead, the Army announced it would design a new combat, camouflage, utility uniform, or what would become the battle dress uniform. In the meantime, the quartermaster expanded the available sizes of the men's durable press fatigue uniform to fit the smaller dimensions needed by many women. The Army then instructed female servicemembers to wear the unisex durable press utility uniform in the field until the battle dress uniform was available.[90]

The women's Army green pantsuit was a comfortable, practical, and welcome addition to the clothing bag in 1976. Planners intended it initially as a Class B uniform for such duties that involved air travel or assignments in Table of Organization and Equipment or field units. The uniform was a loosely fitted long-sleeved jacket and pants of 100 percent polyester. It was to be worn either with a light green knit turtleneck overblouse or a white woven shirt with black neck tab. The Women's Uniform Board approved it for year-round wear.[91]

During the 1970s, the Army Nurse Corps female white duty uniform also changed. The heavily starched white cotton long-sleeved dress, which was replaced by a short-sleeved version and later a synthetic and then a cotton-synthetic-mix short-sleeved dress, subsequently became a polyester short-sleeved pantsuit. The wearing of trousers by women had by then become accepted—indeed, it was an international fashion trend that was both modest and practical. Nonetheless, Dunlap was reluctant to adopt the duty pantsuit. When forced by the majority opinion to do so, Admiral Alene Duerk, director of the Navy Nurse Corps, advised her not to "adopt one that opens in the front because no matter how many regulations you write, you will have a lot of Brigitte Bardots on your staff who will want to open it at the top button." After a small-scale trial of the Navy's pantsuit proved successful, the Army Nurse Corps subsequently adopted the polyester pantsuit with a high neck and back zipper. The Army restricted the wear of the white pantsuit, a duty uniform, to the patient care duty site only.[92]

The white hospital duty uniform worn by male Army Nurse Corps officers had only one major change from the time when men were first authorized commissions in the Corps in 1955 up to the present. Originally, male Army nurses wore a high-necked, heavily starched, cotton uniform top that had cloth knots as buttons across the shoulder and up the collar. Lieutenant John T. Pack found this uniform extremely irritating because the stiff "collar often ended up chaffing your neck so you had to soften it with a bar of soap on the inside."[93] Captain Eugene Cudnohufsky experienced comparable problems with the uniform. He was allergic to the brass that was pinned to the collar in direct contact with the skin of the neck. The brass "would turn [his] neck green and [he] would break out in horrible sores."[94] The collar had a notch centered at the middle of the throat. The men positioned insignia denoting rank and the Army Nurse Corps caduceus on the collar on either side of the notch. Males wore the smock with white cotton drill pants. After 1968, regulations mandated the replacement of the uncomfortable high-necked smock with a more professional look, a white cotton open-necked shirt that buttoned up the front.[95]

By 1972, the women's white duty uniform could also be worn with a green acrylic sweater.[96] At that same time, the Army Nurse Corps was searching for a suitable sweater for male Army nurses to wear on clinical duty. It proved a challenge to find one that looked professional and fit appropriately over the male nurses' smock that was worn loose over the waist.[97] By 1974, regulations allowed men to wear a white cardigan with their hospital duty uniform when cold weather dictated warmer clothing.[98] In 1975, regulations authorized a green acrylic cardigan sweater for wear by male Army Nurse Corps officers.[99] However, few male Army nurses wore this sweater.

Another change in the duty uniform occurred in the 1970s with the evolution of the white starched nurse's cap worn by Army Nurse Corps female officers in the clinical setting. This original headpiece, whose shape was maintained with a white shoelace, was secured to the nurse's head with a bobby pin. In 1972, a button-backed cap replaced the older laced version.[100] As time passed, its wear while on duty became optional. Many civilian nurses were no longer wearing nursing caps with their uniforms, and many civilian collegiate schools of nursing no longer claimed a distinctly styled cap for their individual schools.[101] As a practical matter, with technology moving to the bedside with its attendant bulky equipment such as multiple monitors, ventilators, drainage systems, and infusion pumps, there simply was not enough room to navigate with a cap-covered head. Moreover, the increasing numbers of male nurses in the ranks likely influenced a merging of all nurses' outward physical appearance regardless of gender. In the final analysis, the lines separating nursing practice from medical practice were blurring to some degree. Nurses were undertaking many responsibilities formerly considered the exclusive domain of physicians. As the old demarcations became more obscured, female nurses began to don their traditional starched white garb less frequently. Gradually, the distinctive nurse's cap of the Army Nurse Corps became optional and, with time, disappeared.

Another uniform transformation involved the placement of insignia on the uniform. Previously, female Army Nurse Corps officers had positioned their insignia on the Army green cord, the mint green, and the hospital duty uniforms in a distinctive manner. The rank was pinned on the center of the right collar and positioned perpendicular to the floor. The branch insignia was centered in the same position on the left collar.[102] Army officials questioned this style of brass placement—unique to the Army Nurse Corps—in 1978. At that time, the chief

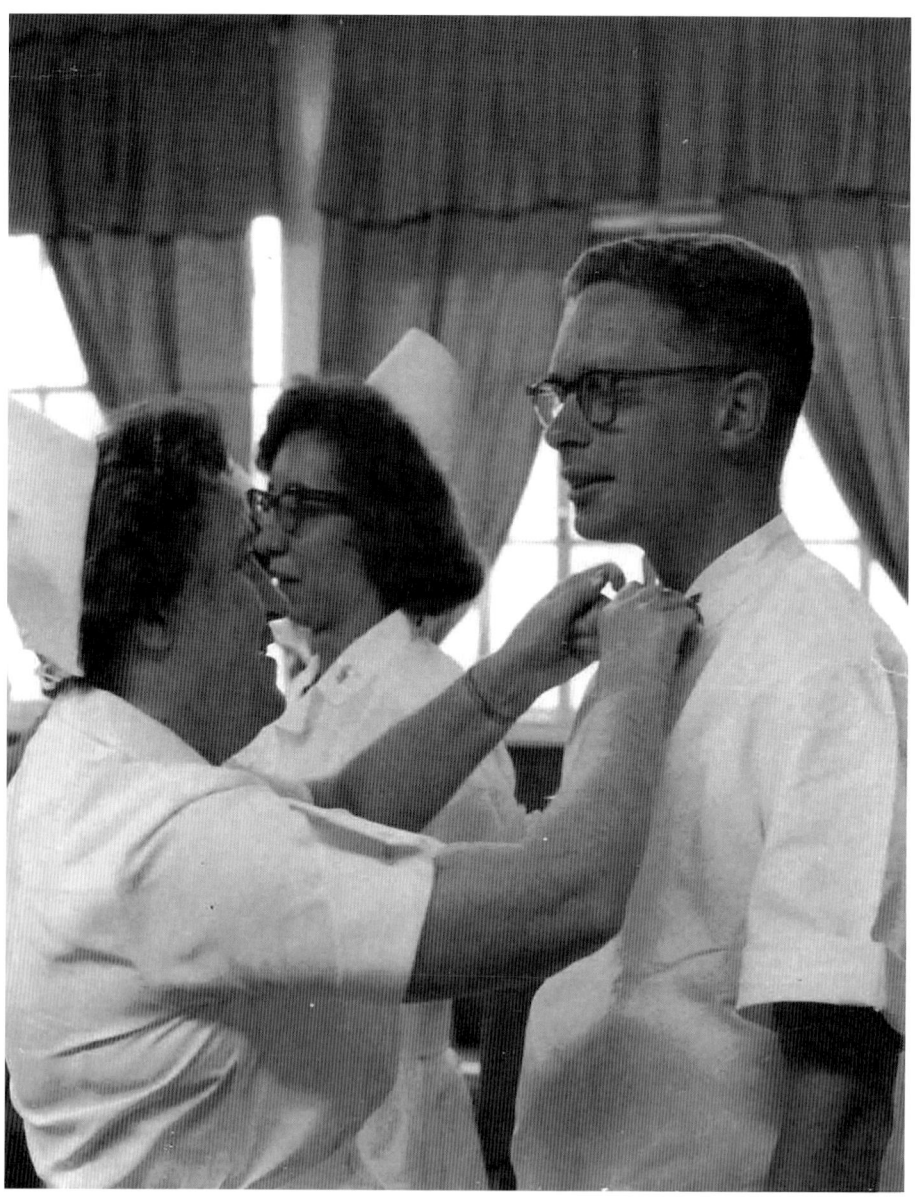

Crisply starched uniforms and Army Nurse Corps caps were the uniform of the day when Lieutenant Colonel Rita Geis (left) promoted First Lieutenant John T. Pack (far right) to captain at the 106th General Hospital in Kishine Barracks, Yokohama, Japan, in the summer of 1967.
Photo courtesy of Major John T. Pack, Fairfield, OH.

of staff of the Army directed the Army Nurse Corps members to reposition their insignia consistent with the rest of the Army—that is, with the insignia positioned parallel with the floor. With characteristic candor, Parks wrote:

> General Rogers, Chief of Staff, has made the decision on how we (all women officers) will wear our brass on the *summer dress* and *suit* and the white hospital *dress* and *pantsuit*. An effective date will be announced later for these changes. Then we will all be wearing our brass like the "WAC's" do now. I fought against this change for 18 months. I lost when the Chief of Staff made his decision.[103]

The nuances in Parks' comments expressed her distress at being forced to implement the new order. It was difficult to dictate such a change to an enduring custom that was long grounded in tradition. The uniform, however, was intended to unify and make all service personnel appear homogeneous. That likely was the rationale for the imposition of the unwelcome change to the Army Nurse Corps insignia placement.

Once regulations allowed pregnant women to remain in service, questions arose about appropriate pregnancy uniforms. A Department of the Army message published in 1975 directed pregnant Army Nurse Corps officers to purchase and wear white commercial maternity dresses or pantsuits as hospital duty uniforms. If the pregnant officer's duty assignment took her away from the AMEDD military treatment facility, such as for a temporary duty assignment, any commercial maternity outfit, "color and style unspecified," was to be worn. The civilian maternity garment was to have no insignia attached. Only a name tag was allowed; it was to include the rank, last name, and the pregnant service member's full, unabbreviated Corps (presumably "Army Nurse Corps" but not "ANC"). These uniforms were expected to be "in good taste" and were to be "approved by the commander." The nurses had to pay for these uniforms.[104]

Change seemed to be among the few constants in the Army Nurse Corps uniform picture in the 1970s. However, more changes loomed on the horizon.

# Notes

1. The active Army fielded 19 divisions in 1969. Three years later it was reduced to 12 2/3 divisions. This trend was partially reversed by the mid-1970s, when the force increased back up to 16 divisions. Vincent Demma, "The Army in the 1970s," Unpublished Information Paper, 27 March 1996, USA Center of Military History, Washington, D.C. From 1969 to 1973, the Army's total strength plunged from 1.5 million down to 0.8 million, virtually a 50 percent cut. Constance J. Moore, "Demobilization of the Army Nurse Corps after World War II, Vietnam, and Operation Desert Storm," Unpublished Information Paper, 2, 30 January 1997, USA Center of Military History, Washington, D.C. From 1969 to 1976, the officer corps, Army-wide, was cut by 74,000. In 1976, the Army was proposing a further cut of 3,800 in AMEDD officer strength. Walter T. Kerwin to E.C. Aldridge, "Manpower Issue Paper," Typewritten Memorandum (TM), 8 July 1976, Army Nurse Corps Collection (ANCC), Office of Medical History (OMH).

2. Richard R. Taylor, "Army Changes Its Ideas, Structure," *U.S. Medicine* 11 (15 January 1975): 55. John E. Haggerty, "Resource Management Presentation, AMEDD Commanders' and Surgeons' Conference," 3, n.d., in "The Surgeon General's Conference for Army Medical Department Surgeons and Commanders," 14–16 November 1973, ANCC, OMH. Charles C. Pixley, "Army Medicine Hurt by MD Shortage," *U.S. Medicine* 15 (15 January 1979): 48.

3. Patricia M. Miller to Lieutenant Colonel James Blair, "Input to Study of Health Care Extender Programs," 2, 17 February 1977, ANCC, OMH.

4. "The Surgeon General's Conference for Army Medical Department Surgeons and Commanders," 14–16 November 1973, Attachment to Colonel Shively, "Officer Strength Authorizations, Distribution and Utilization," Information Paper, 12 November 1973, ANCC, OMH. *Annual Report, The Surgeon General, United States Army, Fiscal Year 1974* (Washington, DC: Office of the Surgeon General, U.S. Army, 1974), 97.

5. J.H. Lindahl, *Army Medical Department, The Surgeon General's Resources Summary 3rd Quarter FY 1974* (Washington, DC: Office of the Surgeon General, Department of the Army, 1974), 21. *Annual Report, The Surgeon General, United States Army, Fiscal Year 1974* (Washington, DC: Office of the Surgeon General, U.S. Army, 1974), 19.

6. J.H. Lindahl, *Army Medical Department, The Surgeon General's Resources Summary 3rd Quarter FY 1975* (Washington, DC: Office of the Surgeon General, Department of the Army, 1975), 19. *Annual Report, The Surgeon General, United States Army, Fiscal Year*

*1975* (Washington, DC: Office of the Surgeon General, U.S. Army, 1975), 60.

7. Madelyn N. Parks, "Information for Key ANC Officers," 2, 24 September 1975, ANCC, OMH.

8. Madelyn N. Parks, "Information for All ANC Officers," 1, 13 July 1976, ANCC, OMH.

9. Madelyn N. Parks, "Information for All ANC Officers," 2, 19 August 1976, ANCC, OMH.

10. Madelyn N. Parks, "Information for All ANC Officers," 1, 29 April 1977, ANCC, OMH.

11. Madelyn N. Parks, "Information for All ANC Officers," 2, 27 March 1978; Madelyn N. Parks, "Information for All ANC Officers," 2, 29 January 1979; and Madelyn N. Parks, "Information for All ANC Officers," 1, 14 August 1979 (all in ANCC, OMH).

12. Madelyn N. Parks, "Information for All ANC Officers," 1, 16 November 1979, ANCC, OMH.

13. *Report of the Surgeon General United States Army Fiscal Years 1976–1980* (Washington, DC: Office of the Surgeon General, Department of the Army, 1988), 39.

14. Madelyn N. Parks, "Recommendations of the Working Conference for Nurse Clinicians," Disposition Form, Inclosure 4, 18–19, 9 March 1977, ANCC, OMH.

15. Constance J. Moore, "Demobilization of the Army Nurse Corps after World War II, Vietnam, and Operation Desert Storm," Information Paper, 2, 30 January 1997, ANCC, OMH.

16. Edith M. Nuttall, "Army Nurse Corps-Clinician Programs," Disposition Form, 18 January 1973, ANCC, OMH.

17. Edith Nuttall, "Presentation to First HSC's Chief Nurses' Conference, Gunter Hotel, San Antonio, Texas," Typewritten Text [TT], 8, 19 April 1974, ANCC, OMH.

18. Edith M. Nuttall, "AMEDD Health Care Extenders," Memorandum for the Record, 1–2, 19 May 1977, ANCC, OMH.

19. Edith Nuttall, "Presentation to First HSC's Chief Nurses' Conference, Gunter Hotel, San Antonio, Texas," TT, 8, 19 April 1974, ANCC, OMH.

20. Constance J. Moore, "Demobilization of the Army Nurse Corps after World War II, Vietnam, and Operation Desert Storm," Information Paper, 2, 30 January 1997, ANCC, OMH.

21. Edith Nuttall, "Presentation to First HSC's Chief Nurses' Conference, Gunter Hotel, San Antonio, Texas," TT, 8, 19 April 1974; and "The Surgeon General's Conference for Army Medical Department Surgeons and Commanders," 6, 14–16 November 1973 (both in ANCC, OMH).

22. Edith M. Nuttall, "AMEDD Health Care Extenders," Memorandum for the Record, 1–2, 19 May 1977, ANCC, OMH.

23. Madelyn N. Parks, "Recruitment for U.S. Army Reserve," Memorandum 3-76, 12 February 1976, ANCC, OMH.

24. *Annual Report, The Surgeon General, United States Army, Fiscal Year 1974* (Washington, DC: Office of the Surgeon General, U.S. Army, 1974), 40. *Annual Report, The Surgeon General, United States Army, Fiscal Year 1975* (Washington, DC: Office of the Surgeon General, U.S. Army, 1975), 60.

25. Edith M. Nuttall, "Conversion of Military Authorizations," Disposition Form, 23 April 1974; Madelyn N. Parks, "Civilianization in the AMEDD Registered Nurse Force," Information Paper, 11 July 1977; and Catherine T. Betz, "VOLAR Planning for FY '73," Disposition Form, 18 February 1971 (all in ANCC, OMH).

26. Doris Frazier, "ANC Fund Requisition for Training, FY 72," Disposition Form,

with attachments, 21 July 1971; "Increase WRAIN Scholarship Grants and Include New Schools in the Program," Typewritten Document [TD], 14 July 1971; "Project: VOLAR Nursing Student Program," n.d., and "Fact Sheet," n.d.; and Doris Frazier, "VOLAR Nursing Student Program," Disposition Form, 5 May 1972 (all in ANCC, OMH).

27. Joan E. Lynaugh, "Nursing's History: Looking Backward and Seeing Forward," in *Enduring Issues in American Nursing*, ed. Ellen D. Baer, Patricia D'Antonio, Sylvia Rinker, and Joan E. Lynaugh (New York, Springer: 2001), 10–24.

28. "Summary of Army Nurse Corps Strength and Distribution," Fact Sheet, 31 October 1973, ANCC, OMH.

29. Joan E. Lynaugh, "Nursing's History: Looking Backward and Seeing Forward," in *Enduring Issues in American Nursing*, ed. Ellen D. Baer, Patricia D'Antonio, Sylvia Rinker, and Joan E. Lynaugh (New York, Springer: 2001), 10–24.

30. "Is There Really a Nurse Shortage?" *Hospitals* (1 November 1979): 104. Letitia Cunningham, "Nursing Shortage? Yes!" *American Journal of Nursing* 79 (March 1979): 469–80.

31. In 1973, a major structure study found that more than 68 percent of young nurses less than 24 years of age expected to leave the Army Nurse Corps, 19 percent were undecided, and only 13 percent intended to remain in the service. This study also revealed that the "highest retention rate, by an overwhelming margin, is among RN's who enter the service through direct appointment from civilian status." John W. Rowen, Ralph B. Swisher, and Patsy B. Saunders, *Executive Summary, Structure Analysis and Program Planning, Study of the Army Nurse Corps (ANC)*, Project No. 431 4487, NBSIR 73-285, 1 October 1973 (Washington, DC: National Bureau of Standards, 1973), 15; and Cassandra M. Smith, "Army Nurse Corps Structure Analysis and Program Planning Studies," Typewritten Briefing Handout, 16 October 1974, Pie Chart labeled "Staying or Leaving by Age" (both in ANCC, OMH).

32. Lillian Dunlap, *33 Years of Army Nursing* (Washington, DC: U.S. Army Nurse Corps, 2001), 235.

33. *Annual Report, The Surgeon General, United States Army, Fiscal Year 1975* (Washington, DC: Office of the Surgeon General, U.S. Army, 1975), 16. *Report of the Surgeon General United States Army Fiscal Years 1976–1980* (Washington, DC: Office of the Surgeon General, Department of the Army, 1988), 204. Virginia L. Brown, "Newsletter to ALL CONUS Chief Nurses," TD, 1, 4 March 1974; and William B. Fulton, "Army Nurse Corps Recruiting," TD, 6 May 1975 (both in ANCC, OMH).

34. Terris Kennedy to Author, 8 November 2002, "Chapter Review for 'A Climate of Change: The Post Vietnam Era,'" Typewritten Letter [TL], ANCC, OMH.

35. Mary K. Kuntz, "Army Nurse Corps Recruiting Mission," TD, n.d., ANCC, OMH.

36. Madelyn N. Parks, "Information for All ANC Officers," Memorandum 2-78, 1, 27 March 1978, ANCC, OMH.

37. Connie L. Slewitzke, "Nurse Corps Can Be Proud," *Army Times* (3 July 1989), n.p., Newspaper Clipping in ANCC, OMH.

38. Madelyn N. Parks, "Recruitment for U.S. Army Reserve," Memorandum 3-76, 12 February 1976, ANCC, OMH.

39. Mary K. Kuntz, "Army Nurse Corps Recruiting Mission," TD, n.d.; and Hazel W. Johnson, "ANC Procurement-Staff Study," Memorandum for the Surgeon General, n.d. (both in ANCC, OMH).

40. Connie L. Slewitzke, Interview by Beverly Greenlee, Transcript, 270, 1988, Army Nurse Corps Oral History Collection, OMH.

41. Mary K. Kuntz, "Army Nurse Corps Recruiting Mission," TD, n.d.; and Hazel W.

Johnson, "ANC Procurement-Staff Study," Memorandum for the Surgeon General, n.d. (both in ANCC, OMH).

42. Mary E. Viehdorfer Frank and Robert V. Piemonte, "The Army Nurse Corps: A Decade of Change," *American Journal of Nursing* 85 (September 1985): 985.

43. Lillian Dunlap, *33 Years of Army Nursing* (Washington, DC: U.S. Army Nurse Corps, 2001), 239. Mary E. Viehdorfer Frank and Robert V. Piemonte, "The Army Nurse Corps since Vietnam," TM, 1, ANCC, OMH.

44. *Annual Report, The Surgeon General, United States Army, Fiscal Year 1974* (Washington, DC: Office of the Surgeon General, U.S. Army, 1974), 89. Richard R. Taylor, "Army Changes Its Ideas, Structure," *U.S. Medicine* 11 (15 January 1975): 56.

45. *Report of the Surgeon General United States Army Fiscal Years 1976–1980* (Washington, DC: Office of the Surgeon General, Department of the Army, 1988), 256.

46. On 1 October 1982, HSC reinstituted inpatient services at Fort Benjamin Harrison. Originally, it had eliminated such services because of "reductions in AMEDD officer authorizations." Bernhard T. Mittemeyer, "Army Medical Department," *Military Medicine* 148 (November 1983): 833–40. *U.S. Army Health Service Command, Annual Historical Review, 1 July 1975 to 30 September 1977* (Fort Sam Houston, TX: Historical Office, HSC, 1979), 106–09.

47. American Nurses Association, *1972–73 Facts about Nursing*, Table I-A-3, 10, Inclosure 2, in Betty Antilla, "ANC Recruiting Staff Study," Disposition Form, 2, 5 April 1976; and Constance J. Moore, "Demobilization of the Army Nurse Corps after World War II, Vietnam, and Operation Desert Storm," Information Paper, 3, 30 January 1997 (both in ANCC, OMH).

48. American Nurses Association, *Facts about Nursing 74–75* (Kansas City, MO: American Nurses Association, 1976), 3.

49. American Nurses Association, *Facts about Nursing 80–81* (New York: American Journal of Nursing Company, 1981), 3–4.

50. Hazel W. Johnson, "ANC Procurement-Staff Study," Memorandum for the Surgeon General, n.d., ANCC, OMH.

51. Betty Antilla, "ANC Recruiting Staff Study," Disposition Form, 2, 5 April 1976, ANCC, OMH.

52. Joan E. Lynaugh and Barbara L. Brush, *American Nursing: From Hospitals to Health Systems* (Cambridge, MA: Blackwell, 1996).

53. Neil Roland, "Army Medicine: On the Mend," *Army Times* (8 November 1982): 1, 10, 43, 56. Neil Roland, "Army, Public Hospitals Similar," *Army Times* (15 November 1982): 1, 8, 19, 34, 62. Neil Roland, "Doctor Upsurge Improves Care," *Army Times* (22 November 1982): 1, 2, 10, 34, 40, 46. Neil Roland, "Army Doctors Inexperienced but Improving," *Army Times* (29 November 1982): 3, 10, 39, 42, 52. Neil Roland, "Health Support Staff Can't Keep Pace," *Army Times* (6 December 1982): 3, 10, 30, 39, 66. Neil Roland, "Equipment Lacks Affect Patients, Exasperate MDs," *Army Times* (13 December 1982): 3, 10, 38, 42, 62. William Mayer, J. Jarrett Clinton, and David Newhall, "A First Report of the Department of Defense External Civilian Peer Review of Medical Care," *Journal of the American Medical Association* 260 (11 November 1988): 2690–93.

54. Beverly Ann K. Glor, "Planning for Quality Assurance: A New Approach for the AMEDD," TM, n.d.; Academy of Health Sciences, U.S. Army, Fort Sam Houston, Texas, *Nursing in Army Hospitals*, Study Guide 310, 76–78, November 1974; and L.J. Eason, "Nursing Audit Workshops," 6 December 1974, in Barbara R. Costello for Virginia L. Brown, "Nursing Information Letter, 3-74," 4 December 1974 (all in ANCC, OMH). Other quality measures recommended by JCAH and introduced by Army nurses included new-

comers' orientation and continuing education, more detailed documentation of care, written policies and procedures, improved patient observation and alarm systems in special care units, and written educational materials for handing out to patients. Virginia L. Brown, "Joint Commission on Accreditation of Hospitals (JCAH)," in "Nursing Information Letter, 2-75," 2–3, 11 July 1975, ANCC, OMH.

55. Academy of Health Sciences, U.S. Army, Fort Sam Houston, Texas, *Nursing in Army Hospitals*, Study Guide 310, 50–51, November 1974, ANCC, OMH.

56. Beverly Ann K. Glor, "Planning for Quality Assurance: A New Approach for the AMEDD," TM, n.d., ANCC, OMH.

57. Department of Nursing, Walter Reed Army Medical Center, "Pri-Team Nursing," Printed Brochure, 11, March 1978, ANCC, OMH. The use of this delivery model was extremely challenging in the Army setting. Its utilization was complicated by the larger proportion of paraprofessionals extant in the AMEDD system and the many extra duties that fragmented duty time for all concerned. Mary Messerschmidt to Author, E-mail Correspondence, 13 August 2002, ANCC, OMH.

58. Department of Nursing, Walter Reed Army Medical Center, "Pri-Team Nursing," Printed Brochure, 5–9, 11, March 1978, ANCC, OMH.

59. Among those involved in the development and testing of Pri-Team were Beverly Glor, Mary Messerschmidt, Fay Ferington, Mary Wise, and Rosemary McCarthy from WRAMC and Doris Frazier, Donna Sylvester and others from DDEAMC. The two factions met monthly at their own expense in Raleigh, North Carolina, to share ideas, carve out their implementation strategy, and fine-tune details. Mary Messerschmidt to Author, E-mail Correspondence, 6 August 2002, ANCC, OMH.

60. Beverly Ann K. Glor, "Planning for Quality Assurance: A New Approach for the AMEDD," TM, n.d., ANCC, OMH.

61. Department of Nursing, Walter Reed Army Medical Center, "Pri-Team Nursing," Printed Brochure, March 1978, ANCC, OMH.

62. Handwritten Note attached to Department of Nursing, Walter Reed Army Medical Center, "Pri-Team Nursing," Printed Brochure, March 1978, ANCC, OMH.

63. Colonel Moore, "Hospital Unit Dose Drug Distribution System (HUDS)," Information Paper, 8 November 1973, ANCC, OMH. Hal B. Jennings, "Hospital Unit Dose Drug Distribution System," Program Change Request, 8 March 1972; and "Letterman General Hospital, Unit Dose Drug Distribution Study," n.d. (both in Record Group 112, Entry 372, Box 1 of 4, National Archives).

64. DA Pamphlet 40-5, 1-1, 1 November 1981; and Mary E. Viehdorfer Frank and Robert V. Piemonte, "The Army Nurse Corps since Vietnam, 1974–1984," Unpublished Manuscript, 7, n.d. (both in ANCC, OMH).

65. "Scope of Professional Nursing Practice," TD, 9, n.d., ANCC, OMH.

66. DA Pamphlet 40-5, 1-1, 1 November 1981; Mary E. Viehdorfer Frank and Robert V. Piemonte, "The Army Nurse Corps since Vietnam, 1974–1984," Unpublished Manuscript, 7, n.d., ANCC, OMH.

67. Robert J.T. Joy to Author, TL, 5, 18 October 2002, ANCC, OMH.

68. Richard R. Taylor to Spurgeon Neel, TL, 29 March 1974, ANCC, OMH. Charles C. Pixley, Interview by John N. Bogart, 66–67, 1985, Research Collection, OMH. Rosemary T. McCarthy pinpointed the date when "the army nurse had officially replaced the ward officer as first-line unit administrator" at 1954. Rosemary T. McCarthy, "Parallels and Paradoxes: Differentiated Nursing Practice," in *Differentiating Nursing Practice into the Twenty-first Century*, ed. I.E. Goertzen (Kansas City, MO: American Nurses Association, American Academy of Nursing, 1991), 361–81.

69. Richard R. Taylor to Spurgeon Neel, TL, 29 March 1974, ANCC, OMH.

70. The six test sites were Brooke and Letterman Army Medical Centers and Martin, Cutler, Raymond Bliss, and Womack Army Hospitals. Philip A. Deffer to Commanders, HSC Installations and Activities, TL, 2 May 1974, ANCC, OMH.

71. Kenneth J. Kiger, "Implementation of Physician-in-Charge Program," TL, 6 June 1974, ANCC, OMH.

72. "Physician-in-Charge Program, Officer Evaluation Report Procedures," Typewritten Paper, n.d., ANCC, OMH.

73. Joan E. Lynaugh and Barbara L. Brush, *American Nursing: From Hospitals to Health Systems* (Cambridge, MA: Blackwell, 1996), 38–40. Joan I. Roberts and Thetis M. Group, *Feminism and Nursing, An Historical Perspective on Power, Status, and Political Activism in the Nursing Profession* (Westport, CN: Praeger, 1995), 221–60.

74. Doris S. Frazier to Lillian Dunlap, TL, 29 May 1974, ANCC, OMH.

75. Ibid.

76. "New Resolution Rejects Physician-in-Charge," *Convention Journal* (11 June 1974): n.p., Newspaper Clipping; and Frazier to Author, E-mail Correspondence, 21 January 2002 (both in ANCC, OMH).

77. Many acknowledged that Frazier was the foremost candidate to become General Lillian Dunlap's successor as chief of the Army Nurse Corps. Most believed that this incident curtailed her career and forced her into an early retirement. Frazier to Author, E-mail Correspondence, 5 February 2002, ANCC, OMH.

78. Lillian Dunlap, *33 Years of Army Nursing* (Washington, DC: U.S. Army Nurse Corps, 2001), 251–54. Philip A. Deffer, "Patient Care Team Program," n.d., ANCC, OMH.

79. Virtually every newsletter generated by the Office of the Chief, Army Nurse Corps, and the chief nurse of HSC during the decade of the 1970s included some degree of direction about new uniforms, correct wearing of uniforms, and miscellaneous other information relating to uniform attire.

80. Men in the Army were and are not allowed to use umbrellas while in uniform.

81. "New Beret in the Future for Women?" *Medcom Examiner* (May 10, 1973): 3. Lillian Dunlap, "Uniforms," *U.S. Army Medical Department Newsletter* 3 (Fall 1972): 23–24; Rose V. Straley, "Questions Pertaining to Uniform," 21 May 1974, in Barbara R. Costello for Virginia L. Brown, "Nursing Information Letter 3-74"; Edith M. Nuttall, "Information on Uniforms," in Madelyn N. Parks, "Information for Key ANC Officers," 24 September 1975; and Marjorie J. Wilson, "Nursing Information Letter 1-77," 3, 1 April 1977 (all in ANCC, OMH). Lillian Dunlap, *33 Years of Army Nursing* (Washington, DC: U.S. Army Nurse Corps, 2001), 304.

82. Rose V. Straley, "Questions Pertaining to Uniform," 21 May 1974, in Barbara R. Costello for Virginia L. Brown, "Nursing Information Letter 3-74"; and Edith M. Nuttall, "Information on Uniforms," in Madelyn N. Parks, "Information for Key ANC Officers," 24 September 1975 (both in ANCC, OMH).

83. "Women in the Army and Sexual Harassment, Historical Milestones," TD, 5, n.d., ANCC, OMH.

84. Lillian Dunlap, *33 Years of Army Nursing* (Washington, DC: U.S. Army Nurse Corps, 2001), 225–26.

85. Rose V. Straley, "Questions Pertaining to Uniform," 21 May 1974, in Barbara R. Costello for Virginia L. Brown, "Nursing Information Letter 3-74," ANCC, OMH.

86. Edith M. Nuttall, "Information on Uniforms," in Madelyn N. Parks, "Information for Key ANC Officers," 24 September 1975, ANCC, OMH.

87. Madelyn N. Parks, "Information for Key ANC Officers," 1, 24 September 1975, ANCC, OMH.

88. Lillian Dunlap, *33 Years of Army Nursing* (Washington, DC: U.S. Army Nurse Corps,

2001), 226–27, 304. Edith M. Nuttall, "Information on Uniforms," in Madelyn N. Parks, "Information for Key ANC Officers," 24 September 1975; and "Wear Policy for the Army Green Pantsuit," DA-TWX Message 181518Z, November 1976, in Madelyn N. Parks, "Information for All ANC Officers," December 1976 (both in ANCC, OMH).

89. "Status of Women's Uniform Items," 11 April 1977, Inclosure 13, in Madelyn N. Parks, "Information for All ANC Officers," 29 April 1977, ANCC, OMH.

90. Patrick R. Lowrey for W.F. Ulmer, "OG 507, Durable-Press, Utility (Fatigue) Uniform for Female Soldiers," 10 January 1979, Inclosure 5, in Madelyn N. Park, "Information for Key ANC Officers," 3, 16 March 1976, ANCC, OMH.

91. Edith M. Nuttall, "Information on Uniforms," in Madelyn N. Parks, "Information for Key ANC Officers," 24 September 1975; "Wear Policy for the Army Green Pantsuit," DA Message, June 1976, in "Nursing Information Letter, 2-76," 8 July 1976; and "Status of Women's Uniform Items," 11 April 1977, Inclosure 13, in Madelyn N. Parks, "Information for Key ANC Officers," 29 April 1977 (all in ANCC, OMH).

92. Lillian Dunlap, *33 Years of Army Nursing* (Washington, DC: U.S. Army Nurse Corps, 2001), 227–28. Virginia L. Brown, "Newsletter to All CONUS Chief Nurses," 2, 4 March 1974, ANCC, OMH.

93. John T. Pack to Author, E-mail Correspondence, 13 December 2002, ANCC, OMH.

94. Eugene Cudnohufsky to Author, E-mail Correspondence, 14 December 2002, ANCC, OMH.

95. Unidentified Chronology of Uniforms, n.d., ANCC, OMH.

96. While acknowledging the need for a sweater for use in cool duty environments, many nurses had reservations about its wear. Some considered the green sweater as a source for transmitting infections from patient to patient in the clinical setting. The white duty uniform was to be changed daily and washed between wearings. But the green sweater, while washable, clearly was not laundered daily. Lillian Dunlap, *33 Years of Army Nursing* (Washington, DC: U.S. Army Nurse Corps, 2001), 255–56. In 1974, Army nurses were cautioned that sweaters were "not to be worn with the white uniform when photographs are taken for publicity purposes." Virginia L. Brown, "Newsletter to All CONUS Chief Nurses," 2, 4 March 1974, ANCC, OMH. It was a functional but not very attractive uniform component.

97. Lillian Dunlap, "Uniforms," *U.S. Army Medical Department Newsletter* 3 (Winter 1972): 29, ANCC, OMH.

98. Rose V. Straley, "Questions Pertaining to Uniform," 21 May 1974, in Barbara R. Costello for Virginia L. Brown, "Nursing Information Letter 3-74," ANCC, OMH.

99. Edith M. Nuttall, "Information on Uniforms," in Madelyn N. Parks, "Information for Key ANC Officers," 24 September 1975, ANCC, OMH.

100. Lillian Dunlap, "Uniforms," *U.S. Army Medical Department Newsletter* 3 (Winter 1972): 29; and Lillian Dunlap, "Uniform Items," *U.S. Army Medical Department Newsletter* 3 (Spring 1972): 27 (both in ANCC, OMH).

101. Lillian Dunlap, *33 Years of Army Nursing* (Washington, DC: U.S. Army Nurse Corps, 2001), 228.

102. Madelyn N. Park, "Information for Key ANC Officers," 3, 16 March 1976, ANCC, OMH.

103. Madelyn N. Park, "Information for All ANC Officers," 1, 18 October 1978, ANCC, OMH.

104. "Authorization of Appropriate Maternity Uniforms for Army Pregnant Female Personnel-Officers and Enlisted," n.d., Inclosure 9, in Virginia L. Brown, "Nursing Information Letter 1-75," 7 March 1975; and Marjorie J. Wilson, "Nursing Information Letter 1-77," 5, 1 April 1977 (both in ANCC, OMH).

*Chapter Six*
# Innovative Roles

Arguably one of the most vital changes of the period, the introduction of the advanced practice movement into the repertoire of the Army Nurse Corps also was one of its most significant challenges. The Army Nurse Corps conceived its Contemporary Practice Program (ANCCPP) as the 1970s began in fiscal year (FY) 1971 and implemented it on 1 January 1972.[1] Several circumstances fostered its inception. Some in the Army Medical Department (AMEDD) viewed it as an answer to the need for physician extenders that was predicted with a future physician shortage.[2] As one source noted, nurses would "extend the arms of the physician," meaning that they would assume some of the physician's responsibilities. The Surgeon General noted that in the future, given the physician shortage crisis, Medical Corps officers would be called on to assume more demanding professional functions such as "open heart surgery, physiological monitoring, vascular surgery, nuclear application[s] in medicine, organ transplantation and highly complex diagnostic and treatment procedures." Army nurses then were among those identified to fill the void created by new demands on Medical Corps officers and assume many of the duties physicians could no longer manage, particularly those in outpatient settings in the fixed facilities.[3]

Others viewed ANCCPP as a vehicle "to promote maximum utilization of Army Nurse Corps officers in the delivery of comprehensive health care to the military community."[4] In that same vein, General Lillian Dunlap affirmed that the program "was established to add a new dimension to patient care in the AMEDD" and "to increase career satisfaction" among Army nurses.[5]

The professional nursing community saw various rationales for the evolution of the national nurse practitioner (NP) movement. Nurse historian Julie Fairman believed that the advanced practice role resulted from a number of "factors such as changes in nursing and medical education and practice, federal entitlement policies, and economics." She theorized that the role evolved "through a process of negotiation rather than delegation."[6] Loretta C. Ford, the founder of the movement, explained that "societal needs and nursing's potential led to this development."[7] She pointed out that the "dearth of physician manpower *provided the opportunity* to test new roles; it was not, however the raison d'être for the initiation of the expanded role."[8] The profession envisioned the advanced practice role as "a nursing model" whose goals were health promotion, monitoring of normal health and development, and disease and disability prevention for communities, especially those underserved by health care providers.[9] Ford and her colleague, Henry Silver, conceptualized and implemented the first such expanded role curriculum, a pediatric nurse practitioner program, at the University of Colorado in Denver in 1965.[10] Just a few years later, the Army Nurse Corps adopted the concept and adapted it to their needs. Initially, the Corps sent Lieutenant Colonels Ruth Kulvi and Mary Condit to the Pediatric Associate Course at the University of Colorado and, in 1968, Kulvi successfully tested the role at Walter Reed General Hospital. There she mainly focused on concerns that arose within the three pediatric units, the newborn nursery, and the surgical recovery unit. She also facilitated the care of pediatric patients in various specialty clinic settings and collaborated in case management with Army health nurses and social workers. Kulvi's "resounding success" in the trial run in the military setting opened the door for nurses to function in the advanced practice role in the AMEDD and served as the basis for the conceptualization of the Army Nurse Clinician Program.[11]

Originally, the plan called for educating 225 nurse clinicians (as nurse practitioners were originally called in the Army Nurse Corps) each year for five years.[12] The plan specified three pathways to "properly qualify nurses as expeditiously as possible through civilian educational programs," by revamping and augmenting existing AMEDD courses and by instituting new training programs internally within the confines of the AMEDD.[13]

At the outset of planning for ANCCPP in 1971, Army Nurse Corps leaders envisaged the need for increased authorizations and fiscal resources to support graduate education in the Long Term Civilian Training program. Planners proposed these academic expenditures "to prepare officers for increased faculty requirements, for planning and teaching duties, and for the significantly increased clinical knowledge" necessary for nurses to undertake "the more complex delegated physician tasks."[14] From FY 1972 to FY 1974, 25, 31, and 36 Army nurses, respectively, attended civilian academic institutions for graduate degrees.[15]

Army nurse educators also expanded five existing courses to incorporate advanced practice skills and knowledge including the intensive care, psychiatric-mental health, Army community health, operating room, and anesthesia nursing courses. By the end of FY 1974, the Army Nurse Corps hoped to produce 130 graduates of these courses.[16]

In FY 1972, the Army Nurse Corps introduced several new courses including the adult ambulatory care, pediatrics, and obstetrics-gynecology clinician courses. The adult ambulatory course convened its first class at Martin Army Hospital, Fort Benning, Georgia, and a few months later at a second location at Silas B. Hays Army Hospital, Fort Ord, California. The first pediatric program met at Fitzsimons

General Hospital, Aurora, Colorado. A short while later, Madigan Army Medical Center, Fort Lewis, Washington, also offered an advanced practice course in pediatrics. The obstetrics-gynecology course took place at Womack Army Hospital, Fort Bragg, North Carolina, and subsequently at William Beaumont Army Medical Center, Fort Bliss, Texas. Additionally, the U.S. Army–University of Kentucky Nurse Midwifery Program began educating nurse midwives in September 1972 at Ireland Army Hospital, Fort Knox, Kentucky. Planners hoped that these 102 nurse clinicians would graduate from these courses. These 102 students coupled with the 130 graduates of already existing courses would—it was expected—produce the intended 225 clinicians. Ultimately however, because of strength reductions levied on the Corps by the Department of the Army, only 50 percent of the original projected goal of 225 new nurse clinicians was met.[17]

The Navy and the Air Force were dealing with comparable issues in this decade, to wit, the need to supplement physicians' efforts in the primary care arena and expand the professional nurse's role.[18] Responding to these realities, the Air Force Nurse Corps (AFNC) similarly sought to augment numbers of nurses in extended roles to 236 at this time. In 1973, it educated 48 obstetrics-gynecology nurse practitioners, and by 1974, 75 Air Force nurses worked in this specialty. The AFNC trained six nurse midwives in an inaugural class at Malcolm Grow U.S. Air Force Medical Center at Andrews Air Force Base, Maryland, in 1973. By 1974, the AFNC had 16 midwives practicing in Air Force facilities and sought to add 30 more within a year. By 1974, the Air Force also had 57 pediatric nurse practitioners who received their advanced practice education in a pilot program at Wilford Hall Medical Center, Lackland Air Force Base, Texas. The Air Force intended to expand that number to 129 "within the next few years." Additional plans called for creating courses to prepare Air Force nurses as practitioners with specialties in "primary care, mental health, aerospace nursing, and visiting nurse services."[19] By March 1974, the Air Force Medical Service entered into an agreement with the University of Arizona to prepare primary care nurse practitioners, counterparts to the Army's adult ambulatory care clinicians. The charter class of 12 Air Force nurses "undertook six months of rigorous didactic education" and subsequently entered into six-month preceptorships with Air Force physicians in various U.S. Air Force facilities. In October 1974, the AFNC established a similar but internal primary care nurse practitioner program with the didactic portion programmed at the U.S. Air Force School of Health Care Sciences at Sheppard Air Force Base, Texas.[20]

By June 1972, the Navy Nurse Corps (NNC) was utilizing newly educated nurse practitioners.[21] However, Medical Corps officers in the Navy Medical Department were somewhat resistant. In 1975, the Navy surgeon general acknowledged that "many among us are just now getting accustomed to the PA [physician assistant] and NP [nurse practitioner] concept," and agreed that "some are less than enthusiastic about the idea."[22] Another source conveyed the impression that the first Navy nurse practitioners "generally [were] well received." Nonetheless, some were not terribly "eager" to accept the new practitioners, and there were "obstacles to overcome."[23] The NNC instituted its first class of six obstetrics-gynecology practitioners in 1971 at the Naval Regional Medical Center in Portsmouth, Virginia. Its interest in Pediatric Nurse Practitioner (PNP) education became manifest in 1972 when it sponsored two Navy nurses in the PNP program at the Bunker Hill Health Center affiliated with the Massachusetts General Hospital. The Navy also began an Ambulatory Care Nurse Practitioner Program in 1974 to educate "providers of primary care to outpatients over the age of 13 years" at the Naval Regional Medical Center in San Diego, California.[24] By 1976, the NNC had "27 family nurse practitioners, 16 pediatric nurse practitioners, and 17 OB/GYN [obstetrics-gynecology] nurse practitioners" actively practicing in their facilities worldwide.[25] The NNC's goal was to employ 255 nurse practitioners by 1978.[26] Actual numbers were just slightly increased by 1977, when the NNC reported that "29 family nurse practitioners, 21 pediatric nurse practitioners, 19 obstetrics/gynecology nurse practitioners, and 5 nurse midwives" were "on board."[27]

Post–Vietnam War economic constraints caused Congress to reduce both fiscal resources and troop ceilings in the Department of Defense. Consequently, Army Nurse Corps authorizations fell steadily from 4,752 at the outset of FY 1972 to 4,106 in the final days of FY 1972 and subsequently to 3,677 by FY 1975 and 3,535 in June 1976. This reduction in numbers was but one threat among many to the continued viability of the ANCCPP. Local commanders and chief nurses had little choice but to shift nurse clinicians from their advanced practice positions and place them on a priority basis in traditional nursing roles. With fewer Army nurses available to provide care in both advanced practice and traditional roles due to the decreased authorizations, and with a marked lack of nonnursing support staff (ward clerks, patient transporters, phlebotomists, dietary aides, etc.), the few remaining Army nurses were stretched to the limit. Excessive and enduring civilianization of registered nurse manpower spaces compounded the predicament. The situation threatened the continued viability of ANCCPP and a state of crisis loomed.[28] But a welcome increase in strength was achieved later in FY 1974 when authorizations rose to a slightly higher level of 3,795.[29]

Planners delegated the responsibilities for the conduct of the various ANCCPP courses to supporting groups. The military treatment facilities (MTFs) where the courses were held provided the "funds, facilities, and related resources for . . . support and to meet the requirements of accrediting bodies." The Academy of Health Sciences (AHS) undertook the tasks of "academic supervision" and "consultative services." AHS also acted as liaison with the University of Texas School of Nursing so that clinician students could be admitted to the university and—if they chose—earn academic credits. The AMEDD Personnel Support Agency, which selected and assigned course directors and instructors, also handpicked students. A three-member board convened annually to consider applicants and select the best-qualified students. Criteria that the selection board scrutinized included scholastic transcripts, performance evaluations, recommendations, Graduate Record Exam or Miller Analogy Test scores, educational preparation, and professional experience. The board also focused on "contingency" factors, such as determining whether an applicant had failed to be promoted to the next grade or whether the individual was overseas and had been in the assignment for the requisite amount of time.[30]

By June 1974, 140 Army nurse clinicians were actively practicing in the Army. Most were assigned to MTFs in the Health Services Command (HSC) including Army nurses in various specialties such as ambulatory care, pediatrics, and obstetrics-gynecology and nurse midwifery.[31] HSC directives required that all nurse clinicians practice under local protocols or written medical standing orders. Responsible local physicians had to sign the parameters of practice that were to be compatible with their own approach to health care and consistent with the amount of responsibility that they judged the nurse clinician capable of shouldering.[32]

Original 1971 program plans estimated that the efforts of each nurse clinician would, on average, replace one-half of a physician's productivity.[33] Another authority predicted that "one nurse clinician will never function as one physician. The exact equivalency is not yet known—i.e., 2, 3, or 4 nurse clinicians to replace one physician."[34] These projections proved to be conservative. Although some variation existed among the clinical specialties, workload data later confirmed that productivity of many of the nurse clinicians approached comparability with the efforts of the physician providers in certain specialties. For instance, in many cases, nurse anesthetists' workload output equaled that of a physician anesthesiologist.[35] Moreover, in Army hospitals at Fort Campbell, Fort Knox, and Fort Hood, nurse midwives delivered from 65 percent to 75 percent of all normal pregnancies.[36] As early as 1973, evidence suggested that, from both a quantitative and qualitative viewpoint, ANCCPP productivity exceeded expectations. By then, a fact sheet generated by the Army Nurse Corps characterized health care services provided through the collaboration of physicians and nurse clinicians as "accessible, comprehensive, continuous and personal." Furthermore, it attributed a "significant reduction in patients' waiting time" to the introduction of nurse clinicians into the health care team.[37]

Workload numbers compiled during the second quarter of FY 1976 for nurse clinicians lent credence to these claims and validated the clinicians' productivity. During that quarter, the average psychiatric mental health nurse clinician provided therapy for a mean total of 318 patients per quarter, devoting a typical time of 57 minutes for each client. Ambulatory care clinicians each provided care for an average of 559 patients per quarter and their visits averaged 31 minutes each. Typical pediatric nurse clinician patient visits lasted 18 minutes and numbered about 820 per clinician for that quarter. Obstetrics/gynecology nurse clinicians assessed and treated an average of 1,220 patients per quarter; their patients were seen for approximately 15 minutes each. These numbers demonstrate the diligence and hard work of the Army Nurse Corps clinicians.[38]

The statistics on the percentage of total clinic visits handled by nurse practitioners during 1978 also provided evidence of the advanced practice nurses' productivity and work ethic. For example, in the busiest of all the Class I facilities (smaller, local post hospitals), at the Fort Hood, Texas, Pediatric Clinic, six

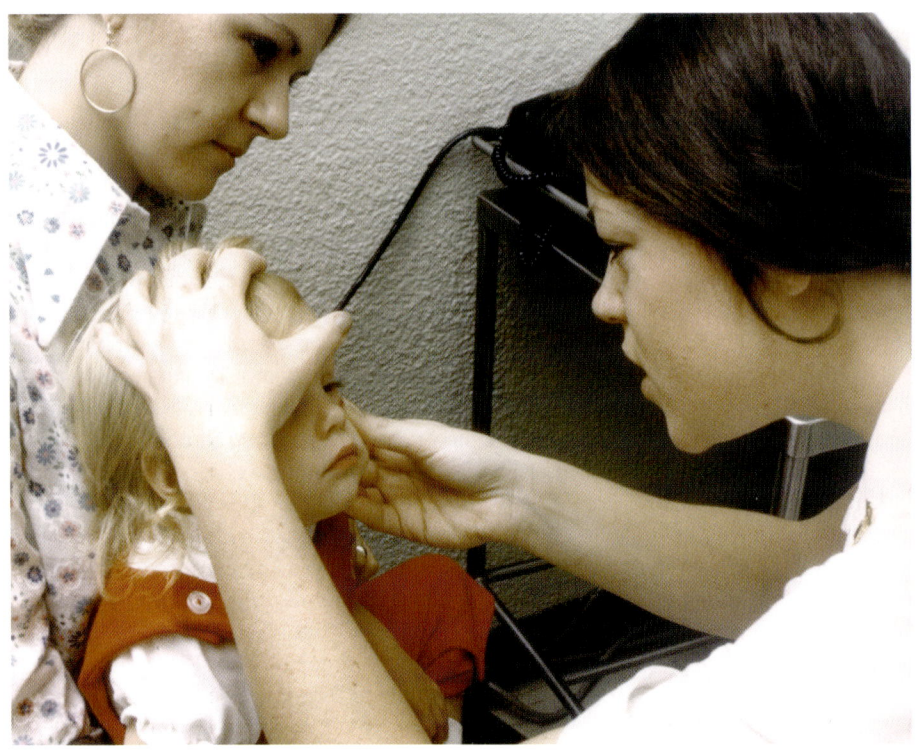

Nurse Clinician Lieutenant M. Wadden assesses an ill child.
Photo courtesy of Army Nurse Corps Archives, Office of Medical History, Falls Church, VA.

pediatricians and one PNP treated 14,370 children during the third quarter of FY 1978. The PNP there handled 20 percent of overall clinic visits and 52 percent of well baby appointments. At Fort Jackson, South Carolina, which reported a workload representative of mid-range activity, two pediatricians and two PNPs were assigned to the Pediatric Clinic. During that same quarter, those two PNPs assumed responsibility for 29 percent of total Pediatric Clinic visits and 92 percent of well child appointments. While reporting the data, Lieutenant Colonel Sarah A. Balkema, the consultant in ambulatory nursing care to The Surgeon General, tactfully cautioned that she was "not drawing any conclusions about physician productivity." Balkema added that what she merely was "saying is that the nurse practitioner *is* seeing such and such percentage of the *reported* clinic workload."[39] In summary, the evidence indicated that PNPs clearly carried their share of the workload.

Statistics such as these were remarkably similar to those in civilian health care settings. In an urban neighborhood health station in Denver, Colorado, for example, PNPs provided care with virtual autonomy for 82 percent of the pediatric population served by the clinic. PNPs referred only about 18 percent of the children for specialist care. Of all the children cared for, 54 percent represented well child visits and 46 percent were sick or injured children.[40]

By 1974, the Nurse Midwifery Program at Fort Knox, Kentucky, consisted of four certified midwives who managed approximately 25 percent of all deliveries. These well-rounded clinicians also taught and served as preceptors for students from the joint U.S. Army–University of Kentucky Nurse Midwifery Program.[41] Ambulatory nurse clinicians served in various settings. Some were staff members of oncology clinics, providing follow-up care, supervising chemotherapy, monitoring patients' lab values, and providing emotional support to both patients and their families.[42]

The expanded practice role of nurses was not limited to Army nurse clinicians functioning in ambulatory, pediatrics, obstetrics-gynecology, or even midwifery settings. The practice scope of Army Community Health Nurses (ACHNs) also widened. AHS revised its Community Health and Environmental Science Course Program of Instruction to include a multidisciplinary block of instruction that covered such topics as "military preventive medicine practices and methods, environmental health procedures and techniques and Army Health nursing activities."[43] The intent of the restructuring was to provide more education for expanded roles.

Generally, local MTF credentialing authorities granted almost all early Army nurse clinicians—regardless of specialty—the privilege of prescribing certain medications for patients in accordance with written practice protocols under some degree of physician supervision.[44] Department of the Army, the Surgeon General's Office, conferred a similar form of prescriptive authority on selected ACHNs. A Department of the Army message directed that applicants for this limited prescriptive authority make a written request for the privilege detailing their educational background and experience. The directive also instructed applicants to attach the pertinent practice protocol. The message limited the credential to the "individual nurse concerned while assigned at the installation where the request originated." The prescriptive credential authorized these ACHNs to order refills for pyridoxine and isoniazid for patients undergoing tuberculosis therapy. However, the credentialed health nurses were not allowed to initiate the therapy. Only physicians could start a patient on antitubercular drugs.[45]

To contribute to the success of the modern volunteer army by enhancing family quality of life, planners envisioned ACHNs staffing "highly visible vans" at all Army posts. They suggested parking these vans at "strategic locations near commissaries, PXs, schools and housing areas" so that nurses might provide health education and offer other health care assistance such as "tuberculin testing, immunizations and other simple health services." However, several restrictions made widespread use of such vans difficult at the outset. For instance, a lack of vehicles and a dearth of funds limited the provision of these mobile services. The few vehicles available to community health nurses at that time could only be used for transportation purposes.[46] Before long, however, ACHNs at Fort Knox, Kentucky,

The Army Health Nurse Mobile Health Van was situated in a housing area at Fort Knox, Kentucky, to provide professional services in the 1970s.
Photo courtesy of Army Nurse Corps Archives, Office of Medical History, Falls Church, VA.

and Fort Hood, Texas, obtained mobile vans to take their services into the communities where their clients resided and worked, thereby increasing access and effectiveness. During July 1975, the "Health on Wheels" van at Fort Hood served more than 400 clients. A few months later in October 1975, the mobile health van at Fort Knox reported 899 client visits.[47] By 1978, the Fort Knox van had logged more than 30,000 odometer miles. The community health nurse and her staff of one, a driver-technician, continued to average about 100 patients weekly, predominantly (88.3 percent) dependents of active duty soldiers. Services rendered included "limited physical examinations, symptomatic treatment of minor illness, immunization checks, cultures, referrals, and health education." The outlay incurred by one patient visit in the mobile health van in 1978 came to $4.05, a significant cost saving over the usual $20.24 expense accrued by a typical patient visit to the Fort Knox MTF.[48]

In Berlin, Germany, ACHNs instituted a community health information program using the Armed Forces Network radio to disseminate health promotion and disease prevention education for their community. Other ACHNs assumed the responsibilities as chief, Health Division and Environment Division, in Army hospitals worldwide.[49]

Although most advanced practice Army nurses functioned beyond the traditional inpatient care wards in ambulatory settings and some even carried out their responsibilities outside the walls of the MTFs, many practiced on a more intense plane within the customary inpatient care wards, particularly in the Intensive Care Units (ICUs). The Army's practice of segregating critically ill patients with complex care needs or those who were "physiologically unstable, at risk, or in danger of dying" in a specialized hospital zone was not a new concept.[50] Louisa May Alcott described a comparable approach used during the Civil War. Furthermore, the shock wards of World War I, World War II, and the Korean War, and the ICUs of the Vietnam War represented contemporary versions of the same concept.[51]

But the widespread introduction of the ICU in both military and civilian settings in peacetime was an innovation of the 1960s. The original modern-day critical care units were an outcome of several interacting forces. One major source was the advent and proliferation of antibiotic use in the 1940s and 1950s. This led to improved treatment of infectious diseases that allowed for greater attention to be focused on cardiovascular diseases such as myocardial infarctions and highly invasive surgeries such as major thoracic and abdominal cases. Patients undergoing these invasive procedures were critically ill and had extreme care needs suitable for management in an ICU environment. As Fairman and Lynaugh concluded, there existed

> . . . an increasingly complex hospital population for whom, at last, more useful treatments could be provided, leading to a change in the professionals' earlier expectations that certain patients were beyond saving. With higher expectations came the recognition that such patients needed more knowledgeable nurses and physicians.[52]

These specialized critical care providers and their patients congregated in the hospitals' ICUs.

The Army recognized the need for nurses with advanced practice skills in the ICU and also acknowledged the need to prepare such nurses for their critical responsibilities. Accordingly in 1970, the Army Nurse Corps began educating nurses to care for ICU patients.[53] The first iteration of many formalized six-month intensive care courses to follow met at Brooke Army Medical Center in 1973. After these seminal classes began and a charter group of educated ICU nurses deployed to the field, the Army Nurse Corps added a second site for the course. In 1974, another intensive care course began at Fitzsimons Army Medical Center. Many applicants enrolled in these courses, whose mission was to "help meet the growing requirement for well-prepared nurses to provide care for critically ill patients."[54] The Department of Nursing at Walter Reed Army Medical Center (WRAMC) subsequently began a similar program in critical care nursing that allowed both military and civil service nurses assigned there to matriculate.

The practice of anesthesia nursing long had exceeded the domains usually considered the traditional sphere of nursing.[55] Lieutenant Colonel Ira P. Gunn recalled that all Army anesthesia students were educated to some degree in "regional anesthesia as a part of their academic program." Gunn added that the majority of Army nurse anesthetists "often managed regional anesthesia cases."[56] Nonetheless, nurse anesthetists now formally sought avenues to widen their responsibilities even further and thus provide even more efficient, enhanced patient care. The long established anesthesia nursing course began to include even greater content related to respiratory care and regional anesthesia.[57] Beginning in May 1973, the course was expanded from 19.5 months to two years to accommodate these and other curriculum changes.[58] This extension of the course was in line with the recommendation of the American Association of Nurse Anesthetists that all entry-level educational programs for nurse anesthetists last two years.[59] Experienced nurse anesthetists also participated in ongoing educational programs to upgrade their knowledge and skills so that they might properly administer local anesthetic agents.[60] HSC charged fully trained anesthesiologists in the MTFs with the responsibility to implement training locally. The HSC commander recommended that the developmental courses conducted at installations include—at a minimum—such topics as anatomy and physiology, pharmacology, indications and contraindications, complications, neurological evaluation, review of individual nerve blocks, and preparation of regional anesthesia sets.[61] However, in spite of all these efforts, only 50 percent of all nurse anesthetists were qualified to administer regional anesthesia by January 1978. General Madelyn N. Parks advised those anesthetists who were not so qualified and had no anesthesiologist to provide the appropriate tutoring locally to "make arrangements to get this done even on TDY," if necessary. Parks noted that the "drastic reduction of anesthesiologists demands that nurse anesthetists be prepared to function in this area . . . *This is urgent*." Parks then added that she wanted "to see 100 percent certification within six to nine months."[62] Eventually all nurse anesthetists did acquire proficiencies in regional anesthesia. Whether they achieved this goal in the specified time frame is not known.

Psychiatric nurses also expanded their roles. Captain Ralph G. Synakowski was assigned as a mental health nurse at the Psychiatry Consultation Service at WRAMC from 1971 through 1973. His experiences typified the practice of psychiatric mental health nurse clinicians of that era. The main components of his role were clinical management, consultation, and education. He carried a panel of about 25 ambulatory patients in individual therapy, offered consultation primarily to other staff members, taught psychiatric mental health nurse clinician students, and participated in staff development programs.[63]

The practice of Lieutenant James Prucha also was state of the art for the times. He served as a psychiatric nurse clinician for the Oncology Service at Brooke Army Medical Center in this same period. Initially, Prucha found his assignment to be "an emotionally charged and draining job." Among his challenges was dealing with patients who expressed "a lack of confidence in the doctor, an overprotective mother, [and] a mother jealous of her dying son's girl friend." He also managed suicidal patients, schizophrenics, and depressed and hostile patients. He worked with cancer patients who expressed "a loss of faith in God" and others who were consumed with guilt feelings. During August 1973, he provided emotional support for 10 terminal patients, allowing them to ventilate their feelings. He assisted a dying patient's family with housing concerns. Additionally, Prucha helped a father explain his imminent death to his two young children.[64]

Infection control and surveillance nursing also was an expanded role that fell under the purview—at least initially—of those carrying the operating room nurse Military Occupational Specialty. The role evolved in both the civilian and military environments in answer to a seemingly unprecedented worldwide wave of staphylococcal infections first recognized in the 1950s. These infections appeared predominantly in the hospital setting in newborn nurseries and in patients with postoperative wound infections or hospital-associated staphylococcal pneumonia, bacteremia, and endocarditis. Investigators attributed the epidemic of hospital-related infections in part to the development of antibiotic-resistant strains of staphylococci and to a lack of guiding protocols and either a complete disregard or careless adherence to infection control techniques. The American Hospital Association's Advisory Committee on Infections issued a recommendation in 1958 that all hospitals implement surveys of nosocomial (hospital-acquired) infections and, in 1970, the Center for Disease Control (now the Centers for Disease Control and Prevention) sponsored a National Nosocomial Infections Surveillance investigation and a Study on the Efficacy of Nosocomial Infection Control. One outcome of these studies was a Centers for Disease Control and Prevention recommendation that health care institutions inaugurate infection control programs that utilized the expertise of an infection control nurse. By 1976, the Joint Commission on Accreditation of Hospitals incorporated extensive standards that addressed principles of infection control for the first time.[65] In 1972, the Army Nurse Corps first assigned infection control nurses to Walter Reed and Brooke general hospitals as a pilot effort.[66] By 1978, it sponsored a curriculum to prepare infection control practitioners that was presented annually at Aberdeen Proving Ground, Maryland. The course, titled "Prevention and Control of Hospital Associated Infections," was the "preferred course" for both military and civilian nurses responsible for the local hospital infection control programs.[67] Fifty-two individuals attended the 1978 course. Among the concerns most frequently brought to the attention of the infection control consultant, Lieutenant Colonel Helen J. Seufert, were queries about the development of local infection control policies and procedures and proper cleaning and disinfection strategies.[68] Nosocomial infections of all types eventually became important quality-of-care issues.[69]

An additional expanded role focused on incorporating nurses' expertise in planning for hospital construction. The health facilities planner became a full-time position in the 1970s when the AMEDD was heavily involved in building new and upgrading older hospitals. Early in 1976, the AMEDD formed the U.S. Army Health Facility Planning Agency, a field operating agency in the Office of The Surgeon General. Its forerunner was the Facilities Branch of the Logistics and

By 1982, attendees at the Prevention and Control of Hospital Associated Infections Course included Army, Navy, Air Force, and Public Health Service nurses. In this photo, course director Colonel Helen Seufert stands in the middle of the first row, holding the course sign.
Photo courtesy of Colonel Mary T. Sarnecky, Carlsbad, CA.

Facilities Division, Directorate of Plans, Supply and Operations, where Lieutenant Colonel Lyndoll L. Wells was the first assigned nursing consultant in 1971. The newly transformed agency administered the Army Health Facility Construction or Modernization Program that by 1980 was managing 20 projects with a combined budget of $500 million. The goal of this massive undertaking was to renovate or replace antiquated, decaying World War II era or older health care facilities.[70]

Army nurses who served in this expanded role as health facility planners shared their expertise and ultimately served to avert physical conditions that "weren't compatible with patient care" or that adversely affected "efficient utilization of staff." Many of the Army nurses who served in this agency were graduates of the U.S. Army–Baylor University Program in Health Care Administration, which awarded master's degrees in hospital administration. Many had previous experience in Army hospitals as Nurse Methods Analysts (NMAs), another role closely aligned with the advanced practice movement.[71]

Although not usually considered advanced practice, the responsibilities of today's Army NMAs clearly were implemented outside of the usual parameters that define nursing practice. Their origins can be traced to 1949 at Valley Forge General Hospital in Phoenixville, Pennsylvania. There, a small group of Army Nurse Corps officers began developing "projects to improve hospital organization

Major Helen Seufert, Infection Control Nurse Clinician, discussed concerns with the head nurse of a nursing unit at the Walter Reed Army Medical Center in 1973.
Photo courtesy of Army Nurse Corps Archives, Office of Medical History, Falls Church, VA.

and administration."[72] From the beginning, NMAs typically were assigned to the hospital comptroller's office. As a result, they found themselves in the equivocal position of answering to two masters—the comptroller and the chief nurse. They owed allegiance to the comptroller by virtue of their location in the organizational structure. At the same time, they had a functional or staff relationship with the hospital chief nurse. This triangular relationship not infrequently dictated the need for discretion, tact, an optimistic outlook, and a pragmatic as well as flexible approach on the part of NMAs.[73]

Originally, these practitioners were referred to as management nurses and subsequently as nursing management analysts. During the 1950s, *management* was dropped from the position title and they became known as Nursing Methods Analysts. The elimination of *management* resulted because the word "tended to convey the impression that nursing service could not manage their activities properly and that efficiency experts—in the guise of Management Nurses—were assigned to tell them what to do and how to do it."[74] In 1984, their designation changed

Lieutenant Colonel Lyndoll L. Wells, left, explains planning details on a model for future Army hospital construction. Wells is briefing from left to right, Brigadier General Anna Mae Hays, Colonel Lillian Dunlap, and Colonel Louise C. Rosasco.
Photo courtesy of Colonel Doris Frazier and Colonel Barbara Davis, Evans, GA.

again—in this case—from that of Nursing Methods Analyst to Nurse Methods Analyst.[75] A new generation of officers promoted this latest designation, reasoning "that the title should reflect exclusivity to nurses." This cohort probably "did not want their expertise to be seen as limited only to 'nursing' but wanted to be viewed as possessing broadly utilizable qualifications as 'methods analysts'."[76]

Included in the responsibilities of this position were conducting studies, assisting "in the determination of personnel requirements," assessing nursing facilities for adequacy and suggesting enhancements, evaluating and developing forms and policies, and judging and approving supplies and equipment for nursing.[77] Among the many far-reaching improvements made by NMAs by the late 1960s was the "centralization of the food service in Army hospitals." Before this time, each individual patient unit or ward in a fixed facility hospital had its own diet kitchen exclusively dedicated to providing nutritional support only for that ward's patients. Furthermore, by then NMAs had begun work on a system to account for workload by categorizing patients according to their nursing requirements. The patient groupings included those with requirements for "intensive, moderate, minimal, and supportive" nursing care.[78] By 1972, there were 12 NMAs assigned to Army hospitals. Of these 12, nine were graduates of the "U.S. Army–Baylor Hospital Administration Course."[79]

Army Nurse Corps support of the Automated Military Outpatient System was another innovative role. This system began in 1969 as an enterprise to expand the medical corpsman's role and evolved into the Triage and Acute Minor Illness clinics at DeWitt Army Hospital, Fort Belvoir, Virginia. The AMEDD subsequently fine-tuned the program at Army MTFs at Fort Meade, Maryland; Fort Bragg, North Carolina; and Fort Hood, Texas. At the Fort Belvoir site, Lieutenant Colonel Margaret E. Weydert and Captain Carolyn C. Knight, the project officers, said it was one effort among many designed to help relieve the shortage of primary health care providers and reduce patient waiting time.[80] The Automated Military Outpatient System Specialists (AMOSISTs), as the enlisted corpsmen involved were called, were to sort "walk-in adult patients by symptoms," input the information into flow sheets, and then, based on feedback, refer these patients "to appropriate treatment areas." They also were expected to treat minor complaints with advice and over-the-counter drugs using comparable algorithms under the direct supervision of the AMOSIST physician.[81] Major Mary Lou Spine, an Army Nurse Corps officer and the HSC Ambulatory Care Division AMOSIST project officer, helped to write the program guides. She explained that, at that time, she was attempting "to standardize how the AMOSISTs would be used and what they would be permitted to do." Such protocols were necessary to achieve appropriate utilization, Spine revealed, because typically "some MDs wanted [the AMOSISTs] to perform major surgery while others wouldn't let them take a temperature!"[82]

To become an AMOSIST, specially selected corpsmen with good communication skills participated in one of several educational programs. They could attend a six- to eight-week course at AHS, participate in local on-the-job training, or engage in a combination of both options.[83] Until 1977, four Army Medical Centers and an assortment of 234 medical facilities used some version of the Automated Military Outpatient System program. However, by 1977, shortages in the numbers of physicians available to oversee the AMOSISTs' performance and reductions in the numbers of corpsmen Army-wide ended the program.[84] Other factors that ultimately contributed to the system's demise were the failures on the part of the AMOSISTs to faithfully use the Triage Manual, the data-collection sheets, and the AMOSIST Manual for every patient; the lack of approved drug lists to complement the treatment protocols; and the fact that the AMOSISTs' autonomy and scope of practice often exceeded accepted standards.[85]

Tentative long-range plans called for Army nurses to practice under similar conditions using automated decision-tree algorithms while caring for patients with "stable, well-defined chronic illnesses." But this computerized approach that "was soon found to be inappropriate to the patients' needs and a poor use of the nurse's skills" halted these plans.[86]

Although the AMOSIST program in its original format vanished, it did lead to other primary health care innovations. From 1973 through 1982, officers at Brooke Army Medical Center refined its concepts, adapted it into a more efficacious format, and extended its use into Troop Medical Clinics. These Medical Corps officers then used it as a foundation for the Army Emergency Medicine residency programs, the Emergency Medicine Program at the Uniformed Services University of the Health Sciences, and the Combat Casualty Care Course (C4). Later, the AMOSIST program served as a model for the development of telephone-based nurse triage systems so prevalent in the civilian health care sector.[87]

Physical therapists, officers of the Army Medical Specialist Corps, also assumed expanded responsibilities including the "initial screening of patients with musculoskeletal disorders." They helped "to maintain the quality of care while freeing the physician . . . to spend more time with the patients requiring their special skill."[88] Army physical therapists also prescribed treatment for minor musculoskeletal ailments.[89] Occupational therapists, also Army Medical Specialist Corps officers, likewise participated in the expanded practice movement and focused on the assessment of musculoskeletal problems of the hands and arms.[90] The expanded practice of Army Medical Specialist Corps officers prepared as dietitians focused primarily on patients involved with the Army's Weight Control Program.[91]

The physician assistant (PA), another new role, also evolved in the AMEDD in 1971. A few years before its integration into the Army, however, civilian physicians had conceptualized the new type of health care provider as another variety of physician extender. The first educational program to prepare PAs met in 1965 at Duke University in North Carolina.[92] For its initial classes, Duke selected military corpsmen who were Vietnam veterans as students because of their unique training, combat experience, and prior exposure to "conflict and controversy."[93] The need for potential PAs to function with skill, discretion, and sangfroid in a difficult climate redolent with hostility and ambiguities proved to be essential.

The Army, with a ready and eager supply of applicants with similar backgrounds, adapted their version of the PA role from the civilian model. The AMEDD's charter class of 60 PA students, warrant officer candidates, started their studies in the summer of 1971 at AHS. In August 1973, 52 neophyte PAs graduated from the two-year curriculum. The Army then promoted the graduates to warrant officer and introduced them into the Army's health care system. Baylor University simultaneously awarded the 52 warrant officers an associate of science degree. The majority of the new PAs' were first assigned to divisional units. Of all the graduates, 36 began their careers as members of tactical organizations, while 16 went to fixed facilities in Army hospitals.[94]

Both variations of PAs, military and civilian, generated impassioned debates and encountered heated resistance from many individual nurses and the profession of nursing at large. For instance, at Duke, when invited to participate or teach in the venture, most professional nurses and nursing administrators in the Medical Center and the faculty of the Nursing School strenuously resisted. They concurred with the American Nurses Association stance, rejecting the PA role for nurses because it would place professional nurses in a subservient rather than a complementary relationship with physicians. Simply put, most professional nurses refused to teach or become PAs. The fires of the controversy stoked even higher when *Look* magazine published an article profiling the innovative PA role and titled the incendiary piece "More than a Nurse, Less than a Doctor."[95]

Many Army Nurse Corps officers had comparable reservations—even spirited objections—to the whole notion of PAs.[96] Some vowed that they would "never take orders from a physician assistant." Dunlap revealed that these Army nurses

> ... pictured the physician assistants giving them orders, supervising nurses. That was not the position I took. My position was that there's plenty of work for everybody as long as we in nursing define nursing's role and how our nurse clinicians will function. Likewise, the physician assistants' roles would be defined. . . . I wanted to go ahead and try it.[97]

When MTF chief nurses met in 1971 in Washington, D.C., they recommended that all "Army nurses respond cooperatively to the concept of the physician's assistant" and reiterated that the PA's "role and functions be clearly defined" jointly by nurses and physicians so that a "professional colleague relationship" be established and maintained.[98]

After a stormy beginning, PAs eventually blended into the AMEDD. Their relationships with Army nurses were sometimes collegial, occasionally distant, and every so often acrimonious. PAs settled primarily into the Troop Medical Clinics and the line units and continued to make their unique contributions to the health of the Army.

At the outset of the ANCCPP introductory period, many Army physicians were resistant or at least uncertain about the use of Army nurses in the extended role. However, their grassroots opposition eventually tapered off and frequently it became enthusiastic acceptance once the nurses demonstrated their skills. Their wholehearted approval led many Medical Corps officers to claim the nurse clinicians (practitioners) as their own. In 1974, Lieutenant Colonel Jean M. Houghton, chief nurse at Munson Army Hospital, Fort Leavenworth, Kansas, wrote that the nurse clinicians "have the judgment to realize the difference between nursing care practice and the practice of medicine." However, she confided, the "bigger dilemma . . . is to make the physicians aware and understand this difference." Captain Richard Harbin, an ACHN assigned to Fort Leavenworth, also practiced in an expanded role at certain times in the Pediatric Clinic. Houghton noted that the clinic pediatricians were "extremely pleased with this concept." She also said that she had "stressed . . . the fact that he is a nurse and not an additional Pediatrician." Captain Nancy Martinkus (McFadin Mueller) pioneered the "chronic care nurse concept in the Ambulatory Care area." There she encountered "almost full blown opposition from some of the internists." Nonetheless, after her precarious start, Martinkus transformed her adversaries into allies after only two months. "The Chief of Medicine, who was originally against the idea[,]" did an about-face "almost to the point the whole concept was his." Soon Martinkus was maintaining her own panel of hypertensive patients.[99]

Patients also were happy with the services the nurse clinicians provided. First Lieutenant Anne Hemme conducted a Well Woman Clinic in the Obstetrics/Gynecology Clinic at Munson Army Hospital, where appointments for her services were available through the Central Appointment Service. At this point Lieutenant Colonel Connie L. Slewitzke was the first woman class president of the Command and General Staff College in the residence course at Fort Leavenworth. Slewitzke often acted as a "sounding board," relaying comments regarding health care provided at Munson Army Hospital. She said "how pleased the women of the community were with [Hemme] and the Well Woman Clinic Nurse idea."[100]

The widespread acceptance accorded Army nurse clinicians (practitioners) in the Army mirrored the patients' perceptions of advanced practice nurses in other military services and in the civilian world. An Air Force spokesman characterized patients' responses to obstetrics/gynecology and pediatric nurse practitioners as "overwhelming." He added that the "nurses are more sympathetic with women and children patients, forming a rapport few male doctors ever achieve." Finally, he disclosed that "in some hospitals . . . the nurse practitioners are booked for Pap smears long before the doctors' schedules are filled."[101] Patient response to the services provided by advanced practice nurses remained consistently excellent in the AMEDD, the military, and civilian health care.

In 1968, Henry Silver investigated the phenomenon of patient satisfaction in a clinic that utilized PNPs in Denver, Colorado, and he noted an almost unanimous acceptance by patients and their families.[102] Two decades later, little had changed. The landmark 1986 Office of Technology Assessment study revealed that advanced practice nurses could efficiently provide care autonomously for 60 to 90 percent of all patients in a primary care setting and that virtually all patients highly valued the services provided by nurse practitioners.[103]

Although, for the most part, Army nurse clinicians (practitioners) were well received and highly satisfied with their professional roles, some inequities, instances of inappropriate utilization, and long-range doubts surfaced. For example, a number of clinicians reported overbooking of their appointments, claiming they were "forced to see patients . . . one per every ten minutes, 8 or more hours per day." Others reported being demoralized because their practice was restricted only to "hundreds of summer camp and 'back to school' physicals," or exclusively "seeing only VD [venereal disease] patients." Still others were disheartened by the scorn certain physicians accorded the nurse clinicians' emphasis on "emotional assistance and health teaching." Some who were oriented to future career opportunities worried about maintaining their advanced practice skills and knowledge while simultaneously feeling pressure to secure promotions and advance.[104] Few simple answers existed for these complex issues and predicaments.

As time passed, ANCCPP was renamed the Army Nurse Clinician Program (AN-CP), sometimes called the Army Nurse Corps Clinician Program, presumably to make the cumbersome acronym pronounceable, and still later it was designated the Army Nurse Practitioner Program. In 1977, the position title of "Nurse

Clinician" was replaced by the designation "Nurse Practitioner" (NP). Moreover, Army Nurse Corps regulations acknowledged another related role, the Clinical Nurse Specialist (CNS), as a new, accepted practice specialty for Army nurses.[105]

The Army Nurse Corps interpretation of the CNS concept differed somewhat from that in the civilian nursing community. Disparities between the CNS and the nurse practitioner in the AMEDD, as described in Army Regulation 40-6, related primarily to educational preparation. Although the regulation required the CNS to have a master's degree in nursing in a clinical specialty area, it expected the NP to have an earned baccalaureate degree and some variation of specialty advanced practice training. The duties of both as described in Army Regulation 40-6 were essentially identical except in the area of ordering patient medications. Only the NP had prescriptive privileges, albeit a circumscribed, limited authority. However, both the CNS and NP would "plan, provide and evaluate" direct and indirect nursing care that involved patient and family assessment, treatment, and follow-on care as well as provide educational services for both patients and other nursing staff members. In addition, both would collaborate with other health care providers and provide an array of consultation services.[106]

The civilian view of the CNS and NP roles was slightly divergent from the Army's concept, especially regarding responsibilities. The nonmilitary model visualized the CNS role with five components: (1) direct hands-on care, (2) consultation, (3) patient and staff education, (4) involvement in research, and (5) leadership. The NP role focused more exclusively and heavily on direct care.[107] Several years later, a survey sample of civilian health care providers reported many "overlapping activities" in all aspects of CNS and NP "role functioning." Respondents judged the two roles to be "more similar than they [were] different." Findings suggested that many NPs and CNSs favored "the merging of clinical nurse specialist and nurse practitioner preparation."[108] Features such as educational preparation and clinical practice indicated the two roles shared many commonalities.[109] Both roles seemed to be fusing.

After the introduction of ANCCPP in the early 1970s, the Army Nurse Corps continually and actively used nurse practitioners and supported a comprehensive advanced practice program. In the early years, most of the preparatory programs—both in the civilian and Army communities—operated as certificate-granting, continuing-education courses that usually did not—although sometimes they could—offer college credit. Most had no relationship with collegiate schools of nursing. The Army, however, took the middle ground when it set up an academic affiliation with the University of Texas, allowing Army graduates the option to apply for 16 graduate credits for their attendance at the certificate-granting course.

The pervasive, nationwide exclusion from the halls of higher education so characteristic during the early years of the NP movement resulted from stands taken by nurse educators in institutions of higher learning and leaders in the professional organizations. They "conceptually divided the health care delivery team into two camps: workers who cured illness and workers who gave sustaining care." These skeptics contended that "the mixed role of the NP who sought to deliver

Major Harriet H. Werley established the Department of Nursing at Walter Reed Army Institute of Research in 1957 and launched the clinical nursing research movement in the Army and likely in the world of professional nursing.
Photo courtesy of Army Nurse Corps Archives, Office of Medical History, Falls Church, VA.

both care and cure-oriented services was suspect." Martha Rogers, an influential nurse theorist, saw the incursion of the NP movement as an effort to lure nurses back into an archaic social order, or as she put it, into "paying obeisance to an obsolete hierarchy." Rogers "wanted nursing to be an independent profession and felt that the NP movement was a step backward and . . . argued that . . . NPs had, in effect, left the nursing profession." These opinions served as "powerful barrier[s] to the early institutionalization of the educational programs within the mainstream of nursing education."[110] Nonetheless, by the mid-1970s, a few universities began to offer graduate degrees in advanced practice roles. These curricula integrated nurse practitioner "philosophy, concept, and processes" in response to overwhelming pressures exerted by "funding agencies, the federal government, . . . students, . . . professional nursing, . . . and changes in state practice laws." Escalating costs and inequities in the distribution of health care professionals also slowly exerted an influence.[111] By the mid-1980s, emerging national trends favoring graduate-level preparation for advanced practice at the master's degree level culminated in the gradual withdrawal of Army-sponsored programs to develop NPs independent of academia. Thereafter, Army nurses received their education for advanced practice primarily in civilian educational institutions.[112]

The sanctioning of independent research activities that studied nursing concerns into the domains of the Army Nurse Corps represented another innovative role. Although Army nurses in the past had participated informally in research activities, the formal origins of nursing research in the Army dated back to 1957 when Major Harriet H. Werley launched the Department of Nursing at the Walter Reed Army Institute of Research (WRAIR). The unit was the first institutional program—probably in the world—dedicated to clinical nursing research. The mission of the fledgling research unit was to develop a program of military nursing research projects oriented to patient care problems and educate a cadre of competent nurse researchers capable of analyzing nursing practices to develop new knowledge for improved patient care. The WRAIR group sponsored research studies, subsidized nursing research conferences, and inaugurated an annual, year-long course to develop Army nurse researchers.[113] The original staff of the Department of Nursing at WRAIR included Werley, Major Clara Duley, and Captain Miriam Ginsberg.[114] Captain Phyllis Verhonick and Major Ruth Greenfield joined the unit six months later. Both Verhonick and Greenfield had just completed their doctorates at Teachers College, Columbia University, under the auspices of the Army Nurse Corps. Ultimately, the combination of senior-level Army Nurse Corps support for the program, Werley's vision and zeal, Verhonick's enthusiasm and wisdom, their collegial relationships with other researchers at WRAIR, and the nurse researchers' diligence produced success beyond the dreams of all concerned.[115]

In the 1960s, the Department of Nursing at WRAIR completed several landmark nursing investigations on various clinical problems such as oral hygiene techniques, reverse isolation, and decubitus ulcers. It sponsored six iterations of the year-long Military Nursing Practice and Research Course.

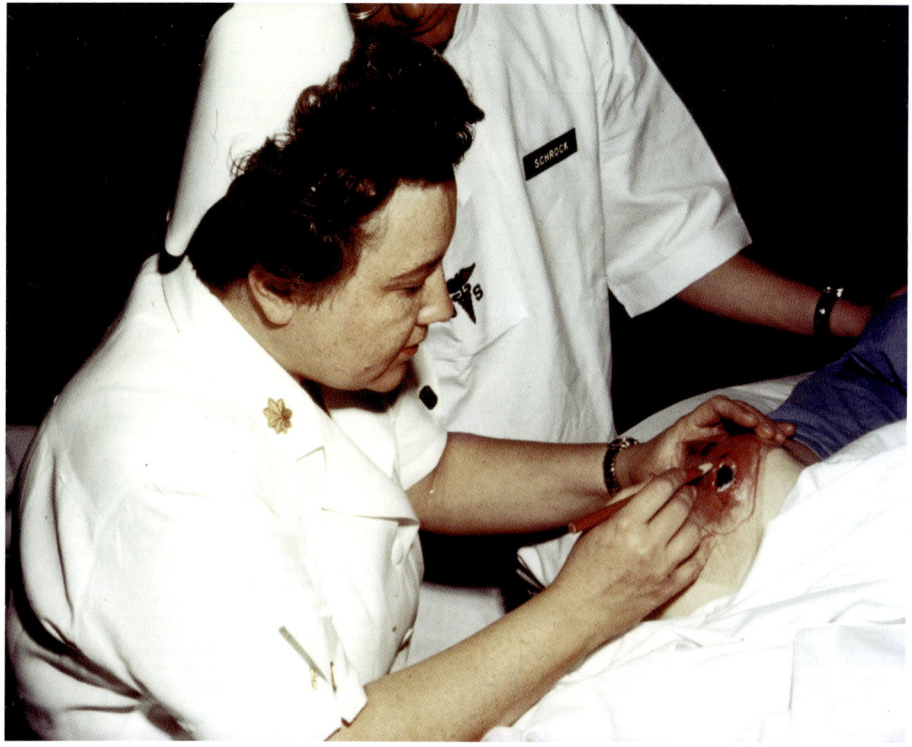

Major Phyllis Verhonick measured the size of a patient's decubitus ulcer. She was renowned globally for her innovative studies of such wounds.
Photo courtesy of Army Nurse Corps Archives, Office of Medical History, Falls Church, VA.

When Werley left WRAIR and was reassigned to Korea in 1963, Verhonick replaced her as department chief. Like Werley, Verhonick had talent, a creative vision, and "possessed a sense of humor that was invaluable in helping overcome the frustrations and obstacles so frequently encountered in research endeavors."[116] A charter member of the American Academy of Nursing, Verhonick

> . . . was known nationally and internationally for research on decubitus and skin care. She persevered in efforts to conduct indepth research in this area and moved from descriptive studies to sophisticated multidisciplinary research involving bioengineering quantitative measures. Her studies were designed to gain greater understanding of phenomena and to develop predictive studies.[117]

In 1968, Verhonick retired from the Army to become a faculty member at the University of Virginia. Lieutenant Colonel Miriam Ginsberg replaced her. That same year, the surgeon general named Lieutenant Colonel Rosemary T. McCarthy as the first nursing research consultant.[118] This appointment formalized the importance of nursing research and set up an easily accessible point of contact for consultation. In 1970, Lieutenant Colonel Glennadee Nichols assumed the senior research position. Among her credentials, Nichols claimed two previous assignments at WRAIR and also a recent doctorate from Teachers College, Columbia University.[119] Nichols' research interests were diverse. In one investigation, she focused on patient satisfaction.[120] Her work revealed that patient dissatisfaction most frequently resulted from problems in communication between patients and hospital staff. The findings became the impetus for the development of an active patient advocacy program at WRAMC in 1974.[121]

In 1973, Lieutenant Colonel Margaret O'Dell became the division's director. At that time, after 15 years under WRAIR, the Division of Nursing sailed into stormy seas. Amongst militarywide retrenchment and personnel shortages, the director of WRAIR substantially reduced the Division of Nursing's budget and its personnel allowances. O'Dell's position remained, but the authorizations for four additional nurse researchers, one administrative specialist, and one secretary were purposely unfilled. Other resources such as office and laboratory space were also pared down. Evidence suggests that personality conflicts between O'Dell and the WRAIR command also contributed to the widening schism.[122]

In the 1970s, Colonel Ed Buescher was director of WRAIR. Buescher objected to the Army Nurse Corps presence in WRAIR, a Medical Research and Development Command unit. Colonel Robert J.T. Joy, WRAIR's deputy director, disclosed that Buescher felt that the nurse researchers at that time "did trivial research, could not write a research protocol, could not put results in decent manuscript format, and did not ask important questions." Joy expanded on other issues that precipitated nursing's eviction from WRAIR. He noted that the nurses were predominantly doing clinical nursing research in an institution (WRAIR) dedicated to "military directed" research. Confusion over funding further complicated matters. WRAIR's budget originated from Program 6, Research and Development dollars, while the nurses' clinical research money came from Program 8, Operations and Maintenance dollars, a funding source foreign to WRAIR. Through his actions, Buescher clearly communicated his disdain. When Nichols left WRAIR in 1973, Buescher refused to see her for an exit interview. Instead, Joy "pinned on her medal in a near private ceremony." Joy remarked, "It was all so sad." He added that Buescher ultimately "ordered that all five nurses be put in one room not quite large enough for five desks; the back row could only be reached by turning sideways and leaning against the wall." This move clearly was the last and most decisive strategy used to remove the nurse researchers from WRAIR. Joy summed up his view of the debacle, stating that the nurse researchers "were nice people wrongly placed in a high-powered biomedical scientific institute."[123]

With the dawning of 1976, nursing research was effectively coerced out of WRAIR. In November 1975, Parks recommended to the surgeon general the transfer of the Division of Nursing at WRAIR to WRAMC, reasoning that nursing research ideally should be conducted in a hospital. The surgeon general concurred with the recommendation in January 1976, thus terminating the WRAIR–nursing

Standing on the steps of the Walter Reed Army Institute of Research (WRAIR) with director, Lieutenant Colonel Harriet H. Werley, are the first four Army nurses to participate in the first 40-week Military Nursing Practice and Research Course launched at WRAIR in the fall of 1961. Front row from left to right: Captain Elenore F. Sullivan, Lieutenant Colonel Harriet H. Werley (director), and Captain Rosemary T. McCarthy. Second row from left to right: Captain Katherine F. Galloway and Major Leonora M. Moseley.
Photo courtesy of Army Nurse Corps Archives, Office of Medical History, Falls Church, VA.

research affiliation, and on 1 April 1976, WRAIR formally relinquished the remaining nursing manpower spaces and funding.[124]

Lieutenant Colonel Elenore Sullivan became the first chief and only staff member of the diminished Nursing Research Service when it settled in its basement office in Building One, the original Walter Reed Hospital building. Fortunately, at the same time, Colonel Katherine Galloway, who was a graduate of the first Military Nursing Practice and Research Course, was chief nurse at Walter Reed. She represented a sympathetic and supportive figure for Sullivan, who sustained the service primarily by facilitating the research endeavors of Army nurse graduate students who were studying in nearby civilian educational institutions. Sullivan expedited the students' data collection in the clinical areas of the hospital. Eventually, the Nursing Research Service staff expanded once again to include four additional nurse researchers.[125]

Major Janet Southby's assignment as the new chief in 1979 injected a healthy and much needed dose of vitality into the service. After earning her doctorate at Catholic University, Southby signed into WRAMC and immediately began developing her researchers, who in turn produced an impressive body of studies. Their investigations focused on diarrhea in tube-fed patients, reducing discomfort from intramuscular injections, health care workers' attitudes toward violence in close relationships, introduction of a post-anesthesia score in the recovery room, and the effectiveness of measures to relieve the pain of episiotomies.[126] Moreover, the hard-working Southby expanded contacts with research consumers and concerned parties on many levels including initiating an annual activity report and publishing and disseminating a newsletter, *Nursing Research Notes*. She encouraged the Nursing Research Service staff to publish in professional, refereed journals that resulted in a renaissance of professional writing within the organization. By 1980, the researchers also took part in hospital committees, presented classes and participated in newcomer orientations, and completed their share of hospital weekend supervision duty.[127] Although most of these responsibilities facilitated exchanges between researcher and clinician and probably were appropriate duties for nurse researchers in a medical center, they did distract the nurses from a total dedication to the exclusive practice of nursing research. Werley had articulated her misgivings about the diversionary nature of such pursuits five years earlier in 1974. She argued:

> In the interest of having the nursing research nucleus group located in a setting conducive to research, I would strongly recommend that the bolstering of the Army Nurse Corps research potential be accomplished within the confines of the Research and Development Command. This is not to say that some of the research will not be worked through with personnel in the clinical setting, but being located within the Research and Development Command, the nursing research nucleus group's work should be facilitated, whether it be basic or applied in nature.[128]

Experience has verified that there is a place for nurse researchers in both hospitals and in purely research institutions. Later, Army Nurse Corps officers would be welcomed back into Army units exclusively dedicated to research.

The climate at the Institute of Surgical Research (ISR), commonly known as the Burn Unit at Brooke Army Medical Center, also was somewhat intimidating for nursing research in the late 1970s. At that time, the Army Nurse Corps assigned Major Hedy Mechanic, a doctoral nurse researcher, to the ISR. Her assignment there "was controversial and short-lived," however, as the ISR commander regarded "nursing research . . . an oxymoron" and "nursing scholarship was considered a punch line." Mechanic defended her role and "clashed with the administrative leadership on research design and methodology and was quickly pushed along out of the area." The milieu was one where "good nurses [knew] their place, [kept] their mouth shut and eyes averted." With time and the influx of new blood, however, the outlook changed. Nonetheless, "the ramp up for nurses to publish or conduct research . . . was steep and arduous initially." The first step on the route to professional recognition and acceptance involved the physicians' acknowledging in writing the nurses' contributions to their investigations and publications. Then the commander/director allowed nurses to publish clinical articles and book chapters and to make presentations. He "spent considerable time reviewing and making changes in manuscripts written by nurses and [the nurses] were grateful to a person for his tutelage and support."[129] But it was only with the passage of the old order and a paradigm shift from patriarchy to collegiality that actual clinical nursing research gained a firm foothold in the ISR. In the late 1990s, Colonel Elizabeth Greenfield received TriService Nursing Research funding to study the efficacy of a new technology—a cap implanted with electrodes to measure pain indirectly in unconscious patients.[130] Another study questioned whether hardiness in burn unit nurses predicted burnout or whether it buffered the effect of caregivers' stress on burnout.[131] An additional investigation implemented by Colonel Linda Yoder probed the long-term outcomes of burn unit patients, focusing on their quality of life and functional status.[132] Although progress was slow and laborious, ISR was moving into the modern age and approaching parity with state-of-the-art nursing research.

In the 1970s, a widespread Army Nurse Corps research agenda emerged. The Army Nurse Corps first assigned nurse researchers to the Health Care Studies Division at HSC. They conducted an assortment of in-depth investigations on research topics such as the foundation studies for the Workload Management System for Nurses, a comprehensive tool for documenting workload and predicting staffing requirements.

The Corps assigned a nurse researcher, Lieutenant Colonel Hazel W. Johnson, to the U.S. Army Research and Development Command's Materiel Development Division for the first time in 1967. She remained there through 1973. Johnson established a nursing role while serving as a project officer for several programs. She recalled:

> I involved myself in a number of opportunities in the Research and Development command when it called for nursing input. I was available to the staff and that was the idea. The other thing, of course, was that I also knew other people out in the Army nursing community who would be available for

consultation. If they needed someone to take a look at something, I might recommend a name of an individual who might be the appropriate person to do that. My major reason for being there was to work on the field sterilization study.[133]

The goal of Johnson's primary work was to develop a field sterilizer, a portable piece of equipment to sterilize instruments in the combat setting. Another of Johnson's initiatives involved creating a system to identify pyrogens (fever-producing substances) in materials such as medications. The system became known as the Pyrogen Identifier, Rapid Response.[134] Johnson also worked at this time with a New York City group studying the need to aerate supplies after gas sterilization, a process used to eradicate all traces of ethylene oxide from instruments and equipment after sterilization and before human use.[135]

The Army Nurse Corps historian, assigned to the U.S. Army Center of Military History, began an important program dedicated to collecting and preserving the oral histories of outstanding Army Nurse Corps senior officers, key leaders, and other Army nurses whose experiences, ideas, and contributions were representative of the majority of the Corps, thus preserving the institutional memory of the Army Nurse Corps. Although not strictly regarded as research, per se, the oral history collection represented a treasury of data upon which many future historical research projects would be based.

Many Army hospitals also created nursing research committees that fostered grassroots research efforts. They disseminated their research findings and those of other health professionals to local health care providers, the ultimate consumers, who used the new knowledge at the bedside.[136]

To identify pertinent, realistic, and appropriate research projects and to ensure that research endeavors addressed the most important and pressing of questions relevant to Army Nurse Corps needs, the Corps established the Nursing Research Advisory Board (NRAB). It initially convened in 1979 and met for three days. The NRAB's membership included the Corps leaders, researchers, and consumers of research products. This gathering bridged the concerns of clinical practitioners with the efforts of nurse researchers. The first NRAB meeting drafted a five-year research plan, outlined a protocol for submitting research proposals, and developed a procedure to assist officers that were implementing research projects while students in civilian academic institutions.[137] Thereafter, NRAB continued to meet every two years to "advise and assist the Chief of the ANC [Army Nurse Corps] in establishing research priorities and to monitor the [p]rogress of nursing research throughout the AMEDD."[138]

The first Phyllis J. Verhonick Research Conference, named after the iconic Army nurse researcher who died in 1979, first occurred in 1981, when the AHS hosted the symposium at Fort Sam Houston, Texas. Forty-five Army nurses attended, 17 of whom presented research reports. Werley, the then-retired leading light of nursing research in the Army, provided the keynote address, while Colonel Rosemary McCarthy eulogized Verhonick, and Colonel Sarah Halliburton spoke on descriptive research designs. Major Susie Sherrod and Captain Judith Kirby became the first recipients of research honors for their award-winning papers.[139]

The conference afforded participants the opportunity "to discuss the current status of research in nursing practice, education, and administration and to explore research methodologies appropriate to nursing research."[140] Following its second meeting in 1982, the symposium thereafter has met once every two years.

In 1988, a group of doctoral military nurses met at the Association of Military Surgeons of the U.S. national conference. This led to the 1991 formation of a Federal Nursing Research Interest Group, later the TriService Nursing Research (TSNR) Group, comprising Army, Navy, and Air Force nurses. The group's initial intent was to foster collaborative research among the three services. Lieutenant Colonel Cindy Gurney was the first Army representative to TSNR, followed later by Colonel Patricia Troumbley. One of TSNR's first actions was to convene a meeting with the corps chiefs and directors and the staff at the National Center for Nursing Research at the National Institutes of Health to obtain advice on "developing a coordinated strategy of nursing research . . . within the military milieu." All participants recognized that the implementation of a program of military nursing research could not advance without funding.

Financial support soon followed in the form of a congressional appropriation sponsored by Senator Daniel Inouye. In FY 1992, Congress appropriated $1 million to support military nursing research. In subsequent FYs 1993 through 1995, military nursing research appropriations grew to $2 million, $3 million, and $5 million, respectively. In FY 1996, the Department of Defense Authorization Act placed the TSNR Program (TSNRP) into the Department of Defense Health Care Program under the auspices of the Uniformed Services University of the Health Sciences.[141]

The Army provided the initial leadership for the TSNRP. In August 1997, Lieutenant Colonel Catherine Schemp became the first program manager for the TSNRP. She administered the by-then $6 million annual appropriation, collaborated with the TSNRP Group (a panel of advisors), and liaised with the chief of the Army Nurse Corps and the directors of the Navy Nurse Corps and Air Force Nurse Corps.[142]

The defining themes of the 1970s were change and renewal. Change significantly influenced Army Nurse Corps officers' roles, numbers, career activities, uniforms, and education. Change, mostly positive, occurred in gender and minority issues. Clinical nursing research and quality assurance activities evolved. Readiness was charged with a new sense of immediacy and vitality, and conditions in the Reserve and National Guard components improved. With the turbulence of change came inevitable disruption, stress, and discontent. But also with change came improvement in services rendered, better overall conditions, and enhanced satisfaction. So marked was the transformation from the early years of the post–Vietnam War period to the later years of the decade that the AMEDD and the Army Nurse Corps grew from a significantly understaffed organization coping with reduced resources to a much improved functional unit.

# Notes

1. Hal B. Jennings, "Army Medical Department," *Military Medicine* 137 (September 1972): 348. Edith M. Nuttall, "AMEDD Health Care Extenders," Memorandum for Record, 1, 19 May 1977, Army Nurse Corps Collection (ANC), Office of Medical History (OMH).
2. Mary E. Viehdorfer Frank and Robert V. Piemonte, "The Army Nurse Corps: A Decade of Change," *American Journal of Nursing* 85 (September 1985): 985–88.
3. Hal B. Jennings and B.C. Lucas, "Program Change Request, Professional Training," Typewritten Document (TD), 1, 5 February 1971, ANCC, OMH.
4. "Army Nurse Corps Goals, Requirements, and Programs," TD, n.d., Box 9, Army Nurse Corps Papers, Archives, U.S. Army Military History Institute, Carlisle Barracks, PA.
5. Lillian Dunlap and Doris Frazier, "Fact Sheet to Deputy Chief of Staff for Personnel, Army Nurse Corps Clinician Program," 1, 27 January 1972, ANCC, OMH.
6. Julie Fairman, "Delegated by Default or Negotiated by Need?: Physicians, Nurse Practitioners and the Process of Clinical Thinking," in *Enduring Issues in American Nursing*, ed. Ellen D. Baer, Patricia D'Antonio, Sylvia Rinker, and Joan E. Lynaugh (New York: Springer, 2001), 309–33.
7. Mathy D. Mezey and Dianne O. McGivern, eds., *Nurses, Nurse Practitioners: The Evolution of Primary Care* (New York: Springer, 1993), 4.
8. Loretta C. Ford, "Nurse Practitioners: History of New Idea and Predictions for the Future, in *Nursing in the 1980s: Crises, Opportunities, Challenges*, ed. Linda H. Aiken and Susan R. Gortner (Philadelphia: Lippincott, 1982), 232.
9. Loretta C. Ford, "Review of *Nurses, Nurse Practitioners: The Evolution of Primary Care*," by Mathy D. Mezey and Dianne O. McGivern, in *Image: Journal of Nursing Scholarship* 18 (Winter 1986): 177–78.
10. Ibid., 178. Mathy D. Mezey and Dianne O. McGivern, eds., *Nurses, Nurse Practitioners: The Evolution of Primary Care* (New York: Springer, 1993), xi, xiii, 4. Jolynn Tumulo, "Controversial, Confident and Committed: How a Close-Knit Group of Believers Launched the NP Profession," *Advance for Nurse Practitioners* 13 (May 2005): 53–54.
11. Lillian Dunlap, "Progress Report: AN-CP," *U.S. Army Medical Department Newsletter* 2 (Fall 1971): 43; "General Jennings, General Neel, Ladies and Gentlemen," Text of Unidentified Presentation, n.d.; and Ruth L. Kulvi to Connie Moore, Typewritten Letter [TL], 29 June 1996 (all in ANCC, OMH).

12. Army Nurse Corps Clinician Program," Fact Sheet addressed to AMEDD Surgeons and Commanders, 2, 1 November 1973, ANCC, OMH.

13. "Army Nurse Corps Goals, Requirements, and Programs," TD, 4, n.d., Army Nurse Corps Papers, Box 9, U.S. Army Military History Institute, Carlisle Barracks, PA.

14. Hal B. Jennings and B.C. Lucas, "Program Change Request, Professional Training," TD, 2, 5 February 1971, ANCC, OMH.

15. Lillian Dunlap and Edith Nuttall, "Progress Report, Program Elements 8.11.13.A, 5 February 1971," Typewritten Disposition Form, 16 September 1974, ANCC, OMH.

16. "Army Nurse Corps Goals, Requirements, and Programs," TD, 5, n.d., Army Nurse Corps Papers, Box 9, U.S. Army Military History Institute, Carlisle Barracks, PA.

17. Army Nurse Corps Goals, Requirements, and Programs," TD, 5, n.d., Army Nurse Corps Papers, Box 9, U.S. Army Military History Institute, Carlisle Barracks, PA. Edith Nuttall, "Progress Report, Program Element 8.11.13.A, 5 February 1972," Disposition Form, 16 September 1974, ANCC, OMH. Richard R. Taylor, "Landmarks Point to Army's Future," *U.S. Medicine* 12 (15 January 1975): 41.

18. Robert A. Patterson, "AF Meets Demand of Volunteer Force," *U.S. Medicine* 10 (15 January 1974): 51. Robert A. Patterson, "Air Force Relies on 'Team' Care," *U.S. Medicine* 11 (15 January 1975): 45. Donald L. Custis, "Navy Sees Crisis as New Incentive," *U.S. Medicine* 10 (15 January 1974): 33. Donald L. Custis, "Rising Demands Face Navy MDs," *U.S. Medicine* 11 (15 January 1975): 27.

19. Robert A. Patterson, "AF Meets Demand of Volunteer Force," *U.S. Medicine* 10 (15 January 1974): 51.

20. Robert A. Patterson, "Air Force Relies on 'Team' Care," *U.S. Medicine* 11 (15 January 1975): 45. Mary C. Smolenski, Donald G. Smith, and James S. Nanney, *A Fit, Fighting Force, The Air Force Nursing Services Chronology* (Washington, DC: Office of the Air Force Surgeon General, 2005), 30, 32–33.

21. Susan H. Godson, *Serving Proudly: A History of Women in the U.S. Navy* (Annapolis: Naval Institute Press, 2001), 241.

22. Donald L. Custis, "Rising Demands Face Navy MDs," *U.S. Medicine* 11 (15 January 1975): 28.

23. Doris M. Sterner, *In and Out of Harm's Way, A History of the Navy Nurse Corps* (Seattle: Peanut Butter Publishing, 1996), 365–66.

24. Ibid., 359–61, 365–66.

25. Another source noted that approximately 100 nurse practitioners were providing services in the Navy in 1975. Susan H. Godson, *Serving Proudly: A History of Women in the U.S. Navy* (Annapolis: Naval Institute Press, 2001), 241.

26. Donald L. Custis, "Navy Vigorously Expands Actions," *U.S. Medicine* 12 (15 January 1976): 31.

27. Willard P. Arentzen, "Advances Logged by Navy Medicine," *U.S. Medicine* 13 (15 January 1977): 34.

28. Lillian Dunlap and Edith Nuttall, "Progress Report, Program Elements 8.11.13.A, 5 February 1971," Typewritten Disposition Form, 3, 16 September 1974; Edith M. Nuttall, Response to Disposition Form "Identification of Study Problems, 11 May 1973," 14 May 1973; "The Effect of Reduction in Authorized Strength, Army Nurse Corps," Fact Sheet, 20 March 1972; "Army Nurse Corps Clinician Program," Fact Sheet addressed to AMEDD Surgeons and Commanders, 1 November 1973, 5–6; Lillian Dunlap, "Area Coordinating Paper-Health Care Delivery," Disposition Form, 14 May 1973; and Madelyn N. Parks, "Recruitment for U.S. Army Reserve," Memorandum 3-76, 12 February 1976 (all in ANCC, OMH). Mary E. Viehdorfer Frank and Robert V. Piemonte, "The Army Nurse

Corps: A Decade of Change," *American Journal of Nursing* 85 (September 1985): 985.

29. "The Surgeon General's Conference for Army Medical Department Surgeons and Commanders," Typewritten Program, 14–16 November 1973, ANCC, OMH.

30. Lillian Dunlap and Doris Frazier, "Fact Sheet to Deputy Chief of Staff for Personnel, Army Nurse Corps Clinician Program," 1–2, 27 January 1972, ANCC, OMH. After July 1974, graduates of the Ambulatory Care, Pediatrics, Obstetrics/Gynecology, Psychiatric-Mental Health, and Intensive Care Nursing courses who qualified for admission into the University of Texas could be awarded 16 graduate credits from that institution. Barbara R. Costello, "Nursing Information Letter 4-74," Typewritten Newsletter, 4 December 1974, ANCC, OMH.

31. *Annual Report, The Surgeon General, United States Army, Fiscal Year 1974* (Washington, DC: Office of the Surgeon General, U.S. Army, 1974), 40–41, 109.

32. CG HSC, "Nurse Clinicians—Parameters of Practice," *USA HSC Commander's Notes*, CG HSC Bulletin No. 1-74 (7 January 1994): 11, RG 112, Entry 455, National Archives.

33. Hal B. Jennings and B.C. Lucas, "Program Change Request, Professional Training," TD, 2, 5 February 1971, ANCC, OMH.

34. Thomas J. Whelan, "Zero Draft and Its Impact on AMEDD," *U.S. Army Medical Department Newsletter* 4 (Winter 1973): 5, ANCC, OMH.

35. Lillian Dunlap and Edith Nuttall, "Progress Report, Program Elements 8.11.13.A, 5 February 1971," Typewritten Disposition Form, 16 September 1974, ANCC, OMH.

36. *Report of the Surgeon General United States Army Fiscal Years 1976–1980* (Washington, DC: Office of the Surgeon General, Department of the Army, 1988), 254.

37. "Army Nurse Corps Clinician Program," Fact Sheet addressed to AMEDD Surgeons and Commanders, 1 November 1973, 2–3, ANCC, OMH. Janet R. Southby, "Primary Care Nurse Practitioners within the Army Health Care System: Expectations and Perceptions of the Role," *Military Medicine* 145 (October 1980): 659–65.

38. Marjorie J. Wilson, "Nursing Information Letter 1-76," 3, 20 April 1976, ANCC, OMH.

39. Sarah A. Balkema to Elenore F. Sullivan, TL with Attached Worksheet, 18 October 1978, in Madelyn N. Parks, "Memorandum 1-79, Information for All ANC Officers," 29 January 1979, ANCC, OMH.

40. Henry K. Silver, "Use of New Types of Allied Health Professionals in Providing Care for Children," *American Journal of Diseases of Children* 116 (November 1968): 486–90.

41. *Annual Report, The Surgeon General, United States Army, Fiscal Year 1974* (Washington, DC: Office of the Surgeon General, U.S. Army, 1974), 107.

42. *Annual Report, The Surgeon General, United States Army, Fiscal Year 1974* (Washington, DC: Office of the Surgeon General, U.S. Army, 1974), 107.

43. Lillian Dunlap, "ANC Officers Attend New Course," *U.S. Army Medical Department Newsletter* 4, (Spring 1973): 23; and Virginia L. Brown, "Nursing Information Letter 1-75," 2, 7 March 1975 (both in ANCC, OMH).

44. In order to prescribe selected medications, HSC required nurse clinicians to be recommended by the hospital Therapeutic Agents Board, reviewed by the Credential Committee, and approved by the hospital commander. "Prescription Writing by Nurses," DA HSC, *Commander's Notes*, CG HSC Bulletin No. 10-75 (October 1975): 5, RG 112, Entry 452, National Archives.

45. Evaline R. Baker, "Review of December 1975 Health Nursing Activities Reports," Typewritten Memorandum [TM] for Record, 3, n.d.; and "Credentialing of Community Health Nurses to Write Refill Prescriptions for Tuberculosis Chemoprophylactic Drugs,"

DA Message, March 1977, Inclosure 1, in Marjorie J. Wilson, "Nursing Information Letter 1-77," 1 April 1977 (both in ANCC, OMH). *Annual Report, The Surgeon General, United States Army, Fiscal Year 1975* (Washington, DC: Office of the Surgeon General, U.S. Army, 1975), 44.

46. "Draft, MVA Memo," 10 June 1971; and Jerome H. Greenberg, "Suggestion for VOLAR-Provision of Mobile Health Units," 23 February 1971 (both TDs in ANCC, OMH). VOLAR stands for "volunteer army."

47. Edith Nuttall, "Progress Report, Program Element 8.11.13.A, 5 February 1972," Disposition Form, 2, 16 September 1974; Amy D. Geissinger, "Review of July 1975 Health Nursing Activities Reports," TM for Record, 15 September 1975; and Amy D. Geissinger, "Review of October 1975 Health Nursing Activities Reports," TM for Record, 17 December 1975 (all in ANCC, OMH). Neil Roland "Some Army Medical Services Unavailable to Most Civilians," *Army Times* 43 (15 November 1982): 62. *Annual Report, The Surgeon General, United States Army, Fiscal Year 1974* (Washington, DC: Office of the Surgeon General, U.S. Army, 1974), 109.

48. David N. Cowan and James J. James, "Mobile Health Units," *Military Medicine* 146 (September 1981): 636–38.

49. Lillian Dunlap, "Expanding the Role of Army Nursing," TD to "provide information for the Surgeon General's Article in *US Medicine*, January 1975," 2, ANCC, OMH. *Annual Report, The Surgeon General, United States Army, Fiscal Year 1974* (Washington, DC: Office of the Surgeon General, U.S. Army, 1974), 109.

50. Julie Fairman and Joan E. Lynaugh, *Critical Care Nursing, A History* (Philadelphia: University of Pennsylvania Press, 1998), 3.

51. Mary T. Sarnecky, *A History of the U.S Army Nurse Corps* (Philadelphia: University of Pennsylvania Press), 14, 106–08, 239, 305, 349.

52. Julie Fairman and Joan E. Lynaugh, *Critical Care Nursing, A History* (Philadelphia: University of Pennsylvania Press, 1998), 5.

53. Hal B. Jennings, "Report from the United States Army Medical Department," *Military Medicine* 136 (October 1971): 774–75.

54. Lillian Dunlap, "Nurse Clinician Courses," *U.S. Army Medical Department Newsletter* 4 (Spring 1973): 23.

55. Ira P. Gunn, "Education for Nurse Anesthetists," Typewritten Manuscript, 25 February 1972, ANCC, OMH.

56. Ira P. Gunn to Author, E-mail Correspondence, 20 May 2002, ANCC, OMH.

57. "Expanding Roles for Nurses Seen Countering Cutback in Army Corps," *U.S. Medicine* (15 February 1972): n.p., News Clipping in ANCC, OMH.

58. Edith Nuttall, "Progress Report, Program Element 8.11.13.A, 5 February 1972," Disposition Form, 1–2, 16 September 1974, ANCC, OMH.

59. Ira P. Gunn, "The History of Nurse Anesthesia Education: Highlights and Influences," *Journal of the American Association of Nurse Anesthetists* 59 (February 1991): 53–61.

60. Katherine Galloway and Edith M. Nuttall, "Non-Funded Training Requirement FY 74," Disposition Form, 7 August 1973, ANCC, OMH.

61. Spurgeon Neel, "Implementing Instructions for Training of Army Nurse Corps Nurse Anesthetists in Regional Anesthesia," TD, 25 July 1975, ANCC, OMH.

62. Madelyn N. Parks, "Information for All ANC Officers," 5, 10 January 1978, ANCC, OMH.

63. Ralph G. Synakowski, "Mental Health Nurse, Psychiatry Consultation Service, Walter Reed Army Medical Center," TM, 2–5, n.d., ANCC, OMH.

64. James F. Prucha, "Report of Monthly Activities, 1-31 August 1973, Psychiatric Nurse Clinician, Oncology Service," TM, 1–3, 8, ANCC, OMH.

65. André J. Nahmias and Theodore C. Eickhoff, "Staphlococcal Infections in Hospitals," *New England Journal of Medicine* 265 (13 July 1961): 74–81. James M. Hughes, "Nosocomial Infection Surveillance in the United States: Historical Perspective," *Infection Control* 8 (November 1987): 450–53. Christopher E. Laxton, "Infection Control: An Idea Whose Time Has Come," *American Journal of Infection Control* 25 (February 1997): 34–37. Elaine Larson, "A Retrospective on Infection Control, Part 2: Twentieth Century—The Flame Burns," *American Journal of Infection Control* 25 (August 1997): 340–49. James D. Whitehouse, Daniel J. Sexton, and Kathryn B. Kirkland, "Infection Control: Past, Present, and Future Issues," *Comparative Therapy* 24 (February 1998): 71–77. Lillian Dunlap, *33 Years of Army Nursing* (Washington, DC: U.S. Army Nurse Corps, 2001), 255.

66. In 1972, Lieutenant Colonel Janie A. Sinclair and Major Helen J. Seufert held full-time assignments as infection control nurses at Brooke General Hospital and Walter Reed General Hospital, respectively. Lillian Dunlap, "Operating Room Nurses: Two Pilot Assignments," *U.S. Army Medical Department Newsletter* 3 (Fall 1972): 22; and Lillian Dunlap, "Expanding the Role of Army Nursing," TD to "provide information for the Surgeon General's Article in *US Medicine*, January 1975," 2 (both in ANCC, OMH).

67. "Courses in Prevention and Control of Hospital Associated Infections," Inclosure 4, in Madelyn N. Parks, "Information for All ANC Officers," TM, 27 March 1978, ANCC, OMH.

68. Helen J. Seufert, to Nursing Consultant, Typewritten Quarterly Report, 18 July 1978, Inclosure 2, in Madelyn N. Parks, "Information for All ANC Officers," 18 October 1978, ANCC, OMH.

69. As early as 1973 the AMEDD considered hospital infection rates as indicators of quality care. Additional quality indicators were data focusing on patients' length of hospital stay, patient complaints, and unusual occurrences. John W. Rowen, Ralph B. Swisher, and Patsy B. Saunders, *Executive Summary, Structure Analysis and Program Planning, Study of the Army Nurse Corps (ANC)*, Project No. 431 4487, NBSIR 73-285, 1 October 1973 (Washington, DC: National Bureau of Standards, 1973), 8–9.

70. Carolyn M. Feller and Debora R. Cox, *Highlights in the History of the Army Nurse Corps, 100th Anniversary Edition* (Washington DC: U.S. Army Center of Military History, 2000), 43. John T. Greenwood and F. Clifton Berry, *Medics at War, Military Medicine from Colonial Times to the 21st Century* (Annapolis: Naval Institute Press, 2005), 154–55.

71. Lillian Dunlap, *33 Years of Army Nursing* (Washington, DC: U.S. Army Nurse Corps, 2001), 258–61. *Report of the Surgeon General United States Army Fiscal Years 1976–1980* (Washington, DC: Office of the Surgeon General, Department of the Army, 1988), 256, 264–76. "Nurse Corps Officers Attend First Methods Analyst Course," *The Military Service News* 60 (15 February 1974): 1. Richard R. Taylor, "Landmarks Point to Army's Future," *U.S. Medicine* 12 (15 January 1975): 39.

72. Among that group were the chief nurse, Lieutenant Colonel Daisy McCommons, and Captains Robena Anderson, Eileen McCarthy, and Ann Witczak. Almost simultaneously, a similar program was established at Walter Reed General Hospital, with Colonel Amelia Jensen and Captain Dorothy Martone spearheading the project. Eileen L. McCarthy to Marguerite A. Holmes, TL, 25 May 1964, ANCC, OMH.

73. Charles F. Bombard, "The Nursing Methods Analyst," 24 October 1972; and John J. Roberts, "Nursing Methods Analyst," 25 March 1969 (both Typewritten Term Papers, ANCC, OMH).

74. John J. Roberts, "Nursing Methods Analyst," Typewritten Term Paper, 1, 25 March 1969, ANCC, OMH.

75. Eileen M. Munn, "NMA Network Newsletter 1" (December 1993): 2, ANCC, OMH.

76. Nickey McCasland to Author, E-mail Correspondence, 14 March 2002, ANCC, OMH. McCasland added that "the universal Army penchant for change for change's sake" also factored into the evolution of the name.

77. "The Role of the Nursing Methods Analyst," TD attributed to Major Stralein at Brooke General Hospital, n.d., ANCC, OMH.

78. "The Future Role of the Nursing Methods Analyst," TD, n.d.; and John J. Roberts, "Nursing Methods Analyst," Typewritten Term Paper, 25 March 1969 (both in ANCC, OMH).

79. Edith M. Nuttall, Untitled TD written in response to what appears to be a proposed TDA (Table of Distribution and Allowances) for Letterman General Hospital, 25 September 1972, ANCC, OMH.

80. Michael R. Soper, Margaret E. Weydert, and Carolyn C. Knight, "The Nurse Practitioner Role at Project AMOS," *U.S. Army Medical Department Newsletter* 3 (Summer 1972): 20–21, ANCC, OMH.

81. "Army Hospitals Elect AMOSISTs," *HSC Mercury* 1 (1 October 1973): 1, 6. Sharon F. Bystran to Author, Handwritten Letter, 15 March 2004, ANCC, OMH.

82. Mary Lou Spine to Author, E-mail Correspondence, 15 March 2002, ANCC, OMH.

83. "Army Hospitals Elect AMOSISTs," *HSC Mercury* 1 (1 October 1973): 1, 6.

84. *Report of the Surgeon General United States Army Fiscal Years 1976–1980* (Washington, DC: Office of the Surgeon General, Department of the Army, 1988), 253–54.

85. One document noted that "AMOSISTs have been observed practicing far too independently, considering the . . . training they have. Such practice places the whole AMOSIST program in jeopardy, and it may only take one unfortunate incident at one facility to cause the entire command to lose this valuable health care extender program." Sarah A. Balkema, "AMOSIST Program," Information Paper for advance distribution to Commanders, HSC Installations and Activities in preparation for 1977 Commanders' Conference in "U.S. Army Health Services Command, Chief Nurses Conference 77, 27–29 September 1977," n.d., ANCC, OMH.

86. Michael R. Soper, Margaret E. Weydert, and Carolyn C. Knight, "The Nurse Practitioner Role at Project AMOS," *U.S. Army Medical Department Newsletter* 3 (Summer 1972): 20–21. Project AMOS Chronic Care Program, DeWitt Army Hospital, Fort Belvoir, Virginia, *Guidelines for Chronic Care, A Reference Manual for Nurse Clinicians*, Printed Manual, June 1973, ANCC, OMH. Michael R. Soper and others, "Evaluation of a New Nurse Practitioner Role in a Medical Clinic," *Military Medicine* 140 (November 1975): 772–76. Barbara R. Costello for Virginia L. Brown, "Nursing Information Letter, 4-74," 2, 4 December 1974, ANCC, OMH.

87. Barry Wolcott to Author, E-mail Correspondence, 28 October 2002, ANCC, OMH.

88. Richard R. Taylor, "Team Work Needed for Army Medicine," *U.S. Medicine* 10 (15 January 1974): 60. Ann M. Ritchie Hartwick, *The Army Medical Specialist Corps, The 45th Anniversary* (Washington, DC: Center of Military History, United States Army, 1993), 38–41.

89. Charles C. Pixley, "Army Medicine Hurt by MD Shortage," *U.S. Medicine* 15 (15 January 1979): 50.

90. Richard R. Taylor, "Landmarks Point to Army's Future," *U.S. Medicine* 12 (15 January 1975): 41.

91. Charles C. Pixley, "Army Medicine Hurt by MD Shortage," *U.S. Medicine* 15 (15 January 1979): 50.

92. Richard A. Smith, M.D., began a similar program, called the Medical Extension (MEDEX) Program, at the University of Washington in 1969. MEDEX became a national demonstration project by 1971 with programs in California, North Dakota, Alabama, New Hampshire, and Utah. C. Emil Fasser, "Historical Perspectives of PA Education," *Journal of the American Academy of Physician Assistants* 5 (October 1992): 663–70. "PAs and the Health Care Revolution: An Interview with Richard Smith, MD," *Journal of the American Academy of Physician Assistants* 6 (January 1993): 54–55. Douglas Condit, "Our Military Heritage," *Physician Assistant* 17 (November 1993): 58, 61–62, 65–67. Richard A. Smith and others, "A Strategy for Health Manpower, Reflections on an Experience Called MEDEX," *Journal of the American Medical Association* 217 (September 6, 1971): 1362–67. Reginald Carter, "Physician Assistant History," *Perspective on Physician Assistant Education* 12 (Spring 2001): 130–32.

93. Natalie Holt, "'Confusion's Masterpiece': The Development of the Physician Assistant Program," *Bulletin of the History of Medicine* 72 (Summer 1998): 246–78. Reginald Carter, "Physician Assistant History," *Perspective on Physician Assistant Education* 12 (Spring 2001): 130–32.

94. Hal B. Jennings, "Physicians' Assistant Program," Program Change Request, 25 February 1971, Record Group 112, Entry 372, National Archives. *Annual Report, The Surgeon General, United States Army, Fiscal Year 1974* (Washington, DC: Office of the Surgeon General, U.S. Army, 1974), 28–29. Rose C. Engelman and Robert J.T. Joy, *Two Hundred Years of Military Medicine* (Fort Detrick, MD: Historical Unit, U.S. Army Medical Department, 1975), 47. Richard R. Taylor, "Team Work Needed for Army Medicine," *U.S. Medicine* 10 (15 January 1974): 60. D. Mallicoat, "Physician's Assistant: The Army's Newest Career Field," *Soldiers* 27 (November 1972): 45.

95. "More Than a Nurse, Less Than a Doctor...," *Journal of the American Academy of Physician Assistants* 5 (October 1992): 711–13. Natalie Holt, "'Confusion's Masterpiece': The Development of the Physician Assistant Program," *Bulletin of the History of Medicine* 72 (Summer 1998): 252, 261–63. Luther Christman, "Advanced Practice Nursing: Is the Physician's Assistant an Accident of History or a Failure to Act?" *Clinical Excellence for Nurse Practitioners* 1 (1997): 337–40.

96. American Nurses Association, "Nurses, in the Extended Role, Are Not Physician's Assistants," developed July 1973, revised 21 July 1976, Inclosure 7, in Madelyn N. Parks, "Information for All ANC Officers," Memorandum 1-78, 10 January 1978, ANCC, OMH.

97. Lillian Dunlap, *33 Years of Army Nursing* (Washington, DC: U.S. Army Nurse Corps, 2001), 221.

98. Hal B. Jennings, "Report from the United States Army Medical Department," *Military Medicine* 136 (October 1971): 774–75.

99. Jean M. Houghton to Edith M. Nuttall, TL, 28 January 1974, ANCC, OMH.

100. Ibid.

101. Sue Toma, "New Plan Extends Nursing Skills," *Air Force Times* (23 January 1974): 1, 6.

102. Henry Silver, "Use of New Types of Allied Health Professionals in Providing Care for Children," *American Journal of Diseases of Children* 116 (November 1968): 486–90.

103. Office of Technology Assessment, United States Congress, *Nurse Practitioners, Physician Assistants, and Certified Nurse-Midwives: A Policy Analysis*, HAS 37 (Washington, DC: Government Printing Office, 1986), 19–20, 39.

104. Patricia M. Miller to James Blair, "Input to Study of Health Care Extender Programs," Memo, 17 February 1977, ANCC, OMH.

105. Mary E. Viehdorfer Frank and Robert V. Piemonte, "The Army Nurse Corps: A

Decade of Change," *American Journal of Nursing* 85 (September 1985): 986. Edith M. Nuttall, "AMEDD Health Care Extenders," Memorandum for Record, 1, 19 May 1977, ANCC, OMH. Rosemary T. McCarthy, "Parallels and Paradoxes: Differentiated Nursing Practice," in *Differentiating Nursing Practice into the Twenty-first Century*, ed. I.E. Goertzen (Kansas City, MO: American Nurses Association, American Academy of Nursing, 1991), 361–81. Sharon F. Bystran to Author, Handwritten Letter, 15 March 2004, ANCC, OMH.

106. "AR 40-6, Army Nurse Corps," 2, 6, 26 October 1977, ANCC, OMH. *Report of the Surgeon General United States Army Fiscal Years 1976–1980* (Washington, DC: Office of the Surgeon General, Department of the Army, 1988), 65.

107. Catherine L. Gilliss, "Education for Advanced Practice Nursing," in *Advanced Practice Nursing: Changing Roles and Clinical Applications*, ed. Joanne V. Hickey, Ruth M. Ouimette, and Sandra L. Venegoni (Philadelphia: Lippincott, 1996), 27.

108. M. Elizabeth Hixon, "Professional Development: Socialization in Advanced Practice Nursing," in *Advanced Practice Nursing: Changing Roles and Clinical Applications*, ed. Joanne V. Hickey, Ruth M. Ouimette, and Sandra L. Venegoni (Philadelphia: Lippincott, 1996), 40.

109. Diane O. McGivern, "The Evolution to Advanced Nursing Practice," in *Nurses, Nurse Practitioners; Evolution to Advanced Practice*, ed. Mathy D. Mezey and Diane O. McGivern (New York: Springer Publishing Company, 1993), 17–20. Mathy Mezey, "Preparation for Advanced Practice," in *Nurses, Nurse Practitioners: Evolution to Advanced Practice*, ed. Mathy D. Mezey and Diane O. McGivern (New York: Springer Publishing Company, 1993), 42–46.

110. Ruth G. Elder and Bonnie Bullough, "Nurse Practitioners and Clinical Nurse Specialists: Are the Roles Merging?" *Clinical Nurse Specialist* 4 (1990), 79. Loretta C. Ford, "Nurse Practitioners: History of a New Idea and Predictions for the Future," in *Nursing in the 1980s: Crises, Opportunities, Challenges*, ed. Linda H. Aiken and Susan R. Gortner (Philadelphia: Lippincott, 1982), 234.

111. Loretta C. Ford, "Nurse Practitioners: History of a New Idea and Predictions for the Future," in *Nursing in the 1980s: Crises, Opportunities, Challenges*, ed. Linda H. Aiken and Susan R. Gortner (Philadelphia: Lippincott, 1982), 236, 239.

112. Julie Fairman, "Delegated by Default or Negotiated by Need?: Physicians, Nurse Practitioners and the Process of Clinical Thinking," in *Enduring Issues in American Nursing*, ed. Ellen D. Baer, Patricia D'Antonio, Sylvia Rinker, and Joah E. Lynaugh (New York, Springer: 2001), 309–33. Mary E. Viehdorfer Frank and Robert V. Piemonte, "The Army Nurse Corps since Vietnam, 1974–1984," Unpublished Manuscript, 5–6, n.d., ANCC, OMH.

113. Harriet H. Werley, "Promoting the Research Dimension in the Practice of Nursing through the Establishment and Development of a Department of Nursing in an Institute of Research," *Military Medicine* 127 (March 1962): 219–32. Mary T. Sarnecky, "Inventing Nursing Research," *Nursing Research* 42 (September/October 1993): 318–19. Mary T. Sarnecky, "Nursing Research in the Army, Thirty Years of Leadership, 1957–1987," Unpublished Manuscript, 1991. Joanne S. Stevenson, "Forging a Research Discipline," *Nursing Research* 36 (January/February 1987): 60–63.

114. Miriam G. Rothchild, Interview by James D. Vail, 17 November 1983, Army Nurse Corps Oral History Collection, OMH.

115. Mariam K. Ginsberg, "Years of Nursing Research at the Walter Reed Army Institute of Research," *Military Medicine* 132 (March 1967): 219–23.

116. Harriet H. Werley and Rosemary T. McCarthy, "In Memoriam. Phyllis J. Verhon-

ick: Practitioner, Researcher, Teacher, and Scholar," *Research in Nursing and Health* 2 (June 1979): vi.

117. Ibid.

118. Terris E. Kennedy, "The Evolution of Nursing Research in the Army Nurse Corps," *Military Medicine* 159 (November 1994): 680–83.

119. Mary T. Sarnecky, "Nursing Research in the Army, Thirty Years of Leadership, 1957–1987," Unpublished Manuscript, 1991.

120. Glennadee A. Nichols and others, "Patient's Perceptions of Important, Satisfying and Dissatisfying Aspects of Army Hospitalization," *Military Medicine* 139 (November 1974): 869–76.

121. Glennadee A. Nichols, Interview by Larry Hamer, 22 September 1983, Army Nurse Corps Oral History Collection, OMH.

122. Lillian Dunlap, *33 Years of Army Nursing* (Washington, DC: U.S. Army Nurse Corps, 2001), 263–66. Margaret O'Dell, Rosemary McCarthy, and Cassandra Smith, "Future Directions of the Division of Nursing, WRAIR," TD, 22 May 1974; and Lieutenant Colonel O'Dell to Colonel Nuttall, Telephone or Verbal Conversation Record, 21 March 1974 (both in ANCC, OMH). This latter documentation suggests that O'Dell failed to keep her superiors in the Army Nurse Corps informed and was unable to respond to unspecified charges levied by the director of WRAIR. It also reports that the director of WRAIR, Colonel Buescher, asked, for whatever reason, that "younger nurses" be assigned to the organization.

123. Robert J.T. Joy to Author, TL, 4, 18 October 2002, ANCC, OMH.

124. Madelyn Parks to Richard Taylor, "Nursing Research, Walter Reed Army Medical—Decision Memorandum," 6 November 1975, ANCC, OMH. Five officer and one civilian space and the budget of $4,000 for FYs 1976 and 1977 and a total budget of $14,000 for FYs 1978–1981 all shifted to WRAMC, the gaining command. Director of Resource Management, Disposition Form, 3 February 1976, ANCC, OMH.

125. Elenore Sullivan, Telephone Interview by Author, 9 October 1991.

126. "Activity Summary for Nursing Research Service," TD, 11 October 1979, ANCC, OMH.

127. Janet R. Southby, "Activities Summary for Nursing Research Service, 13 March 1980," TD, ANCC, OMH.

128. Harriet H. Werley to Lillian Dunlap, TL, 20 June 1974, ANCC, OMH.

129. Brian S. Jordan to Author, E-mail Correspondence, 13 January 2003; Brian S. Jordan to Author, E-mail Correspondence, 14 January 2003; and Linda Yoder to Author, E-mail Correspondence, 17 January 2003 (all in ANCC, OMH).

130. Linda Yoder to Author, Telephone Conversation, 24 January 2003.

131. Charlotte L. DePew and others, "The Relationship of Burnout, Stress, and Hardiness in Nurses in a Military Medical Center: A Replicated Descriptive Study," *Journal of Burn Care & Rehabilitation* 20 (November/December 1999): 515–22.

132. Linda Yoder to Author, Telephone Conversation, 24 January 2003.

133. Hazel W. Johnson-Brown, Interview by Charles F. Bombard, 75–76, 106–07, 1984, Army Nurse Corps Oral History Collection, OMH.

134. Hazel W. Johnson to Lillian Dunlap "Activities of Project Officer, Consultant to the Surgeon General for Centralized Materiel Services," Disposition Form, 8 September 1971; "Army Nurse Specializes in Research," *Pentagram News* (16 March 1972): n.p., News Clipping; and Hazel W. Johnson-Brown, Interview by Charles F. Bombard, 74–80, 1984 (all in ANCC, OMH).

135. Hazel W. Johnson-Brown to Author, E-mail Correspondence, 27 June 2002; and

Hazel W. Johnson-Brown, Interview by Charles F. Bombard, 76–78, 1984 (both in ANCC, OMH).

136. Mary E. Viehdorfer Frank and Robert V. Piemonte, "The Army Nurse Corps since Vietnam, 1974–1984," Unpublished Manuscript, 6, n.d., ANCC, OMH. Rita K. Chow and others, "Historical Perspectives of the United States Air Force, Army, Navy, Public Health Service, and Veterans Administration Nursing Services," *Military Medicine* 143 (July 1978): 457–62. Bernice L. Shaw, "Current Therapy for Burns," *RN* 34 (March 1971): 33–42.

137. Madelyn N. Parks, "Information for All ANC Officers," Memorandum 2-79, 1, 1 May 1979; and Department of the Army, Office of the Surgeon General, "OTSG Reg 15-58," 17 April 1980 (both in ANCC, OMH). Rosemary T. McCarthy, Interview by Author, 5 November 1991.

138. *Nursing Research Notes* (Spring 1982): 3, ANCC, OMH.

139. Sherrod's paper was titled "The Nursing Care Hour Standards Study" and was the precursor work on the Workload Management System for Nurses; and Kirby's project title was "A Study of Variation in Measurement of Doses of Nitroglycerin Ointment." Janet Southby, *Proceedings of the First Phyllis J. Verhonick Nursing Research Symposium 1-5 June 1981* (Washington, DC: WRAMC Pam 601-2, 1981); and "Phyllis J. Verhonick Nursing Research Symposium," *Nursing Research Notes* (Summer 1981): 1, 3 (both in ANCC, OMH).

140. "Phyllis J. Verhonick Nursing Research Symposium," *Nursing Research Notes* (Summer 1981): iii, ANCC, OMH. Terris E. Kennedy, "The Evolution of Nursing Research in the Army Nurse Corps," *Military Medicine* 159 (November 1994): 681.

141. Institute of Medicine, Committee on Military Nursing Research, *The Program for Research in Military Nursing: Progress and Future Direction* (Washington, DC: National Academy Press, 1996): 17–21.

142. Carolyn M. Feller and Debora R. Cox, eds., *Highlights in the History of the Army Nurse Corps* (Washington, DC: U.S. Army Center of Military History, 2000), 70.

*Chapter Seven*
# Humanitarian Relief and Assistance Missions in the 1970s

In the post–Vietnam era, particularly in the early days of the 1970s, many aspects of Army Nurse Corps life were less than ideal. Moreover, the warweary American populace was firmly opposed to supporting overseas combat operations. Nonetheless, when the call came to participate in relief or humanitarian missions, Army Nurse Corps officers responded quickly and with enthusiasm. They made worthwhile contributions to the disaster relief operations in Nicaragua and Guatemala and in Operations New Arrivals and New Life. They also readily shared their expertise and acumen when asked to do so by U.S. international allies and friends.

Just after midnight on 23 December 1972, an earthquake shook the Nicaraguan capital city of Managua. Although the temblor measured in the moderate to serious range at 6.25 on the Richter scale, several factors intensified the effects of the shock and created a disaster with significant destruction and casualties. The effect of the earthquake was even more devastating because of the location of the epicenter in a vulnerable, heavily populated downtown area; the fragile mortar-and-tile construction of dwellings; the unfortunate timing, when most citizens were indoors asleep; and the ensuing fire that raged unchecked for days because of high winds and a disrupted water supply.

The Nicaraguan government immediately asked the United States to provide some measure of medical assistance because all local hospitals in Managua were destroyed. U.S. Southern Command responded to the call by deploying two field hospitals—an Air Force Tactical Hospital based at MacDill Air Force Base, Florida, and 100 beds of the Army's 21st Evacuation Hospital, garrisoned at Fort Hood, Texas.[1] General Lillian Dunlap handpicked Lieutenant Colonel Jane High to serve as chief, Nursing Service, for the 21st Evacuation Hospital Team. The Army Nurse Corps placed 23 Army nurses and 30 enlisted nursing staff from Darnall Army Hospital at Fort Hood on alert. With many personnel on holiday leave, selection of staff was complicated by concerns about reducing the fixed facility's staffing to a dangerous level. Nonetheless, by 1800 hours on 23 December 1972, the Corps had notified nearly all of the deploying personnel. Throughout the night, those deploying completed necessary preparations, such as making finance arrangements, receiving immunizations, and reviewing personnel records. Local staff issued field clothing and equipment to the minority of Army nurses who did not have such gear, but summer-weight fatigues—so important for comfort in the expected hot and humid environment—were unavailable for issue. At noon on Christmas Eve, the first of several groups of the hospital's staff and its equipment departed from Texas and arrived in Managua by dusk that same day. The first three Army nurses and a number of enlisted service members then bunked down at a staging area adjacent to the rubble of what was formerly the Managua General Hospital. Other cohorts of the 21st Evacuation Hospital arrived in Managua in subsequent sorties. The original contingent arose at 0600 hours on Christmas morning and, before eating, began erecting their tentage. By noon, the hospital was operational and admitted its first patients, two children with meningitis and a two-year-old postoperative nephrectomy patient. At the end of the first day, the inpatient census numbered 35 patients. By 1 January 1973, five wards with 20 beds each were functional. At that time, the total census averaged 49 patients per day. Army nurses worked 12-hour shifts, either from midnight to noon or from noon to midnight. This arrangement allowed both shifts to enjoy a few hours of sleep in relatively cool temperatures. After a week, High wanted to close some wards and consolidate patients so that the work shifts could be shortened. However, the hospital commander elected to maintain the status quo, feeling that closed wards would require posting guards to protect equipment and supplies from looters.

As the first week passed, several more Army nurses arrived in Nicaragua, including three officers from Reynolds Army Hospital at Fort Sill, Oklahoma. At peak, 30 Army Nurse Corps officers participated in the effort. By the beginning of the new year, Nicaraguan doctors and nurses gradually began to replace their American counterparts. The focus of the workload then shifted from the inpatient to the outpatient setting, where the ambulatory workload averaged 385 patients daily. Finally, on 5 January 1973, Health Services Command (HSC) released all Army Nurse Corps officers from the mission and redeployed them back to their home units in the continental United States.

The overall mission in Nicaragua was generally successful, although several minor setbacks surfaced. For example, the x-ray facility lacked a darkroom in which to develop film. Since the majority of patients presented with fractures, they could only be immobilized until the film could be developed. The functioning of the operating room was delayed by the need to process instruments. Essential surgical instruments, originally received in depot packs, came coated with cosmoline, a petroleum jelly-like rust preventive agent. They had to be cleaned by hand before use. The Central Material Section could not operate its autoclaves because no 220-volt cable was available. Deficiencies in all types of supplies were an added complication. Although aircraft efficiently delivered supplies as planned, the medical logistic warehouse was overwhelmed, understaffed, or disorganized and was unable to locate and deliver specific supplies and pieces of equipment. Furthermore, the US Southern Command was unprepared to resupply needed expendable items. Over the course of the mission, it filled only one supply requisition and responded with "due outs" for the 10 additional typewritten pages of requisitions.

The type of supplies also conflicted with the mission requirements. Although there were many pediatric and obstetrics patients, planners had included no pediatric or obstetrics supplies or medications in the original supply issue. The preponderance of the supplies naturally was geared instead to the demands of combat medicine, not disaster relief. Other deficiencies included a lack of field safes to store narcotics and valuables securely; too few military police for crowd control; limited shower and laundry facilities; and inadequate blood supplies, vaccines, water, fuel pods, generators, organic mess facilities, and vehicles. The minimal care ward was unexpectedly inundated with individuals with supportive care needs, like geriatric patients, the debilitated, the blind, and paraplegics. Caring for these patients called for adjustments in expectations, staffing, and equipment. Weather was equally trying. Dusty winds gusted constantly. Oppressive heat intensified the state of affairs.[2]

Although difficulties arose in the work setting, off-duty living conditions were correspondingly annoying. All 35 officers and enlisted women assigned to the unit were initially billeted in a cramped general purpose medium tent and subsisted on C-rations for the entire duration of the mission.[3] Creature comforts such as personal space and appetizing meals certainly raise morale, and their absence has an equal and opposite reaction. Nonetheless, conditions in the field can hardly be expected to approach the standard of living enjoyed at home.

Despite hardships, there was some good news. The first maternity case at the hospital produced a baby girl whose parents named Christina. The news media highlighted this human interest story and labeled the operational site "Camp Christina, Fort Hood, South." Excursions to the nearby Pacific coast beach for a few staff chosen by lottery also helped to boost spirits.[4]

Operational conditions experienced during the disaster relief operations in Nicaragua seemed to ignore the imperative for adequate preparations and provisions, a lesson relearned in the mid-1960s in Vietnam and once again promptly forgotten. The success achieved by the task force deployed to Nicaragua can be attributed in large part to the adaptability and field expedient skills of participating Army nurses and other dedicated service members and to the relatively brief mission, just under two weeks. Sad to say, the Nicaraguan experience was a microcosm of the shortcomings of the Army Medical Department (AMEDD) and the Army in the immediate post–Vietnam era.

A few years later, Army nurses received another call to provide assistance. In the spring of 1975 after the fall of Vietnam, more than 100,000 South Vietnamese fled their homes and lands in Southeast Asia, attempting to escape the threat of marauding North Vietnamese Communists. Forced to leave their country with few or no possessions, they sought refuge. In the spirit of humanitarianism, the U.S.

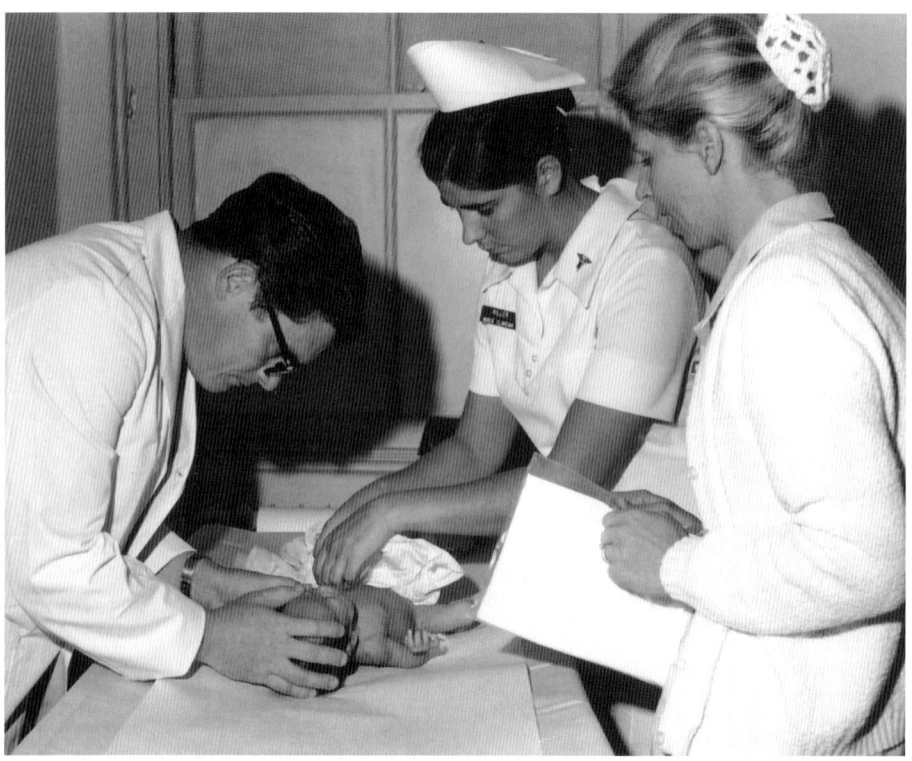

Army nurse clinician Captain Miller provides care for a newborn Vietnamese baby during operations New Life and New Arrivals. An Army physician stabilizes the baby's head while a civilian nurse shares her observations.
Photo courtesy of Army Nurse Corps Archives, Office of Medical History, Falls Church, VA.

government aided them and subsequently initiated a massive effort to resettle the displaced Vietnamese.[5]

Hence, in April 1975, Operation New Life began. At that time, the Department of Defense (DoD) established refugee reception centers at Orote Point on the island of Guam; at Fort Chaffee, Arkansas; and later at Fort Indiantown Gap, Pennsylvania, all supported by the Army. Ultimately, the Army processed 55 percent of all the refugees at the latter two sites. The Navy maintained a similar immigrant station at Camp Pendleton, California; and the Air Force was responsible for another such refugee center at Eglin Air Force Base, Florida. The center on Guam was the initial screening point for all refugees. They then were channeled to one of the four continental U.S. sites for more extensive services.[6] Operation New Life became Operation New Arrivals on 1 May 1975.[7]

Because a large percentage of the boat people were in poor health, with many suffering from various maladies common to developing countries, DoD delegated

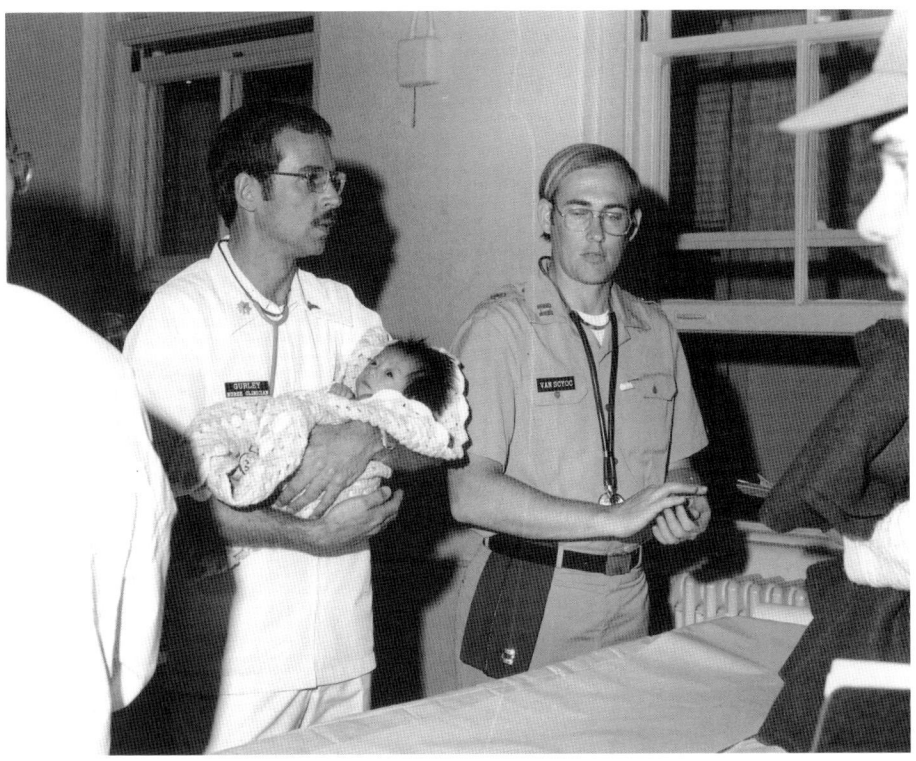

Army nurse clinician Major Gurley holds a Vietnamese infant while discussing the child's condition with its attentive Vietnamese parents during operations New Life and New Arrivals. An Army physician listens to the conversation.
Photo courtesy of Army Nurse Corps Archives, Office of Medical History, Falls Church, VA.

to HSC the responsibility to provide the refugees with certain health care services in the Army-sponsored centers. In all, about 97 Army Nurse Corps officers participated in the overall mission, with nine officers assigned to Guam, 50 to Fort Chaffee, and 38 to Fort Indiantown Gap.[8] Several nurse clinicians (Army Nurse Corps nurse practitioners) participated in operations New Life and New Arrivals and provided primary care in the refugee camps. This was the first instance where the AMEDD augmented field units with advanced practice nurses.[9]

The chief of the Army Nurse Corps selected Lieutenant Colonel Jeanne Hoppe to deploy from Hawaii to serve as the chief nurse of the 1st Medical Group on Guam. With the initial flood of refugees, Hoppe was in dire straits with too few staff.[10] To augment the nursing staff, she asked the Red Cross, local hospitals, and the civilian population for assistance. Many volunteers responded. As a result, Hoppe had two to three additional nurses every day, including several who were formerly medical missionary nurses in Vietnam. Transportation initially was a

Although assigned to the 702nd Medical Clearing Company on Orote Point, the westernmost point on the mainland of Guam, Army Nurse Corps officer Lieutenant Colonel Jeanne Hoppe, second from right, pauses with three medical missionary nurses. The three had formerly served in Vietnam. All of these nurses volunteered to care for refugees during operations New Life and New Arrivals.
Photo courtesy of Army Nurse Corps Archives, Office of Medical History, Falls Church, VA.

problem, but one quickly resolved when the commander of the 1st Medical Group made a vehicle available, allowing Hoppe to travel to supervise staff. Originally, everyone was working 12-hour shifts. But when the flood of immigrants subsided, eight-hour shifts with days off became the routine. Patient loads included both outpatients and inpatients, with 90 percent of the latter being pediatric cases.[11] Hoppe assigned the medical-surgical nurses to clearing companies that treated 1,800 ambulatory patients per day at the outset of the deployment and, by June 1975, treated approximately 800 to 900 patients per 24-hour period. Although Hoppe concluded that "all the nurses . . . performed in an outstanding manner," she expressed some dismay with the nurses' lack of preparation to function in a field setting.[12] She observed that "TOE [Table of Organization and Equipment] training in CONUS 'is inadequate'."[13] The Army mission on Guam concluded on 15 July 1975.[14]

HSC support at Fort Chaffee spanned from 29 April to 22 December 1975. In all, 50 Army nurses served there under chief nurses Lieutenant Colonel Velma J. Barkley and later Lieutenant Colonel Maurine Hill.[15] The Fort Chaffee health care facility, which was vacant for nine years, was a wood-frame World War II cantonment configuration with separate ward buildings connected by open-sided ramps.[16] The structure had been maintained in fair condition as a contingency for future mobilizations, but it initially required extensive cleaning. Soon after the buildings were occupied, structural and engineering problems materialized.[17]

When First Lieutenant Stephanie Velsmid reported in to the 47th Field Hospital, which had deployed to Fort Chaffee, and helped to open the obstetrics ward, she spent the "first two days . . . cleaning and scrubbing walls and floors." Then the exposed plumbing pipes and fixtures began to leak, and Velsmid explained that the staff spent "half the time mopping up these little puddles. Last night the ceiling pipes let loose and flooded the whole hallway!" As always, supplies were problematic. Although pitocin was available, ergotrate and methergine were somehow unobtainable. Neither were medication cards available. Velsmid took to "tearing up small pieces of paper to make med cards!"[18]

Meanwhile, operating room nurse Captain Diane McDermott wrote that they desperately needed 5 percent dextrose in water in liter bags for intravenous administration. Instead, they were "swamped" with saline, an unsatisfactory substitute. McDermott vowed that "someday, sometime, I'll look back on this mission and smile; but I think it will be a long time from now."[19]

On a more positive note, the hospital's first delivery was a little girl weighing 7 lbs. and 1 oz. on 7 May 1975. At the baby's birth, the father emotionally exclaimed, "I have lost all of my possessions but now I have gained a new joy!" Velsmid remarked that the refugees were "very kind and grateful for every little thing we do for them. Their attitude . . . is surprisingly optimistic for people who have lost family, most of their possessions, and their country."[20]

Conditions in the upper administrative echelons were little better than those on the ward level. As days of little irritants passed into months of ongoing hassles with no resolution on the horizon, compounded by the stress of being away from home in a situation where everyone had to make do with what little was available, conflicts and personality clashes emerged. As late as August 1975, no one assigned to the 47th Field Hospital understood the unit's mission. With no unifying mission and no common goal, varied ends resulted in disparate means. The hospital commander refused to allow Lieutenant Colonel Maurine Hill, the 47th Field Hospital's chief nurse, to comply with guidelines passed down from the Forces Command chief nurse. He forbade Hill to go on consultation visits to community health nurses in the Vietnamese village or to the outlying Vietnamese dispensaries. Patient care concerns and dispositions were equally difficult. One patient, diagnosis unknown, was hospitalized, probably unnecessarily, for 80 days. Several malaria patients were hospitalized for several weeks. A schizophrenic patient regularly fled the ward, causing frustration for all concerned. Several patients on the infectious ward had provisional diagnoses of tuberculosis, a dreaded disease that few of the younger nurses had previously encountered.[21]

The challenges met by the five Army Community Health Nurses (ACHNs) deployed to Fort Chaffee contributed significantly to the mission's success. One ACHN supervised American Red Cross volunteer nurses in the initial reception center. There both volunteers and ACHNs dispensed "advice, fluids, infant needs, and minor analgesics." These nurses also "identified and questioned pregnant women, the elderly and disabled, and those who appeared ill." In addition, the preventive medicine officer assigned one ACHN to each of three cantonment areas where refugees were housed. These ACHNs dealt with minor medical problems, provided care for convalescents or those with chronic illnesses, implemented case findings by seeking those who were ill but unable to reach out for help, supported epidemiologic investigations, and sponsored health education offerings. They later organized and supervised minor illness clinics in each of the three living areas and staffed the clinics with Vietnamese health professionals. The preventive medicine officer assigned the fifth ACHN to the epidemiology section. In this role, the ACHN carried out "epidemiologic surveillance and investigations." This effort involved "collecting and tabulating medical screening, inpatient, and outpatient data; . . . providing follow-up for medical screening; . . . conducting contact tracing and interviewing; and . . . investigating disease outbreaks." The ACHNs' interventions yielded various positive outcomes that contributed to the atmosphere of welcome, monitored sanitary conditions, enhanced refugees' quality of life, provided day-to-day comforts, maintained family cohesiveness, and prevented large-scale morbidity and mortality.[22] The ACHNs' role was key to the mission's success.

In retrospect, the minor, daily aggravations of deploying to the field did not eclipse the yeoman's service provided by those members of the AMEDD that participated in the relief mission at Fort Chaffee. In spite of daunting circumstances that persisted for 90 days for many deployed personnel, they provided high-quality health care for the 36,000-plus refugees who passed through the center.[23]

When the refugee center at Fort Chaffee, Arkansas, reached its capacity of 24,000 evacuees, DoD had to find an alternate site.[24] On 22 May 1975, another center opened its doors at Fort Indiantown Gap, Pennsylvania, and remained in operation until 15 December 1975.[25] Indiantown Gap accommodated more than 17,000 refugees in World War II era barracks painted white with green trim and situated on 22,000 acres of gravel and grass in Pennsylvania's Blue Mountains.[26]

The 42nd Field Hospital deployed from Fort Knox, Kentucky, and initially catered to the health care needs for the population at Fort Indiantown Gap. Lieutenant Colonel Vera Nolfe served as the unit's chief nurse.[27] The 42nd Field Hospital settled into the installation's cantonment hospital building that had been mothballed since 1953. Here, too, preparations involved significant elbow grease. Major Louis Tardif, a nurse anesthetist, who deployed with the 42nd Field Hospital from Walter Reed Army Medical Center, remarked that the staff searched in storage areas there and found an operating room table and cabinets that were "basic, operational, and simple." They scrubbed the table "down every morning, whether we plan[ned] on using it or not." As of 20 June, the total number of operative cases included one appendectomy and several births.[28]

Lieutenant Colonel Mary Dewan was an ACHN whose home unit also was Walter Reed Army Medical Center. On Mondays, Wednesdays, and Fridays, De-

A group of Vietnamese refugees carrying their few belongings enter their assigned living quarters at Fort Chaffee Refugee Center in Arkansas on 5 June 1975.
U.S. Army photograph released by Department of Defense, Washington, DC.

wan could be found in one of two *tram te tuu dong*, or mobile health clinics, set up in an Army van. The "tailgate medicine" vans brought basic primary care to the refugee quarters that were located a few miles from the hospital. Through the doors of the vehicle, staff distributed over-the-counter preparations, helped to screen patients for common maladies, and set up clinic appointments for the refugees.[29] The two mobile health clinics provided assistance for an average of 700 patients daily. Fortunately, Dewan had a competent interpreter to facilitate her communications with her clients. For the remaining two days of the work week, Dewan and her associate conducted home visits to patients recently discharged from the hospital.[30]

Forces Command and the Office of the Surgeon General agreed on a 90-day rotation policy for staff. However, the average overall time spent by the AMEDD personnel on temporary duty at the camps was 71 days. The purpose of the rotation policy was to mitigate personnel difficulties by replacing partial or total units assigned to the relief mission.[31] Thus, as summer ended, the 15th Combat Support Hospital from Fort Belvoir, Virginia, replaced the 42nd Field Hospital.

The incoming unit subsequently reduced itself to a 10-bed holding facility and operated a community medical center for routine outpatient obstetrics, optical, and dental appointments. When a medical officer judged that a refugee required hospitalization, an ambulance transferred the patient to nearby institutions such Hershey Medical Center in Hershey, Pennsylvania, or other hospitals in nearby Baltimore, Maryland.[32] As the number of expatriates decreased and requirements for care declined, the commander refused to reduce the staff correspondingly, perhaps fearing that another influx of immigrants might overwhelm a diminished staff. Although nursing administrators felt that the facility was overstaffed, the commander insisted on maintaining a one-for-one replacement system as outgoing staff returned to their home units. With very little to do, 13 Army Nurse Corps and five Medical Corps officers remained more or less idle, a state of affairs that seemed incomprehensible to many in an era when Army Nurse Corps assets were at an all-time low.[33] Nevertheless, the 15th Combat Support Hospital stayed at Fort Indiantown Gap until the mission closed at the end of calendar year 1975.[34]

Also among the tribulations of Fort Indiantown Gap was the emergence of a large number of cases of respiratory illness. The refugees were accustomed to the tropical climate of Southeast Asia. With impaired immune systems plus the stress of monumental change and a lifelong exposure to war and poverty, many succumbed to infectious diseases, pneumonias being the most serious.[35]

In the final analysis, operations New Life and New Arrivals cost the AMEDD much but yielded great benefit in assisting a deserving population of displaced persons. On the debit side, financial expenditures for medical supplies, equipment, and other health care costs from the massive humanitarian enterprise totaled more than $2.5 million in 1975 dollars, excluding personnel costs.[36] Effects felt in selected HSC medical treatment facilities as a consequence of the absent personnel included random increases in patient appointment waiting times, cancelled leaves for nurses, consolidated wards, and some 12-hour duty shifts for personnel. At Fort Campbell, Kentucky, the commander suspended activities of ACHNs for two weeks.[37] The intangible emotional losses of those that deployed and were consequently separated from their loved ones, families, and friends must not be ignored. These costs are not easily quantifiable but are a noteworthy feature of any such mission.

Overall, significant advantage came from the operation. The large-scale humanitarian assistance provided to the great masses of displaced Vietnamese refugees who were in truly dire straits ranks first. The AMEDD also learned valuable lessons about the conduct of these missions that had applicability to future, as yet unanticipated, combat missions. Operations New Life and New Arrivals tested and refined the AMEDD's emergency operation plans and highlighted areas of readiness that clearly needed improvement.[38] Many of those mobilized, for instance, were not Process for Overseas Rotation qualified. Furthermore, most of the senior Army nurses lacked the lightweight summer fatigue uniform. Many could not obtain these uniforms at their home stations, in which case the Academy of Health Sciences issued the uniforms to the senior officers.[39] Finally, participation in this disaster relief situation undoubtedly paid substantial dividends "in the peacetime mission of patient care through deepened and improved competencies in nursing practice."[40]

In a related effort, AMEDD personnel cared for hundreds of Southeast Asian orphan babies at various HSC installations in April 1975. Referred to as Operation Babylift, the humanitarian relief mission involved the air evacuation of children, mostly orphans, from Indochina after the collapse of the South Vietnamese government. The state department, DoD, and various volunteer American relief agencies collaborated to place these children with adoptive families within the United States. Along the way, nurses and other personnel at military treatment facilities cared for the infants, many of whom were suffering from a variety of illnesses, such as conjunctivitis, otitis media, skin diseases, chicken pox, malnutrition, dehydration, upper respiratory infections, and pneumonia. AMEDD personnel at Tripler Army Medical Center, Letterman Army Medical Center, Madigan Army Medical Center, Fitzsimons Army Medical Center, and Fort Benning, Georgia, cared for the children both in hospital settings and in centers outside hospitals specifically set up to house the evacuees.[41]

Tragically, one of the Air Force air evacuation flights that transported the Vietnamese babies crashed when taking off from Ton Son Nhut Airbase in Vietnam in April 1975. Many of the orphans and two of the medical crew died in the accident. One of those who perished in the line of duty was an Air Force flight nurse, Captain Mary T. Klinker. Operation Babylift concluded on 6 May 1975.[42] The short-term venture was but one of many contributions made by military nurses in the name of good will and humanitarianism.

In this same period, the AMEDD once again answered the call to provide humanitarian relief assistance to earthquake victims, this time in Guatemala. On 4 February 1976, a massive earthquake measuring 7.5 on the Richter scale struck; its epicenter was approximately 38 miles east of Guatemala City. The state department originated the request for foreign medical assistance, and Forces Command, HSC, and the Office of The Surgeon General coordinated the type of support to deploy. They opted for the 100-bed 47th Field Hospital from Fort Sill, Oklahoma, as a suitable unit to participate in the mission, perhaps because the 47th Field Hospital had a considerable amount of recent field experience. Six months before the Guatemalan disaster, the 47th Field Hospital had spent four months (from April to August 1975) at Fort Chaffee providing health care for the Southeast Asian refugees. When the earthquake struck, the 47th Field Hospital was conducting a field exercise. HSC immediately put personnel on alert, and they mobilized quickly. An advance team flew without delay to Guatemala and selected the hospital site on a picnic grove at the edge of a mountain lake near Chimaltenango, a small Indian village 31 miles southwest of Guatemala City. The main echelon followed straightaway, and the 47th began operations on the evening of 6 February 1976.[43]

Most of the 26 Army Nurse Corps officers who joined the unit came from the Fort Sill, Oklahoma, Medical Department Activity. However, HSC pulled others,

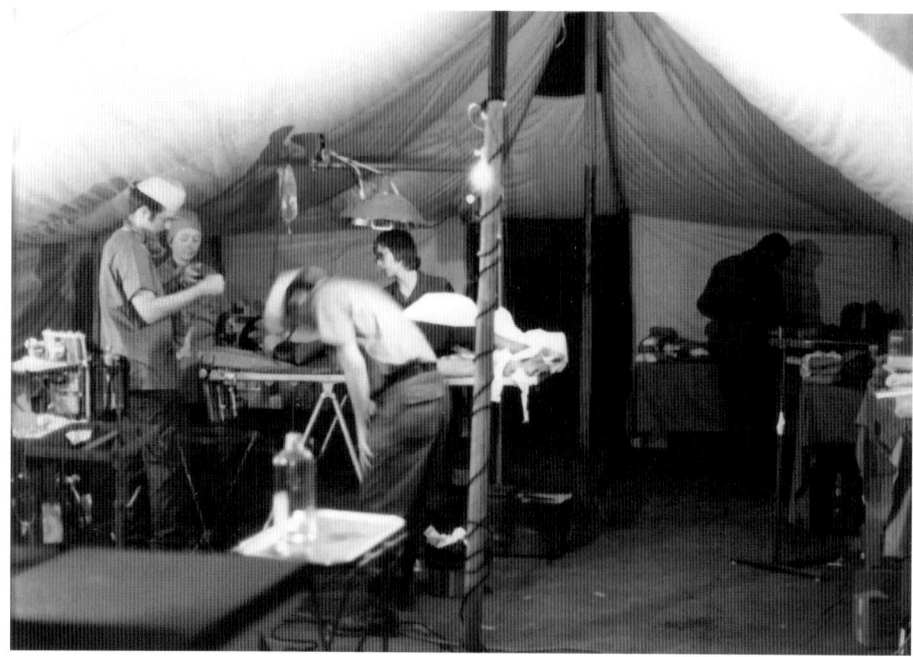

In this photo, Captain Margaret Kulm lends a hand with a native patient who sustained crushing injuries during the Guatemala earthquake of February 1976. Although she was head nurse of the 47th Field Hospital's pediatric ward, Kulm and all the multitalented Army Nurse Corps officers who deployed to Guatemala assisted and provided care wherever help was needed.
Photo courtesy of Colonel Peggy Jane Newman, Great Falls, VA.

including the chief nurse, from units at Fort Sam Houston, Texas.[44] Among the nursing personnel who deployed to Guatemala were two ACHNs who worked with the preventive medicine staff and three nurse clinicians (practitioners). Two of the three clinicians, prepared as adult ambulatory care specialists, functioned in the dispensary and were deemed "extremely effective." Little demand existed for the services of the third, an obstetrics/gynecology clinician, so she worked as a staff nurse on the obstetrics/pediatric ward.[45]

The majority of casualties cared for at the tent hospital had suffered orthopedic injuries. About 30 percent of those treated carried a diagnosis of a fractured pelvis.[46] Other cases involved various crushing injuries, other fractures, and lacerations.[47] A number of babies, including a set of twins, also were delivered at the hospital.[48] Captain Margaret Kulm, head nurse on the pediatric ward, noted that a few of the newborns were premature, but all of the infants thrived. The older children on the pediatric ward bore emotional as well as physical wounds and would "often wake screaming from nightmares." Frequent aftershocks also distressed the smaller tots.[49] Reassurance and comfort played a large part in the treatment regimen of these patients.

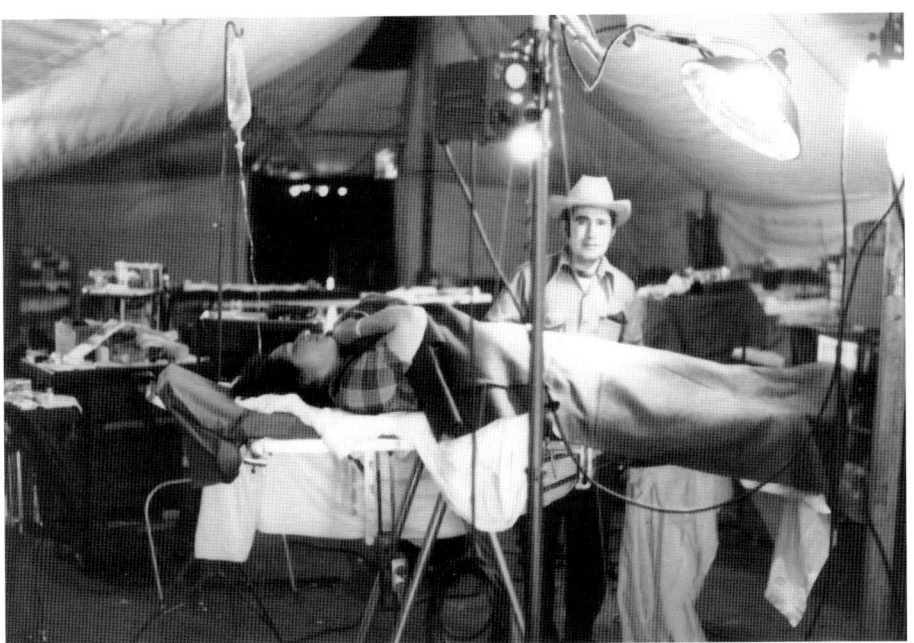

This Guatemalan couple share a quiet moment immediately after birth of their twins at the 47th Field Hospital during the Guatemalan earthquake of February 1976. Staff observed that the period of labor was quite precarious with the new mother lying on a flimsy field bed. The sparsely equipped hospital also had only one isolette, so both newborns closely shared their first external accommodation. Photo courtesy of Colonel Peggy Jane Newman, Great Falls, VA.

A number of operational snags emerged during the mission. Supply deficits were again a major concern. Much needed items that were in insufficient quantity or nonexistent included plaster, Ace bandages, slings, x-ray film, pediatric anesthesia equipment, surgical instruments, gloves, suture, urinary drainage systems, chest tubes, intravenous fluids, needles, administration sets, and replacement light bulbs.

The unexpected cool weather precipitated other difficulties. Before deployment, the unit failed to issue any TA-50 equipment, and thus members of the 47th were not protected from the elements.[50] Captain Sandra Hamper recalled that no one had anticipated cool weather, with nights as low as 28° F and afternoons lower than 70° F, and many were uncomfortably cold.[51]

Public relations was among the many frustrating issues that surfaced with this mission. The chief nurse, Lieutenant Colonel Marbeth Michael, perceived a need for a public information officer in future deployments because many individuals wanting to explore the hospital appeared on the scene "and occasionally they were disrespectful."[52] The commander added that these individuals were major irritants. They were the "curiosity-seekers and reporters . . . and Americans who turn[ed] up and demand[ed] to be fed because they are taxpayers." The commander made it a policy to furnish meals for "only those volunteers who work[ed] alongside his men and women, such as two medical students and a Guatemalan woman who [was] a trained nurse."[53]

Cultural differences and communication problems also emerged. A throng of family members wishing to visit hospitalized victims caused substantial strife and misunderstanding. To deal with the crowds, hospital authorities asked Guatemalan soldiers to restrict entry into the hospital compound, an action that "seemed absurd to local peasants." An American physician who had resided and practiced among the Indians in the neighboring villages for 14 years disclosed the natives' view of the American presence. He explained that a number of families wished "to take their relatives out of the Army hospital because . . . the Americans don't speak their language, don't understand them and never explain anything." This expatriate American physician allowed that the 47th Field Hospital "was 'doing a good job' and 'keeping a low profile'." Notwithstanding, he concluded that the Army "practiced a medicine unadapted to the customs and lives of the people it served." Other observers summarized their viewpoints by stating that the American contributions to the relief effort were "overstaffed, overorganized, and slow."[54]

A total of 69 officers and enlisted medics from 19 HSC organizations deployed to Guatemala and provided disaster relief.[55] The 47th Field Hospital spent a total of 12 days in Guatemala and cared for about 700 patients, most of whom were treated on an outpatient basis.[56] Like all relief missions, it too was an amalgam of unfortunate and worthwhile components.

Although the humanitarian assistance operations of the 1970s seemed to be plagued by difficulties, they were—in the final accounting—significantly constructive. Not only did the mission provide "succor [to] countless victims of nature's wrath who might not otherwise have received help," but they also were a source of growth and development for the AMEDD institution and fulfillment for those who personally furnished the relief. Army historian Gaines M. Foster concluded:

> Civilian emergencies provided more realistic experience in the care of mass casualties than most training exercises, and participating units learned a great deal about operating in an environment that resembled combat. Moreover, the personnel felt a sense of accomplishment that came from helping people in need and using the skills they had worked to develop. Successful disaster relief missions, in sum, improved technical skills while they increased morale and esprit. They thereby strengthened the Army Medical Department as well as aided civilians.[57]

The Military Training Team (MTT) effort that involved sending two Army Nurse Corps officers to Jordan was another type of foreign assistance. The Jordanian government and the AMEDD jointly conceived and implemented the MTT to educate approximately 40 senior Royal Jordanian Medical Corps nurses in the current trends in "nursing administration, methods of instruction and hospital management and operation." The goal of the MTT was "to provide the Jordanian nurses with enough 'know-how' so they [could] form their own cadre of teachers"

Two non-English speaking members of the Guatemalan protective forces flank Army Nurse Corps officers Major Nancy Nooney, left, and Captain Peggy Jane Newman, right, on the picnic grounds where the 47th Field Hospital erected its tents near Chimaltenango, Guatemala, after the February 1976 earthquake. The local militia guarded the hospital compound.
Photo courtesy of Colonel Peggy Jane Newman, Great Falls, VA.

to pass on their acquired knowledge and skills.[58]

The Army Nurse Corps selected two officers, Colonel Marian C. Barbieri and Major Mary Lou Spine, to participate because of their extensive backgrounds in the education of military nurses.[59] They departed from their respective home stations, Fort Dix, New Jersey, and Letterman Army Medical Center, California, on 14 November 1976 for orientation at HSC, Fort Sam Houston, Texas, from 15 to 19 November 1976.[60] Then they went to Jordan, arriving in Amman on 21 November 1976.[61] The two settled into their lodging, a spacious but no-frills second-floor flat, and began their work as expeditiously as possible.[62]

Barbieri and Spine spent an initial assessment period observing at the Princess Muna College of Nursing (a three-year diploma program and an 18-month practical nurse course), at the King Hussein Medical Center, at the 1st and 2nd Field Hospitals, and at the Amman Military Hospital. After the initial assessment process, the two U.S. Army nurses presented several iterations of a two-day lecture series on the basics of nursing administration and principles of teaching. This didactic program was followed by a practicum geared to the individual needs of the particular faculty and staff members.[63] By February 1977, the two made other significant contributions, such as assisting the Jordanians to write job descriptions and administrative procedures and helping their hosts to restructure the existing nursing department. They also were setting up a staff development program and helping the college faculty to implement a new curriculum.[64] As of March 1977, Barbieri and Spine had prepared suggestions for the professional development of members of the Royal Jordanian Nurse Corps. These recommendations included tentative plans for Jordanian Army nurses to participate in observer training programs with selected counterparts in the U.S. Army Nurse Corps and in educational offerings such as the operating room, intensive care, and nurse clinician courses sponsored within the United States by the U.S. Army Nurse Corps.[65] By the midpoint of the six-month temporary duty, Barbieri noted that the "feedback we do receive is our best reward and serves as an incentive to plug ahead. Our hope is to build a bit of self-confidence for . . . our counterparts. . . . We hope to encourage self-reliance."[66] In April 1977, the pair "oriented the staff of one of the Field Hospitals to the intricacies of process audit." They noted that they "would have preferred to do [a] retrospective audit but discovered nursing notes, if they exist, are not made a permanent part of the chart."[67] One of the team's final efforts was to promote and set up a supervisory level of employees in the King Hussein Medical Center hierarchy between the matron and the head nurses to improve supervision and coordination in the large, widely dispersed facility. Many of the staff were unwilling to accept this change. One new supervisor was markedly unenthusiastic because she feared "that if the need arose for her to correct" one of her assigned head nurses, "the disciplined person would complain to the supervisor's mother." At first the American nurses could not fathom this Jordanian nurse's way of thinking. However, the supervisor's concern was sincere. "In the light of the very strong family influences that prevail[ed] in this culture," Barbieri and Spine realized that the new supervisor's apprehension about the "possibility of someone tattling on her to her mother" was indeed a terrifying prospect.[68] The pair ironed out many similar cultural wrinkles while they were in the Hashemite Kingdom of Jordan.

The two Army Nurse Corps officers' copious correspondence shows that their days were saturated not only with professional activities, educational offerings, and consultation, but also with various social events and extensive sightseeing. Local Jordanians, the embassy staff, and other American military families assigned to Jordan entertained Barbieri and Spine in a series of dinners, teas, receptions, and parties. They attended the Royal Jordanian Military Academy's commencement ceremony and shopped in bazaars and souks, finding a variety of native arts and crafts. They also visited the ruins of a first-century city called Jerash, picnicked on the edge of the Dead Sea in view of the city of Jericho and the Mount of Olives, and visited Damascus and bought tablecloths. Barbieri and Spine realized a special dream when they toured Egypt and the Holy Land in

April. In their last days in Jordan, they spent some time with Bedouin families in their desert tents "to assess health needs of the nomadic tent dwellers." In February 1977, Spine was promoted to lieutenant colonel. The Americans arranged for the promotion ceremony to take place in the Princess Muna College of Nursing with Jordanian Army dignitaries, college staff and students, and U.S. military attachés from the embassy in attendance. Barbieri and the chief of the Royal Jordanian Nurse Corps pinned the silver leaves on Spine's uniform. A reception that followed featured "tea and sweets."[69] Barbieri and Spine took advantage of many opportunities while serving in the Middle East, and they lived every minute of their six-month temporary duty in Jordan to the fullest.

The duo wrote in their final communiqué that they were beset "with ambivalent feelings." They explained that although they were

> ... pleased to be returning to our family and friends on US soil, we were saddened to leave behind our foster family and newly acquired friends on desert sands. In six months we became very close with the Jordanians with whom we worked and felt that we had just reached an optimum level of productivity where concepts and ideas were beginning to be transferred into action. This phase is always the most satisfying but leave it we must with hopes that the seeds we planted take hold and continue to grow.[70]

Six years later, the Army Nurse Corps provided additional support to the Jordanian Army. From 12 February to 12 March 1983, Major Annette R. Aitcheson, an Army nurse from the U.S. Army Institute of Surgical Research at Brooke Army Medical Center, Texas, advised the staff of the Jordanian Army Burn Treatment Centre. While in Amman, Jordan, Aitcheson presented lectures to Jordanian physicians and nurses on various aspects of care for "the thermally injured patient"; demonstrated specialized equipment such as the Laminar Flow Isolator, the Clinitron Air Fluidized Bed, and the IVAC infusion pump; and helped the nurses to develop policies and job descriptions. However, one of the greatest challenges for the mission arose from the fact that the Jordanian Army Burn Treatment Centre was not yet operational. Without actual burn patients, "the clinical application of the didactic and theoretical data" was impossible.[71]

Professional and cultural conditions Aitcheson encountered in Jordan were marked by vivid contrasts. On the one hand, some of the physical facilities were state of the art. The Queen Alia Heart Centre, for instance, was "one of the best equipped and clean" institutions that Aitcheson had ever seen.[72] Also, the Jordanians billeted Aitcheson at a four-star hotel, a first-rate establishment that served gourmet meals, and provided her with transportation and "afforded [her] every possible courtesy and respect." On the other hand, there was a complete "absence of Standards of Nursing Practice."[73] Additionally, nursing documentation was sparse to nonexistent, and nursing care plans were not used at all.[74] When a protracted snowfall happened during Aitcheson's visit, employees failed to report to work and staffing levels were inadequate. Those nurses already on duty were forced to work "two to three additional shifts" to maintain coverage.[75]

At the conclusion of her visit, Aitcheson made several recommendations. She proposed appropriate staffing levels, training, supplies, and equipment necessary for quality care in the Jordanian Army Burn Treatment Centre. She suggested that several Jordanian Army nurses spend three months at the U.S. Army Institute of Surgical Research to learn necessary skills for caring for critically burned patients. Finally, Aitcheson advised that a MTT consisting of a burn nurse administrator, a critical care staff nurse, and 91C licensed practical nurse revisit Jordan in the future to evaluate the "prior training" and build on these previous educational efforts.[76]

One year later, a team consisting of Aitcheson, Major Kathryn Robertson, and Staff Sergeant Joe Constantine returned to Jordan and discovered numerous improvements in practice, such as the use of standard nursing care plans and evidence of better nursing documentation, both of which bore witness to the motivation and diligence of the Jordanian nurses. However, Aitcheson noted that "if the nurses write too much [on their nursing notes] then the Records Department complains and the chart must be thinned out (permanently)."

Overall objectives for this 1984 mission included striving to improve the quality of nurses notes, changing "the nurses' attitude of patient care from a task . . . to an holistic orientation," implementing a "multidisciplinary approach to burn care" involving physical therapy and social work in the patient care effort, and developing "a diet that will meet the increased nutritional demands of the burn injured patient." However, some disappointment inevitably accompanied progress. Aitcheson wrote:

> Everyday when we think we have a good grasp of the situation, the realities of the culture and the economic conditions rocks us on our heels. Today we had to sit down, again, and decide what it is we can and cannot change.[77]

The trio of U.S. Army visitors managed some diversion and rest with a trip to Azrat, an oasis in the nearby desert, but even that adventure was rife with challenges. They attempted to camp out with a Jordanian nurse on a cold 30° F night. Aitcheson revealed that "like true soldiers we tried to brave the freezing temperature and howling winds as we huddled around the barbecue grill . . . in two and three blankets." Eventually, however, they "packed up and spent the night in the rest house." In the morning, the band of intrepid campers awoke to a desert dust storm. Aitcheson philosophically remarked "so much for our first adventure."[78]

Several years later Aitcheson articulated her guiding philosophy, writing:

> As nurses, we each have a responsibility to assist in the growth of nursing throughout the world. Nurses in the United States can participate in developing nursing colleagues in third world nations. It is only through consistent and knowledgeable practices throughout the world that nursing will be recognized as the sole authority on nursing care.[79]

Although challenges were many and progress was slow, long-term gains were significant. Much credit can be attributed to the optimism of those altruistic Army Nurse Corps officers who traveled to Jordan and shared their knowledge and expertise in spite of attendant hardships. Moreover, the Jordanian nurses' willingness to internalize the proffered advice and their enthusiastic efforts to improve their professional practice were laudable. Few, if any, other allied military nurses were eager to endure the trauma inherent in the professional growth process.

No Army Nurse Corps officers participated in combat operations during the immediate post–Vietnam War era. At that time, the prevailing state of affairs dictated that deployments not exceed the boundaries that defined the term 'operations other than war.' However, the more or less peaceful operations that occurred at that juncture exhibited many telling attributes. For example, the readiness planning that occurred before the deployments in the 1970s was nominal and lacking in refinements. The deficient levels of readiness were similar to those that existed just before the onset and during the early days of Vietnam and other prior wars. Army nurses coped with the deficits that were one consequence of meager planning by functioning with ingenuity and implementing field expedient strategies. In the final analysis, the missions of that time generally were successful, furnishing the required amenities and assistance to the populations they served. The deployments also profited those who provided the support and the Army organization as a whole by supplying very useful, practical field experience. Finally, the deployments triggered essential development and underscored the imperative to improve readiness planning on a regular basis. Readiness planning as an ongoing process would be acknowledged as a prime necessity in the years to come.

# Notes

1. Raymond L. Coultrip, "Medical Aspects of US Disaster Relief Operations in Nicaragua," *Military Medicine* 139 (December 1974): 879–83. Gaines M. Foster, *The Demands of Humanity; Army Medical Disaster Relief* (Washington, DC: Center of Military History, U.S. Army, 1983), 168–70.

2. Jane High, "Information Copy, Nursing Service, Managua, Nicaragua Disaster," Typewritten Document (TD), 22 January 1973; and Jane High to Madelyn Parks, Handwritten Letter, 1 January 1973 (both in Army Nurse Corps Collection [ANCC], Office of Medical History [OMH]).

3. The general purpose medium tent measured 32 feet long and 16 feet wide. http://www.imsplus.com/ims66b.html (accessed 28 June 2005). Jane High, "Information Copy, Nursing Service, Managua, Nicaragua Disaster," TD, 22 January 1973; and Jane High to Madelyn Parks, Handwritten Letter, 1 January 1973 (both in ANCC, OMH).

4. Ibid.

5. Department of State, Bureau of Public Affairs, Office of Media Services, "Humanitarian Aid to Viet-Nam," News Release, 15 April 1975; and Department of State, Bureau of Public Affairs, Office of Media Services, "Indochina Refugee Resettlement," News Release, August 1975 (both in ANCC, OMH).

6. *Report of the Surgeon General United States Army Fiscal Years 1976–1980* (Washington, DC: Office of the Surgeon General, Department of the Army, 1988), 165–67. Richard R. Taylor, "Landmarks Point to Army's Future," *U.S. Medicine* 12 (15 January 1975): 46. Robert Shaw, "Health Services in a Disaster: Lessons from the 1975 Vietnamese Evacuation," *Military Medicine* 144 (May 1979): 307–11.

7. Carolyn M. Feller and Debora R. Cox, *Highlights in the History of the Army Nurse Corps, 100th Anniversary Edition* (Washington, DC: U.S. Army Center of Military History, 2000), 48.

8. *Report of the Surgeon General United States Army Fiscal Years 1976–1980* (Washington, DC: Office of the Surgeon General, Department of the Army, 1988), 165–67. The Army Nurse Corps After Action Report stated, "over 100 ANC officers participated in this mission." Virginia L. Brown, "After Action Report—Operation NEW ARRIVALS," Typewritten Disposition Form, 26 January 1976, ANCC, OMH.

9. Richard R. Taylor, "Landmarks Point to Army's Future," *U.S. Medicine* 12 (15 January 1975): 41.

10. As of 9 June 1975, seven Army nurses were in Guam. They included Hoppe; the two Army Community Health Nurses, Lieutenant Colonel Anna Frederico and Captain Mary L. Criswell, who were assigned to an epidemiology detachment, the 152nd Medical Detachment; captains June Sekiguchi and Mary F. Faupel; and first lieutenants Ollie B. Gray and Rebecca Atwood, who were assigned either to the 423rd or the 702nd Medical Company (Clearing). Jean Hoppe to Edith Nuttall, Typewritten Letter (TL), 9 June 1975, ANCC, OMH.

11. Edith Nuttall, "Nursing Activities, 1st Medical Group, Guam," Telephone Conversation Record from dialogue with Jeanne Hoppe, 6 June 1975, ANCC, OMH.

12. The MOS (Military Occupational Specialty) for Medical-Surgical Nurse at that time was 3438. Other MOSs in existence then were 3430, Nurse Administrator; 3431, Community Health Nurse; 3437, Psychiatric/Mental Health Nurse; 3442, Pediatric Nurse; 3443, Operating Room Nurse; 3445, Nurse Anesthetist; 3446, Obstetric and Gynecologic Nurse; and 3449, Clinical Nurse, or one who "functions in first level nursing care activities." The specific digits had meaning as well. The first digit, 3, indicated an AMEDD MOS. The second digit, 4, specified an ANC or AMSC officer. The final two digits identified the specialty with the ANC. Academy of Health Sciences, U.S. Army, "Nursing in Army Hospitals," Study Guide 310, 102–12, November 1974, ANCC, OMH. Jean Hoppe to Edith Nuttall, TL, 9 June 1975, ANCC, OMH.

13. Edith Nuttall, "Nursing Activities, 1st Medical Group, Guam," Telephone Conversation Record from dialogue with Jeanne Hoppe, 6 June 1975, ANCC, OMH.

14. *Report of the Surgeon General United States Army Fiscal Years 1976–1980* (Washington, DC: Office of the Surgeon General, Department of the Army, 1988), 167. *U.S. Army Health Service Command, Annual Historical Review, 1 July 1975 to 30 September 1977* (Ft. Sam Houston, TX: Historical Office, HSC, 1979), 120.

15. *Report of the Surgeon General United States Army Fiscal Years 1976–1980* (Washington, DC: Office of the Surgeon General, Department of the Army, 1988), 166–67. Carolyn M. Feller and Debora R. Cox, *Highlights in the History of the Army Nurse Corps, 100th Anniversary Edition* (Washington, DC: U.S. Army Center of Military History, 2000), 48. Edith Nuttall, "Information, 47th Field Hospital, Fort Chaffee, Arkansas," Telephone Conversation Record from dialogue with Maurine Hill, 5 August 1975, ANCC, OMH.

16. Joel C. Gaydos and others, "A Preventive Medicine Team in a Refugee Relief Operation—Fort Chaffee Indochina Refugee Camp (April–July 1975)," *Military Medicine* 143 (May 1978): 318–21.

17. Lillian Dunlap, *33 Years of Army Nursing* (Washington, DC: U.S. Army Nurse Corps, 2001), 292. James B. Dalton, "Conditions at Fort Chaffee Refugee Camp," TL, 12 June 1975, ANCC, OMH.

18. Stephanie Velsmid to Ward 7, Handwritten Letter, 8 May 1975, ANCC, OMH.

19. Diane McDermott to Lieutenant Colonel Carr, Handwritten Letter, 11 May 1975, ANCC, OMH.

20. Stephanie Velsmid to Ward 7, Handwritten Letter, 8 May 1975, ANCC, OMH.

21. Edith Nuttall, "Information, 47th Field Hospital, Fort Chaffee, Arkansas," Telephone Conversation Record from dialogue with Maurine Hill, 5 August 1975, ANCC, OMH.

22. Joel C. Gaydos and others, "A Preventive Medicine Team in a Refugee Relief Operation—Fort Chaffee Indochina Refugee Camp (April–July 1975)," *Military Medicine* 143 (May 1978): 318–21.

23. Department of State, Bureau of Public Affairs, Office of Media Services, "Indochina Refugee Resettlement," News Release, 2, August 1975, ANCC, OMH.

24. Ibid. Lillian Dunlap, *33 Years of Army Nursing* (Washington, DC: U.S. Army Nurse

Corps, 2001), 292.

25. *Report of the Surgeon General United States Army Fiscal Years 1976–1980* (Washington, DC: Office of the Surgeon General, Department of the Army, 1988), 167.

26. Department of State, Bureau of Public Affairs, Office of Media Services, "Indochina Refugee Resettlement," News Release, 2, August 1975; and Ann Butler, "Waiting for Acceptance," *Pittsburgh Press Roto* (26 October 1975): n.p., Newspaper Clipping (both in ANCC, OMH).

27. Connie L. Slewitzke, "Indian Town Gap Military Reservation," Memorandum for Record, 21 May 1975, ANCC, OMH.

28. Vickey Mouze, "Ft. Indiantown Gap: WRAMC Personnel Doing Their Part to Improve, Restore Health of Refugees," *The Stripe* (20 June 1975): 6.

29. OTC preparations are medications that can be purchased without a prescription. Certain cough and cold remedies, aspirin, and specific ointments are examples of OTC items.

30. Vickey Mouze, "Ft. Indiantown Gap: WRAMC Personnel Doing Their Part to Improve, Restore Health of Refugees," *The Stripe* (20 June 1975): 6.

31. *Report of the Surgeon General United States Army Fiscal Years 1976–1980* (Washington, DC: Office of the Surgeon General, Department of the Army, 1988), 166–67.

32. John Romer, "Refugee Work: A New Experience," *Army Times* (3 December 1975): n.p., Newspaper Clipping, ANCC, OMH.

33. Edith Nuttall, "Information from Chief Nurse, Indiantown Gap, PA," Telephone Conversation Record from dialogue with Dorothy Nelson, 9 October 1975, ANCC, OMH. Lillian Dunlap, *33 Years of Army Nursing* (Washington, DC: U.S. Army Nurse Corps, 2001), 293.

34. John Romer, "Refugee Work: A New Experience," *Army Times* (3 December 1975): n.p., Newspaper Clipping, ANCC, OMH.

35. Lillian Dunlap, *33 Years of Army Nursing* (Washington, DC: U.S. Army Nurse Corps, 2001), 292–93.

36. *Report of the Surgeon General United States Army Fiscal Years 1976–1980* (Washington, DC: Office of the Surgeon General, Department of the Army, 1988), 167.

37. Virginia L. Brown, "After Action Report—Operation NEW ARRIVALS," Typewritten Disposition Form, 26 January 1976, ANCC, OMH.

38. Lillian Dunlap, *33 Years of Army Nursing* (Washington, DC: U.S. Army Nurse Corps, 2001), 294–95.

39. Virginia L. Brown, "After Action Report—Operation NEW ARRIVALS," Typewritten Disposition Form, 26 January 1976, ANCC, OMH.

40. Academy of Health Sciences, U.S. Army, "Nursing in Army Hospitals," Study Guide 310, 96, November 1974, ANCC, OMH.

41. Virginia L. Brown, "Impact Statement on Vietnam Orphans," Typewritten Document, 11 April 1975; "Arrival of Sea Orphan Evacuees, Fort Benning, GA," Memorandum for Record, 11 April 1975; Virginia L. Brown, "Information on "Operation Baby-Lift" in CONUS," Telephone Conversation Record from dialogue with Edith M. Nuttall, 14 April 1975; Ron Taylor, "Benning's Babes, 171 Vietnamese Orphans Find Temporary Home," Newspaper Clipping from *Columbus (GA) Journal-Constitution*, n.p., n.d. (all in ANCC, OMH). "Operation Babylift," *Army Times* (30 April 1975): 27.

42. Mary C. Smolenski, Donald G. Smith, and James S. Nanney, *A Fit, Fighting Force, The Air Force Nursing Services Chronology* (Washington, DC: Office of the Air Force Surgeon General, 2005), 33–34.

43. *Report of the Surgeon General United States Army Fiscal Years 1976–1980* (Washington, DC: Office of the Surgeon General, Department of the Army, 1988), 172–74.

Gaines M. Foster, *The Demands of Humanity; Army Medical Disaster Relief* (Washington, DC: Center of Military History, U.S. Army, 1983), 170–71. Richard B. Taylor, "Army's Programs Fitted to Mission," *U.S. Medicine* 13 (15 January 1977): 49. "Massive Quake Smashes Guatemala," *Washington Star* (4 February 1976): A-1. "GIs Ease Quake Victims' Pain," *Los Angeles Herald-Examiner* (20 February 1976): A-10.

44. Marbeth G. Michael, "Nursing Service After Action Report," TL to Thomas C. Birk, 15 March 1976, ANCC, OMH. Gaines M. Foster, *The Demands of Humanity; Army Medical Disaster Relief* (Washington, DC: Center of Military History, U.S. Army, 1983), 171. "HSC's Medical People Help Field Hospital Care for Guatemala's Earthquake Victims," *HSC Mercury* 3 (April 1976): 4–5.

45. Marbeth G. Michael, "Nursing Service After Action Report," TL to Thomas C. Birk, 3, 15 March 1976, ANCC, OMH.

46. "Five Brooke Nurses Weather Shocks, Cold to Aid Victims," *HSC Mercury* 3 (April 1976): 5.

47. "HSC's Medical People Help Field Hospital Care for Guatemala's Earthquake Victims," *HSC Mercury* 3 (April 1976): 5. Gaines M. Foster, *The Demands of Humanity; Army Medical Disaster Relief* (Washington, DC: Center of Military History, U.S. Army, 1983), 171.

48. "GIs Ease Quake Victims' Pain," *Los Angeles Herald-Examiner* (20 February 1976): A-10.

49. "Five Brooke Nurses Weather Shocks, Cold to Aid Victims," *HSC Mercury* 3 (April 1976): 5.

50. TA-50 is the field equipment issued prior to deployment. It can include any number of objects, such as web gear, canteens, ponchos, and helmet liners, to name but a few crucial items. Marbeth G. Michael, "Nursing Service After Action Report," TL to Thomas C. Birk, 1–3, 15 March 1976, ANCC, OMH.

51. "Five Brooke Nurses Weather Shocks, Cold to Aid Victims," *HSC Mercury* 3 (April 1976): 5.

52. Marbeth G. Michael, "Nursing Service After Action Report," TL to Thomas C. Birk, 4, 15 March 1976, ANCC, OMH.

53. "GIs Ease Quake Victims' Pain," *Los Angeles Herald-Examiner* (20 February 1976): A-10.

54. Gaines M. Foster, *The Demands of Humanity; Army Medical Disaster Relief* (Washington, DC: Center of Military History, U.S. Army, 1983), 171–72.

55. Spurgeon Neel, "HSC Guatemala Earthquake Assistance," in Department of the Army, Headquarters, U.S. Army Health Services Command, *Commander's Notes*, CG HSC Bulletin No. 4-76 (April 1976): 1, Record Group 112, Entry 452, National Archives.

56. *Report of the Surgeon General United States Army Fiscal Years 1976–1980* (Washington, DC: Office of the Surgeon General, Department of the Army, 1988), 174. Gaines M. Foster, *The Demands of Humanity; Army Medical Disaster Relief* (Washington, DC: Center of Military History, U.S. Army, 1983), 171.

57. Gaines M. Foster, *The Demands of Humanity; Army Medical Disaster Relief* (Washington, DC: Center of Military History, U.S. Army, 1983), 174–75.

58. U.S. Army Health Services Command, Public Affairs Office, "Army Nurses Depart for Jordan," News Release No. 470, 19 November 1976, ANCC, OMH.

59. Marian C. Barbieri, Interview by Susan Steinfeld and Wynona Bice-Stephens, 10, 11, 14–16, and 19–20, 12 May 1988, U.S. Army Center of Military History, Washington, D.C., ANCC, OMH.

60. Marian C. Barbieri, "Effectiveness of Training Report (RCS CSGPO-125)," Typewritten Report, ANCC, OMH.

61. Marian C. Barbieri, "Nursing Administration and Education MTT-JO-0025-77, Interim Report—20 January 1977," Typewritten Report, ANCC, OMH.

62. Barbieri and Spine sent regular letters to Brigadier General Madelyn Parks full of candid, humorous details chronicling their circumstances, challenges, and experiences. Their letter dated 2 December 1976 tells of their hospitable welcome, spartan living conditions in a "cold water flat," erratic transportation provided by a chauffeur who carried a sidearm and spoke no English, social engagements, and their initial efforts to educate. Marian C. Barbieri and Mary Lou Spine to General Parks, TL, 2 December 1976, ANCC, OMH.

63. Marian C. Barbieri, "Nursing Administration and Education MTT-JO-0025-77, Interim Report—20 January 1977," Typewritten Report, ANCC, OMH.

64. Marian C. Barbieri and Mary Lou Spine to General Parks, TL, 2 February 1977, ANCC, OMH.

65. Marian C. Barbieri and Mary Lou Spine to General Parks, Typewritten Letter, 7 March 1977; and Marian C. Barbieri and Mary Lou Spine to Director, Royal Medical Services, JAF, "Suggested Plan for Further Education for Royal Jordanian Nursing Services Personnel," TD, 5 March 1977 (both in ANCC, OMH).

66. Marian C. Barbieri to General Parks, Handwritten Letter, 12 March 1977, ANCC, OMH.

67. Marian C. Barbieri to General Parks, TL, 1 April 1977, ANCC, OMH.

68. Marian C. Barbieri to General Parks, TL, 10 May 1977, ANCC, OMH.

69. Marian C. Barbieri and Mary Lou Spine to General Parks, 2 December 1976; Marian C. Barbieri and Mary Lou Spine to General Parks, 15 December 1976; Marian C. Barbieri and Mary Lou Spine to General Parks, 20 January 1977; Marian C. Barbieri and Mary Lou Spine to General Parks, 2 February 1977; Marion C. Barbieri to General Parks, 26 April 1977; and Marion C. Barbieri and Mary Lou Spine to General Parks, 10 May 1977 (all TLs in ANCC, OMH).

70. Marian C. Barbieri and Mary Lou Spine to General Parks, TL, 10 May 1977, ANCC, OMH.

71. Annette R. Aitcheson, "RCS CSGPO-125 (Effectiveness of Training of Mobile Training Team)," TD, 5 April 1983, ANCC, OMH.

72. Annette R. Aitcheson, "Annex (Unofficial Report)," TD, n.d., ANCC, OMH.

73. Annette R. Aitcheson, "RCS CSGPO-125 (Effectiveness of Training of Mobile Training Team)," TD, 5 April 1983, ANCC, OMH.

74. Annette R. Aitcheson to General Slewitzke, Handwritten Letter, 11 March 1984, ANCC, OMH.

75. Annette R. Aitcheson, "Annex (Unofficial Report)," TD, n.d., ANCC, OMH.

76. Annette R. Aitcheson, "RCS CSGPO-125 (Effectiveness of Training of Mobile Training Team)," TD, 5 April 1983, ANCC, OMH

77. Annette R. Aitcheson to General Slewitzke, Handwritten Letter, 11 March 1984, ANCC, OMH.

78. Ibid.

79. Annette R. Aitcheson, "US Army Burn Nurse Consultant Assignment Jordan," *Medical Bulletin of the US Army, Europe* 43 (September/October 1986): 45.

*Part Two*

A Decade of Change

*Chapter Eight*
# New Leadership and Expanding Horizons

Having navigated the troubled waters of the 1970s with fair success, the Army Nurse Corps entered into an even more complex decade in the 1980s as it dealt with both traditional and unprecedented issues of equal intensity. A blend of new and familiar perplexities also confronted the Army and the Army Medical Department (AMEDD).

The 1980s was a time of difficult transitions. Most of the evolving issues had their roots in the 1970s and amplified with the new decade. The shortage of nurses was the most obvious challenge, but improving quality of care and readiness also consumed much time and energy. Army Nurse Corps leaders were creative and innovative when dealing with these dilemmas.

At the same time that the Army Nurse Corps was coping with these demands, it also was slowly expanding its practice frontiers. Increasing numbers of Army nurses were accepting nontraditional assignments and pushing back long-established boundaries. They were bellwethers of the paradigm shift from strictly traditional roles to unprecedented command positions for Army nurses. From the Cuban Relief Mission reminiscent of 1970s field missions, to the checkered campaign of Operation Urgent Fury, to the more streamlined execution of Operation Just Cause, the AMEDD and the Army Nurse Corps advanced out of the post–Vietnam War doldrums into the era of the all-volunteer army. The 1980s represented sweeping change, reform, and modernization for the U.S. Army. Conversely, growth in numbers of women in the active Army slowed in relation to the prior decade.[1]

A total of 12,542 female officers and soldiers served in the active force during fiscal year (FY) 1960.[2] Ten years later, during FY 1970, the numbers remained constant, with 12,500 women in active service.[3] Across the 1970s, however, a large number of women joined the Army and, by FY 1980, the Army counted 68,966 officer and enlisted women in its ranks.[4] After the 1980s, a decade of comparatively minimal growth for the Army, some 83,600 women were on active duty, as of FY 1989.[5] Feminist scholars specializing in military women's issues posit that the senior Army and Air Force hierarchy encouraged the Reagan administration early in 1981 to put a damper on the numbers of women in military, who they believed hindered military efficiency. This movement became known as "womanpause."[6] The entry of large numbers of women soldiers into the Army was not issue-free. Fierce debate over topics such as degraded unit readiness because of pregnancies, women's failure to complete their enlistments, and a lack of physical endurance and upper extremity strength led to the formation of a Policy Review Group on Women in the Army in April 1981.[7] In November 1982 this task force recommended that enlisted women be restricted to service in 93 percent of all enlisted military occupational specialties (MOSs), basing the decisions on the Direct Combat Probability Coding system. To set up this system, a team scrutinized and graded each MOS on a scale of P1 to P7, with P1 indicating the greatest probability of involvement in direct combat.[8] The Army banned female soldiers from any MOS that fell into the category of P1, essentially the combat arms, which also offered career soldiers the best opportunities for promotion, command, and awards. Controversy and challenges led to minor modifications to the Direct Combat Probability Coding rating system in the following years.[9] The changes, interestingly enough, did not liberalize standards, perhaps because a mostly male backlash followed the large-scale introduction of women into the military.[10] The reaction may also have represented another illustration of womenpause. By 1989, Army enlisted women were eligible for only 86 percent of MOSs, although the Army deemed female officers eligible for 95 percent of all officer specialties. Women could also qualify for 91 percent of all warrant officer roles. The Army's official attitude was that the Direct Combat Probability Coding system reflected the implied intent of the Congress.[11] This meant Army policy, not congressional legislation, dictated the service's utilization of women. The Navy, however, relied on statutes, not policy, to prohibit the permanent service of Navy women on combat ships and aircraft. Similar restrictions applied to women serving in the Marine Corps. Legislation likewise proscribed Air Force women's presence on combat aircraft. However, the law exempted Air Force women in the medical professions and the chaplaincy from the prohibition. Of all the uniformed services, women in the Coast Guard enjoyed the greatest latitude. They had no restrictions or embargoes imposed. Every role in that service was open to women.[12] Perhaps this liberal stance could be traced to the fact that the Coast Guard was a small service, not an element of the Department of Defense, but under the Treasury Department, and not in the front line of combat.

The greater presence of women in the Army had a variety of effects on the daily concerns of the Army Nurse Corps. In many cases, more females in the Army meant better overall treatment for women in general and for the women in the Army Nurse Corps in particular. Moreover, with many more women service members as patients, it also added a new dimension to health care that often transcended gender and affected the nature of the health service support provided by Army Nurse Corps officers.[13]

Although old-school traditionalists decried the greater inclusion of women into the Army organization, they simultaneously applauded the adoption of a new philosophy, the Army of Excellence. The Army as an institution became committed to turn the so-called Army of Excellence into a reality to confront "a powerful and dangerous Soviet adversary, a global defense mission, an ongoing major cycle of weapon modernization, and an inflexibly capped Army end strength too small for the force needed."[14] Meanwhile, defense funding was increased to modernize the force with the Abrams tank, the Patriot Missile system, the Bradley fighting vehicle, the Apache helicopter, and the Multiple Launch Rocket System—the "Big Five." The Army also invested significant money and energy into enhancing quality of life by promoting equality of opportunity, preventing substance abuse, and bolstering a number of morale and welfare projects. These efforts restored "confidence, self-esteem, and a strong sense of professionalism within the Army that did much to erase the Army's tarnished image of a decade earlier."[15] The crescendo of modernization climaxed with the fall of the Berlin Wall in 1989 and the subsequent dissolution of the Soviet Union.[16]

In synchrony with the organizational, doctrinal, and equipment transformations ongoing within the Army, the AMEDD also was undergoing a sizeable evolution. During this period of fast-paced change and technological innovation, one of the greatest dilemmas facing the military health care system was the need to provide the best possible health care for troops at a time of rising health care costs, stringent fiscal controls, and limited financial resources. To address the predicament, the Department of Defense launched and the Army surgeon general supported cost-reduction projects that relied on information management systems such as the Defense Enrollment Eligibility Reporting System, Tri-Service Medical Information System, and Composite Health Care System, automated patient health data systems that helped to reduce personnel costs and overhead.[17] The Army surgeon general also gave closer scrutiny to the burgeoning Civilian Health and Medical Program of the Uniformed Services expenditures in an effort to hold down patient costs.[18] The AMEDD contracted for services from outside sources to augment health care delivery, a move believed to be cost effective. In the summer of 1985, the first Primary Medical Care for the Uniformed Services Clinic opened in Fairfax County, Virginia, with civilian vendors in charge. Private contractors offered primary health care along with limited laboratory and pharmacy services to military patients.[19] By 1989, many more Primary Medical Care for the Uniformed Services Clinics were operational.[20] Although these initiatives contributed to alleviating the difficult situation, the chiefs who led the Army Nurse Corps during the 1980s also were instrumental in solving enormous problems. During their four-year terms, they faced hectic times and demanding issues.

On 1 September 1983, Colonel Connie L. Slewitzke was promoted to brigadier general and became the 17th chief of the Army Nurse Corps. Her most recent assignments had been as assistant chief of the Army Nurse Corps, chief nurse of 18th Medical Command in Korea, and chief, Department of Nursing, at Letterman Army Medical Center in San Francisco, California.

Slewitzke's tenure coincided with a very challenging time for the AMEDD and

Pictured is Brigadier General Connie L. Slewitzke, who served as the 17th Chief of the Army Nurse Corps from 1983 to 1987.
Photo courtesy of Army Nurse Corps Archives, Office of Medical History, Falls Church, VA.

the Army Nurse Corps. She capably dealt with issues of readiness, nursing shortages, retention problems, promotion delays, the physical fitness standards, and backlash against growing numbers of women in the Army. Slewitzke advocated for greater educational opportunities, more nurse autonomy, and increased input from Army Nurse Corps officers into the business of the AMEDD. She promoted the AMEDD Officer Structure Study, the publication of a history of the Army Nurse Corps, the introduction of information systems, the refinement of the standards of nursing practice, and quality improvement incentives. Additionally, she successfully lobbied for a general officer position for an Army nurse in the Army Reserve/Army National Guard, strengthening those components' stature, inclusion, and effectiveness. She created and sponsored the Army Nurse Corps fellowship in the Chief of the Corps Office, the preceptorship for newly graduated second lieutenant Army nurses, and the Workload Management System for Nurses. She began the program to collect oral histories of former chiefs of the Corps. She worked for across-the-board exposure to field nursing for all Army nurses, improved the Professional Officer Filler System and Mobilization Designee programs, expanded the Individual Mobilization Augmentee matrix, oversaw the widespread introduction of Army Nurse Corps officers into Forces Command roles, and assigned officers to key positions in the Army Reserve and Army National Guard. She actively monitored the activities and conditions experienced by Army nurses assigned to temporary duty in Central America and presided over Army Nurse Corps participation in Operation Urgent Fury. Slewitzke and her assistant chief, Colonel Eily P. Gorman, managed all of these pressing concerns while simultaneously interfacing with the whole of the Army, the other uniformed services, the civilian nursing community, and the retired Army nurse population and while attending to the routine, everyday leadership requirements inherent in managing a corps of thousands of Army nurses—Active, Reserve, and National Guard. Slewitzke retired after the completion of her four-year tenure in 1987. Following her retirement, she actively supported the efforts to build the Women in Military Service for America Memorial at the gateway to Arlington Cemetery.

On 1 September 1987 Brigadier General Clara Adams-Ender became the 18th chief of the Army Nurse Corps. She had been the chief, Department of Nursing, at Walter Reed Army Medical Center and, before that, chief of the Army Nurse Corps Division of the U.S. Army Recruiting Command. Throughout her career, Adams-Ender consistently broke new ground. She was the first female soldier to earn the Expert Field Medical Badge and to graduate with a master of military art and science degree from the Command and General Staff College. Additionally, she was the first chief of the Corps to choose a male Army Nurse Corps officer, Colonel John M. Hudock, to be the assistant chief of the Corps. Adams-Ender became the first chief to wear two hats, serving concurrently as chief of personnel for the AMEDD and the Chief of the Army Nurse Corps. She remained on active duty after her four-year term as chief of the Corps to assume command of a major Army installation, Fort Belvoir, Virginia, and become the deputy commanding general for the Military District of Washington.

Pictured is Brigadier General Clara L. Adams-Ender, who served as the 18th Chief of the Army Nurse Corps from 1987 to 1991.
Photo courtesy of Army Nurse Corps Archives, Office of Medical History, Falls Church, VA.

Adams-Ender faced a serious and debilitating nursing shortage and embarked on many ventures to recruit and retain both civilian and military nurses, such as the Army Nurse Candidate Program, the Accession Bonus Program, incentive pay for certified registered nurse anesthetists, greater numbers and varieties of Reserve Officers' Training Corps scholarships, the AMEDD Enlisted Commissioning Program, and a selection of plans to bolster the U.S. Army Reserve and Army National Guard. Adams-Ender also encouraged the development of novel organizational configurations to enhance the efficiency of Army hospitals' nursing departments. Unwilling to degrade the Army Nurse Corps educational credentials, she maintained existing standards and gained input into legislation and policy formulation by beginning the practice of testifying annually before Congress with her Navy and Air Force counterparts and arranging for Army Nurse Corps officers to serve in congressional fellowships. Adams-Ender also led the Corps through the thorny challenges of Operation Just Cause and the massive demands of operations Desert Shield and Desert Storm while simultaneously responding to the substantial personnel requirements that these campaigns created.

To tackle the tremendous complexities of the 1980s, Army Nurse Corps leaders conceived and implemented imaginative strategies that paid unexpected dividends. They developed Army Nurse Corps officers, augmented the services they provided, and broadened their horizons beyond usual parochial limits. Two important programs were the introduction of Army Nurse Corps officers into the White House and the halls of Congress.

The Army Nurse Corps affiliation with the White House dated to 1970, when First Lady Patricia Nixon asked that women officers be allowed to serve as White House social aides. Formerly, only male officers served in this capacity. Major Susanne Philips Crowe was the first Army nurse to assume these extra duties while she was stationed concurrently at Walter Reed Army Medical Center.[21] Subsequently, from 1973 to 1979, Major Janet Rexrode (Southby) represented the Army Nurse Corps as a senior White House social aide.[22] Rexrode made her contributions in the limelight while simultaneously pursuing her doctorate at the Catholic University of America.[23]

Strict criteria applied to selection as a White House aide. Applicants had to be single and between 24 and 37. Height requirements were at least 5'10" for male officers and 5'2" for female officers. The officer's military assignment had to be within 25 miles of the White House, and aides needed to have 18 months remaining on their tour of duty in the National Capital Region. Applicants also underwent an intensive scrutiny involving several detailed interviews, recommendations by a supervisor or commander, background checks, and a security appraisal. Only a few candidates survived the rigorous process.

One of Rexrode's classic duties was to attend formal state dinners where maintaining appropriate protocol and decorum were most important. She had to get "the right people to the right place at the right time." On a scheduled evening, Rexrode typically received her assignment and a briefing on the expected events and guests at about 6:00 P.M. She then greeted and escorted the visitors to the East

Before a White House state dinner in May 1979, Army Nurse Corps officer Major Janet Rexrode (Southby) conversed with President and Mrs. Jimmy Carter. Since she was marrying soon, Rexrode (Southby) also was concluding her tenure as a senior military social aide at that time.
Photo courtesy of Army Nurse Corps Archives, Office of Medical History, Falls Church, VA.

Room in the White House, where they were formally announced to the president, given predinner drinks, and handed their dinner cards. She next shepherded the guests to the receiving line and later "toed the carpet," lining up with the other aides along the grand hallway leading to the state dining room. Aides did not drink or dine with the guests but were "encouraged to mingle while retaining an air of separateness." Rexrode compared these interactions to those between nurse and patient, "meeting guests while working is much like nursing—meeting and talking with someone doesn't necessarily mean that you also see them socially." As with nursing, Rexrode found the greatest returns were intrinsic ones. She had the opportunity to observe the shifting White House ambiance with three successive presidential administrations. The Nixon administration's tone was very formal, while the Fords enjoyed dancing, and so the guests and aides went home late. At the other extreme, the Carters went to bed early, and so the guests departed promptly as did the aides. Rexrode also participated in ceremonial presidential signings of agreements or bills into law, and she witnessed the signing of the Panama Canal Treaty in 1978.[24]

In 1979, another group of Army Nurse Corps officers stepped through the White House portals to offer their professional skills as White House nurses. These officers staffed the White House Medical Clinic and occasionally traveled with the president to provide any health care needed during the journey.[25] Navy nurses were the first military nurses to serve in this role beginning in 1961. Eleven years later, in 1972, the Air Force assigned nurses to the White House Medical Clinic. By 1990 the staffing mix of military nurses changed so that at any one time, six military nurses, two from each service, worked together in this setting.[26]

Three years later, an Army nurse assumed a different role in the White House, when Major Sharon Richie became the first Army Nurse Corps officer to be one of 14 White House fellows. The intent of the White House fellowship was to familiarize the participant with the nuts and bolts workings of the government on a national level and to encourage networking among fellows who came from such diverse venues as the military, the business world, the civil service, and so on.[27]

Richie was the first nurse selected in the history of the 18-year program. However, instead of functioning in a nursing role, she served in the White House Office of Intergovernmental Affairs.[28] Her experience in the Old Executive Office Building involved contact with high-level public figures and observation of important decision making and was anything but a relaxed, tranquil duty. The hectic schedule involved conferences, document writing, and research, as Richie contributed to special projects that affected the nation's large and small municipalities. Travel and working groups with important government and business leaders also fostered Richie's professional development, as she "met so many people from different walks of life and learned so much from them."[29] Years later, Richie reflected on her year as a White House fellow as an incredible and unique educational experience.[30] Although these fellowships were associated with the White House, other Army nurses found comparable opportunities in the Congress.

The Congressional Fellowship Program for Army Nurse Corps officers began in 1988, but Adams-Ender unintentionally laid the groundwork for the opportunity several years earlier. During her assignment as chief nurse of Walter Reed Army Medical Center, she initiated an acquaintance with Senator Daniel Inouye while he was a patient on that facility's very important persons unit. Inouye was then the powerful chairman of the Senate Appropriations Committee and the two conferred on strategies to place an Army nurse in his office on Capitol Hill to furnish input on nursing and health care concerns. However, before that juncture and throughout her career, Adams-Ender

> . . . observed many occasions in which we nurses lost many battles because others (mostly MSCs [Medical Service Corps officers] and MCs [Medical Corps officers]) were carrying our messages to the high places (e.g., DA [Department of Army] staff, DoD [Department of Defense] staff and to the Congress). Many times, when that message was carried and received, it was NOT the one that the nurses had originally sent, so we were often told that we lost an issue, when in effect, THE BOYS decided against us because we were not there to make our own case.

On 1 September 1982, President Reagan welcomed the White House Fellows Class of 1982–1983 with a certificate in recognition of their selection for this honor at a ceremony in the White House Rose Garden. On Major Richie's right is her classmate Daniel T. Oliver (Admiral, USN, retired and later President of the Naval Postgraduate School).
Photo courtesy of Army Nurse Corps Archives, Office of Medical History, Falls Church, VA.

When she later became chief of the Corps, Adams-Ender encouraged participation by Army nurses in the political process on every echelon, starting with their place of work.[31]

At about this same time, Majors Susan Connor and Patricia Wise were attending graduate school at the University of Maryland and seeking practicums for their health policy courses. Connor secured an internship in Senator John Glenn's office early in January 1989. Wise simultaneously interviewed with Inouye and began her fellowship in his office. Wise impressed the senator so much with her outstanding performance that he resolved subsequently to request participation by Air Force and Navy nurses as well.

Immediately thereafter in 1989, the Congressional Liaison Office approached the Army Nurse Corps for another Army nurse to work with the House Armed Services Committee. In response, the Army Nurse Corps nominated two individuals to job share the requested full-time position, after obtaining the concurrence of their university programs. Both were doctoral students, one at Catholic University and the other at George Mason University. Lieutenant Colonel Loretta Forlaw and Major Christine Galante began their practicums in the House of Representatives in February 1989.[32] Adams-Ender had Forlaw and Galante provide her with firsthand information about legislation, assess situations, and advise her about "when it was time . . . to weigh-in on an issue" about the Army Nurse Corps. In one key instance, Forlaw and Galante personally thwarted an attempt to dilute Army Nurse Corps quality. Adams-Ender recalled the details:

> During a congressional mark-up of a defense bill, a political appointee in the Army was hell-bent on changing the requirements for active duty Army Nurses to have a baccalaureate degree. Chris Galante was tasked to write the language for the final bill. When it was published, this fellow was sure that he had changed the law so that it would be so. He called me over to his office to personally give me a copy of the language and to "rub it in" that he had won. Chris had already provided me with a copy of the bill and it was written so that the requirement [for the BSN (bachelor of science in nursing)] remained. When I arrived at the Pentagon, I pointed this fact out to my "political friend," and he was livid. Afterward, he made an attempt to have all of the nurses removed from Congressional offices. However, by this time, we were firmly entrenched because of our work ethic, attention to detail and knowledge of the issues.[33]

Adams-Ender summarized the far-reaching effects of this innovative approach:

> The influence of those nurses in nursing and health policymaking was powerful and set the stage for a new era of nursing leadership in . . . military health care. We were able to get incentive pay for nurse anesthetists, which was a good start. Also, Senator Inouye decided that the nurse corps chiefs should testify before his committee, . . . in 1989. The MSCs [Medical Service Corps officers] who worked in legislative liasion [sic] on the Hill called it a "love-in."[34]

After negotiating the congressional ramparts for the first time, Army Nurse Corps involvement on the Hill subsequently expanded. In 1994, Lieutenant Colonel Patricia Saulsbery was selected for the highly competitive Army Congressional Fellowship. She served for one year as a congressional liaison staff officer for the assistant secretary of the Army for manpower and reserve affairs. That same year, Lieutenant Colonel Barbara Scherb participated in a nurse-specific fellowship, once again in Inouye's office.[35] This program evolved into a tri-service rotation with military nurses from the Army, Navy, and Air Force serving sequential one- to two-year terms also in Inouye's office.[36] When Lieutenant Colonel Nancy Gilmore-Lee was a congressional fellow in 1998, she worked on legislation that dealt with special incentive pay for military nurse practitioners and nurse anesthetists, funding for the Graduate School for Nursing at the Uniformed Services

Senator Daniel K. Inouye and Army Nurse Corps fellow, Lieutenant Colonel Barbara J. Scherb, pause for a moment in Inouye's office in the Senate's Hart Office Building.
Photo courtesy of Colonel Barbara J. Scherb, Franklin, NC.

University of the Health Sciences, appropriation of TriService Nursing Research monies, and the reimbursement of advanced practice nurses under the Medicare program.[37] The benefits of the congressional programs included the integration of a distinctive viewpoint of military nursing into the legislative process that became an advantage for the Army Nurse Corps and the AMEDD when dealing with legislation and appropriations.[38]

No longer were Army nurses found exclusively on hospital wards. Their widening involvement in high-level policy formulation led to greater self-determination, branch immaterial positions, and command assignments for nurses in the not-too-distant future. More important, Army nurses gained greater influence in the legislative and political processes that actually controlled their unique destiny and evolution.

Another innovative element for dealing with the strategic issues of the day was the AMEDD Personnel Proponency Division (APPD). Several years earlier, most of the Army had decentralized this function, but within the AMEDD the responsibility for officers' proponency remained an exclusive tasking for the Corps chief of each branch.[39] However, in 1987, the AMEDD established its own decentralized officers' APPD.

Regulations tasked APPD with structuring AMEDD branches into viable organizations with supporting staff compatible with war and peace requirements. This had to be done within the parameters of Department of the Army allocated budgeted end strength and authorizations. APPD also was accountable for doctrine, regulations, force structure analysis, and life-cycle development issues.[40]

Like the rest of the Army, the AMEDD located APPD at its "schoolhouse," initially at the Academy of Health Sciences and later at the AMEDD Center and School, to comply with requirements for each proponent to have an integrating center. The integrating center's role ensured homogeneity, unity of purpose, synergy of effort, reduction of needless duplication, and a means to resolve differences of opinion among the various AMEDD branch proponents.[41]

In 1988, the Army Nurse Corps first assigned an officer as its representative to APPD and later each representative became known as a Corps Specific Branch Proponency Officer.[42] Lieutenant Colonel Theresa Washburn, the first Army nurse assigned to APPD, faced many challenges when she reported for duty in July 1988 following a stint in graduate school at George Mason University. Washburn's first-ever staff position was in a newly created billet with no precedents and no job description. She recalled that her "early days were exciting, frustrating, overwhelming," and fearsome as she learned and understood "totally foreign concepts like Force Structure, TDA [Table of Distribution and Allowances], TOE [Table of Organization and Equipment]," in the context of the total Army, the AMEDD and Army Nurse Corps Active Force, National Guard, and the Reserve. Washburn rose to the challenge and contributed to numerous projects such as the AMEDD Leader Development Study, an analysis of war and peacetime area of concentration requirements, a review of all senior Army Nurse Corps positions to gauge the necessity for War College preparation, and an intense scrutiny of the organizational structure of departments of nursing worldwide.[43]

Other Corps Specific Branch Proponency Officers who followed Washburn worked closely with the chief of the Corps as well on issues such as developing plans to deal with critical care nurse shortages in all components, analyzing the force configuration, reviewing the Forward Surgical Team structure, planning the large personnel downsizing of the 1990s, eliminating the pediatric area of concentration, and establishing a distance learning system.[44] But innovation and enthusiastic service were not only the exclusive domain of those Army nurses actively serving, but also characteristic of the retired community.

In 1976, 38 retired Army nurses met informally in San Antonio, Texas, to form an organization whose objectives were to carry Army Nurse Corps comradeship into retirement and maintain communication among the Corps retirees. The following year the Retired Army Nurse Corps Association (RANCA) was incorporated.[45] The founding members chose—after considerable reflection—to devise two forms of membership. The first, according to Colonel Doris Cobb, RANCA's initial president, was regular status, and included retired Army nurses from the Active, Guard, or Reserve components. The second, or associate, membership consisted of Army nurses on active duty or those who had served previously and were honorably discharged but not retired from the service. Several charter members suggested inviting Navy and Air Force Nurse Corps officers into the organization, making it a "Military Nurse Association," but the group rejected this idea, fearing that it would promote competition with other wide-ranging military retiree organizations. Hesitancy about adding retirees from other services with differing backgrounds and priorities also contributed to the decision.

RANCA's original dues were $5 annually, but several charter group members donated an additional $1 or more each to pay mailing expenses to recruit new members and fund the costs associated with creating a nonprofit organization. In anticipation of incorporation in 1976, the group elected its first officers and directors, each one intended to represent one of five geographical regions across the United States.[46]

It also organized the Army Nurse Corps Foundation to acquire donations for the construction of the U.S. Army Medical Museum at Fort Sam Houston, Texas.[47] Since its founding, RANCA has donated more than $75,000 and countless volunteer hours to the establishment and daily operations of the museum. It also assisted in collecting and compiling selected Army Nurse Corps oral histories from various eras of service, sponsored the Army Nurse Corps Medal that was awarded to an exceptional Army nurse graduate of each Officer Advanced Course, and supported a medallion to bestow on an exemplary mid-level Army Nurse Corps officer annually as the RANCA Advanced Military Practice Award.[48]

In 2000, RANCA metamorphosed into the Army Nurse Corps Association (ANCA). Although the name changed, the group's composition, activities, and purposes remained, and ANCA continued to offer membership to past or current commissioned officers in all three components, the Active, Guard, and Reserve, of the Army Nurse Corps. ANCA preserved the tradition of biennial conventions

Pictured is the Colonel Florence A. Blanchfield Army Community Hospital at Fort Campbell, Kentucky. Photo courtesy of Army Nurse Corps Archives, Office of Medical History, Falls Church, VA.

in various locations throughout the nation, and the organization's newsletter, *The Connection*, continued its quarterly publication. ANCA maintained RANCA's original goals as they had evolved, namely to furnish communication and social occasions for the membership, collaborate in the maintenance of Army Nurse Corps history, provide scholarships for students in collegiate nursing programs, and develop a means for regular interaction among Army nurses.[49] Many of these objectives converged into one major effort in 1978, as a movement to name the new hospital facility at Fort Campbell, Kentucky, after a revered Army nurse gained impetus.

Early in 1978, General Madelyn N. Parks resolved to honor Colonel Florence A. Blanchfield, the respected chief of the Army Nurse Corps during the challenging World War II era, in a meaningful way.[50] She asked for RANCA's support to commemorate Blanchfield's special contributions to the Army by naming the newly erected Fort Campbell, Kentucky, hospital in her memory. RANCA enthusiastically responded after Cobb initially contacted about 125 members, who in turn notified their friends and acquaintances. The letter-writing crusade snowballed and an avalanche of letters filled the mailboxes of the surgeon general (Lieutenant General Charles Pixley), the post commander (Major General John A. Wickham), and numerous congressmen and senators.[51] Wickham, who would make the final decision, did not ignore the tidal wave of requests. As he told the hospital commanding officer, he received so much mail from Army nurses who he would be terrified to call the institution anything but the Blanchfield Hospital.[52] Wickham decided in March 1978 to name the institution as a permanent memorial to Blanchfield.[53] This was not the first instance of an Army hospital bearing the name of an Army nurse, but it was the only existing facility so named.[54] Army nurses, both active and retired, then pursued raising funds to subsidize a portrait and a bust of Blanchfield for the military treatment facility's lobby.[55] The surgeon general (Lieutenant General Bernhard T. Mittemeyer) and a host of dignitaries and Blanchfield family and friends officially dedicated the Colonel Florence A. Blanchfield Army Community Hospital on 17 September 1982.[56] The state-of-the-art facility remains a testament to the contributions of Blanchfield and all Army Nurse Corps officers.

Collaboration, mutual support, and advancement were themes that emerged from the various innovations of the 1980s. This unity of purpose was but one of many factors that helped the Army Nurse Corps to meet its mission during the 1980s.

# Notes

1. Paula L. Potts, "Women in the Military," *Military Lifestyle* 21 (October 1989): 38–42, 45, 50. Paula L. Potts, "Do Women Belong in the Military: A Debate," *Military Lifestyle* 21 (October 1989): 46–49.

2. William Joe Webb, *Department of the Army Historical Summary, Fiscal Year 1988* (Washington, DC: Center of Military History, United States Army, 1993), 33.

3. Mary L. Haynes, *Department of the Army Historical Summary, Fiscal Year 1987* (Washington, DC: Center of Military History, United States Army, 1995), 16.

4. Karl E. Cocke and others, *Department of the Army Historical Summary, Fiscal Year 1981* (Washington, DC: Center of Military History, United States Army, 1988), 98.

5. Vincent H. Demma, *Department of the Army Historical Summary, Fiscal Year 1989* (Washington, DC: Center of Military History, United States Army, 1998), 129–30.

6. Roxine C. Hart, *Women in Combat* (Patrick Air Force Base, FL: Research Division, Defense Equal Opportunity Management Institute, 1991), 14. Jeanne Holm, *Women in the Military, An Unfinished Revolution*, revised edition (Novato, CA: Presidio, 1992), 387–97. Les Aspin, "Manning the Military: The Female Factor," *Minerva, Quarterly Report on Women and the Military* 2 (Summer 1984): 133–51. "Utilization of Women Slows under Reagan," *Minerva, Quarterly Report on Women and the Military* 3 (Spring 1985): 18. Feminist scholars later refuted the notion that the inclusion of women "damaged military effectiveness" by citing the largely successful use of women in the 1980s Middle East peacekeeping efforts and in the combat support operations in Grenada and Panama. In these operations, they argued, "males and females all got the job done together." Lorry M. Fenner, "Moving Targets: Women's Roles in the U.S. Military in the 21st Century," in *Women in Combat, Civic Duty or Military Liability?* ed. Lorry M. Fenner and Marie E. deYoung (Washington, DC: Georgetown University Press, 2001), 41–42.

7. Karl E. Cocke and others, *Department of the Army Historical Summary, Fiscal Year 1981* (Washington, DC: Center of Military History, United States Army, 1988), 96–97. Rosemarie Skaine, *Women at War, Gender Issues of Americans in Combat* (Jefferson, NC: McFarland & Company, Inc., 1999), 62. Roxine C. Hart, *Women in Combat* (Patrick Air Force Base, FL: Research Division, Defense Equal Opportunity Management Institute, 1991), 13–15.

8. In 1982, the Army defined direct combat as "engaging any enemy with individual or crew-served weapons while being exposed to direct enemy fire, a high probability of

direct physical contact with the enemy's personnel, and a substantial risk of capture." It added that "direct combat takes place while closing with the enemy by fire, maneuver, or shock effect in order to destroy or capture him, or while repelling his assault by fire, close combat or counterattack." Rosemarie Skaine, *Women at War, Gender Issues of Americans in Combat* (Jefferson, NC: McFarland & Company, Inc., 1999), 29.

9. Mary Ellen Condon-Rall, *Department of the Army Historical Summary, Fiscal Year 1983* (Washington, DC: Center of Military History, United States Army, 1990), 60–62. Karl E. Cocke, *Department of the Army Historical Summary, Fiscal Year 1985* (Washington, DC: Center of Military History, United States Army, 1989), 22. Women's Research and Education Institute, "Facts about Women in the Military, 1980–1990," Fact Sheet, 2, n.d.; and "Women in the Army," Information Paper, 2 October 1989 (both in Army Nurse Corps Collection [ANCC], Office of Medical History [OMH]).

10. The backlash as a reaction to the feminist movement was not restricted to the military. There also was a "return to a more conservative political agenda" nationwide at this time. Thetis M. Group and Joan I. Roberts, *Nursing, Physician Control, and the Medical Monopoly* (Bloomington: Indiana University Press, 2001), 273.

11. "Direct Combat Probability Coding (DCPC) Policy," Information Paper, 16 July 1989; and Major Habitzreuther, "Women in the Army," Information Paper, 29 September 1989 (both in ANCC, OMH).

12. Women's Research and Education Institute, "Facts about Women in the Military, 1980–1990," Fact Sheet, 6–10, n.d.; and Soldier Policy Branch, Human Resources Division, Office of the Deputy Chief of Staff for Personnel, "Women in the Army," Briefing Slides, n.d. (both in ANCC, OMH). Title 10, U.S.C. 3012. Title 10, U.S.C. 6015. Title 10, U.S.C. 8549. The Coast Guard also was the most progressive in its approach to pregnancy and parenthood issues. Its "Care of Newborn Child Program" allowed any new parent, regardless of gender, to "leave the service for up to a year with the assurance that when they return, they will have the same rank and occupational specialty as when they left." Georgia Clark Sadler, "From Women's Services to Servicewomen," in Francine D'Amico and Laurie Weinstein, *Gender Camouflage: Women and the U.S. Military* (New York: New York University Press, 1999), 43–44.

13. Bette S. Mahoney, "1989 Department of Defense Women's Health Survey," Typewritten Report, 28 October 1989, ANCC, OMH.

14. John L. Romjue, *The Army of Excellence: The Development of the 1980s Army* (Fort Monroe, VA: Office of the Command Historian, United States Army Training and Doctrine Command, 1997), xiii.

15. Vincent Demma, "The Army in the 1970s," Information Paper, 6–7, ANCC, OMH. Robert H. Scales, *Certain Victory* (Washington, DC: Office of the Chief of Staff, United States Army, 1993), 16–20. Frank N. Schubert and Theresa L. Kraus, eds., *The Whirlwind War, The United States Army in Operations Desert Shield and Desert Storm* (Washington, DC: Center of Military History, United States Army, 1993), 28–33.

16. John L. Romjue, *The Army of Excellence: The Development of the 1980s Army* (Fort Monroe, VA: Office of the Command Historian, United States Army Training and Doctrine Command, 1997), 1–2. *225 Years of the Army* (Tampa, FL: Faircount, LLC, 2000), 302.

17. "Army Medical Department ADP Master Plan, FY 71–78," n.d., Record Group 112, Entry 372, Box 2 of 4, National Archives. Gar Yip, "Composite Health Care System (CHCS)," Information Paper, 3 March 1988, ANCC, OMH.

18. Dwight Oland, *Department of the Army Historical Summary, Fiscal Year 1984* (Washington, DC: Center of Military History, United States Army, 1995), 195. William Joe Webb, *Department of the Army Historical Summary, Fiscal Year 1988* (Washington,

DC: Center of Military History, United States Army, 1993), 30. Vincent H. Demma, *Department of the Army Historical Summary, Fiscal Year 1989* (Washington, DC: Center of Military History, United States Army, 1998), 168. Frank F. Ledford, "Surgeon General Outlines Priorities for AMEDD Action," *HSC Mercury* 16 (March 1989): 2.

19. Terrence Gough, *Department of the Army Historical Summary, Fiscal Year 1986* (Washington, DC: Center of Military History, United States Army, 1989), 23, 94. Dennis Steele, "Patients First," *Soldiers* (January 1987): 28–33.

20. There were two PRIMUS Clinics each in Northern Virginia; Fort Stewart, Georgia; Fort Hood, Texas; and Fort Ord, California. One clinic was providing care in the Fort Benning, Georgia, and Fort Bragg, North Carolina, environs. Frank F. Ledford, "Army 'Innovative' in Use of Funds," *U.S. Medicine* 25 (January 1989): 41–42.

21. Janet R. Southby to Author, E-mail Correspondence, 28 June 2004; and Constance J. Moore to Major Fox Johnson, Typewritten Letter (TL), n.d. (both in ANCC, OMH).

22. Major Leslie Dempsey Brousseau followed Southby in this role after 1979. Janet R. Southby to Author, E-mail Correspondence, 28 June 2004, ANCC, OMH.

23. Carolyn M. Feller and Debora R. Cox, *Highlights in the History of the Army Nurse Corps* (Washington, DC: U.S. Army Center of Military History, 2000), 50.

24. Dorothy Dee, "White House Social Aides," Typewritten Manuscript, October 1978, ANCC, OMH.

25. Among those who served were Captain Vicky Sheldon, Major Dianne Capps, Captain Ann Treleven, Major Barbara Eller, Lieutenant Colonel Paula Trivett, Major Arthur Wallace, Major Leana Fox-Johnson, Captain Maureen Donohue, Captain Vinette Gordon, Captain Greta Krapohl, Major Brenda C. McDaniel, Major Rene Katial, and Captain Stacy Usher. Leana Fox-Johnson "History of Army Nurses Assigned to the White House," Memorandum, 3 December 1994, ANCC, OMH. Carolyn M. Feller and Debora R. Cox, *Highlights in the History of the Army Nurse Corps* (Washington, DC: U.S. Army Center of Military History, 2000), 86.

26. "The White House Nurse Directory," May 1995, ANCC, OMH. Major Arthur Wallace was the first male and the first emergency nurse to serve in the White House Medical Clinic.

27. Clara L. Adams-Ender to Author, Handwritten Note, 3 October 2003, ANCC, OMH. Former Secretary of State General Colin Powell was a White House fellow from 1972 to 1973. http://www.whitehousefellows.gov/home.html (accessed on 5 February 2004).

28. "Richie at White House," *HSC Mercury* 10 (November 1982): 4. Carolyn M. Feller and Debora R. Cox, *Highlights in the History of the Army Nurse Corps* (Washington, DC: U.S. Army Center of Military History, 2000), 54.

29. Pamela Noel, "White House Fellows," *Ebony* 38 (March 1983): 107, 108, 110, 112.

30. Jan Murphy, "US Seeks Movers, Shakers," *Sentinel* (18 September 1987): C1.

31. Clara L. Adams-Ender to Author, E-mail Correspondence, 4 July 2003, ANCC, OMH.

32. John M. Hudock, "Congressional Nursing Practicums," Information Paper, 12 October 1989; and John M. Hudock, Routing and Transmittal Slip to BG A-E, 12 October 1989 (both in ANCC, OMH).

33. Clara L. Adams-Ender to Author, E-mail Correspondence, 4 July 2003, ANCC, OMH.

34. Ibid.

35. A Navy nurse, Nancy Lescavage, preceded Scherb, who in turn was followed by an Air Force nurse. Terris Kennedy to Author, E-mail Correspondence, n.d., ANCC, OMH.

36. Michelle Kohl, Untitled Typewritten Document (TD), 12 November 1996; Daniel K. Inouye to Robert P. McAleer, TL, 20 May 1994; Nicolai Timenes to Daniel K. Inouye, TL, 20 June 1994; Nancy R. Adams to Daniel K. Inouye, TL, n.d.; and Daniel K. Inouye to

Nancy R. Adams, TL, 29 July 1993 (all in ANCC, OMH).

37. Nancy Gilmore-Lee, "A Year on Capitol Hill," *Army Nursing Newsletter* 99 (January 1999): 7, ANCC, OMH.

38. Untitled TD addressed to COL Mc[Call], n.d., ANCC, OMH.

39. Kathleen Srsic-Stoehr to Author, 24 May 2003; Clara L. Adams-Ender to Author, 11 July 2003 (both E-mail Correspondence, ANCC, OMH). Connie L. Slewitzke, Interview by Beverly Greenlee, 210, 457–62, n.d., USAWC/USAMHI Senior Officer Oral History Program, Project No. 88-8, ANCC, OMH. Headquarters, Department of the Army, Army Regulation 5-22, "The Army Proponent System," 3 October 1986.

40. Thomas Pozniak, Information Paper, 22 September 1992, Attachment to E-mail from Kathleen Srsic-Stoehr to Author, May 2003, ANCC, OMH. Tracy E. Strevey and Quinn H. Becker, "Army Medical Department Personnel Proponent System," Memorandum of Understanding between the Surgeon General, Department of the Army and the Commander, U.S. Army Health Services Command, 23 October 1987, ANCC, OMH. The eight life-cycle functions were structure, acquisition, distribution, sustainment, professional development, individual training and education, unit deployment, and separation. Kathleen Srsic-Stoehr, "AN Consultants Conference-'The Winds of Change: Nursing Opportunity for Leadership,' 13–17 July 1992: AN Management Study Workgroup," Memorandum for Record, 5 August 1992, ANCC, OMH.

41. Timothy Jackman, "Management of Proponency in the AMEDD," Draft Concept Proposal, 23 February 1993, ANCC, OMH.

42. The first Army Nurse Corps representative to the APPD was Lieutenant Colonel Theresa Washburn. Lieutenant colonels Lee Perry, Kathleen Srsic-Stoehr, Carol Reineck, Dena Norton, Stephanie Marshall, and Deborah Gustke followed. Kathleen Srsic-Stoehr to Author, 24 May 2003; John Hudock to Author, 11 July 2003; Stephanie Marshall, Interview by Mary T. Sarnecky, Transcript, 19–22, July 2003, Army Nurse Corps Oral History Collection; Carol Reineck, "To Provide Information on Role Development for Corps Specific Branch Proponent Officer (CSBPO), Army Nurse Corps," Information Briefing, 29 May 1996 (all in ANCC, OMH).

43. Theresa Washburn to Author, E-mail Correspondence, 30 September 2003, ANCC, OMH.

44. Kathleen Srsic-Stoehr, "Input for Legion of Merit Award," TD, April 1994; and Carol Reineck, Interview by Mary T. Sarnecky, Transcript, 36–38, May 2003, Army Nurse Corps Oral History Collection (both in ANCC, OMH).

45. http://e-anca.org/ANCAHist.htm (accessed 14 July 2003). "Retired Army Nurse Corps Association, Background Information," TD, November 1997. Demonstrating significant growth from its embryonic numbers, the organization had more than 500 members by November 1977. Doris M. Cobb to Dorothy Zalabak, TL, 28 November 1977, ANCC, OMH. By early 1978, RANCA claimed a total of 1,450 members. Lois Haase, "Shot in the Ego for Army Nurses," *San Antonio Express* (14 April 1978), 1-C.

46. The first officers were Doris M. Cobb, president; Sally H. Rawlins, vice president and treasurer; and Marian A. Tierney, secretary. Other charter board members were Alma B. Anderson, Marion K. Kennedy, Ann B. Cost, Edith B. Whitelaw, and Augusta L. Short. Doris M. Cobb to Retired Army Nurse Corps Officers, Former ANC Officers, TL, October 1977; and Mary Messerschmidt to Author, E-mail Correspondence, 5 August 2003 (both in ANCC, OMH).

47. Doris M. Cobb to Retired Army Nurse Corps Officers, Former ANC Officers, TL, October 1977, ANCC, OMH.

48. "Retired Army Nurse Corps Association, Background Information," TD, November

1997, ANCC, OMH. "The R.A.N.C.A. Advanced Military Practice Award," Standard Operating Procedure, 1 November 1998, ANCC, OMH.

49. "The Army Nurse Corps Association History Page," http://e-anca.org/ANCAHist.htm (accessed 14 July 2003).

50. Madelyn N. Parks, "Information for All ANC Officers," 3, 27 March 1978, ANCC, OMH.

51. Doris M. Cobb, "RANCA Newsletter," 1, April 1978, ANCC, OMH.

52. Lillian Dunlap, *33 Years of Army Nursing, An Interview with Brigadier General Lillian Dunlap* (Washington, DC: United States Army Nurse Corps, 2001), 316.

53. Madelyn N. Parks, "Information for All ANC Officers," Typewritten Newsletter, 1, 27 March 1978; and Doris M. Cobb, "RANCA Newsletter," 1, April 1978 (both in ANCC, OMH).

54. In World War II, Gardiner General Hospital in Chicago, Illinois, memorialized the contributions of Second Lieutenant Ruth M. Gardiner, an Army nurse who perished in a plane crash in Alaska. Mary T. Sarnecky, *A History of the U.S. Army Nurse Corps* (Philadelphia: University of Pennsylvania Press, 1999), 262. Knute A. Tofte-Nielsen to Raymond H. Bishop, TL, 6 October 1982, ANCC, OMH.

55. Patricia Silvestre, "US Colonel Florence A. Blanchfield Army Hospital Memorialization Committee," TL, 12 October 1978, Inclosure 1, in Madelyn N. Parks, "Information for All ANC Officers," 18 October 1978; and Rose V. Straley, "Colonel Florence A. Blanchfield Memorial Fund," TL, 19 August 1980, Inclosure 7, in Hazel W. Johnson, "Information for All ANC Officers," 12 September 1980 (both in ANCC, OMH). "Surgeon General Set as Dedication Speaker," *Fort Campbell Courier* (16 September 1982): 1A.

56. "Colonel Florence A. Blanchfield Army Community Hospital," Dedication Program, 17 September 1982, Blanchfield Collection, Army Medical Department Museum. "New Hospital Takes Nurse's Name," *HSC Mercury* 9 (October 1982): 1. Charles F. Bombard, Wynona M. Bice-Stephens, and Karen L. Ferguson, "The Soldiers' Nurse: Colonel Florence A. Blanchfield," *Minerva, Quarterly Report on Women and the Military* 6 (Winter 1988): 43–49.

*Chapter Nine*
# Refining Quality of Care Strategies

The Army Medical Department (AMEDD) dedicated even more attention to quality issues in the 1980s by building on the efforts of the 1970s.[1] This pursuit of quality paralleled the efforts of the Army of Excellence.[2] In keeping with this theme, the Army Nurse Corps introduced measures to enhance the delivery of nursing care in the 1980s.

During the 1980s, the Army Nurse Corps supported many efforts to improve the quality of Army nurses' practice. In 1981, work began to improve paper forms to document nursing care. One objective was to reduce the burden on nurses' time during personnel shortages and thus allow nurses to attend to their most important duties, direct patient care. Another objective was to prevent malpractice cases caused by deficiencies in the documentation of nursing activities.[3] Many Army nurses also were generally dissatisfied with available records and forms and requested approval to use overprints.[4]

A 1981 ad hoc committee recommended testing of newly revised forms, and the project later included scrutiny of every inpatient form in active use under the umbrella of the "Clinical Nursing Records Study." This became part of the fiscal year 1984 AMEDD Study Program, with the Health Care Studies and Clinical Investigation Activity at Fort Sam Houston, Texas, as proponent. Study questions addressed how the Army Nurse Corps could best organize its documentation of inpatient nursing activities to comply with AMEDD, Joint Commission on Accreditation of Hospitals, and quality assurance requirements, and what approaches would make inpatient nursing documentation more efficient. The gathered data, from various sources, such as practicing Army nurses, other military nursing services, the Health Services Command Inspector General Team, civilian "magnet" hospitals, and several civilian institutions recommended by a Joint Commission on Accreditation of Hospitals nurse surveyor, indicated that the Army Nurse Corps forms for documenting nursing history/assessment, problem list/nursing diagnosis, and nursing orders complied with Joint Commission on Accreditation of Hospitals standards and were state of the art philosophically and conceptually. However, a major discrepancy emerged with progress notes. In prestigious civilian institutions, the use of progress notes was multidisciplinary. In the AMEDD, the nursing notes were separate, not integrated into the progress notes, the venue where most other health care providers recorded their observations, plans, and interventions. The working group then developed revised forms based on their findings and deliberations, pilot and field tested the forms, and made recommendations for implementation.[5]

The Clinical Nursing Records Study suggested adopting four of the 14 modified and tested forms, namely a revised Nursing History and Assessment form, its continuation sheet, a Nursing Care Plan with Draft Design Changes, and a Nursing Discharge Summary also with design changes. The Office of the Chief, Army Nurse Corps, then implemented the corresponding regulation changes.[6] In spite of difficult circumstances in the 1980s, the Army Nurse Corps successfully improved its administrative practice, documentation, and delivery of patient care.

The Corps also implemented, refined, and expanded its Standards of Nursing Practice in the 1980s. The Corps followed the lead of the American Nurses Association, which had first published generic standards in 1973.[7] "Standards," the American Nurses Association explained, "provide a means by which a profession clearly describes the focus of its activities, the recipients of service, and the responsibilities for which its practitioners are accountable."[8] The Army Nurse Corps identified its Standards of Nursing Practice as the fulfillment of "the profession's obligation to assess, provide, evaluate, and improve nursing practice." The Corps also intended the standards to "serve as a documentation tool to assist in the audit and evaluation process."[9] Although the intent behind the standards was straightforward, initially many misinterpreted and rejected the document.

Considerable confusion, anger, and frustration greeted the introduction of the Army Nurse Corps Standards of Nursing Practice. General Hazel Johnson thought that some Army nurses "felt as though we were asking them to do more than they should be doing," and reported that a handful of individuals wrote to the surgeon general to say that "we had our nerve." Several Medical Corps officers also penned "some very nasty letters to the Surgeon General." Semantics was one aspect of the problem. For example, the word *diagnose* set off alarms because professional nurses at this time were assuming a diagnostic role, meaning this function was no longer the exclusive domain of physicians.[10] Johnson mused, "What do we have here. People who own words. Who owns this word that we can't use without having copyright on it." However, she decided if the surgeon general asked her to delete the word *diagnose* from the standards at the behest of Medical Corps officers, she then would replace that word with *assessment*. She rationalized that it was "the same identical thing. It is exactly, precisely the same identical thing." Johnson refused to let the criticisms upset her. Her standard reply to such disparagements was, "Fine, we'll take that into consideration when we put the next edition out."[11] The word *diagnose*, however, did disappear from the Standards of Nursing Practice. Reactions to the introduction of the standards took many forms.

Captain Freida J. Sadler, a head nurse at Kimbrough Army Hospital, Fort Meade, Maryland, aired her response in a poem that illustrated her misgivings.

> There are so many changes
> How can I adjust
> To doing SOAPIE [Subjective data, Objective data, Assessment, Plan, Implementation, Evaluation] charting
> On all this nursing stuff?
>
> It seems so overwhelming
> I'm approaching it with dread
> How can I do an assessment
> With such confusion in my head?
>
> Assessments, problem lists, etcetera
> There seems so much to do
> And I can't even tell the difference
> Between S & O and Problem #2
>
> I must listen to the patient
> I must hear and understand
> I must palpate and auscultate
> And initiate my plan
>
> It's almost 1430
> The 24 hour report is due
> There are two more admissions
> And, I need to assess them too
>
> I must develop a nursing diagnosis
> And, long and short term goals
> Along with nursing orders and discharge plans
> Oh, won't you give me a hand?[12]

Nine months later, Sadler once again described in doggerel her total involvement in the new standards and her good-natured acceptance of them that was characteristic of many Army nurses:

> The change was imminent
> The front office declared
> The first month was tough
> I was threatened and scared
>
> Inservices were held
> Nursing articles were read
> As we learned to assess
> And plan ahead
>
> We had to implement
> We strived to succeed
> Everyone struggled, every one asked
> Why are you doing this to me?

> Several months passed by
> As we all persevered
> We began to see progress
> And our thoughts also cleared
>
> SOAP [Subjective data, Objective data, Assessment, Plan] notes were written
> Problem lists were made
> Consults were sent
> The plan of care was laid
>
> We followed nursing orders
> We understood the patient's needs
> We became more involved
> We were growing, indeed
>
> It's not so overwhelming now
> I do know what to do
> What is most perplexing though
> Is that I'm never through
>
> Taped reports have helped a lot
> Along with peer review
> Research will soon be done
> To evaluate what we do
>
> Patients are much happier
> Care is much improved
> Staff receives more thanks
> For the efforts they pursue
>
> It's been a good experience
> Much knowledge I have gained
> I'm glad I've had a part in it
> And imagine! I'm still sane![13]

Over time, several Army Nurse Corps nursing specialties and interest groups augmented and improved the original Standards of Nursing Practice. A 1983 supplement that identified nursing quality assurance guidelines appeared in print, and the community health nurses published their practice standards as an adjunct to the Department of Army Pamphlet.[14] In 1986, Change 2 to the AMEDD Standards of Nursing Practice, Department of Army Pamphlet 40-5, added standards for occupational health nursing.[15] That same year, a group of Army nurse practitioners developed practice standards geared to their specialty issues, such as the provision of patient care, professional development, and care supervision. They devised a checklist based on the standards for use in chart audits and peer review.[16] By 1987, the various nurse consultants all had developed standards of practice for the Army Nurse Corps nursing specialties.[17]

Publication of the Army Nurse Corps Standards of Nursing Practice sparked additional reflection and other standards development. Lieutenant Colonel James D. Vail called on nurse anesthetists to develop anesthesia practice standards rela-

Lieutenant Colonel James D. Vail served as Chief, Nursing Research Service at Walter Reed in 1985. Photo courtesy of Nursing Research Service, Walter Reed Army Medical Center, Washington, DC.

tive to clinical practice in all settings. He also advocated an anesthesia-oriented compilation of process criteria and recommended testing, refinement, and implementation of the criteria as an instrument to evaluate anesthesia practice.[18]

The 13th Evacuation Hospital, a unit of the Wisconsin Army National Guard, saw the wisdom and need to develop standards and criteria for routine peacetime training responsibilities and wanted a template for organized review that was appropriate for a nonhospital setting. The purpose of the "Quality Assurance Plan for Nursing Service" was to improve unit level performance and efficiency. These guardsmen hoped that their work could be emulated by other Army Reserve and Army National Guard units to achieve higher levels of effectiveness and competence that in turn would improve combat readiness, contribute to individual satisfaction, and increase retention rates.[19]

As one relatively small but unified element in the larger civilian and military nursing cosmos, the Army Nurse Corps was in the vanguard in developing and publishing both general and specific Standards of Nursing Practice.[20] In part, the achievement owed much to the Corps members' advanced educational background, the specialty nurse consultants' keen insight, the senior leaders' determination, and the realization of a critical mass—a large organization moving forward with virtual unity on a significant piece of work. As the world of nursing evolved, conditions in the Army also changed, and the standards were widely accepted and duplicated. With that goal accomplished, the Army Nurse Corps no longer regarded publication and dissemination of the standards as a priority.

In November 1998, the Army Nurse Corps rescinded Department of the Army Pamphlet 40-5, the Standards of Nursing Practice. The rationale determined by a team of senior officers was that the Corps then based its practice on the American Nurses Association Standards of Nursing Practice and standards of the specialty nursing organizations.[21] At that time, as Simmons' assistant, Colonel Susan McCall recognized, the Department of Defense (DoD) was eliminating unnecessary regulations, pamphlets, and circulars.[22] Cost containment became the AMEDD watchword as the 1980s ended. In the meantime, several other innovations emerged in the pursuit of excellence.

The arduous process of developing and implementing a patient classification system was another effort initiated—in part—to improve the quality of nursing care delivered in the AMEDD.[23] Specific reasons for the creation of the system included the need to have a valid and reliable method to determine appropriate and adequate amounts of staff, have acuity data available for the Force Development Division to calculate safe levels of personnel, and be able to compute the correct mixture of staff—both professional and paraprofessional—to provide care in any given nursing unit.[24]

Before the 1980s, nursing administrators in Army hospitals staffed nursing units primarily on the basis of patient census, reasoning that units with more patients—regardless of acuity—needed more staff. In a changing health care climate characterized by "increasingly complex technology, growth in specialization, provision of more time consuming tasks, increased emphasis on health teaching, personalization of service to patients, and ongoing evaluation of performance," a better method was needed to determine staffing needs based on the aggregate number of nursing care hours required by patients on a unit.[25]

Early in the 1970s, the Army Nurse Corps recognized the need for such a system and considered assigning the herculean task to the Division of Nursing at Walter Reed Army Institute of Research. At the same time, however, the Army Nurse Corps leadership acknowledged that nurse researchers then assigned to that unit possessed "limited research ability" and were in a "precarious posture" in an organization that rendered them demoralized and "non-productive." Coupled with the fact that the division's operating budget was limited to a mere $100 a month, leaders decided not to ask nurse researchers in the Division of Walter Reed Army Institute of Research to develop and test a patient classification instrument.[26] Instead, Colonel Beverly Glor, assigned at Madigan Army Medical Center, Washington, and Lieutenant Colonel Susie Sherrod, assigned at Health Care Studies Division, Fort Sam Houston, Texas, worked on projects that had comparable goals but disparate approaches.[27] Glor's effort, the Madigan Army Medical Center Acuity Based Patient Classification Subsystem, quantified direct and nondirect nursing care in medical-surgical and specialty areas and included a yardstick to determine numbers and mix of personnel required.[28] Sherrod's approach, the Nursing Care Hour Standards Study, measured the standard time required to complete 352 operationally defined, direct nursing care tasks in six military treatment facilities (MTFs) of differing sizes over two years. It gauged the frequency of direct nursing care tasks in various specialty areas, such as medical-surgical, intensive care, obstetrics, newborn, pediatric, and psychiatric units, and computed the ideal numbers and types of nursing personnel. To evaluate the two studies and solicit recommendations, the Army Nurse Corps hired Health Management Systems, a consulting firm. Health Management Systems recommended rejection of the weaknesses of both plans and consolidation of their best features to create one ideal system. The new plan included the Nursing Care Hour Standards System's time standards and task frequencies and the Madigan Army Medical Center Acuity Based Patient Classification Subsystem's instrument and nondirect care components. At approximately the same time, the Navy Nurse Corps, then working on a patient classification system for its hospitals, joined forces with the Army Nurse Corps to conduct validity and reliability studies in medical-surgical specialties. This further revised, improved, and expanded the tool, and the system's new designation became the Workload Management System for Nurses (WMSN).

In 1983, a team of investigators used a self-tutoring program to familiarize nurses with the WMSN at five selected Army MTFs. Charge nurses and team leaders subsequently tested the system by classifying patients every day on every work shift for four months. Then the team returned to the MTFs to appraise the system, basing their evaluations on criteria of comprehensiveness, data output and input, validity and reliability, implementation, and cost. The results were used to fine-tune the WMSN.[29] The Army Nurse Corps required all nursing departments at all MTFs to use the WMSN beginning on 1 January 1985.[30] By August of that year, the WMSN was used throughout the Army Nurse Corps. Lieutenant Colonel Jude Larkin, a nurse researcher at the Walter Reed Army Medical Center (WRAMC), pondered the implications.

> The question then becomes how to use these data for increased efficiency and political gains. That is, at the local intra-departmental and departmental level, ANC [Army Nurse Corps] wide and for validating our manpower needs to others within the Army and on Capitol Hill. With automation, we would be derelict if we didn't explore full use of the WMSN....[31]

The Army Nurse Corps continually upgraded the system. Private contractors developed commercial software to support automation for data input at the unit level. The Army Nurse Corps coordinated the interface of WMSN with Uniform Chart of Accounts for Personnel.[32] By 1989, all nursing units had computers for data input.[33] Various Army Medical Department Activities and Army Medical Centers published regulations based on the WMSN, and the Department of the Army issued a Field Manual to guide its use.[34] The Corps then planned to expand the WMSN to include utilization in ambulatory care clinics, labor and delivery settings, the postanesthesia care units, and emergency departments.[35]

The Corps did not implement any research to determine whether a relationship existed between the use of the WMSN and patient outcomes. Thus, its impact on variables such as adverse patient events, length of hospital stay, or improvements in care was unknown. Colonel Bonnie Jennings, who spent several years testing and implementing the tool, noted that, in the Army, the presumption existed that if enough staff was available, quality care would follow. However, no scientific evidence affirmed that premise. Jennings admitted that the staffing mix in the military—so heavily influenced by the demands of readiness—was another consideration. The blend of professional nurses, practical nurses, and nursing assistants differed significantly from the mix in a civilian hospital setting. Nonetheless, she considered the WMSN as good as any acuity tool available nationwide. Jennings recalled that, in her later exposure to the WMSN as a chief nurse, it served primarily as a demonstration of the process used to make staffing decisions during Joint Commission for the Accreditation of Healthcare Organizations accreditation visits. Whether those decisions were valid was yet another untested question.[36]

The WMSN usually justified the need for significant numbers of additional professional and paraprofessional nursing staff, a state of affairs that threatened and irritated other departments within MTFs who feared that—in the balance—they would lose staff. The outcomes were a series of bureaucratic battles for funds and people.

General Connie L. Slewitzke remembered a skeptical physician who doubted that it took 20 minutes to give a bed bath to an intensive care patient, as if a patient festooned with drainage tubes, infusion lines and pumps, ventilator systems, and other miscellaneous technological paraphernalia made bathing a simple operation. Many Medical Corps officers were suspicious of the WMSN's statistics and resisted its implementation. Slewitzke had a conversation with Major General Lewis Mologne, WRAMC commander, when he came to realize that the WMSN

Refining Quality of Care Strategies 197

Lieutenant Colonel Jude Larkin served as Nurse Researcher, Nursing Research Service at Walter Reed in 1985.
Photo courtesy of Nursing Research Service, Walter Reed Army Medical Center, Washington, DC.

Colonel Carol Reineck served as Chief Nurse, Darnall Army Community Hospital, Fort Hood, Texas in 1998.
Photo courtesy of Colonel Carol Reineck, San Antonio, TX.

was "really predicated on orders the doctors write." His illogical conclusion was that "we can fix that. We do not need all these nurses—doctors can put in NG [nasogastric] tubes, doctors can put in IVs." Slewitzke replied, "Yes, . . . but who watches that IV? Who continually calibrates it, who observes the patient, who charts it, who manages that NG tube, . . . ?"[37]

Other problems surfaced when nurse staffing, as calculated by the WMSN, was unavailable, which then precipitated bed or entire ward closures. The closures affected physician internship and residency instruction, since they decreased the pool of available patients. This development, in turn, had Graduate Medical Education implications and became a serious issue for the Medical Corps. According to Colonel Carol Reineck, "doctors pooh poohed the system when they just plain wanted to fill beds and did not like to have a 'system' say no."[38] Major General John E. Major, Health Services Command commander, may have had this situation in mind when he editorialized about the WMSN in the *HSC Mercury*. "None of us can afford to use this tool as either a weapon or an encumbrance," he wrote, "since the WMSN was the best way to offer quality care at reasonable cost. The AMEDD should not abdicate its long-established team spirit," Major advised, "because a nurse-doctor schism would only hurt patients by limiting or diminishing care."[39]

Several nurses also had reservations about the WMSN. They lamented the amount of time required to enter the WMSN numbers into the system, particularly during the 1980s, when staffing levels regularly fell below accepted levels and nurses' time was a precious commodity.[40] Simplistic answers to the puzzle of calculating adequate staffing abounded but few if any easy solutions resolved the question. Nonetheless, the WMSN served for two decades as the best available instrument for the purpose.

Another hurdle to overcome was the Air Force Nurse Corps reluctance to accept and use the WMSN.[41] The Army Nurse Corps wanted the WMSN as the DoD patient classification standard so that statistics could be compared across the services and as a means for all services to demonstrate a unified need to support a claim with DoD and Congress for more personnel. The Air Force Nurse Corps, however, preferred to use its own 20-year-old patient classification system, which lacked supporting statistical documentation, as a foundation for its staffing system. Slewitzke shared the WMSN with General Carmelita Schimmenti, chief of the Air Force Nurse Corps, to convince her to adopt its use; Schimmenti remained unconvinced. She perceived the WMSN not as a means to justify more personnel but as a way to better distribute available staff. Slewitzke was disappointed, having expected Schimmenti to be excited when she learned of the system's success. That did not happen. In 1987, Slewitzke believed it unlikely the Air Force could continue to use its own outdated system.[42] She was right. By 1988, implementation of the WMSN began "in several Air Force Hospitals."[43] On 21 March 1989, the deputy secretary of defense signed a directive ordering the utilization of the WMSN by all services. It then became an accepted DoD-wide system.[44]

The use of automated information systems in both civilian and military health care institutions to improve quality and enhance efficiency began in the 1970s. However, the trend became a major force in the 1980s. Army Nurse Corps officer Major Mary Messerschmidt accepted an assignment to work in a full-time role focusing on automated hospital support systems when the information management program was in its infancy. Her involvement with this project began in 1973 with an assignment to U.S. Army Health Services Data Systems Agency at Fort Detrick, Maryland. Originally, Messerschmidt collaborated with a team to formulate the automatic data processing specifications for the new WRAMC, then under construction, which involved providing recommendations on nursing requirements, assessing technological and professional input, identifying reasonable objectives, and determining appropriate operational concepts.[45] By 1975, however, DoD directed that all automation efforts be jointly developed and standardized among the three military hospital systems, and the Tri-Service Medical Information System (TRIMIS) was born.[46]

Thus, the tri-service effort to begin using computers to improve health care and eventually nursing care in the three military services originated in the mid-1970s with the establishment of TRIMIS. The assistant secretary of defense (health affairs) charged the TRIMIS Program Office with developing functional applications to enhance health care delivery, manage medical information, and integrate functional and management applications. The purpose ultimately was to create a prototype of a replicable system to be implemented originally in a demonstration hospital and later expanded throughout the system.[47] The tri-services translated functional requirements into procurement packages and developed procurement contracts with commercial firms for pilot tests of automated systems to support pharmacy, laboratory, radiology, appointment, and logistics services.[48]

In 1982 the Army Nurse Corps assigned Captain Elizabeth Weathington as part of the two-person TRIMIS Nurse Consultant Team.[49] One of their projects was to survey 33 Army nurses who had some computer expertise to evaluate the current status of on-the-job computer use. Twenty-two Army nurses responded to the questionnaire, almost all answering that they had no computers or software to support their nursing roles. Most expected computers in the near future and hoped to use them for compiling staff work schedules, documenting education, preparing monthly/quarterly reports, managing laboratory data and Central Materiel Supply levels, and so forth. Most chief nurses had a positive attitude about computerization (77 percent), while 16 percent were indifferent, and 5 percent were negative. The study's sample size was too small to provide valid and reliable conclusions but it did suggest the lack of experience Army nurses as a whole had with computers. However, those surveyed had a fairly accurate understanding of the role that automated systems might play in managing nursing information in the future.

Lieutenant Colonel Gar Yip was the Army Nurse Corps consultant on the TRIMIS team in 1988. She played a major role in the development and implementation of the Composite Health Care System (CHCS). Planners conceived CHCS to facilitate the exchange of patient health information with related services like dietetics, patient administration, radiology, pharmacy, laboratory, and the patient appointment system.[50] The TRIMIS staff organized CHCS to support quality assurance activities, as well as managing resource, mobilization, and mass casualty requirements.

TRIMIS contracted with outside sources to process CHCS from concept to application. It awarded Stage I contracts in 1986 to three bidders to design and install their assigned CHCS components in one of three MTF locations, or alpha sites: (1) Camp Lejeune, North Carolina; (2) Fort Knox, Kentucky; and (3) Sheppard Air Force Base, Texas. After evaluating the performance of Stage I contractors, TRIMIS awarded contracts for an improved CHCS at 14 beta sites, including three Army MTFs, Eisenhower Army Medical Center, Georgia; Tripler Army Medical Center, Hawaii; and the Nürnberg Medical Department Activity, Germany. Stage II called for development of capabilities to automate nursing patient documentation, physiological monitoring, personnel scheduling, resource management, nursing reports and minutes, and educational endeavors.[51]

These expectations were not fully met because serious flaws appeared in the $1.6 billion system. Contractors were unable to complete their requirements on time or within budget. Two critical but unsolved issues were multiple files of identical patient records and difficulties with archiving patient records.[52] Other significant inherent problems were a nonfunctional module for entry of doctors' orders, a character-based computer user interface as opposed to the user-friendly Windows or Macintosh graphic-based operating systems, an acquisition strategy that failed to deliver a computer-based patient record, no modules for nursing documentation, and other critical system performance concerns.[53] *Inside the Pentagon*, a commercial publication, cited numerous other flaws in CHCS, such as "cost overruns, system development delays, slow response times and 'breakdowns in medical care'." The Defense Medical Systems Support Center rebutted the charges and continued tests to solve problems and eliminate bugs.[54] In the final analysis, the only successful modules were those tangential to nursing and applicable to operations such as laboratory, pharmacology, radiology, and appointment scheduling.[55]

Another issue relating to good quality of care had to do with the requirement for all Army nurses to pass the National Council of State Boards of Nursing Licensure Examination (NCLEX) following their graduation from an accredited collegiate school of nursing. A successful score on this examination, which became the professional standard in 1978, was a requirement for professional licensure and for commissioning in the Army Nurse Corps.[56] By 1981, probably because of the pressing need for more nurses, the Army Nurse Corps was commissioning "by exception" both direct accessions and Reserve Officers' Training Corps graduates before they received a NCLEX passing grade.[57] If the newly commissioned officer subsequently failed the examination, Johnson instructed chief nurses to refer the officer to remedial courses to better prepare him or her for the next testing opportunity. She also thought it would be helpful for the officer to work in the specialty field that correlated with the section of the test that he or she failed and directed that the officer take the next NCLEX offered.[58] After the first failure to pass the NCLEX, Joint Commission for the Accreditation of Hospitals standards dictated that the nurse in question should not be allowed to perform professional nursing activities before retesting.[59] DoD Directive 6025.6 specified that any care provided by these graduate nurses *not* be given independently but only "under the direct supervision of an appropriate licensed health care provider of the same discipline."[60] The Army discharged direct commissioned officers who failed the NCLEX a second time. Reserve Officer Training Corps graduates who failed the examination twice were transferred from the Army Nurse Corps to another branch in the Army to fulfill their service commitment. Johnson expedited the discharge or branch transfer.[61] A memorandum granted Army Enlisted Commissioning Program graduates 60 days of study time to prepare for and take the NCLEX. After those first 60 days, Army Enlisted Commissioning Program participants had to work in a local military unit in enlisted status while awaiting exam results and before attending the Officer Basic Course.[62]

In yet another effort to improve quality, the Army Nurse Corps conceived and implemented a novel and unique departmental-level matrix. It first developed a new Department of Nursing Organizational Model in 1988 "to prepare . . . for efficient and effective operations during the 21st century."[63] In 1989, the annual Professional Development Course's primary commission was designing the model's prototype.[64] The draft model elevated Army Medical Center and Medical Department Activity chiefs, Department of Nursing, to the level of deputy commander for nursing.[65] This new configuration would render the deputy commander for nursing on a par with the deputy commander for clinical services, formerly the chief, professional services, and the deputy commander for administration, formerly the executive officer, and would also furnish the deputy commander for nursing with direct access to the commander. The deputy commander for nursing had the ultimate responsibility and authority for nursing services within the institution. The next subordinate echelon, referred to as the chief, nursing administration, would more closely and directly supervise all nursing activities in the MTF, such as the clinical nursing coordinators on days, evenings, and nights; the standard nursing support and productivity services; and the case managers (usually clinical nurse specialists) who established and monitored the patients' critical paths and outcomes and coordinated the health care team group effort.

Course participants described the model as patient centered, collaborative, functional in peace and war, capable of managing both cost and quality concerns, consumer driven, outcome focused, and flexible.[66] Over time, several MTFs implemented some of its features. The position title of chief, Department of Nursing, for instance, virtually disappeared during the 1990s, to be replaced by variations on the deputy commander model. Yet, the ideas in the organizational model were so broad that little if any reorganization occurred based on the original prototype.[67] Some questioned whether the organizational reconfiguration influenced good quality care to any degree. They argued that the changes did little to improve Army nurses' status and were a contributing factor to a loss of professional identity.[68] Still, it was a harbinger of future organizational configurations.

Some Army Nurse Corps leaders were simultaneously developing and testing a paradigm to clarify the delivery of nursing care in the Army. For them, the Army Nursing Practice Model was an amalgam of several "civilian practice models," such as functional, team, primary, or case management nursing. The actual delivery model depended on variables such as patients' acuity; numbers and mix of staffing; the practice milieu; the manner in which the organization's values, goals, objectives, and philosophy were operationalized; and whether the care setting was a combat or a peacetime environment. Its architects envisaged an adaptable, expandable, and resilient model that was not static but instead dynamic. This meant there was no single right nursing delivery model suitable for all exigencies. The basic premise was that the chosen blend of nursing care delivery models should produce positive patient outcomes and satisfaction, retain premium staff, and improve organizational finances.[69] It accurately portrayed the philosophy and practice environment of contemporary Army nursing.

Five years later, after careful scrutiny and with considerable deliberation, Colonel Terris Kennedy, Major Elizabeth Hill, Brigadier General Nancy Adams, and Colonel Bonnie Jennings expanded the practice model as a "Conceptual Model of Army Nursing Practice." In keeping with the accepted definition of a conceptual model, they proposed "a symbolic depiction in logical terms of an idealized, relatively simple . . . structure."[70] They assumed Army Nurse Corps officers were unique in their readiness to provide nursing care in various contingencies. At the model's heart were concentric triangles symbolizing Army nurses' duty to provide care, comfort, and cure. This occurred in a framework of administration, education, and research support embellished by professional efforts in traditional nursing care, advanced practice nursing care, and clinical case management. The model's intent was to direct nursing practice, to guide development of professional nursing, and to prepare Army Nurse Corps officers for the demands of future deployments and health care provision.[71] This was an example of evolving doctrine and theory development within the Army Nurse Corps whose purpose was to explain and improve Army nursing practice and to expand the professional knowledge unique to military nursing.

The Army Nurse Corps used numerous tactics to improve the knowledge base of its officers, another aspect of the movement to enhance the quality of care provided. In the 1980s, the Corps offered a variety of educational courses to improve officer professionalism. Some of these classes had existed for decades, while others were innovations. Their objectives were to enhance nursing specialty knowledge and skills, develop military acumen, and provide orientation to unfamiliar role expectations or new care settings.[72]

For many years, the Army Nurse Corps offered its members various types of specialty education. During the 1980s, the Corps sponsored a specialty course in Psychiatric Mental Health Nursing at Eisenhower Army Medical Center in Georgia, courses in Obstetrical and Gynecological Nursing and Pediatric Nursing at Tripler Army Medical Center in Hawaii, and courses in Operating Room Nursing at Brooke Army Medical Center, Madigan Army Medical Center, and Beaumont Army Medical Center. As a recruiting incentive, applicants for Army Nurse Corps commissions could request that they be allowed to participate in the course of their choice. They then were guaranteed enrollment at the course within their first year of service.

More experienced Army Nurse Corps officers enjoyed additional educational opportunities. They could apply for advanced studies, such as the Principles of Military Preventive Medicine Course given at Fort Sam Houston, Texas; the Critical Care Nursing Course held at Brooke and Fitzsimons Army Medical Centers; in some cases, a follow-on Renal Dialysis Course conducted at Brooke Army Medical Center; and the Nurse Practitioner Course held at Fort Ord, California. Also available were two-week Professional Management Courses, such as the Clinical Head Nurse Course, Principles of Advanced Nursing Administration, and the Preventive Medicine Program Management Course.[73] In 1984, the Army

Nurse Corps sponsored the first course to prepare Army nurses for roles as chiefs, nursing education and training services. The first such class met at the Academy of Health Sciences (AHS).[74]

Additionally, Army nurses could apply for Army-sponsored graduate education in civilian academic institutions as a part of the Long Term Civilian Training Program. Army degree programs could focus on many nursing specialty areas. Career officers could also take advantage of graduate education in health care administration and receive a master's degree in health care administration from Baylor University, with the classroom instruction at the AHS. They also could pursue graduate education in anesthesia nursing.

Although the overall topical content of course curriculums remained relatively constant, the Army Nurse Corps and the faculty continually improved and refined offerings. For instance, in 1981, the anesthesia course became a graduate program.[75] Originally, the State University of New York at Buffalo awarded a master's degree to Army nurses who successfully completed the anesthesia course.[76] In 1984, the Army transferred its anesthesia affiliation from the State University of New York to the Texas Wesleyan College.[77] By 2000, the Army again shifted its program affiliation, this time to the University of Texas at Houston Health Science Center. The repeated affiliation changes resulted from the competitive bidding process required for contract awards. Many civilian universities expressed interest in contracting with the Army Nurse Corps to provide anesthesia education.[78] As the century waned, candidates for anesthesia education could alternatively choose to attend the nurse anesthesia program at the Uniformed Services University of the Health Sciences.[79]

Other classes had military topics as their focus. The first two foundation military education courses were the AMEDD Officer Basic Course and the AMEDD Officer Advanced Course, both of which were in most cases mandatory. Opportunities for attendance in residence at the Combined Armed Services Staff School, the Command and General Staff College, and the Senior Service College, or its counterpart, the Army War College Corresponding Studies Course, were successively fewer and rationed to the most promising officers. The Corps gave preference to nurses assigned to Forces Command units for attendance at the Combat Casualty Care Course at Fort Sam Houston, Texas; the Medical Defense against Biological Warfare and Infectious Diseases Course given at Fort Detrick, Maryland; and the curriculum that dealt with Medical Management of Chemical Casualties at Aberdeen Proving Ground, Maryland.[80]

For many years, organized nursing acknowledged that newly graduated professional nurses, particularly those educated at the baccalaureate level, were susceptible to "reality shock" when moving from the role of student to that of full-time employment as a graduate nurse. Collegiate graduates were especially vulnerable because their demanding academic requirements left little time to gain hands-on experience from actual clinical practice. Possessing much theoretical knowledge, graduates had fewer clinical skills. The frustrated novice nurses, confronted by the reality of professional nursing as opposed to the ideal presented in their educational programs, often changed careers.[81]

To thwart reality shock and to ease the transition from collegiate student to Army Nurse Corps officer, the Corps created a preceptorship program for newly graduated second lieutenants in 1981.[82] The Corps intended the program to stimulate recruitment by the U.S. Army Recruiting Command and to enhance retention by "mitigating negative affective states."[83] Designed by the Nursing Science Division at AHS, the program concentrated on three key areas: (1) socializing the new officer to identify with the nursing profession and the Army; (2) sharpening clinical skills; and (3) teaching entry-level managerial skills. The chief, Nursing Education and Training Section in the MTF normally was responsible for the program, whose original length was tailored to meet individual needs with an optimum goal of 120 days of developmental mentoring. The chief, Nursing Education and Training Section assigned the new officer to an experienced Army Nurse Corps preceptor who served as a role model in one of several clinical areas. The pair frequently worked together with identical schedules. The preceptee also rotated through several other clinical areas, usually medical and surgical units and recovery and emergency departments, with about one week spent in ancillary services. After completing each clinical element, the unit's head nurse and the preceptor submitted a written evaluation of the preceptee's performance using an AHS-designed form.[84]

Over time, the Army Nurse Corps fine-tuned its Preceptor Program. By 1987, the curriculum, as implemented at William Beaumont Army Medical Center, was a wide-ranging experience anchored in certain behavioral objectives that integrated nursing theory and practice with pragmatic leadership principles and skills needed in military organizations. However, the Beaumont nurse educators subsequently shortened the time allocated to the program, perhaps as a result of the shortage of nursing resources or possibly because the additional time was superfluous to the new graduates' needs. Preceptees participated in the two-week Professional Orientation Program attended by all professional nurses new to the institution, which was followed by a four-week clinical experience under the direct supervision of a preceptor from the nursing unit to which the new officers would be permanently assigned. At intervals during the four weeks, the new officer spent eight hours in the emergency department and four hours each in the operating and recovery rooms, the laboratory, and the electrocardiogram clinic. The newcomer participated in classes on the Officer Efficiency Report, career planning, head nurse and wardmaster expectations, how to sponsor newcomers, and a group discussion of expectations and perceptions. The standard Officer Efficiency Report format guided the evaluation of the preceptee's performance in the program, although its contents did not become part of the preceptee's official military record. Rather, it was considered when preparing the preceptee's mandatory initial 120-day Officer Efficiency Report.[85]

Four years earlier, in October 1977, the Air Force Nurse Corps began a program similar to the Army Nurse Corps Preceptorship Program. It ran for 20 weeks and aided in the transition from civilian life of about 100 new nurses every six months at nine Air Force Base hospitals in the continental United States. Patterned after comparable civilian programs, the Air Force Nurse Internship Program included classroom lessons on topics such as clinical procedures, techniques for the emergency department, pharmacology, and nursing practice standards. For actual, hands-on clinical experience, the Air Force Nurse Corps paired the new nurse with an experienced partner who was to be both mentor and friend.[86]

In 1984, Slewitzke started another innovative program, the Army Nurse Corps Fellows Program, to develop mid-grade officers. She expected the fellowship to familiarize officers with the complex administrative activities involved in daily operations of the Office of the Chief and also to implement special projects.[87] The Dental Corps offered a similar yearlong fellowship, but the Army Nurse Corps had no personnel allocations or funds for such a lengthy venture. Thus, Slewitzke sponsored Army nurses locally assigned in the Military District of Washington for participation in the Army Nurse Corps three-month mentorship program.[88] Various Military District of Washington chief nurses in the Washington, D.C. area nominated the fellows, and Slewitzke made the final selection. Reservists initially filled in for the participating officers at their duty sites, but this practice quickly drew criticism. Chief nurses did not want reservists in some of these key positions, recalled Slewitzke, and the WRAMC commander, General Mologne, complained about nurses in his medical center working somewhere else even when a reservist replaced them.[89] The first two participants were Major Dena Norton and Major Kathleen Srsic-Stoehr.[90] Norton came from the Nursing Research Service at WRAMC, and her special project was to survey civilian anesthesia schools and students to gauge interest in a tuition assistance plan. The National Guard eventually funded a tuition assistance program based on her findings.[91] Srsic-Stoehr sat in on high-level meetings and reviewed and analyzed manpower databases—both civilian and military—as her special project. She described the interplay of the senior officers' personalities in the chief's office. Slewitzke, for example, was passionate about issues. Srsic-Stoehr recognized how much Slewitzke cared for the Corps and fought to keep it in the forefront. The assistant chief of the Corps, Colonel Eily P. Gorman, was perceptive, conscientious, and inquisitive, and she always asked the right questions and saw beyond the obvious. Colonel Audre McLoughlin, the Army Nurse Corps consultant in the Consultant's Branch, was knowledgeable in both an academic and a practical sense.[92]

Several years later, in 1986–1987, Lieutenant Colonel Gar Yip served in the three-month fellowship and also carried out a number of projects such as developing the hospital white duty uniform, evaluating a 600-response civilian nurse survey, and analyzing the Workload Management System for Nursing.[93] During her fellowship, Major Nancy Molter devised an Army-wide questionnaire seeking to modify the criteria for the critical care nurse skill identifier. The data gathered stimulated innovative regulation change. No office space was available for Molter, so she typically would sit at the desk of anyone who was not present. If all were there, she occupied a cupboard down the hall with a Canadian dental officer. The location of the Office of the Chief of the Corps explained the cramped quarters.

A while after her fellowship concluded and Major Kathleen Srsic-Stoehr, right, returned to duty at Fort Belvoir, she escorted Brigadier General Connie Slewitzke, left, who was making an official visit to DeWitt Army Community Hospital at Fort Belvoir, Virginia.
Photo courtesy of Colonel Kathleen Srsic-Stoehr, McLean, VA.

It was situated in the E-Ring, prime real estate in the Pentagon. On a lighter note, Molter set a personal goal to beat Gorman to work in the morning, but no matter how early she arrived, Gorman was always there. The best she could do was get there at 6:10 one morning only to find her senior officer already making the coffee. She never got there before her![94]

The enthusiasm and resolve of all involved ultimately made the fellowship productive. The fellows' participation furnished them with a personal insight into the attitudes of the senior officers working under conditions of intense pressure

While Major Nancy Molter was serving as the Army Nurse Corps fellow, she was promoted to lieutenant colonel. Brigadier General Connie Slewitzke (left) and Colonel Elizabeth Finn (right) pinned on Molter's new rank insignia in December 1984.
Photo courtesy of Army Nurse Corps Archives, Office of Medical History, Falls Church, VA.

generated by the immediacy of multiple complex issues. The fellowship in the Office of the Chief, Army Nurse Corps, continued into the 1990s, at which time the Corps expanded the program to a year. This change was dictated by the fact that the original participants consumed the first four weeks of their three-month fellowship orienting themselves and feeling comfortable enough to do the work. Major Kathleen Tracy was the first Army nurse to serve in the extended fellowship.[95]

Not all the issues relating to Army Nurse Corps education and the development of its officers, however, were positive and encouraging. Some challenges to the educational status quo threatened the Corps overall high quality. Such was the case with the entry-level education issue.

Driven by the persistent shortages, external forces again tested the Army Nurse Corps 1974 regulation mandating that all its active duty officers have a minimum of a baccalaureate degree in nursing.[96] In July 1989, the House of Representatives Armed Services Committee approved a bill authorizing the three military nursing services to again accept nurses with an associate degree or a diploma in nursing from a hospital school.[97] The Navy Nurse Corps, with its most critical shortages, supported the legislation. However, the Air Force Nurse Corps and the Army Nurse Corps General Clara L. Adams-Ender vigorously opposed it. Of course Adams-Ender would support the mandate if it became law, but she insisted on maintaining professional nurse quality and believed that accepting a lesser educational level was a step backward.[98] She reasoned that with a baccalaureate-educated nurse, the Army knew what it was getting and what it could do with the officer.[99] Opposing the legislation, Adams-Ender relied on an interesting strategy. She wrote, "In these situations . . . you have to fake it until you make it, [and] sometimes you are faking it up to the last minute." She told legislators that she considered the Corps already in compliance with the intent of the bill because it accepted less than baccalaureate graduates into the Army Reserve and Army National Guard, just not in the active component. Once they earned their bachelor's degrees, these Army nurses were then eligible for active duty. She argued for "the best folks I can have. I can't be mixing them up with all sorts of other kind of folks."[100] All the former chiefs of the Army Nurse Corps, representing almost a half-century of leadership in Army nursing, objected to the measure. Collectively, they wrote to Senator Daniel Inouye, member of the Defense Subcommittee and long-time advocate of military nursing, asking his support in defeating the bill in the Senate.[101] Inouye replied favorably, and through his efforts the bill failed to become law.[102] In 1992, Adams-Ender recalled:

> That was 2 years ago and we did not have any further discussion on the BSN [bachelor of science in nursing] thing. I really wanted to know how to put that to rest once and for all. Things that are important in management and leadership are one, get people into positions where you don't have to worry about whether or not they can do their job, and two, find out how you can fix something so it will stay fixed. Those two things are tough, because you don't have full control. . . . [103]

This was but one of a series of perennial efforts that had the potential to degrade the caliber of the Army Nurse Corps. At best it was an attempt to overcome a severe nurse shortage. At worst it represented a covert effort to limit the Corps quality, authority, and influence. In any case, it failed. Fortunately the Corps stature remained inviolate and regrettably the serious shortfall of Army Nurse Corps officers persisted throughout the 1980s.

# Notes

1. William Mayer, J. Jarrett Clinton, and David Newhall, "A First Report of the Department of Defense External Civilian Peer Review of Medical Care," *Journal of the American Medical Association* 260 (11 November 1988): 2690–93. An AMA official offered a critique of the foregoing DoD computerized system used to assess quality in John T. Kelly, "Assessing Quality," *Journal of the American Medical Association* 260 (11 November 1988): 2715–16.

2. Bernhard T. Mittemeyer, "Quality Assurance: Major Army Focus," *U.S. Medicine* 20 (15 January 1984): 55–59.

3. Connie L. Slewitzke, "Memorandum from the Chief, U.S. Army Nurse Corps," 2, October 1984, Army Nurse Corps Collection (ANCC), Office of Medical History (OMH).

4. The use of "overprints" involved augmenting standard forms with additional printed information in a local MTF. The intent was to add data routinely recorded on a common group of patients and thereby save time and effort.

5. Martha R. Bell, "Field Test Clinical Nursing Records Study," Information Paper, 1 February 1984, Inclosure 6, in Charles J. Reddy, "Nursing Newsletter Number 84-1," 1 February 1984, ANCC, OMH.

6. Eily P. Gorman, "DASG-CN Newsletter," n.d.; and Clara L. Adams-Ender, "Memo from the Chief Army Nurse Corps," 4–5, 30 September 89 (both in ANCC, OMH).

7. American Nurses Association, *Standards of Nursing Practice* (Kansas City, MO: ANA, 1973).

8. American Nurses Association, *Standards of Clinical Nursing Practice*, second ed. (Kansas City, MO: ANA, 1998), vii.

9. Headquarters, Department of the Army, "Army Medical Department Standards of Nursing Practice," Department of the Army Pamphlet 40-5, November 1981, Change 2, 15 May 1986, 1-1.

10. Hazel W. Johnson-Brown, Interview by Charles F. Bombard, 1984, 130–33, USAWC/USAMHI Senior Officer Oral History Program, Project No. 84-15, ANCC, OMH. This issue was an outward sign of what Aiken referred to as "fundamental incompatibilities in the . . . social contract between nurses and physicians." Prevalent hospital trends in the 1980s, such as more acutely ill patients, decreased physician presence, and physician subspecialty practice with no one physician at the helm, could "result in costly and dangerous duplication or omission." All this contributed to the expansion of independent roles for

hospital nurses, of which diagnosis was a component. Aiken argued that the social contract between these two health disciplines that defined clinical decision making had to be renegotiated. Linda H. Aiken, "The Impact of Federal Health Policy on Nurses," in *Nursing in the 1980s, Crises, Opportunities, Challenges*, ed. Linda H. Aiken and Susan R. Gortner (Philadelphia: J.B. Lippincott, 1982), 3–20.

11. Hazel W. Johnson-Brown, Interview by Charles F. Bombard, 1984, 130–33, USAWC/USAMHI Senior Officer Oral History Program, Project No. 84-15; and Darlene K. McLeod, "Revisions to Standards of Nursing Practice," Memorandum for Brigadier General Johnson, n.d. (both in ANCC, OMH).

12. Freida J. Sadler, "The Standards & Primary Nursing," 1979, in Virginia L. Brown for Hazel W. Johnson, "Information for All ANC Officers," TD, 8 May 1980, Inclosure 6, ANCC, OMH.

13. Freida J. Sadler, "A Change of Life," 1979, in Virginia L. Brown for Hazel W. Johnson, "Information for All ANC Officers," TD, 8 May 1980, Inclosure 6, ANCC, OMH.

14. Marie O'Neil, "Highlights in the History of the Army Nurse Corps," Typewritten Memorandum (TM), 29 June 1990, ANCC, OMH. Bernhard T. Mittemeyer, "Army Medical Department," *Military Medicine* 148 (November 1983): 834. Carolyn M. Feller and Debora R. Cox, *Highlights in the History of the Army Nurse Corps* (Washington, DC: U.S. Army Center of Military History, 2000), 55.

15. Department of the Army, "Army Medical Department Standards of Nursing Practice," DA Pamphlet 40-5, Change 2, 15 May 1986; Hazel W. Johnson, "Notes from the Chief, Army Nurse Corps," Typewritten Newsletter, 5, March 1983; and Marie O'Neil, "Highlights in the History of the Army Nurse Corps," TM, 29 June 1990 (all in ANCC, OMH).

16. Eileen M. Sperling and Heidi L. Wesley, "Standards of Nurse Practitioner Practice: A Foundation for Peer Review," *Medical Bulletin of the US Army, Europe* 43 (September/October 1986): 14–17.

17. Connie L. Slewitzke, Interview by Beverly Greenlee, 79, n.d., USAWC/USAMHI Senior Officer Oral History Program, Project No. 88-8, ANCC, OMH.

18. James D. Vail, "Accountability of Anesthesia Nursing through Standards of Practice," *Military Medicine* 150 (November 1985): 582–86.

19. Diane M. Ebersberger, "13th Evacuation Hospital Nurses Develop a Quality Assurance Program," *National Guard* 40 (September 1986): 22–26.

20. Connie L. Slewitzke, Interview by Beverly Greenlee, 78, 79, n.d., USAWC/USAMHI Senior Officer Oral History Program, Project No. 88-8, ANCC, OMH.

21. The team contributing to the decision consisted of Brigadier General Nancy Adams, Colonels Terris Kennedy, Bettye Simmons, Dianne Bechtold, Claudia Bartz, and Dena Norton, and Lieutenant Colonel Donna Wright. All agreed unanimously to rescind Pamphlet 40-5. Carol I. Reineck to Colonel Bettye Simmons and others, E-mail Correspondence, 5 January 1995, ANCC, OMH. Mary Eichhorn to Emily Court, E-mail Correspondence, 24 March 2003, ANCC, OMH.

22. Susan McCall to Author, E-mail Correspondence, 24 March 2003, ANCC, OMH.

23. Although the quest for quality was a major reason for development of an Army Nurse Corps classification system, no research-based proof linking the use of such a system to quality outcomes then existed. Phyllis Giovannetti, "Understanding Patient Classification Systems," *Journal of Nursing Administration* 9 (February 1979): 4–9. However, it seemed reasonable to assume empirically that there was such a relationship.

24. Development of a Standard Patient Classification System for Use throughout the Army Medical Department, (AMEDD)," Typewritten Statement of Work, 12 March 1982; and James D. Vail, "Workload Management System for Nursing (Patient Classification and

Staffing Guide)," Monograph, 1–2, January 1986 (both in ANCC, OMH).

25. Susie M. Sherrod, "Patient Classification System: A Link between Diagnosis-Related Groupings and Acuity Factors," *Military Medicine* 149 (September 1984): 506–11. James D. Vail and Elizabeth A. Rimm, "Testing of a Patient Classification System for Army-Wide Use," Information Paper, 10 March 1983, Inclosure 3, in Hazel W. Johnson, "Notes from the Chief, U.S. Army Nurse Corps," August 1983; James D. Vail, "Workload Management System for Nursing (Patient Classification and Staffing Guide)," Monograph, 1–2, January 1986 (both in ANCC, OMH).

26. Rosemary T. McCarthy, "Categorization Scheme (Acuity Index) Project Proposal," Disposition Form, 18 March 1975, ANCC, OMH.

27. Rosemary T. McCarthy, "Patient Classification System Currently Utilized by Madigan Army Medical Center, Department of Nursing (MAMC-DON)," Disposition Form, 21 December 1981; and James J. James to Connie L. Slewitzke, Typewritten Letter (TL), 14 January 1982 (both in ANCC, OMH).

28. Direct patient care activities, such as administering a medication or health teaching, required an observable, behavioral interaction between nurse and patient. Indirect care activities were those carried on in behalf of the patient but usually away from the bedside, such as documenting care or ordering a diet tray for the patient. Susie M. Sherrod, "Patient Classification System: A Link between Diagnosis-Related Groupings and Acuity Factors," *Military Medicine* 149 (September 1984): 506–11.

29. James D. Vail and Elizabeth A. Rimm, "Testing of a Patient Classification System for Army-Wide Use," Information Paper, 10 March 1983, Inclosure 3, in Hazel W. Johnson, "Notes from the Chief, U.S. Army Nurse Corps," August 1983; James D. Vail, "Workload Management System for Nursing (Patient Classification and Staffing Guide)," Monograph, 1–6, January 1986; "Workload Management System for Nursing: A Tri-Service Staffing Standard," *Army Nurse* 3 (1990): 3; and Susie Sherrod to Author, E-mail Correspondence, 26 March 2003 (all in ANCC, OMH).

30. Connie L. Slewitzke, "Memorandum from the Chief U.S. Army Nurse Corps," October 1984; and "ANC Annual Historical Report FY 85," 8 (both in ANCC, OMH).

31. Jude Larkin, "Army Nurse Corps Personnel Management Practice Study," Information Paper, 2 August 1985, ANCC, OMH.

32. Connie L. Slewitzke, "Memorandum from the Chief U.S. Army Nurse Corps," 7–8, December 1986; and Gar Yip, "After Action Report of ANC Fellowship for LTC Gar Yip, 17 Nov 1986–13 Feb 87," Memorandum for Record, 13 February 1987 (both in ANCC, OMH). UCAPERS (Uniform Chart of Accounts for Personnel) was a system employed by the Army "using uniform accounting principles and performance indicators, standardized terminology, common expense classification procedures, and standard statistical definitions" to capture workload. Vernon McKenzie, "Department of Defense," *Military Medicine* 144 (September 1979): 569–72. The WMSN captured the workload of nurses. When these two systems were linked, the ability to accurately project nursing manpower standards was enhanced. Gar Yip to Author, E-mail Correspondence, 12 February 2003, ANCC, OMH.

33. Betty C. Jones, "Ways to Increase Job Productivity for Army Nurses," Memorandum for LTC Wil Nieves, 26 May 1989, ANCC, OMH.

34. Karl H. Pfaehler, TL, 12 December 1988, ANCC, OMH. FM 8-501, November 1990; and Clara L. Adams-Ender, "Memo from the Chief Army Nurse Corps," 5, 30 September 1989 (both in ANCC, OMH).

35. Connie L. Slewitzke, "Topics for the Army Study Program," TM, 3 August 1987; John M. Hudock, "US Army Nurse Corps Nursing Research Advisory Board (NRAB),

2–4 November 1987," Typewritten Meeting Minutes, 3; Jeffrey P. Moon and James M. Georgoulakis, "Input Regarding AMEDD Study Program—Ambulatory Care Classification Project," TM, 10 August 1988; and "Synopsis of Nursing Research from Health Care Studies and Clinical Investigation Activity," in Barbara S. Turner, "Nursing Research Activities Report, 1988–1989," n.d. (all in ANCC, OMH).

36. Bonnie M. Jennings to Author, E-mail Correspondence, 30 January 2004, ANCC, OMH.

37. Connie L. Slewitzke, Interview by Beverly Greenlee, 241–43, n.d., USAWC/USAMHI Senior Officer Oral History Program, Project No. 88-8, ANCC, OMH.

38. Carol Reineck to Author, E-mail Correspondence, 8 March 2003, ANCC, OMH.

39. John E. Major "Commander Calls Nurses Vital Part of Team," *HSC Mercury* 16 (May 1989): 2.

40. Carol Reineck to Author, E-mail Correspondence, 8 March 2003, ANCC, OMH.

41. Brigadier General Connie Slewitzke firmly believed that the WMSN was the best available instrument. "Outside consultants" and "another Corps" (the Navy Nurse Corps) confirmed its validity. General Slewitzke shared that she "was so proud of Susie's [Sherrod] statistics. They could not question our data. . . ." Connie L. Slewitzke, Interview by Beverly Greenlee, 240–41, n.d., USAWC/USAMHI Senior Officer Oral History Program, Project No. 88-8, ANCC, OMH.

42. Connie L. Slewitzke, Interview by Beverly Greenlee, 20–23, n.d., USAWC/USAMHI Senior Officer Oral History Program, Project No. 88-8, ANCC, OMH.

43. "Military Nurses Task Force Report on the Military Nursing Shortage," Department of Health and Human Services, Secretary's Commission on Nursing, VI-12, December 1988, ANCC, OMH.

44. Clara L. Adams-Ender, "Memo from the Chief Army Nurse Corps," 5, 30 September 1989; Clara L. Adams-Ender, "Memo from the Chief Army Nurse Corps," 7, 31 December 1989; Clara L. Adams-Ender, Interview by Virginia Ruth Cheney, 152, 1992, Project 92-3, U.S. Army Military History Institute, Senior Officer Oral History Program; and "Workload Management System for Nursing: A Tri-Service Staffing Standard," *Army Nurse* 3 (1990): 3 (all in ANCC, OMH). Sunnie Scarlett, "Statistics Prove Need for Nurses," *HSC Mercury* 16 (August 1989): 4.

45. Mary L. Messerschmidt, Officer Efficiency Reports, DA Form 67-7, 11 December 1973, 1 September 1974, Typewritten Documents (TDs), ANCC, OMH.

46. While Army nurses were the key players in TRIMIS, Air Force nurses also actively participated. Navy nurses, however, remained on the sidelines. The Army and Air Force nurses had many spirited discussions about informatics and sometimes the battles were "not pretty." Mary L. Messerschmidt to Author, 30 January 2004; Mary L. Messerschmidt to Author, 2 February 2004 (both E-mail Correspondence in ANCC, OMH).

47. Robert N. Smith, "Department of Defense," *Military Medicine* 142 (August 1977): 585–90. Philip A. Deffer, "Tri-Medical Information System (TRIMIS)," in Department of the Army, Headquarters, U.S. Army Health Services Command, *Commander's Notes*, CG HSC Bulletin No. 1-75 (January 1975): 9, Record Group 112, Entry 452, National Archives.

48. Vernon McKenzie, "Department of Defense," *Military Medicine* 144 (September 1979): 571. John H. Moxley, "Department of Defense," *Military Medicine* 145 (September 1980): 608–11. John H. Moxley, "Military Medicine Programs Progress," *U.S. Medicine* 17 (15 January 1981): 14. John H. Moxley, "Department of Defense," *Military Medicine* 146 (September 1981): 626–30. John H. Moxley, "Department of Defense," *Military Medicine* 147 (November 1982): 943–48.

49. Connie L. Slewitzke for Hazel W. Johnson, "Notes from the Chief, US Army Nurse Corps," 3, December 1982, ANCC, OMH.

50. Developers created CHCS as an information system based in hospitals to manage clinical patient data. The Workload Management System for Nurses was developed to gauge nursing workload and make staffing determinations. The two systems were never linked, conceptually or operationally. Gar Yip to Author, E-mail Correspondence, 29 January 2004, ANCC, OMH. Sunnie Scarlett, "Army Experts Say CHCS 'Can Do'," *HSC Mercury* 17 (June 1990): 7. Harry Noyes "Computer System Gets Go-Ahead," *HSC Mercury* 20 (May 1993): 12.

51. Gar Yip, "Composite Health Care System (CHCS)," Information Paper, 3 March 1988, ANCC, OMH. "Knox Tests New Health Care Computer System," *HSC Mercury* 15 (June 1988): 7. "CHCS Computers Online at All DoD Hospitals," *The Mercury* 25 (October 1997): 7.

52. United States General Accounting Office, Information Management and Technology Division, *Medical ADP Systems: Composite Health Care System Is Not Ready to Be Deployed*, GAO/IMTEC-92-54 (Washington, DC: United States General Accounting Office, 1992).

53. Anonymous to Author, E-mail Correspondence, 22 March 2003, ANCC, OMH.

54. Sunnie Scarlett, "Army Experts Say CHCS 'Can Do'," *HSC Mercury* 17 (June 1990): 7.

55. Anonymous to Author, E-mail Correspondence, 22 March 2003, ANCC, OMH.

56. Jennifer Petersen, Untitled TD whose subject was the NCLEX, ANCC, OMH. Another unique requirement for commissioning in the Army Nurse Corps specified that an applicant be a graduate of a nursing program recognized by the U.S. Secretary of Education or accredited by the National League for Nursing and acceptable to the Department of the Army. Headquarters, Department of the Army, Army Regulation 135-101, "Appointment of Reserve Commissioned Officers for Assignment to Army Medical Department Branches," 10–11, 15 February 1984. Prior to 1978, different states used various locally prepared paper and pencil tests.

57. Department of the Army, AR 135-101, "Appointment of Reserve Commissioned Officers for Assignment to Army Medical Department Branches," 15 July 1979.

58. Hazel W. Johnson, "Information for All ANC Officers," 7 November 1980, Inclosure 9, ANCC, OMH.

59. Eily P. Gorman, "Implementation of Licensure Requirements for Army Nurse Corps Officers and Other Nurses," Information Paper, 3 February 1986, ANCC, OMH.

60. Department of Defense, DoD Directive 6025.6, "Licensure of DOD Health Care Providers," 18 July 1985.

61. Hazel W. Johnson, "Information for All ANC Officers," 2, 27 November 1981, ANCC, OMH. Headquarters, Department of the Army, Army Regulation 135-101, "Appointment of Reserve Commissioned Officers for Assignment to Army Medical Department Branches," 10–11, 15 February 1984.

62. "Scope of Practice for NCLEX-RN Failures," Information Paper, n.d., ANCC, OMH.

63. Clara L. Adams-Ender, "Department of Nursing Organizational Model," 6 November 1989, ANCC, OMH.

64. Claudia Bartz, "After Action Summary for the Course," TM, 27 July 1989, ANCC, OMH.

65. This position eventually had differing titles in different institutions. For instance, Tripler Army Medical Center nurses suggested using the appellation "Deputy Commander

Patient Care Services (DCPCS)." "Optimal Organizational Structure for the Department of Nursing in U.S. Army Medical Treatment Facilities," TD, 15 May 1989, ANCC, OMH.

66. LTC Bomberger, "Outcomes of the Professional Development Course, 12–16 June 1989 — Bethesda, Maryland," TD, ANCC, OMH.

67. Claudia C. Bartz to Author, E-mail Correspondence, 1 February 2003, ANCC, OMH.

68. Terris Kennedy to Author, E-mail Correspondence, n.d., ANCC, OMH.

69. Clara L. Adams-Ender, Bonnie Jennings, Claudia Bartz, and Richard Jensen, "Nursing Practice Models, The Army Nurse Corps Experience," *Nursing & Health Care* 12 (March 1991): 120–23.

70. J.P. Riehl and C. Roy, "Theory and Models," *Conceptual Models for Nursing Practice*, second ed. (New York: Appleton-Century-Crofts, 1980), quoted in Terris E. Kennedy and others, "A Conceptual Model of Army Nursing Practice," *Nursing Management* 27 (October 1996): 33–36.

71. Terris E. Kennedy and others, "A Conceptual Model of Army Nursing Practice," *Nursing Management* 27 (October 1996): 33–36.

72. "Classes Scheduled FY81," 7 February 1981, Inclosure 4, in Hazel W. Johnson, "Information for All ANC Officers," 9 February 1981; and "Army Nurse Corps Course Schedules, FY 82," Inclosure 5, in Connie L. Slewitzke for Hazel W. Johnson, "Information for All ANC Officers," 27 November 1981 (both in ANCC, OMH).

73. Before 1982, the Army Nurse Corps called the Principles of Advanced Nursing Administration Course the Chief Nurse Orientation Course. Carolyn M. Feller and Debora R. Cox, *Highlights in the History of the Army Nurse Corps* (Washington, DC: U.S. Army Center of Military History, 2000), 53.

74. Carolyn M. Feller and Debora R. Cox, *Highlights in the History of the Army Nurse Corps* (Washington, DC: U.S. Army Center of Military History, 2000), 58.

75. The Air Force Nurse Corps began their transition to a graduate program in 1987. They closed their nurse anesthetist residency program at Wilford Hall Air Force Medical Center in San Antonio, Texas, that year and began sending 20 students to the University of Texas Health Science Center's School of Nursing in San Antonio in 1989 to complete a master's program in anesthesia. They also instituted a master's degree affiliation in nurse midwifery with Georgetown University in September 1988. The nurse midwife students took part in a clinical practicum at Malcolm Grow USAF Medical Center at Andrews Air Force Base, Maryland. Mary C. Smolenski, Donald G. Smith, and James S. Nanney, *A Fit, Fighting Force, The Air Force Nursing Services Chronology* (Washington, DC: Office of the Air Force Surgeon General, 2005), 42, 43, 44. Monte B. Miller, "Air Force Launches 'New Approaches'," *U.S. Medicine* 25 (January 1989): 45–46, 48.

76. Bernhard T. Mittemeyer, "Army Medical Department," *Military Medicine* 147 (November 1982): 919.

77. Kathleen Srsic-Stoehr, "AN Educational Opportunities," Information Paper, October 1988, ANCC, OMH. "Nurse Graduates Get Degree," *HSC Mercury* 15 (November 1987): 4. Carolyn M. Feller and Debora R. Cox, *Highlights in the History of the Army Nurse Corps* (Washington, DC: U.S. Army Center of Military History, 2000), 53.

78. John Sherner to Author, E-mail Correspondence, 11 August 2003, ANCC, OMH.

79. Carolyn R. Bulliner, "U.S. Army Nurse Corps Programs in Anesthesia Nursing, FY 00 Application Guidelines," Printed Brochure, n.d., ANCC, OMH.

80. U.S. Army Forces Command was the major command that included continental United States-based TO&E, or go-to-war, units. Kathleen Srsic-Stoehr, "AN Educational Opportunities," Information Paper, October 1988, ANCC, OMH.

81. Marlene Kramer, *Reality Shock: Why Nurses Leave Nursing* (St. Louis: Mosby, 1974). Claudia Schmalenberg and Marlene Kramer, *Coping with Reality Shock: The Voices of Experience* (Wakefield, MA: Nursing Resources, Inc., 1979), 1–30. Robin Isaak Chagares, "The Nurse Internship Question Revisited," *Supervisor Nurse* 11 (November 1980): 22–24.

82. Kathleen Srsic-Stoehr, "Transition to Practice: The Army Nurse Corps Preceptorship Program," Unpublished Manuscript, n.d., ANCC, OMH. The 1980 ANC Professional Development Workshop advanced the recommendation for such a preceptorship on 3 November 1980. Hazel W. Johnson, "Information for All ANC Officers," 7 November 1980, Inclosure 1, ANCC, OMH.

83. Bruce C. Allanach and Bonnie M. Jennings, "Evaluating the Effects of a Nurse Preceptorship Programme," *Journal of Advanced Nursing* 15 (1990): 22–28.

84. Major (P) Kennedy, "ANC Preceptorship Program," Information Paper, 21 March 1983, ANCC, OMH.

85. Jane Y. Yaws, "The Army Nurse Corps Preceptorship Program," *Military Medicine* 152 (August 1987): 411–13.

86. Don Washington, "Nurse Internship Program Eases Transition to AF," *Air Force Times* 49 (24 October 1988): 21. Paul W. Myers, "Air Force Holding Optimistic Outlook," *U.S. Medicine* 17 (15 January 1981): 61–62. Randall H. Smith, "The Air Force Nurse Intern Program," *Military Medicine* 156 (August 1991): 417–19. Mary C. Smolenski, Donald G. Smith, and James S. Nanney, *A Fit, Fighting Force, The Air Force Nursing Services Chronology* (Washington, DC: Office of the Air Force Surgeon General, 2005), 36.

87. Connie L. Slewitzke to Author, E-mail Correspondence, 21 January 2003, ANCC, OMH.

88. Connie L. Slewitzke, Interview by Beverly Greenlee, 386–87, n.d., USAWC/USAMHI Senior Officer Oral History Program, Project No. 88-8; and Connie L. Slewitzke to Author, E-mail Correspondence, 21 January 2003 (both in ANCC, OMH).

89. Connie L. Slewitzke, Interview by Beverly Greenlee, 387–89, n.d., USAWC/USAMHI Senior Officer Oral History Program, Project No. 88-8, ANCC, OMH.

90. Connie L. Slewitzke to Author, E-mail Correspondence, 21 January 2003, ANCC, OMH. Other participants included Major Charlene Walker, Lieutenant Colonel Jude Larkin, and Major Frances Davison in 1985. "ANC Annual Historical Report FY 85," 2, ANCC, OMH. In 1986, additional fellows included Captain Rita Schulte, Lieutenant Colonel Dennis Rieker, Lieutenant Colonel Jean Reeder, Major Elaine Mayo, and Lieutenant Colonel Gar Yip. "Army Nurse Corps (ANC) 1986 Annual Historical Report," 3, ANCC, OMH.

91. Connie L. Slewitzke, Interview by Beverly Greenlee, 389, n.d., USAWC/USAMHI Senior Officer Oral History Program, Project No. 88-8, ANCC, OMH.

92. Kathleen Srsic-Stoehr to Author, E-mail Correspondence, 16 January 2003, ANCC, OMH.

93. Gar Yip, "After Action Report of ANC Fellowship for LTC Gar Yip, 16 November 1986–13 Feb 1987," Memorandum for Record, 13 February 1987, ANCC, OMH.

94. Nancy Molter to Author, E-mail Correspondence, 13 March 2003, ANCC, OMH.

95. "ANC Staff Officer Fellow Orientation," Memorandum for Record, 30 January 1986; and Clara L. Adams-Ender, "Management Fellow, Office of the Chief, Army Nurse Corps," Memorandum for Record, 6 January 1988 (both in ANCC, OMH). Clara L. Adams-Ender, "Management Fellow, Office of the Chief, Army Nurse Corps," TM for Record, 2 October 1990, ANCC, OMH. Carolyn M. Feller and Debora R. Cox, *Highlights in the History of the Army Nurse Corps* (Washington, DC: U.S. Army Center of Military History, 2000), 58. Connie L. Slewitzke, Interview by Beverly Greenlee, 390, n.d., USAWC/USAMHI Senior

Officer Oral History Program, Project No. 88-8, ANCC, OMH.

96. Department of the Army, AR 601-100, paragraph 2-61, October 1974; and Department of the Army, DA Circular 01-68, "Army Nurse Corps Active Duty Program Fiscal Year 1977 through 15 January 1978," 13 October 1977 (both in ANCC, OMH).

97. H.R. 2461. "Plan Would Lower Nurse Education Standards," *Army Times* 49 (10 July 1989): 18. Vincent H. Demma, *Department of the Army Historical Summary, Fiscal Year 1989* (Washington, DC: Center of Military History, United States Army, 1998), 167.

98. The Air Force had required a bachelor of science in nursing for all newly accessed officers since 1979. However, in 1987, it accepted applicants for commissioning with an associate degree or a diploma in nursing if the applicant had a baccalaureate degree in another health science field as well. Linda J. Stierle, "Presentation to the Committee on Appropriations, Subcommittee on Defense, United States Senate," April 1998, ANCC, OMH. Colonel John Hudock recalled that "the *minimum* requirement for all other Army active duty commissioned officers was a baccalaureate degree. Why should the ANC be any different? Because the 'hidden' agenda here was that if we took less than BSN on active duty, we would then be forced to have less than commissioned officer nurses—i.e., warrant officers again!" John Hudock to Author, Handwritten Letter, 15 September 2003, ANCC, OMH.

99. "Plan Would Lower Nurse Education Standards," *Army Times* 49 (10 July 1989): 18. Clara L. Adams-Ender, Interview by Virginia Ruth Cheney, 90, 1992, Project 92-3, U.S. Army Military History Institute, Senior Officer Oral History Program, ANCC, OMH.

100. Clara L. Adams-Ender, Interview by Virginia Ruth Cheney, 93–95, 1992, Project 92-3, U.S. Army Military History Institute, Senior Officer Oral History Program, ANCC, OMH.

101. Ruby F. Bryant and others to Daniel K. Inouye, TL, 4 October 1989, ANCC, OMH.

102. Daniel K. Inouye to Clara L. Adams-Ender, TL, 6 November 1989, ANCC, OMH. John Hudock to Author, Telephone Interview, 7 March 2003.

103. Clara L. Adams-Ender, Interview by Virginia Ruth Cheney, 95–96, 1992, Project 92-3, U.S. Army Military History Institute, Senior Officer Oral History Program, ANCC, OMH.

*Chapter Ten*
# The Shortage Intensifies

One major and recurring issue that the Army Medical Department (AMEDD) faced during the 1980s was a critical, wide-ranging shortage of personnel. Severe shortages of physicians and nurses existed in all components—Active, National Guard, and Reserve—for almost the entire decade. A shortage of enlisted medical specialists, the paraprofessionals who provided assistance and support services, exacerbated the situation. Inadequate training of enlisted service members and their lack of satisfactory qualifications also worsened the state of affairs. These trends also appeared in every echelon of the Army and the AMEDD and permeated the affairs of the Army Nurse Corps. The Surgeon General judged the disparity in pay between the military and civilian sectors as responsible for these shortages and deficiencies.[1] However, the dearth of personnel was not only limited to the Army but also was a worrisome issue in the civilian health care system.

In the 1980s, professional nursing literature reported dire staffing circumstances in the civilian world.[2] The nurse shortages were so profound that the U.S. Department of Health and Human Services Division of Health Professions Analysis studied the issues, conferred with stakeholders, compiled statistics, and published a report in 1981 that would serve "in a broad interpretive context" as a framework to enhance understanding and expand the dialogue and scrutiny of pertinent issues.[3] Its findings oversimplified the economic interpretation of a highly complex problem and were predicated on the fact that nursing was a predominantly female profession highly sensitive to pay trends. The study revealed that nurses participated in the workforce at about the same rate as women in other analogous career fields and experienced approximately the same number of problems as did those in similar occupations with a significant ratio of female to male workers. When nurses' salaries steadily rose in the late 1960s after the introduction of Medicare, according to the report, the supply of nurses correspondingly increased. This trend continued until 1976 when, inexplicably, nurses' wages became static in relation to those of other predominantly female professions. By 1978, there was a definite decrease in entrants into nursing educational programs, probably because females then took advantage of other professional options virtually denied them in the past. The report forecast that the continued shortage of professional nurses would endure until relative wages improved. This meant that little could "be done either to hasten the market processes that must unfold or to dampen the cyclical fluctuations in the nurse labor market."[4]

Intensifying the nurse shortage, the numbers of college students considering a nursing career dwindled in the 1980s and also created a situation with long-range implications for Army Nurse Corps recruiting. In 1984, 63,257 students expected to become nurses. In 1985, that number fell to 53,321, a 16 percent decrease. In 1986, only 42,846 college students planned to major in nursing, approximately a 20 percent reduction, or an overall decrease of 33 percent from 1984 to 1986.[5]

Shortages of available nurses worsened over the years. The American Hospital Association claimed in 1987 that nationwide nurse vacancy rates stood at 13.5 percent and had more than doubled within a year.[6] Contributing to the problem were decreased interest among young women in nursing as a career, the ill-advised use of nurses by administrators for nonnursing tasks, and low wages despite an individual nurse's expanding educational level or increased experience.[7]

The AMEDD attributed the crisis within the military to the competition for nurses in a market where civilian hospitals were providing outstanding improvements in work scheduling, better staffing ratios, and enhanced benefit packages.[8] Baptist Medical Center in Columbia, South Carolina, for instance, offered a $1,200 bonus to new hires. Employees who recruited another nurse also received $1,200. Providence Hospital in Columbia, South Carolina, offered similar enticements and paid nurses who worked two 12-hour weekend shifts the same amount as a 40-hour week.[9] Some hospitals in Denver, Colorado, relied on benefits such as no-cost child care and free cars to attract nurses.[10]

The shortages prevalent in the civilian sector were much worse in the Army Nurse Corps. The Army considered the shortfalls a "war stopper," meaning the deficits were so dire that they would prevent or seriously inhibit the Army from going into combat.[11] In fiscal year (FY) 1981 there was a slight incongruity between the Army Nurse Corps actual and authorized year-end strengths, 3,833 and 3,859, respectively. Still, the Corps perceived a pressing need for more nurses because manpower team surveys calculated huge discrepancies between authorized levels and required strength numbers. The Air Force Nurse Corps (AFNC) found itself in similar circumstances. In 1981, it reported an actual year-end strength of 4,149 officers vis-à-vis an authorized total of 4,141. It too predicted that more nurses would be required as the Air Force physician shortage resolved because more physicians generated a need for more nurses.[12] The AFNC traditionally had more officers than the Army, and its professional staffing was "plush"—in part, because it did not rely on licensed practical nurses to any great extent, and having smaller hospitals required proportionately larger staffs to maintain than bigger hospitals.[13] In other words, those hospitals that operated fewer beds usually were less efficient personnel wise than larger hospitals.[14]

By 1982, the Army Nurse Corps authorized year-end strength increased slightly to 3,891. However, at that time, manpower survey teams calculated personnel requirements at 6,343.[15] Authorizations increased slightly again in 1983 and 1984 to 4,038 and 4,142, respectively.[16] Nonetheless, the glaring incongruities between authorized and required numbers not only persisted, but also the gap steadily widened.[17] In FY 1988, the Army Nurse Corps requirements for the active component stood at 7,417, with the authorizations set at 5,018.[18]

Also affecting the problem was the fact that during the 1980s, the Army Nurse Corps transitioned from using the Health Services Command manpower survey team as a tool for calculating requirements to using the Workload Management System for Nurses. The former, the Health Services Command manpower survey team, used a staffing guide—outdated even in the 1970s—with yardsticks as standards and extra personnel allowances based on added missions, greater acuity of patients, and physical facility factors. These criteria guided the local appraisal, conducted every two years, which was at best a subjective assessment to arrive at nursing requirements. The Workload Management System for Nurses, however, was an objective system that portrayed more accurately the required numbers of nurses needed to handle the workload. Other factors that caused the requirements to surge in the 1980s were the greater level of patient acuity, advanced technological complexity, and larger patient censuses.[19]

In 1986, 1987, and 1988, the Army Nurse Corps recruited only 26.2 percent, 38 percent, and 21.4 percent of its goals, respectively. Analogous statistics for the Navy Nurse Corps showed an 89.6 percent attainment in 1986, 97.9 percent in 1987, but a dramatic plunge to 17.5 percent in 1988 as the shortage intensified. The AFNC achievement of recruiting goals, recorded as 39.9 percent, 39.2 percent, and 36.9 percent during the same time, demonstrated the greatest consistency.[20] After recruitment but before commissioning, almost half of Army Nurse Corps applicants withdrew because the salary for beginning second lieutenants was about $3,000 less annually than starting salaries offered in civilian hospitals. Compounding the servicewide shortage was the significant numbers of nurses who chose to leave the military after their first tour, most citing better civilian-sector pay as their reason for departing.[21] From 1986 to 1988, the Army documented retention rates (the percentage of Army nurses who chose to remain in the Army after their first commitment) at 66 percent, 62 percent, and 62 percent.[22] The Navy reported similar statistics of 66 percent, 54 percent, and 57 percent. The Air Force kept a slightly larger percentage of their nurses, 70 percent in 1986 and 1987 and 69 percent in 1988. Adding to the staffing woes were the unfilled civilian nurse positions. In 1988, the Army had a civilian vacancy rate of 10 percent; the Navy, 20 percent; and the Air Force, 6 percent.[23] By 1990, the statistics revealed improvements in the nurse corps officer retention. That year, the AFNC reported 90 percent retention, the Army cited 70 percent retention, and the Navy Nurse Corps had only a 60 percent rate of retention for civilian nurses.[24]

Planners in the Department of Defense (DoD) Office of Reserve Medical

Planning also predicted huge mobilization shortfalls in the ranks of military reserve nurses. Post–Vietnam War reserve forces doctrine specified that, in times of war, reserve components would assume the bulk of responsibility for care of sick and wounded combatants.[25] Doctrine allocated responsibility for 70 percent of the AMEDD's field hospitals and 90 percent of the Air Force's medical evacuation crews to the U.S. Army Reserve (USAR) or Army National Guard (ARNG). In the event of a large-scale war, planners projected a need for 43,500 nurses across the three military services. However, as of March 1982, only 20,500 (or 47 percent) of the required Active, Guard, Reserve total force nurses were available. Shortages were most marked among numbers of operating room nurses and anesthetists. Surgical specialties in all DoD reserve component units were 60 percent below authorizations for operating room nurses and 59 percent below authorizations for nurse anesthetists.

To obtain more reservists, a DoD task force recommended that these specialists be allowed to participate in military-sponsored professional courses, offered financial assistance to underwrite anesthesia education, and encouraged to actively participate in professional nursing organizations, presumably during their active duty for training time. The services also eliminated the red tape in the reserve application process, thereby reducing the lag time from submission of request to commission as an Army Nurse Corps officer from three to four months to 30 days.[26] These measures failed to avert the looming crisis. The Army Nurse Corps saw little improvement in the reserve numbers. By 1987, the Corps had only 35 percent of nurse anesthetists and 50 percent of operating room nurses required for mobilization.[27]

One strategy to bridge the gap was to employ civilian registered nurses in Army Nurse Corps positions. The situation was so serious that the Corps dropped its long-held reservations regarding the use of civilian professional nurses. Nonetheless, the supply of Army-employed civilian nurses also failed to meet demand. As of September 1981, 2,162 civil servants were working as professional nurses in Army health care facilities worldwide.[28] By FY 1984, however, the AMEDD's Civil Service Registered Nurse (CSRN) workforce had a vacancy rate of 18 percent and a voluntary resignation rate of 12.6 percent, which rose to 19.1 percent in FY 1987.[29] By 1990, the vacancy rate for CSRNs exceeded 24 percent and turnover was a turbulent 20 percent.[30] Upon resignation, CSRNs revealed various satisfaction or dissatisfaction factors either in questionnaires or comments. Satisfaction factors included practicing in a patient-focused environment—most notably with professional and clinical autonomy—providing care for a challenging population of patients, and working under the clear command and control structure in the military.[31] Dissatisfaction factors included the unsettling and frequently changing duty shift rotations, bleak career-development prospects, recurrent conflicts with military nurses, supervisors' inattention to the federal civil service system, and salary rates.[32] In 1987, outgoing Assistant Chief of the Corps Colonel Eily P. Gorman—with characteristic keen insight—advised the incoming chief, Brigadier General Clara L. Adams-Ender, that there were some correctable

Pictured is Colonel Eily P. Gorman, Assistant Chief of the Army Nurse Corps (1987). Photo courtesy of Army Nurse Corps Archives, Office of Medical History, Falls Church, VA.

issues, specifically the work and time schedules and interpersonal relationship difficulties. She emphasized, however, that nurse administrators needed to be encouraged to address the concerns. Gorman acknowledged that the austere career development opportunities for CSRNs made for a difficult situation:

> We can hardly stand (in terms of recruiting and retaining green suiters) to have fewer opportunities for ANC development, nor to have RNs [CSRNs] with lower educational attainment, in supervisory role[s] over persons [Army nurses] with higher edu[cational] level[s]. But we should have our perfor-

mance standards for [the] ANC written so that differences in education—as well as in rank—can be seen to make a difference in responsibilities and patient care.[33]

Gorman noted that some installations had already begun writing such standards and recommended that an ad hoc group examine the issues.[34] Subsequently, a Civil Service Task Force composed of both military and civilians met in 1988 to develop a lateral progression of opportunities for career advancement for CSRNs.[35] The task force's consensus was that the Army Nurse Corps should develop incentives that were *individually* based to facilitate lateral progression" or CSRN recognition. The task force hoped that incentives would motivate the individual's professional development and ultimately improve patient care. Thus, the task force recommended civil service grade and step increases for deserving employees. Criteria such as the employee's work toward educational advancement, participation in continuing professional education, personal improvement through specialty training, credentialing or certification, research activities, writing for publication, contributions to hospital committees, and active membership in professional organizations were the basis for justifying advancement.[36]

The CSRNs' pay issues were most difficult to resolve. Title 5, U.S. Code, the General Schedule (GS) pay scale, dictated a fixed salary for CSRNs in military hospitals. In contrast, the Veterans' Administration hospitals and later the National Institutes of Health employed nurses under the authority of Title 38, U.S. Code, which allowed "flexibility . . . for entry level salaries to be established to remain competitive with civilian medical facilities wage and salary schedules."[37] For economic reasons, civilian registered nurses gravitated to Veterans' Administration hospitals because they offered more equitable and generous salaries for comparable duties compared with military hospitals.

DoD supported various pieces of legislation to attract and retain CSRNs. Some bills never became law and others took years to be enacted.[38] Nonetheless, the Army did obtain legislative approval to grant special pay categories for civilian nurses in high-cost areas, for those who functioned as charge nurses, and for those who practiced in critical-care settings.[39] To cut the lengthy application and hiring process, the U.S. Office of Personnel Management granted direct-hire authority to local military installations for nurses at the levels of GS-5, GS-7, and GS-9.[40] Moreover, Health Services Command advertised in national publications to attract more civilians. In the early 1980s, the Army Nurse Corps also authorized civilian participation in Area of Concentration courses and incorporated instruction about Department of Army Civilian issues into the Program of Instruction for the Officer Basic Course in April 1988.[41] These improvements failed to alleviate the CSRN shortage.[42] Clearly, CSRNs were an essential element of the nursing force in Army hospitals. The unsafe dearth in their numbers seriously affected the ability of the Army to provide quality nursing care.

Adams-Ender, chief of the Army Nurse Corps from 1987 to 1991, referred to CSRNs as "Army nurses in disguise."[43] Actually, many CSRNs were simultaneously Army nurses in the USAR or ARNG. Colonel John M. Hudock recalled that when "attempting to identify the numbers upon mobilization, many MTFs in

Colonel John M. Hudock, left, Assistant Chief of the Army Nurse Corps from 1987 to 1991, accepts the Legion of Merit award from General Clara L. Adams-Ender, right, on the occasion of his retirement in September 1991.
Photo courtesy of Colonel John Hudock, Hazleton, PA.

CONUS [military treatment facilities in the continental United States] would be short civilian nurses because they mobilized as Army Nurses." Hudock noted that when he retired in 1991, civilian personnel offices "were still trying to sort out the numbers. The nurse shortage problem was actually amplified by the 'double counting'." Like the CSRNs, many contract nurses served in dual roles. While they worked as temporary or agency nurses in Army hospitals, they also were Army Nurse Corps officers in the USAR or ARNG.[44]

On a grassroots level, Army nurses worked diligently to compensate for the insufficient staff. At Moncrief Army Community Hospital, Fort Jackson, South Carolina, shortages were particularly grave in 1988. Local staffing agencies could not provide Moncrief Army Community Hospital with contract nurses to supplement the permanent staff, and no replacements were available for the 7.5 civilian nurse vacancies. Fifteen Army Nurse Corps officers transferred from the hospital that year but it received only eight replacements, none of whom were the urgently needed company grade (captain or lieutenant) medical-surgical nurses.[45] One medical ward and the labor and delivery suite were forced into 12-hour shifts. Nursing supervisors admitted and discharged patients, transcribed orders, and did what they could to actively help the ward staff. Even in these difficult circumstances, nurses continued to draw blood samples after the laboratory staff made their daily morning rounds and they continued to transport patients throughout the hospital. Most department of nursing employees were extremely dissatisfied and resigned their positions when they could.[46]

At Fitzsimons Army Medical Center (FAMC) in Aurora, Colorado, staff frustration underscored the extreme shortages of personnel and funding. Brigadier General Thomas Geer, the FAMC commander, admitted to sending patients to local civilian hospitals for care on a daily basis because there were not enough nurses. Major William Marx, a surgeon, acknowledged that often he did not know who would have surgery until the last minute, adding that FAMC had patients lined up "outside the operating room door, waiting to see who will get in and who won't." Major Kate Robertson, head nurse of the Surgical Intensive Care Unit, lamented that if there was insufficient nursing staff, "someone's brain surgery or heart surgery gets postponed."[47] Marx affirmed that FAMC was "top-heavy with doctors, but we can't get enough nurses." Consequently, nurses worked doubly hard. Major Sheila Harris, head nurse of the Coronary Care Unit, asserted that the nurses gave "110 percent constantly. You do more than should really be expected of you." The military nurses also carried most of the overtime burden. Since the hospital had to "pay overtime to the civilian nurses but not military nurse officers, the latter [were] asked to work extra hours when necessary." Marx concluded that "just to maintain, we abuse our military nurses."[48]

Similarly bleak working conditions existed at other Army medical centers. An unflattering investigative report published in *Reader's Digest* divulged that personnel shortages compelled the commander of the Walter Reed Army Medical Center (WRAMC) to close four of 17 operating rooms at one point during the 1980s.[49] In the summer of 1985, WRAMC had to close 80 beds, or two average-sized wards, because of shortfalls in the numbers of nurses and administrative staff.[50] In this same period, the Joint Commission for the Accreditation of Hospitals threatened to rescind its accreditation of Madigan Army Medical Center, Tacoma, Washington, because of staffing deficiencies, particularly intensive care nurses. A second civilian health care professional panel reviewed the situation at Madigan and declared the ratio of professional nurses "to lesser trained staff" was unacceptable.[51] At Brooke Army Medical Center, similar unsatisfactory circumstances existed. There, patients languished, waiting in a queue for about three months to be hospitalized for orthopedic surgery.[52]

Navy nurses also had concerns. A study quoted one Navy nurse: "I believe it is very dangerous, with 2 nurses on a 40-bed ward, with corpsmen staff . . . to supervise closely, but cannot, due to overworked nurses." Another complaint about "always being asked to do more with less (people, supplies, etc.) is very discouraging. . . . Administrators seem more concerned with paperwork . . . than they are with the population we are trying to serve."[53]

A 1988 Air Force study revealed that 46 percent of Air Force nurses worked 50 hours or more a week and 59 percent considered their nursing unit understaffed. Moreover, 53 percent of the Air Force nurses responding to the questionnaire believed that "the compensation received is 'less' to 'much less' than the contribution they make toward health care service in the Air Force."[54]

A draft study report written by the Association of the United States Army, an unofficial, independent organization, concluded:

> The Army has not exactly covered itself with glory in its treatment of nurses compared to other professions in the AMEDD. The accession, utilization and promotion policies of the Nurse Corps indicate a lack of imagination, image and fulfillment.[55]

It added:

> The mixture of military nurses and civilian nurses seemingly helps solve the problem. It also exacerbates the problem. From a labor relations point of view, the mixing of military, civilian, general schedule, civilian personnel contract, and other civilian contract personnel would try the patience of Job and require the labor acumen of Samuel Gompers, John L. Lewis, and Sidney Hilsman combined.
>
> How the Army does as well as it does with the nurses it has is a tribute to the dedication of these great people.[56]

Although the dimensions of the Army nurse shortage were overwhelming for a while, they were not insurmountable. A combination of evolving conditions in the civilian nursing world, a tincture of time, and a collection of ingenious strategies ultimately rectified that particular iteration of the nurse shortage problem. Both Brigadier General Connie L. Slewitzke and her successor, General Clara L. Adams-Ender, as Chief, Army Nurse Corps, worked to improve recruitment and retention. They initiated a large-scale survey of Army Nurse Corps officers to gather opinions, solicit ideas for solutions, and gauge levels of satisfaction.[57] They also convened focus groups to strategize on the issues. In addition, they conferred with the sister services, the Navy Nurse Corps and AFNC, to create a unified approach.[58]

Slewitzke and Adams-Ender also directed the concentrated intelligence of the annual Army Nurse Corps Strategic Planning Conference to brainstorm on issues and their solutions.[59] They supported unit-level efforts in the military treatment facilities to find answers to the shortages.[60] They answered numerous inquiries about the shortage from congressional and Department of Army levels.[61] They also enlisted the support of the Defense Advisory Committee on Women in the Services that in turn recommended "that the Secretary of Defense take timely and positive action to resolve nurse accession, retention, compensation, promotion, and motivation issues."[62] Finally, they implemented their carefully considered plans to augment numbers in the Active Army (COMPO 1), the ARNG (COMPO 2), and the Reserve (COMPO 3).[63]

At congressional direction, the Army Nurse Corps conceived, recommended, and carried out several recruitment and retention strategies. Major incentives to improve recruitment of Army nurses to the active component and make the Corps competitive with civilian hospitals included the Army Nurse Candidate Program and the Army Nurse Corps Accession Bonus Program.

The Army paid nursing students in the Army Nurse Candidate Program $500 monthly for the final two years of their collegiate program and subsequently awarded them a one-time $5,000 accession bonus when they were commissioned. In return, candidates agreed to serve on active duty for no fewer than four years. This program started in May 1990. By 1993, 91 nursing students were enrolled, and program participation grew steadily every year.[64]

The Army Nurse Corps Accession Bonus Program also offered a one-time $5,000 accession bonus to any eligible registered nurse who accepted a commission and agreed to serve on active duty for at least four years. As early as May 1990, the Army was processing 186 application packets for these programs.[65] The Army also implemented the program on a test basis for USAR recruiting in selected states. By 1993, the Army Nurse Corps leadership justifiably considered the program successful. In those states included in the test program, almost all available vacancies in the USAR were filled. Based on these results, the leadership speculated, expanding the program across the country would be a worthwhile venture.[66]

Another proposal to open a collegiate nursing program at the Uniformed Services University of the Health Sciences (USUHS) surfaced as an option to deal with the militarywide nursing shortage in the late 1980s.[67] This was an old idea. In April 1974, the Army considered closing the Walter Reed Army Institute of Nursing (WRAIN) because of the limited budget. At that time, The Surgeon General asked the USUHS Board of Regents to consider assuming responsibility for a baccalaureate program in nursing. The board rejected this proposal because of the lackluster retention rate of WRAIN graduates. Of the 925 students who began the WRAIN program between 1964 and 1969, only 562 (61 percent) completed the course, and among graduates, only 232 (41 percent) fulfilled their service commitment. By 1974, only 51 (22 percent) of those who fulfilled their obligation were still on active duty.[68] In 1976, when WRAIN was closing, USUHS reconsidered the proposal.[69] A USUHS Feasibility Study Group for a School of Nursing composed of nurse officers from all the federal services analyzed the issues and proposed options.[70] The group's most favored solution was to subsidize education in civilian institutions to achieve "a varied program selection, cheaper cost, less drain on available manpower, and cross fertilization resulting from exposure to diverse philosophies of education." If that option was unacceptable, an alternative was to establish a USUHS School of Nursing as a two-year upper-division course or a three-year accelerated baccalaureate program. All "other options considered would prove most difficult to justify and defend in any budget hearing."[71] Since the shortage in military nurse accessions was gradually resolving, the board of regents did not act, concluding that although "the University stands ready to discuss any future need, it did not plan to become involved in nursing education at that time."[72] Because nursing shortages are cyclical, so too are repetitive solutions, and this idea resurfaced about a decade later.

In 1989, Army Nurse Corps leaders collaborated with the other uniformed services to again probe the feasibility of a baccalaureate program in nursing at USUHS. An AMEDD Office of The Surgeon General task force had recommended to the secretary of the Army the restoration of an educational program that would allow the Army to educate its own baccalaureate nurses."[73] Jay P. Sanford, the dean of USUHS's medical school, responded by appointing Rear Admiral Faye G. Abdellah, a nurse who had served as the deputy surgeon general of the U.S. Public Health Service, to chair an ad hoc committee composed of representatives from the federal nursing services. Sanford instructed them to investigate the possibility of setting up a college of nursing within USUHS. The task force recommended a program "that would combine both academic and professional education with operational readiness, allow for multiple entry and exit options, and provide both baccalaureate and graduate programs." Members proposed admitting sufficient full-time students to graduate 300 nurses annually for the uniformed nursing services. Graduates would agree to active duty and reserve service in exchange for their education.[74] The Army, Navy, and Air Force surgeons general were reluctant to endorse the plan, however, predicting that, once more, low retention rates would plague the program. Consequently, the board of regents rejected the task force's recommendations.[75] The veto of the surgeons general was strange. Since May 1978, Army regulations prohibited female officers from having their service obligations for educational subsidies forgiven by reason of pregnancy, the usual cause for attrition in females in the past.[76]

However, other factors were involved. Brigadier General Hazel Johnson, the last director of WRAIN, thought that a baccalaureate program "would have been a costly effort in terms of personnel." "Then again," she added, "did we want an undergraduate school in a school where all other students were in graduate education." She judged it better to handpick students from across the country and subsidize their education with the Reserve Officers' Training Corps (ROTC) in civilian institutions rather than opening a school and moving all the students there. Johnson emphasized the importance of a "diversity of philosophies which has been a strength of the Corps, bringing together people from a variety of backgrounds to work together."[77] Moreover, by the early 1990s, there were adequate numbers of military nurses and some even saw a glut, a dramatic upswing typical in the aftermath of nursing shortages. Furthermore, all three military nursing branches, like their services, were appreciably reducing personnel. Taken together, these factors contributed to the rejection of an undergraduate college of nursing at USUHS. The concept of having a permanent military entry-level nursing program fell victim to the circumstances of the post–Cold War period—budget constraints, difficulties in starting a new program when the Army was cutting divisions, high attrition rates, insufficient faculty, a lack of educational diversity, a dearth of clinical practicum sites, and unpredictability in the supply of nurses.

Having failed to gain the approval to establish a baccalaureate program, the planning group instead deliberated about opening a graduate program to educate family nurse practitioners, nurse anesthetists, and nurse midwives for the uniformed services. Senator Daniel K. Inouye was the strongest congressional ally for the Graduate School of Nursing (GSN) at USUHS. Through his efforts, Congress appropriated funds to support the school's opening and operation.[78] The charter class of three family nurse practitioner students—all affiliated with the U.S. Public Health Services—began their studies in the summer of 1993. When the nurse anesthetist program earned academic accreditation in 1994, eight students matriculated in that advanced practice specialty.[79] The original demand for family nurse practitioners emanated from the U.S. Public Health Service. The push to open a facility to educate nurse anesthetists came from the U.S. Air Force because these specialists were in great demand in the smaller Air Force hospitals. Both the U.S. Public Health Service and the Air Force encountered great difficulty in recruiting and retaining these specialties.[80] In these early days, the Army did not participate in these programs.

According to the Army surgeon general, Lieutenant General Alcide LaNoue (1992–1996), the AMEDD would not furnish faculty for the school because Army nurses were in short supply as a result of Army-wide personnel reductions. Nor could the AMEDD sponsor Army students at USUHS, particularly in the anesthesia program, because it was supporting its own nurse anesthesia education program for direct accession applicants. AMEDD treatment facilities could not offer the USUHS students hands-on anesthesia clinical experience because their own internal anesthesia program was making full use of clinical facilities in the Washington, D.C., area.[81]

Brigadier General Nancy R. Adams, chief of the Army Nurse Corps (1991–1995), adopted a similar position regarding the GSN at USUHS. Adams was concerned that active participation in the GSN program would detract from the Corps ability to support students in civilian educational curriculums, adding that Army nurses' attendance in civilian venues showcased the Army Nurse Corps talent to its civilian counterparts and helped to recruit new officers. Adams also favored

Several Army nurses served as the commandant of the Graduate School of Nursing at the Uniformed Services University of Health Sciences. One of those was Colonel Constance J. Moore. Photo courtesy of Colonel Constance J. Moore, El Paso, TX.

the exposure to a wide diversity of civilian programs that ultimately contributed to the Corps diverse pool of professional knowledge but conceded that using the USUHS facilities for the didactic phase of anesthesia education made sense because of the exposure afforded to the cutting-edge science courses already made available for the medical students. Still, she had significant reservations about the proposed advanced practice programs at USUHS because of the intense competition for practicum sites in the D.C. area and her reservations "about the influence of the medical model for the preparation of advanced practice nurses."[82] Adams believed that a "strong nursing component was lacking" at USUHS because the school was "essentially isolated from a mainstream academic setting" of nursing. She was convinced that "the motivation to have a nursing program was an attempt to increase the support of the school to make it more difficult to close." During President Clinton's administration, several attempts surfaced favoring the closure of USUHS. Their overriding objective was to save money. Within one year, the U.S. Senate successfully countered the first proposal spearheaded by Vice-President Albert Gore, Jr. Senator Russell Feingold subsequently introduced another legislative attempt to close USUHS. Senators Daniel Inouye and Sam Nunn effectively laid that scheme to rest with the dissemination of a highly favorable 1995 GAO (Government Accountability Office) report.[83]

With new Army Nurse Corps leadership in 1996 and the continuing evolution of the GSN, the Army Nurse Corps relationship with the GSN at USUHS changed. The new chief of the Corps, General Bettye Simmons, sent a few Army students to USUHS to maintain the educational diversity of the Corps while simultaneously demonstrating Army support of USUHS in "deed as in word." The Army Nurse Corps then found the program "sound." Colonel Susan McCall, the new assistant chief of the Corps, saw a faculty linked with mainstream academia and publishing in professional journals. The Army Nurse Corps began to assign officers as faculty, and even the commandant of the GSN was an Army Nurse Corps officer. McCall and Simmons envisioned the GSN at USUHS as an opportunity to offer graduate education to more Army nurses when educational funding was diminishing. Henceforth, the Army Nurse Corps participated and supported the institution. Shortages among the ranks of nurse anesthetists and nurse practitioners were important factors in the establishment of the GSN. However, the Army Nurse Corps also implemented other measures to recruit and retain these and other specialists.

To relieve the extreme shortages of nurse anesthetists, Congress approved incentive pay for Certified Registered Nurse Anesthetists (CRNAs) in 1989. The Army Nurse Corps offered eligible CRNAs as much as $6,000 annually as incentive special pay to remain on active duty.[84] This was the first time Congress passed legislation to award special pay bonuses to Army Nurse Corps officers.[85]

By 1994, it became clear that compensation in the form of incentive pay was failing to retain CRNAs.[86] In the 1989 "Proud to Care" survey, Army Nurse Corps anesthetists cited monetary compensation as their most important point of dissatisfaction. Many expressed their unhappiness by leaving the service. In FY 1992 and FY 1993, an alarming 50 and 40 percent of the CRNAs, respectively, resigned their commissions before eligibility for retirement and immediately after fulfilling their active duty service obligation.[87] Consequently, Congress passed and the president signed another bill into law that authorized an increase in the maximum amount of incentive pay available for payment to certain specialists, including CRNAs, to $15,000 annually.[88] Adams noted this measure's ultimate success in affecting the retention of CRNAs, reporting that in FY 1995, 25 such specialists were eligible to separate from active duty after completing four years of obligated service. Of the 25, only three decided to leave active duty.[89] Moreover, other nonphysician health care providers in all three military services became eligible to apply for the benefit, newly referred to as Board Certification Pay (BCP). To qualify for the pay, the nurse provider needed a master's degree in the appropriate specialty, board certification, and local hospital privileging in the specialty. The applicant for BCP also had to substantiate years of creditable service because computation of the pay was based on years of service in the specialty.[90] By May 1997, 309 Army Nurse Corps officers were receiving BCP. The group included 210 nurse anesthetists, 25 family nurse practitioners, 27 adult nurse practitioners, 23 pediatric nurse practitioners, 11 obstetrics/gynecology nurse practitioners, and 13 midwives. Certain Army community health nurses and clinical nurse specialists also became eligible for BCP in 1997. At that time, one psychiatric clinical nurse specialist privileged by WRAMC to prescribe and refill certain psychotropic drugs applied for and was awarded BCP.[91]

In another effort to augment the supply of Army nurses, the Army Nurse Corps also increased the number of ROTC scholarships offered to collegiate nursing students. However, this effort did not produce many more ROTC cadets. In school year 1988–1989, it made available 40 four-year, 89 three-year, and 37 two-year ROTC scholarships. In school year 1989–1990, the number of four-year scholarships increased to 293; three-year scholarships increased to 174; and two-year scholarships increased to 69. Nevertheless, several students declined ROTC scholarships, leaving some scholarships unused.[92] From 1988, numbers of ROTC cadets on scholarships fell for the next two years.[93] To reinvigorate the program, the ROTC Cadet Command implemented "Operation Golden Gale," a program designed to spark the interest of high school students in Army nursing. In 1989, ROTC had available 750 Golden Gale scholarships for nursing students. The Army Nurse Corps also assigned four additional recruiters to find potential cadets. By 1989, 13 Army Nurse Corps officers were actively recruiting for ROTC, including the ROTC command chief nurse, four regional chief nurses, and eight nurse counselors.[94]

The ROTC Command also used the Green to Gold program to educate more nurses for the Army. With the assistance of local commanders, the AMEDD Green to Gold Operation identified those enlisted soldiers in the AMEDD that demonstrated the potential to become officers and facilitated their transition from active military service into civilian collegiate nursing programs by simultaneously recruiting them into ROTC.

The Army discharged enlisted soldiers who participated in this program and ended all previous pay entitlements and allowances. The discharged soldiers then received ROTC scholarships augmented by the new GI bill or the Army College Fund. A ROTC counterpart battalion and the in-service recruiters assisted participants in completing applications for ROTC scholarships. Soldiers had to have served at least two years on active duty to be eligible and apply for an early release for entry into the ROTC Nursing Program.

For the two-year scholarship, a Green to Gold participant needed the equivalent education of a college junior and, for a three-year scholarship, sophomore standing. The Army required students requesting a four-year scholarship to have freshman standing. Applications for the Green to Gold program required letters of acceptance from the appropriate college admissions office and from the school's professor of military science. The applicant had to be an American citizen no older than 25 years of age, had to achieve designated Scholastic Aptitude Test, American College Testing, or General Technical scores, and comply with weight and fitness standards. Scholarships covered tuition assistance, expenses, fees, required books, supplies, and equipment as well as a stipend of as much as $1,000 annually.[95]

In school year 1988–1989, ROTC offered nine Green to Gold scholarships and it offered 57 in the next year.[96] Major Cory V. Perkins, ROTC enrollment officer at the University of Texas at San Antonio, remarked that the students—mostly former 91Cs, Army practical nurses—were older and more mature than the typical student and sometimes needed waivers for age. Nonetheless, they were fine soldiers and goal-directed students.[97] Cadet Lisa A. Toven, for example, had served several years as an enlisted operating room technician in the AMEDD. She entered the Green to Gold program at Seton Hall University School of Nursing, where she completed 21 to 23 credits every semester of her two years in the program. Toven was on the Dean's List for her entire time at Seton Hall and graduated magna cum laude. She earned many awards, such as the Association of the United States Army ROTC Medal, the Pallas Athene Award, the George C. Marshall Award, and Seton Hall's Military Science Medal. The nursing faculty nominated her for membership in Sigma Theta Tau, the international nursing honor society. In 1991, Toven received the prestigious Hughes-Lambert Trophy at the Pentagon, distinguishing her as the most outstanding ROTC graduate in the nation.[98] She continued with an exemplary career in the Army, serving as an operating room nurse in subsequent assignments and as company commander with the 28th Combat Support Hospital at Fort Bragg, North Carolina.[99] Toven's achievements highlighted the wisdom and advantages of investing in the skills, knowledge, and credentials of a few, select, top-notch performers within the organization. The investment the Army made in this fine soldier nurse yielded significant dividends.

The AMEDD Enlisted Commissioning Program (AECP), originally called the Medic to RN Program, was another effort to educate potential Army nurses that began in September 1990. In this program, selected AMEDD enlisted soldiers could complete educational requirements for a bachelor of science in nursing degree. Participating soldiers had to already have completed two years of general education credits before entering the program. As students, AECP participants received their normal pay and allowance for up to two years, and the Army paid their tuition. Upon completion of their studies and after passing the National

Senior ROTC Cadet Lisa Toven, right, accepts the George C. Marshall Award at the George C. Marshall ROTC Award Seminar in April 1991. Seminar officials, Colonel McDevitt, center, and Command Sergeant Major Hills, left, presided at the award ceremony.
Photo courtesy of Lieutenant Colonel Lisa A. Toven, Oakton, VA.

Council of State Boards of Nursing Licensure Examination, the state licensing examination for professional nurses, the Army Nurse Corps commissioned the AECP participants.

These nurses agreed to serve three years in return for the first year of Army support in school and to serve two more months for every month spent in school in the second academic year, not to exceed a total obligation of four years. Originally, the Army funded the first year of the program for up to 100 participants. The following year, the Army Nurse Corps, with the approval of the vice chief of staff of the Army, raised the quota to 125 participants.[100] In May 1992, the Army Nurse Corps commissioned the first cohort of 65 registered nurses who participated in the AECP.[101] By 1992, a total of 370 enlisted soldiers had participated, while 77 had been commissioned. Corps leaders projected that number would rise to 88 commissioned by 1993.[102] Although the program worked well for the Army Nurse Corps in the short term, it had serious long-term consequences for the participants.

After only a few years, the military careers of almost all the Army Nurse Corps officers who took advantage of the AECP were in jeopardy. By 1996, the Berlin Wall was rubble, the Cold War was only a memory, and the Army was in the midst of a massive downsizing. That year, the AMEDD instructed a selection board to accept fewer than 50 percent of those applying for voluntary indefinite status.[103] The board accordingly failed to select many of the individuals, by then mostly first lieutenants, who took advantage of the AECP, effectively ending their active duty careers. Their options were to revert to their prior enlisted status, leave active duty and shift to the reserve components, transfer their commissions to another service, or separate and accept a lump sum payment as severance pay. Nearly all the AECP graduates did not initially qualify to retire as commissioned officers because the law specified that an officer must accrue 10 years of active commissioned officer service to retire as a commissioned officer after 20 years. The Army Nurse Corps pursued a one-time exception to the law and this exception was granted, thereby preserving the careers of a number of AECP graduates.[104]

But as this process was unfolding, most of the AECP cohort was unsurprisingly disillusioned and angry. First Lieutenant Mary Andrews was bitter. Andrews had been in the Army since she was 17 and found it unbelievable that the Army "would do this to me now, at this point." Andrews' frustration was understandable, as one board denied her voluntary indefinite status while another selected her for a promotion to captain, almost simultaneously.[105] Army requirements, as usual, took priority over individual needs and preferences, with results that were irrational and overwhelming on a personal level.

The Army Nurse Corps used many strategies to recruit new officers. One inducement first made available early in the 1980s offered guarantees for certain area of concentration courses. If applicants accepted a commission, the Army Nurse Corps granted them the opportunity to attend full-time, on-duty classes at certain military treatment facilities and learn critical care, operating room, pediatric, psychiatric mental health, or obstetrics/gynecology nursing. When completed, the courses would qualify graduates to hold the appropriate area of concentration credentials and function in those specialties.[106]

Other actions taken to retain Army Nurse Corps officers involved making full use of the personnel quotas for definite term extensions and expanding the conditional voluntary indefinite selection rates. In FY 1988, the Health Service Division, Army Nurse Corps Branch, added 100 slots for officers who chose to extend their service beyond their initial obligation for a specific time, which was referred to as a definite term extension. In FY 1989, it added 66 more slots and increased the conditional voluntary indefinite selection rate to almost 100 percent.[107] This allowed more Army nurses to remain on active duty beyond their initial obligation.

Another strategy to improve morale, update skills and knowledge, and encourage retention was to protect the funds appropriated for continuing health education from the Army's budget ax. In FYs 1988 and 1989, the AMEDD approved the Army Nurse Corps Professional Development Funding Package for full funding.[108]

With such adverse conditions, the Army Nurse Corps considered any and all strategies to obtain new officers. The accession of foreign nurse graduates was one such option that Colonel Claudia Bartz explored in detail, although Immigration and Naturalization Service regulations, licensure requirements, language difficulties, and educational discrepancies ultimately led the Corps to reject the option.[109]

The Army Nurse Corps also attempted to achieve relief from the constraints of the Defense Officer Personnel Management Act (DOPMA) grade tables to improve recruitment and retention. DOPMA mandated that Army Nurse Corps officers be managed by year groups.[110] But year groups, especially those consisting of field grade officers, were over strength because of the practice of awarding constructive credit (increased rank) for civilian experience and education upon recruitment to what were referred to as "non–due course" officers.[111] With such huge year groups, too many officers found themselves in the zone of consideration for promotion at any one time, and the keen competition significantly decreased their chance for promotion. The practice of awarding constructive credit did improve Army Nurse Corps recruitment and professional quality but became a disincentive to retention.[112]

While participating in the AMEDD Officer Structure Study, a task force formed on 1 March 1985 to examine topics such as structure and inventory, the Army Nurse Corps realized that the problem was not in DOPMA but in the Corps "broken" structure. It concluded that it could "not get well in [the] short term without [an] increase in field grade allocations" and recognized that the medical grade table for AMEDD officers contained in Army Regulation 611-101 was obsolete, inaccurate, and undergraded for Army Nurse Corps officers.[113] For example, DOPMA directed that 4.7 percent of all active duty personnel be colonels, but the medical grade table allowed only about 1 percent of the Army Nurse Corps to be colonel. In other words, the problem with the Army Nurse Corps structure was that the template used to assign grades to various positions did not consider increases in the complex scope of responsibility, span of control, and requisite education and experience required in those positions.[114] Some thought that the inequities in the allocation of colonel authorizations to the Army Nurse Corps occurred because the Corps was a predominantly female branch and traditional practices restricted grade advancement or even permanently assigning advanced grades to female officers.[115] The problem eventually was corrected, but only after a prodigious three-year struggle.[116]

To rectify imbalances, the Army Nurse Corps asked its senior officers to apply their professional expertise to evaluate and regrade all the Corps positions. They identified approximately 100 additional colonel allocations. The Army Nurse Corps then approached the Army deputy chief of staff for personnel through the Office of the Surgeon General and requested and received the additional allocations. These new allocations authorized the promotion of a sizable number of Army nurse colonels and broke the promotion logjam. As Colonel John Hudock, assistant chief of the Army Nurse Corps, observed, each one of these promotions was—in effect—three promotions. When the Army promoted a lieutenant colonel to colonel, that promotion produced a ripple effect, because a major could be promoted to lieutenant colonel and a captain to major.[117] Rank restructuring brought the Army Nurse Corps into compliance with DOPMA's configuration, allowed the Corps to continue awarding constructive credit for recruitment purposes and overall quality, enhanced morale, improved retention, opened up promotions, preserved the existing end strength, and conferred the appropriate rank for the specific responsibilities on principal Army Nurse Corps positions. The Army Nurse Corps achieved its AMEDD Officer Structure Study purpose, "to develop an AMEDD officer structure for the future that will serve Army needs and provide career progression opportunities on a parity with the Total Active Army Force."[118]

During the 1980s, the Army implemented initiatives to increase the numbers of nurses in the USAR and ARNG. It relaxed the policy governing training schedules, thus making training requirements more flexible and adaptable for individual needs.[119] It also allowed constructive credit for a nurse's education and civilian experience. The Army extended the maximum age to 52 for the initial appointment to the ARNG and USAR, and it collaborated with national nursing organizations in a direct-mail campaign and a media blitz to publicize the opportunities available with reserve service.[120]

The team dedicated to recruiting Army Nurse Corps reserve components grew. Program Budget Guidance authorized 140 additional Army Guard and Reserve nurse recruiters.[121] It also authorized 77 more civilians to support Army Nurse Corps recruitment and retention. The USAR also established the National AMEDD Augmentation Detachment to retain those AMEDD officers who found it impossible to train with units "on a regular basis."[122] Operating room nursing, anesthesia, and medical-surgical nursing specialties were the areas of greatest need, and so the three services requested and Congress funded financial incentives for these specialists.[123]

The Army implemented the New Specialized Training Assistance Program to increase personnel in the surgical specialties in the USAR. In 1988, this program subsidized educational expenses for reservists in Troop Program Units and the Individual Ready Reserve at the rate of $664 and $332 a month, respectively. In return, the Army required these reservists to serve two years in the reserves for every year of funding. The Army likewise financed those in the Individual Ready Reserve who were pursuing a bachelor of science in nursing degree at $100 a month. All of these grants had an annual per-soldier expenditure ceiling of $7,900.[124]

Another program, the Health Professional Loan Repayment Program, was an incentive for the same nursing specialties—operating room nurses, anesthetists, and medical-surgical nurses. The Army repaid a participant's outstanding student loans in the amount of $3,000 for each year served in the Selected Reserve.[125] The total loan forgiveness package could not exceed $20,000.[126] Anecdotal feedback provided hints as to the success of this program. These unconfirmed reports indicated that some nurses chose to accept a reserve rather than an active commission for the generous loan repayment program.[127]

The Army Nurse Corps also encouraged local programs to relieve the nurse shortage. In 1987, Tripler Army Medical Center in Hawaii surveyed nurses' attitudes. Based on the investigational findings, the Department of Nursing adjusted work scheduling to accommodate nurses' personal preferences whenever feasible and expanded training opportunities and staff recognition. The effort reduced staff turnover from 40 percent to 20 percent. By April 1988, registered nurse staffing was at 102 percent.[128]

At Blanchfield Army Community Hospital at Fort Campbell, Kentucky, Colonel Charles Bombard set up a nursing pool of 13 civilian nurses to work when more nurses were needed on nursing units. The civilian nurses could be hired either as intermittent employees on an on-call basis, as part-time employees working from 16 to 32 hours weekly, or as full-time staffers.[129]

Colonel Sandrah Johnson, the chief nurse at FAMC in Aurora, Colorado, awarded $50 prizes to individual nurses who excelled in one of 14 areas, such as education, training, or community service. The purpose was to keep and reward nurses and to attract new employees from the local area. Within six months Johnson had already awarded $1,000.

Advertising to create interest in employment was also an effective recruitment tool. The chief nurse at Gorgas Army Community Hospital in Panama, Colonel Randall L. Oliver, invested $4,000 to publicize the benefits of employment in the Canal Zone. The advertisements, published in a number of national nursing journals, touted features such as "a 15 percent tropical pay differential, a good-sized overseas housing allowance, [and] the opportunity to ship a car" to the Central American country.

Another chief nurse, Colonel Janet Southby, put up a poster in the Fort Belvoir, Virginia, One-Stop Employment Center, to recruit nurses who might then seek employment at DeWitt Army Community Hospital. The poster displayed the advantages of employment at DeWitt, such as working intermittently, job sharing, preferential scheduling, or tuition subsidies.

The tuition assistance program also served as a magnet at Eisenhower Army Medical Center at Fort Gordon, Georgia. There, Colonel Marilyn DiGirol, chief of nursing education and staff development, reported that the hospital discussed the benefits with about 20 potential employees and received four applications for employment within weeks as a result of the tuition assistance program.[130]

The Fort Leonard Wood, Missouri, Medical Department Activity held a nurse information day in 1989, inviting 51 civilian nurses from the local area to learn about the post's employment opportunities. Coordinated by Lieutenant Colonel Ann Stanton and Major Niranjan Balliram, the day's activities included presentations and tours of the hospital guided by civilian nurses already employed by the institution. Eight new civilian employees soon filled vacant nursing positions.[131]

All of these creative and mostly unprecedented programs contributed to the eventual resolution of the profound and long-term nurse shortage of the 1980s. As the 1980s ended, the strength of the Army Nurse Corps improved conspicuously.

When DoD hospitals were unable to provide nursing coverage by either Nurse Corps officers or CSRNs, they relied on contract nurses as a last resort.[132] Variously referred to as temporary, agency, or contract nurses, these providers relieved certain employee vacancies, served as an entire staff, or lent support where additional resources have not been allocated.[133] The contract nurses worked for proprietary agencies that paid their nurse employees directly and in turn were reimbursed for expenses according to their contracts with the specific military hospital.[134] The use of contract nurses had both disadvantages and advantages. The financial cost of using such workers was steep as compared to the expense of employing CSRNs, and their temporary employment could adversely affect continuity of care.[135] Contract nurses were not allowed to serve in leadership roles, that is, as a charge nurse or team leader, thus limiting their overall utility. There was also a heavy investment in time by the permanent nursing staff that had to devote many hours to various issues such as negotiating contracts and setting proficiency standards for the contract employees. The better pay and more convenient hours accorded contract nurses influenced some of the permanent staff to resign their civil service employment or their active commissions in the Army Nurse Corps to become contract nurses. On the plus side, Colonel Mary Messerschmidt, who had extensive exposure to contract nurses while chief, Department of Nursing, at WRAMC, recalled that many of the contract nurses were former CSRNs or junior officers who separated from the service. These former civil servants and junior officers required little to no orientation and proved to be dependable employees. Moreover, if they failed to deliver high-quality service, it was not difficult to remove them. The hospital simply told the agency not to schedule that particular temporary nurse to work in that institution anymore. Messerschmidt observed that these workers were venturesome in ways that many CSRNs were not. Nonetheless, they were "certainly not anywhere near as adventuresome as someone who joins the military and stays" in the service.[136] Another chief nurse at WRAMC, Colonel Clara Adams-Ender, remembered that some of the contract nurses "liked what we were doing and sometimes would decide to join the Army or Civil Service and become salaried people on our staff."[137] In the final analysis, the use of contract nurses was an unwelcome expedient used in very straitened circumstances.

By 1989, the military Nurse Corps began to see positive results from the many incentive programs implemented across the decade. In FY 1989, the Army Nurse Corps met recruitment goals and accessed 524 new officers for the active component. Voluntary recalls to active duty numbered 47, a striking increase from FY 1988's total of 15 returnees. The chief nurse of the U.S. Army Recruiting Command, Colonel Susan (Shipley) Christoph observed that this statistic reflected the growing propensity for former Army nurses to return to active duty after observing working conditions, salary, and benefits in civilian institutions. The ARNG also accessed 297 Army nurses, and the USAR commissioned 1,600 Army Nurse Corps officers.[138] By 1990, the Army Nurse Corps was only 27 officers short of its 4,551 authorizations. The AFNC exceeded its 5,352 nursing billets by 57 officers. However, the Navy Nurse Corps had a shortage of 476 officers, or only 3,000 nurses against 3,476 authorizations.[139] In the early 1980s, the Navy surgeon general acknowledged that the Navy Medical Department had always functioned "with fewer monetary and manpower assets than the Army or Air Force." It subsequently made concerted attempts to correct "those inadequacies" through the addition of "sufficient manpower and monies and an efficient command structure."[140] But success was long in coming.

In the context of a nationwide shortage of professional nurses, an exponentially growing demand for more care providers, and stringent military budget constraints, it was the imagination and hard work of many dedicated individuals who enabled the Army Nurse Corps to maintain an adequate force. The concentrated attention and insight of Army Nurse Corps leaders, the support of officials in Congress and the Department of Army, the collaboration with sister services, the herculean efforts of recruiters, and the day-to-day commitment of the rank and file of the Army Nurse Corps and the Army all contributed to the positive outcome.

# Notes

1. Vincent H. Demma, *Department of the Army Historical Summary, Fiscal Year 1989* (Washington, DC: Center of Military History, United States Army, 1998), 166–67.

2. Maryann F. Fralic, "Nursing Shortage: Coping Today and Planning for Tomorrow," *Hospitals* 54 (1 May 1980): 65–67. Patricia K. Munshaw, "Solve Nurse Shortage with Dual Attack," *Modern Healthcare* 10 (July 1980): 99. Linda H. Aiken, Robert J. Blendon, and David E. Rogers, "The Shortage of Hospital Nurses: A New Perspective," *Annals of Internal Medicine* 95 (September 1981): 365–72. Ann L. Steck, "The Nursing Shortage: An Optimistic View," *Nursing Outlook* 29 (May 1981): 302–04. E. Ginzberg, J.A. Patray, and M. Ostow, "Nurse Discontent: The Search for Realistic Solutions," *Journal of Nursing Administration* 12 (November 1982): 7–11. D.R. Smith, "Nursing Shortage: Some Practical Response Please!" *Nursing Management* 14 (November 1983): 38–40. M.L. Barer, A.J. Star, and C. Kinnis, "Manpower Planning, Fiscal Restraint and the Demand for Health Care Personnel," *Inquiry* 21 (Fall 1984): 254–65. B. O'Brien, K.E. Knutson, and L.B. Welch, "Nursing Shortage or Transition, Three Perspectives," *Health Progress* 68 (May 1987): 36–40. L.L. Curtin, "A Shortage of Nurses: Traditional Approaches Won't Work This Time," *Nursing Management* 18 (September 1987): 7–8. C.M. Fagin, "Why the Quick Fix Won't Fix Today's Nurse Shortage," *Inquiry* 25 (Fall 1988): 309–14. "Nursing Organizations Propose Solutions to the Shortage," *Michigan Nurse* 61 (December 1988): 3–4. S.S. Blanchett, "The Shortage: Medicine Speaks Out," *Nurse Educator* 14 (May–June 1989): 5. J.M. Keith, "A Temporary Solution to the Nursing Shortage," *Health Progress* 70 (December 1989): 76–77. P.L. King and T. Sherman, "Recruitment Target: The Guidance Counselor Connection," *Nursing Management* 21 (May 1990): 38–39, 42, 44. S. Watras, "Solutions to the Nursing Shortage," *Imprint* 37 (November 1990): 86–87.

3. Howard V. Stambler, *The Recurrent Shortage of Registered Nurses, A New Look at the Issues* (Washington, DC: U.S. Department of Health and Human Services, Public Health Service, Health Resources Administration, Bureau of Health Professions, Division of Health Professions Analysis, 1981): ii.

4. Howard V. Stambler, *The Recurrent Shortage of Registered Nurses, A New Look at the Issues* (Washington, DC: U.S. Department of Health and Human Services, Public Health Service, Health Resources Administration, Bureau of Health Professions, Division of Health Professions Analysis, 1981): iii, 23.

5. "Hospitals Need More Nurses; Trend Shows Supply Declining," *HSC Mercury* 14 (March 1987): 4. American Association of Colleges of Nursing, "Nursing Shortage Fact Sheet," 2, n.d., Army Nurse Corps Collection (ANCC), Office of Medical History (OMH).

6. In 1988, civilian nurse vacancies in DoD were estimated at 15–16 percent. "Military Nurses Task Force Report on the Military Nursing Shortage," Department of Health and Human Services, Secretary's Commission on Nursing, December 1988, VI-7, ANCC, OMH.

7. Tamar Lewin, "Sudden Nurse Shortage Threatens Hospital Care," *New York Times* (7 July 1987): A1. Linda H. Aiken and Connie Flynt Mullinix, "The Nurse Shortage, Myth or Reality?" *New England Journal of Medicine* 317 (3 September 1987): 641–45. John K. Iglehart, "Problems Facing the Nursing Profession," *New England Journal of Medicine* 317 (3 September 1987): 646–51.

8. Eily P. Gorman, "To Provide Information to BG Rumbaugh in Preparation for His Visit to DCCS Conference," Information Paper, 21 September 1987, ANCC, OMH.

9. Mobashir Salahuddin, "Bonuses Have Hospitals Competing for Nurses, *Columbia State* (30 July 1988): 1-A, 2-A.

10. Steven Eisenstadt, "Money, Nurse Shortages Deal Hospitals a One-Two Punch," *Army Times* 48 (28 March 1988): 1, 8.

11. Esther J. Segler, "What Are We Doing about Nurse Shortage," *HSC Mercury* 16 (February 1989): 2. "TSG Meeting with CSA," Typewritten Outline, 2 July 1987, ANCC, OMH.

12. "Briefing, DoD Nurses' Meeting, Status of Air Force Nurse Corps," Briefing Slides, 12–13, 21 October 1981, ANCC, OMH.

13. Connie L. Slewitzke, Interview by Beverly Greenlee, 20, 28, n.d., USAWC/USAMHI Senior Officer Oral History Program, Project No. 88-8, ANCC, OMH.

14. *U.S. Army Health Service Command, Annual Historical Review, 1 July 1975 to 30 September 1977* (Ft. Sam Houston, TX: Historical Office, HSC, 1979), 107, ANCC, OMH.

15. Karl E. Cocke and others, *Department of the Army Historical Summary, Fiscal Year 1981* (Washington, DC: Center of Military History, United States Army, 1988), 83.

16. Dwight D. Oland, *Department of the Army Historical Summary, Fiscal Year 1984* (Washington, DC: Center of Military History, United States Army, 1995), 198.

17. Charles J. Reddy, "Nursing Newsletter Number 83-2," 1, 1 November 1983, ANCC, OMH.

18. John Hudock, "Army Nurse Corps and Civil Service Registered Nurse Structure and Strength," Information Paper, 19 October 1989, ANCC, OMH.

19. Nickey McCasland to Author, E-mail Correspondence, 19 January 2004, ANCC, OMH. Department of the Army, Headquarters, U.S. Army Health Services Command, "Manpower Management, Manpower Survey Program, Fiscal Year 1974," HSC Circular No. 570-1, 30 April 1973, Record Group 112, National Archives.

20. Carmelita Schimmenti, "Point Paper on Military Nursing," Typewritten Document (TD), 4 February 1988, ANCC, OMH.

21. John Hudock, "Nationwide Shortage of Registered Professional Nurses Is Impacting on the Retention of Army Nurse Corps Officers," Information Paper, 14 July 1988, ANCC, OMH. Deborah L. Finfgeld, "What Does a Military Nursing Shortage Mean to Us?" *Nursing Economics* 9 (January–February 1991): 44–47.

22. A preferred retention rate was about 85 percent. John Hudock, "The Registered Nurse Shortage," Information Paper, n.d., ANCC, OMH. The retention rate for the Army Nurse Corps for FY 1989 was a slightly improved 69 percent. Clara Adams-Ender, "Hearing before the Senate Appropriations Committee, Subcommittee on Defense," Transcript of Testimony, 16 March 1989, ANCC, OMH.

23. Carmelita Schimmenti, "Point Paper on Military Nursing," TD, 4 February 1988, ANCC, OMH. Don Winingham, "Nursing Chief Battles Shortages, Discontent," *Air Force Times* 49 (14 November 1988): 14.

24. Sid Balman, "Rx for Nurses," *Air Force Times* 50 (19 February 1990): 14–16.

25. "Military Nurses Task Force Report on the Military Nursing Shortage," Department of Health and Human Services, Secretary's Commission on Nursing, December 1988, VI1-5, ANCC, OMH.

26. "Wartime Nurse Shortage Expected to Total 23,500," *Army Times* 43 (27 December 1982): 30. John H. Moxley, "Military Medicine Programs Progress," *U.S. Medicine* 17 (15 January 1981): 9, 11, 12, 14. "U.S. Army Medicine, from the Ferment, Profound Changes," *Army* 36 (March 1986): 43.

27. "Nurses No Longer Servants," *Stars and Stripes* (17 June 1987): 17.

28. Karl E. Cocke and others, *Department of the Army Historical Summary, Fiscal Year 1981* (Washington, DC: Center of Military History, United States Army, 1988), 127.

29. Daniel M. Clawson, "Review of Recruitment/Retention Issues—Army Medical Department (AMEDD) Civil Service (CS) Registered Nurses (RN)," Draft Memorandum for the Surgeon General, n.d., ANCC, OMH.

30. John Hudock, "The Registered Nurse Shortage," Information Paper, n.d.; Clara Adams-Ender, "Hearing before the Senate Appropriations Committee, Subcommittee on Defense," Transcript of Testimony, 16 March 1989; Wil Nieves, "Status of Nursing Shortage Initiatives," Information Paper, 4, 5, 19 July 1989; and Clyde R. Cunningham, "Civilian Registered Nurse Task Force," Information Paper, 14 March 1989 (all in ANCC, OMH). John E. Burick, "Army Civilian Nurse Jobs Still Hard to Fill," *HSC Mercury* 17 (May 1990): 4.

31. Gar Yip, "Civilian Nurse Survey Results," Typewritten Memorandum (TM), 1–3, 11 March 1987; and "Recruitment and Retention—AMEDD Civilian Registered Nurses," TD, n.d. (both in ANCC, OMH).

32. Daniel M. Clawson, "Review of Recruitment/Retention Issues—Army Medical Department (AMEDD) Civil Service (CS) Registered Nurses (RN)," Draft Memorandum for the Surgeon General, n.d., ANCC, OMH.

33. Eily P. Gorman, Handwritten Note to BG AE, 9 September 1987, ANCC, OMH.

34. Ibid.

35. Career ladders for professional nurses also were virtually nonexistent in the civilian milieu. Civilian nurse leaders debated the wisdom of establishing "a salary differential based on experience, ... education, ... [and] competence in direct care." Susan R. Gortner, "Commentary," in *Nursing in the 1980s, Crises, Opportunities, Challenges*, ed. Linda H. Aiken and Susan R. Gortner (Philadelphia: J.B. Lippincott, 1982), 495–502. Most other trades and professions had such criteria that, when met, qualified the worker for enhanced salary or benefits. Strangely, such was not the case for nursing even in otherwise modern times. The archaic one-size-fits-all mentality may have been a vestige of the paternalistic, hospital-based culture of the past where, in many cases, nurses were considered virtually indentured servants.

36. Kathleen M. Tracy, "Minutes of Civil Service Registered Nurse (CSRN) Task Force," Memorandum for Record, 26 April 1988, ANCC, OMH.

37. "Department of Defense Report on the Military Nursing Shortage," Typewritten Draft Copy of Report, 12, n.d.; "Military Nurses Task Force Report on the Military Nursing Shortage, Prepared for Department of Health and Human Services, Secretary's Commission on Nursing," December 1988, VI-7; Clyde R. Cunningham, "Lack of Competitive Pay for Civilian Medical Occupation Positions," Information Paper, 14 March 1989; and John

Hudock, "Contract Nurses," Information Paper, 7 August 1990 (all in ANCC, OMH).

38. Many of the bills failed to become law for a variety of reasons. In some instances they were not considered as important as other pressing concerns. Alternately, budgetary constraints precluded their passage. Some of the bills did not have strong advocates to shepherd them through the law-making process. P.L. 99-103 sought to match Veterans' Administration (VA) and civilian hospital salaries. Congress formulated the Wolf-Trimble bill to authorize bonuses and special pay rates. The Ackerman bill was another effort to raise pay, authorize bonuses, and test "alternative pay systems." None of these bills became law. Tracy E. Strevey, "Civilian Registered Nurse (RN) Shortage," TM, 2, 18 April 1988, ANCC, OMH. The Office of Personnel Management (OPM) and Senator John Glenn also proposed bills to change the wage system for nurses. Tom Shoop, "Wage Wars," *Government Executive* (June 1990): 40–44, 46.

39. CSRNs working in the D.C. area; Letterman, Fitzsimons, and Eisenhower Medical Centers; Fort Ord; Fort Monmouth; Fort Jackson; Fort Knox; and the U.S. Military Academy had special salary rates. Clyde R. Cunningham, "Civilian Registered Nurse Task Force," Information Paper, 14 March 1989, ANCC, OMH. The AMEDD effected the promotion of ICU nurses to GS-10 and GS-11 "in recognition of the level of complexity and authority for these special skills." Tracy E. Strevey, "Civilian Registered Nurse (RN) Shortage," TM, 2, 18 April 1988, ANCC, OMH.

40. Tracy E. Strevey, "Civilian Registered Nurse (RN) Shortage," TM, 2, 18 April 1988, ANCC, OMH.

41. The Army Nurse Corps added "one civilian slot per course per iteration" in Area of Concentration courses. The civilian slot was an addition "not a replacement for an AN [Army Nurse] slot." The purpose of this action was "to give the civilian nurses career progression." John M. Hudock, "US Army Nurse Corps, Nursing Research Advisory Board (NRAB), 24–26 July 1989," Typewritten Minutes, 4, ANCC, OMH. Sunnie Scarlett, "Four Army Civilian Nurses Will Attend Military Courses," *HSC Mercury* 16 (September 1989): 3.

42. John Hudock, "The Registered Nurse Shortage," Information Paper, n.d.; Clara Adams-Ender, "Hearing before the Senate Appropriations Committee, Subcommittee on Defense," Transcript of Testimony, 16 March 1989; Wil Nieves, "Status of Nursing Shortage Initiatives," Information Paper, 4, 5, 19 July 1989; and "Army Nurse Corps Strategic Plan Summary," TD, 7, December 1988 (all in ANCC, OMH).

43. Clara L. Adams-Ender, Interview by Virginia Ruth Cheney, 155, 1992, Project 92-3, U.S. Army Military History Institute, Senior Officer Oral History Program, ANCC, OMH.

44. John Hudock, "Chapter Two-1980s's Review," Handwritten Comments, 15 September 2003, ANCC, OMH.

45. Surgical specialties also were the Medical Corps areas of greatest need. In 1982 and 1983, The Surgeon General authorized increased procurement efforts to bring orthopedists, neurosurgeons, general surgeons, and otolaryngologists into the AMEDD. These specialties were the most challenging to recruit and retain. Bernhard T. Mittemeyer, "Army Medical Department," *Military Medicine* 147 (November 1982): 918–28. Bernhard T. Mittemeyer, "Army Medical Department," *Military Medicine* 148 (November 1983): 833–40.

46. Karl H. Pfaehler, Typewritten Letter (TL), 12 December 1988, ANCC, OMH.

47. Steven Eisenstadt, "Money, Nurse Shortages Deal Hospitals a One-Two Punch," *Army Times* 48 (28 March 1988): 1, 8. Some civilian hospitals reported similar circumstances. One publication noted that the nursing shortage "resulted in delays in scheduling elective surgery." Also, "hospital administrators have been frustrated by disruptions in the day-to-day operation of their institutions, revenue lost from beds closed" attributable to a lack of nurses. *Nursing in the 1980s, Crises, Opportunities, Challenges*, ed. Linda H.

Aiken and Susan R. Gortner (Philadelphia: J.B. Lippincott, 1982), 57, 58.

48. Steven Eisenstadt, "Money, Nurse Shortages Deal Hospitals a One-Two Punch," *Army Times* 48 (28 March 1988): 1, 8.

49. Donald Robinson, "The Mess in Military Medicine," *Reader's Digest* 126 (February 1985): 49–53.

50. Judy E. Fox, "Army May Gain Funds Easing Staff Shortages," *U.S. Medicine* 21 (1 December 1985): 1, 20.

51. Ibid.

52. Donald Robinson, "The Mess in Military Medicine," *Reader's Digest* 126 (February 1985): 49–53.

53. "Individual Organizational and Job Factors Affecting the Quality of Work Life among Navy Nurse Corps Officers," quoted in "Summary Analysis of the Following Studies," TD, n.d., ANCC, OMH.

54. "Vital Signs: A Survey of the Air Force Nurse Corps," quoted in "Summary Analysis of the Following Studies," TD, n.d.; and Lt. Col. Black, "Talking Paper on Vital Signs: A Survey of the USAF Nurse Corps," 26 October 1988 (both in ANCC, OMH).

55. Association of the United States Army, "The Army Medical Department—An Assessment," Typewritten Draft Report compiled under the auspices of the Institute of Land Warfare, August 1989, n.p., in chapter titled "The Nurse Problem," ANCC, OMH.

56. Association of the United States Army, "The Army Medical Department—An Assessment," Typewritten Draft Report compiled under the auspices of the Institute of Land Warfare, August 1989, n.p., in chapter titled "The Nurse Problem," ANCC, OMH. These comments did not appear in the final report of the following study: Jack N. Merritt, *The Army Medical Department, Caring for the Troops in War and Peace*, Special Report (Arlington, VA: Association of the United States Army, 1989).

57. The "Proud to Care" survey had an 80 percent response rate from the active component nurses. It revealed that key elements affecting Army nurses' decisions to remain on active duty were "time for personal and family life," job satisfaction, and pay and benefits. Valerie E. Biskey and others, "The Army Nurse Corps Proud to Care Survey," Executive Summary, December 1991; and Clara Adams-Ender, "Hearing before the Senate Appropriations Committee, Subcommittee on Defense," Transcript of Testimony, 16 March 1989 (both in ANCC, OMH).

58. Department of Health and Human Services, Secretary's Commission on Nursing, "Military Nurses Task Force Report on the Military Nursing Shortage," December 1988, ANCC, OMH.

59. "Army Nurse Corps Strategic Plan Summary," December 1988; and "Army Nurse Corps Strategic Plan Summary," March 1989 (TDs, both in ANCC, OMH).

60. Tracy E. Strevey, "Civilian Registered Nurse (RN) Shortage," TM, 2–3, 18 April 1988, ANCC, OMH. G.A. Vidis, "Tripler Keeps Nurses with Job Satisfaction," *HSC Mercury* 15 (December 1987): 6. Charles Bombard, "Civilian Nurses Fill Campbell Gaps," *HSC Mercury* 12 (July 1985): 6. Sunnie Scarlett, "Chief Nurses Find Publicity Attracts More RNs," *HSC Mercury* 16 (April 1989): 9. "Wood Greets New Nurses," *HSC Mercury* 16 (February 1989): 12.

61. In 1987, the assistant chief and the chief of the Army Nurse Corps wrote it was "most unfortunate that despite congressional expectations that nurses should be exempt from reductions, they must undergo review. In fact the ANC and PAs get singled out for an additional 20 percent reduction in training. Almost daily, DASG-CN [chief of the Corps office] must deal with issues related to the nurse shortage from AMEDD sources and others such as DA, DOD, etc." John M. Hudock for Clara L. Adams-Ender, "Officer End Strength

Reduction—Authorizations," TM, 9 December 1987, ANCC, OMH. Undoubtedly, crafting justifications to respond to unrealistic proposals about reductions in numbers and to explain the dire necessity for more and better-educated Army nurses detracted from the time available to concentrate on other important concerns, such as quality issues or career matters. It seems counterintuitive that the upper echelons of the Army and DoD behaved in such a manner.

62. "DACOWITS 2000 Spring Conference, History of Recommendations, 1951–1999," Printed Brochure, n.d., ANCC, OMH.

63. COMPO 1 is all active duty personnel and is priority funded. COMPO 2 consists of the National Guard. COMPO 3 is made up of the United States Army Reserve. COMPO 4 comprises unresourced structure—that is, units that exist on paper but have no funding. However, COMPO 4 potentially can be activated and subsequently funded. "This is how the Army structures itself . . . to meet requirements." It is laid out in the Total Army Analysis (TAA), a part of the entire budget process, and is calculated annually. Jennifer Petersen to Author, E-mail Correspondence, 20 May 2003, ANCC, OMH.

64. "Statement of Brigadier General Nancy R. Adams, Chief, Army Nurse Corps," 1, 5 May 1993, ANCC, OMH. Carolyn M. Feller and Debora R. Cox, *Highlights in the History of the Army Nurse Corps* (Washington, DC: U.S. Army Center of Military History, 2000), 62.

65. Clara L. Adams-Ender, "Legislative Awareness," *Memo from the Chief, Army Nurse Corps* (31 December 1989): 1; John Hudock, "Army Nurse Corps (ANC) Active Component (AC) Recruitment Bonus," 28 August 1989; and John Hudock, "Nursing Shortage," 8 May 1990 (Information Papers, all in ANCC, OMH). Mary C. Smolenski, Donald G. Smith, and James S. Nanney, *A Fit, Fighting Force, The Air Force Nursing Services Chronology* (Washington, DC: Office of the Air Force Surgeon General, 2005), 44.

66. "Nurse Corps Testimony Issues," TD, 3, n.d., ANCC, OMH.

67. Soraya S. Nelson, "Initiatives May Help Ease Nursing Shortage," *Army Times* 50 (18 December 1989): 18. Soraya S. Nelson, "Federal Nursing School Concept Being Studied," *Navy Times* 39 (18 December 1989): 8. Soraya S. Nelson, "Federal Nursing School Plan Advances," *Air Force Times* 50 (22 January 1990): 14. Soraya S. Nelson, "Federal Nursing School Plan Clears First Hurdle," *Navy Times* 39 (29 January 1990): 18. "Military Nurse Chiefs Fight for Federal Nursing College," *American Journal of Nursing* 90 (March 1990): 96. Mary C. Smolenski, Donald G. Smith, and James S. Nanney, *A Fit, Fighting Force, The Air Force Nursing Services Chronology* (Washington, DC: Office of the Air Force Surgeon General, 2005), 42.

68. David Packard, "Minutes of the Board of Regents of the Uniformed Services University of the Health Sciences," Amendment to Minutes of 13 May 1974, 9 July 1974, 54; and "Uniformed Services University of the Health Sciences, School of Nursing Feasibility Study," Typewritten Draft, June 1989 (both in ANCC, OMH).

69. "Minutes of the Board of Regents of the Uniformed Services University of the Health Sciences," 171, 18–19 October 1976.

70. Hazel W. Johnson to Madelyn N. Parks, TL, 26 July 1977, ANCC, OMH.

71. "Final Report, Uniformed Services University of the Health Sciences (USUHS) School of Nursing Feasibility Study Committee," TD, June 1997, ANCC, OMH.

72. "Uniformed Services University of the Health Sciences, School of Nursing Feasibility Study," Typewritten Draft, June 1989, ANCC, OMH.

73. Christine M. Galante, "Staff Study Report, Program to Increase Use of Certain Nurses, Section 706, HR 2461/Report #101-121, National Defense Authorization Act for Fiscal Years 1990–1991, Committee on Armed Services, Subcommittee on Military Per-

sonnel and Compensation, House of Representatives, 101st Congress," TD, 16, n.d.; and Wil Nieves, "Status of Nursing Shortage Initiatives," Information Paper, 2, 19 July 1989 (both in ANCC, OMH).

74. "USUHS College of Nursing Feasibility Study Task Force Report," 24 September 1990, in Alma S. Woolley, *Good Nursing in Difficult Places: The First Eight Years of the Graduate School of Nursing, Uniformed Services University of the Health Sciences* (Bethesda, MD: privately printed, 2001), 5.

75. "USUHS College of Nursing Feasibility Study Task Force Report," 24 September 1990, in Alma S. Woolley, *Good Nursing in Difficult Places: The First Eight Years of the Graduate School of Nursing, Uniformed Services University of the Health Sciences* (Bethesda, MD: privately printed, 2001), 5–6.

76. "Pregnant Officers Must Serve Out Obligations," *Pentagram News* (27 April 1978): 13, Newspaper Clipping and Inclosure 8, in Madelyn N. Parks, "Information for ANC Officers," Memorandum, 5 July 1978, ANCC, OMH.

77. Hazel W. Johnson-Brown, Interview by Charles F. Bombard, 111–12, 1984, USAWC/USAMHI Senior Officer Oral History Program, Project No. 84-15, ANCC, OMH.

78. "USUHS College of Nursing Feasibility Study Task Force Report," 24 September 1990, in Alma S. Woolley, *Good Nursing in Difficult Places: The First Eight Years of the Graduate School of Nursing, Uniformed Services University of the Health Sciences* (Bethesda, MD: privately printed, 2001), 8–9.

79. Eugene Levine, "Needs Assessment for Advanced Practice Nurses for the Uniformed Services," *Military Medicine* 159 (October 1994): 50–54. "USUHS College of Nursing Feasibility Study Task Force Report," 24 September 1990, in Alma S. Woolley, *Good Nursing in Difficult Places: The First Eight Years of the Graduate School of Nursing, Uniformed Services University of the Health Sciences* (Bethesda, MD: privately printed, 2001), 15–16.

80. Robert J.T. Joy to Author, TL, 24 November 2003, ANCC, OMH.

81. "USUHS College of Nursing Feasibility Study Task Force Report," 24 September 1990, in Alma S. Woolley, *Good Nursing in Difficult Places: The First Eight Years of the Graduate School of Nursing, Uniformed Services University of the Health Sciences* (Bethesda, MD: privately printed, 2001), 18–19.

82. The term medical model referred to the typical physician approach of diagnosing and treating illness. It was disease focused. The nursing model viewed the patient as a social being within the context of the environment and focused on caring for the patient by identifying and fulfilling needs. *Mosby's Medical, Nursing, & Allied Health Dictionary*, fifth ed. (St. Louis: Mosby, 1998), 1001. Often these paradigms were encapsulated into a cure/care dichotomy. Many nurses viewed the medical model with repugnance and expressed reservations about advanced practice nurses who functioned within both paradigms. Nancy R. Adams to Author, E-mail Correspondence, 28 February 2003, ANCC, OMH.

83. Robert J.T. Joy to Author, TL, 24 November 2003, ANCC, OMH. "USUHS College of Nursing Feasibility Study Task Force Report," 24 September 1990, in Alma S. Woolley, *Good Nursing in Difficult Places: The First Eight Years of the Graduate School of Nursing, Uniformed Services University of the Health Sciences* (Bethesda, MD: privately printed, 2001), 19–22. John Sherner to Author, E-mail Correspondence, 11 August 2003, ANCC, OMH.

84. Prior to being eligible for incentive pay, military CRNAs were required by DoD to complete the pay-back service time for their anesthesia education that was subsidized by the military services. Usually the pay-back period encompassed 4–4½ years for 2–2½ years of anesthesia education. "Incentive Special Pay for Certified Registered Nurse Anes-

thetists," 19 May 1995, in "Statement of Rear Admiral Joan M. Engel, Nurse Corps, Director, Nurse Corps, United States Navy before the Subcommittee on Defense of the Senate Appropriations Committee," Transcript, ANCC, OMH. John Hudock, "Army Nurse Corps (ANC) Active Component (AC) Incentive Pay," 28 August 1989; and John Hudock, "Nursing Shortage," 8 May 1990 (Information Papers, both in ANCC, OMH). Mary C. Smolenski, Donald G. Smith, and James S. Nanney, *A Fit, Fighting Force, The Air Force Nursing Services Chronology* (Washington, DC: Office of the Air Force Surgeon General, 2005), 44.

85. Clara L. Adams-Ender, "Legislative Awareness," *Memo from the Chief, Army Nurse Corps* (31 December 1989): 1, ANCC, OMH.

86. Office of the Assistant Secretary of Defense (Health Affairs), "Certified Registered Nurse Anesthetists Incentive Special Pay Study," Report, March 1994, ANCC, OMH.

87. Terris Kennedy, "Retention Issues," Information Paper, 26 July 1993, ANCC, OMH.

88. While Congress *authorized* the $15,000 ISP in 1994, it did not, however, immediately *appropriate* the dollars to fund the legislation. Michael J. Foster, "Minutes of the Army Nurse Corps Staff Meeting on 4 January 1994," Typewritten Minutes, 2, 6 January 1994, ANCC, OMH.

89. "Statement by Brigadier General Nancy R. Adams, Chief, Army Nurse Corps, Army Medical Department, before the Defense Subcommittee, Committee on Appropriations, United States Senate, 1st Session, 104th Congress, Health Programs, 13 June 1995," Record Version, 7, ANCC, OMH.

90. House of Representatives, 103rd Congress, 2nd Session, "National Defense Authorization Act for Fiscal Year 1995, Report of the Committee on Army Services, House of Representatives, on H.R. 4301, Together with Additional and Dissenting Views (Including Cost Estimate of the Congressional Budget Office)," Report 103-499, Section 611, 251, 10 May 1994. Michele L. Kohl, "Board Certification Pay for Army Nurse Corps Health Care Providers," Memorandum, 1 November 1996; and Carolyn Bulliner, "PERSCOM Update," *The Army Nursing Newsletter* (October 1999): 5 (both in ANCC, OMH).

91. Monica A. Secula, "Board Certification Pay for Psychiatric and Community Health Clinical Nurse Specialists," Memorandum, 6 May 1997, ANCC, OMH.

92. Charlene Peterson, "Nursing Scholarship Update," Information Paper, 28 August 1989, ANCC, OMH. One primary reason that nursing students failed to accept scholarships had to do with curriculum and constructive credit problems. Collegiate nursing students typically carried a heavier load of academic and clinical course work than most other students. At the same time, many nursing schools refused to award credit for the additionally required military science courses for ROTC cadets, even for elective requirements. The Army Nurse Corps, the Recruiting Command, and the ROTC Command responded by educating individual nursing school faculties and deans about the applicability of ROTC studies to nursing and education in general. Their efforts eventually rectified the injustice, and most schools subsequently awarded constructive credit for ROTC courses. Another serendipitous outcome of the recruiters' outreach was the recruitment of many faculty members into the Army Reserve. Clara L. Adams-Ender to Author, E-mail Correspondence, 26 January 2004, ANCC, OMH.

93. John Hudock, "The Registered Nurse Shortage," Information Paper, n.d., ANCC, OMH.

94. Wil Nieves, "Status of Nursing Shortage Initiatives," Information Paper, 19 July 1989; and Charlene Peterson, "Annual Historical Report Input," TM, 18 December 1989 (both in ANCC, OMH). "Soldiers Go 'Green to Gold' to Become Nurses," *HSC Mercury* 16 (March 1989): 7.

95. "Operation AMEDD Green to Gold," Fact Sheet, 28 August 1989, and attached briefing slides; "Soldiers Can Swap Army Green for Officers' Gold Bars," *USA Today*, n.d., n.p., Newspaper Clipping; and Lorraine Fritz to Jennifer Petersen, "ROTC History Questions," E-mail Correspondence, 8 December 2003 (all in ANCC, OMH).

96. Charlene Peterson, "Nursing Scholarship Update," Fact Sheet, 28 August 1989; and Frank F. Ledford, "Nurse Action Plan—INFORMATION MEMORANDUM," 21 September 1989 (both in ANCC, OMH).

97. "Soldiers Go 'Green to Gold' to Become Nurses," *HSC Mercury* 16 (March 1989): 7.

98. "Lieutenant Gets 'Green-to-Gold' Award," *Pentagram* (21 May 1992): 7, 13. Jeri Chappelle, "Nurse Earns Honor as U.S.'s Best ROTC Cadet," *HSC Mercury* 19 (May 1992): 7.

99. Lisa A. Toven, "Curriculum Vitae," n.d., ANCC, OMH.

100. John Hudock, "Nursing Shortage," Information Paper, 8 May 1990; Clara Adams-Ender, "Hearing before the Senate Appropriations Committee, Subcommittee on Defense," 16 March 1989, Transcript of Testimony; and Clara L. Adams-Ender, "Legislative Awareness," *Memo from the Chief, Army Nurse Corps* (31 December 1989): 2 (all in ANCC, OMH). "Program Helps Medics Get Nurse Commissions," *HSC Mercury* 17 (March 1990): 3.

101. Carolyn M. Feller and Debora R. Cox, *Highlights in the History of the Army Nurse Corps* (Washington, DC: U.S. Army Center of Military History, 2000), 64.

102. "Statement of Brigadier General Nancy R. Adams, Chief, Army Nurse Corps," 5 May 1993, 1, ANCC, OMH.

103. VI was a level of officer career status that followed an obligated tour but preceded Regular Army status. Several years after VI became available, Conditional Voluntary Indefinite (CVI) became a preliminary option conferred before VI status. A board selected Army nurses for VI, and the number chosen was "dependent upon how many vacancies recruiting would not be able to fill." CVI evolved into being the Army Nurse Corps "way of hedging [their] bets about candidates who were not the most stellar performers." It also was a bolt hole for officers who "were only staying in to see if they could get a certain assignment or if they were applying for specialty training/school." Darlene McLeod to Author, E-mail Correspondence, 12 June 2003, ANCC, OMH. For a while, an officer had to be in CVI status before applying for VI. Later, however, certain officers could apply directly for VI. Gail Croy to Author, E-mail Correspondence, 29 July 2003, ANCC, OMH.

104. "AMEDD Enlisted Commissioning Program (AECP)," *Memo from the Chief, Army Nurse Corps* (December 1993): 3; Terris M. Kennedy, Interview by Constance J. Moore, Transcript, 302–03, 25 October 1995; Terris M. Kennedy, Interview by Constance J. Moore focusing on "One Moment in Time," Briefing Slides, Transcript, 25, 11 February 1997; Terris Kennedy to Author, E-mail Correspondence, 24 January 2004; Nancy Adams to Author, E-mail Correspondence, 30 January 2004; and Stephanie Marshall to Author, E-mail Correspondence, 2 February 2004 (all in ANCC, OMH).

105. G.E. Willis, "Feelings of Betrayal Abound as Drawdown Hits Nurses," *Army Times* 57 (16 September 1996): 3. Colonel John Hudock noted that these inequities happened frequently. Sometimes an Army nurse had just completed graduate school at Army expense and immediately failed to be selected for promotion. He explained that "the criteria for selection does vary slightly for schooling, voluntary indefinite, promotion, etc., and perceptions of board members vary, not to mention that there are cutoff points to be made. The concept of *best qualified* versus *fully qualified* sometimes leaves good people behind." John Hudock to Author, Handwritten Letter, 15 September 2003, ANCC, OMH.

106. Frank F. Ledford, "Nurse Action Plan—Information Memorandum," 21 September

1989; Wil Nieves, "Status of Nursing Shortage Initiatives," Information Paper, 19 July 1989; and Clara L. Adams-Ender, "If You Have an AOC/SI Producing Course Guarantee," *Memo from the Chief, Army Nurse Corps* (31 December 1989): 4–5 (all in ANCC, OMH).

107. Conditional voluntary indefinite (CVI) was "the preferred method" for extension of active duty service beyond the officer's initial obligated tour. It conferred "career status" on the officer. To apply for CVI, officers had to have completed two years of Active Federal Commissioned Service (AFCS). A selection board met twice yearly to recommend officers for CVI, basing their decisions on the officers' performance, recommendations of superiors, and compliance with the fitness regulations and weight standards. CVI status obligated officers to one year of Active Duty Service Obligation (ADSO) but allowed them to continue through eight years of AFCS if they so desired. Clara L. Adams-Ender, "Lieutenant's Corner," *Memo from the Chief, Army Nurse Corps* (31 December 1989): 3–4, ANCC, OMH. At the seventh year of AFCS, an Army nurse could apply for VI (Voluntary Indefinite) status. Applicants could be considered for CVI two times. They could be considered only once for VI. Clara L. Adams-Ender, *Memo from the Chief, Army Nurse Corps* (30 June 1990): 2, ANCC, OMH.

108. Frank F. Ledford, "Nurse Action Plan— Information Memorandum," 21 September 1989; Wil Nieves, "Status of Nursing Shortage Initiatives," Information Paper, 2, 19 July 1989; and Clara L. Adams-Ender, "ANC Branch, Health Services Division, PERSCOM (TAPC-OPH-AN)," *Memo from the Chief, Army Nurse Corps* (31 December 1989): 5 (all in ANCC, OMH).

109. Claudia Bartz, "Foreign Nurse Accession into the Army Nurse Corps," Staff Study, 4 October 1989, ANCC, OMH.

110. A year group was a collection of due course officers whose entry date on active duty occurred within the same fiscal year. The officers were sorted into year groups as a way of managing promotions and other board actions. Jennifer L. Petersen to Author, E-mail Correspondence, 30 January 2004, ANCC, OMH.

111. Due course officers entered the Army as second lieutenants and were promoted according to a set schedule. They never were selected above or below the zone for promotion, never had a break in service, and received no constructive credit upon commissioning. "AMEDD Officer Structure Study (AMOSS)," Briefing Slides, n.d.; and Clara L. Adams-Ender, *Memo from the Chief, Army Nurse Corps* (30 June 1990): 2–3 (both in ANCC, OMH).

112. Untitled TD, no author, n.d., that used an "Issue, Question, Answer, Rationale" format to strategize on recruitment and retention topics; Delbert L. Spurlock, "Army Medical Department Promotions," Memorandum for Chief of Staff, United States Army, 1 October 1985; and "Field Grade Structure in the Army Nurse Corps," Information Paper, 5 December 1991 (all in ANCC, OMH). "From the Ferment, Profound Changes," *Army* 36 (March 1986): 42.

113. Colonel Audre McLoughlin served as the study group's deputy director. Lieutenant Colonel John Hudock and Major Dena Norton were the Army Nurse Corps representatives. Connie L. Slewitzke, "Memorandum from the Chief, Army Nurse Corps," Typewritten Newsletter, 2, March 1985, ANCC, OMH. John M. Hudock, "Revision of Medical Grade Table AR 611-101," Action Summary Sheet, 18 September 1986, ANCC, OMH. DA Pam 611-21, "Military Occupational Classification and Structure," 21 March 1999, superseded AR 611-101, "Commissioned Officer Classification System."

114. John Hudock to Author, 7 Telephone Interview, March 2003. "AMEDD Officer Structure Study (AMOSS)," Briefing Slides, n.d., ANCC, OMH.

115. John Hudock to Author, Telephone Interview, 12 March 2003. Connie L. Slewitzke,

Interview by Beverly Greenlee, 146–49, n.d., USAWC/USAMHI Senior Officer Oral History Program, Project No. 88-8, ANCC, OMH.

116. John Hudock to Author, E-mail Correspondence, 6 March 2003, ANCC, OMH.

117. John Hudock to Author, Telephone Interview, 7 March 2003. "AMEDD Officer Structure Study (AMOSS)," Briefing Slides, n.d.; and Clara L. Adams-Ender, *Memo from the Chief, Army Nurse Corps* (30 September 1989): 3 (both in ANCC, OMH).

118. "AMEDD Officer Structure Study (AMOSS)," Briefing Slides, n.d.; and Clara L. Adams-Ender, *Memo from the Chief, Army Nurse Corps* (30 September 1989): 3 (both in ANCC, OMH).

119. Marie P. Alire, "Input to Readiness Issue on ANC Strategic Plan," TM, June 1988; and Craig L. Urbauer, "Strategic Planning Recommendations," Information Paper, 1 June 1988 (both in ANCC, OMH).

120. The maximum age for the initial appointment in the Navy and the Air Force reserves was 47 years old. Annie R. Spurlin and Donna F. Owen, "What Nurses Ask about the Military Reserves," *American Journal of Nursing* 89 (October 1989): 1311–12. Donna F. Owen, "Direct Mail Campaign for Physicians and Nurses with Critical War Time Skills," Fact Sheet, 6 January 1988, ANCC, OMH. Sunnie Scarlett, "Army Needs Nurses, Supply Shrinks," *HSC Mercury* 16 (January 1989): 1, 6, 7.

121. Active, Guard, Reserve (AGR) recruiters were members of the National Guard who came on active duty to fill certain positions that required full-time staffing. Their pay could come from federal coffers (Title 10) or from state funds (Title 32). Jennifer L. Petersen to Author, E-mail Correspondence, 30 January 2004, ANCC, OMH.

122. PBG 698A; and Wil Nieves, "Status of Nursing Shortage Initiatives," Information Paper, 19 July 1989, 3, 4 (both in ANCC, OMH).

123. "Nursing Shortage Hits Guard, Reserves," *The American Nurse* 20 (March 1988): 18. "Military Reserves Offer Nurses Opportunities, Benefits, Options," *The American Nurse* 20 (March 1988): 20.

124. Clara L. Adams-Ender and John Hudock, "Nurse Recruiting, SA-3-1," 18 July 1988, ANCC, OMH. "Nursing Shortage Hits Guard, Reserves," *The American Nurse* 20 (March 1988): 18. "Military Reserves Offer Nurses Opportunities, Benefits, Options," *The American Nurse* 20 (March 1988): 20.

125. A similar loan repayment program for active duty members failed to garner legislative approval in 1989. Lark A. Ford, "Active Duty Loan Repayment Program for Army Nurse Corps: Status Report of Legislative Proposal," TD, 18 May 1994, ANCC, OMH.

126. Clara L. Adams-Ender and John Hudock, "Nurse Recruiting, SA-3-1," 18 July 1988, ANCC, OMH. "Nursing Shortage Hits Guard, Reserves," *The American Nurse* 20 (March 1988): 18. "Military Reserves Offer Nurses Opportunities, Benefits, Options," *The American Nurse* 20 (March 1988): 20. Annie R. Spurlin and Donna F. Owen, "What Nurses Ask about the Military Reserves," *American Journal of Nursing* 9 (October 1989): 1311–12. Committee on Armed Services, House of Representatives, Title 10, United States Code, Armed Forces (as Amended through April 21, 1987), §2172.

127. "Nurse Corps Testimony Issues," TD, 3, n.d.; and "Active Component Health Professionals Loan Repayment Program for Nurses," Information Paper, 6 May 1993 (both in ANCC, OMH).

128. Tracy E. Strevey, "Civilian Registered Nurse (RN) Shortage," TM, 2–3, 18 April 1988, ANCC, OMH. G.A. Vidis, "Tripler Keeps Nurses with Job Satisfaction," *HSC Mercury* 15 (December 1987): 6.

129. Charles Bombard, "Civilian Nurses Fill Campbell Gaps," *HSC Mercury* 12 (July 1985): 6. Charles F. Bombard and Terris E. Kennedy, "An Aid to Temporary Staffing Short-

ages: The Nursing Pool," *Military Medicine* 152 (March 1987): 136–38. When Kennedy was a University of Colorado graduate student in 1980, she and Major Ed Kurlansick, the Nurse Methods Analyst at Fitzsimons Army Medical Center, created a very successful internal float pool with Hire Lag Funds. Later, Kennedy implemented a similar program in Korea. Terris L. Kennedy to Author, Typewritten Comments on 1980s chapter, n.d., ANCC, OMH.

130. Sunnie Scarlett, "Chief Nurses Find Publicity Attracts More RNs," *HSC Mercury* 16 (April 1989): 9.

131. "Wood Greets New Nurses," *HSC Mercury* 16 (February 1989): 12.

132. Charlotte Asch, "Increased Authorizations to Relieve Army Nurse Shortage," *HSC Mercury* 13 (August 1986): 4.

133. "Military Nurses Task Force Report on the Military Nursing Shortage, Prepared for Department of Health and Human Services, Secretary's Commission on Nursing," December 1988, VI-10, ANCC, OMH.

134. Patricia A. Prescott, "Supplemental Agency Employment of Nurses," in *Nursing in the 1980s, Crises, Opportunities, Challenges*, ed. Linda H. Aiken and Susan R. Gortner (Philadelphia: J.B. Lippincott, 1982), 399–417.

135. The Army paid the agencies about $60 per hour for the nurses. The nurses then earned approximately $35 hourly. John Hudak to Author, E-mail Correspondence, 9 September 2003, ANCC, OMH. In FY 1989 the Army funded $2,529,800 for contract nurses at Walter Reed Army Medical Center. In FY 1990, that allocation rose to $5,575,759. John Hudak, "Contract Nurses," Information Paper, 7 August 1990, ANCC, OMH. Connie L. Slewitzke, Interview by Beverly Greenlee, 266–67, n.d., USAWC/USAMHI Senior Officer Oral History Program, Project No. 88-8, ANCC, OMH.

136. Mary Messerschmidt to Author, E-mail Correspondence, 11 February 2003, ANCC, OMH.

137. Clara L. Adams-Ender, Interview by Virginia Ruth Cheney, 156, 1992, Project 92-3, U.S. Army Military History Institute, Senior Officer Oral History Program, ANCC, OMH.

138. Clara Adams-Ender, "Hearing before the Senate Appropriations Committee, Subcommittee on Defense," Transcript of Testimony, 16 March 1989; and Susan B. Christoph, "Chief, ANC Division's Comments on ANC FY 90 Communications Plan," TD, 2 October 1989 (both in ANCC, OMH).

139. Sid Balman, "Rx for Nurses," *Air Force Times* 50 (19 February 1990): 14–16. Soraya S. Nelson, "Initiatives May Help Ease Nursing Shortage," *Army Times* 50 (18 December 1989): 18.

140. Lewis H. Seaton, "Navy Medical Department," *Military Medicine* 148 (November 1983): 841–44.

*Chapter Eleven*
# Preparing for Action

A major theme dating from the 1970s that grew significantly stronger in the 1980s was the Army's clear-cut determination to better prepare for future combat. The major components of this movement involved maintaining proper physical fitness and improving the overall readiness of the Army.[1]

A Healthy and Fit Force was the first pillar of the Health Service Support Air-Land Battle, the doctrine for contemporary combat service support derived from lessons learned from World War II to the campaign in Grenada.[2] The Honorable John O. Marsh, secretary of the Army, espoused the belief that readiness began with physical fitness and encompassed all aspects of total fitness. General E.C. Meyer, the chief of staff of the Army, insisted that each individual was personally responsible for developing and maintaining lifestyles for themselves and their soldiers to meet the rigors of military service, affirming that appropriate physical training and proper nutritional habits affected professional competency. General Hazel Johnson explained that the components of a total fitness routine for Army nurses included eating a sensible diet, coping with stress, controlling weight, eschewing substance abuse, participating in regular physical exercise, and preventing disease. Johnson instructed all Army nurses to begin such an all-encompassing program, and advised them that failure to do so would adversely affect their Army career.[3]

One indication of the Army's intent to promote all soldiers' fitness was its increased emphasis on successful completion of the Army Physical Fitness Test and compliance with the height and weight standards twice yearly.[4] Meeting the standards significantly affected selections for promotion, continuation on active duty, and schooling opportunities. The Army required officers to meet the fitness standards before it approved their attendance at educational courses. Those who did not meet standards had their course attendance delayed. General Clara L. Adams-Ender advised officers that the "rationale for the delay is for the benefit of you, the officer." Attaining the standards was part of course completion requirements, and so not meeting them could precipitate a student's failure in a specific course or could result in a poor academic efficiency report.[5] This could adversely impact selection for promotions and other opportunities. The Army's emphasis on the fitness benchmarks meant failure to meet them could doom a career.

The Army Medical Department (AMEDD) officers occasionally singled out Army Nurse Corps officers for their failure to meet the fitness requirements. Colonel Charles J. Reddy, chief of the Nursing Division at the Health Services Command (HSC), allowed that much was written and said about Army nurses who did not meet weight standards, but only 5 percent (151 of 2,999) of Army Nurse Corps officers assigned to the U.S. Army HSC exceeded weight standards. Less known and publicized were the pounds that Army Nurse Corps officers shed to conform to benchmarks. The majority of Army nurses were complying with the weight standards, passing the Army Physical Fitness Test, living healthy lives, and excelling in athletics.[6]

Army Nurse Corps officers also worked to improve overall Army fitness levels. They succeeded beyond anyone's expectations. Many of them obtained graduate degrees and experience as cardiac rehabilitation clinical nurse specialists or as critical care nurses.[7]

In March 1984, Captain Leslie Brousseau became the health fitness consultant to Europe's 7th Medical Command. In that role, she wrote a monthly health and fitness column for the command newspaper and served as a project officer for many health promotion activities, such as the European Command's Great American Smokeout, a tobacco-cessation program, and high blood pressure month. She also coordinated health fairs and health fitness conferences in Europe.[8]

Captain Jeanne Picariello was another Army nurse involved in improving fitness. She was a member of the U.S. Army Pentathlon Team from 1975 to 1978, the first woman and Army nurse to participate.[9] Picariello was program director of the Army Staff Corporate Fitness Program in 1985 and 1986. She worked with two other Army nurses, a health risk appraisal and intervention coordinator, and the surgeon general's nursing consultant on fitness to gauge the cost effectiveness of health promotion activities of 6,000 military and civilian Pentagon employees. As a part of the project, volunteers underwent a preliminary physiological assessment of current fitness levels and then started physical conditioning. Based on individual needs, volunteers could enroll in classes on smoking cessation, weight control, and stress management. With control and experimental groups, the researchers measured and statistically analyzed the variables of work productivity, reductions in health care expenses, job absenteeism, and turnover/retraining costs.[10] The study demonstrated a positive physiological advantage from structured cardiovascular screening and health education classes.[11] Picariello concluded that the program was cost effective and well accepted. Using civilian staff, the Department of Defense (DoD) continued the program for the Pentagon workforce over the succeeding years.[12] Picariello later served as commandant of the U.S. Army Physical Fitness School at Fort Benjamin Harrison, Indiana, from 1994 to 1997, where she oversaw the Army's studies on the Army Physical Fitness Test

Pictured is Colonel Charles Reddy, Chief Nurse, Health Services Command, 1985.
Photo courtesy of Army Nurse Corps Archives, Office of Medical History, Falls Church, VA.

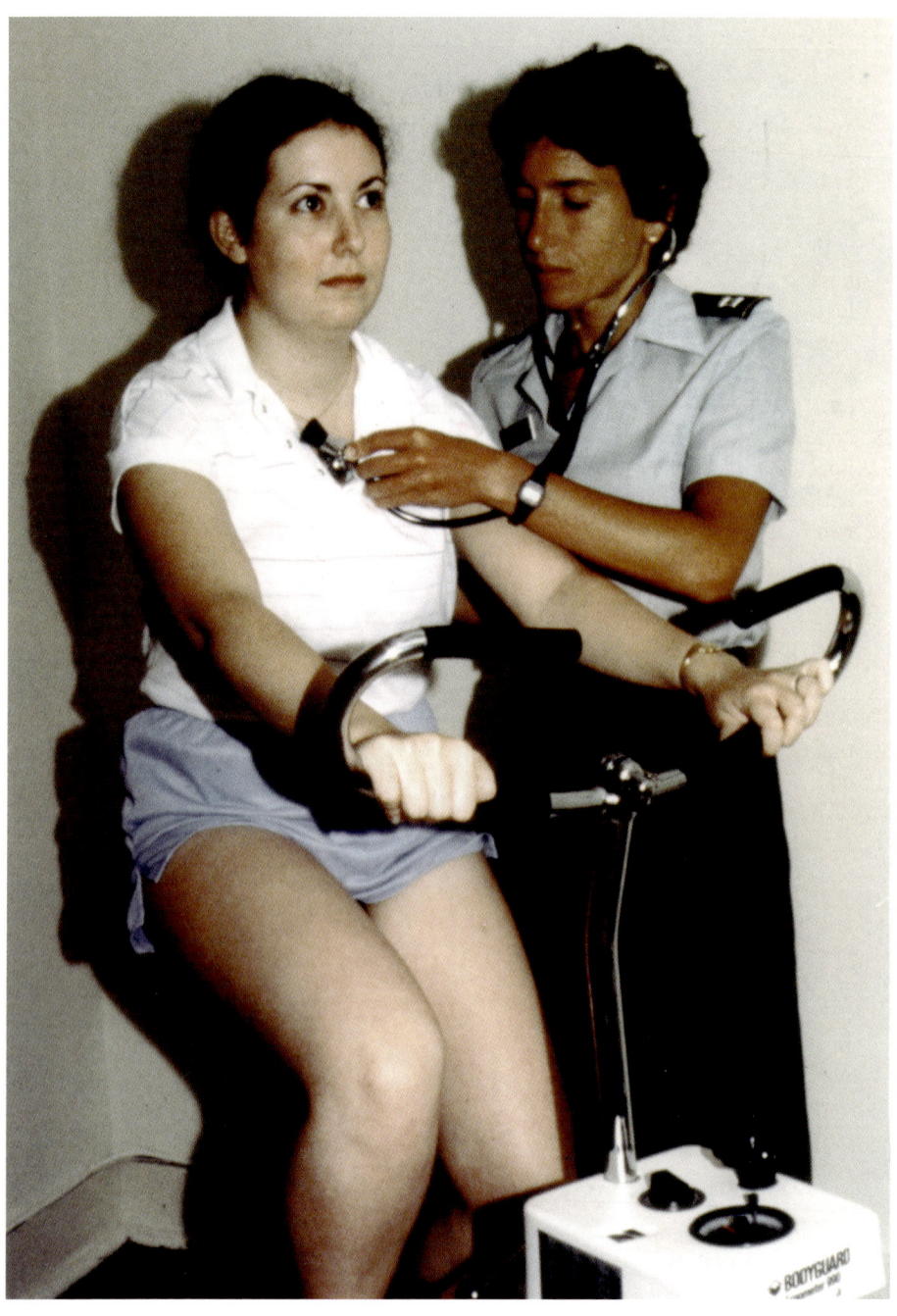

Captain Jeanne Picariello assesses a participant in the Army Staff Corporate Fitness Program in the Pentagon in 1985.
Photo courtesy of Army Nurse Corps Archives, Office of Medical History, Falls Church, VA.

standards that led to revisions in the existing benchmarks.[13]

In 1987, Lieutenant Colonel Antoinette Hagey, a health promotions nurse specialist, made her contribution to the Army fitness program. She oversaw the development and implementation of the health risk assessment component of the Army Health Promotion Program. Hagey concurrently served on the DoD Health Promotion Coordination Committee and tested and selected materials for education on smoking cessation and hypertension.[14]

Fitness was a key component of readiness. Without soldiers fit to fight, readiness was a difficult if not impossible state to achieve on both a personal and unit level.

AMEDD leaders defined readiness as the ability to immediately deploy qualified military medical personnel in support of combat.[15] Other elements also determined readiness. A multidimensional construct, readiness presupposed unit cohesion or a state where soldiers worked efficiently in unison for a common goal. Achieving the goal required physical agility, mental power, psychological aptitude, and effective leadership.[16] Appropriate Table of Organization and Equipment (TO&E) equipment, adequate levels of training, and personnel strength also influenced readiness. For Lieutenant General Quinn Becker, the surgeon general, readiness demanded the integration of finely honed medical skills with the logistical ability to get the right equipment and people to the appropriate place at the necessary time.[17]

As the AMEDD entered the 1980s, serious readiness problems existed. In 1982, Assistant Secretary of Defense (Health Affairs) (ASD[HA]) John Beary warned that the military medical services could provide surgery for only one in 10 wounded combatants in the event of war.[18] By the mid-1980s officials described the level of medical readiness as extremely critical. Speaking in 1985, ASD(HA) William E. Mayer shared his dour assessment with the nation's physicians:

> I regret to tell you that if we entered a major conventional war today, the system could not render an adequate level of emergency surgery and resuscitation to the wounded in action. Morbidity and mortality rates could be high.[19]

One year later, in 1986, Mayer wrote of steady improvements, although the military health care system was still not up to par. In the event of war, Mayer wrote, "scarcely three out of ten wounded [would] receive the prompt care that can spell the difference between life and death."[20]

At the same time, medical readiness became a high-profile issue that proved embarrassing when details became public.[21] Both civilian and military newspapers and magazines chronicled readiness deficiencies from the level of DoD all the way down to the AMEDD. In 1985, *Reader's Digest* quoted a U.S. Air Force physician who believed that were the United States to go to war prior to 1991, "a lot of people are going to die unnecessarily."[22] Around the same time, a former Navy physician proclaimed in the *Washington Post* that the entire military medicine system should be abolished, with resultant annual savings of hundreds of millions of dollars by the elimination of medical department salaries and by the sale of military medical facilities, located on prime real estate around Washington, D.C., California, and Hawaii.[23] In 1986, *U.S. News & World Report* characterized readiness of the military medical services as substandard, recounting that only 30 percent of infantrymen wounded in battle could rely on prompt medical care because of personnel and logistical deficits.[24] *Army* magazine acknowledged that Army medicine was the object of intense controversy because of its lack of readiness for combat.[25] The *Department of Army Historical Summary* added its voice to the calamity, recording that the "ability to provide wartime medical support has been severely limited by a shortage of the medical equipment and professional medical personnel."[26] Everyone realized shortcomings had to be corrected. Fortunately, plans for improving and upgrading medical combat support were already in the works.

In 1982, the acting ASD(HA), Beary, instructed the three military services' medical departments to use only field health facility systems developed by a quad-service task force, the Military Field Medical Systems Standardization Steering Group, and approved by Beary's office. His aim was to improve the services' medical support levels and logistical capability.[27] Becker, the Army surgeon general, opposed Beary's dictum, questioning the wisdom of a joint, strictly homogeneous approach. Becker saw the mandate as an attempt to take control away from the Army and allow DoD to dictate the size and configuration of the medical departments of the services. Without the destiny of the entire AMEDD in his hands, Becker saw only trouble ahead.[28] Nonetheless, the Deployable Medical System (DEPMEDS), as it came to be known, moved forward. By 1984, the Military Field Medical Systems Standardization Steering Group had agreed on the use of the TEMPER, as the standardized fabric wall (exterior side of the tent) for the chosen single-system DEPMEDS. The fabric design incorporated a layer of air that served as insulation to counter extremes of hot or cold weather. All the military services tested the new equipment at Fort Hood, Texas, in November 1984 and determined that the DEPMEDS was able to carry out the mission, as long as improvements were made to make it more easily transportable.[29]

During the next few years, Congress funded 30 sets of DEPMEDSs for the AMEDD, and the Army erected a complete prototype hospital at Camp Bullis, Texas, in August 1987.[30] The DEPMEDS' cost for a 60-bed mobile army surgical hospital (MASH) in 1987 was $8.2 million and $16.6 million for a 1,000-bed general hospital.[31]

In February 1988, the 8th Evacuation Hospital at Fort Ord, California, became the first TO&E unit to field DEPMEDSs. It deployed to Fort Hunter Liggett, California, and set up a 400-bed DEPMEDS hospital, staffing it with 85 Professional Officer Filler System personnel.[32] The assigned staff implemented a Department of the Army–directed assessment and validation of the equipment and forwarded their findings to the Test and Experimentation Command. Field testing did validate the utility of DEPMEDS equipment. In January 1989, the 8th Evacuation Hospital deployed to Honduras with its DEPMEDS facility to support Fuertes Caminos 89.[33] The detachment in Honduras treated the first surgical case and delivered the first baby in a DEPMEDS. Active Army, Army National Guard, and Army, Navy, and Air Force Reserve units took part in the deployment.[34] By 1990, the Army had fielded 46 DEPMEDS hospital sets and expected to equip a total of 129 hospitals in the near future.[35]

DEPMEDS used modules that offered almost unlimited potential for configuration.[36] The hard-walled containers, referred to as ISO containers, housed the operating room, radiology, laboratory, pharmacy, and central supply elements. The TEMPER, soft-sided tents, contained the triage area, intensive care units, and inpatient wards.[37]

The DEPMEDS model had both advantages and disadvantages. Its many advantages were its fuel efficiency compared to the Mobile Unit, Surgical, Transportable (MUST) facility, its relative ease in assembly and disassembly, its flexible configuration, its improved level of lighting, and its standardized medical and nonmedical equipment.[38] The nonmedical standardized items in DEPMEDS were electrical generators, dietary systems, water distribution and utilities support equipment, bathing facilities, oxygen-generating mechanisms, water-production systems, power distribution infrastructure, and environmental-control components.[39] These advantages outweighed the major problem of the sets: their immobility and excessive weight.

The size and weight of the DEPMEDS forced Colonel Jerome Foust, Medical Services Corps (MSC), commander of the 44th Medical Brigade, to reduce the bulk of combat support hospitals and MASHs during Operation Desert Storm. This enabled the DEPMEDS to move with organic vehicles and keep pace with the combat units.[40] In turn, that led to the dual development of a mini-MASH and to the creation of a Contingency Medical Force. The mini-MASH downsized the MASH unit from 60 beds to a 30-bed intensive surgical hospital. Adoption of the Contingency Medical Force, first utilized in the Balkans during the 1990s, further streamlined combat medical support.[41] The DEPMEDS facility also was vulnerable to biological and chemical warfare attack. After the first Gulf War, planners debated hardening the DEPMEDS equipment to protect against biological and chemical warfare, but the added weight and complexity would render its use extremely difficult for a field unit. However, in the immediate aftermath of the war, planners created an insert for the TEMPER tents and retrofitted a filter for the air handlers to lessen the threat from biological and chemical warfare.[42]

DoD arrived at medical logistical standardization of DEPMEDS by convening 23 panels of expert clinicians to identify therapeutic regimens to treat more than 300 combat-related diagnoses based on actual combat data. The Task/Time/Treater database, as it was known, detailed precise supplies and equipment required to provide each diagnosis-specific treatment.[43] The Defense Medical Standardization Board (DMSB) gradually assumed the overall responsibility for obtaining equipment and determining staffing levels for the DEPMEDS.[44]

DEPMEDS began as a logistical system, a physical field hospital, but with time it also became a personnel element.[45] A subunit of the DMSB, the Joint Services Nursing Advisory Group, a tri-service task force with Army Nurse Corps representation, originally calculated the required nursing assets needed in theater.[46] However, the DMSB slashed the Joint Services Nursing Advisory Group's recommendations, rejecting the proposed numbers and mix of nursing staff because field staffing had to be "austere but adequate."[47] Nurses countered that while the DMSB's staffing levels were austere, they were neither adequate nor safe. General Connie Slewitzke felt that the Medical Corps and Medical Service Corps officers never took nurses seriously when they talked about safe staffing levels. Many time-consuming and acrimonious sessions justified and rejustified staffing.[48] Only after several years of struggle could the Army Nurse Corps produce firm evidence demonstrating the amount of time each nursing procedure consumed based on Sherrod's previously described Nursing Care Hour Standards Study. With the established estimates of the potential types and numbers of different patients requiring care at the DEPMEDS facility calculated against the known care needs for these patients, the Army Nurse Corps used Sherrod's statistics to show an accurate picture of the numbers and types of nurses required.[49] Without Sherrod's hard work, the Army Nurse Corps, in Slewitzke's words, would "really have been behind the eight ball."[50]

By the 1990s, however, even these more realistic staffing levels seemed inadequate for cutting-edge, adequate medical care. At that time, the Army Nurse Corps recognized that basing mobilization staff numbers on the task times of the Workload Management System for Nurses (WMSN), as then recommended by a Manpower Requirements Criteria document, created unrealistic and insufficient numbers of staff. General Nancy Adams wrote that even a modified WMSN was inappropriate for staff forecasting in mobilization situations. Corps leaders concluded the WMSN had been developed many years in the past and needed updating. The system, moreover, was never intended for use in a combat setting. Field conditions such as reduced communications, limited electrical power, inadequate climate control, lack of plumbing, poor automation, and restricted infrastructure resources dramatically increased a nurse's time to do even the simplest tasks. Combat nursing staff necessarily spent more time and energy building and maintaining the hospital, and on duties relating to nuclear, biological, and chemical concerns, sentry duty, field sanitation chores, staff officer and driver duty, erecting and maintaining bunkers, filling sandbags, and many other unanticipated responsibilities. There were many other arguments against using the WMSN to gauge staffing. For instance, there was the erroneous belief that the administration of multiple antibiotics, the standard of care for trauma patients with contaminated combat wounds, would be underestimated and counted in the WMSN as only one task. In reality, the administration of multiple antibiotics would actually require more time because limited pharmacy support was available to prepare the medications. Also, assumptions that less nursing care was needed with limited technological equipment failed to comprehend the certainty that less-sophisticated equipment increased the need for one-on-one care, demanding a more labor-intensive effort. The WMSN presupposed that nurses were working five eight-hour shifts (40 hours) a week, but mobilization staffing assumed that personnel would

Throughout her assignment as chief nurse of the 121st Evacuation Hospital and the 18th Medical Command in Korea, as pictured here, and in her subsequent role as assistant chief of the Corps, Colonel Terris Kennedy used her wealth of practical knowledge about personnel strength issues and readiness concerns to improve the ability of the Army Nurse Corps to support future combat operations. Photo courtesy of Colonel Terris Kennedy, Onancock, VA.

work longer shifts with less time off duty. Adams believed that it was unrealistic in times of continuous operations to require nurses to work at their peak for lengthy periods without time off and wanted flexibility built into the system. Her office stayed dedicated to creating rational, meaningful, and validated Manpower Requirements Criteria standards for combat nursing.[51] Colonel Terris Kennedy, the assistant chief of the Corps, subsequently recommended that the Health Care Studies/Clinical Investigations Agency at Fort Sam Houston validate and document actual nursing care requirements for mobilization. Until such a study was completed, the Army Nurse Corps had no way of knowing if its field staffing requirements were accurate and if the discrepancies identified with Manpower Requirements Criteria's numbers would be resolved.[52]

Many Army Nurse Corps officers spent a great deal of time with the DEPMEDS project developing an improved field facility with functional equipment and supplies and appropriate nursing staff levels. Lieutenant Colonel Collette Keyser, an operating room nurse, became the first military nurse to work with DEPMEDS as a staffer in the Health Care Operations Office in the Surgeon General's Office in 1983. Keyser meticulously computerized information and lists of supplies required for Operating Room/Central Materiel Supply sets and trays. Since no other military service had assigned a nurse that early to the DEPMEDS project, the sister services had to accept Keyser's recommendations.[53] Lieutenant Colonel Roger Hopkins, who had been assigned to the Academy of Health Sciences and worked with the Manpower Requirements Criteria process and had experience with TO&E matters, chose ward equipment.[54] Colonel Eily P. Gorman collaborated on the quad panels. Lieutenant Colonel Diane Corcoran, while assigned to the Proponency Office of the Directorate of Training and Development at the Academy of Health Sciences, did extraordinary work to justify numbers of nursing staff for the DEPMEDS.[55] This was crucial because Colonel Demetrios G. Tsoulous, a key project officer, drastically underestimated nurse staffing requirements. For instance, he believed a total staff of two people could manage the holding ward 24 hours a day/seven days a week. Slewitzke's comeback was that they could, but "they aren't going to get any sleep." When Tsoulous failed to adjust his computations, Corcoran would notify the Army Nurse Corps leadership in Washington, D.C., about what was happening by back channel, thus providing senior officers with information to fight for the cause of adequate, safe, levels of staff. Slewitzke's office worked closely with Corcoran defending requirements and providing rationale that in turn she would communicate to Tsoulous. The Army Nurse Corps regained some—but not all—of its authorized nursing slots.[56] Lieutenant Colonel Elizabeth Wanersdorfer later carried on the effort when she served as chief, hospital nursing, and DEPMEDS nurse consultant at Medical Research and Development Command. There she monitored more than 5,000 items of medical supplies and equipment and chaired the Quad-Service Nursing Panel that defined intensive, intermediate, and minimal care patients for the mobilization doctrine, developed mobilization standards of practice, and reviewed and revised the DEPMEDS nursing database consisting of nursing tasks, times, and treaters.[57] At the end of the tumultuous period in 1988, Slewitzke reflected:

> We are able to keep on hammering home our point so that we don't lose. As I said many times over, we are the patients' advocate. If we don't do it, there won't be anyone there that will do it for the patients . . . there is no way under God's name that our people would not be stressed out because of the category of the patient that we are taking care of. We fought many iterations. . . . We have done an awful lot of work.[58]

With attention sharply focused on readiness issues, the Army Nurse Corps responded to the imperative to better prepare nurses for field operations. Johnson ordered a review of all Army Nurse Corps courses to identify deficiencies that needed to be remedied in subjects such as field skills and knowledge.[59] She expanded the emphasis already being placed on field nursing in the Army Nurse Corps Officer Basic Course and Officer Advanced Course at Fort Sam Houston, Texas.

In July 1983, the Army Nurse Corps initiated a Field Nursing Course at the Academy of Health Sciences and at Camp Bullis, Texas. The first class met for two weeks, but budget constraints forced the Army Nurse Corps to shorten the course to one week the following year. TO&E chief nurses and staff nurses received priority for attendance. Any further vacancies were sequentially allocated to Table of Distribution and Allowances/Augmentation chief nurses, senior Army Nurse Corps officers, and finally, fixed unit staff nurses.[60] Faculty included selected TO&E chief nurses, such as Major Lynne Connelly, who taught classes on the care of nuclear, biological, and chemical patients. Others provided tutelage on various other aspects of field care. Classes were held in tents, and field training exercises were the preferred method of instruction. Gradually, more nurses attended the Combat Casualty Care Course (C4). However, because much of the material in the Field Nursing Course Program of Instruction replicated that of C4, Army Nurse Corps leaders discontinued offering the Field Nursing Course.[61]

Both the Navy Nurse Corps and the Air Force Nurse Corps sponsored similar courses in combat nursing. The Naval Health Sciences Education and Training Command offered a nurse operational readiness course for its nurses for the first time in September 1981 to provide information and practice for fleet and field activities. Originally, the Navy limited the course to classroom activities but later expanded the curriculum to Camp Lejeune, North Carolina, and Camp Pendleton, California, to provide more realistic exercises.[62] The Air Force graduated the first class of its quarterly Battlefield Nursing Course in July 1982. The course was held for five days to prepare nurses for treating battlefield casualties and to develop patient management skills in the field. Instruction relied on seminars and laboratory and field work.[63] All the military nursing services were striving to improve levels of combat readiness.

Another major effort to prepare tri-service personnel for their combat roles was the C4 program. In the early 1980s, the Joint Medical Readiness Education Committee, composed of the surgeons general and the president of the Uniformed Services University of Health Sciences, established this educational opportunity to instruct health care professionals in techniques of casualty care on the integrated battlefield during a mid- to high-intensity conflict. The eight- to ten-day course at Camp Bullis, Texas, taught Advanced Trauma Life Support skills, care of casualties in deployed hospitals, the fundamentals of triage, management of nuclear, biological, and chemical casualties, patient evacuation, combat roles, prevention of environmental problems in combat, selection of field sites, and field living conditions.[64] In 1985, the Joint Medical Readiness Education Committee implemented an improved curriculum, the C4A, designed to focus on medical treatment facilities

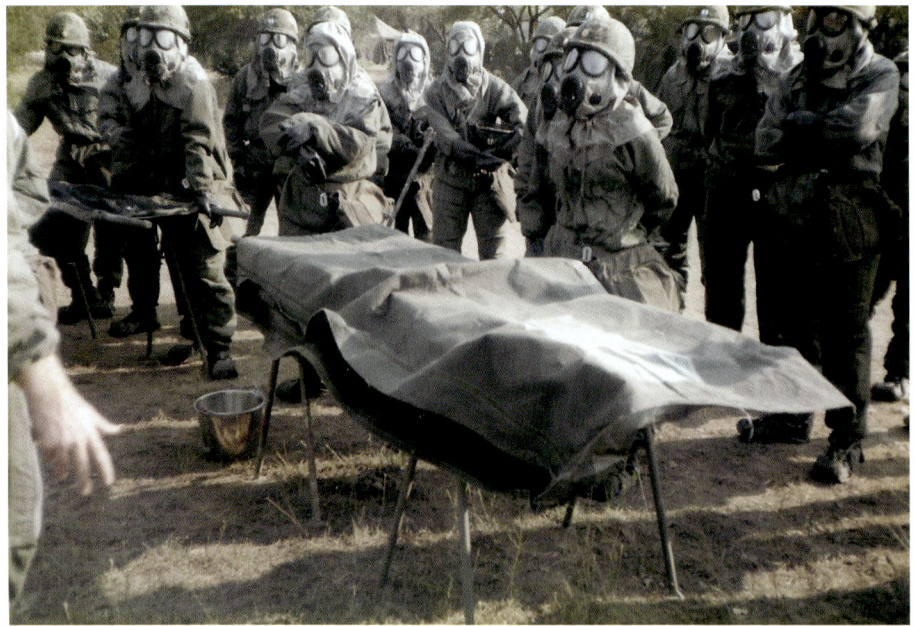

Major Lynne M. Connelly teaches a class focusing on the decontamination of patients in the field during a 1984 iteration of the Field Nursing Course at Camp Bullis, Texas. Here the students are in Mission Oriented Protective Posture 4 gear with gas masks.
Photo courtesy of Colonel Lynne M. Connelly, Basehor, KS.

in the rear guard.[65] It was similar to its precursor, with added subjects such as communications and management of medical resources.[66]

At first only active component Medical Corps officers attended the C4. But the "One Army" concept relied heavily on the reserve components (RCs) and could not deploy on a major mission without reserve augmentation. Because the reserves were essential, DoD began to include a few RC officers in the course. Dentists, nurses, veterinarians, and physician assistants were later assigned to the course, testimony to its growing success.[67] Major Barbara J. Smith was the first Army Nurse Corps officer to attend the C4 course in January 1983.[68]

Soon, more RC officers had to attend the C4 than there were slots available. Consequently, the Office of the Surgeon, Army National Guard (ARNG), established its own Combat Nursing Course, with instruction paralleling that of the C4. Colonel Amelia J. Carson, who was instrumental in setting up this program, organized the first class of nurses at Fort Meade, Maryland, where she contracted with the University of Maryland for Advanced Trauma Life Support training. The course also later welcomed RC Medical and Dental Corps officers and physician assistants.[69]

Although developing readiness skills and knowledge in a structured learning environment was an important approach the Army also understood the value of

Pictured is Colonel Amelia J. Carson, the first Chief Nurse of the Army National Guard (1983). Photo courtesy of Army Nurse Corps Archives, Office of Medical History, Falls Church, VA.

fostering local grassroots efforts to upgrade readiness among individual soldier nurses. The Army Nurse Corps repeatedly emphasized the need for its officers to maintain familiarity with skills associated with mobilization. Readiness featured prominently at the 1980 Professional Development Workshop, where participants recommended that Professional Officer Filler System officers and Mobilization Designees, those active and RC Army nurses who were preassigned to units on a contingency basis, train with their units.[70] This would create an awareness of the unit's capability and how its personnel and equipment functioned. Participants also proposed that more Army Nurse Corps officers attend the Officer Advanced Course in residence status to strengthen their wartime skills. A consensus emerged that it was essential for all regular Army nurses to finish the Resident Advanced Course between their fourth and ninth year of service.[71]

Slewitzke reaffirmed that the primary combat roles involved duties normally assumed by nurse administrators, operating room nurses, anesthetists, and medical-surgical nurses, but upon mobilization almost all pediatric, obstetrics/gynecology, psychiatric mental health, and community health nurses would take on the medical-surgical role. She insisted that all Army nurses be ready to competently function during war or peace and asked that Army community health nurses receive in-hospital training at least two weeks annually to maintain competence in nursing tasks such as intravenous therapy and the operation of equipment. Slewitzke asserted that all Army nurses needed adequate field training with a TO&E unit to competently carry out their wartime responsibilities.[72]

Misunderstandings and discontent surfaced about the need to gain or renew medical-surgical nursing aptitudes. A few nurses, particularly U.S. Army Reserve (USAR) officers with highly specialized skills deemed irrelevant to combat roles, voiced dissatisfaction with the requirement. In civilian life, USAR Captain Mark O. McMorris was an obstetrics and gynecology practitioner in a highly specialized civilian practice. His military superiors ordered him to reserve duty at Eisenhower Army Medical Center on a medical-surgical unit. McMorris felt uncomfortable in this role and objected to his assignment, citing patient safety and quality care issues and concerns about professionalism and jeopardizing his nursing license. As a consequence of his reservations, McMorris' reserve unit asked for his resignation. Officials at HSC verified that USAR nurses had to be prepared for mobilization assignments.[73]

Major Christine E. Cobb, a nurse counselor (recruiter), responded to McMorris' predicament by affirming that "nurses are seeking Reserve and Active Duty nursing because of and not in spite of its perceived challenges." Cobb listed the challenges as "potential mobilization, the probability of cross-training in a different specialty, and the need to creatively utilize nursing's tight resources."[74]

A few months later, another USAR obstetrics/gynecology nurse practitioner in circumstances comparable to those of McMorris spoke out on a more positive note. First Lieutenant M. Denise Palmer accepted that in times of war she had to be ready, according to her understanding of the responsibilities inherent in her commission:

Not only do I agree with this policy, I appreciate the diversity. Membership in the Army Nurse Corps offers many benefits and incentive programs, along with many challenges. It is not easy, nor is it meant to be, but it is worthwhile. Patriotism, leadership, team work, discipline and dedication are attributes we can all admire; my experience in the Army Reserve has given me a sense of purpose and individual growth beyond my initial expectations of a "part-time job."[75]

Skills in obstetrics/gynecology, pediatrics, and other unique specialties proved invaluable in subsequent deployments to Grenada, Panama, the Persian Gulf, Bosnia, Kosovo, and Haiti. Nonetheless, a firm foundation in medical-surgical nursing was essential for all Army nurses.

To boost nurses' readiness at Walter Reed Army Medical Center, Lieutenant Colonel Sharon Bystran, chief of nursing education and staff development, developed a practical tool to serve as a guide and a gauge of personal preparedness. Bystran's comprehensive inventory detailed planning the mobilized officer should make, specifying legal responsibilities, personal military equipment, clothing, comfort items, and immunizations. It stressed the imperative for advanced groundwork, included practical packing hints, and provided an extensive checklist for the Army spouse who would remain behind.[76] It is likely that Bystran's efforts facilitated the mobilization of many Army nurses, such as those who deployed soon thereafter in Operation Desert Shield/Operation Desert Storm.

Another innovative plan that improved readiness while relieving the shortage of Army nurses came to fruition in 1984. That year, the Army Nurse Corps assigned 180 additionally authorized officers to Forces Command (FORSCOM) units with a Memorandum of Understanding (MOU) detailing the agreement in writing. In general, the MOU specified that the FORSCOM nurses would participate in an orientation to their field unit after first signing in to a post and subsequently would work on a more or less permanent basis at the co-located military treatment facility. The MOU obliged military treatment facility commanders to release these FORSCOM nurses from their fixed facility responsibilities when their field unit conducted field training exercises or upon deployment.[77]

A controversial point surfaced in the MOU negotiations. All parties finally achieved a consensus on the issue, but only after extensive dialogue. The area of dissent had to do with officer efficiency report rating chains. FORSCOM wanted the Army nurses, mostly junior officers, to have their performance evaluated by the local FORSCOM commanders, usually an MSC officer. Slewitzke opposed this idea, preferring that other nurses (in the fixed facilities) rate the nurses on their clinical nursing performance rather than MSC officers from the field units rate them on their field nursing skills. She based her objection on a fear that some of the junior officers' careers would be adversely affected because the "MSC . . . commanders in the unit[s] were sometimes a problem." In the end, Slewitzke prevailed but only after making a personal visit to FORSCOM at Fort McPherson in Atlanta, Georgia, to clarify her position. Her vision of the officer efficiency report rating scheme ultimately became reality.[78]

But another glitch also had to be resolved. Not infrequently, the FORSCOM nurses held key positions, such as that of clinical head nurse in the fixed facilities.

As chief of nursing education and development, Colonel Sharon F. Bystran, right, had many diverse responsibilities. Here she is depicted celebrating on Nurses' Day, 1989, at Walter Reed Army Medical Center with Colonel Jane L. Hudak, left, and Colonel Brooke Serpe-Ingold, center, wearing old Army Nurse Corps uniforms.
Photo courtesy of Colonel Sharon Bystran, Aptos, CA.

Administrators in the fixed facilities expressed some foreboding about a possible mass exodus resulting in widespread vacancies in these vital positions when future deployments would occur. Despite the administrators' reservations, Slewitzke insisted on placing Army nurses into head nurse positions because their careers would be negatively affected if they were not afforded leadership opportunities.⁷⁹ Slewitzke optimistically acknowledged that "there will be some 'growing pains' with the new system but we are confident they can be worked out through good communication."⁸⁰ In the final analysis, she concluded that field exposure significantly improved Army nurses' ability to function in general. Before the FORSCOM program, almost all Army nurses had a "big shock" when confronted with the use of post–World War II field equipment in the field hospitals. Although with time the nurses adapted, made do, and learned to improvise, preemptively avoiding such crises was a judicious approach.⁸¹ In spite of the inevitable wrinkles that had to be ironed out, the FORSCOM scheme greatly enhanced readiness.

Another aspect of the readiness picture had to do with retired Army Nurse Corps officers, a largely unknown quantity of relatively untapped resources for use in future emergencies. In 1986, the Health Care Studies and Clinical Investigation Activity at Fort Sam Houston surveyed retired Army nurses younger than age 60 to determine their personal and professional readiness for mobilization. The overall response rate to the questionnaire was 81.7 percent, or 748 retirees. Of the total sample, 93 percent were cognizant of their potential to be recalled, 80 percent had "hip pocket" orders, and 75.4 percent were willing to be recalled if they were physically able.⁸² Almost all (93 percent) still maintained a nursing license but 82 percent felt they needed about six weeks to become clinically competent. Among the anesthetists who responded, 71 percent continued to hold specialty certification in anesthesia and, of those, 77.2 percent were actively practicing in that specialty field.⁸³ This study furnished the Army Nurse Corps with an estimate of the numbers of retirees who would be available to answer the call in times of national need. Most were remarkably willing to serve in such an emergency.

Like the retirees, those Army nurses assigned to USAR or ARNG units, the citizen soldier nurses, also stood ready and committed to activate when called to the service of their nation. Both Army and the Health Service Support Air Land Battle doctrine assigned a significant mobilization role and an increased readiness function to the RCs in the post–Vietnam Army. The Surgeon General acknowledged, however, that the medical RC units were in bad shape in terms of mobilization.⁸⁴ Slewitzke concurred after reviewing the findings of a survey she sent to 3,000 USAR and ARNG officers in 1982.⁸⁵ The quality of chief nurse leadership was a major problem. Some senior officers, many educated with less than a baccalaureate degree, had remained in their positions for almost 20 years, thwarting any kind of upward mobility for better-educated, younger Army nurses. Slewitzke implemented a regulation that limited the tenure of RC chief nurses, but by that time the stagnation had already led many more junior officers to abandon their reserve commissions.⁸⁶ Clearly, the USAR and the ARNG had to revamp their organization as well as their readiness levels. The Individual Mobilization Augmentee (IMA) program was one effort to achieve this end.

As of 1983, the Reserve Components Personnel and Administration Center had assigned 81 Individual Ready Reserve Army Nurse Corps officers to specific positions that they would occupy upon mobilization. Colonel Charles Reddy, the chief, Nursing Division, HSC, encouraged all military treatment facility chief nurses to make full use of their IMAs in their assigned positions during annual training.[87] The numbers of IMAs slowly increased over the years, and by 1988, there were about 144 Individual Ready Reserve Army nurses slotted into IMA assignments.[88]

Many talented, accomplished professionals served in IMA roles, such as Lieutenant Colonel Margaret McClure, who in civilian life was executive director of nursing at New York University Medical Center and president of the American Organization of Nurse Executives. McClure's IMA mobilization position was as a senior staff officer at HSC. On active duty, she familiarized herself with specific role responsibilities and implemented special projects, including one on the recruitment of civilian nurses that capitalized on her doctorate in research administration. McClure was uniquely qualified to carry out a research project focusing on the recruitment of civilian nurses.[89] Later, McClure would serve as the IMA to the assistant chief of the Army Nurse Corps.

The IMA program, however, had some problems. Sometimes chief nurses did not actively support the concept. At one large medical center, for instance, Slewitzke identified about 100 potential IMA positions, but the institution had only two IMAs assigned despite repeated guidance to justify more. Active Army prejudice against reservists persisted, although the majority of reservists could work wonders with proper guidance.[90] As chief nurse at Letterman Army Medical Center, then-colonel Slewitzke relied on reservists to the greatest possible extent. When one particular reservist came for a two-week annual training period, she assigned the individual as chief of ambulatory care. The next year, she made the same assignment and allowed the Army nurse who normally held that position to go on leave. She reasoned that there was always someone around to prevent the IMA from failing. At the Fort Bragg hospital, an entire reserve unit took over the facility while the permanent active component hospital staff did their field training.[91]

Another measure taken to enhance RC readiness placed officers full-time in key USAR and ARNG positions. Johnson posted an active component War College graduate, Colonel Amelia J. Carson, to the ARNG Surgeon's Office as its chief nurse. Slewitzke increased the staff at the Army Reserve Personnel Center, formerly the Reserve Components Personnel and Administration Center, from one Army Nurse Corps officer to five, a number more appropriate to deal with the personnel issues of almost 7,000 RC nurses. She justified a position at FORSCOM to manage RC concerns and arranged RC positions in the Office of The Surgeon General, Quality Assurance, and Procurement.[92] Another USAR officer, Lieutenant Colonel Donna Owen, served on the staff of the ASD(HA) in the Directorate of Manpower, Personnel, and Training as the deputy director for reserve affairs in January 1987.[93]

During the last year of Slewitzke's tenure as chief of the Corps, she directed her IMA, Colonel Catherine Foster, to prepare and propose legislation to create an Army Nurse Corps general officer position for the reserves. In 1988, Congress approved the new position.[94] Brigadier General Dorothy B. Pocklington became the first reserve Army nurse and the first female reserve officer to become a brigadier general.⁹⁵ Pocklington served as the IMA to Adams-Ender, the chief of the Army Nurse Corps, assisting her on mobilization issues as they applied to both the USAR and ARNG.⁹⁶ She represented the chief in boards and meetings; assisted in the formulation of RC integration and mobilization policy; participated in RC recruitment, retention, and training activities; and increased RC visibility.⁹⁷

After three years in her IMA position, Pocklington pioneered another unusual assignment by assuming responsibilities of a non-branch-specific position as deputy chief for public affairs on the Department of the Army level. At first, Pocklington considered her new responsibilities in public affairs as worlds apart from her former role as a nurse. After considering it, however, she concluded there were similarities between the two missions because survival was the crucial attribute of both these disciplines. In the AMEDD, Pocklington envisioned survival of the soldier as fundamental, while in public affairs the focus was the survival of the Army's reputation. This approach provided her with a framework through which to view her responsibilities and allowed her to make use of her AMEDD background to enhance her contributions in public affairs. Pocklington was the first female and nurse to serve in this atypical role and the first general officer Army nurse to fill a position not in the AMEDD.⁹⁸

In 1993, Brigadier General Sharon Vander Zyl blazed a parallel trail in the Army National Guard. Vander Zyl, likewise the first female general officer in the ARNG, served as special assistant to the chief of the Army Nurse Corps.⁹⁹ Many talented Army Nurse Corps officers in the Active Component, Reserve, and National Guard helped to widen the access to future branch immaterial and command positions for Army nurses.

During the 1980s, the Army Nurse Corps made an effort to improve the quality of RC training to enhance readiness skills. As early as 1981, Major Diane Corcoran, chief of the Nursing Education and Training Service (NETS) at Fitzsimons Army Medical Center, and Sergeant First Class David Steffenson, Non-Commissioned Officer in Charge, NETS, tackled readiness issues on a unit level when reservists arrived at their installation for training. Corcoran observed that the reservists typically felt that their annual two-week active duty for training assignment did not furnish them with what they needed, indeed, they "weren't even sure what they were supposed to accomplish."¹⁰⁰ Consequently, the pair formulated a reserve training program, the Systematic Modular Approach to Realistic Training (SMART), to educate officers and enlisted troops about their actual wartime responsibilities. Previously, the reservists provided peacetime health care services during their annual training time.¹⁰¹ This improved routine nursing skills but did not enhance combat nursing proficiencies. SMART was one answer to that problem. It began with a program briefing. Next, NETS furnished the participants with booklets that delineated learning objectives and assignments in specific roles, such as wardmaster, head nurse, practical nurse, or medic. The booklets explicitly outlined clinical and administrative tasks and specified individual and unit training responsibilities. The reserve units became accountable for each soldier's implementation of the training and tasks, while NETS provided assistance

Pictured is Brigadier General Dorothy B. Pocklington, the first reserve Army nurse and the first female reserve officer to serve in the grade of brigadier general (1988).
Photo courtesy of Dorothy Pocklington, Ellicott City, MD.

Pictured is Brigadier General Sharon Vander Zyl, the first female general officer in the Army National Guard who served as the Special Assistant to the Chief Army Nurse Corps for Mobilization and Guard Affairs (1993).
Photo courtesy of Army Nurse Corps Archives, Office of Medical History, Falls Church, VA.

on an as-needed basis.[102] Also, an evaluation of the soldier's performance served to document training and capabilities. By 1984, after three years of using SMART, both Fitzsimons staff and reservists agreed that SMART fostered a higher level of training and better utilization of active component and ARNG/USAR personnel.[103] Nonetheless, SMART had its detractors among hospital commanders. In fact, some of the commanders created "a lot of flak" about the program.[104] Some observers felt the added RC support in meeting the everyday needs of providing health care in fixed facilities in times of peace was viewed as more important than enhancing combat readiness knowledge and skills.

From 1987 to 1989, USAR nurses participated in a number of practical field exercises. They erected a pre-positioned, 1,000-bed hospital in Great Britain and field tested its equipment, e.g., ventilators, infusion pumps, and suction machines.[105] The nurses fine-tuned an evacuation plan in a combined British–U.S. Air Force exercise. They also repacked the facility so that it could be put to use quickly if the reserve forces mobilized. Other realistic training occurred in the summer of 1988, when Army Nurse Corps officers and others assigned to the 399th Combat Support Hospital staffed a field hospital during a 15,000-soldier ARNG two-week field training exercise at Fort Hood, Texas. The Army nurses cared for approximately 1,500 patients, about 75 of the soldiers being admitted to the hospital for treatment of illness or injury.[106]

Throughout the 1980s, Army Nurse Corps officers committed themselves to improving readiness and built on the progress achieved earlier in the immediate post–Vietnam War years. Army nurses' preparedness steadily improved and, whether relief mission or combat operation, Army nurses were ready to provide care.

# Notes

1. Karl E. Cocke, and others, *Department of the Army Historical Summary, Fiscal Year 1982* (Washington, DC: Center of Military History, United States Army, 1988), 81–82. Dwight D. Oland, *Department of the Army Historical Summary, Fiscal Year 1984* (Washington, DC: Center of Military History, United States Army, 1995), 196–197. William Joe Webb, *Department of the Army Historical Summary, Fiscal Year 1988* (Washington, DC: Center of Military History, United States Army, 1993), 29. Bernhard T. Mittemeyer, "Army Medical Department," *Military Medicine* 148 (November 1983): 833.

2. AirLand Battle doctrine, a combined arms concept, involved a number of innovations in operations, training, and joint air-ground operations. It emphasized the operational level of war and stressed maneuver warfare, fostered a major change in education and training with opposing forces exercises at the National Training and Combat Training Centers, and emphasized coordination between Training and Doctrine Command and the Tactical Air Command of the Air Force. Harry G. Summers, *On Strategy II: A Critical Analysis of the Gulf War* (New York: Dell, 1992), 139–50. Frank N. Schubert and Theresa L. Kraus, eds., *The Whirlwind War, The United States Army in Operations Desert Shield and Desert Storm* (Washington, DC: Center of Military History, United States Army, 1993), 26–28. Health Service Support AirLand Battle was the template for the AMEDD's wartime structure. Emerging Medical Force 96 and Medical Force 2000 later replaced Health Service Support AirLand Battle and served to outline the 21st century field medical doctrine and force structure. Frank F. Ledford, "Surgeon General Outlines Priorities for AMEDD Action," *HSC Mercury* 16 (March 1989): 2. Medical Force 2000 proposed reducing the structure from seven hospitals down to a medical holding company and four hospitals. The four hospital units were a Mobile Army Surgical Hospital, a Combat Support Hospital, a Field Hospital, and a General Hospital. Richard V.N. Ginn, *The History of the U.S. Army Medical Service Corps* (Washington, DC: Office of the Surgeon General and Center of Military History, United States Army, 1997), 376, footnote 7, 411. "MF2K Medical Units," Printed Handout, n.d., Army Nurse Corps Collection (ANCC), Office of Medical History (OMH). Basic tenets of Medical Force 2000 doctrine included "far-forward surgical care; a focus on returning soldiers to duty from as far forward as possible; increased intensive care capability in the combat zone; new medical logistics systems that incorporate blood distribution capabilities; improved ground and air evacuation capabilities; and improved management of combat stress." Frank F. Ledford, "Army 'Innovative' in Use of Funds," *U.S. Medicine*

25 (January 1989): 41–42. "HSSALB: New Medical Operational Doctrine Receives Approval," *Medical Soldier's Outlook, Army Medical Department Enlisted Training News* 3 (Spring 1986): 1. Frank F. Ledford, "Army Medicine Balancing Needs with Resources," *Army* 40 (October 1990): 180–83, 185. Frank F. Ledford, "Medical Support for Operation Desert Storm," *The Journal of the US Army Medical Department*, PB8-92-1/2 (January/February 1992): 4. The other five pillars of Health Service Support AirLand Battle were "prevention, immediate far-forward care, a hospital structure which is deployable and mobile, a timely dedicated evacuation system and a continental U.S. support base." Raymond Leahey, "Implementing 'Pillars of Wellness/Fitness and Prevention'," *Army* 36 (March 1986): 46–47. "Health Service Support, Futures," AHS White Paper, Final Draft, i-ii, March 1989, ANCC, OMH.

3. Hazel W. Johnson, "Notes from the Chief, US Army Nurse Corps," 1, March 1983, ANCC, OMH.

4. The APFT consisted of three components. It involved a timed two-mile run and a prescribed number of push-ups and sit-ups. The regulation based the minimum acceptable number of items in each event on the gender and age of the participant. Joseph Knapik, "The Army Physical Fitness Test (APFT): A Review of the Literature," *Military Medicine* 154 (June 1989): 326–29. Department of the Army, Field Manual 21-20, "Physical Fitness Training" (Washington, DC: Department of the Army, 1985). Prior to 1982, the Army allowed only soldiers under the age of 40 to take the Army Physical Fitness Test, fearing that its widespread implementation across the age spectrum would contribute to increased numbers of sudden cardiac death. To prevent such catastrophes, the Army began screening active component soldiers over age 40 in 1982, evaluating their cardiac risk factors and subjecting them to physical exams. The reserve components implemented the Over-40 Medical Screening Program in 1987. Bernhard T. Mittemeyer, "Facing Challenges, Army Goals Endure," *U.S. Medicine* 18 (5 January 1982): 41–42. Bernhard T. Mittemeyer, "Army Medical Department," *Military Medicine* 148 (November 1983): 833. Bernhard T. Mittemeyer, "Army Total Fitness Program a Success," *U.S. Medicine* 19 (15 January 1983): 29–34. Karl E. Cocke, and others, *Department of the Army Historical Summary, Fiscal Year 1982* (Washington, DC: Center of Military History, United States Army, 1988), 81–82. Dwight D. Oland, *Department of the Army Historical Summary, Fiscal Year 1984* (Washington, DC: Center of Military History, United States Army, 1995), 196. Donna Bolinger, "Reserve Components to Get Same Over-40 Screening as Active Duty," *HSC Mercury* 14 (February 1987): 8.

5. Clara L. Adams-Ender, "Memo from the Chief, Army Nurse Corps," 4, 31 December 1989, ANCC, OMH.

6. Charles Reddy, "Nursing Newsletter Number 84-1," 1, 1 February 1984, ANCC, OMH.

7. "Army Nursing in the 1990's (NLN Conf)," Typewritten Text for Speech, June 1985, ANCC, OMH.

8. "ANC Annual Historical Report FY 85," 5, n.d., ANCC, OMH.

9. "Army Nurse Aims for World Games," *HSC Mercury* 4 (May 1977): 11. Carolyn M. Feller and Debora R. Cox, *Highlights in the History of the Army Nurse Corps* (Washington, DC: U.S. Army Center of Military History, 2000), 48.

10. Connie L. Slewitzke, "Memorandum from the Chief, Army Nurse Corps," 4–5, March 1985; Connie L. Slewitzke, "Memorandum from the Chief, Army Nurse Corps," 5–6, July 1986; and "ANC Annual Historical Report FY 85," Typewritten Document (TD), 11–12, n.d. (all in ANCC, OMH).

11. Quinn H. Becker, "Medical Readiness Primary Army Focus," *U.S. Medicine* 22

(January 1986): 39–40.

12. Other Army nurses who actively participated in various phases of the program were captains Sandy Yaney, Catherine Schemp, Jill Phillips, and Leslie Dempsey Brousseau, majors Carolyn Bernheim and Mary C. Davis, and lieutenant colonels Antoinette Hagey and Susanne Allen. Jeanne Picariello to Author, E-mail Correspondence, 24 March 2003; and "Army Nurse Corps (ANC) 1986 Annual Historical Report," 24 (both in ANCC, OMH).

13. Jeanne Picariello to Author, E-mail Correspondence, 24 March 2003. Alcide M. LaNoue to Barry R. McCaffrey, 6 April 1994; Jerry A. White to Alcide M. LaNoue, 5 May 1994; Nancy R. Adams to Jerry A. White, 20 May 1994 (all Typewritten Letters in ANCC, OMH). Some time later, the Army Panel on Sexual Harassment's findings of unfairness instigated the setting of new, higher Army Physical Fitness Test standards for women soldiers. The existing women's standards, dating back to 1986, became more stringent and more closely approximated those set for men soldiers. "Army to Raise Fitness Standards for Women," *Minerva's Bulletin Board* (Summer 1997): 3. "New Army Fitness Test Imposes Higher Standards of Women," *Minerva, Quarterly Report on Women and the Military* 4 (Spring 1986): 72–73.

14. "Army Nurse Corps (ANC) FY 87 Annual Historical Report," 10, ANCC, OMH.

15. Hudak and Mouritsen identified readiness as "the overriding reason for [the] AMEDD's existence." Ronald P. Hudak and Paul B. Mouritsen, "Improving the Army's Primary Care Delivery System," *Military Medicine* 153 (June 1988): 282–86.

16. Rosemarie Skaine, *Women at War, Gender Issues of Americans in Combat* (Jefferson, NC: McFarland & Company, Inc., 1999), 154.

17. Quinn H. Becker, "The 'We Care People' in Army Medicine," *Army* 36 (October 1986): 240–43.

18. "Medical Readiness of the Armed Services, Hearings before the Subcommittee on Manpower and Personnel of the Committee on Armed Services, United States Senate, 97th Congress, 2nd Session, May 4, 26, 1982" (Washington, DC: U.S. Government Printing Office, 1982), 2.

19. William E. Mayer, "Medical Readiness DoD Top Priority," *U.S. Medicine* 21 (15 January 1985): 7–10. "Hearings before a Subcommittee of the Committee on Appropriations, House of Representatives, 99th Congress, 1st Session," Part 3 (Washington, DC: U.S. Government Printing Office, 1985), 1022, 1026–27, 1069.

20. William E. Mayer, "DoD Not Medically Ready for War Needs," *U.S. Medicine* 22 (January 1986): 13–14.

21. "Hearings before a Subcommittee of the Committee on Appropriations, House of Representatives, 99th Congress, 1st Session," Part 3 (Washington, DC: U.S. Government Printing Office, 1985), 1022–23.

22. Donald Robinson, "The Mess in Military Medicine," *Reader's Digest* 126 (February 1985): 52.

23. Lawrence H. Fink, "Military Medicine Is a Terminal Case; It's Time to Pull the Plug," *Washington Post* (24 November 1985): C1, C4. A number of writers, including the Army surgeon general, penned letters to the *Washington Post* editor countering this extreme viewpoint. Quinn Becker, Edward Weiss, Eileen Matthews, and Nicholas Dunlap, "Letters," *Washington Post* (30 November 1985): A25.

24. David Whitman, "Under Attack: Military Care," *U.S. News & World Report* (27 January 1986): 69.

25. "U.S. Army Medicine, from the Ferment, Profound Changes," *Army* 36 (March 1986): 22.

26. Terrence Gough, *Department of the Army Historical Summary, Fiscal Year 1986*

(Washington, DC: Center of Military History, United States Army, 1989), 61.

27. John F. Beary, "Department of Defense," *Military Medicine* 148 (November 1983): 857–63. John F. Beary, "Medical Readiness DoD's Main Goal," *U.S. Medicine* 19 (15 January 1983): 9–12. "Medical Readiness of the Armed Services, Hearings before the Subcommittee on Manpower and Personnel of the Committee on Army Services, United States Senate, 97th Congress, 2nd Session, May 4, 26, 1982," (Washington, DC: U.S. Government Printing Office, 1982), 5, 27–28.

28. "U.S. Army Medicine, from the Ferment, Profound Changes," *Army* 36 (March 1986): 23.

29. Bernhard T. Mittemeyer, "'Volatile' Year Sees Army Medical Gains," *U.S. Medicine* 21 (15 January 1985): 15, 16, 21. Dwight D. Oland, *Department of the Army Historical Summary, Fiscal Year 1984* (Washington, DC: Center of Military History, United States Army, 1995), 197. "Hearings before a Subcommittee of the Committee on Appropriations, House of Representatives, 99th Congress, 1st Session," Part 3 (Washington, DC: U.S. Government Printing Office, 1985), 1071. "DEPMEDS the Latest in Portable Medical Care," *Army Reserve Magazine* 33 (Fourth Issue of 1987): 26–27. Kevin Ropp, "Review Hits DEPMEDS Shortages," *HSC Mercury* 17 (June 1990): 10. Academy of Health Sciences, *Deployable Medical Systems Users' Manual, Final Draft* (Fort Sam Houston, TX: 1989), 1–4, Smith Collection, U.S. Army Medical Department Museum. Quinn H. Becker, "Medical Readiness Primary Army Focus," *U.S. Medicine* 22 (January 1986): 39–40.

30. Terrence Gough, *Department of the Army Historical Summary, Fiscal Year 1986* (Washington, DC: Center of Military History, United States Army, 1989), 61. "Medics Train in New Field Hospital," *HSC Mercury* 14 (October 1987): 12. By 1990, the Army had fielded more than 40 DEPMEDS facilities with 17,560 beds. Captain Clyburn, "Status of Deployable Medical Systems (DEPMEDS) Fieldings," Information Paper, 28 February 1990, ANCC, OMH.

31. "DEPMEDS the Latest in Portable Medical Care," *Army Reserve Magazine* 33 (Fourth Issue of 1987): 26–27.

32. Department of the Army, Headquarters, U.S. Army Health Services Command, Medical Services, "AMEDD Professional Officer Filler System," Memorandum No. 40-2, 13 November 1973, Record Group 112, National Archives. The Professional Officer Filler System (PROFIS) program's intent was to predesignate officers "for forward deployed and deploying units" so as "to hasten the mobilization process." Bernhard T. Mittemeyer, "Facing Challenges, Army Goals Endure," *U.S. Medicine* 18 (5 January 1982): 41–42. Dwight Oland and Jeffrey Greenhut, *Report of the Surgeon General, United States Army Fiscal Years 1976–1980* (Washington, DC: Office of the Surgeon General, U.S. Army, 1988), 301. Nelia Schrum, "PROFIS Puts Providers There When Needed," *The Mercury* 24 (May 1997): 12. Cleo Brennan "PROFIS Soldiers Offer Two-For-One Service," *The Mercury* 26 (January 1999): 12. By 1982, the system had slotted 3,600 physicians and nurses into vacancies for combat roles. "Medical Readiness of the Armed Services, Hearings before the Subcommittee on Manpower and Personnel of the Committee on Army Services, United States Senate, 97th Congress, 2nd Session, May 4, 26, 1982" (Washington, DC: U.S. Government Printing Office, 1982), 25.

33. Fuertes Caminos ("strong roads" in Spanish) was an annual Army Reserve and National Guard rotation that implemented nation-building projects, such as the planning and paving of roads, the construction of schools, the distribution of clothing, and medical outreach in Central and South America. John D. Sherwood, "U.S. Army Operations Other Than War since 1989," 5–6, 7 April 1995, ANCC, OMH.

34. Carolyn M. Feller and Debora R. Cox, *Highlights in the History of the Army Nurse*

*Corps* (Washington, DC: U.S. Army Center of Military History, 2000), 61.

35. Frank F. Ledford, "Army Medicine Balancing Needs with Resources," *Army* 40 (October 1990): 180–83, 185.

36. "Medics Train in New Field Hospital," *HSC Mercury* 14 (October 1987): 12.

37. "Operation Desert Shield/Storm, Lessons Learned—DEPMEDS," TD, n.d., ANCC, OMH. Kevin Ropp, "Review Hits DEPMEDS Shortages," *HSC Mercury* 17 (June 1990): 10.

38. "Medics Train in New Field Hospital," *HSC Mercury* 14 (October 1987): 12.

39. "Standard Field Equipment Coming This Year," *HSC Mercury* 14 (April 1987): 1.

40. An organic vehicle is a piece of equipment permanently assigned to a unit based on the Table of Organization and Equipment (TO&E) for that type of unit. Richard V.N. Ginn, *The History of the U.S. Army Medical Service Corps* (Washington, DC: Office of the Surgeon General and Center of Military History, United States Army, 1997), 435. United States General Accounting Office, *Military Personnel and Compensation, Committee on Armed Services, House of Representatives, Operation Desert Storm, Full Army Medical Capability Not Achieved*, GAO/NSIAD-92-175 (Washington, DC: GAO, August 1992), 4, 40–43.

41. Colonel Jerome V. Foust, Interview by Captain Donald Hall, March 29, 1991, Typewritten Transcript, 10, 22, Richard V.N. Ginn Collection, OMH. "Army Identifies 'Lessons Learned' from Desert Storm," *U.S. Medicine* 28 (February 1992): 1, 3, 26, 27. Frank Best and Nancy Tomich, *Medicine in the Gulf War* (Washington, DC: U.S. Medicine, 1991), 6, 8, 9. Ingeborg Sosa, "The Journal Interviews—MG Michael J. Scotti, Jr., MC, Commanding General, 7th Medical Command, Europe," *The Journal of the US Army Medical Department*, PB8-92-1/2 (January/February 1992): insert between pages 34 and 35. Ingeborg Sosa, "The Journal Interviews—LTG Frank F. Ledford, Jr., Surgeon General, United States Army," *The Journal of the US Army Medical Department*, PB8-92-3/4 (March/April 1992): insert between pages 30 and 31. William R. Smith and Philip Lisagor, "Experience of the 31st Combat Support Hospital in Operation Desert Shield and Desert Storm, A Commander's Story," *The Journal of the US Army Medical Department*, PB8-92-11/12 (November/December 1992): 4–10.

42. "Operation Desert Shield/Storm, Lessons Learned—DEPMEDS," TD, n.d., ANCC, OMH.

43. "Medics Train in New Field Hospital," *HSC Mercury* 14 (October 1987): 12. Academy of Health Sciences, *Deployable Medical Systems Users' Manual, Final Draft* (Fort Sam Houston, TX: 1989), 1–3, Smith Collection, U.S. Army Medical Department Museum.

44. The Defense Medical Standardization Board became the Joint Readiness Clinical Advisory Board in the 1990s. Kathryn L. Boehnke, "Slot Authorization for Army Nurse Corp [sic] Officer at JRCAB/(DMSB)," Typewritten Letter, 16 June 1998, ANCC, OMH.

45. Connie L. Slewitzke, Interview by Beverly Greenlee, 354, n.d., USAWC/USAMHI Senior Officer Oral History Program, Project No. 88-8, ANCC, OMH.

46. Eily P. Gorman, "Joint Services Nursing Advisory Group (JSNAG)," Typewritten Memorandum, 10 March 1988; John W. Funk, "Joint Services Nursing Panel of Clinical Experts," Typewritten Letter, 22 February 1988; Alcide M. Lanoue, "Request for Additional Health Care Planning Factors," Typewritten Memorandum, 13 January 1988; Walter F. Johnson, "Request for Additional Health Care Planning Factors," Typewritten Memorandum, 15 January 1988; Alcide M. Lanoue, "Request for Additional Health Care Planning Factors," Typewritten Memorandum, 30 October 1987; and Susie Sherrod to Author, E-mail Correspondence, 26 March 2003 (all in ANCC, OMH).

47. Bernhard T. Mittemeyer, "Quality Assurance: Major Army Focus," *U.S. Medicine* 20 (15 January 1984): 55–59. As well as austere but adequate, the new U.S. Army's Deployable Medical System was intended to be "affordable, maintainable, and relocatable." Acad-

emy of Health Sciences, *Deployable Medical Systems Users' Manual, Final Draft* (Fort Sam Houston, TX: 1989), 1–2, Smith Collection, U.S. Army Medical Department Museum.

48. Connie L. Slewitzke, Interview by Beverly Greenlee, 346, 349, n.d., U.S. Army War College/U.S. Army Military History Institute Senior Officer Oral History Program, Project No. 88-8, ANCC, OMH.

49. Connie L. Slewitzke, Interview by Beverly Greenlee, 355, n.d., U.S. Army War College/U.S. Army Military History Institute Senior Officer Oral History Program, Project No. 88-8; and Susie Sherrod to Author, E-mail Correspondence, 26 March 2003 (both in ANCC, OMH).

50. Connie L. Slewitzke, Interview by Beverly Greenlee, 360, n.d., U.S. Army War College/U.S. Army Military History Institute Senior Officer Oral History Program, Project No. 88-8, ANCC, OMH.

51. Nancy R. Adams, "Coordination Draft Manpower Requirements Criteria (MARC) Study Document (MSD) for Hospital Ward Nursing (AOC 66J/H, MOS 91B/C), MCN SO4," Memorandum for DASG-HCD-O, TD, 14 January 1992; and Jeannette S. James, "Manpower Requirements Criteria (MARC)," Briefing Slides, n.d. (both in ANCC, OMH).

52. Terris E. Kennedy, "Coordination Draft MARC for Hospital Ward Nursing," Memorandum for DASG-HCD-D, TD, 8 March 1993, ANCC, OMH.

53. Connie L. Slewitzke, Interview by Beverly Greenlee, 354–55, n.d., USAWC/USAMHI Senior Officer Oral History Program, Project No. 88-8, ANCC, OMH. Carolyn M. Feller and Debora R. Cox, *Highlights in the History of the Army Nurse Corps* (Washington, DC: U.S. Army Center of Military History, 2000), 55.

54. Connie L. Slewitzke, Interview by Beverly Greenlee, 343, 344, 345, n.d., U.S. Army War College/U.S. Army Military History Institute Senior Officer Oral History Program, Project No. 88-8, ANCC, OMH.

55. "ANC Annual Historical Report FY 85," 3, ANCC, OMH.

56. Connie L. Slewitzke, Interview by Beverly Greenlee, 345, 347, 372, n.d., U.S. Army War College/U.S. Army Military History Institute Senior Officer Oral History Program, Project No. 88-8, ANCC, OMH.

57. "Army Nurse Corps (ANC) 1986 Annual Historical Report," 16–17; and Elizabeth Wanersdorfer, "ANC Highlight Update," Typewritten Memorandum, 11 July 1990 (both in ANCC, OMH).

58. Connie L. Slewitzke, Interview by Beverly Greenlee, 373, n.d., U.S. Army War College/U.S. Army Military History Institute Senior Officer Oral History Program, Project No. 88-8.

59. "Nurses Work to Respond to Readiness," *HSC Mercury* 8 (March 1981): 5.

60. Carolyn M. Feller and Debora R. Cox, *Highlights in the History of the Army Nurse Corps* (Washington, DC: U.S. Army Center of Military History, 2000), 56. Charles D. Matthews, "Memorandum for RC Chief Nurses," Information Paper, 26 September 1983, ANCC, OMH; Bernhard T. Mittemeyer, "Army Total Fitness Program a Success," *U.S. Medicine* 19 (15 January 1983): 29–34. Bernhard T. Mittemeyer, "Quality Assurance: Major Army Focus," *U.S. Medicine* 20 (15 January 1984): 55–59.

61. Lynne T. Connelly to Author, E-mail Correspondence, 1 July 2003, ANCC, OMH.

62. Lewis H. Seaton, "Navy Medical Department," *Military Medicine* 148 (November 1983): 842. J. William Cox, "Navy Transition Brings Progress," *U.S. Medicine* 19 (15 January 1983): 73, 74, 76.

63. Max B. Bralliar, "Air Force Medical Service," *Military Medicine* 148 (November 1983): 850. Mary C. Smolenski, Donald G. Smith, and James S. Nanney, *A Fit, Fighting Force, The Air Force Nursing Services Chronology* (Washington, DC: Office of the Air

Force Surgeon General, 2005), 38–39.

64. Office of the Assistant Secretary of Defense (Health Affairs), "Plan for Expanding the Combat Casualty Care Course," TD, 2, December 1987, ANCC, OMH. Dale C. Smith, "Military Medicine," in *Encyclopedia of the American Military*, ed. John E. Jessup and Louise B. Ketz (New York: Charles Scribner's Sons, 1994), 1625.

65. Jim Markiewicz, "Course Teaches Medical Leadership," *HSC Mercury* 13 (November 1985): 12.

66. Office of the Assistant Secretary of Defense (Health Affairs), "Plan for Expanding the Combat Casualty Care Course," TD, 3, December 1987, ANCC, OMH.

67. Office of the Assistant Secretary of Defense (Health Affairs), "Plan for Expanding the Combat Casualty Care Course," TD, 2, December 1987, ANCC, OMH.

68. Carolyn M. Feller and Debora R. Cox, *Highlights in the History of the Army Nurse Corps* (Washington, DC: U.S. Army Center of Military History, 2000), 55. Barbara J. Smith, Interview by Constance J. Moore, Transcript, 2 March 1995, Army Nurse Corps Oral History Collection, OMH, 12.

69. Connie L. Slewitzke, "Memorandum for the Chief, US Army Nurse Corps," 4, July 1986, ANCC, OMH; and Connie L. Slewitzke, Interview by Beverly Greenlee, 470, n.d., U.S. Army War College/U.S. Army Military History Institute Senior Officer Oral History Program, Project No. 88-8 (both in ANCC, OMH).

70. The Mobilization Designees "were usually Reservists and National Guard . . . who were activated as backfill and to fill existing vacancies created by [the] mission." Frank Metcalf to Author, E-mail Correspondence, 25 April 2003, ANCC, OMH. Bruce Aron, "All You Ever Wanted to Know about the Reserves," *HSC Mercury* 9 (October 1982): 7.

71. "1980 ANC Professional Development Workshop," in Hazel W. Johnson, "Information for All ANC Officers," 7 November 1980, Inclosure 2, ANCC, OMH.

72. Connie L. Slewitzke, "Memorandum for the Chief, US Army Nurse Corps," 10–11, October 1984; and Connie L. Slewitzke, "Memorandum for the Chief, US Army Nurse Corps," 11, December 1986 (both in ANCC, OMH).

73. Mark O. McMorris, "Nurse Training," Letters to the Editor, *HSC Mercury* 16 (May 1989): 2.

74. Christine E. Cobb, "Nurse Training," Letters to the Editor, *HSC Mercury* 16 (July 1989): 2.

75. M. Denise Palmer, "USAR Nurse Comments on Training," Letter to Editor, *HSC Mercury* 16 (October 1989): 2.

76. Sharon Bystran, "Deployment Checklist," 1986; and Connie L. Slewitzke, "Memorandum from the Chief, US Army Nurse Corps," 8, December 1986 (both in ANCC, OMH).

77. Charles J. Reddy, "Nursing Newsletter Number 83-2," 1 November 1983; Hazel W. Johnson, "Notes from the Chief U.S. Army Nurse Corps," 3, March 1983; and Terris M. Kennedy, Interview by Constance J. Moore, Transcript, 217–19, 24 October 1995 (all in ANCC, OMH).

78. Connie L. Slewitzke, Interview by Beverly Greenlee, 40–42, n.d., USAWC/USAMHI Senior Officer Oral History Program, Project No. 88-8, ANCC, OMH.

79. Connie L. Slewitzke, Interview by Beverly Greenlee, 353, n.d., USAWC/USAMHI Senior Officer Oral History Program, Project No. 88-8, ANCC, OMH.

80. Connie L. Slewitzke, "Memorandum from the Chief US Army Nurse Corps," 1, October 1984, ANCC, OMH.

81. Connie L. Slewitzke, Interview by Beverly Greenlee, 41–42, n.d., USAWC/USAMHI Senior Officer Oral History Program, Project No. 88-8, ANCC, OMH.

82. The Army issued some officers, upon their retirement, hip pocket orders that assigned them to a particular duty at a specific post in the event of a national emergency. The hip pocket orders included a Unit Identification Code that specified a mobilization station.

83. Terry R. Misener, Martha R. Bell, Hedy Mechanic, and Valerie P. Biskey, "Mobilization Readiness of Retired Army Nurse Corps Officers," Report #HR86-002 (Fort Sam Houston, Texas: United States Army Health Care Studies and Clinical Investigation Division, 1986), ii-iii.

84. The Surgeon General Lieutenant General Quinn Becker reiterated that 70 percent of the Army's medical support was destined to come from the Army Reserve and National Guard. "U.S. Army Medicine, from the Ferment, Profound Changes," *Army* 36 (March 1986): 43. "TSG Meeting with CSA, 2 July 1987," Typewritten Outline, ANCC, OMH.

85. Another result of this survey was the 1986 establishment of a policy barring reserve nurse promotions above the rank of major without a baccalaureate degree in nursing. General Slewitzke was able to implement this standard because educational funding was available to support reservists in their pursuit of the degree. Connie L. Slewitzke to Author, Typewritten Comments, 29 September 2003; and "Army Nurse Corps (ANC) 1986 Annual Historical Report," 20 (both in ANCC, OMH).

86. Connie L. Slewitzke, Interview by Beverly Greenlee, 464–65, n.d., U.S. Army War College/U.S. Army Military History Institute Senior Officer Oral History Program, Project No. 88-8, ANCC, OMH.

87. Charles J. Reddy, "Nursing Newsletter Number 83-2," 3, 1 November 1983, ANCC, OMH. "ARPERCEN and RCPAC, What Do They Do?" *Army Reserve Magazine* (Winter 1985): 10–11.

88. COL Blake, "Practice Requirements for USAR Nurse Corps Officers," Typewritten Memorandum, 4 January 1988, ANCC, OMH.

89. "Program Boosts Reserve Readiness," *HSC Mercury* 13 (December 1985): 5. Jerry Harben, "Competition for Nurses Gets Tough," *HSC Mercury* 16 (August 1989): 6.

90. Connie L. Slewitzke, Interview by Beverly Greenlee, 393–94, n.d., U.S. Army War College/U.S. Army Military History Institute Senior Officer Oral History Program, Project No. 88-8, ANCC, OMH.

91. Connie L. Slewitzke, Interview by Beverly Greenlee, 396, n.d., U.S. Army War College/U.S. Army Military History Institute Senior Officer Oral History Program, Project No. 88-8, ANCC, OMH. Wesley G. Byerly, "A Mutual Support Program between a 1,000 Bed TDA Augmentation Reserve Hospital and an Active Component Army Community Hospital," *Military Medicine* 149 (October 1984): 565–69. James H. Carter, "Mutual Support and Mobilization Preparedness: The Method of an Army Reserve Hospital," *Military Medicine* 155 (August 1990): 379–81.

92. The officer in OTSG was Lieutenant Colonel Marie P. Alire. Marie P. Alire, "Input to Readiness Issue on ANC Strategic Plan," Typewritten Memorandum, June 1988, ANCC, OMH. Connie L. Slewitzke, Interview by Beverly Greenlee, 466–68, n.d., U.S. Army War College/U.S. Army Military History Institute Senior Officer Oral History Program, Project No. 88-8, ANCC, OMH. Clara L. Adams-Ender and Amelia J. Carson, "Capabilities of Army Nurse Corps Officer Graduates of the United States Army War College," *Medical Bulletin of the US Army, Europe* 43 (September/October 1986): 27–29.

93. Donna F. Owen, "Annual Historical Report," Typewritten Memorandum, 2 December 1989, ANCC, OMH.

94. Lorraine Mirabella, "Army Reserve General Wears One Star but Two Hats," *Howard County Sun* (6 August 1989): 4.

95. "Nurse Named Brigadier General," *Army Times* 50 (21 August 1989): 2.

96. Dorothy Pocklington to Author, E-mail Correspondence, 3, 22 August 2003; and Dorothy Pocklington to LTC Mittelstaedt, Typewritten Letter, 13 January 1995 (both in ANCC, OMH).

97. Dorothy Pocklington, "BG Pocklington's OER Support Objectives & Contributions," TD, March 1988–June 1991, ANCC, OMH.

98. Dorothy Pocklington to Author, E-mail Correspondence, 4, 22 August 2003, ANCC, OMH.

99. Michael J. Foster, "Minutes of the Army Nurse Corps Staff Meeting on 2 April 1993," TD, 5, 5 May 1993, ANCC, OMH.

100. Sonnie Scarlett, "Academy, FORSCOM Develop a Smart Training Plan," *HSC Mercury* 15 (January 1988): 1.

101. Diane Corcoran to Author, Telephone Conversation, 9 April 2003.

102. "Reserve Training Program," Information Paper, 2 July 1985, Enclosure 5, in Connie L. Slewitzke, "Memorandum from the Chief, US Army Nurse Corps," April 1986, ANCC, OMH.

103. Connie L. Slewitzke, "Memorandum from the Chief, US Army Nurse Corps," 10, October 1984, ANCC, OMH.

104. Connie L. Slewitzke, Interview by Beverly Greenlee, 471, n.d., USAWC/USAMHI Senior Officer Oral History Program, Project No. 88-8, ANCC, OMH.

105. The AMEDD termed this notion of pre-positioning a hospital the "warm-base concept." It involved "the remote storage of a general hospital set at the intended site of its wartime use. As a minimum, the hospital core [was] established, including the operating rooms, central material service, laboratory, radiology and 100 intensive care beds. The remainder of the equipment [was to be] stored contiguously to facilitate expansion to the full 1,000 bed capacity." Quinn H. Becker, "Medical Readiness: Army's Top Priority," *U.S. Medicine* 24 (January 1988): 45–46.

106. Barbara Jo Foley and Joseph E. Foley, "On Worldwide Call to the Army," *American Journal of Nursing* 89 (October 1989): 1310.

*Chapter Twelve*
# Refugee and Humanitarian Operations During the 1980s

Army Nurse Corps readiness met its first field test for the new decade in the spring of 1980 with a humanitarian mission, the Cuban Refugee Operation. In April 1980, Cuban leader Fidel Castro allowed a mass emigration of Cubans, and many absconded from the communist country. President Jimmy Carter in turn resolved to accept the tens of thousands of immigrants who landed on the U.S. shores, many of whom were described as unwanted social elements, such as career criminals, those with psychiatric illnesses, and mentally deficient individuals.[1]

Carter delegated the responsibility for coordinating the reception of refugees to the newly organized Federal Emergency Management Agency, which directed the U.S. Public Health Service (USPHS) to provide health assessments and medical treatment for the displaced persons. The USPHS, however, was unable to respond fully to the mission because the charge was beyond its capabilities. Consequently, the Federal Emergency Management Agency approached the Department of Defense, asking it to help provide the required services.[2] Because the Army had been so successful in managing a similar processing operation for Vietnamese refugees in 1975, the Department of Defense named the secretary of the Army as the defense executive agent of the "Freedom Flotilla," or "Mariel Boatlift," as the operation was labeled.[3] The Army Medical Department (AMEDD) subsequently provided support at the Miami, Florida, Reception Center and furnished the bulk of the medical services at the processing centers located at Fort Chaffee, Arkansas; Fort McCoy, Wisconsin; and Fort Indiantown Gap, Pennsylvania; with the assistance of USPHS personnel, as available. Health care support encompassed hospitalizations early in the mission and extensive outpatient, preventive medicine, and environmental engineering services and aeromedical evacuation throughout the operation. The USPHS later contracted with local civilian hospitals to care for most of the immigrants who required further hospitalization.[4]

The first hospital unit to mobilize for the Cuban relief mission was the 47th

Field Hospital garrisoned at Fort Sill, Oklahoma. On 7 May 1980, Forces Command (FORSCOM) alerted the 47th to deploy to Fort Chaffee, Arkansas. The main elements of the 47th Field Hospital arrived at Fort Chaffee by truck convoy on 8 May 1980. Professional Officer Filler System staff from Reynolds Army Hospital at Fort Sill arrived the next day, and the hospital commenced operation. By 11 May 1980, 4,000 refugees were living in the resettlement camp at Fort Chaffee.[5] The camp population peaked at 19,200 on 18 May 1980, when the last group of refugees arrived.[6] From 11 May until 28 June 1980, at which point most of the 47th returned to Fort Sill, the hospital dealt with one case of meningococcal meningitis, an outbreak of staphylococcal food poisoning, and three refugee births.[7]

The tenor of the operation was neither humdrum nor tranquil. On 26 May 1980, "refugee discontent" devolved into rioting, turmoil, and the escape of hundreds of refugees. Although the 47th Field Hospital activated its mass casualty plan, in this instance there were no injuries from the revolt. On 1 June 1980, however, another uprising ended in mayhem and bloodshed.[8] Several hundred Cubans escaped from Fort Chaffee, rioted in the local streets, and marched down a highway chanting "Libertad! Libertad!" In response, Governor William Clinton activated the state police and National Guard. Confrontations between authorities and demonstrators left 67 injured, "mostly Cubans, some of whom had their heads cracked open with billy clubs." Residents living around Fort Chaffee were "incensed at the Carter administration's hellbroth of Cuban refugees invading their neighborhood."[9] The 47th Field Hospital treated 46 emergent patients, five suffering from gunshot wounds and 13 others with knife wounds and blunt-trauma injuries. Most of the 47th Field Hospital's personnel left Fort Chaffee on 28 June 1980, but some clinical staff, including a psychiatric nurse, remained behind to augment the USPHS efforts.[10]

There were 14 Army Nurse Corps officers detailed to the 47th Field Hospital.[11] Lieutenant Colonel Esther Segler, the chief nurse, individually selected the nurses, basing her choice on their specialty skills, their professional experience, and the anticipated population of care recipients, not simply on Modified Table of Organization and Equipment (MTO&E) requirements. As patient care needs became clearer, the command requested additional Army Nurse Corps officers and sent others back to their home units because their specialty services proved less essential. Early in the mission, Segler asked for a senior Army nurse to undertake the responsibilities of assistant chief nurse because her usual day was consumed by a plethora of responsibilities, such as answering questions pertaining to the assembly of the tent hospital and organizing support staff in a "constantly changing situation which fluctuated by the hour."[12] When her assistant arrived, Segler redirected her own attention to other essential chores, such as coordinating meetings with the USPHS, press briefings, escorting both military and congressional VIPs, touring the mothballed hospital, and attending innumerable staff meetings. Her redirection allowed others to engage requisite daily activities necessary for mission success.

Many of those Army nurses who arrived after the mission began, especially those coming from Puerto Rico's 369th Station Hospital, were fluent in Spanish. Besides nursing duties, they translated for the staff and shared insights on the refugees' cultural perceptions. They remained for only eight days and, after their departure, the accuracy and quality of staff communication with patients plummeted dramatically. Other units also reinforced the 47th Field Hospital's efforts. On 12 May 1980, the 675th Medical Detachment and 676th Medical Detachment deployed from Fort Benning, Georgia, and operated a 24-hour dispensary. They remained at Fort Chaffee until 22 June 1980.

After the long days spent erecting tents and organizing and equipping wards at Fort Chaffee, duty shifts settled into a routine of 10-hour days. Eight days into the mission, the hospital moved from mobile Army surgical hospital tentage into the previously mothballed cantonment facility and began eight-hour shifts.[13] There were—no doubt—exceptions to the routine schedules, and Army nurses worked extended shifts when necessary. During the rioting, when a higher alert level was in place and workload increased, the commander telephoned the deputy chief of staff, operations, at Health Services Command (HSC), reiterating previously written pleas for more nurses. Lieutenant Colonel Carns expressed concern that HSC was unaware that Army Nurse Corps officers were covering 24-hour shifts every day.[14] A week later, his persistent demands paid off, when five medical-surgical nurses and a psychiatric nurse arrived to augment the 47th Field Hospital. However, their arrival was offset by the almost simultaneous departure of five other nurses. With the exception of this one crisis, however, staffing seemed adequate and working hours acceptable.

Topping the list of lessons learned were the all-too-familiar logistical deficiencies. Nurses from Reynolds Army Hospital fortunately had the good sense to bring supplies like bassinets, a fetoscope, Halothane, a laryngoscope, baby shirts, and so forth along with them. Nonetheless, many essential items, such as intravenous equipment, syringes, blood tubes, tape, gauze, and medications, were unavailable when the 47th Field Hospital began operation. There also were not enough field sinks, and those that were available proved unreliable.

Coordination between the Army nurses who predominantly operated the inpatient services and the USPHS nurses who staffed the dispensaries was poor and the USPHS nurses rotated in and out of Fort Chaffee every two weeks.[15] Newly arrived USPHS nurses required a few days for orientation and a few more for out-processing at the beginning and end of their two-week duty period, thereby limiting their productivity.[16]

Control of the displaced persons in the camp also presented problems. The camp was spread over a wide area and a labyrinthine layout forced nurses to escort refugees moving between sections of the hospital. Patients also strayed from their wards and were disinclined to settle down at night. Control of patient visitors was another demanding task. Thievery was prevalent. Then another wholly unforeseen cultural complication surfaced. In the field setting, the nurses wore their fatigue uniforms, but their olive drab clothing reminded the patients of Castro's militia, who wore similar-looking uniforms. Patients suspected the fatigue-clad nurses were somehow in league with their former leader.[17]

Another point realized during the Fort Chaffee mission was the imperative to review and upgrade the MTO&E/TO&E system to include facilities, structure, and function. True readiness and field efficiency depended on new doctrine, better facilities, and improved staffing. The 47th Field Hospital's After Action Report documented that "gross inadequacies which require immediate attention exist in the areas of personnel staffing, equipment, medical supply, and power distribution." Transportation of the field hospital highlighted further shortcomings. When the 47th Field Hospital deployed for the Cuban Refugee Operation, only 16 percent of its basic load of equipment could be moved on its own trucks.[18] The expedient practice of depending on other units for transportation potentially jeopardized this and future operations.

The second processing center to receive the Cuban refugees began operation on 11 May 1980 at Fort Indiantown Gap, Pennsylvania, where in 1975 displaced Vietnamese immigrants were processed. The Fort Indiantown Gap director of personnel and community activities in-processed the Cuban refugees, assisting them in filling out Immigration and Naturalization Service paperwork, distributing meal and identification cards, and providing billeting assignments and medical screening. As of 31 May 1980, FORSCOM relinquished control of the center to the Immigration and Naturalization Service, U.S. Department of State, and volunteer agencies, which then assumed responsibility for resettling the Cubans. Over the 20-day span from 11 May to 31 May 1980, 19,094 refugees arrived at Fort Indiantown Gap.[19]

The 42nd Field Hospital, home based at Fort Knox, Kentucky, provided medical support for the refugee camp at Fort Indiantown Gap. Unit conditions before deployment were reminiscent of those prevalent in the 1970s.[20] While in garrison at Fort Knox, the Medical Service Corps unit commander delegated many duties to the chief nurse, including the significant responsibility of logistics officer, and assigned many of the enlisted nursing staff to nonnursing duties. When Captain Wilfredo Nieves, the garrison chief nurse, prepared to step aside as Lieutenant Colonel Mary J. Wise assumed the chief nurse responsibilities upon deployment, the garrison hospital commander objected to Wise's assignment and reminded Nieves that he still worked for the commander and that Nieves' officer efficiency report was pending.[21] The commander's statements seemed to suggest that Nieves should resist his replacement or face the possibility of a substandard job performance evaluation. When Wise arrived at Fort Indiantown Gap and took charge, she met with blatant opposition from the garrison commander and found that many of the enlisted nursing personnel were filling slots in the motor pool, ambulance section, and x-ray department, and one was even a driver for the commander. For the entire deployment of 28 days, Wise exerted prodigious efforts to correct the assignments and the command and control channels. Still, she had little authority over the enlisted nursing staff. At the same time, she characterized her rapport with the Medical Corps officer who assumed command of the hospital in the field as exceptional and her relationship with Nieves collegial. Wise considered Nieves an outstanding officer and credited him with making the operation a success. She recommended that in the future TO&E units be assigned to the local Table of Distribution and Allowances (TDA) hospital commander to encourage cross-training and improve individual readiness of both TO&E and TDA personnel.[22] Although TO&E personnel were not subsequently assigned to TDA units as Wise suggested, Professional Officer Filler System nurses eventually did train with their designated mobilization units, and TO&E enlisted personnel did gain clinical experience in co-located TDA hospitals under the Medical Proficiency Training program. Later, when a sizable number of Army nurses was assigned to FORSCOM but were attached to HSC (TDA) hospitals, they expanded their versatility and gained a foothold in both camps, improving their skills and establishing important professional relationships.

When Fort Indiantown Gap neared its capacity of 20,000 immigrants, a consortium made up of Department of Defense, Federal Emergency Management Agency, and the General Services Administration designated a third camp, Fort McCoy, Wisconsin, to accommodate Cuban refugees.

Fort McCoy, Wisconsin, opened on 29 May 1980 and processed a total of 14,360 refugees through 3 November 1980, when it ceased operation. Those processed at Fort McCoy included a higher percentage of criminals and mentally ill individuals than at the other two centers.[23] This reality made more violence inevitable, and the Army had to deploy mechanized infantry from Fort Carson, Colorado, and airborne air assault troops from Fort Campbell, Kentucky, to control the violence.[24] Additionally, the overall health of these immigrants was significantly worse than that of the first immigrants. A FORSCOM historian later concluded that "Communist Cuba's highly vaunted and even more highly publicized socialized medical care delivery system did not, in fact, extend to every member of the population."[25]

The 86th Combat Support Hospital, garrisoned at Fort Campbell, Kentucky, arrived with its Mobile Unit, Surgical, Transportable (MUST) equipment at Fort McCoy on 23 May 1980. Professional Officer Filler System staff signed in the following day, and Lieutenant Colonel Maria L. Flecha, the chief nurse, went to work. She assigned patients to nursing units based on their diagnoses. She conferred with the preventive medicine officer and outlined procedures for isolation, infectious waste disposal, and contaminated linen handling. Flecha assigned her 18 Army Nurse Corps officers, selecting head nurses and detailing others to their individual responsibilities. Elective surgeries were not scheduled daily, so Flecha had the nurse anesthetist and operating room nurse work in the emergency room while remaining on call for unscheduled operative cases. Patients hospitalized or treated in the emergency room included refugees who were dehydrated, asthmatics, hypertensives, psychiatric cases, those with infected wounds, victims of animal bites, those suffering with acute skin conditions, trauma patients, and a few with cardiac and respiratory arrest. The command soon found it expedient to delegate unanticipated medical duties to nursing personnel. Two Army nurses, for example, became responsible for triaging refugees disembarking from incoming flights. Four other Army nurses served at the in-processing center doing health screenings and referrals as needed. When the command established two Troop Medical Clinics, nursing staff took charge. They set up the Troop Medical Clinics, scrubbed the facilities, oversaw installation of partitions, and requisitioned and organized equipment and supplies. Spanish-speaking Army nurses staffed the Troop Medical Clinics. Not surprisingly, during the first three weeks of the deployment, all of the nursing staff worked 12-hour shifts.[26]

FORSCOM announced retrospectively that the AMEDD failed to deploy enough people to Fort McCoy to meet demands for refugee medical care. Health care services greatly exceeded the capability of the one Combat Support Hospital and the two Preventive Medicine Detachments deployed. Originally, however, the Office of The Surgeon General and HSC had planned to limit their support to emergency treatment, hospitalization, and preventive medicine, but other missions materialized with the arrival of the refugees. Additional missions were support at the airfield at LaCrosse, Wisconsin, screening new arrivals, ambulance transportation, and the operation of two TMCs. There also were requirements for emergency care, hospitalization, preventive health measures, urgent dental care involving extractions and emergency oral surgery, and a considerable amount of psychiatric care, including specialized psychiatric assessments called for by the Immigration and Naturalization Service.[27] The leadership of the 86th Combat Support Hospital disputed the shortcomings alleged by FORSCOM. Flecha's After Action Report read:

> Another major area of concern affecting the mission was the inability of the United States Public Health Service (USPHS) to effectively plan and execute the organization of the overall Cuban Refugee Program. The 86th Combat Support Hospital was deployed to provide inpatient and emergency room care. Due to the inability of USPHS to recruit and hire sufficient personnel to staff all areas of the operation, the 86th CSH was required to take on the added responsibilities of airfield support, in-processing and medical screening, and the opening and staffing of two refugee dispensaries.[28]

FORSCOM ordered the 86th Combat Support Hospital to end operations by 29 June 1980 and directed the unit to disassemble its MUST equipment for shipment back to Fort Campbell. The USPHS then made accommodations for the Cuban refugees requiring hospitalization to receive care in local civilian institutions. Authorities directed the USPHS to set up and staff an emergency room, which it was unable to do. Instead, the 86th Combat Support Hospital staff designed and coordinated the facility and organized the equipment, supplies, and drugs in the new emergency room. They also gave an orientation to USPHS staff working in the emergency room.[29] Whether because of inadequate numbers or lack of experience, the USPHS could not conduct its assigned mission. Instead, a group of Army Nurse Corps officers were there and filled the void.

Flecha's After Action Report criticized the unfamiliar and obsolete equipment and the unavailability of medical items to treat the various ailments of the refugees. She recommended that the Army update the medications, supplies, and equipment prescribed for combat support hospitals. Flecha viewed the lackluster medical proficiency of most of the assigned TO&E enlisted staff as a larger problem. They neither could immediately respond to emergencies nor meet the needs of patients or physicians. Senior non-commissioned officers needed to improve their management skills to oversee wards and clinics, establish supply levels, and teach and supervise the junior enlisted staff. Consequently, Flecha recommended that the AMEDD devote additional time and energy to augment the training for its troops. Army nurses in fixed facilities likewise should instruct the personnel assigned to field facilities because—in Flecha's opinion—the AMEDD had to stress field training for all professional personnel. These kind of assessments and lessons learned from all the deployed field hospitals gave impetus for the radical reform and modernization of TO&E structure and function in the approaching decade.

The field hospitals that deployed for the Cuban Refugee Operation played an important role, and without them, the undertaking had the potential to become an embarrassing debacle. At the least, conditions would have been more chaotic. Several Army Nurse Corps officers who participated were Vietnam War veterans and others had recent field experience. Their professional knowledge and experience were vital to the mission.

Another significant foreign mission took place in the summer of 1983. At that time, President Ronald Reagan ordered joint and combined military exercises with Honduras and El Salvador in Central America to demonstrate the U.S. commitment against a growing Marxist guerilla threat.[30] The objectives of the Big Pine II maneuvers, Ahuas Tara I, Ahuas Tara II, and Granadero I, were to improve host-nation readiness, counter Communist expansion, and to demonstrate an American presence and interest.[31]

Most of the aforementioned exercises took place in Honduras, a developing Central American nation. In support of these training missions, elements of the 41st Combat Support Hospital from Fort Sam Houston, Texas, deployed to that country in September 1983 and in 48 hours erected a 60-bed facility in a muddy, insect-ridden field. This humble beginning evolved into the Medical Element (MEDEL) of Joint Task Force (JTF) Bravo, Honduras. U.S. Army, Navy, and Air Force medical personnel staffed the MEDEL, whose missions were to support the joint field exercises and provide humanitarian assistance to local Hondurans. JTF Bravo staff rotated regularly. In March 1984, the 47th Field Hospital from Fort Sill, Oklahoma, arrived for its temporary duty in support of the mission. While there, the staff also supported Medical Civilian Assistant Programs, also referred to as Medical Readiness Training Exercises, three times a week.[32]

Lieutenant Colonel Nancy Nooney was chief nurse in Honduras for several months in 1984. She characterized the climate there as so unbearably hot that even tropical-weight fatigues were uncomfortable. Despite the miserable weather, the Army Nurse Corps officers made their contributions. An assigned nurse midwife working for Nooney participated in Medical Civilian Assistant Programs and evaluated expectant mothers—seemingly every local female inhabitant older than 12 years of age.[33] The midwife also conducted a gynecological clinic twice weekly and was a great asset in controlling venereal disease. Additionally, a Spanish-speaking Army nurse and two enlisted medics taught a Combat Medic Course for 35 Honduran soldiers. When the 82nd Airborne Division scheduled an air drop about seven miles away, the MEDEL went into a Mass Casualty posture but fortunately had to treat only one minor injury. Overall, the nurses provided good safe care and did a considerable amount of teaching under exceedingly difficult circumstances.[34]

Captain Nelly Aleman-Guzman also provided state-of-the-art nursing care and taught rudimentary nursing skills to local nationals in Honduras in 1984. Her instruction focused variously on the knowledge and skills necessary to carry out cardiopulmonary resuscitation, infusion therapy, and the application of tourniquets. She participated in 134 Medical Civilian Assistant Programs treating upward of 400 patients daily on her visits to rural villages and regarded her time in Honduras as "a once-in-a-lifetime experience." Aleman-Guzman's fluent Spanish facilitated her one-on-one interactions with locals and made her the obvious choice as an interpreter for her English-speaking counterparts as well.[35]

When General Connie L. Slewitzke visited JTF Bravo with a group of general officers in 1987, she found troubling issues.[36] The operating room staff, for example, routinely allowed contaminated drainage to flow through a hole in the floor, and years of seepage left a noxious odor and even larger quality issues. Slewitzke rejected the attitude that the Hondurans did it this way and insisted on maintaining North American standards while adapting to the local realities. Although the rough conditions gave the Army nurses experience in operating in an austere environment, Slewitzke had some doubts about the real value of the mission, believing the participating nurses were engaged in work more suitable for the Peace Corps.[37]

In 1992 when Lieutenant Colonel Cindy Gurney was chief nurse at the MEDEL, some conditions had improved but many had not. By then, the facility had become a network of wooden hooches (semipermanent huts) connected by boardwalks, "a remarkable cross of wild west and polynesian [sic] village." The nursing office shared a hooch with the Patient Administration Division. The operating room, central material supply, x-ray, and laboratory were housed within the Deployable Medical System equipment. The facility's single ward had a 12-bed capacity. Gurney's quarters consisted of a small room in a one-story building with shared communal baths.

Security at the compound was exceptionally strict. Helicopters carried those participating in the Medical Readiness Training Exercises, morale shopping activities, and recreational trips from the camp. Travel over land demanded heightened security and special precautions because of possible guerrilla threats. Personnel traveled in groups of at least two vehicles with a minimum of four people per vehicle. When a third vehicle was added to the group, they moved in convoy formation accompanied by a Joint Security Forces vehicle loaded in the front and rear with M60 automatic weapons.[38]

When Gurney arrived at a nearby orphanage to participate in a Medical Readiness Training Exercise one Saturday morning, boys and girls darted out from

Lieutenant Colonel Cindy Gurney, chief nurse at the Medical Element in Honduras in 1992, is pictured here with a three-year-old local child, Omar. The pair became good friends.
Photo courtesy of Colonel Cindy Gurney, Clifton Park, NY.

every direction. Gurney organized the children, who ranged in age from toddlers to adolescents, into a medical assembly line. First, a Honduran liaison physician determined the child's chief medical complaint. Then a physician assistant did a brief assessment of that problem and prescribed a medication. Two pharmacy technicians dispensed the appropriate medications and Gurney administered deworming medication to each child, the amount depending on the youngster's age and weight. The children's health problems varied from simple complaints to serious syndromes, and teams treated everything from runny noses, inflamed ears, headaches, and dermatitis to malaria, cardiac anomalies, and cerebral palsy. A three-year-old latched onto Gurney.

> When I couldn't carry him, he hung on my pockets. I didn't need to speak to him. He didn't try to speak to me. We couldn't understand each other except for the primitive understanding that passes when two souls touch and tickle and giggle together.[39]

There was great personal gratification in the work because it involved a satisfying blend of altruism and mission accomplishment.[40]

Although these outreach activities—common to many foreign missions of any sizable extent—were undoubtedly well intentioned, there were those who believed that they rarely yielded long-term positive effects. Advances in health status were realized but they may have suggested to the local inhabitants that their own government was incapable of providing basic health care. Once the Americans left, the population's health had the potential to revert quickly to its previous precarious state. Such conditions in Honduras bore a noteworthy resemblance to comparable activities during the Vietnam War, about which Wilensky suggested the priority instead "should be on developing capability, not providing service." He added that "this process of education requires a long standing commitment" and is challenging for typically task-oriented, hands-on, American health care providers who must stand back "while others attempt to provide health care who are less able and work far slower."[41]

The MEDEL staff in Honduras usually kept quite busy. On one occasion, a jump of 190 troops from the 82nd Airborne into an area of broken terrain after a nightlong flight from Fort Bragg created scores of casualties. Air evacuation helicopters flew the casualties to the MEDEL, where the staff treated numerous fractures, including those of two paratroopers requiring immediate surgery. Shortly afterward, another soldier arrived from a remote listening post suffering burns sustained while incinerating trash. The staff stabilized him and arranged his evacuation to the Burn Unit, Institute for Surgical Research, at Fort Sam Houston, Texas. Next, four Hondurans appeared at the gate seeking care. The four were accompanied by three family members who also required lodging. By day's end, the facility was operating at full capacity, with four surgical procedures scheduled for the next morning.[42]

The command designated Saturdays as force protection days. They began with formations followed by training sessions. Soldier skills such as vehicle maintenance and disassembling and cleaning and reassembling small arms were the topics for classes on one particular Saturday. The following Saturday called for a five-mile road march with full Load Bearing Equipment and weapons.[43] All Army Nurse Corps officers not on hospital duty participated in the weekly training.

The temporary assignment of Army Nurse Corps officers to the MEDEL at JTF Bravo in rotations just short of six months continued for decades. The Army nurses provided health care for JTF troops, offered humanitarian assistance for Honduran nation building, performed civic actions, accrued valuable training experience, learned to adapt health care provision to developing nations, and probably improved the image of the United States in Central America.[44] At the same time, Army nurses served in advisory roles in another Central American country, El Salvador.

The efforts of Army Nurse Corps officers during the bloody civil war years in El Salvador were another expression of U.S. diplomacy whose goals were to promote human rights, support democracy, challenge Soviet and Cuban leftist influence, and bolster U.S. security interests in that developing nation.[45]

While many Army nurses actively provided hands-on care in Honduras, the role of their counterparts in neighboring El Salvador was different. In El Salvador, Army Nurse Corps officers were limited to giving professional advice to local

Captain Charlotte Scott stands ready to provide care for incoming mass casualty patients during an exercise at the Medical Element of Joint Task Force Bravo in Honduras.
Photo courtesy of Colonel Cindy Gurney, Clifton Park, NY.

caregivers. Captain Juan Sandoval was one such Army nurse.

In 1983, Sandoval became the first Army nurse to serve on temporary duty in El Salvador as a member of a Medical Mobile Training Team that deployed to bolster that nation's military medical establishment because the national army of El Salvador lacked an organized field medical system. Survival statistics for combat wounded were grim, with more than 45 percent dying of their battlefield wounds. Sandoval's charge was to evaluate health services and requirements in the El Salvador army's garrison and consult with those who trained military medics. As an operating room nurse with that specialty's unique mindset, Sandoval reduced the local hospital's infection rate and improved infection control practices by encouraging good aseptic technique, especially when caring for the high number of land mine amputees.[46] Sandoval spent a productive three months in El Salvador.

Duty in El Salvador was dangerous. Flying into the country was somewhat like arriving in Vietnam in the 1960s. Small arms fire provided an ominous welcome. Visiting officers wore civilian clothing and changed into different vans as they traveled from site to site.[47] Captain Nelly Aleman-Guzman, who was teaching a five-month intensive care course to 21 El Salvador nurses in 1989, carefully observed these precautions and a few more. She never ate in public restaurants, avoided going out at all, and traveled different routes every day to work with her bodyguard. She carried a 9-mm Beretta pistol with ammunition and slept with her M16 rifle. Her quarters had a high fence and round-the-clock guards. None of these safeguards protected her from guerillas' bullets when on 21 November 1989 rebels attacked her quarters. Aleman-Guzman suffered gunshot fragment wounds to her face and chest. Her housemates, a physical therapist, two physicians, and a paramedic, rendered immediate first aid but were unable to move her to the hospital until the siege ended 48 hours later. Despite her wounds, Aleman-Guzman completed her tour in El Salvador and returned to her home post in the United States in January 1990. Nearly five years later, in ceremonies held at the Pentagon, Brigadier General Nancy Adams presented the Purple Heart to Aleman-Guzman for wounds suffered in El Salvador. She was the first female Army Nurse Corps officer to be so decorated since the Vietnam War.[48] One author attributed the unusually lengthy five-year delay from time of wounding to formal recognition with the Purple Heart to the Reagan administration's political agenda that directed that a low profile be maintained regarding American presence in El Salvador.[49] Many of the campaigns of the 1980s featured both humanitarian and hostile actions.

## Notes

1. The approximate number of refugees processed in the three main reception centers as totaled from statistics appearing in this text was 52,654. However, the Office of the Deputy Chief of Staff for Operations noted on page E-III-2 of its *Annual Historical Review of 1980* that the refugees numbered "over 55,000." The commander of the U.S. Army Center of Military History estimated the number of refugees at 44,000. BG Harold Nelson, "The Army and the Cuban Refugee Problem, 1980–1981," Information Paper, 4 December 1991, Army Nurse Corps Collection (ANCC), Office of Medical History (OMH). Frank W. Pew, "The Role of FORSCOM in the Reception and Care of Refugees from Cuba in the Continental United States," FORSCOM Historical Monograph Series (Fort McPherson, GA: Military History Office, Office of the Chief of Staff, U.S. Army Forces Command, 1984), 1. Robert L. Scheina, "The Cuban Exodus of 1980," *United States Naval Institute Proceedings* (October 1980): 44–51.

2. Charles C. Pixley, "Significant Strides Recorded by Army," *U.S. Medicine* 17 (15 January 1981): 37–38, 43, 46. Dwight Oland and Jeffrey Greenhut, *Report of the Surgeon General, United States Army Fiscal Years 1976–1980* (Washington, DC: Office of the Surgeon General, U.S. Army, 1988), 168.

3. Frank W. Pew, "The Role of FORSCOM in the Reception and Care of Refugees from Cuba in the Continental United States," FORSCOM Historical Monograph Series (Fort McPherson, GA: Military History Office, Office of the Chief of Staff, U.S. Army Forces Command, 1984), 2.

4. Charles C. Pixley, "Significant Strides Recorded by Army," *U.S. Medicine* 17 (15 January 1981): 37–38, 43, 46. Dwight Oland and Jeffrey Greenhut, *Report of the Surgeon General, United States Army Fiscal Years 1976–1980* (Washington, DC: Office of the Surgeon General, U.S. Army, 1988), 168.

5. Edwin H. J. Carns, "After Action Report, 47th Field Hospital, Cuban Refugee Operation Resettlement, 8 May–28 June 1980," Typewritten Report (TR), 2–5, 1 December 1980, Army Nurse Corps Collection, Office of Medical History. Frank W. Pew, "The Role of FORSCOM in the Reception and Care of Refugees from Cuba in the Continental United States," *FORSCOM Historical Monograph Series* (Fort McPherson, GA: Military History Office, Office of the Chief of Staff, U.S. Army Forces Command, 1984), 9–10.

6. Frank W. Pew, "The Role of FORSCOM in the Reception and Care of Refugees from Cuba in the Continental United States," *FORSCOM Historical Monograph Series* (Fort

McPherson, GA: Military History Office, Office of the Chief of Staff, U.S. Army Forces Command, 1984), 4–5.

7. Parents of the first child born named him "Jimmy Fred Guerro-Ruiz" in honor of the United States president and the physician who assisted at the birth, Fred A. Simon, M.D. Edwin H. J. Carns, "After Action Report, 47th Field Hospital, Cuban Refugee Operation Resettlement, 8 May–28 June 1980," TR, 4, 1 December 1980, ANCC, OMH.

8. Edwin H. J. Carns, "After Action Report, 47th Field Hospital, Cuban Refugee Operation Resettlement, 8 May–28 June 1980," TR, 2–5, 1 December 1980, ANCC, OMH. Frank W. Pew, "The Role of FORSCOM in the Reception and Care of Refugees from Cuba in the Continental United States," *FORSCOM Historical Monograph Series* (Fort McPherson, GA: Military History Office, Office of the Chief of Staff, U.S. Army Forces Command, 1984), 9–10.

9. Douglas Brinkley, *The Unfinished Presidency* (New York: Viking, 1988), 354–55.

10. Edwin H. J. Carns, "After Action Report, 47th Field Hospital, Cuban Refugee Operation Resettlement, 8 May–28 June 1980," TR, 2–5, 1 December 1980, ANCC, OMH. Frank W. Pew, "The Role of FORSCOM in the Reception and Care of Refugees from Cuba in the Continental United States," *FORSCOM Historical Monograph Series* (Fort McPherson, GA: Military History Office, Office of the Chief of Staff, U.S. Army Forces Command, 1984), 9–10.

11. The charter group included Lieutenant Colonel Esther Segler, majors Kathryn Deuster and Loraine Dayton, captains Jackie Saye, Audrey Walding, Joel Messing, William Bester, Sheila Clarke, Naomi Foody, and Dora Deal, and lieutenants Patricia Simon, Cynthia Pinski, Pamela Hummel, and A. Medina-Muniz. HSPE-MO, "Cuban Refugee Support, Ft Chaffee," Typewritten List, 16 May 1980, ANCC, OMH.

12. The assistant chief nurse assigned was Lieutenant Colonel Adolfo Rosado. Esther Segler, Telephone Conversation with Author, 3 June 2003.

13. Edwin H. J. Carns, "After Action Report, 47th Field Hospital, Cuban Refugee Operation Resettlement, 8 May–28 June 1980," TR, I-1 to I-3, 1 December 1980, ANCC, OMH.

14. Lieutenant Colonel Carnes [sic] to Lieutenant Colonel Wahl, "Request for ANC Personnel, 47th Fld Hosp," Telephone or Verbal Conversation Record, 28 May 1980, ANCC, OMH.

15. Edwin H.J. Carns, "After Action Report, 47th Field Hospital, Cuban Refugee Operation Resettlement, 8 May–28 June 1980," TR, I-5 to I-6, 1 December 1980, ANCC, OMH.

16. Frank W. Pew, "The Role of FORSCOM in the Reception and Care of Refugees from Cuba in the Continental United States," *FORSCOM Historical Monograph Series* (Fort McPherson, GA: Military History Office, Office of the Chief of Staff, U.S. Army Forces Command, 1984), 227, 233–34.

17. Edwin H.J. Carns, "After Action Report, 47th Field Hospital, Cuban Refugee Operation Resettlement, 8 May–28 June 1980," TR, I-6 to I-7, 1 December 1980, ANCC, OMH.

18. Ibid., 6.

19. Frank W. Pew, "The Role of FORSCOM in the Reception and Care of Refugees from Cuba in the Continental United States," *FORSCOM Historical Monograph Series* (Fort McPherson, GA: Military History Office, Office of the Chief of Staff, U.S. Army Forces Command, 1984), 6–7.

20. Madelyn N. Parks to Lillian Dunlap, Typewritten Letter (TL), 19 June 1973, ANCC, OMH.

21. "Army Nurse Corps Key Officer Assignments," 14, 1 February 1980, ANCC, OMH.

22. Mary J. Wise to Eunice Kennedy, "Field Training Units," TL, 24 September 1980,

ANCC, OMH.

23. Frank W. Pew, "The Role of FORSCOM in the Reception and Care of Refugees from Cuba in the Continental United States," *FORSCOM Historical Monograph Series* (Fort McPherson, GA: Military History Office, Office of the Chief of Staff, U.S. Army Forces Command, 1984), 6–8. Many Cubans had arrived on America's shores in the years before the Mariel Boatlift. A federal official who had "worked with the earlier waves of exiles" noted that those who arrived first were "the elite, next the professional class and now the lower class." David M. Alpern and others, "Carter and the Cuban Influx," *Newsweek* (26 May 1980): 22.

24. Frank W. Pew, "The Role of FORSCOM in the Reception and Care of Refugees from Cuba in the Continental United States," *FORSCOM Historical Monograph Series* (Fort McPherson, GA: Military History Office, Office of the Chief of Staff, U.S. Army Forces Command, 1984), 6–8.

25. Ibid., 226–27.

26. Maria L. Flecha, "After Action Report, Cuban Refugee Mission," Typewritten Document, 1-4, n.d., ANCC, OMH.

27. Frank W. Pew, "The Role of FORSCOM in the Reception and Care of Refugees from Cuba in the Continental United States," *FORSCOM Historical Monograph Series* (Fort McPherson, GA: Military History Office, Office of the Chief of Staff, U.S. Army Forces Command, 1984), 226–27.

28. Maria L. Flecha, "After Action Report, Cuban Refugee Mission," Typewritten Document, 4, n.d., ANCC, OMH.

29. Ibid., 5. Frank W. Pew, "The Role of FORSCOM in the Reception and Care of Refugees from Cuba in the Continental United States," *FORSCOM Historical Monograph Series* (Fort McPherson, GA: Military History Office, Office of the Chief of Staff, U.S. Army Forces Command, 1984), 234.

30. Scott M. Hines, *Joint Task Force-Bravo—The U.S. Military Presence in Honduras: U.S. Policy for an Evolving Region* (College Park: University of Maryland, School of Public Affairs, 1994).

31. The objective of Big Pine II (August 1983 to February 1984) was to demonstrate the United States' military ability to operate in Central America and to convince the Sandinista government of Nicaragua to cease fostering insurrection in the area. In January 1983, U.S. and Honduran military forces carried out Operation Ahuas Tara I near Puerto Lempira, Honduras. Granadero I took place in Cucuyagua, Honduras. Dwight Oland, *Department of the Army Historical Summary, Fiscal Year 1984* (Washington, DC: Center of Military History, United States Army, 1995), 39–40.

32. Cindy Gurney, "Preliminary History of the Medical Element, Joint Task Force-Bravo, Soto Cano Air Base, Honduras," September 1992, ANCC, OMH. Bernard T. Mittemeyer, "Quality Assurance: Major Army Focus," *U.S. Medicine* 20 (15 January 1984): 56. Bernard T. Mittemeyer, "'Volatile' Year Sees Army Medical Gains," *U.S. Medicine* 21 (15 January 1985): 16. Arthur C. Wittich, "The Medical Care System and Medical Readiness Training Exercises (MEDRETEs) in Honduras," *Military Medicine* 154 (January 1989): 19–23. Charles H. Hood, "Humanitarian Civic Action in Honduras, 1988," *Military Medicine* 156 (June 1991): 292–96.

33. One account stated that in Honduras, over a woman's reproductive life span, "nine-plus pregnancies per woman is the rule (9.5), with about 7 live births." Charles H. Hood, "Humanitarian Civic Action in Honduras, 1988," *Military Medicine* 156 (June 1991): 292.

34. Nancy Nooney to Connie L. Slewitzke, Handwritten Letter, 21 March 1984, ANCC, OMH.

35. "Honduras Called Good Experience," *HSC Mercury* 11 (August 1984): 12.

36. Accompanying General Slewitzke were generals Tracy Strevey, Lewis Mologne, Richard Travis, James Rumbaugh, and Wally Johnson. Several reserve generals and SG consultants also made up the party. Connie L. Slewitzke, Interview by Beverly Greenlee, 50–51, n.d., USAWC/USAMHI Senior Officer Oral History Program, Project No. 88-8, ANCC, OMH.

37. Connie L. Slewitzke, Interview by Beverly Greenlee, 42–46, n.d., USAWC/USAMHI Senior Officer Oral History Program, Project No. 88-8, ANCC, OMH.

38. Cindy Gurney, "Howdy!" TL, 16 March 1992, ANCC, OMH.

39. Cindy Gurney, "Greetings from Lake Soto Cano!" TL, 29 June 1992, ANCC, OMH.

40. General William Westmoreland had another motive for encouraging the MEDCAPs in another earlier operation in Vietnam. General Westmoreland believed that "medical personnel, used to working, get surly if they have nothing to do." He saw the MEDCAPs as a way of keeping the AMEDD busy. Westmoreland wrote that he observed discontent in medical personnel and they "even feel misused, when they are not occupied with their specialty." Robert J.T. Joy to Author, TL, 24 November 2003, ANCC, OMH. William C. Westmoreland, *A Soldier Reports* (New York: Doubleday & Company, 1976), 82, 266–67. However, Honduras was not Vietnam. JTF Bravo was an operation of armed diplomacy, and MEDCAPs had a higher priority there as opposed to those in Vietnam, which was a combat operation.

41. Robert J. Wilensky, "The Medical Civic Action Program in Vietnam: Success or Failure?" *Military Medicine* 166 (September 2001): 815–19.

42. Cindy Gurney, "Greetings from Honduras!" TL, 24 March 1992, ANCC, OMH.

43. Ibid.

44. Angela Williams, "Joint Task Force—Bravo," *Army Nurse Corps Newsletter* (July 2000): 17–18. Charles H. Hood, "Humanitarian Civic Action in Honduras, 1988," *Military Medicine* 156 (June 1991): 292–96. Arthur C. Wittich, "The Medical Care System and Medical Readiness Training Exercises (MEDRETEs) in Honduras," *Military Medicine* 154 (January 1989): 19–23. Cindy Gurney, "Preliminary History of the Medical Element, Joint Task Force-Bravo, Soto Cano Air Base, Honduras," September 1992, ANCC, OMH. Frank F. Ledford, "Army 'Innovative' in Use of Funds," *U.S. Medicine* 25 (January 1989): 41–42.

45. Richard A. Haggerty, ed., *El Salvador, A Country Study*, Headquarters, Department of the Army, DA Pamphlet 550-150 (Washington, DC: U.S. Government Printing Office, 1990). James S. Corum, "The Air War in El Salvador," *Airpower Journal* 12 (Summer 1998): 27–44. Shawn Sullivan, "The Reagan Administration and El Salvador, 1981–1984: Bureaucratic and Domestic Politics Revisited," *Low Intensity Conflict & Law Enforcement* 8 (Summer 1999): 33–57.

46. "Medical Survey Team, El Salvador," After Action Report, August–September 1980; "Report on the Effectiveness of Training, US Army Humanitarian Medical MTT El Salvador (Phase I), 23 May–19 Dec 83," TR, 20 January 1984; Juan M. Garcia, "Effectiveness of Training Mobile Training Team, RCS CSGPO-125," Typewritten Report, 17 August 1984; Robert H. Buker, "Progress of Humanitarian Medical Mobile Training Team (Med MTT), El Salvador," Information Memorandum, 2 June 1988; Mr. Gonzales, "Medical MTT-El Salvador," Information Paper, 7 March 90; Felipe Casso, "U.S. Army Humanitarian Medical Assistance in El Salvador," TR, 3–5, February 1990; "Medical Mobile Training Team (MTT) Accomplishments—El Salvador," Information Paper, 31 December 1991; and Connie L. Slewitzke, Interview by Beverly Greenlee, 46–47, n.d., USAWC/USAMHI Senior Officer Oral History Program, Project No. 88-8 (all in ANCC, OMH). Bernard T. Mitte-

meyer, "'Volatile' Year Sees Army Medical Gains," *U.S. Medicine* 21 (15 January 1985): 16. Russ Zajtchuk, F. William Brown, and James H. Rumbaugh, "Medical Success in El Salvador," *Military Medicine* 154 (February 1989): 59–61. Carolyn M. Feller and Debora R. Cox, *Highlights in the History of the Army Nurse Corps* (Washington, DC: U.S. Army Center of Military History, 2000), 55.

47. Connie L. Slewitzke, Interview by Beverly Greenlee, 47–50, n.d., USAWC/USAMHI Senior Officer Oral History Program, Project No. 88-8, ANCC, OMH.

48. Gilda A. Herrera, "Walter Reed Nurse Earns Purple Heart," Typewritten Press Release, 16 November 1994; Award Certificate, 17 August 1994; Gregory R. Walker to Colonel Terris Kennedy, TL, March 8, 1994; Ronald M. Tolls, "Substantiation of Soldier's Injuries," Typewritten Memorandum, 10 March 1994; and Nelly Aleman-Guzman, Interview by Jennifer Petersen, 11–35, 22 January 2004 (all in ANCC, OMH). Gilda A. Herrera, "Walter Reed Nurse Earns Purple Heart," *Stripe* (4 November 1994): 6, 11. Greg Walker, "Vets of Clandestine Central American War Rate Recognition," *VFW* (April 1994): 20–22. Carolyn M. Feller and Debora R. Cox, *Highlights in the History of the Army Nurse Corps* (Washington, DC: U.S. Army Center of Military History, 2000), 67.

49. Greg Walker, *At the Hurricane's Eye: U.S. Special Operations Forces from Vietnam to Desert Storm* (New York: Ballantine Books, 1994), 114–15.

*Chapter Thirteen*
# Additional Deployments in the 1980s

In October 1983, the Army Medical Department (AMEDD) deployed to the Caribbean island of Grenada. The United States responded to a takeover of the government on Grenada by a Soviet-backed coup with ties to Cuba. Grenada's Caribbean neighbors and Washington interpreted the military revolutionaries' leftist philosophy as a serious Communist threat. A large number of American expatriates as well as a group of U.S. medical students were on the island, and fears for their safety and the possibility of their becoming hostages of the revolutionary regime also spurred American intervention. The military code-named the mission that commenced on 25 October 1983 to restore democratic government to Grenada "Operation Urgent Fury."[1]

Contingency operations like Operation Urgent Fury and the 1989 Operation Just Cause were carried out by ready reaction force units, most positioned at Fort Bragg, North Carolina; Fort Campbell, Kentucky; Fort Ord, California; and Fort Stewart, Georgia. Such units were expected to deploy anywhere with less than 18 hours' notice.[2] Army Nurse Corps officers also participated in Operation Urgent Fury. Most of these women and men were Professional Officer Filler System (PROFIS) personnel, and many came from other U.S. installations and units to Fort Bragg, North Carolina, the staging site for the mobilization.[3] Several of these individuals replaced Army nurses at the Fort Bragg Medical Department Activity who subsequently mobilized. A small contingent deployed with two Table of Organization and Equipment units, the 307th Medical Battalion and the 5th Mobile Army Surgical Hospital (MASH).[4]

This was the first combat experience for the Army and the Army Nurse Corps since Vietnam, and numerous difficulties cropped up throughout the mission. Some could be attributed to the rapid tempo of the mission. Some were caused by the untested PROFIS system that clearly required modification. Some could be blamed on poor planning and misplaced priorities.[5] Finally, some could be ascribed to lingering prejudice against women in combat.[6]

After Operation Urgent Fury, the press in particular was highly critical of the conduct of the operation, focusing on planning, intelligence, equipment, and interservice cooperation.[7] Operational medical support also was criticized. During the mission's abbreviated (four-day) predeployment phase, there was little communication among the various echelons of the chain of command. The original plan was to use Navy ships for health service support to reduce ground medical assets. The Navy was prepared medically for these responsibilities, but may have had difficulty with joint operations (having never jointly trained with the AMEDD) if no training occurred. Although fully qualified in their specialties, the AMEDD PROFIS physicians had little knowledge of the principles of combat medicine. Few—if any—had the opportunity to attend the Combat Casualty Care Course.[8] Anecdotal allegations charged that surgeons had immediately sutured battlefield wounds rather than using the accepted combat technique of delayed primary closure. Later, Colonel John E. Hutton, chief of surgery at Walter Reed Army Medical Center, confirmed that battlefield surgeons closed the minor wounds of three of 28 casualties prematurely.[9] Major General Eugene Trobaugh, 82nd Airborne Division commander, chose to reduce already austere medical assets to get more combat and combat service elements into Grenada. It was 48 hours into the operation before the medical elements began trickling onto the island. No vehicles were earmarked to evacuate casualties, so the AMEDD relied on military or commercial vehicles to transport the wounded. Air ambulances did not arrive on the island until 72 hours after the invasion. This forced the staff to rely on U.S. Air Force cargo planes that circumvented the useless Navy medical support. Tactical commanders ignored proper field sanitation, failed to enforce water consumption, and overloaded their soldiers with excessive weight. Illness and heat injuries multiplied. No plans existed to treat the pressing medical assistance needs of the civilian population.[10] Lieutenant Colonel Donn Richards, an Army physician, evaluated Operation Urgent Fury as follows:

> It was a tribute to the versatility and flexibility of the individual doctors, nurses, corpsman [sic], and administrators that a bad situation did not turn into a disastrous event. Whatever medical success [was] achieved in this operation was in spite of and not due to the actions of the senior leadership of the services. Overall the senior leadership showed a lack of planning and inattention to medical needs.[11]

Lieutenant Colonel Patricia A. Diskin, the chief nurse of the 44th Medical Brigade, identified problems nursing staff encountered, including nonfunctional medical equipment, lack of spare parts for equipment, and staffs' inability to set up or use field gear. She recommended that the Table of Organization and Equipment staff participate in more training in the use of medical equipment. Those who were proficient with equipment had little ability to handle basic patient care like obtaining routine vital signs, bathing patients, providing oral hygiene, or changing linens. Command and control was chaotic. On the Green Ramp at Pope Air Force Base, lists with numbers and names rarely matched up. Loadmasters called 32 names and 32 voices responded, but only 29 actually boarded the plane. After the plane arrived in Grenada in the dead of night, they could not account for all personnel. Names were called, buses left, and many got left behind. Protective masks were unusable and small-size masks were not available. Some of the masks only had training filters. But there were worse blunders.

Trobaugh forbade female soldiers to deploy with their support units, a prohibition that disregarded the Army's policy on women in combat.[12] The Direct Combat Probability Coding system barred women from combat positions where they were judged to be at risk for direct contact with the enemy, not from an entire operation.[13]

One of the Army nurses excluded was Major Shirley A. Davis, head nurse on a medical unit at Womack Army Community Hospital, Fort Bragg, North Carolina. Davis first learned on 25 October 1983 that she was assigned since July 1983 as PROFIS to the 5th MASH. Unprepared for the impending deployment, Davis drove that same October morning to the 44th Medical Brigade Headquarters at Fort Bragg and went through the Process for Overseas Rotation.[14] This involved the usual legal and administrative matters, such as assigning power of attorney to a civilian nurse friend, receiving a meal card, completing a post office change-of-address card, and verifying her identification card and dog tags. Personnel and finance records had to be reviewed, but they could not be located at Davis' company. She had to buy a third pair of Battle Dress Uniforms from the clothing sales store and then retrieved her medical and dental records, which remained in her field pack for the duration of the deployment. The next day, Davis received six immunizations because—since she was unaware of her PROFIS assignment—she had not kept her vaccinations up to date. On 30 October 1983 at 0200 hours, the final alert call came and Davis reported into the 5th MASH, where a staff member issued her a flak jacket and a poorly fitting protective mask. Some personnel also received weapons but no ammunition.[15] At the company, Davis received her chalk number—that is, the soldier's number on a list of the personnel and equipment to be loaded on a particular aircraft. She next boarded a bus bound for the Green Ramp at Pope Air Force Base, North Carolina. When ordered to board the plane, Davis recalled, some answered while others did not. Some heard the call and others just were not ready to go.[16]

Trobaugh banned military women, including Army nurses, from the island. He ordered that all female soldiers assigned to the invasion force remain on the nearby island of Barbados. Despite this directive, seven women (four officers and three enlisted) arrived on Grenada at 2200 hours on 30 October as a result of the confusion on the Green Ramp.

Upon their arrival on Grenada, a flabbergasted, harried officer directed the uninvited women to sleep on the tarmac of the Port Salinas Air Field.[17] Next morning, the women overheard rumors that generals were unhappy about the unexpected presence of women and the logistical challenges it posed in Grenada.[18] A Black Hawk helicopter took the seven women soldiers to Barbados, far from the action.[19] Fortunately, C Company of the 307th Medical Battalion, a small advance party comprising an orthopedic surgeon, a 91C licensed practical nurse, and four corpsmen were able to stabilize the first few casualties with their basic load of equipment.[20]

The women stayed on Barbados for only a short time. The 5th MASH, with its full complement of male and female personnel, departed from Barbados after one day and arrived on Grenada at 0200 hours on 2 November 1983. The first casualty they treated was a young soldier suffering head and back trauma from falling down a hill while on patrol. After that, the unit treated patients with minor injuries and illnesses, such as lacerations, gastroenteritis, eye injuries, sunburn, and skin rashes. The 15-bed facility was fully operational by 5 November 1983.[21]

On 7 November, the hospital received an eight-year-old Grenada boy, injured when a hand grenade a friend was playing with detonated. The child spent seven hours in the operating room for the repair of a lacerated liver, bowel perforations with evisceration, an open fracture of an ankle, and a fragment wound of the eye.[22] Only one urinary catheter that came close to the appropriate gauge was available, and when it fell out of the patient, the nurses were compelled to soak the drainage tube in Betadine and reinsert it. The only available ventilator had no intermittent manual ventilation and, when not sedated, the boy fought the respirator, attempting to breathe on his own. The laboratory had no reagents available to test blood gases. Few pediatric supplies were available.[23] Two days later the child was evacuated to Naval Hospital Roosevelt Roads, Puerto Rico. An Army Nurse Corps anesthetist, Major Flint Gullet, ventilated the boy by hand, bagging for the entire flight.[24]

The injured child received state-of-the-art care but only because the staff could improvise. Had the 5th MASH received a large influx of wounded soldiers, the inadequate medical supplies and equipment might have cost lives. When C Company, 307th Medical Battalion, first deployed, it packed five Gama Goat vehicles filled to capacity with supplies.[25] Only three arrived with the initial deployment, the other two appearing five days later.[26]

Only a few seriously ill patients required combat care. Thus, many Army nurses were able to offer their assistance at the island's civilian St. George's Hospital, displaying their usual concern for local nationals. There, the vast differences between health care in a developing nation and the level of care provided in the Army medical system presented a sharp contrast.[27]

It soon became apparent that the Army Nurse Corps officers were not the only female soldiers on the island. Ultimately, about 170 military women served across the span of the entire operation in diverse combat support roles, such as perimeter guards, sergeants of the guard, Military Police, and cargo handlers. Major Ann Wright, for example, was responsible for ensuring compliance with the Geneva and Hague conventions in the Cuban Prisoner of War camps, served on the Foreign Claims Commission, liaised with the Agency for International Development, and participated on the Engineering Team that surveyed the Point Salinas International Airport.[28]

Major Rosamond Shepard, an obstetrics/gynecology nurse practitioner, was assigned to the 5th MASH and her knowledge and skills were very useful. She cared for several female soldiers and a few of the local nationals.[29] Shepard also treated both male and female soldiers for skin irritation and chafing caused by the wear of poorly fitting, winter-weight Battle Dress Uniform pants in the tropical island's heat and humidity. When jungle fatigues became available, the problems lessened. Women also had significant difficulty gaining access to showering facilities. Shepard reported:

> Shower hours were arbitrarily changed and many times no notification was given. When complaints were lodged no apparent action was taken. The excuse "well there were so many more men that we needed to use the female shower; only 20 women showed up for showers, etc." Of course if the showers were only available when the women were on duty [they] could not utilize them. Furthermore, if you arrived at the shower hour announced the night before and it had been changed to the previous hour it was impossible to take a shower.[30]

A daily shower was one of only a few comforts in a hot, dirty, field setting, and the denial of this small indulgence was a blow to morale.

Army nurse Major Jack L. McNeil also detected subtle gender discrimination in the way various combat service and combat service support units treated their female soldiers. The women were dropped off for treatment at the MASH and were not transported back to their units. It seemed their units forgot about them.[31]

Many line officers, non-commissioned officers, and soldiers thought women had no place in the invasion force destined for Grenada. The antagonistic attitude of senior officers contributed to this sentiment. Army nurses were a concentrated and visible element in hospital units, so they were easy targets for derision. Lieutenant Colonel Patricia A. Diskin shared her view of the gender discrimination and conflicts that surfaced in Operation Urgent Fury:

> The issue of when women deploy with CS [combat support] and CSS [combat service support] units into a potential combat area needs to be addressed. . . . The impact on readiness is substantial since women comprise as much as 30-40% in some units and frequently are in leadership positions. Historically, women especially nurses, have been confronted with the need to do their jobs in a potentially hostile environment (most recently Vietnam) and have taken these risks willingly. Any future conflict will necessarily involve large numbers of women deploying . . . and any effort to restrict or delay their participation will seriously degrade the ability of . . . units to carry out their mission. If decisions restricting participation by women can be made at a local level, the Army should remove these MOSs [Military Occupational Specialties] from consideration for women.

She insisted that the Army continue to train and deploy women on combat missions and recommended only the service secretary, i.e., the secretary of the Army, have the authority to exclude women soldiers from operations.[32]

By mid-November senior officials ordered the MASH to be reduced to a clearing company. Most of the AMEDD participants left the island soon thereafter.[33] Six Army Nurse Corps officers received awards for their service in Operation Urgent Fury.[34]

Although many aspects of Army Nurse Corps participation in Operation Urgent Fury were troublesome, many other features were almost flawless. The relationships between the Table of Organization and Equipment and PROFIS staffs were generally agreeable and productive.[35] Major Grace Johnson wrote that she found the unit responsive and cohesive, with "no prima donnas, no drunks, no doctors who thought they were God's gift to women and no slouches." The arrival of a military exchange boosted morale because the PX stocked both feminine hygiene supplies along with the Skoal and Red Man chewing tobacco favored by Army Rangers.[36] Captain Teresa Milie was impressed with the efficiency in setting up the field facility. The 5th MASH personnel built a large, well-appointed, technologically advanced, comprehensive hospital. Despite their long, drawn-out, arduous days, they also found time to explain details and help the PROFIS staff.[37]

Strangely, the general impression communicated by those who did not deploy was that the nurses on Grenada had been on vacation. This was far from the reality, and difficult personal conditions did not abate with the operation's end. Soon, returning nurses experienced sleep disturbances and other ailments such as diarrhea.[38] When Major Shirley Davis returned home, she woke up in the middle of the night and was surprised to see furniture in her tent. She added that it "took a while to figure out that I was indeed in my home, with a bed, privacy, carpets, running water, and flush toilets."

Reflecting on her experience, Davis acknowledged the importance of maintaining her immunization status when assigned as PROFIS to a rapid deployment unit. She came to understand the deployment process, became aware of what to bring on deployments, and acquired a "field-sense." Finally, she realized that high-quality care was possible in the field.[39]

Operation Urgent Fury was a wake-up call for the Army that underscored the need to improve readiness capabilities, refine contingency operations, and establish channels for interservice communication and collaboration. It spurred the development of new approaches for Health Service Support, better and lighter field medical supplies and equipment, more joint training and rehearsals, and new personnel configurations to provide health care on the battlefield. It added one more spark to the revitalization and modernization of the AMEDD.

Women soldiers deployed subsequently with almost every major Army operation but never again faced such wholesale discrimination and blatant exclusions by senior commanders. Both female and male Army Nurse Corps officers participated in the brief but fierce campaign in Panama in 1989.

Operation Just Cause began on 20 December 1989 in the Republic of Panama but its roots reached back to May 1988 when the Joint Chiefs of Staff debated the use of military intervention to deal with Panamanian dictator Manual Noriega.[40] The Joint Chiefs of Staff originally code-named the Panama operation "Operation Prayer Book/Blue Spoon" and envisioned it as a gradual, piecemeal military operation. Over time, the plan changed to a "surgical strike" favored by Lieutenant General Carl Stiner, the XVIII Airborne Corps commander. His plan was to surprise the enemy and attack during the night with overwhelming force that paralyzed the opposition's defenses, in effect a blitzkrieg.[41] This approach required a thick shroud of operational security, but the secrecy in turn complicated planning and execution of the mission.[42] With Joint Chiefs of Staff approval, the chief of staff of the Army stated the objectives for Operation Just Cause included prevention of harm to U.S. citizens, strengthening of Panamanian democracy, safeguarding of the unimpeded passage of vessels through the Panama Canal, removal of

Noriega, and the ending of his massive cocaine-trafficking business.[43]

Health service support planning for Operation Just Cause also claimed moderately deep roots. The relatively lengthy time available for careful planning, intensive training exercises, and rehearsals contributed significantly to the operation's success. For several years before the operation, the 44th Medical Brigade had been developing a prototype compact element, the Forward Surgical Team (FST), a light, mobile unit designed for contingency operations.[44] The concept had an extensive history but originated in recent times from the lessons learned in Grenada. During that campaign, it took 27 transport aircraft to deploy the 5th MASH.[45] Operation Urgent Fury task force commanders refused to give up that many aircraft because they needed to fly combat units to the island. To avoid a recurrence of the same problem, the 44th Medical Brigade devised a light, agile, exceptionally competent team that could provide resuscitative surgery and intensive, professional pre- and post-operative care. Army nurses and physicians consulted on equipment and team capabilities, blending common sense with pragmatic expectations. The combination of practicing professionals and skilled soldiers was key to the success. The final product, the FST, required just one aircraft for deployment.[46]

The FST was intended as an expedient until the entire MASH would arrive in theater, and its capacities were ordered in keeping with its short-term life span.[47] The FST could support 125 Advanced Trauma Life Support (ATLS) and about 60 surgical patients before resupply became necessary. Organic holding capability was 12 casualties.[48] Developers envisioned the 18-person staff of the FST as able to maintain professional levels of competence for 36 to 48 hours before fatigue diminished their capabilities.[49]

During development, officers in the AMEDD's Fort Sam Houston-based Combat Developments Branch declined to support the FST, judging there was no "valid requirement" for such a team. Refusing to be stymied, the FST developers subsequently presented the idea to Surgeon General Frank Ledford, who approved it and provided $50,000 to purchase specialized equipment commercially. These were small, state-of-the-art pieces such as a little ventilator, a pulse oximeter, oxygen concentrators, and basic cots that permitted raising the patient's head.[50] They then tested the equipment for durability by air-drop. In the main, the equipment proved capable of enduring abuse and staying operational. Planners next identified the equipment that could be carried on a single pallet together with the team. The entire set-up, equipment and team members, could unload from the aircraft tail and soon be ready to function in the field.[51] If a secure landing site was available, the entire assembly could be flown into theater on a USAF C-130 or C-141 aircraft, and the tents, supplies, and equipment subsequently could be loaded on a 2.5 ton truck with a half-ton trailer (air-land delivery). To relocate the entire FST after aerial insertion, the team would use the sling load delivery technique. In this case, tentage, equipment, and supplies were placed in cargo nets and lifted by a single CH-47 helicopter or two UH-60 rotary wing aircraft. With this method, the tent poles, fluorescent lights, and 18-man team would travel within the helicopter. Another choice would be a five-ton truck with the 18-man team following in another vehicle.[52]

Based on the notion that repetition enhances skills and performance, the team continually rehearsed their tasks and responsibilities over a two-year period, and the enlisted members cross-trained in a variety of roles. Their versatility enabled them to perform their duties independent of outside support. All were airborne qualified and proficient in survival skills. Everyone knew everyone else and their capabilities on this cohesive team.[53]

Operation Just Cause planners never intended to use Gorgas Army Hospital, a U.S. Army Medical Department Activity in Panama, for supplementary Health Service Support.[54] It was close to the fighting and key buildings of Noriega's Panamanian Defense Forces, making access very hazardous.[55] Furthermore, some of the hospital staff that were local nationals had allegiance to Noriega or his Panamanian Defense Forces, and these divided loyalties had the potential to jeopardize the mission.[56] These factors plus the limited capacity of the FST led to the decision to use a zero-day evacuation policy, that is, casualties would be evacuated out of the combat zone in less than 24 hours.[57]

All the Army Nurse Corps officers who were members of the two FSTs that deployed to OJC were male.[58] McCall did this on purpose, considering the female nurse fiasco of Operation Urgent Fury. Her goal was to first establish the teams' credibility before getting into other issues because she did not want the mission sidetracked or scrubbed because of gender concerns. After the initial operation, she planned to integrate female nurses in an incremental fashion. McCall, however, accompanied the teams as chief nurse, and her presence was the first step in putting women on the FSTs.[59] However, in the end, no female Army Nurse Corps officers were assigned to FSTs during Operation Just Cause. Conversely in Operation Desert Storm, both male and female Army nurses were part of the FSTs.[60]

The 5th FST, a forward echelon of the 5th Mobile Army Surgical Hospital, received its initial warning orders at 2100 hours on 17 December 1989. FST members boarded a C-141B at Pope Air Force Base at 2345 hours on 18 December 1989 and arrived in Panama at 0430 hours the following morning.[61] Both FSTs set up on a parking tarmac at Howard Air Force Base, Panama, the site of the Joint Casualty Collection Point (JCCP) and the Air Force Mobile Aeromedical Staging Facility.[62] The 5th FST was operational several hours before H-hour (the time of onset of hostilities).[63] Its professional complement included a general and an orthopedic surgeon, an operating room nurse, a nurse anesthetist, and an operations officer who was a Medical Service Corps officer.[64]

The initial alert for the 1st FST of the 274th Medical Detachment (KA) came on 18 December 1989. Rain, sleet, and snow delayed their departure from Pope Air Force Base until the evening hours of 19 December. They arrived in the country at H-hour by air-land delivery and set up their facility adjacent to the 5th FST.[65] In addition to its other staff, this unit had two nurse anesthetists and an intensive care unit nurse.[66]

Augmenting the staff of the two FSTs were a team of six Army nurse anesthetists who functioned with the Joint Special Operations Task Force. They did not administer anesthesia but provided ATLS and airway management before casualties were admitted to the FSTs for treatment and surgery.[67]

A complex of several Health Service Support facilities occupied the tarmac on Howard Air Force Base, the JCCP. The two FSTs, an ATLS tent, a pair of holding tents, and an aeromedical evacuation tent were the most important.[68] The operation ran smoothly, and staff from the Army, Navy, and Air Force collaborated in a model of joint (purple) teamwork.[69] A Navy team provided triage services, while Army personnel from the 44th Medical Brigade and Air Force representatives from the 1st Aeromedical Evacuation Squadron and the Howard AFB Clinic carried out their responsibilities.[70] One particular FST provided a communication specialist, while the other included a biomedical repair specialist, both of whom were cross-trained in other medical specialties and worked wherever the need was greatest, no matter the unit or military service.[71] The Army surgeon general later remarked that, "cooperation was outstanding among task force medical units."[72]

One General Purpose large tent housed each FST. Triage of incoming casualties took place outside the tents. Inside near the entrance, two litters rested on stands, surrounded by ATLS equipment. Further inside, there was an operating table, and if necessary, staff swiveled one of the ATLS litters, converting it into an operating table. Thus, one nurse anesthetist could care simultaneously for two patients undergoing emergency surgery. A cold (chemical) sterilization point existed just beyond the operating table. The rear of the tent had eight intensive care beds with patient care and monitoring equipment.

Strict blackout conditions were in effect and the only lighting available for the triage teams shone from the pen lights imbedded in the miners' helmets worn by the staff. There was light inside the tents but the sides were rolled down to enforce the blackout. The tents were hot and sultry, a distinct contrast to the frigid winter conditions the team had left just a few hours before. Outside the tents were portable toilets and a "water buffalo."[73] In the middle of the tents was an open area where the triage team placed expectant category patients, those judged not likely to survive their wounds.

McCall encountered a young Navy SEAL corpsman on a litter, alone in the expectant area. Despite a bullet wound in one leg, he had continued to care for his team but later suffered a gunshot wound to the head, which he promptly bandaged himself. Then he was evacuated to the JCCP. The severity of his head wound—large enough to insert a hand, with exposed brain tissue—and his untimely arrival with a large number of casualties led the triage team to assign him to the expectant category. McCall sat down and talked to him:

> The patient was alert and awake. . . . He had an IV going. . . . I said to him, "So what's your name?" He said, "My name is Macho Camacho." I said, "Well Macho, where are you from?". . . He said, "I'm from Dallas." I said, "Oh, do you know where you are?" He said, "Yes, I'm in hell." I said, "No you are not in hell. You are at an air base." He said, "No, I'm in hell. My head is on fire and you have to put some water on my head."[74]

The one attendant in the expectant area, a Navy corpsman, asked McCall if he should administer morphine. Macho interrupted, "You can't give me morphine. I have a head injury." Taken aback at his awareness, McCall said to herself, "This kid is much too alert to be placed in the expectant category." A medical officer was summoned and concurred with her assessment and promptly put Macho on the second evacuation mission out of Panama to San Antonio, Texas. McCall thought the young SEAL probably had died en route but later discovered that he was a patient at Audie Murphy Memorial VA Hospital in San Antonio. She contacted him and learned that he was awaiting surgery to insert a plate under his scalp. Meanwhile, he wore a bicycle helmet as protection for his head. He suffered some residual neurological deficits (partial vision loss and paralysis), but during rehabilitation, he volunteered at an elementary school and read stories to students, thereby contributing to his own healing and providing a meaningful service to his adopted community. Later he and his wife led support groups for families of service members deployed overseas during Operation Desert Storm and Operation Desert Shield. Macho's wife subsequently went to medical school. McCall believed that his life was saved for a greater purpose.[75]

Preliminary statistics from the two FSTs showed that they cared for 341 casualties and performed 73 operative procedures. One patient died in the FST following a traumatic arm amputation and the severe mangling of his other arm. With hindsight, the staff concluded that he had lost too much blood before reaching the JCCP. His condition underlined the need to have written standard operating procedures to dig soakage pits for body fluids and drainage and similar protocols to deal with severed body parts. McCall carefully checked to ensure that the detached arm had no wedding ring. As she stood in the middle of the tent holding his arm in her hands, she realized that no one had arranged to dispose of amputated body parts. As an expedient, she later used the laboratory at Gorgas to dispose of the torn limb.[76]

On 29 December 1989, the 1st FST left Panama and returned to Fort Bragg.[77] The 5th FST departed two days later on New Year's Eve.[78] Throughout the operation, there were conflicting numbers of reported evacuations and casualties. The Air Force reported to have evacuated 261 patients between 20 December 1989 and 26 January 1990.[79] Another source calculated the numbers of evacuees at 284.[80] Some of the inaccurate numbers and accountability problems were attributed to operational security requirements that proscribed divulging identification or personal information, which in turn caused problems in regulating casualties.[81] The Air Force evacuated most casualties to two military hospitals in San Antonio, Texas—Wilford Hall Air Force Medical Center and Brooke Army Medical Center (BAMC).

Early in the morning on 20 December 1989, nursing staff at BAMC received the alert notice that every Army nurse expects to get sooner or later. The telephone caller told them that battlefield casualties would soon be arriving. Lieutenant Colonel David Tranel, the chief of BAMC's Critical Care Nursing Section and a Vietnam veteran, heard the news at 0245 hours that morning. After donning his Battle Dress Uniform and arriving at his duty station at Beach Pavilion, he informally took over and tried to organize the personnel and supplies available there. Headquarters first notified Tranel that patients would be arriving almost instantaneously. Then they said there would be an eight-hour delay, reverting to a four-hour holdup, then a 12-hour arrival time. Amid the uncertainty, Tranel set up four teams, each with a field grade nurse and three to four enlisted staff, to deal with the expected influx of patients. These teams would admit the patients, obtain physicians' orders, and settle the patients into the nursing unit. Another team then would assume responsibility for the patients' requirements. Tranel subsequently confirmed the availability of physician, x-ray, and laboratory support. Time passed, everyone was ready, but still no patients appeared. Not until 22 hours later did the first admissions arrive. In the interim, Tranel recognized that 100 percent of his staff was on standby and there was no backup for anyone. He released part of the staff but placed them on call. Others slept in the ward area until patient arrivals were imminent. At first, the mood was positive, but with each additional delay, frustration mounted. When the patients ultimately did arrive, the staff provided excellent care. Some casualties suffered jump-related orthopedic injuries, but most were heat casualties, while some were victims of extreme fatigue. They did not need intensive care nursing, just a telephone to contact their families, some privacy, and a little quiet time to reflect on their experiences. The nursing staff, however, found themselves responsible for controlling an almost continuous stream of visiting VIPs, an unexpected duty. The huge crowds of visitors and their entourages, while well intentioned, interfered with patient care and represented a threat to security.[82]

Major Jennifer J. Wiggall was the clinical head nurse of the Emergency Medical Service at BAMC. She arrived at her post just after 0400 hours on 20 December 1989 and immediately activated the unit's Mass Casualty plan. She designated one nurse and a medic for every one or two emergency beds. Each dyad assembled the equipment and supplies they expected to use and discussed individual responsibilities. The chief of the Department of Emergency Medicine assigned a physician to each nurse/medic team. By 0900 hours, no casualties had arrived, so Wiggall released her night staff. The Emergency Medical Service nurses worked 12-hour shifts, and they had to be back on duty at 1900 hours that night, so it seemed a prudent measure. That same morning the first air-evacuation mission landed at Kelly Air Force Base and delivered all 63 patients to Wilford Hall while the Emergency Medical Service staff at BAMC were sitting and waiting. After the second plane landed, BAMC received notification at about 1800 hours that patients would arrive.[83]

The onset of casualties brought unexpected assistance when a group of general surgeons appeared in the unit. The surgeons were not familiar with the decisions previously made or the plans for assigning responsibilities. Confusion ensued. After the first push, the staff discussed what to change with the next surge of patients. Everyone resolved to calm down, show the surgeons what the process was, and reassure the patients with better explanations of their conditions. After this baptism by fire, routines were refined. Nonetheless, after every push, time was set aside to discuss and evaluate performance. With each additional wave of arriving patients, the staff's approach was honed and perfected. The team nurse greeted each incoming casualty, explained where they were, made clear that a triage and assessment would first take place, and ensured that the patient was stable. The nurse then queried the casualty about allergies and medications, verified that the IV line was patent, did a head-to-toe assessment, drew lab work, and coordinated other services and specialty referrals. For seven days, a steady stream of casualties arrived. The greatest volume of incoming casualties occurred during the first three days.[84]

The staff's experience in BAMC's level-one trauma center, their training in Combat Casualty Care Course with its emphasis on triage and the care of combat patients, and their ATLS and/or Advanced Cardiac Life Support certification were instrumental in the positive outcome. All were unstinting in their praise of the excellent care the casualties received in Panama and during air-evacuation. Most presented with dry dressings, patent IV lines, and were clean and tidy. In retrospect, the nursing staff was amazed at the extreme youthfulness of their patients. They also were surprised by the young troopers' stoicism. Finally, the staff was astonished by their own overwhelming sense of satisfaction and their feelings of real accomplishment and contribution to the mission.[85]

Because of their minimal care needs and good physical condition, most of the patients were discharged within two to three days. Administrative problems, however, complicated their disposition from the hospital. For example, the soldiers needed Class A uniforms for travel, and the Air Force kept changing the requirements for airlift.[86] Colonel Charles Bombard, the chief, Department of Nursing, felt the Air Force demanded too much trivial detail about the conditions of the patients, most of whom were able to return to duty, had no need for medical attention, and were fit to fly. Still, the Air Force refused to manifest these soldiers until BAMC forwarded information about their height, weight, hemoglobin, hematocrit, and electrolyte levels, and a host of other information. Bombard talked with an Air Force medical officer who was an orthopedic resident at BAMC. He too expressed frustration over the senseless minutiae and phoned Wilford Hall, discovering they were not required to furnish any of the information required of BAMC. Having worked for the Armed Services Medical Regulating Office at Scott Air Force Base, Illinois, this physician knew that the information required of Wilford Hall was all that the Armed Services Medical Regulating Office needed. He could not understand why BAMC was asked for such inconsequential data.[87]

Skewed San Antonio media coverage also hurt Army/Air Force relations.[88] Many Army personnel believed that local press and TV coverage that focused almost exclusively on the contributions of Wilford Hall neglected BAMC and its participation. The BAMC staff thought both services deserved credit. Some Army casualties that were admitted to BAMC did not understand why their friends were being cared for in an Air Force hospital. One entrepreneur began selling T-shirts reading "BAMC—We also served Operation JUST CAUSE." The general feeling was that BAMC had not received due recognition for its contributions.[89]

Overall, medical support for Operation Just Cause was successful. Still, the Army leadership evaluated performance to find what went well and what needed improvement.[90] Several broad categories such as medical supply, communications, evacuation, resuscitation, patient accountability, and the restrictions imposed on the size and composition of the medical task force needed improvement. The complexity of Operation Just Cause, an airborne/air assault operation, its nocturnal timing, its setting in urban, mountain, and jungle terrain, and the heavy security that hampered planning explained some of the shortcomings.[91]

Planners set to work to rectify the shortcomings, but many issues remained unresolved when Iraqi dictator Saddam Hussein's invasion of Kuwait in 1990 brought a swift and powerful reaction. With time, however, many of these deficiencies also achieved resolution.

During the 1980s, Army Nurse Corps officers participated in numerous noncombat overseas missions. Their expertise and knowledge proved of great assistance to allied countries. The Army Nurse Corps normally selected only one Army nurse or at most a small team for these missions, during which the nurse or team members served to further diplomatic policy objectives of the U.S. government.

Major Paul Farineau participated in a three-month assignment in Egypt as a member of Project Hope in 1982. He assisted the local medical establishment in devising a curriculum to teach emergency medical care.[92] A trio of Army Nurse Corps officers traveled overseas to the Sinai to operate several health clinics that same year. As members of a United Nations peacekeeping force, Captains Patrick M. Schretenthaler and Delois Daniels and Second Lieutenant Paul Escott helped to staff two health clinics and provided emergency care to members of the multinational force, to United Nations observers, and to civilian contract employees. They later cared for a group of Bedouins—desert nomads—who lived in the region.[93]

Also in 1982, the U.S. Army Material Development and Readiness Command sent Lieutenant Colonel Charles Bombard to Saudi Arabia to oversee the contracting of nursing services for a new 500-bed hospital. He provided assistance and expertise to members of the Saudi Arabian National Guard.[94] The Army Nurse Corps furnished additional consultation for the Saudi Arabian forces when Major Gary Naleski spent 11 months in Taif, Saudi Arabia, in 1984 helping the Saudi armed forces to develop doctrine, implement educational programs, and choose options for the proper allocation of resources.[95] Although many missions were humanitarian or focused on nation building, a few—such as Operation Brightstar—added another element. They also served as field exercises.

Seven Army Nurse Corps officers constituted the nursing complement of the 5th MASH that took part in Operation Brightstar, held from 12 to 28 August 1983. This multinational joint exercise took place at Cairo West Airbase, Egypt. The hospital deployed with prototype Deployable Medical System TEMPER equipment and cared for American forces afflicted with dysentery, asthma, renal calculi, and minor orthopedic problems. The most significant group of casualties was 24 soldiers who came down with shigella-induced dysentery and experienced chills, fever, and diarrhea in the second week of the operation. Their admission to the small 30-bed 5th MASH facility was regarded as a Mass Casualty situation.

Throughout this mission, women's issues proved taxing. Local customs forbade women from wearing shorts for physical training or even in their living areas. Women also had to keep communications with men on duty to a minimum and not speak with them at all in social settings. Egyptian troops involved in the operation regarded the women soldiers as prostitutes.[96] The cultural shock of female soldiers' participation in Operation Brightstar was unexpected. It was a prime example of diverse national and ethnic expectations and values, a not-uncommon occurrence encountered by women in the Army when deployed on foreign soil. American cultural norms about the position, decorum, and role of American women soldiers clashed with Middle East expectations concerning the status of women, proper attire, alcohol consumption, and other customs. These thorny issues and circumstances called for adjustments on both sides.[97]

Also in 1983, Lieutenant Colonel Dorothy Clark crafted contingency plans for hospitals that were designated for wartime activation at the United Kingdom Plans Division in Burtonwood, England. She provided consultation on issues such as adequate hospital staffing, proper equipment, and appropriate locations for combat hospitals.[98]

In 1985, Captain Karen Keller served with a Medical Mobile Training Team in the African nation of Liberia. She assessed learning needs, developed a Program of Instruction, and taught programs for medical corpsmen in the armed forces of Liberia. Keller's assignment lasted 168 days.[99] Also in 1985, seven Army nurses deployed with the 42nd Field Hospital from Fort Knox, Kentucky, to Morocco to support 300 U.S. Army soldiers training there. The 75-member element of the Medical Readiness Exercise set up tents to house an intensive care unit, an operating room, and various other facilities in the desert environment. They admitted five patients and performed two minor surgical procedures. The staff also evaluated some 300 Moroccan citizens and treated their maladies. The team worked under hardship conditions with outdated and substandard equipment and medications in hot, dusty tents. They encountered a dubious welcome from the Moroccans, who seemed to believe that their own local medical facilities were adequate for their particular needs. Major Linda Henson, the 42nd Field Hospital's chief nurse, agreed, suggesting that when a country believes its level of medical care is satisfactory, a Medical Readiness Exercise is unnecessary. Before deployments, she recommended authorities need to ascertain the host country's actual opinions about intervention by U.S. medical elements.[100]

In 1986, the Philippine government asked for an AMEDD team to evaluate its health care facilities. Lieutenant Colonel Ronald Oliver participated and made contributions with that team. That same year Lieutenant Colonel Franklin Metcalf served as a nurse advisor to the Saudi Arabian National Guard. Metcalf's primary focus was the King Fahad National Guard Hospital in Riyadh, where he helped to select nurse applicants for hire from other countries, made daily inspection trips through the facility, observed at committee meetings, and advised on nursing issues. One of his most taxing responsibilities was the hiring of foreign nurses to

Lieutenant Colonel Franklin Metcalf, center, with Ann Kartley, left, a nurse consultant from the United States, and Suleiman Al Zakr, right, await their turns to brief incoming foreign nurses about Saudi customs at the King Fahad National Guard Hospital in 1986.
Photo courtesy of Colonel Franklin Metcalf, Hopkinsville, KY.

work in the facility, a significant challenge, because few nurses were willing to live and work in such a politically unstable area. Metcalf helped to prioritize vendors whom the government would select to provide nurses, experiencing firsthand the frustrations and uncertainty of waiting for lengthy periods while the government slowly deliberated on the merits of the various contractors.

While in Saudi Arabia, Metcalf and his family enjoyed unique travel opportunities and on one occasion attended a camel race of epic proportions. More than a thousand camels took part in the 12-mile contest where the first prize was a water tanker. After the race, the Metcalf family and their hosts shared a capsa, a traditional meal, consisting of a quartered goat or sheep on a bed of rice. All the diners sat or knelt around the main dish and—using no plates or utensils—ate with their right hands.[101]

Ten Army nurses participated in a humanitarian mission with the Public Health Service, Air Force, and Navy aboard the USNS *Mercy* in February 1987. The vessel visited ports in the Philippines, Tonga, Fiji, and the Gilbert Islands, mostly performing corrective surgery on children with congenital deformities. Those who participated felt that their contributions to the mission were far exceeded by the personal rewards of experiencing cross-cultural nursing, a high level of

Lieutenant Colonel Franklin Metcalf, extreme left, shares a traditional Saudi meal (capsa) of rice and roasted goat with American soldiers (in camouflage uniforms) and Saudi soldiers (in solid-color uniforms). The two men not in uniform were contract workers.
Photo courtesy of Colonel Franklin Metcalf, Hopkinsville, KY.

interservice collaboration, professional advancement, and opportunities to hone their field expedience skills. One Army nurse, Lieutenant Ronald Kirkconnell, lost his life in a helicopter crash while in support of the mission.[102]

The Army dispatched several relief missions in 1989. At the U.S. Department of State's request, Major Jimmie Keenan and Captains Andrea Coenen and Dennis Driscoll joined a burn team from the Institute of Surgical Research to care for about 100 patients suffering from thermal injuries as a result of a train wreck and subsequent gas explosion in the Ural Mountains near Ufa, Russia.[103] Responding to another state department appeal in 1990, Captain Elizabeth Hill accompanied two physicians to Sweden to advise health care workers there about the use of high containment equipment to care for a patient suffering with Ebola/Marburg fever.[104]

When the Philippine volcano Mount Pinatubo erupted in 1991, another Army Nurse Corps officer, Major Daniel Jergens, deployed with the 25th Infantry Division. He cared for Philippine nationals affected by the volcanic eruption.[105] The following year, operating room nurses and anesthetists from 7th Medical Command in Europe deployed on a nation-building mission to upgrade the skills of local hospital staff in Tbilisi in the Georgian Republic and Bishkek in Kirghizstan.[106] Finally, in 1999, two Army Nurse Corps officers participated in Operation Provide Hope in Kharkiv, Ukraine. They provided training for hospital staffs in the use of equipment and supplies donated by the U.S. Department of State, U.S. Department of Defense, and private organizations. Captain Johnnie Koch oriented the local medical personnel to operating room equipment and supplies. Captain Pablito Gahol focused on intensive care unit equipment, teaching health care providers in the new independent state of the former Soviet Union about cardiac monitors, defibrillators, crash carts, and pulse oximeters.[107]

The optempo (operations tempo), the volume and increasing frequency of peacemaking and peacekeeping activities, with Army Nurse Corps participants grew with the passage of time. As part of military operations other than war, these efforts promoted peace, deterred war, resolved conflict, and supported civil authorities responding to national crises.[108] Army nurses also became involved in civic action and nation-building missions. Although such endeavors were not new for Army Nurse Corps officers, during the decade of the 1980s they became routine, normal missions. They were successfully conducted despite nursing shortages, readiness issues, quality concerns, and the establishment of new, innovative patient care roles. These missions did improve conditions in developing nations and strengthened relationships with allies. Through participation in these operations, nurses gained much experience that better prepared them for future responsibilities.

# Notes

1. Dwight D. Oland, *Department of the Army Historical Summary, Fiscal Year 1984* (Washington, DC: Center of Military History, United States Army, 1995), 237–45. Peter M. Dunn and Bruce W. Watson, eds., *American Intervention in Grenada: The Implications of Operation "Urgent Fury"* (Boulder, CO: Westview Press, 1985). Mark Adkin, *Urgent Fury, The Battle for Grenada* (Lexington, MA: Lexington Books, 1989). Thomas E. Broyles, "A Comparative Analysis of the Medical Support in the Combat Operations in the Falklands Campaign and the Grenada Expedition," Masters Thesis, 81–84, U.S. Army Command and General Staff College, 1987. Richard V.N. Ginn, *The History of the U.S. Army Medical Service Corps* (Washington, DC: Office of the Surgeon General and Center of Military History, United States Army, 1997), 423–25.

2. "Health Service Support Observations, Operation Just Cause," Typewritten Report (TR) 19–20, 28 June 1990, Army Nurse Corps Collection (ANCC), Office of Medical History (OMH).

3. A total of 35 Army Nurse Corps officers participated. Twelve came from Fort Bragg and the remaining 23 were pulled from other HSC installations within CONUS. "AMEDD ANC PROFIS Support for Military Operation in Grenada," Typewritten List, n.d., attached to Kim M. Cowden to ANC Historian, "ANC Award Recipients in Grenada," Typewritten Letter, 12 September 1984, ANCC, OMH.

4. "AMEDD ANC PROFIS Support for Military Operation in Grenada," Typewritten List, n.d., attached to Kim M. Cowden to ANC Historian, "ANC Award Recipients in Grenada," Typewritten Letter, 12 September 1984, ANCC, OMH. Carolyn M. Feller and Debora R. Cox, *Highlights in the History of the Army Nurse Corps* (Washington, DC: U.S. Army Center of Military History, 2000), 57.

5. Donn R. Richards, "Medical Trends: An Evaluation of Medical Care Given in Vietnam, Grenada, Panama, and Desert Storm," Study Research Project, 6 April 1999, U.S. Army War College, Carlisle Barracks, PA.

6. Roxine C. Hart, *Women in Combat* (Patrick Air Force Base, FL: Research Division, Defense Equal Opportunity Management Institute, 1991), 14.

7. Daniel P. Bolger, "Operation Urgent Fury and Its Critics," *Military Review* 66 (July 1986): 57–69.

8. Donn R. Richards, "Medical Trends: An Evaluation of Medical Care Given in Vietnam, Grenada, Panama, and Desert Storm," Study Research Project, 17–18, 6 April 1999,

U.S. Army War College, Carlisle Barracks, PA. Thomas E. Broyles, "A Comparative Analysis of the Medical Support in the Combat Operations in the Falklands Campaign and the Grenada Expedition," Masters Thesis, 92, U.S. Army Command and General Staff College, 1987. Dale C. Smith, "Military Medicine," in *Encyclopedia of the American Military*, ed. John E. Jessup and Louise B. Ketz (New York: Charles Scribner's Sons, 1994), 1625.

9. Nancy Tomich, "Beirut, Grenada: Scenarios Unfolding," *U.S. Medicine* 19 (1 December 1983): 1, 8.

10. Donn R. Richards, "Medical Trends: An Evaluation of Medical Care Given in Vietnam, Grenada, Panama, and Desert Storm," Study Research Project, 17–21, 6 April 1999, U.S. Army War College, Carlisle Barracks, PA. Thomas E. Broyles, "A Comparative Analysis of the Medical Support in the Combat Operations in the Falklands Campaign and the Grenada Expedition," Masters Thesis, 96–108, U.S. Army Command and General Staff College, 1987. James M. Dubik and Terrence D. Fullerton, "Soldier Overloading in Grenada," *Military Review* 67 (January 1987): 38–47. Mark Adkin, *Urgent Fury, The Battle for Grenada* (Lexington, MA: Lexington Books, 1989), 222, 290.

11. Donn R. Richards, "Medical Trends: An Evaluation of Medical Care Given in Vietnam, Grenada, Panama, and Desert Storm," Study Research Project, 20, 6 April 1999, U.S. Army War College, Carlisle Barracks, PA.

12. Patricia A. Diskin, "After Action Report 'Urgent Fury'," Typewritten Document (TD), 3, n.d., ANCC, OMH. Diskin revealed that Trobaugh "wanted a medical unit minus its females. The commanding officer of the HQs above the 44th Med Brigade was adamant that the unit go as is," or with its female contingent intact. Patricia A. Diskin to Author, E-mail Correspondence, 6 March 2004, ANCC, OMH. Diskin noted that the female commander of an MP detachment was forbidden to accompany her troops. Patricia A. Diskin to Author, E-mail Correspondence, 6 March 2004, ANCC, OMH. Despite the prohibition, four female Military Police actually deployed to Grenada on 29 October 1983. One day later, the ground commander (Trobaugh) ordered them returned to the States. They deployed a second time when commanders determined their units could not meet their mission without the women. Female Air Force officers piloted C-141 Starlifter transport planes with full troop loads into Grenada as well. Ann Wright, "The Roles of US Army Women in Grenada," *Minerva, Quarterly Report on Women and the Military* 2 (Summer 1984): 103–13. William Proxmire, "Three Myths about Women and Combat," *Minerva, Quarterly Report on Women and the Military* 4 (Winter 1986): 105–12. Lorry M. Fenner, "Either You Need These Women or You Do Not: Informing the Debate on Military Service and Citizenship," in *Women in the Military*, ed. Rita James Simon (New Brunswick, NJ: Transaction Publishers, 2001), 5–32. Lorry M. Fenner, "Either You Need These Women or You Do Not: Informing the Debate on Military Service and Citizenship," *Gender Issues* 16 (Summer 1998): 5–34.

13. William Joe Webb and others, *Department of the Army Historical Summary, Fiscal Years 1990 and 1991* (Washington, DC: Center of Military History, United States Army, 1997), 41–42.

14. POR can also refer to "Processing for Overseas Readiness." Susan C. McCall, Interview by Constance J. Moore, Transcript, 7, 23 January 1997, Army Nurse Corps Oral History Collection, OMH.

15. Differing viewpoints about the necessity and wisdom of issuing weapons to Army nurses have been articulated. While on the aircraft bound for Grenada, an engineer queried Davis about why some nurses had no weapons. He asked if she was not "nervous about going to war without a weapon." Davis later confided that she "did not have the nerve to inform him those carrying weapons did not have any ammunition assigned." Shirley A.

Davis, "Comments on Grenada Experience, Urgent Fury," TD, 1, 3–5, 18 October 1988, ANCC, OMH. During Operation Just Cause, Lieutenant Colonel Susan McCall did carry a 9-mm sidearm with 200 rounds of ammunition. She decided later that it was not such a good idea; in fact, it created a hazardous situation for "all of these medical folks with limited amount of training running around with [loaded] weapons. . . . That's just another thing that you have to keep up with. You constantly have to be aware of where that weapon is and I think it distracts from your ability to move about and take care of patients. . . . It was cumbersome and for the value added I think it was not necessary." Susan C. McCall, Interview by Constance J. Moore, Transcript, 8–9, 23 January 1997, Army Nurse Corps Oral History Collection, OMH.

16. Shirley A. Davis, "Comments on Grenada Experience, Urgent Fury," TD 1–3, 18 October 1988, ANCC, OMH.

17. Grace C. Johnson, "Reflections on Grenadian Experience, Urgent Fury" TD, 21, 18 October 1988; Shirley A. Davis, "Comments on Grenada Experience, Urgent Fury," TD, 5, n.d.; Susan M. Keller, Untitled TD, 1, 23 February 1984; and Teresa Milie, Untitled TD, 1, n.d. (all in ANCC, OMH).

18. Teresa Milie, Untitled TD, 1, n.d., ANCC, OMH.

19. Shirley A. Davis, "Comments on Grenada Experience, Urgent Fury," TD, 6, 18 October 1988, ANCC, OMH.

20. Donn R. Richards, "Medical Trends: An Evaluation of Medical Care Given in Vietnam, Grenada, Panama, and Desert Storm," Study Research Project, 18–19, 6 April 1999, U.S. Army War College, Carlisle Barracks, PA. On 27 October, a Ranger assault on Camp Calivigny ended in disaster. Three Black Hawk helicopters crashed, killing three and critically injuring four Rangers. Sergeant Stephen Trujillo, a medic, rushed into the melee, removed the injured, and saved lives. President Reagan subsequently awarded him the Silver Star before a joint session of Congress. Mark Adkin, *Urgent Fury, The Battle for Grenada* (Lexington, MA: Lexington Books, 1989), 278–85.

21. Joel Messing, "After Action Report Grenada Deployment," 2–3, n.d., ANCC, OMH.

22. Patricia Diskin, "Notes on Grenada," TD, 4, n.d., ANCC, OMH.

23. Shirley A. Davis, "Comments on Grenada Experience, Urgent Fury," TD, 10, 18 October 1988, ANCC, OMH.

24. Patricia Diskin, "Notes on Grenada," TD, 4, n.d., ANCC, OMH.

25. The M561 Gama Goat was a multipurpose "six wheel drive amphibious 1 1/4 ton Cargo truck." The derivation of its name came from Roger Gamaunt, who designed its articulated section, and from the fact that it could go anywhere, like a goat. "The rear portion of the vehicle was attached with a coupling mechanism; the front and rear mechanisms allowed the carrier part of the truck to roll and pitch. The high level of gravity did result in roll-overs." The HMMWV (Humvee) later replaced the Gama Goat. Vicki R. Odegaard to Author, E-mail Correspondence, 10 June 2003, ANCC, OMH.

26. Cecil Stack, "Movable Medicine," *Soldiers* 41 (June 1986): 24–25.

27. Shirley A. Davis, "Comments on Grenada Experience, Urgent Fury," TD, 7–8, n.d.; and Jack L. McNeil, "Grenada Diary," TD, 3, n.d. (both in ANCC, OMH).

28. Ann Wright, "The Roles of US Army Women in Grenada," *Minerva, Quarterly Report on Women and the Military* 2 (Summer 1984): 103–13. William Proxmire, "Three Myths about Women and Combat," *Minerva, Quarterly Report on Women and the Military* 4 (Winter 1986): 105–12. Lorry M. Fenner, "Either You Need These Women or You Do Not: Informing the Debate on Military Service and Citizenship," in *Women in the Military*, ed. Rita James Simon (New Brunswick, NJ: Transaction Publishers, 2001), 5–32. Lorry M. Fenner, "Either You Need These Women or You Do Not: Informing the Debate on Military

Service and Citizenship," *Gender Issues* 16 (Summer 1998): 5–34.

29. Rosamond R. Shepard, "After Action Report, OB/GYN Nurse, Project Urgent Fury," TD, 1, 23 February 1984, ANCC, OMH.

30. Rosamond R. Shepard, "After Action Report, OB/GYN Nurse, Project Urgent Fury, Oct–Nov 83," TD, 2, 23 February 1984, ANCC, OMH.

31. Jack L. McNeil, "Grenada Diary," TD, 4, n.d., ANCC, OMH.

32. Patricia A. Diskin, "After Action Report, 'Urgent Fury'," TD, 3, n.d., ANCC, OMH.

33. Jack L. McNeil, "Grenada Diary," TD, 4, n.d.; and Joel Messing, "After Action Report Grenada Deployment," TD, 3, n.d. (both in ANCC, OMH).

34. Among the six was Lieutenant Colonel Patricia Diskin, who received the Joint Services Commendation Medal. The remaining five were awarded the Army Commendation Medal. They included majors Jack McNeil, Flint Gullet, and Rosamond Shepard; Captain Joel Messing; and First Lieutenant Teresa Milie. Kim M. Cowden to ANC Historian, Typewritten Letter, 12 September 1984, ANCC, OMH.

35. Shirley A. Davis, "Comments on Grenada Experience, Urgent Fury," TD, 10, 18 October 1988, ANCC, OMH.

36. Grace C. Johnson, "Reflections on Grenadian Experience, Urgent Fury" TD, 4, 18 October 1988, ANCC, OMH.

37. Teresa Milie, Untitled TD, 3, n.d., ANCC, OMH.

38. Ibid., 3. One study noted that 20 percent of a sample of 684 Urgent Fury veterans "reported abdominal pain and/or diarrhea during or after the action." The investigators attributed a significant number of these cases to hookworm infection. Patrick W. Kelley and others, "An Outbreak of Hookworm Infection Associated with Military Operations in Grenada," *Military Medicine* 154 (February 1989): 55–59.

39. Shirley A. Davis, "Comments on Grenada Experience, Urgent Fury," TD, 11–12, 18 October 1988, ANCC, OMH.

40. William Joe Webb and others, *Department of the Army Historical Summary, Fiscal Years 1990 and 1991* (Washington, DC: Center of Military History, United States Army, 1997), 41–42. "Operation Just Cause, The Untold Tale," *Army Times* 52 (30 December 1991): 12–14, 16, 18–19, 46. Clarence E. Briggs, *Operation Just Cause: Panama, December 1989: A Soldier's Eyewitness Account* (Harrisburg, PA: Stackpole Books, 1990). Thomas Donnelly, Margaret Roth, and Caleb Baker, *Operation Just Cause: The Storming of Panama* (New York: Maxwell Macmillan, 1991). Malcolm McConnell, *Just Cause: The Real Story of America's High-Tech Invasion of Panama* (New York: St. Martin's Press, 1991).

41. "Operation Just Cause, The Untold Tale," *Army Times* 52 (30 December 1991): 13–14.

42. George E. Hammond, "Operation Just Cause Lessons Learned Report," 2, 1 June 1990, ANCC, OMH.

43. Office of the Secretary of the Army, "Operation Just Cause Fact Sheet," 1, n.d., ANCC, OMH. Kevin Buckley, *Panama, The Whole Story* (New York: Simon & Schuster, 1991). Carl E. Vuono, "Initial Observations of Operation Just Cause," TD, n.d., ANCC, OMH.

44. Susan C. McCall, Interview by Constance J. Moore, Transcript, 3, 23 January 1997, ANCC, OMH. Charlotte Hough, Michael Sadler, and Patricia Patrician, "Military Nursing at the ForeFront: The Army Forward Surgical Team," *Critical Care Nursing Clinics of North America* 15 (June 2003): 193–200. Susan C. McCall, "Lessons Learned by Army Nurses in Combat, A Historical Review," USAWC Military Studies Program Paper, 27, n.d., ANCC, OMH.

45. The FST concept can be traced back to the 18th century. Its American origins resided

in World War I, with the surgical teams positioned at forward field hospitals. During World War II, it was exemplified in the Auxiliary Surgical Teams at Division Clearing Stations and in the Southwest Pacific Theater, where the PASH (Portable Army Surgical Hospital) was employed in the jungle. During the Korean War, the Mobile Army Surgical Hospital (MASH) served as an expression of the concept. Robert J.T. Joy to Author, Typewritten Letter, 24 November 2003, ANCC, OMH. Dale C. Smith, "Military Medicine," in *Encyclopedia of the American Military*, ed. John E. Jessup and Louise B. Ketz (New York: Charles Scribner's Sons, 1994), 1615, 1621.

46. Susan C. McCall, "Lessons Learned by Army Nurses in Combat, A Historical Review," USAWC Military Studies Program Paper, 27–28, n.d., ANCC, OMH. At the behest of Colonel Bruce T. Miketinac, commander of the 44th Medical Brigade, Lieutenant Colonel Susan McCall headed up the team that designed the FST. Others involved on the ad hoc planning group were Captain Stephen Janney, a nurse anesthetist, and a surgeon, Major David Rivera. The team looked at the Korean War–era MASHs, the British version utilized in the Falklands War, and the French Surgical Parachute Teams. "They bounced the[ir] ideas off of" McCall and Colonel Kim, the brigade S3, operations and training officer. Susan C. McCall, Interview by Constance J. Moore, Transcript, 35–36, 23 January 1997; Lee Porisch to Author, E-mail Correspondence, 7 July 2003; and "Army Nurse Corps (ANC) 1986 Annual Historical Report," 19 (all in ANCC, OMH).

47. Susan C. McCall, "Lessons Learned by Army Nurses in Combat, A Historical Review," USAWC Military Studies Program Paper, 27–29, n.d., ANCC, OMH.

48. "5th MASH, Operation 'Just Cause' AAR," TD, 1, n.d., ANCC, OMH.

49. Lee A. Porisch, "Basic Logistical Considerations for Rapid Medical Deployment," *Military Medicine* 156 (May 1991): 215–18.

50. The oxygen concentrators allowed the FST to eliminate "compressed medical gases as the power and oxygen source." This was the "major logistical burden that impeded previous medical units from being as mobile and logistically independent as the forces they support[ed]." Lee A. Porisch, "Basic Logistical Considerations for Rapid Medical Deployment," *Military Medicine* 156 (May 1991): 215–18.

51. Susan C. McCall, Interview by Constance J. Moore, Transcript, 13–14, 23 January 1997, ANCC, OMH.

52. Lee A. Porisch, "Basic Logistical Considerations for Rapid Medical Deployment," *Military Medicine* 156 (May 1991): 215–18.

53. Susan C. McCall, "Lessons Learned by Army Nurses in Combat, A Historical Review," USAWC Military Studies Program Paper, 28–29, n.d., ANCC, OMH. Frank F. Ledford, "Army Medicine Balancing Needs with Resources," *Army* 40 (October 1990): 180–83, 185.

54. OPSEC dictated that staff at Gorgas be kept uninformed about the mission. When the battle commenced, the Gorgas staff could not comprehend why they were not being allowed to treat American casualties. "The vast majority of people [they] treated were Panamanian Defense Forces and Dignity Battalion members." Ralph A. Franco, "Officer Tells Story of 'Just Cause'," *HSC Mercury* 17 (March 1990): 6.

55. Lee A. Porisch, "Basic Logistical Considerations for Rapid Medical Deployment," *Military Medicine* 156 (May 1991): 215–18.

56. Susan C. McCall, Interview by Constance J. Moore, 16–17, 23 January 1997; and "Health Service Support Observations, Operation Just Cause," TR, 8, 28 June 1990 (both in ANCC, OMH).

57. Donn R. Richards, "Medical Trends: An Evaluation of Medical Care Given in Vietnam, Grenada, Panama, and Desert Storm," Study Research Project, 23, 6 April 1999, U.S.

Army War College, Carlisle Barracks, PA.

58. The two teams were the FST, 5th MASH, and the FST, 274th Medical Detachment. George E. Hammond, "Operation Just Cause Lessons Learned Report," 1, 1 June 1990, ANCC, OMH. Susan C. McCall, "Lessons Learned by Army Nurses in Combat, A Historical Review," USAWC Military Studies Program Paper, 27–29, n.d., ANCC, OMH.

59. Susan C. McCall, Interview by Constance J. Moore, Transcript, 12–13, 23 January 1997, ANCC, OMH.

60. Barbara J. Smith, Interview by Constance J. Moore, Transcript, 35, 2 March 1995, Army Nurse Corps Oral History Collection, OMH.

61. "5th MASH, Operation 'Just Cause' AAR," TD, 2, 3, n.d., ANCC, OMH.

62. JCCP was also referred to as the Joint Casualty Control Point. Courtney Scott, "The Impact of Strategic Aeromedical Evacuation in Operation Just Cause," TD, 4–7, June 1991, ANCC, OMH. "Health Service Support Observations, Operation Just Cause," TR, 3, 28 June 1990; and Susan C. McCall, Interview by Constance J. Moore, Transcript, 3–4, 23 January 1997 (both in ANCC, OMH).

63. "5th MASH, Operation 'Just Cause' AAR," TD, n.d., ANCC, OMH. Lee A. Porisch, "Basic Logistical Considerations for Rapid Medical Deployment," *Military Medicine* 156 (May 1991): 215–18.

64. Captain (P) William F. Wadford was the OR nurse and Captain William Watson was the nurse anesthetist. "5th MASH, Operation 'Just Cause' AAR," TD, 6, n.d., ANCC, OMH. "Panama Action Proves Surgical Teams' Value," *HSC Mercury* 17 (March 1990): 7.

65. Lee A. Porisch, "Basic Logistical Considerations for Rapid Medical Deployment," *Military Medicine* 156 (May 1991): 215–18. Susan C. McCall, Interview by Constance J. Moore, Transcript, 6, 23 January 1997, ANCC, OMH.

66. The two 1st FST nurse anesthetists were Major Lee Porisch and Captain Robert Yates. The ICU nurse was Captain Steve Hendrix. Lee Porisch to Author, 13 June 2003; and Lee Porisch to Author, 7 July 2003 (both E-mail Correspondence, ANCC, OMH).

67. These Army Nurse Corps officers were LTC Stan Strzelecki, Major (P) Larry McDade, Major Ronald Ostmann, Major Robert Conneen, CPT Marty Godwin, and CPT Steve Allen. "Military History of the Army Nurse Corps," Typewritten Memorandum, 5 June 1990; and Lee Porisch to Author, E-mail Correspondence, 29 June 2004 (both in ANCC, OMH).

68. "5th MASH, Operation 'Just Cause' AAR," TD, 3, n.d., ANCC, OMH. Courtney Scott, "The Impact of Strategic Aeromedical Evacuation in Operation Just Cause," TD, 4–7, June 1991, ANCC, OMH.

69. The purple suit concept referred to a recurring proposal to combine all DoD medical personnel "into a single consolidated agency," thus eliminating the Army, Navy, and Air Force medical departments as separate entities. Some conjectured that the staff of this agency would wear a purple suit, or a uniform whose colors were a combination of the Army green and the Navy and Air Force blues. Most AMEDD personnel opposed the purple suit concept. Richard V.N. Ginn, "Of Purple Suits and Other Things: An Army Officer Looks at Unification of the Department of Defense Medical Services," *Military Medicine* 143 (January 1973): 15–24. Richard V.N. Ginn, "Organization of the Military Health Care System," *Military Medicine* 151 (June 1986): 299–307. Charles C. Pixley, Interview by John N. Bogart, Transcript, 61, 1985, Oral History Collection, OMH.

70. Courtney Scott, "The Impact of Strategic Aeromedical Evacuation in Operation Just Cause," TD, 4, June 1991; and Susan C. McCall, Interview by Constance J. Moore, Transcript, 11, 18, 23 January 1997 (both in ANCC, OMH). Frank F. Ledford, "War, Peace Roles: Army Measures Up," *U.S. Medicine* 27 (January 1991): 27–28. Monte Miller, "Air

Force Handles the 'Unexpected'," *U.S. Medicine* 27 (January 1991): 35–37. Soraya S. Nelson, "Just Cause Nurses Urge More Training," *Air Force Times* (3 December 1990): 8.

71. "5th MASH, Operation 'Just Cause' AAR," TD, 3, n.d., ANCC, OMH.

72. Frank F. Ledford," Army Medicine Balancing Needs With Resources," *Army* 40 (October 1990): 180–83, 185.

73. The water buffalo was a tank welded on a wheeled trailer whose usual function was to hold and dispense potable water. However, it could contain any kind of liquid. Also referred to as the M149A2 trailer mounted water tank, it had a 400-gallon capacity and was constructed of either stainless steel or fiberglass. It could be towed to keep pace with a moving Army.

74. Susan C. McCall, Interview by Constance J. Moore, Transcript, 18–26, 23 January 1997, ANCC, OMH.

75. Ibid.

76. Ibid., 28–29.

77. Lee A. Porisch, "Basic Logistical Considerations for Rapid Medical Deployment," *Military Medicine* 156 (May 1991): 215–18

78. "5th MASH, Operation 'Just Cause' AAR," TD, 5, n.d., ANCC, OMH.

79. "24th Medical Group Operation Just Cause, After-Action Report," 4 April 1990, Annex B, in George E. Hammond, "Operation Just Cause Lessons Learned Report," 1 June 1990, ANCC, OMH.

80. "U.S. Military Casualties Evacuated to Kelly AFB," TD, n.d., Inclosure 1, in Robert F. Elliott, "After-Action Report, Operation Just Cause," Typewritten Memorandum, 15 January 1990, ANCC, OMH.

81. Robert F. Elliott, "After-Action Report, Operation Just Cause," Typewritten Memorandum, 2, 15 January 1990, ANCC, OMH.

82. David A. Tranel, Interview by Barbara G. Covington, Transcript, 3–4, 8–21, 20 July 1990, ANCC, OMH.

83. Jennifer J. Wiggall, Interview by Barbara G. Covington, Transcript, 2–7, 14–16, n.d., ANCC, OMH.

84. Ibid., 17–18, 25–26, 33.

85. Ibid., 37, 43, 45–46.

86. David A. Tranel, Interview by Barbara G. Covington, Transcript, 20–21, 20 July 1990, ANCC, OMH.

87. Charles F. Bombard, "First Impressions—Operation Just Cause," Typewritten Memorandum, 5, 18 January 1990, ANCC, OMH.

88. Throughout the 1980s, an intense, fiery debate raged about the need to build a new facility for BAMC and the precise number of beds required. Igniting further discord, the GAO vetoed the new BAMC construction at one point, positing that the Air Force's Wilford Hall Hospital could handle all the San Antonio military patient population. Later, William Mayer, President Reagan's ASD(HA), ordered the two services to combine staffs and establish a Joint Military Medical Command (JMMC) in San Antonio with the Air Force assuming the leadership roles. This joint endeavor ultimately failed. Acrimony and rancor festered among the Air Force, Army, and civilian sectors of the community as a result of the decade-long turmoil. Bob Richter, "BAMC, Wilford Hall Merger Plans Ordered," *San Antonio Express-News* (19 July 1986), 1-A, 16-A. "Events Chronicled in Five Years of BAMC Debate," *San Antonio Express-News* (22 July 1986), 1-A. Jim Michaels, "Today's the Day: Future of BAMC is on the Line," *San Antonio Light* (26 September 1986), A1, A14. Jim Michaels, "Mayer Says Smaller BAMC Won't Affect Jobs or Care," *San Antonio Light* (27 September 1986), A1, A16. Don Driver, "Air Force Expected to Direct New Mili-

tary Medical Center," *San Antonio Express-News* (26 November 1986), 8-D. Major Maher, "Impact of JMMC on AMEDD Training," Information Paper, 6 February 1987; and Milton E. Turner, "Scope of Practice Differences between Army and Air Force Nonphysician Medical Specialties in the San Antonio Joint Military Medical Command (JMMC)," Disposition Form, 26 August 1987 (both in ANCC, OMH). Bruce Davidson, "Delay Sought in BAMC Graduate Program Merger," *San Antonio Express-News* (7 October 1987), 5A. "BAMC Downsizing Needs Another Look," *San Antonio Express-News* (7 October 1987), 5A. Bruce Davidson, "Amendment Fails to Halt Further BAMC Transfers," *San Antonio Express-News* (30 October 1987), 1C. M. Grace Johancen, "Downsized BAMC Cannot Handle Training," Letter to Editor, *San Antonio Light* (31 October 1987), B5. Paul N. Biediger, "Joint Medical Command Should be Disbanded," Letter to Editor, *San Antonio Light* (5 April 1988). Charles J. Reddy, Interview by Mary T. Sarnecky, Transcript, 55–58, 9 January 2002, Army Nurse Corps Oral History Collection, OMH.

89. Jennifer J. Wiggall, Interview by Barbara G. Covington, Transcript, 57–58, n.d., ANCC, OMH. One source documented that of the total of 284 OJC casualties evacuated to Kelly AFB, 172 were admitted to Wilford Hall and 112 were admitted to BAMC. "U.S. Military Casualties Evacuated to Kelly AFB," TD, n.d., Inclosure 1, in Robert F. Elliott, "After-Action Report, Operation Just Cause," Typewritten Memorandum, 15 January 1990, ANCC, OMH.

90. George E. Hammond, "Operation Just Cause Lessons Learned Report," 1–30, 1 June 1990, ANCC, OMH.

91. "Health Service Support Observations, Operation Just Cause," TR, 1, 28 June 1990, ANCC, OMH.

92. Carolyn M. Feller and Debora R. Cox, *Highlights in the History of the Army Nurse Corps* (Washington, DC: U.S. Army Center of Military History, 2000), 53.

93. Ibid., 54.

94. Ibid., 54.

95. Ibid., 57.

96. Paula J. Lowney, "After-Action Report on Operation Brightstar '83," TR, n.d. Inclosure 1, Joan Snell to Chief, Army Nurse Corps, Typewritten Letter, 26 October 1983, ANCC, OMH.

97. Ibid.

98. Carolyn M. Feller and Debora R. Cox, *Highlights in the History of the Army Nurse Corps* (Washington, DC: U.S. Army Center of Military History, 2000), 55.

99. Ibid., 59. "ANC Annual Historical Report FY85," 2, ANCC, OMH.

100. Linda C. Henson to Cynthia A. Gurney, Typewritten Letter, 31 March 1986, ANCC, OMH.

101. "ANC Annual Historical Report FY 85," 4, n.d., Inclosure 3, ANCC, OMH.

102. The 10 Army nurses were lieutenants Debra L. Ferguson, Judith A. Murray, Ronald Kirkconnell, and Donna S. Priest, captains Mary P. Rubbert, Elizabeth Stewart, Robert J. Mele, and Russell L. Lazarus, and majors Gary D. Hix and Edwin D. Reed. Pentagon Operations Directorate, "Pers for USN Mercy Hospital Mission," Official Orders, January 1987; and "Army Nurse Corps (ANC) FY 87 Annual Historical Report," 14, n.d. (both in ANCC, OMH). Susan H. Godson, *Serving Proudly: A History of Women in the U.S. Navy* (Annapolis: Naval Institute Press, 2001), 271.

103. "Highlights in the History of the Army Nurse Corps (USAMRDC)," TD, n.d., ANCC, OMH. Carolyn M. Feller and Debora R. Cox, *Highlights in the History of the Army Nurse Corps* (Washington, DC: U.S. Army Center of Military History, 2000), 62.

104. "Highlights in the History of the Army Nurse Corps (USAMRDC)," TD, n.d.,

ANCC, OMH.

105. "Somalia Operation Just One of Many Demands on US Military Medicine," *Journal of the American Medical Association* 269 (6 January 1993): 11–12. Carolyn M. Feller and Debora R. Cox, *Highlights in the History of the Army Nurse Corps* (Washington, DC: U.S. Army Center of Military History, 2000), 63.

106. Carolyn M. Feller and Debora R. Cox, *Highlights in the History of the Army Nurse Corps* (Washington, DC: U.S. Army Center of Military History, 2000), 65.

107. Pablito Gahol, "Operation Provide Hope," *Army Nursing Newsletter* (November 1999): 6–7.

108. Linda H. Yoder and Sandra L. Brunken, "Peace Making/Peace Keeping Missions Role of the U.S. Army Nurse," *Critical Care Nursing Clinics of North America* 15 (June 2003): 265–73.

*Part Three*

The Concluding Decade of a
Century of Service

*Chapter Fourteen*
# The Post Cold War Period

The 1990s witnessed extraordinary transformations within the Army, the Army Medical Department (AMEDD), and the Army Nurse Corps. Unchanging, however, was the Army's fundamental mission of organizing, training, and equipping soldiers to execute ground combat operations, to deter aggression and—when required—win the nation's wars.[1] The AMEDD's core mission and functions also stayed constant as it provided world-class health care for the Army and, as directed, for other agencies, organizations, and sister services anytime, anywhere, and under any conditions.[2] Core functions required an ability to deploy a healthy force, to deploy the medical support force, and to manage the care of all beneficiaries.[3] Likewise, the role played by Army nurses was unaltered as they provided quality nursing services to active, retired, and family members in peacetime or contingency operations within the professional military health care system. Army Nurse Corps officers executed their mission by functioning within the four pillars of professional nursing—clinical practice, administration, research, and education.[4] While most of these fundamentals remained constant, momentous change predominated all around.

By the early 1990s, the Soviet Union had disintegrated, the Iron Curtain had collapsed, and the Cold War along with its strategy of containment ended. With the threat seemingly eliminated, there was significant political pressure to reduce the U.S. national debt and balance the federal budget by a comprehensive wave of military retrenchment. The nation sought to apply the peace dividend of previously committed fiscal resources from the Department of Defense (DoD) to other areas of national need, such as welfare reform and health care. In 1993, President William Clinton, with the approval of Congress, cut the DoD budget, which had peaked at $303.6 billion in fiscal year (FY) 1989, to a belt-tightening $255.2 billion by FY 1994. In this austere climate, the Army struggled to maintain its combat edge while navigating a precipitous downsizing from an 18-division, armor-heavy organization to a 10-division, light, highly mobile force. Army leaders developed new doctrine, Force XXI, which emphasized use of innovative technology to implement information age warfare that—it was expected—would enhance the speed and precision of combat. The Army honed a new military strategy focused on dealing with two regional threats simultaneously with forces garrisoned mainly within the United States by means of strategic deterrence and defense, forward presence, crisis response, and reconstitution.[5]

While the Army was changing, the AMEDD too was undergoing a startling transformation, some facets of which reflected the revolution exploding within the national health care industry. One of the most significant determinants of the crisis was the exponential rise of health care costs. Between 1970 and 1990, health care spending escalated at a rate greater than twice that of inflation. In 1980, health care expenditures represented 9 percent of the gross national product. By 1990, this figure rose to 12.5 percent. Health care costs soared again in 1993 to 14 percent of the gross national product and economists projected they would consume 17 percent of the gross national product by 2000.[6]

Overwhelming pressures for a major overhaul of the nation's health care system resonated in the military health care system. Issues such as excessive costs, limited access, inappropriate allocation of scarce resources, unnecessary care (often implemented to protect against a potential lawsuit), and high administrative and overhead costs added to the confusion. Richard Southby summarized the pervasive challenges faced by the military health care system: the need for enhanced health care quality and better administrative management, the need to contain exorbitant costs, the difficulties in recruiting and retaining personnel, the mandate to accentuate health promotion and disease prevention, the necessity to expand discharge planning and patient education, the imperative to develop and pay for new technology, and the requirement to expand information management systems.[7] Another dilemma centered on the massive personnel and budget reductions imposed on the military and the Army and in turn on the AMEDD at a time of expanding responsibilities, a rapidly changing health care environment, the transformation of health care into a business model, and a significant revamp of the AMEDD organizational structure.[8] The AMEDD had to do much more with much less.

To survive and thrive despite these many challenges, the AMEDD revitalized itself into a more efficient, cost-effective organization in September 1991, adopting a new delivery approach called Gateway to Care (GTC), as conceived by the Surgeon General, Lieutenant General Alcide LaNoue. The exclusively Army GTC model, based on the concept of managed medical care, involved using specific primary care clinics to coordinate beneficiaries' health care requirements within a defined catchment area and to arrange for specialized care for patients when appropriate.[9] Thus, the responsibility for obtaining and coordinating care shifted from the patient to the larger comprehensive health care delivery system, with the local hospital commander determining whether the care would be provided in a military or civilian facility. If civilian care proved necessary, the commander would negotiate with the civilian provider for the most reasonable fee.[10] Within months after the Army's launch of GTC, expenses incurred by local medical commanders for nonmilitary civilian-based medical care (through CHAMPUS) saw a significant decrease. During March 1992, reductions in Army CHAMPUS claims totaled $4.1 million, while in May 1992 claims were $33.4 million less when compared to the corresponding months in the previous year, 1991.[11] Evidence of improved access appeared in the dramatic reduction of patient waiting time for appointments at Army hospitals. GTC, however, was an interim measure utilized only by the Army until the implementation of DoD's Coordinated Care Program (CCP).[12]

Congress mandated the next-generation health care delivery model—DoD's CCP—when it directed DoD to maintain access to quality care for its beneficiaries while stabilizing costs and maintaining efficient use of resources. CCP replicated many of the provisions of GTC.[13] Its major features were decentralized control and administration by local medical commanders, patient enrollment, utilization of primary care managers, employment of utilization management and quality assurance measures, the establishment of specialized treatment facilities, and increased emphasis on health promotion and disease prevention activities.[14] As the CCP became the model for DoD's managed care system, Colonel Bonnie Jennings, the Army Nurse Corps consultant, articulated the need to develop and define the role nurses would assume in this new care delivery model. She devised five potential templates to define nurses' participation. These templates involved using nurse practitioners as primary care providers, explicating bedside nurses' patient care roles, delineating ambulatory care nurses' unique responsibilities, maintaining the contributions of clinical nurse specialists, and fully utilizing nurses as case managers.[15]

In March 1995, DoD initiated an aggressive implementation plan that transformed CCP into TRICARE, an updated umbrella program for all managed care programs. DoD subdivided the TRICARE organization into 12 geographical regions, each administered by a lead agent who was a flag/general officer assigned to a military medical center. Implementation began on the West Coast and gradually migrated to the East. All TRICARE regions were operational by the end of FY 1998. TRICARE merged the precepts of managed care; the joint resources of the Army, Navy, and Air Force medical departments; and civilian contractors to provide health care for all DoD beneficiaries. Choice was a key concept, and patients could opt to receive their care from a military provider or a civilian subcontractor, participating in one of three options: (1) TRICARE Prime, a health maintenance organization; (2) TRICARE Extra, a preferred provider organization; or (3) TRICARE Standard, a fee-for-service option.[16] By 1998, the Department of Veterans Affairs, the Army, and TRICARE agreed to share selected resources to provide more efficient, less costly care. Moreover, some VA facilities participated as TRICARE providers.[17]

Change also was a hallmark within the profession of nursing in the 1990s. The dramatic increase in health care costs was a major factor precipitating change. Skyrocketing costs motivated health care administrators to implement measures

Colonel Bonnie M. Jennings (left) made many contributions to the Army Nurse Corps and to the world of professional nursing. The American Academy of Nursing recognized her substantial accomplishments and inducted her as a fellow in November 1991. Nancy Fugate Woods, PhD, RN, FAAN, then-president of the organization (right), presided at the induction ceremony.
Photo courtesy of Colonel Bonnie Jennings, Evans, GA.

such as programs affecting nurse-patient ratios, decreasing patients' length of hospital stays, downsizing staff, merging functions, and replacing registered nurses with unlicensed ancillary workers.

In 1990, the American Medical Association was actively implementing plans to introduce a new breed of health care worker, the Registered Care Technician, who would carry out physician orders and return control of bedside nursing to the physician. This movement, vehemently opposed by organized nursing and the military nursing services, threatened patient safety, health care quality, and nurse autonomy. Ultimately, the American Medical Association's Registered Care Technician proposal failed, largely due to opposition of the American Nurses Association and the Army and Air Force Nurse Corps.[18]

Simultaneously, health maintenance organizations proliferated in the civilian sector and managed care became a standard delivery format. Hospitalized patients were usually acutely ill, while many patients with less serious conditions who formerly were cared for in hospitals received care in skilled nursing facilities or at home. Because hospitals had downsized nursing staffs, the numbers of critically ill patients overtaxed the fewer nurses who remained as hospital employees. As patients shifted from the acute care hospital environment, more nurses practiced in outpatient settings. The nursing shortage of the 1980s gave way in the early 1990s to a brief period of surplus, while predictions of a higher demand for nurses to care for victims of the AIDS epidemic, the growing geriatric population, and the increased need for community-based care seemed ominous. However, the reversal of the shortage was brief, and deficit conditions returned in the mid-1990s.[19] All these external phenomena influenced conditions faced by Army Nurse Corps officers on a daily basis within the AMEDD.

Reductions in forces have followed every war and the end of the Cold War and conclusion of Operation Desert Storm proved no exceptions. In a series of incremental waves, the Clinton administration cut a swath through the strength of the Army that affected the AMEDD and the Army Nurse Corps during the 1990s. By 1994, the Army Nurse Corps had forecasted that its budgeted year-end strength would fall 13.4 percent, losing 615 officers from 4,576 in FY 1989 to 3,961 in FY 1998. Since the Army initially planned an overall decrement of 25 percent, and the AMEDD's downsizing would be at least 19 percent to as much as 22 percent, the Army Nurse Corps leadership accepted the inevitable downsizing as their share of the overall Army decrement.

Brigadier General Nancy Adams, the chief of the Army Nurse Corps, and her assistant chief, Colonel Terris Kennedy, worked prodigiously to stop or at least moderate the losses beyond that level. They explained to the surgeon general, the chief of staff of the Army, and the secretary of the Army the serious consequences the cuts would exert on Army nurses' ability to care for patients. They noted that the Air Force and Navy Nurse Corps would sustain significantly fewer personnel losses than the Army Nurse Corps even though the smaller Army Nurse Corps cared for the largest population of beneficiaries in comparison to its sister services and had the fewest active duty assets to fill authorized deployment (Table of Organization and Equipment [TO&E]) positions. The few cognoscenti privately acknowledged that internal politics could have worsened the situation even further had Adams not battled to maintain nurse authorizations.[20] Most of the lost positions resulted from the closure of hospitals in Europe and the United States as a result of the Base Realignment and Closure (BRAC) Commission recommendations. This served to mitigate slightly the deleterious effect the drawdown could have on the delivery of health care.

Over time, however, even deeper, previously unimagined cuts loomed on the horizon, and Army Nurse Corps apprehensions intensified. Some predicted reductions of almost 30 percent by 1998. The reality was only slightly less alarming, because by FY 1998 the budgeted year-end strength of the Army Nurse Corps fell to 3,405, a decrease of 1,171 authorizations, or about 26 percent from FY 1989 numbers.[21] Of all the AMEDD officer branches, the Dental Corps sustained the highest percentage of cuts, at 31 percent at this time, followed by the Army Nurse Corps at 26 percent and the Army Medical Specialist Corps with a 20 percent decrease.[22] The decrements threatened the Army Nurse Corps' ability to provide safe, quality care both on the field of combat and in the peacetime setting and also affected morale.

In the early 1990s, the Army contemplated the use of several measures to adjust its numbers to conform to declining strength authorizations and personnel fiscal constraints. These included limiting Army Nurse Corps accessions, restricting the numbers of officers who would be selected for career Voluntary Indefinite (VI) or Conditional Voluntary Indefinite (CVI) status, lowering the selection rate for promotions (meaning fewer promotions) convening yearly Selective Early Retirement Boards (SERBs) for senior officers, obtaining legislation for severance pay for specific officers who would voluntarily separate, and waiving the three-year lock-in for promotion requirement among lieutenant colonels and colonels.[23] To one degree or another, the Army Nurse Corps used all of these measures, along with the rest of the Army, to downsize its personnel base.

Limiting accessions to support the drawdown—an Army-wide concept—was pointless in the early 1990s because in FYs 1991 and 1992 the Army Nurse Corps failed to recruit enough new Army nurses to meet its recruiting goals.[24] Recruiters identified disparities between civilian wages and those paid to new second lieutenants as a primary cause for recruiting failures.[25] Perhaps because of the difficulties in recruiting direct accessions (fully educated and qualified registered nurses), the Army Nurse Corps shifted its emphasis to the accession of students, who incurred an obligation to serve by their participation in Army civilian education programs, such as Reserve Officers' Training Corps, the Army Nurse Candidate Program, and the AMEDD Enlisted Commissioning Program. In FY 1993, the Army Nurse Corps met its recruitment target of 580; however, projected accessions were lowered after that time as a consequence of the Army drawdown.[26] Accessions continued to decrease from FYs 1994 through 1998, totaling 497, 457, 310, 290, and 300, respectively. Retention of junior officers, however, was at a five-year high, which Adams considered an outcome of these officers' appreciation for the collective worth and vision of the Army Nurse Corps.[27]

During the 1990s, as the Army Nurse Corps recruiting mission decreased, the size of the recruiting force correspondingly diminished. In FY 1994, the director of Health Services Recruiting for the Army Medical Department, Colonel Sharon I. Richie, expected the recruiting mission for active duty Army Nurse Corps officers to fall by approximately 75 per year.[28] Consequently, the Army made plans to reduce the numbers of recruiters from 148 to about 88 recruiters, nurses, and support staff.[29]

On comparable issues, the Air Force Nurse Corps (AFNC) presented a somewhat divergent picture. In FY 1992, the AFNC exceeded its recruitment goal of 425 new accessions, but the specialties of those recruited did not match the AFNC's requirements. For example, while the AFNC set a goal of recruiting 15 Certified Registered Nurse Anesthetists, it accessed only two. At the same time, the AFNC had only 71 percent of its requirements for Certified Registered Nurse Anesthetists. The AFNC also hoped to recruit pediatric and obstetrics/gynecology nurse practitioners but here again accessions failed to meet its expectations. The entire AFNC's retention rate also slipped during FY 1992. In response, Air Force nurse leaders planned to implement a strategic marketing plan to help improve the retention of quality, career-oriented professional nurses and reverse the unwelcome trend.[30] The Navy Nurse Corps picture also varied slightly from its sister services. From FY 1985 to FY 1991, the Navy Nurse Corps was unable to fill all its recruiting requirements. This state of affairs improved significantly in FY 1992, when the Navy fully met its recruitment goals and welcomed 400 new ensigns into the service.[31] The Navy achieved this about-face by expanding the numbers and increasing the types of scholarships to support nurse recruiting. They offered Health Sciences Collegiate Program scholarships, formerly restricted to Navy Medical Service Corps officers, to potential Navy nurses and augmented the numbers of Navy Reserve Officers' Training Corps scholarships. Additional incentives included specialty bonuses for nurse anesthetists and bonuses for new accessions.[32]

Another method to contribute to the drawdown involved reducing the selection rates of VI boards.[33] The Army intended this strategy to limit the numbers of junior officers who passed from their first obligated tours into VI career status. In FYs 1994 and 1995, VI selection rates were 85 percent and 60 percent, respectively. The 1996 VI board had a selection rate of only 35 percent. The remaining 65 percent of those requesting consideration by the board for VI, but passed over, were involuntarily released from the Army Nurse Corps. The 1997 board had equally stringent guidelines replicating the 35 percent selection rate. This harsh process cost the Army many fine junior officers with excellent potential. Many nurses felt betrayed and frustrated because they could no longer have an Army career. A few transferred their commissions to other federal nursing services.[34] The dismal and demoralizing VI board results were better in 1998 when the targeted selection rate rose to 49 percent.[35] In 1999, the selection rate doubled to 98 percent and the Army Nurse Corps leadership declared that the drawdown was completed, signaling the end of a particularly painful era of Army Nurse Corps history.[36]

The SERBs took place annually from 1992 to 1995, resulting in the involuntary retirement of a small number of senior officers. In FYs 1992 through 1994, for example, 12 Army Nurse Corps colonels were SERBed annually. In FYs 1993 and 1994, 33 and 23 lieutenant colonels also were SERBed.[37] The AMEDD planned a SERB that would involve Army Nurse Corps officers for FY 1998 as well but canceled it when sufficient officers voluntarily retired.[38]

The details of the SERB that met in December 1993 for FY 1994 offer a picture of the collective process. In a manner similar to promotion boards, the SERB convened to consider colonels, certain lieutenant colonels, and majors for involuntary retirement.[39] The Army planned the numerical officer losses to size and shape year groups that would in part support the smaller Army Nurse Corps projected for FY 1996.[40] Those Army Nurse Corps officers selected by the FY 1994 SERB received a mandatory retirement date of 1 July 1994. Certain Army nurses holding critical specialties, such as anesthesia nursing, were exempt from the SERB involuntary retirement.[41] Although the number of those required to retire involuntarily was small, the impact of this initiative was enormous.

The SERB process had disturbing overtones both in its human dimensions and its effect on readiness.[42] Receiving notification of a pending SERB was shocking and painful for virtually all those selected and frequently carried unfounded negative connotations about the officer's career, contributions, and personal characteristics. In January 1993, when the Army Nurse Corps notified officers affected by the FY 1992 SERB, the leadership stressed the need for all Army nurses to maintain the confidentiality of the process, respect the individual's privacy, be sensitive about the gravity of the news, and support those involved when indicated.[43] Nonetheless, the aftereffects of all the SERBs were noticed. Institutional morale suffered and the process cast a pall over units with involuntarily retired officers. The focus of everyone's concern was the loss of the SERBed officers, the curtailment of working relationships, and the end of career dreams and confidence in the organization by everyone involved. The SERBs did bring the actual numbers into alignment with strength objectives and contributed to the rightsizing of the Army Nurse Corps.[44] The SERB also eliminated a number of senior officers who were less than effective. Without the SERB program, retained ineffective senior officers had the potential to tie up promotions, send a negative message to junior officers, and adversely affect the organization.[45] The SERB process did result in some positive effects but at a measurable cost to morale, trust, and unit cohesion.

Other avenues for officers to leave active duty also reduced Army Nurse Corps personnel numbers. One option was the 15-year retirement. Officers usually had to serve a minimum of 20 years to become eligible for full retirement benefits. The new program available in 1993 allowed those who had at least 15 years of active service to retire with reduced benefits. Eligible officers had to be serving in the grade of captain through colonel and meet certain criteria to take advantage of the program.[46] By October 1993, 31 officers had requested retirement from active duty under this program. One anesthetist applied for the early retirement but was denied.[47] The early retirement option continued for several years. By 1997, the Army Nurse Corps assigned priority for approval of the 15-year retirement to majors and lieutenant colonels not selected for promotion. All other majors and lieutenant colonels with at least 15 years of service also could apply on a first-come, first-served basis.[48]

By FY 1994, it was clear that the Army Nurse Corps needed to reduce its strength in the company grade levels, that is, the ranks of lieutenant and captain. To achieve this objective, the Army offered monetary Voluntary Separation Incentives and the Special Separation Benefit to certain Army Nurse Corps officers to encourage them to leave active duty.[49] One of the criteria was that eligible officers had to have more than six but fewer than 20 years of active service, with five of those years continuous service prior to separation. Army nurses passed over by the selection board that considered them for VI career status were among those eligible to apply for the bonus. Also, the Voluntary Separation Incentive Program targeted captains who were passed over one time for promotion to major. By April 1994, 22 Army Nurse Corps officers took advantage of the Voluntary Separation Incentive Program, and the Army expected 128 more applications before the program expired on 15 June 1994. The Army Nurse Corps used this initiative to rightsize its force structure and to provide "a compassionate system" that facilitated Army nurses' departure from the service, allowing them to enter the civilian job market with some financial security.[50]

The Army staff repeatedly proposed the unacceptable alternative of replacing more Army nurses with civilian nurses and converting the existing Army Nurse Corps authorizations to positions in the combat arms. Army Nurse Corps leaders regularly rejected this idea, believing that it threatened to degrade overall unit readiness.[51] Furthermore, the Army was having problems filling the authorizations it currently had for civilian nurses. In 1992, for instance, the civilian nurse vacancy rate exceeded 24 percent. At the same time, civilian nurse authorizations comprised about 40 percent of the peacetime nurse strength in the Army. In spite of several liberal programs that authorized special salaries, greater positional authority, and educational benefits, civilian nurses seemed uninterested in Army employment in the 1990s.[52] Further complicating the picture was the fact that an unknown number of civil service nurses also were reservists, which represented another threat to readiness.[53] By 1996, the picture became bleaker because civilian nurses accounted for even more—50 percent—of the Army's total nursing assets. Yet by 1997, the Army staff inexplicably planned a 32 percent reduction of civilian nurses. When viewed together with the proposed 30 percent reduction in numbers of Army Nurse Corps officers by 1998, questions arose whether there would be sufficient personnel resources to support the "redesigned, resource-efficient, wellness focused health care delivery system."[54] Simply put, conditions were approaching the point where the level of readiness as well as the delivery of safe health care services was open to serious question.

The large-scale drawdown of the 1990s created unexpected consequences of enormous proportions. It cast grave doubts about the AMEDD's capacity to field successfully the most effective medical forces to support future medical operations in foreign lands, either combat missions or Operations Other Than War. It created uncertainties about the AMEDD's ability to provide health care for its large group of beneficiaries in the United States and overseas installations.[55] Numerous other undesirable repercussions with implications for force readiness are thought to follow large-scale organizational downsizing.[56] Typically, the members of the affected organization demonstrate plummeting morale, a dulling of initiative, more guarded behavior, and an overall risk avoidance. Loyalty to the organization suffers, productivity drops, recruiting becomes onerous, public image tarnishes, and stress-related symptoms proliferate.[57]

When rumors of downsizing spread in the late 1980s, individual Army nurses felt threatened by the potential loss of their jobs and their accustomed Army way of life. Army Nurse Corps leaders sought to allay fears across every echelon of the Corps.[58] By 1995, the drawdown was creating even greater tensions within the ranks of Army Nurse Corps officers. Incoming chief of the Army Nurse Corps, Brigadier General Bettye Simmons, and her assistant, Colonel Susan McCall, implemented a transition survey and polled a sample of Army nurses and noncommissioned officers. The results confirmed that the ongoing drawdown was the most important and most frequently identified concern of 33 percent of the study sample. Many thought its effects carried over to the clinical setting. Numerous survey participants articulated the belief that the drawdown had negatively impacted patient care, while others asserted that they were short-staffed and rarely had the time or opportunity to mentor junior staff. The respondents expressed the feeling that the Army considered them expendable cogs and that they were approaching the breaking point of no longer being able to "do more with less." Others commented that even outstanding officers had doubts that they could advance in their Army careers. Still others believed that the Army Nurse Corps had degenerated into a cutthroat operation. One officer observed that the downsizing did not promote the retention of the best and the brightest soldiers. Neither did it increase productivity. Instead, it fostered an atmosphere of detrimental competition and a stressful working climate.[59]

Nurses, their fellow officers and coworkers, and their patients all tried to cope with the stress engendered by the drawdown. Some used euphemisms to put a positive spin on the cuts, referring not to the "drawdown" or "downsizing" but to "rightsizing," "force sculpting," or "force tailoring." Others used black humor, labeling the "downsizing" as a "capsizing." Some coped by openly acknowledging their pending involuntary retirement status, focusing on their work and staff responsibilities, or planning for their future career or family obligations. Social support, in the form of encouragement and assistance from peers and family, facilitated the adaptation process. Many found sustenance in spirituality or by framing their involuntary retirement with various philosophical attitudes and approaches.[60]

With the dawning of 1998, Simmons announced that the Corps had successfully met its downsizing targets, although the accomplishment was fraught with "uncertainty, professional challenges and disappointments and hard decisions."[61] She added that "the chaos and turmoil" were "a reflection of the shift in national priorities" and the upheaval in the country's health care system and acknowledged that the drawdown had been "personally hurtful to many." Simmons called for a fresh start, observing that "it is now time to dust ourselves off and move into the new year."[62]

In a complementary approach to the personnel drawdown, DoD also implemented the mandates of the BRAC Commission to further decrease infrastructure costs. Political appointees of the BRAC Commission recommended various base closures and adjustments and forwarded them to DoD. The secretary of defense then released to the president and Congress the list of facilities to be closed, realigned, disbanded, or relocated. Congress reserved final approval authority for the BRAC lists and had to either accept or reject the secretary's recommendations in their entirety.[63]

Consistent with the new doctrine of posting fewer troops overseas and emphasizing regional deployability, the U.S. Army, Europe (USAREUR), instituted significant reductions. From September 1991, the end of Desert Storm, to 30 September 1994, USAREUR planned a reduction of troop strength from 214,000 to 92,200 personnel.[64] Although the Army cut almost 60 percent of its troops in Europe, USAREUR 7th Medical Command (MEDCOM) was to lose only about 40 percent of its personnel inventory.[65] As a part of the overall plan, however, a number of 7th MEDCOM facilities would close.

The BRAC Commission recommendations degraded the 5th General Hospital at Bad Cannstatt, near Stuttgart, Germany, to a clinic in the summer of 1992, and many of the 46 Army Nurse Corps officers assigned there were uneasy about their immediate future and concerned about their next assignments. Change and uncertainties were among the few constants.[66] Moreover, fears were not confined to Bad Cannstatt or to Army Nurse Corps officers. Civilian nurses, frequently spouses of military personnel assigned to Europe, also voiced their apprehensions. Many worried that they would be laid off without any warning.[67] By 1993, the BRAC Commission mandate closed Army hospitals at Bremerhaven and Augsberg, Germany, and Brussels, Belgium, or downgraded them to clinics, giving rise to similar concerns. Hospitals located in Nürnberg, Berlin, and Frankfurt, Germany, and Vicenza, Italy, also were scheduled for potential downgrading or closure. TO&E units faced comparable uncertainties. The 128th and 32nd Combat Support Hospitals (CSHs) were pegged to deactivate in November 1991. The 30th Medical Group would cease operations in January 1992.[68] By the fall of 1993, the 502nd Mobile Army Surgical Hospital (MASH) would be shuttered.[69] Whether going through closure or radical alterations, the staff of all these units lived with ambiguity and uncertainty in their personal and professional lives.

The few hospitals that remained in Europe underwent a transition from TO&E units with Table of Distribution and Allowances (TDA) augmentation to the configuration of CSHs.[70] The drive to improve readiness was the impetus for this large-scale transformation. By 1998, the Army wanted all its TDA assets to be unequivocally related to the TO&E either through the Professional Officer Filler System or the U.S. Army Forces Command (FORSCOM) Nurse Programs.[71] Medical Force 2000 doctrine guided this transition, intending to make hospital TO&E units more mobile and deployable. The restructuring of field medical support was an outcome of lessons learned during Operation Desert Shield/Operation Desert Storm.[72] Accordingly, the Nürnberg Medical Department Activity (MEDDAC), formerly the 98th General Hospital, became the 3rd CSH, staffed with nurses who were assigned based only on mobilization areas of concentration.[73] This raised the question of who would provide care for the existing specialty cases, such as maternal-child patients, represented in the statistic of an average of 42 births monthly.[74] Army nurses with the medical-surgical specialty doubtless stepped in to fill the void and likely some had a background and experience in the required specialties. Several years later, the Nürnberg hospital closed permanently. Another facility undergoing transformation was the Frankfurt Army Regional Medical Center, formerly the 97th General Hospital, which became the 51st CSH. It, too, subsequently closed. The Würzburg MEDDAC merged into the 67th CSH.[75] At Heidelberg, the 95th CSH was integrated into the existing MEDDAC.[76] The Landstuhl Army Regional Medical Center, previously the 2nd General Hospital, remained a fixed facility and the only Medical Center in Europe. The first of a group of 288 Air Force personnel augmented the Landstuhl Army Regional Medical Center staff in April 1993, and it became known as Landstuhl Regional Medical Center.[77]

As of 1997, three fixed hospitals and 29 health clinics remained in Germany, Italy, or Belgium. Many Army Nurse Corps officers assigned to Europe had dual responsibilities and divided their duty time between fixed medical facilities and TO&E units. Army nurses assigned to the 212th MASH at Wiesbaden, Germany, for example, filled positions at the Heidelberg hospital when not deployed or participating in training. Similarly, Army nurses of the 67th CSH worked at the Würzberg MEDDAC. A contingency plan, Operation Backbone, stipulated the process for maintaining fixed facility operations when the TO&E staff deployed. It identified backfill requirements by rank and specialty when staff deployments with their TO&E units exceeded two weeks. The Army implemented Operation Backbone in 1995 and again in 1996, when it mobilized hundreds of reservists from across the United States for 140-day rotations to backfill the Landstuhl Regional Medical Center, the Würzberg MEDDAC, and the Heidelberg hospital.[78]

Change likewise occurred in Korea and the 18th MEDCOM. The 121st Evacuation Hospital in Seoul continued to operate a 150-bed fixed facility that was expandable to 500 beds using Deployable Medical System equipment stored in country. The 43rd MASH, a TO&E unit whose mission was to provide far forward resuscitative surgery in support of the 2nd Infantry Division, retired its colors in March 1997. In its stead, the division activated the 127th and 135th Forward Surgical Teams (FSTs) to provide a far forward, rapidly deployable, urgent, initial surgical service. Both of these FSTs were attached to the 121st Evacuation Hospital. Two medical-surgical nurses, two nurse anesthetists, and an operating room nurse served on each team along with other AMEDD personnel.[79] Army Nurse Corps officers also were assigned to multiple roles in the 168th Medical Battalion. They provided ambulatory care in Troop Medical Clinics throughout the peninsula and were also chief nurses for headquarters support, A Company and B Company, answering to the 18th MEDCOM commander and chief nurse for administrative and clinical management of the Area Support Medical Companies. They were also principal nursing advisors to the company commanders. One Army Community Health Nurse was assigned to each company in the 168th Medical Battalion. Additionally, Camp Casey, 40 miles north of Seoul, was the worksite for a handful of Army nurses who supported 2nd Infantry Division soldiers. They served in positions such as chief nursing consultant to the division surgeon, head nurse of the Camp Casey Troop Medical Clinic, obstetrics/gynecology nurse practitioner, or community health nurse.[80]

Other overseas installations also closed. The USA MEDDAC Panama, Gorgas Army Community Hospital, was inactivated in June 1997. This institution's roots reached back to 1882, when the French government opened a hospital on the same location. The French hospital later became the Ancon Hospital and then the Canal Commission Hospital. Finally, it became an Army hospital named in honor of Major William C. Gorgas, who eradicated yellow fever within the Panama Canal Zone from 1904 to 1914, making it feasible for Army engineers to construct the Panama Canal across the Isthmus of Panama.[81]

In addition, the BRAC Commission dictated that several major hospitals within the continental United States (CONUS) close. Throughout the 20th century, historic Letterman Army Medical Center, situated on the Presidio of San Francisco, remained a robust, busy hospital. At the turn of the century, it received and cared for soldiers evacuated from the Philippines during and after the Spanish-American War. It cared for sick and wounded soldiers who arrived from the Pacific theater during World War II. During the Vietnam era, it also provided care for many of that war's casualties. Early in the 1990s, the Army incrementally reduced the medical center into the 100-bed Letterman U.S. Army Hospital and later in June 1993 into clinic status. Letterman closed permanently on 31 July 1994, with all equipment and personnel departed by 30 September 1994. The hospital's mission, many of its specialty staff, and other personnel transferred to Madigan Army Medical Center in Tacoma, Washington, where a new facility had recently opened.

Throughout the dismantling process initiated by the BRAC Commission, the Letterman staff and patients faced enormous stress and uncertainties. Major problems were a seemingly perpetual dearth of information from higher authorities, reduced ability to provide a diverse range of required patient services, and the need to carry on daily operations and maintain quality of care vis-à-vis a steadily diminishing level of administrative and logistical support. Another challenge was the accelerated departure of civilian employees. Once closure became a certainty, the civil service staff—as could be expected—sought other jobs, promptly leaving the organization as soon as alternative positions became available in the civilian community. In normal situations, the civilian force exerted a stabilizing effect. But these were unusual times and the military staff of Letterman quickly discovered that in a BRAC situation, the exodus of the civilian workforce further undermined already declining operations and contributed to the sense of anxiety and confusion. To cope with the evolving organizational change, the hospital contracted with a group of management consultants who worked with the staff on a regular basis.[82]

Faced with the pending dissolution at Letterman, nursing staff also conducted strategic planning to facilitate transition and ease the pain of shutting down the institution and terminating its services. Most of the beneficiaries who received their care at Letterman were retired personnel and their families, over 65 years of age, and eligible for Medicare. Many had multiple health problems. To complicate matters, a significant number of beneficiaries had failed to sign up for Medicare Part B, which generally compensated for outpatient care, when they were first eligible. The Letterman staff exerted significant efforts to negotiate inclusion in Medicare Part B for these beneficiaries, allowing them to enroll without incurring a financial penalty for their late applications. In addition, the staff devoted much time and energy in referring these beneficiaries to suitable civilian health care providers.[83]

The 1995 BRAC Commission recommendations also directed that Fitzsimons Army Medical Center in Aurora, Colorado, close its doors primarily because there was no longer a major Army presence in the area. Significant pain resulted. The pre-World War I facility, designated for many years as a tuberculosis treatment center in the first half of the 20th century, downgraded into a clinic in June 1996 and closed entirely soon thereafter. The 14 tenant units on the grounds realigned to other existing locations. The only remaining Army elements were 11 reserve units housed in the McWethy Reserve Center. The 50,000 to 70,000 military retirees who formerly received health care at the hospital felt bitter, disillusioned, and abandoned by the military that had promised retirees free medical benefits for life.[84] After the AMEDD's almost total departure from the Fitzsimons grounds, the University of Colorado Health Science Center created a bioscience research park in its place.[85] In 2004, the educational institution opened the Anschutz Inpatient Pavilion, a state-of-the-art hospital facility, on the former Fitzsimons Army Medical Center site.[86]

Other facilities faced inactivation as a result of the BRAC process. Noble Army Community Hospital at Fort McClellan, Alabama, closed. Additionally, Kimbrough Army Community Hospital at Fort Meade, Maryland, and Kenner Army Community Hospital at Fort Lee, Virginia, downgraded to clinic status.[87] Cutler Army Community Hospital at Fort Devens, Massachusetts, claiming 75 years of service to the nation, also closed.[88] Furthermore, TO&E hospitals within CONUS were not exempt from the downsizing. In September 1993, the Army inactivated the 8th Evacuation Hospital at Fort Ord, California.[89] The 93rd Evacuation Hospital at Fort Leonard Wood, Missouri, the 42nd Field Hospital at Fort Knox, Kentucky, and the 46th Combat Support Hospital at Fort Devens, Massachusetts, also closed in FY 1994.[90] During the summer of 1995, the 16th MASH at Fort Riley, Kansas, and the 2nd MASH at Fort Benning, Georgia, cased their colors.[91]

In 1998, the surgeon general noted that of 168 field hospitals existing in 1990—both active and reserve—only 52 remained. He expected that number to drop even further in the future.[92] The numbers of fixed TDA facilities—both overseas and within the United States—fell from 49 in 1988, 14 outside of CONUS and 35 within CONUS, to 27 by 1999, with five overseas and 22 within CONUS.[93]

The long-term effects of the drawdown of the 1990s remain unclear. Nonetheless, several of the readiness concerns articulated in May 1994 by Brigadier General Dorothy Pocklington, the first female and nurse to be promoted to brigadier general in the U.S. Army Reserve (USAR), seemed prophetic. When discussing readiness, she observed that "a lot of things may not be in place before the next major conflict begins" and optimistically hoped that the situation would not adversely impact on recruitment and retention. Pocklington added that with the downsizing of the active component and the increased dependence on the reserves and National Guard, retention would be adversely affected if the USAR and Army National Guard units were repeatedly mobilized.[94]

In the time frame that commenced in the aftermath of the Cold War, serious challenges, critical issues, and thorny dilemmas proliferated. Chief among these were the draconian cuts levied on the Army Nurse Corps, making it difficult—if not virtually impossible—to provide safe, quality care. Fortunately, the three chiefs of the Corps who sequentially served in these troubled times were equal to the task.

Brigadier General Nancy R. Adams became the 19th chief of the Army Nurse Corps in November 1991 and led the Corps for four challenging years until December 1995. Before this most senior leadership role, she served as Army Nurse Corps consultant and previously was chief nurse of the Frankfurt Regional Army Medical Center in Germany. Colonel Terris E. Kennedy served as Adams' assistant chief of the Corps.

During her tenure, Adams assumed various roles and responsibilities. In the first months of her administration, she held three positions, serving as chief of the Corps, the assistant surgeon general for nursing, and director of AMEDD Personnel. In the summer of 1994 she assumed command of the U.S. Army Center for Health Promotion and Preventive Medicine at Edgewood Arsenal, Maryland.

Adams' contributions were many and diverse. She developed a conceptual model of Army nursing practice that optimized the role of the advanced practice nurse in clinical case management and managed care. She encouraged individual Army nurses to design and implement innovative programs and processes that resulted in significant cost avoidance, better access to care, and improved quality of care. She took the lead with Kennedy's assistance to revamp the face of nursing research in the Army, supporting the TriService Nursing Research program, restructuring the organization of nursing research into local regions with imbedded consultants, assigning officers to the Medical Research and Materiel Command to manage the multimillion-dollar Breast Cancer Research Program, creating the Persian Gulf War Illness Task Force to add clinical input and media coordination, and instituting research fellowships at the Walter Reed Army Institute of Research. She furnished nursing informatics experts to work on the development of clinical information systems within DoD. Adams adopted a proactive approach to the USAR and Army National Guard components. She assigned regional training coordinators who integrated and scheduled unit training that improved care in military treatment facilities, enhanced readiness, and led to the establishment of recognized Active, Guard, Reserve positions within the Health Service Support Areas. Adams also worked tirelessly to minimize and mitigate the loss of Army Nurse Corps authorizations within the context of a massive Army drawdown. In 1995, she assumed command of the Southwest Health Service Sup-

Pictured is Brigadier General Nancy R. Adams, who served as the 19th Chief of the Army Nurse Corps from 1991 to 1995.
Photo courtesy of Army Nurse Corps Archives, Office of Medical History, Falls Church, VA.

port Area and later command of the William Beaumont Army Medical Center. In 1998, the president of the United States nominated Adams for promotion to major general, a first for an Army Nurse Corps officer. She then assumed command of Tripler Army Medical Center and the Pacific Regional Medical Command. She also served as command surgeon of the U.S. Army, Pacific. Adams retired from active duty in 2002.

Following her retirement, she served in the Senior Executive Service in Aurora, Colorado, as senior advisor to the director of TRICARE management activity. She subsequently accepted an appointment as regional director for the TRICARE North Regional Office in Falls Church, Virginia.

The 20th chief of the Army Nurse Corps was Brigadier General Bettye H. Simmons. She served in this most senior leadership position from December 1995 to January 2000. Before her selection as chief of the Corps, Simmons discharged the responsibilities of chief nurse, U.S. Army Medical Command, and filled the role of consultant to the Army surgeon general for nursing administration. Previous to these assignments, she was chief nurse at the U.S. Army MEDDAC, Fort Polk, Louisiana. Colonel Susan C. McCall was Simmons' assistant chief of the Corps from November 1995 to September 1998. Following McCall's retirement, the assistant chief's position remained vacant for more than a year.

When Simmons assumed her duties as chief of the Army Nurse Corps, the surgeon general simultaneously directed her to fill the position of deputy commandant of the AMEDD Center and School at Fort Sam Houston, Texas, with San Antonio, Texas, being the location of her principal office. McCall's office, however, remained within the National Capital Region at Fort Belvoir, Virginia. Some 18 months later, Simmons departed from Fort Sam Houston and reported in to Fort McPherson, Georgia, to become the command surgeon of FORSCOM. Two years later, she completed her tour of duty as FORSCOM command surgeon and assumed command of the U.S. Army Center for Health Promotion and Preventive Medicine.

As chief of the Army Nurse Corps, Simmons left a significant legacy. She created a managed loss plan designed to reduce corps strength to mandated numbers with the least possible adverse influence on mission accomplishment. Simmons also used a variety of strategies to enhance relationships and build a cohesive team of enlisted medics, licensed military practical nurses, and professional nurses in the Army. She presided over a revamp of the Army Nurse Corps specialty mix, implementing an Emergency Nurse Course to improve combat nursing skills, and combined the four specialties of nurse practitioner roles into one generalist nurse practitioner, the family nurse practitioner, thereby providing a flexible health care provider for virtually every patient population in almost any contingency. Simmons collaborated with the reserve components to craft a postdeployment medical care package that employed nurse case managers with physician support to triage injured soldiers to the proper level of care before demobilization. She also sponsored an Active Component/Reserve Component Chief Nurse Strategic Planning Summit that convened to develop a long-range plan to drive future Active

Pictured is Brigadier General Bettye H. Simmons, who served as the 20th Chief of the Army Nurse Corps from 1995 to 2000.
Photo courtesy of Army Nurse Corps Archives, Office of Medical History, Falls Church, VA.

Pictured is Brigadier General William T. Bester, who served as the 21st Chief of the Army Nurse Corps from 2000 to 2004.
Photo courtesy of Army Nurse Corps Archives, Office of Medical History, Falls Church, VA.

Component/Reserve Component initiatives. Simmons retired from active duty in January 2000 and became the director of the Leadership Institute at Hampton University in Norfolk, Virginia.

Brigadier General William T. Bester succeeded Simmons as the 21st chief of the Army Nurse Corps, serving in this role from 2000 to 2004. Bester was the first male Army Nurse Corps officer to hold this position in the century-long history of the Army Nurse Corps. Colonel Deborah Gustke served as the assistant chief of the Army Nurse Corps and simultaneously as the Corps-specific branch proponency officer at the AMEDD Center and School at Fort Sam Houston, Texas, at this time. Before becoming chief of the Army Nurse Corps, Bester served as advance party commander when deploying to Taszar, Hungary, in support of Operation Joint Endeavor. For the 60 days before his departure from that theater of operations, he functioned as the Medical Task Force commander, shouldering responsibility for all medical assets in Hungary and Croatia. Immediately before his selection as chief of the Corps, he commanded Moncrief Army Community Hospital at Fort Jackson, South Carolina.

Upon selecting Bester to be chief, Army Nurse Corps, the surgeon general simultaneously assigned him as the assistant surgeon general for force projection and deputy chief of staff for operations, health policy, and services, with an office in the Pentagon. In the spring of 2002, he left these positions and assumed command of the U.S. Army Center for Health Promotion and Preventive Medicine.

While chief of the Army Nurse Corps, Bester faced the challenge of recruiting and retaining adequate numbers of Army nurses while the nation was undergoing a severe nursing shortage. He marshaled an array of initiatives such as the critical skills retention bonus for nurse anesthetists and operating room nurses and the $18 million Health Loan Repayment Program for the accession and retention of Army nurses with six to 96 months of active duty service. He championed expanding Reserve Officers' Training Corps scholarships for nurses to almost 200 colleges and universities nationwide and enlarged the Army Enlisted Commissioning Program for Nursing from 55 to 75 slots. Bester sought and obtained congressional approval for direct hire authority for civilian registered nurses, reducing the length of the hiring process from an average of 101 to 21 days.

Bester retired from active duty in March 2004. Following his retirement, he accepted a faculty position at the University of Texas at Austin, teaching both undergraduate and graduate students. Still later he joined the staff of the Graduate School of Nursing at USUHS.

## Notes

1. The United States Army: Strategic Force-Strategic Vision, Executive Summary, n.d., Army Nurse Corps Collection (ANCC), Office of Medical History (OMH).
2. "The United States Army Medical Department Mission," Briefing Slide, in "1993 Army Medical Department Functional Review, Army Medical Department (AMEDD) Overview," 1 November 1993, ANCC, OMH. Alcide M. LaNoue, "Army Medical Department: Staying Ahead of the Curve," Army 45 (October 1995): 135–36, 138, 140. Ronald R. Blanck, "Army Approaches Being 'The Best'," U.S. Medicine 33 (January 1997): 16–17.
3. Jerry Harben, "Commander Draws Up Blue Print for '97," The Mercury 24 (January 1997): 3.
4. "Statement by Brigadier General Nancy R. Adams, Chief of the Army Nurse Corps, before the Subcommittee on Defense, Committee on Appropriations, United States Senate, 2nd Session, 103rd Congress, Health Services and Infrastructure," 2, 14 April 1994; and "Statement by Brigadier General Bettye H. Simmons, Chief, Army Nurse Corps, Army Medical Department, before the Subcommittee on Defense, Committee on Appropriations, United States Senate, 2nd Session, 104th Congress, DoD Health Care Programs," 2, 5 June 1996 (both in ANCC, OMH).
5. Gordon R. Sullivan, "Total Army, Total Victory," Typewritten Address presented to Eisenhower Luncheon, Annual Meeting of AUSA, Washington, D.C., 15 October 1991. Gordon R. Sullivan, "The Return to History," Typewritten Address presented to National Security Seminar, U.S. Army War College, Carlisle Barracks, PA, 1 June 1992. Gordon R. Sullivan, Untitled Typewritten Address presented to Army Session Luncheon, ROA Mid-Winter Conference, Washington, D.C., 21 January 1992. Gordon R. Sullivan, *America's Army, Into the Twenty-First Century* (Cambridge, MA: Fletcher School of Law and Diplomacy, Tufts University, 1993). Army Initiatives Group, Office of the Deputy Chief of Staff for Operations and Plans, "State of America's Army on its 218th Birthday," Printed Report, 1993. Laurence Jolidon, "Military, Clinton at Odds," USA Today (8 February 1993): 4. Stephen Conley, "Downsizing the U.S. Military," USA Today (8 February 1993): 4. Gordon R. Sullivan, America's Army (Cambridge, MA: Institute for Foreign Policy Analysis, 1993). Edward D. Martin, "Danger, Opportunity Challenge for DoD," U.S. Medicine 30 (January 1994): 7–8. "Military Operations, Force XXI Operations, A Concept for the Evolution of Full-Dimensional Operations for the Strategic Army of the Early Twenty-First Century," TRADDOC Pam 525-5, 1 August 1994. Mark Newell, "Force XXI, A Revolution

and Evolution in Military Affairs Proceeds," n.d., http://www.wolfson.ox.ac.uk/~floridi/forcexxi.htm (accessed 15 August 2004). L. Martin Kaplan, *Department of the Army Historical Summary, Fiscal Year 1994* (Washington, DC: Center of Military History, United States Army, 2000). Earl H. Tilford, "Implications for the Army," in *World View: The 1996 Strategic Assessment from the Strategic Studies Institute*, ed. Earl H. Tilford, Jr., (Carlisle Barracks, PA: Strategic Studies Institute), 53–58. Douglas A. MacGregor, *Breaking the Phalanx, A New Design for Landpower in the 21st Century* (Westport, CN: Praeger, 1997). A. Christopher St. Jean, "Managing the Drawdown's Human Side," *Military Review* 77 (November/December 1997): 63–65. Edward Drea to Author, E-mail Correspondence, 30 April 2004, ANCC, OMH.

6. 50 Years at the Division of Nursing, United States Public Health Service, April 1997, 25, 30, ANCC, OMH. "How to Fight Killer Health Costs," *U.S. News & World Report* (23 September 1991): 50–52, 54, 56–58. Joseph Owen, "Medical Chief Urges Use of Local Hospitals," *Stars and Stripes* (13 May 1992): n.p., Newspaper Clipping in ANCC, OMH.

7. Richard F. Southby, "Military Health Care in the 21st Century," *Military Medicine* 158 (October 1993): 637–40. LTC Smith, "Department of Defense Plan to Bring Military Health Care into Harmony with the President's Proposed American Health Security Act of 1993," Information Paper, 9 November 1993, Inclosure 8, Memo from the Chief, Army Nurse Corps (December 1993), ANCC, OMH.

8. In 1997, the Surgeon General observed that missions were expanding as the force was shrinking. At that time, 37,000 active component and 20,000 reserve component service members were soldiering in 51 foreign countries. David Stanley, "LTG Blanck's Focus for the Army Medical Department," Information Paper, 1, 1 October 1996, ANCC, OMH. Ronald R. Blanck, "Army Approaches Being 'The Best'," *U.S. Medicine* 33 (January 1997): 16–17. David Stanley, "LTG Blanck's Focus for the Army Medical Department," Information Paper, 1, 1 October 1996, ANCC, OMH. Jerry Harben, "Commander Draws Up Blue Print for '97," The Mercury 24 (January 1997): 3. "Posture Statement by Major General John J. Cuddy, Deputy Surgeon General, United States Army, before the Committee on Appropriations, National Security Subcommittee, U.S. House of Representatives, 2nd Session, 104th Congress," Typewritten Record Version, 24 April 1996, ANCC, OMH. General Accounting Office, "Defense Health Care: Issues and Challenges Confronting Military Medicine," GAO/HEHS-95-104, 1–3, 22 March 1995.

9. Managed care is considered virtually synonymous to coordinated care. It is a system to provide quality care on a cost-effective basis that is anchored in principles of accountability, communication, and collaboration between provider and patient. Planners designed managed care to enhance the business practices of the health care industry. Its objective was to "achieve optimal and specific patient outcomes, within fiscally responsible timeframes, and with an appropriate utilization of resources." Bonnie M. Jennings, "Nursing Implications of the Department of Defense Coordinated Care Program," *Military Medicine* 158 (December 1993): 823–27. Susan I. Reinhart and others, "Managed Care at Eisenhower Army Medical Center: An Initial Experience," *Military Medicine* 160 (August 1995): 384–88. Bettye H. Simmons, "Professional Development and Readiness Guide," 2–3, 7 May 1997, ANCC, OMH.

10. William Joe Webb and others, Department of the Army Historical Summary Fiscal Years 1990 and 1991 (Washington, DC: Center of Military History, United States Army, 1997), 52–53. Harry Noyes, "Army Opens 'Gateway' for Patients," *HSC Mercury* 18 (March 1991): 1, 12. "Gateway to Care," *HSC Mercury* 18 (July 1991): 12. Andrew B. Cornell, "Downsizing the US Army Medical Corps," *Military Review* (January 1992): 82–84. Harry Noyes, "Gateway to Care Opens Soon," *HSC Mercury* 19 (March 1992):

1, 12. Dennis Dohanos, "Experience Guides Managed-Care Policies," *The Mercury* 23 (December 1995): 12.

11. "Statement by Lieutenant General Alcide M. LaNoue, The Surgeon General, Department of the Army, before the Subcommittee on Defense, Committee on Defense, House of Representatives, 1st Session, 103rd Congress, DoD Medical Programs," 8, 29 April 1993, Draft Record Version, ANCC, OMH.

12. "Statement by Lieutenant General Alcide M. LaNoue, The Surgeon General, Department of the Army, before the Subcommittee on Military Forces and Personnel, Committee on Army Services, House of Representatives, 1st Session, 103rd Congress, Department of the Army Medical Programs," 6–7, 11 May 1993, ANCC, OMH.

13. D.J. Atwood, "Strengthening the Medical Functions of the Department of Defense," Memorandum, 1 October 1991; and William T. Gray, "'Gateway to Care' Interaction," Memorandum, 3 January 1991 (both in ANCC, OMH). Susan I. Reinhart and others, "Managed Care at Eisenhower Army Medical Center: An Initial Experience," *Military Medicine* 160 (August 1995): 384–88. Dwight D. Oland and David W. Hogan, *Department of Army Historical Summary Fiscal Year 1992* (Washington, DC: Center of Military History, United States Army, 2001), 170–71.

14. Enrique Mendez, "Implementation of the Coordinated Care Program," Memorandum, 8 January 1992; Assistant Secretary of Defense (Health Affairs), "Coordinated Care Program," Printed Document, 8 January 1992; Frank F. Ledford, "Implementation of the Coordinated Care Program," Action Memorandum, 8 April 1992; and "Outlook for Coordinated Care," n.d., Enclosure 5, in Memo from the Chief, Army Nurse Corps (January 1993) (all in ANCC, OMH). Bonnie M. Jennings, "Nursing Implications of the Department of Defense Coordinated Care Program," *Military Medicine* 158 (December 1993): 823–27. Dwight D. Oland and David W. Hogan, *Department of Army Historical Summary Fiscal Year 1992* (Washington, DC: Center of Military History, United States Army, 2001), 170–71.

15. Bonnie M. Jennings, "Nursing Implications of the Department of Defense Coordinated Care Program," *Military Medicine* 158 (December 1993): 823–27.

16. Lieutenant Colonel Smith, "TRICARE Initiatives," Information Paper, 8 November 1993; Lieutenant Colonel Smith, "Military Health Care Moving Towards National Health Care Reform," Talking Paper, 9 November 1993; "Department of Defense Medical Program, FY 1997, Statement by Stephen C. Joseph, M.D., M.P.H., Assistant Secretary for Defense for Health Affairs, Submitted to the Subcommittee on Defense, Committee on Appropriations, United States Senate, 2nd Session, 104th Congress," Typewritten Document (TD), 7, 5 June 1996; and Bettye H. Simmons, "Professional Development and Readiness Guide," 2–3, 7 May 1997 (all in ANCC, OMH). Alcide M. LaNoue, "Army Medicine: 'Caring Beyond the Call of Duty'," *Army* 46 (October 1996): 151–52, 154, 157. "Strategic Thinking Assumptions, Health Affairs and the MHSS in 1998," http://www.ha.osd.mil/ppc/assump.html (accessed 18 April 1998). Bonnie M. Jennings and Lori A. Loan, "Patient Satisfaction and Loyalty among Military Healthcare Beneficiaries Enrolled in a Managed Care Program," *Journal of Nursing Administration* 29 (November 1999): 47–55. Bonnie M. Jennings and others, "What Really Matters to Healthcare Consumers," *Journal of Nursing Administration* 35 (April 2005): 173–80. Patricia Golson, TRICARE Management Agency, Telephone Interview, 24 August 2005.

17. "Statement by Lieutenant General Ronald R. Blanck, The Army Surgeon General, on Health Care in the United States Army," Printed Document, 23, n.d.; and Ronald R. Blanck, "TSG Update #26," E-mail Correspondence, 17 August 1999 (both in ANCC, OMH).

18. The AMA solicited but failed to garner the military nursing services' support for their RCT proposal. Colonel John Hudock and the USAF chief nurse flew to Chicago, Illinois,

and attended an AMA-sponsored session at the Drake Hotel. Hudock wrote, "We effectively distanced ourselves from this proposal and supported the ANA position." Hudock added that he and the USAF chief "articulated that 'medics' were trained, supervised, and evaluated by Professional Nurses, not physicians (or others). Medics practiced under our license—end of case." John Hudock to Author, Handwritten Notes, 1, 5 July 2005, ANCC, OMH.

19. Pew Health Professions Commission, "Health Professions Education for the Future: Schools in Service to the Nation," Printed Report, 30, 83–90, February 1993; Sheila R. Schultz and Kristina M. Brown, "Nursing in the Nineties: Profile of a Profession at the Crossroad," Printed Report, 29–30, Human Resources Research Organization, 24 January 1994; and 50 Years at the Division of Nursing, United States Public Health Service, April 1997, 30, 31 (all in ANCC, OMH). Joan E. Lynaugh and Barbara L. Brush, *American Nursing: From Hospitals to Health Systems* (Cambridge MA: Blackwell Publishers, 1996), 57–64. Beverly L. Malone and Geri Marullo, Workforce Trends among U.S. Registered Nurses, A Report for the International Council of Nurses (ICN) Workforce Forum, Stockholm, Sweden, September 21–October 1, 1997, http://www.nursingworld.org/readroom/usworker.htm (accessed 31 December 1997). Thelma M. Schorr and Maureen S. Kennedy, *100 Years of American Nursing, Celebrating a Century of Caring* (Philadelphia: Lippincott, 1999), 179–80. Thetis M. Group and Joan I. Roberts, *Nursing, Physician Control, and the Medical Monopoly* (Bloomington: Indiana University Press, 2001), 273, 359–61.

20. Terris E. Kennedy, Interview by Constance J. Moore, Transcript, 301–02, 356–59, 31 October 1996, ANCC, OMH. "AMEDD General Officer Position Descriptions," n.d., ANCC, OMH.

21. Nancy R. Adams, "Message from the Chief," Memo from the Chief, Army Nurse Corps (January 1992): 1, ANCC, OMH. Livian Mack, "Nurse Corps Chief Predicts Good Future for Nursing," *HSC Mercury* 19 (June 1992): 7. Nancy R. Adams, "Message from the Chief," Memo from the Chief, Army Nurse Corps (July 1992): 1, ANCC, OMH. Harry Noyes, "Chief Sees Opportunities in Nurse Corps Future," *HSC Mercury* (October 1992): 12. Chet Nunley, "Army Corps Chief Visits Fort Hood, DACH Nurses Told Their Jobs Are Secure," Unidentified Newspaper Clipping, n.d.; Nancy R. Adams, "Downsizing of the Army Nurse Corps," Information Paper, 22 July 1994; "AMEDD Reorganization Manpower Briefing, Presented to General Peay," Briefing Slides, 4 February 1994; "AMEDD Manpower Update, Presented to USAMEDCOM Board of Directors," Briefing Slides, 11 May 1994; "Statement by Brigadier General Bettye H. Simmons, Chief, Army Nurse Corps, Army Medical Department, before the Subcommittee on Defense, Committee on Appropriations, United States Senate, 2nd Session, 104th Congress, DoD Health Care Programs," 5–6, 5 June 1996; LTC David Stanley, "LTG Blanck's Focus for the Army Medical Department," Information Paper, 1, 1 October 1996; "Army Nurse Corps Branch Briefing," Briefing Slides, October 1997; "Combined Clinical Conference, AN Branch Update, 20 March 1998," Briefing Slides; and "Posture Statement by Lieutenant General Ronald R. Blanck, The Surgeon General, United States Army, for the Appropriations Committee, United States Senate, 2nd Session, 105th Congress, Health Care," 2–3, 1 April 1998 (all in ANCC, OMH).

22. In a decreasing order of reductions, the Medical Corps and Medical Service Corps sustained losses of 19 percent each. The Veterinary Corps and Physician Assistants each decreased by 10 percent. "AMEDD Manpower/Personnel Drawdown," 7, Briefing Slides presented to MSC Commanders, 12 February 1998, Box 455, OTSG/Medical Command, OMH.

23. Lowering the selection rate resulted in more pass-overs. A pass-over occurred when a board failed to select an officer for promotion. Officers who had two successive pass-overs were mandated to separate from the service with some severance pay. Usually an

officer had to serve in grade for three years in order to retire in that grade. For instance, if a lieutenant colonel wanted to retire and receive lieutenant colonel retirement pay, she would had to have been promoted to lieutenant colonel three years prior to her retirement date. Tom Wilson, "Officer Force Reductions in the Future," Officers' Call (January–February 1990): 19–21. "Personnel Boss Foresees Force Outs," *HSC Mercury* 19 (October 1991): 1. LTC Kitsopoulos, "AMEDD Selective Early Retirement Boards, FY94," Information Paper, 4 May 1993, ANCC, OMH. Jim Tice, "Medical Dept. Begins Its Officer Drawdown," *Army Times* 58 (2 March 1998): 5. Dwight D. Oland and David W. Hogan, *Department of Army Historical Summary Fiscal Year 1992* (Washington, DC: Center of Military History, United States Army, 2001), 117–19.

24. "Statement by Brigadier General Nancy R. Adams, Chief of the Army Nurse Corps, Army Medical Department, before the Subcommittee on Defense, Committee on Appropriations, United States Senate, 1st Session, 103rd Congress, DOD Medical Programs," 1, 5 May 1993; and Michael J. Foster, "Minutes of the Army Nurse Corps Staff Meeting on 2 April 1993," Memorandum for Record, 4, 5 May 1993 (both in ANCC, OMH).

25. One recruiter noted that, dating back to 1987, Army pay had been highly competitive. However, by 1992 it had lost its competitive edge. Patricia M. Forest, "Army Nurse Accession Strategy," Memorandum for Record, 4 May 1992, ANCC, OMH.

26. "Army Nurse Corps Branch Briefing," Briefing Slides, October 1997, ANCC, OMH.

27. "Statement by Brigadier General Nancy R. Adams, Chief of the Army Nurse Corps, Army Medical Department, before the Subcommittee on Defense, Committee on Appropriations, United States Senate, 1st Session, 103rd Congress, DOD Medical Programs," 1, 5 May 1993; Theresa M. Tominey for Sharon I. Richie, "Congressional Testimony," Memorandum for PAE, 1, 22 April 1993; and "Army Nurse Corps Branch Briefing," Briefing Slides, October 1997 (all in ANCC, OMH).

28. The recruiting mission actually fell from 497 to 457 (a discrepancy of 40) between FYs 1994 and 1995. However, the mission decreased more significantly between FYs 1995 and 1996, from 457 to 310 (a decrease of 147). In the subsequent FYs 1997 and 1998, the recruiting missions stabilized at 290 and 300, respectively. "Army Nurse Corps Branch Briefing," Briefing Slides, October 1997, ANCC, OMH.

29. Theresa M. Tominey for Sharon I. Richie, "Congressional Testimony," Memorandum for PAE, 2, 22 April 1993, ANCC, OMH.

30. "Statement of Brigadier General Sue E. Turner, Director, Nursing Services, Air Force Nurse Corps," Draft Copy of Testimony, n.d., ANCC, OMH.

31. Draft copy of testimony presented by RADM Stratton to Congress, n.d., ANCC, OMH.

32. Jan K. Herman to Author, 6 September 2005; and Jan K. Herman to Author, 7 September 2005 (both E-mail Correspondence, ANCC, OMH).

33. VI was a level of officer career status that followed an obligated tour but preceded Regular Army status. Several years after VI became available, Conditional Voluntary Indefinite (CVI) became a preliminary option conferred before VI status. A board selected Army nurses for VI, and the number chosen was "dependent upon how many vacancies recruiting would not be able to fill." CVI evolved into being the Army Nurse Corps' "way of hedging [its] bets about candidates who were not the most stellar performers." It also was a bolt hole for officers who "were only staying in to see if they could get a certain assignment or if they were applying for specialty training/school." Darlene McLeod to Author, E-mail Correspondence, 12 June 2003, Army Nurse Corps Archives, OMH. For a while, an officer had to be in CVI status before applying for VI. Later, however, certain officers could apply directly for VI. Gail Croy to Author, E-mail Correspondence, 29 July 2003, Army Nurse

Corps Archives, OMH.

34. G.E. Willis, "Feelings of Betrayal Abound as Drawdown Hits Nurses," *Army Times* 57 (16 September 1996): 3. Michele L. Kohl, "Trip Report, Installation Visited: Tripler Army Medical Center, Honolulu, Hawaii, 29 July–2 Aug 1996," Memorandum, 2, 15 August 1996; and "Army Nurse Corps Branch Briefing," Briefing Slides, October 1997 (both in ANCC, OMH).

35. Carolyn Bulliner, "PERSCOM Update," *The Army Nursing Newsletter* (January 1998): 2, ANCC, OMH

36. Carolyn Bulliner, "PERSCOM Update," *The Army Nursing Newsletter* (December 1998): 2, ANCC, OMH.

37. Michael J. Foster, "Minutes of the Army Nurse Corps Staff Meeting on 6 October 1993," Memorandum for Record, 5, 14 October 1993; "SERB History, AN," and "SERB History, AMEDD," n.d., Presentation Slides attached to "Statement by Brigadier General Nancy R. Adams, Chief of the Army Nurse Corps, before the Subcommittee on Defense, Committee on Appropriations, United States Senate, 2nd Session, 103rd Congress, Health Services and Infrastructure," 14 April 1994; and Michele Kohl, "PERSCOM Update," Memo from the Chief, Army Nurse Corps (1 September 1997): 2 (all in ANCC, OMH). Deborah Funk, "Medical Dept. Under Drawdown Fire," *Army Times* 58 (1 September 1997): 3. Jim Tice, "Medical Dept. Begins Its Officer Drawdown," *Army Times* 58 (2 March 1998): 5. Dwight D. Oland and David W. Hogan, *Department of Army Historical Summary Fiscal Year 1992* (Washington, DC: Center of Military History, United States Army, 2001), 129.

38. Jerry Harben, "Some MC, NC, MSC Officers Face SERB," *The Mercury* 24 (September 1996): 1. Tranette Ledford, "Medical Officer Drawdown Gets Reprieve," *Army Times* 58 (12 January 1998): 3.

39. The lieutenant colonels and majors considered by the SERB had been passed over or nonselected for promotion to the next grade.

40. A year group was a collection of due course officers whose entry date on active duty occurred within the same fiscal year. The officers were sorted into year groups as a way of managing promotions and other board actions. Jennifer L. Petersen to Author, E-mail Correspondence, 30 January 2004, ANCC, OMH.

41. LTC Kitsopoulos, "AMEDD Selective Early Retirement Boards, FY94,"Information Paper, 4 May 1993; Nancy R. Adams, "AMEDD FY94 Early Retirement Programs," Memorandum for DASG-PTM, n.d.; and Alan I. Fox, "Fiscal Year 1995 Drawdown Messages," Memorandum for See Distribution, 19 May 1994 (all in ANCC, OMH).

42. A. Christopher St. Jean, "Managing the Drawdown's Human Side," *Military Review* 77 (November/December 1997): 63–65.

43. Michael J. Foster, "Minutes of the Army Nurse Corps Staff Meeting on 7 January 1993," Memorandum for Record, 7, 27 January 1993, ANCC, OMH. Deborah Funk, "Medical Dept. Under Drawdown Fire," *Army Times* 58 (1 September 1997): 3.

44. Sharon I. Richie, "The Effects of the Selective Early Retirement Board (SERB) Process on Field-Grade Army Nurses," Ph.D. dissertation, George Washington University, 1998, 121.

45. John Hudock to Author, Handwritten Notes, 2, 5 July 2005, ANCC, OMH.

46. "15 Year Retirement Option," Memo from the Chief, Army Nurse Corps (August 1993): 3–4. Laura Browning, "Medical Drawdown," *Army Times* 58 (2 March 1998): 5.

47. Michael J. Foster, "Minutes of the Army Nurse Corps Staff Meeting on 6 October 1993," Memorandum for Record, 5, 14 October 1993, ANCC, OMH.

48. Michele Kohl, "PERSCOM," Memo from the Chief, Army Nurse Corps (May 1997):

1, ANCC, OMH.

49. Complicated formulas determined the amount paid for VSI and SSB. The VSI computation equaled 2.5 percent multiplied by the final base pay times 12 months and then multiplied by years of service. Those who took advantage of VSI were "paid for twice the number of years served." SSB recipients' pay equaled 15 percent times their final base pay that then was multiplied by 12 months and years of service. These individuals also received the "same transition benefits as involuntary separations." "Voluntary Separation Incentive (VSI) and Special Separation Benefit (SSB)," Briefing Slide, September 1994, ANCC, OMH.

50. Jim Tice, "Voluntary Separation Incentives," *Army Times* 58 (2 March 1998): 5. Michael J. Foster, "Minutes of the Army Nurse Corps Staff Meeting on 1 February 1994," Memorandum, 3; "Recruitment/Retention, VSIP/VERP," TD, 12 April 1994; and "Voluntary Separation Incentive (VSI) and Special Separation Benefit (SSB)," Briefing Slide, September 1994 (all in ANCC, OMH). L. Martin Kaplan, *Department of the Army Historical Summary Fiscal Year 1994* (Washington, DC: Center of Military History, United States Army, 2000), 43.

51. Nancy R. Adams, "Message from the Chief," Memo from the Chief, Army Nurse Corps (January 1992): 1, ANCC, OMH. While Army nurses were ready and able to deploy on combat missions or Operations Other Than War, civilian nurses could not be utilized in this manner. Thus, with greater numbers of civilian nurses, fewer numbers of nurses were available to deploy on these operations. This would create a negative impact on overall readiness.

52. Wilfredo Nieves, "FY 92–97 Program Objective Memorandum, Program Decision Package," n.d .; and "Statement by Brigadier General Nancy R. Adams, Chief of the Army Nurse Corps, Army Medical Department, before the Subcommittee on Defense, Committee on Appropriations, United States Senate, 1st Session, 103rd Congress, DOD Medical Programs," 2, 5 May 1993 (both in ANCC, OMH).

53. John Hudock to Author, Handwritten Notes, 2, 5 July 2005, ANCC, OMH.

54. "Statement by Brigadier General Bettye H. Simmons, Chief, Army Nurse Corps, Army Medical Department, before the Subcommittee on Defense, Committee on Appropriations, United States Senate, 2nd Session, 104th Congress, DoD Health Care Programs," 5–6, 5 June 1996; and Defense Manpower Data Center, OASD Health Affairs, "Department of Defense Health Manpower Personnel Data System, Fiscal Year 1996 Statistics," 2, 46, Format 1, Format 12 (both in ANCC, OMH).

55. Gary Cecchine and others, *Army Medical Strategy, Issues for the Future* (Santa Monica, CA: RAND, 2001), Box 171, OTSG Files, OMH. Lois M. Davis and others, *Army Medical Support for Peace Operations and Humanitarian Assistance* (Santa Monica, CA: RAND, 1996), http://www.rand.org/publications/MR/MR773/ (accessed 6 July 2004).

56. Soraya S. Nelson, "Report to Set Limit to Medical Drawdown," *Army Times* 56 (6 November 1995): 31.

57. A. Christopher St. Jean, "Managing the Drawdown's Human Side," *Military Review* 77 (November/December 1997): 63–65. Rick Maze, "Drawdown Legacy: Stress," *Army Times* 58 (11 March 1996): 12, 15.

58. Chet Nunley, "Army Corps Chief Visits Fort Hood, DACH Nurses Told Their Jobs Are Secure," Unidentified Newspaper Clipping, n.d., in ANCC, OMH.

59. "Army Nurse Corps Transition Survey," Typewritten Summary, n.d., ANCC, OMH. Carol A. Reineck, Lynne M. Connelly, and Linda H. Yoder, "Transition to the Future: The Chief, ANC Asks the Field," *U.S. Army Medical Department Journal*, PB 8-96-1/2 (January–February 1997): 2–5.

60. Sharon I. Richie, "The Effects of the Selective Early Retirement Board (SERB) Process on Field-Grade Army Nurses," Ph.D. dissertation, George Washington University, 1998, 84, 181–82. "Statement of Brigadier General Linda J. Stierle, Director of Medical Readiness and Nursing Services, Office of the Surgeon General, Department of the Air Force," 20, April 1998, ANCC, OMH.

61. The budgeted end strength actually dropped by another 25 Army nurses in FY 1999 from 3,406 to 3,381. "Army Nurse Corps Annual Historical Report, Calendar Year 1999," 9 June 2000, 2, ANCC, OMH.

62. Bettye H. Simmons, "Notes from the Chief, Army Nurse Corps," *The Army Nursing Newsletter* 1-2, December 1997, ANCC, OMH.

63. Mike Buckley, "Closing Bases, Opening Doors," *Soldiers* 53 (November 1998): 16–20.

64. By December 1992, USAREUR had moved 94,129 service members from targeted units, 122,368 of their family members, and 28,050 household pets. The command also had shipped 34,828 privately owned vehicles (POVs). The destination of most was CONUS. U.S. Army Europe, The Right Force for a Changing World, Printed Brochure, n.d., ANCC, OMH.

65. Joseph Owen, "Medical Chief Urges Use of Local Hospitals," *Stars and Stripes* (13 May 1992): n.p., Newspaper Clipping, ANCC, OMH. Stephen E. Everett and L. Martin Kaplan, *Department of the Army Historical Summary Fiscal Year 1993* (Washington, DC: Center of Military History, United States Army, 2002), 100–01.

66. Dorothy J. Clark, "Trip Report: Medical/Surgical Conference; Willingen, Germany; 14–20 September 1991," Typewritten Memorandum (TM), ANCC, OMH.

67. Nancy R. Adams, "Trip Report for Visit to Germany, 9–20 May 1992," TM, 28 June 1992, ANCC, OMH.

68. Dorothy J. Clark, "Trip Report: Medical/Surgical Conference; Willingen, Germany; 14–20 September 1991," TM; Dorothy J. Clark, "After Action Report Europe, 25 May 1992–5 June 1992," TM; Michele L. Kohl, "Army Nurse Corps Distribution Conference, FY 94," Memorandum for Chief, Army Nurse Corps, 1–2, 3 October 1993; and "7th Medical Command," Memo from the Chief, Army Nurse Corps (January 1993): 11–12 (all in ANCC, OMH).

69. Michele L. Kohl, "Army Nurse Corps Distribution Conference, FY 94," Memorandum for Chief, Army Nurse Corps, 1, 3 October 1993, ANCC, OMH.

70. Nancy R. Adams, "Message from the Chief," Memo from the Chief, Army Nurse Corps (July 1992): 1, ANCC, OMH.

71. Carol A. Reineck, Lynne M. Connelly, and Linda H. Yoder, "Transition to the Future: The Chief, ANC Asks the Field," *U.S. Army Medical Department Journal*, PB 8-96-1/2 (January–February 1997): 2–5. Karen Jowers, "One Drawdown Ending; Medical Cuts Just Beginning," *Army Times* (6 February 1995): 22.

72. Stephen E. Everett and L. Martin Kaplan, *Department of the Army Historical Summary Fiscal Year 1993* (Washington, DC: Center of Military History, United States Army, 2002), 100–01.

73. The mobilization AOCs (Areas of Concentration) were 66C, 66H/66J, 66E, and 66F, or Psychiatric Nurse, Medical-Surgical Nurse, Operating Room Nurse, and Nurse Anesthetist, respectively. The 66J AOC, normally awarded to a neophyte Army Nurse Corps officer, typically was upgraded to 66H after a year of service.

74. Nancy R. Adams, "Trip Report for Visit to Germany, 9–20 May 1992," TM, 28 June 1992, ANCC, OMH.

75. "7th Medical Command," Memo from the Chief, Army Nurse Corps (January 1993): 11–12, ANCC, OMH. "Annual Historical Report, AMEDD Activities, RCS-MED41 (R-4), 01 Jan 93–31 Dec 93, Department of the Army, Headquarters, 7th Medical Command,

APO AE 09102," Section I, 1, Section XVII, 1, Box 166A, OTSG Files, OMH.

76. Nancy R. Adams, "Army Nurse Corps Statistical Abstract," December 1994, ANCC, OMH.

77. Michele L. Kohl, "Army Nurse Corps Distribution Conference, FY 94," 2, 3 October 1993, Memorandum for Chief, Army Nurse Corps, ANCC, OMH. "Annual Historical Report, AMEDD Activities, RCS-MED41 (R-4), 01 Jan 93–31 Dec 93, Department of the Army, Headquarters, 7th Medical Command, APO AE 09102," Section XVII, 2, Box 166A, OTSG Files, OMH. William R. Addison, Selfless Service, a 50-Year History of Landstuhl Regional Medical Center (Landstuhl, Germany: Landstuhl Regional Medical Center, 2003), 151.

78. In 1995, the pilot test of Operation Backbone took place. At that time, CONUS backfill personnel deployed to Europe to take the place of U.S. Army, Europe, troops and units who deployed to Grafenwoehr, Germany, to participate in Exercise Mountain Eagle. Officials deemed the trial run "very successful." "Backfill Keeps Hospitals Open in Germany," *The Mercury* 23 (December 1995): 7. The 1996 iteration of Operation Backbone deployed USAR personnel to assume the fixed facility responsibilities of active component soldiers who deployed with tactical medical units to the Balkans. Harry Noyes, "New Reservists Go to Germany for Backfill," *The Mercury* 23 (May 1996): 1. Harry Noyes, "Reservists in Europe Fill Gaps While Hospital Staffers Deploy," *The Mercury* 24 (December 1996): 1. Bettye H. Simmons, "Professional Development and Readiness Guide," 3–14, 7 May 1997, ANCC, OMH. "Backfill Keeps Hospitals Open in Germany," *The Mercury* 23 (December 1995): 7. Harry Noyes, "New Reservists Go to Germany for Backfill," *The Mercury* 23 (May 1996): 1. Harry Noyes, "Reservists in Europe Fill Gaps While Hospital Staffers Deploy," *The Mercury* 24 (December 1996): 1.

79. The FST provides far forward surgical support for a brigade, 1,200 to 1,700 soldiers. It usually has a staff of 10 officers and 10 enlisted soldiers. Among the staff of 20 are three trauma surgeons, an orthopedic surgeon, two nurse anesthetists, an operating room nurse, one medical-surgical nurse, one critical care nurse, one field medical officer (MSC), four EMTs, three surgical technologists, and three practical nurses. It can be housed in a GP tent or a Deployable Ready Assembly Surgical Shelter (DRASH). As of 2003, the Active Army claimed 13 FSTs, while the Army Reserve had 23. Members of these units honed and maintained their skills at the Army Trauma Training Center at Jackson Memorial Hospital's Army Trauma Training Center in Miami, Florida. Charlotte Hough, Michael Sadler, and Patricia A. Patrician, "Military Nursing at the Forefront, The Army Forward Surgical Team," *Critical Care Nursing Clinics of North America* 15 (2003): 193–200. Harry K. Stinger and Robert M. Rush, "The Forward Surgical Team: The Army's Ultimate Lifesaving Force," *Infantry Magazine* 92 (Winter 2003): 11–13. John T. Greenwood and F. Clifton Berry, *Medics at War, Military Medicine from Colonial Times to the 21st Century* (Annapolis: Naval Institute Press, 2005), 172. "Forward Surgical Teams," http://www.armymedicine.army.mil/about/tl/95-factsfst.htm (accessed 2 September 2005). "801st Forward Surgical Team," http:// members.aol.com/rotkiv1/fst/ (accessed 2 September 2005).

80. Bettye H. Simmons, "Professional Development and Readiness Guide," 3-15, 3-16, 7 May 1997, ANCC, OMH.

81. Nancy Woolnough, "Panama," Memo from the Chief, Army Nurse Corps (May 1997): 10. Rose C. Engelman and Robert J.T. Joy, *Two Hundred Years of Military Medicine* (Fort Detrick, MD: USA MEDD Historical Unit, 1975), 15. Marie D. Gorgas and Burton J. Hendrick, *William Crawford Gorgas: His Life and Work* (Philadelphia: Lea and Febiger, 1924). John M. Gibson, *Physician to the World: The Life of General William C. Gorgas* (Durham, NC: Duke University Press, 1950).

82. Claudia M. Mundy, "The Challenge of Closure," *Journal of Nursing Administration* 23 (April 1993): 35–36. Nancy R. Adams, "Trip Report for Visit to the Annual Meeting of the American Association of Nurse Anesthetists (AANA) and to Letterman US Army Health Clinic, 16–19 August 1993," Memorandum for the Surgeon General, 10 September 1993; and Michael J. Brennan, "BRAC Lessons Learned," Memorandum for BG Adams, 18 August 1993 (both in ANCC, OMH).

83. The penalty incurred for not signing up for Medicare Part B when first eligible at age 65 was 10 percent for each 12-month period that the beneficiary could have had coverage but did not sign up for it. In the year 2000, the penalty would have been $546 for every year of noncoverage. "AUSA Resolution #C-8-01-1," 26 September 2000, ANCC, OMH. Claudia M. Mundy, "The Challenge of Closure," *Journal of Nursing Administration* 23 (April 1993): 35–36. Nancy R. Adams, "Trip Report for Visit to the Annual Meeting of the American Association of Nurse Anesthetists (AANA) and to Letterman US Army Health Clinic, 16–19 August 1993," Memorandum for the Surgeon General, 10 September 1993; and Michael J. Brennan, "BRAC Lessons Learned," Memorandum for BG Adams, 18 August 1993 (both in ANCC, OMH).

84. "Base Closure Plan, FAMC," Initial Draft, May 1995; and Leslie M. Burger, "Base Realignment and Closure (BRAC) Actions on Military Healthcare Delivery," Information Paper, n.d. (both in ANCC, OMH). Nicke Adde, "Fitzsimons Closing Brings on Sadness, Anger," *Army Times* 56 (24 June 1996): 18. "The MEDCOM," *The Mercury* (Fall 1996): 21.

85. Mike Buckley, "Closing Bases, Opening Doors," Soldiers 53 (November 1998): 16–20.

86. Melissa Knopper, "Trends in Health Care, Creature Comforts for Hospital Patients," *Clinician News* 8 (October 2004): 11–12.

87. Stephen C. Joseph, "Bosnia Deployment Tests DoD Training," *U.S. Medicine* 32 (January 1996): 8–10.

88. Michael J. Foster, "Minutes of the Army Nurse Corps Staff Meeting on 4 February 1993," Memorandum for Record, 2–3, 23 February 1993, ANCC, OMH.

89. Stephen E. Everett and L. Martin Kaplan, *Department of the Army Historical Summary Fiscal Year 1993* (Washington, DC: Center of Military History, United States Army, 2002), 100.

90. Susan McCall, "FORSCOM," Memo from the Chief, Army Nurse Corps (April 1994): 11, ANCC, OMH.

91. Susan McCall, "Forces Command," Memo from the Chief, Army Nurse Corps (August 1995): 18, ANCC, OMH.

92. "Posture Statement by Lieutenant General Ronald R. Blanck, The Surgeon General, United States Army, for the Appropriations Committee, United States Senate, 2nd Session, 105th Congress, Health Care," 2–3, 1 April 1998, ANCC, OMH.

93. "As the World Turns," Briefing Slides for Head Nurse Course, 1 February 1999, ANCC, OMH.

94. "Summary of Key Issues, Interview with BG Pocklington, 14 May 1994," TD, ANCC, OMH.

*Chapter Fifteen*
# Revamping the Medical Department and Army Nursing

Another consequence of the Base Realignment and Closure process was the overall restructuring of the Army Medical Department (AMEDD) that transpired in the 1990s. The Quicksilver downsizing initiative, a part of the 1990 Base Realignment and Closure plan, recommended the elimination of Health Services Command (HSC) and its replacement by a new Medical Major Command (MACOM) commanded by The Surgeon General (TSG). This would ultimately restore the TSG's authority lost during the HSC reorganization in the early 1970s and render it commensurate with the position's responsibilities. It would also centralize accountability for all health care delivery in the Army with TSG. Original plans called for co-locating the MACOM within the Office of The Surgeon General (OTSG) in the National Capital Region (NCR). This did not materialize. Given a recent political controversy about the construction and bed size of a new Brooke Army Medical Center in San Antonio, Texas, and the Texas congressional delegation's concerns, planners deemed it unwise to shift assets from Fort Sam Houston, Texas, at that time. Additionally, constraints limited assigning additional manpower and resources within the NCR.[1] The new MACOM, the U.S. Army Medical Command (MEDCOM), thus located its headquarters at Fort Sam Houston, Texas.

On 1 July 1991, the Army officially authorized the organization of the U.S. Army Medical Department Center and School (AMEDD C&S), formerly known as the Academy of Health Sciences, at Fort Sam Houston. This was the first phase of the MEDCOM's reorganization within the changing Army.[2] The AMEDD C&S was the AMEDD's schoolhouse and think tank. A combined staff and faculty of 1,800 manned the institution and provided education for 31,000 resident students enrolled annually in some 150 courses. Another 25,000 students participated in correspondence courses each year. The AMEDD C&S also developed military medical doctrine, supported research, and was responsible for AMEDD personnel proponency.[3]

By 1 October 1993 the reorganization plan for the Medical Command (Provisional), as approved by Department of the Army, was in progress. The fully activated command commenced operations on 2 October 1994 and featured more precise lines of authority, more realistic spans of control, and improved use of resources in relation to the previous structure and function of HSC. The surgeon general became the principal medical adviser to the chief of staff of the Army and commander of the MEDCOM. A smaller OTSG staff, Army Staff, in the NCR, and a MEDCOM in San Antonio served as Army medicine's center of gravity.[4] The MEDCOM had a strategic focus, while the Medical Treatment Facilities' (MTFs') approach was tactical. Functioning between the MEDCOM and the MTFs were seven medical regions, originally called Health Services Support Areas (HSSAs) but later designated Regional Medical Commands (RMCs) in July 1996.[5] The HSSAs/RMCs had an operational focus and managed readiness, supervised education and training, and coordinated all health care delivery operations within each geographical region. The HSSAs strove to integrate the assets of the reserve components "into a seamless, combat-ready force." Since 70 percent of the AMEDD's assets were in the U.S. Army Reserve or the Army National Guard, this initiative allayed some of the readiness concerns that had surfaced during Operation Desert Storm.[6]

Army Nurse Corps officers held various staff positions in the HSSAs and added their unique clinical nursing perspective. Medical Center chief nurses typically served as chief nurses of the HSSAs and advised on the assignments of Army nurses to the HSSA, usually in the areas of coordinated care, education and training, and resource management, or wherever the HSSA need or health care mission dictated.[7] By 1 December 1993, seven HSSAs were operational at each of the seven Medical Centers.[8] By 1996 the RMCs were headquartered at Brooke, Eisenhower, Madigan, Tripler, Landstuhl, Beaumont, and Walter Reed Army Medical Centers.[9] The HSSAs or RMCs were Major Subordinate Commands of the MEDCOM along with the AMEDD C&S, the Dental and Veterinary Commands, and the Army Environmental Hygiene Agency, which became the U.S. Army Center for Health Promotion and Preventive Medicine in 1994 with responsibility for force health protection—physical fitness, health promotion, and preventive medicine.[10] The Medical Research and Materiel Command was another Major Subordinate Command. It subsumed the former Medical Research and Development Command and field operating activities whose functions were the development and acquisition of supplies and equipment, health facility planning, informatics, and the production and distribution of medical materiel. Table of Organization and Equipment and overseas units were also included under the MACOM.[11]

To enhance planning and review, refine the concept plan, and implement the transition of the proposed reorganization, Lieutenant General Alcide M. LaNoue established Task Force Aesculapius (TFA) in 1992 as one of his first objectives as surgeon general.[12] [Note: Aesculapius was a Greek god of medicine; his staff with a snake entwined around it is a symbol of the medical profession.] TSG directed the group to redesign the AMEDD's mission, function, and structures "into a streamlined, flattened organization" to support its strategic mission. LaNoue also instructed TFA to prepare an implementation plan for the proposed transformation. TFA's guiding principles were to draft the organizational design with clear accountability linked with authority, have the right people implementing the proper tasks at the appropriate level, and avoid duplication and redundancy. The basis for the TFA effort was Elliott Jacques' untested theory, "requisite organization," that advanced the notion that organizational structure transcends personalities within a corporation, and a detailed focus on precise roles and responsibilities yields greater employee satisfaction and efficiency.[13]

The TFA process, however, often was difficult and represented some of the most challenging days within OTSG. TSG's mandate to avoid parochialism and the omnipresent need by individual corps representatives to strongly support the reorganization yet preserve their roles were countervailing forces that resulted in considerable acrimony among the task force members. The conflict contributed to some of the flawed TFA recommendations.

The group arrived at a number of puzzling conclusions whose implementation fundamentally changed the structure and function of the AMEDD and whose cost/benefit ratio seemed skewed. The unintended consequences of the changes were not always predominantly constructive. For instance, a TFA decision obliterated the Consultants' Division in OTSG, in which the Army Nurse Corps chief consultant was a key player with a strong voice, and replaced it with the Clinical Policy Division with minimal if any nurse input. Like her predecessors, the last chief nurse consultant, Colonel Bonnie Jennings, studied and often resolved a number of wide-ranging concerns with implications for nursing and improved patient care, such as case management, female hygiene during deployment, epidural analgesia for all deliveries, and anesthesiologist/anesthetist practice issues. When the chief nurse consultant position disappeared, resolution of such matters was undermined. Thereafter, "decisions were made [without] the input of nurses that had huge ramifications for nursing and patient care. The clinical voice of nursing was weakened."[14]

Another aftereffect emerged with the elimination of the chief nurse consultant position. The central figure to coordinate nursing innovations and a vital repository for ideas ceased to exist and function.[15] Previously, the Army Nurse Corps consultant had clinical oversight AMEDD-wide. Various Army MTFs transmitted new and successful ideas to the consultant, who investigated them and, if they proved valid and worthwhile, promulgated the information to Army facilities around the globe. After TFA recommendations were implemented and the "hub of the clinical wheel" disappeared, high-quality nursing practice in the Army became less homogeneous and standardized.[16] The negative effects of eliminating the chief nurse consultant position outweighed its cost-saving advantages. Although organizational efficiency and economy may have been enhanced, quality suffered in the long run.

Major General Girard Seitter originally led the TFA group.[17] After his retirement, Colonel Stephen Xenakis succeeded Seitter and then Brigadier General

Russ Zajchuk led the group.[18] Colonel Mary Messerschmidt served as the Army Nurse Corps representative on TFA.[19]

As an integral component of the AMEDD, the Army Nurse Corps was a target for restructuring. Various plans proposed numerous organizational modifications, some of which were implemented. The intent of the proposed changes was to provide leadership experience to develop Army Nurse Corps officers' aptitude for future command and branch immaterial positions. An early proposal would have located the chief of the Army Nurse Corps away from the Washington, D.C., area. In 1992, an abortive plan surfaced to name the Army Nurse Corps chief as the deputy commandant at the AMEDD C&S in Texas. General Nancy Adams disagreed with this proposal because such a move would leave nursing in an obscure organizational element, diminish the effectiveness of the chief of the Corps, and disenfranchise the chief from health care's national policy-making levels. She added that such action ran counter to the congressionally encouraged movement toward jointness, or interservice collaboration, by hampering interface with the other military nurse corps chiefs whose positions were firmly entrenched in the NCR. Removing the Army Nurse Corps chief to Texas would also physically distance the Army Nurse Corps from the civilian professional organizations, most of which had offices in the Washington, D.C., metropolitan area. Surgeon general, LaNoue, accepted Adams' analysis and instead assigned another AMEDD general officer to the AMEDD C&S position.

At the same time, Adams also recommended that the Army Nurse Corps general officer serve as an assistant surgeon general for nursing, directly under the authority of the surgeon general. This would ensure that nursing remained identified as a separate functional element rather than one subsumed within other organizational entities. The position would call attention to nursing's vital organizational role in readiness, team building, and customer advocacy as well as allow availability for future additional functional roles for the Army Nurse Corps general officer.[20] The surgeon general approved this initiative in December 1992. By that time Adams wore three hats: (1) chief of the Army Nurse Corps, (2) assistant surgeon general for nursing, and (3) director of AMEDD Personnel.[21] This multifaceted role expansion was consistent with the AMEDD's changing vision of corps chiefs' responsibilities. By the 1990s, corps chiefs were increasingly assuming noncorps-specific corporate-level responsibilities while delegating the day-to-day operational management of their corps to their assistants at the colonel level.[22]

General Clara L. Adams-Ender observed that the corps chiefs' roles also were changing as a consequence of the reduction in the overall force that included a corresponding drop in the total number of general officers. The chief of staff of the Army directed that a general officer's functions, duties, and responsibilities "be in an operational position and not a personnel position like Chief of a Corps." Adams-Ender added that the line Army had functioned "this way for years because they had no specifically designated branch Chief positions in the law."[23]

In 1993, the surgeon general asked Adams to build the prototype HSSA, or the first region in his massive restructuring plan at Fitzsimons Army Medical Center.

She would then assume command of the Fitzsimons HSSA. Adams noted the limitations in this assignment, believing that in order to command the HSSA, she also needed to command the Fitzsimons Army Medical Center installation. Without this latter responsibility, Adams felt she would not establish command identity or credibility but would merely serve as a resource manager in a coordination/integration capacity that did not intrinsically reflect command authority. Additionally, General Gordon Sullivan did not approve this assignment for Adams, basing his decision on the notion that the AMEDD had not provided proper leader development for her to assume this command. Thus, a second plan to relocate the chief of the Army Nurse Corps away from the NCR did not come to fruition. Although Adams was not in favor of the HSSA assignment, she confided that she momentarily did regret the lost opportunity to command. However, she was consoled by the realization that in her existing tripartite role, she had ample opportunity to participate in the mainstream of AMEDD business and incorporate the agenda of the Army Nurse Corps into the transcending framework of the AMEDD.[24]

Adams' opportunity to command materialized in the summer of 1994, when she became the commander of the U.S. Army Center for Health Promotion and Preventive Medicine at Edgewood Arsenal, Maryland.[25] The function of this new command was to integrate health promotion and preventive medicine (a vital component of a trained and ready Army) with the existing environmental and occupational health responsibilities of the Army Environmental Hygiene Agency that it replaced.[26] Sullivan would not allow Adams to relocate to Edgewood Arsenal, so she commuted from the Washington, D.C., area one to two days weekly to do her U.S. Army Center for Health Promotion and Preventive Medicine work.[27]

Other changes related to the major AMEDD reorganization continued within the Office of the Chief of the Army Nurse Corps. By 1995, plans specified that the chief of the Army Nurse Corps would no longer be the assistant surgeon general for nursing but instead become an Army Staff general officer. The assistant chief of the Army Nurse Corps then became the assistant to TSG for nursing and served as the primary staff officer for all Army nurse operations at the corporate level. The Corps converted the Army Nurse Corps management fellow position into a nurse staff officer and eliminated the nurse consultant position, along with its responsibilities for multiple practice and patient care issues and its interface with the Department of Defense (DoD) and professional organizations. The Army Nurse Corps decentralized the consultant's functions to other elements such as the Army Staff, nursing subspecialty consultants, and quality assurance at the MEDCOM. Other OTSG nurse staff officer positions transferred to the MACOM, AMEDD C&S, Personnel Command, Forces Command, and the U.S. Army Recruiting Command.[28] Plans also called for eliminating the slots for Army Nurse Corps officers who dealt with community health nursing, drug and alcohol issues, coordinated care, manpower, and quality assurance within OTSG. The Army Nurse Corps procurement position consolidated with the U.S. Army Recruiting Command at Fort Knox, Kentucky. The Nursing Education Branch moved to the AMEDD C&S, and two Health Education and Training Division positions shifted to Personnel Command in the Hoffman Building in Alexandria, Virginia.[29]

Nursing elements within HSC/MEDCOM also changed with the Army significantly reducing authorizations and assignments. The new organization, the MEDCOM, no longer showed a Nursing Division. In the spring of 1994, Colonel Bettye Simmons transitioned from being the chief of the Nursing Division into the new role of chief nurse, Clinical Operations Directorate, MEDCOM.[30] Several other positions disappeared with the reorganization from HSC to MEDCOM. The nurse staff officer and the Army nurses assigned to ambulatory care and the inspector general positions vanished from the organizational chart.[31]

The downsizing of the Army Nurse Corps and shrinking health care dollar left the organization of a number of MTFs along with their nursing elements in a state of flux. Departments of nursing at Moncrief Army Community Hospital (MACH) at Fort Jackson, South Carolina; General Leonard Wood Army Community Hospital at Fort Leonard Wood, Missouri; Munson Army Community Hospital at Fort Leavenworth, Kansas; Evans Army Community Hospital at Fort Carson, Colorado; and Ireland Community Hospital at Fort Knox, Kentucky, were undergoing change.[32] The organizational paradigm shift at MACH, for example, aimed to set up a matrix organization made up of three teams (Medicine, Nursing, and Administration) that would function with organizational parity in a flexible hierarchy.

With this framework, HSC approved a one-year pilot test beginning in May 1992 for MACH to reorganize its Department of Nursing. The concept envisaged the senior Army Nurse Corps officer without the title of chief nurse but instead claiming the position of the deputy commander for nursing, which later evolved into the deputy commander for hospital services, with authority and responsibility for all nursing activities, all hospital education and training, and hospital quality management.[33] The change refocused the role of the chief nurse from inward-looking departmental parochialism to an orientation encompassing the entire command and exemplified the trend of preparing selected Army Nurse Corps officers for future command and branch immaterial responsibilities. With this change came a metamorphosis for the assistant chief nurse (or chief, nursing administration, days), whose title became chief, Department of Nursing.

Other organizational changes at MACH eliminated the chief, Ambulatory Care Nursing Service, and the assistant chief wardmaster positions and substituted the chief, nursing administration for evenings and nights, position with a newly conceptualized role, the senior charge nurse on evenings and nights. The senior charge nurse performed clinical duties on a nursing unit when not carrying out supervisory responsibilities, such as resolving staffing issues, providing staff relief, furnishing emergency response, completing reports and administrative rounds, evaluating patient care, and resolving equipment and supply issues.

MACH plans also consolidated the chief positions for Medical Nursing and Surgical Nursing, eliminating the role of the special projects officer and changing the title of the clinical head nurse to unit nurse manager, which, it was thought, more accurately portrayed the job's responsibilities and levels of accountability. MACH nurses also established a Same Day Surgery Unit or Ambulatory Surgery

Unit that by September 1993 accounted for 54 percent of all surgical cases. Six nurse case managers were on staff by September 1993, and they developed their positional job descriptions; collected workload data on parameters such as cost abatement, length of stay, and readmissions; and created critical clinical pathways for procedures and diagnoses such as mastectomy, prostatectomy, bowel resection, reactive airway disease, and chest pain.

All the nursing staff practicing in the ambulatory setting were realigned from the Department of Nursing to positions under the chiefs of the departments under which they served—Medicine, Surgery, or Primary Care. Originators of the plan expected this change would enhance accountability, better define leadership responsibilities, and facilitate the implementation of coordinated care. It placed physicians in the nurses' rating chains, however, creating a need to educate the Medical Corps officers about performance evaluation procedures and priorities. Furthermore, it violated the long-standing principle that only a senior Army Nurse Corps officer should evaluate nurses' performance.

To evaluate the efficacy of the reorganization, the staff at MACH scrutinized productivity measures, including workload, cost, contract, and overtime data. It also considered risk management variables such as patient falls and medication errors. Findings revealed that personnel utilization was more consistent with workload and acuity demands. Moreover, many administrative nursing positions shifted to the hands-on clinical area. The architects of the plan viewed this flattening of the hierarchy as an auspicious change, but in fact, little improvement occurred in operating costs, and the manpower requirements remained unchanged. Similarly, numbers of unusual occurrences and patient complaints/concerns remained relatively stable.[34]

The team that implemented the restructuring saw the benefits of the new configuration in improved access to care, better staff development, more efficient management of patient care, the integration of Army nurses into multidisciplinary leadership roles, and more efficient actualization of case management. They identified lessons learned, including the need to implement the new structure in a series of carefully considered steps, evaluate outcomes sequentially before implementing further change, and mitigate title confusion.[35]

When Major General Richard Cameron, the commander of HSC, deputized the HSC Inspector General Team to evaluate the ongoing reorganization in MTFs—all based on patterns similar to MACH—their study uncovered similar pitfalls. The team found less-than-ideal communication patterns throughout the systems that caused "a high level of patient misunderstanding and staff aggravation." Cameron added that the absence of precedents for transformations intensified difficulties encountered in integrating the changes, as planners were navigating previously uncharted waters. Resistance to change was significant and the temptation to continue business as usual was widespread. Nonetheless, the accrued benefits seemed to outweigh the attendant problems. Cameron concluded that the overall advantages of the restructuring were twofold, specifically an expanded patient focus and a greater empowerment of those who delivered patient care.[36]

The senior leaders of the Army Nurse Corps expressed reservations about the remodeling of departments of nursing within certain MTFs' organizational structures as well. Adams echoed the thoughts of a visionary, Dr. Tim Porter-O'Grady, who predicted that nursing would not survive as a profession if its members did not soon publicly acknowledge and more authentically convey nursing values.[37] Adams reiterated his misgivings, emphasizing that, with the new organizational configurations, nurse leaders may have abdicated their allegiance and obligations to professional nursing to gain new, more impressive titles and widen the scope of their management duties. As a consequence, she cautioned, patient care could suffer. Adams warned that nurses should function as nurses and the patient care role should trump organizational roles. Colonel Terris Kennedy also succinctly advanced a parallel notion, remarking that Army nurses must not lose sight of what it is they do and who they are.

Doubtless referring to the notion of assigning nurses working in the ambulatory environment to the aegis of medical departments, Adams reaffirmed her stance that the medical model was not an appropriate paradigm to guide nursing practice and patient care responsibilities and reasoned that the traditional "nursing structure should not be replaced and subsumed by a medical organization (e.g., pediatric service, medical team, surgical team, etc.)."[38] Within a few years, however, this concept of aligning multidisciplinary teams along product lines that transcended the boundaries of inpatient and ambulatory settings of the organization became an accepted norm throughout the AMEDD.[39] A key difference with the product line model was that it provided nurses with the opportunity to be in charge, in contrast to multidisciplinary teams who previously had assumed the physician was in charge.[40] Similar patterns of change, revamping, and reorganization also surfaced in the civilian practice realms.

Despite rapid and sometimes chaotic change, the shift of patient workload from the inpatient to the ambulatory setting, the substantial cuts in numbers of nurses, and the painfully tightened fiscal resources, Army Nurse Corps officers found creative solutions to unprecedented challenges in whatever setting they practiced.

In a 1994 study that looked at the utilization of registered nurses in the ambulatory setting, investigators Colonel Carol Reineck, Lieutenant Colonel Donna Wright, and Captain Sheila Jones found that the nurses they polled were fulfilling some 17 roles, predominantly nontraditional for the AMEDD, at 10 selected MTFs. The most frequently cited positions were in the workplace setting of the Same Day Surgery Unit and Pre-Admission Unit. Other commonly reported roles among the 17, some unprecedented, some long-established, were as clinical case managers, coordinated care nurse, health care advisor, automation nurse, patient educator, and nurse researcher. A few nurses also were serving as project officers for new hospital construction, Joint Commission for the Accreditation of Healthcare Organizations preparation, with the Composite Health Care System, as a bed control manager or a third-party collection agent.[41] These nurses were fulfilling progressive roles in a variety of cutting-edge programs. Their assignments were another expression of the expanding boundaries that defined nursing, and they served as leadership development activities and preparation for future branch immaterial roles.

Around the same time, as the locus of care shifted from the acute facility to the ambulatory setting, the Army Nurse Corps initiated a Primary Care Demonstration Project to support health care delivery and to pinpoint the Army Nurse Corps personnel requirements needed for the approaching transformations expected to emerge with the new AMEDD health care delivery model. The program featured a redistribution of Army nurses from inpatient to outpatient roles, thereby preserving Army Nurse Corps authorizations that had been predicted to disappear with the anticipated dwindling numbers of hospitalized patients. Primary care teams comprising a primary care physician and a nurse practitioner or physician assistant would meet the expected increased demand for primary health care at selected installations, such as Fort Belvoir, Virginia; Fort Bragg, North Carolina; and Fort Lewis, Washington.[42] A subsidiary study in part justified the new model, concluding that the physician, nurse practitioner, or physician assistant provider team combination was efficient. The investigation also revealed that all three categories of providers merged into an effective team capable of providing quality adult, non-obstetrical primary care. Patient outcomes were not adversely affected. Moreover, the model's use of lower-priced nurse practitioners and physician assistants cut expenses and was more cost effective when compared with an all-physician-provider arrangement.[43] Army Nurse Corps leaders judged that the use of a multidisciplinary primary care team resulted in better patient access to services, greater cost efficiency, preservation of quality care, and improved patient satisfaction.[44]

In 1989, the Department of Nursing at Tripler Army Medical Center (TAMC) in Honolulu, Hawaii, proposed a novel demonstration program and subsequently secured a total of $7.5 million in congressional appropriations for fiscal years 1990 to 1995 to underwrite what was termed the Nursing Productivity Study. The study's purpose was to test the belief that the augmentation of nursing staff with ancillary personnel would result in improved nursing productivity and job satisfaction and ultimately would enhance patient care. The proposal called for hiring escorts/couriers, custodial workers, supply clerks, ward clerks, dietary aides, and phlebotomists to do non-nursing tasks previously performed by nurses and, in theory, increase the amount of time professional nurses spend with patients.

Numerous difficulties and unanticipated variables plagued the study from its inception. Staff turbulence during Operation Desert Shield/Operation Desert Storm interfered with the progress of the study. A DoD hiring freeze thwarted the planned employment of ancillary staff. The simultaneous introduction of the Composite Health Care System, an automated patient health data system, at TAMC skewed the findings. With time, the researchers identified basic flaws in the study design. As the study progressed, the investigators consequently revamped the methodology, outcome variables, and study sample to improve the project's scientific merit and organizational relevance. All these circumstances profoundly invalidated the study outcomes.

The addition of the ancillary workers, however, did demonstrate that nurses had more time available to spend in direct contact with patients. A January 1990 pre-investigation baseline tabulated nurses spending 62.2 percent of their time with patients. By January 1991, with the supplementation of ancillary workers, that statistic increased to 75.5 percent. When the study concluded in 1995, nurses' contact time with patients had increased by some 12 percent.[45]

Another TAMC endeavor with more favorable outcomes was the Ambulatory Care Clinic, later called the Specialized Nursing Care Center. Among the first of its kind in the military health care system, the Ambulatory Care Clinic was established in 1991 as a multidisciplinary-staffed, nurse-managed unit that offered an alternative for selected patients who formerly would have required a hospital admission. The Ambulatory Care Clinic had virtually no patient waiting time and operated beyond normal duty hours seven days a week, making it convenient for patient access after work or school. It offered services on an outpatient basis that had previously been restricted to an inpatient venue, such as hydration, blood transfusions, chemotherapy, antibiotics administration, wound care, dressing changes, patient education, observation after selected procedures, and Pain Clinic support.[46] The clinic avoided more than 900 expensive inpatient bed days and served approximately 600 patients each month in 1994. The next year, the Specialized Nursing Care Center was supporting more than 650 patients monthly, with bed costs of $2.7 million averted that year. The Specialized Nursing Care Center recaptured $36,000 in health insurance reimbursements from civilian third-party payers during fiscal year 1995. This cost-effective, collaborative, customer-oriented effort resulted in better quality care and enhanced patient and staff satisfaction.[47]

The TAMC Pre-Admission Unit (PAU) was another cost-sparing, quality-enhancing, access-improving, nurse-managed initiative that opened its doors in 1992 as a collaborative effort of the TAMC departments of Nursing and Surgery. It had three components. The first, the preadmission multidisciplinary conference, screened all potential PAU patients and coordinated all pre-operative documentation and diagnostic procedures for all preadmission surgical patients with a one-stop customer service approach. The second, the Ambulatory Surgery Center (ASC), eliminated the need for hospitalization before and after minor surgery. Patients who took advantage of this service reported to the ASC on the day of their procedure, subsequently went to the operating and recovery rooms, then returned to the ASC for a further brief recovery period, and finally went home with an escort, all on the same day. The ASC saved a minimum of two occupied bed days, the pre- and post-operative days. The Same Day Admission Unit was the third component of the PAU. Planners designed it for patients who could be admitted on the day of surgery but required post-operative hospitalization. These patients were admitted to the Same Day Admission Unit and went that same day to the operating and the recovery rooms. Once cleared from the recovery room, they spent the requisite time on the inpatient nursing unit and at least one day later were discharged home. This option saved one occupied bed day, the day before surgery.

The PAU's nursing staff made post-operative follow-up contact by telephone with 98 percent of all patients who participated in the PAU's programs, completing the care cycle and contributing to a trouble-free convalescence.

The PAU exerted a positive effect on staff and patient satisfaction. Of all patients scheduled for surgical procedures at TAMC, 84 percent used some aspect of PAU services. The PAU also reduced waiting time for surgery by 55 percent, resulting in improved patient satisfaction and better access to care. The PAU's efficiency meant fewer cancellations of surgical procedures as a result of patient noncompliance. The PAU netted an impressive cost avoidance of more than $18 million in its first 30 months of operation.[48]

In 1991, the command group at Bassett Army Community Hospital (BACH) at Fort Wainwright, Alaska, inaugurated a Certified Nurse Midwives Service. The Army Nurse Corps promptly assigned two Certified Nurse Midwives (CNMWs) to BACH. These two officers provided nearly all routine antenatal and postpartum care, presided over approximately 50 percent of normal labor and delivery cases, and served as first assistants at caesarean sections. They established a well-woman clinic that met during evening hours and set up a nurse-led perinatal bereavement support group to provide counseling and follow-up care for patients and families who experienced the devastation of pregnancy loss. With this comprehensive level of support, medical officers were free to offer specialty consultation and concentrate on complex gynecological surgery. These measures resulted in significant paring of costs, expanded access to care, and enhanced quality of care. Annual cost avoidance generated by the Certified Nurse Midwives Service, for example, totaled $800,000. Surveys confirmed that the increased patient satisfaction was attributable to the care provided by CNMWs at BACH. Among other benefits accrued from the introduction of CNMWs at BACH was the improved level of maternal/child health in Alaska. The CNMWs sponsored and presented lectures for annual conferences in the community's civilian hospital and in a statewide midwifery conference. They provided obstetrical instruction in the interior of Alaska and furnished clinical mentoring for nurse midwifery students enrolled in an educational program affiliated with the Frontier Nursing Service and Case Western Reserve University.[49] The introduction of CNMWs at BACH was a noteworthy contribution not only to the welfare of the command's beneficiaries but also for prenatal health across the state.

The CNMWs and Women's Health Nurse Practitioners (WHNPs) at Blanchfield Army Community Hospital answered the call to broaden their existing range of ambulatory services by expanding their practice at Fort Campbell, Kentucky. They used two approaches, the Daily Walk-In Clinic and its subsidiary, the Active Duty Pap Program, to achieve their objectives. Each duty day, one assigned CNMW or WHNP conducted the Daily Walk-In Clinic and provided care for about 15 to 20 prenatal or postnatal patients with various health needs involving urinary, respiratory, neurological, musculoskeletal, or gastrointestinal problems, or other issues associated with pregnancy, and that needed to be addressed before the patient's next routine obstetrics/gynecology appointment. As patients arrived at the clinic, receptionists inserted their charts in a box affixed to the nurse's door. On a very busy day, when many patients came to the clinic and the chart box was full, records were piled on a cart outside the nurse's door. This state of affairs became known as the "cart sign" and was the signal for all available CNMWs and WHNPs to assist with patients. One of the CNMWs noted that the positive spirit of teamwork unified the staff and improved the morale of both staff and patients. The Daily Walk-In Clinic also eased the workload in the hospital emergency department and provided patients with a more appropriate venue for dealing with their health concerns. The Active Duty Pap Program was another feature of the Daily Walk-In Clinic. Every active duty female soldier signing into Fort Campbell processed through a specified Troop Medical Clinic. One aspect of the process was a health record screen to verify the existence of a normal Pap smear within the past six months. If the soldier had no such documentation, the Troop Medical Clinic personnel referred the female soldier to the Daily Walk-In Clinic for assessment. This type of referral also provided the CNMW or WHNP with a timely opportunity to offer the female soldiers health education on contraception, disease prevention, and health promotion.[50]

Military nurses assigned to Landstuhl Regional Medical Center in Landstuhl, Germany, launched several innovations to improve quality of care, facilitate optimal functioning despite a more stringent budget, and expand access to care. They established a voluntary Mother/Baby Early Discharge Program in January 1995 that usually allowed the earlier hospital discharge of 41 percent of all patients from 24 to 48 hours after delivery. An Air Force nurse who was a perinatal clinical nurse specialist served as this program's case manager and educated expectant mothers, beginning at 34 weeks of gestation, on infant and postpartum care. This anticipatory guidance better prepared expectant families for impending labor and delivery and approaching parenthood. It doubtless eased prenatal fears and anxiety. The case manager routinely contacted new mothers one day after discharge to answer queries, gauge the family's state of well-being, and coordinate a pediatric follow-up for the infant at three days of age. Program evaluations revealed that the staff liked the concept, patient satisfaction exceeded 99 percent, and the small number of infant readmissions and emergency department visits affirmed the protocol's success. After a year, the program's estimated savings generated by reduced inpatient bed costs approached $750,000.

The Landstuhl nurses also began a Preadmission Clinic in January 1995. The clinic's two staff nurses and four paraprofessionals completed all preliminary diagnostic work required for patients scheduled for surgery, implemented preoperative teaching, and processed patients for admission through the Patient Administration Division. Nurse anesthetists also completed their pre-operative assessments in this setting. In its first year of operation, the Preadmission Clinic served 3,264 patients and avoided the expenditure of almost $4.4 million.[51]

Nurses serving in the Walter Reed Health Care System implemented innovative approaches in response to changing circumstances.[52] They opened an Ambulatory Procedure and Processing Center in January 1996 that provided preadmission services, day of surgery in-processing, and short-term recovery from conscious sedation. The Ambulatory Procedure and Processing Center coordinated with 18 in-house and two outlying clinics. By July 1997, Kimbrough Ambulatory Care Center at Fort Meade, Maryland, became the product line manager for same day surgeries in the Walter Reed Health Care System. The staff at Kimbrough Ambulatory Care Center streamlined the admission process; coordinated with pharmacy, laboratory, radiology and PAD services; cross-trained nursing personnel to improve effectiveness; simplified documentation; and developed a system for patient follow-up. Surgeons and staff members were highly satisfied with the program and, more important, patients rated the care they received as efficient, personalized, professional, and caring.

The Walter Reed Army Medical Center (WRAMC) nurses also established a Limb Preservation Clinic to aid patients with peripheral vascular disease or other conditions that threatened their extremities' viability. Based in part on the premise that reducing hospitalizations saved on operating costs, the clinic staff aimed to preserve the health of this population, maintain them as outpatients, and decrease the likelihood of complications that could lead to amputation. The goal of the resourceful, nurse-run Well Watch Clinic at WRAMC was to improve the accessibility of health services and to encourage cost avoidance through patient education and early detection of disease. The clinic furnished preventive health and clinical services such as patient's immunization review, health risk appraisal, health counseling by nurses, and self-help resources.[53]

At Madigan Army Medical Center (MAMC) in Tacoma, Washington, nurses played key roles in a unique, collaborative, interdisciplinary approach that centered around the patient rather than on the provider of services. This perspective led to improved patient outcomes and decreased costs by avoiding hospitalizations. MAMC Dialysis Unit physicians, nurses, and technicians offered an outpatient infusion service, administering blood products, antibiotics, and selected other medications to other than dialysis patients who in the past would have required hospital admission.

In another model endeavor, a nurse practitioner had charge of the multidisciplinary MAMC Congestive Heart Failure Clinic. This clinic focused on about 35 high-risk Congestive Heart Failure patients, all of whom had a history of repeated admissions with heart failure. Jennings, the MAMC assistant chief nurse, reported that—as a result of the clinic's aggressive approach—the patients' health status and quality of life were significantly improved and hospitalizations prevented.[54]

In the summer of 1997, nurse practitioners assigned to General Leonard Wood Army Community Hospital at Fort Leonard Wood, Missouri, established and managed a Health Promotion Clinic. Two nurse practitioners, a pharmacist, and a dietician managed a group of patients with diagnoses like diabetes, hypertension, or hyperlipidemia, and others on anticoagulant therapy. The generous appointment time of 30 to 45 minutes furnished the staff with the opportunity to reduce the complications resulting from these conditions. In its first six months of operation, the clinic cared for about 300 patients. Annually reviewed protocols guided the staff's practice, while a medical officer reviewed about 10 percent of all charts for quality assurance. The Health Promotion Clinic was a subunit of the Health Promotion Center, an educational/marketing endeavor that offered classes and services on a variety of health issues such as self-care, stress management, smoking cessation, weight management, and back pain.[55] These strategies were an expression of the Army's emphasis on preventing disease and promoting health, designing initiatives to enhance quality of life, improving readiness, and saving fiscal and personnel resources.

In the early 1990s, the AMEDD encouraged multidisciplinary clinical case management in MTFs to support the provision of cost-effective, quality care. In the clinical aspect of managed care, nurse case managers dealt with high-risk, high-volume, or high-cost groups of patients to achieve optimal outcomes. The clinical case managers devised critical pathways (protocols with timelines or yardsticks to measure patient progress) that delineated intermediate goals for patients whose course of recovery was predictable. The critical pathway outlined steps as the patient progressed from a certain condition, procedure, or diagnosis along the road to regaining health and the best possible function. Variance analysis was another component of the AMEDD's clinical case management. This process involved identifying patients who failed to meet recuperation goals at predicted times and were possible candidates for individual case management. Case managers used this rigorous approach when a patient's course was unpredictable and complicated. An expert nurse case manager worked with other health care team members, the patient, and/or the family to assess, educate, plan, coordinate, and often deliver suitable care across the care continuum from hospitalization to ambulatory, outpatient status. Often the case manager made referrals when the patient relocated. The final phase of clinical case management evaluated predetermined goals such as better patient outcomes, improved quality, wider access, and/or reduced costs.[56]

By 1997, at least nine MTFs were actively using case management for high volume or long length-of-stay patients to avoid repeated hospitalizations and to contain costs. Their achievements were impressive. At Walter Reed Army Medical Center (WRAMC), the case management of four conditions, including percutaneous cardiovascular procedures, circulatory disorders, back and neck procedures, and medical back problems, led to $800,000 in cost avoidance by reducing bed days and disposition rates. At Keller Army Community Hospital at the U.S. Military Academy at West Point, New York, case management netted $12,000 in cost savings and $22,000 in cost avoidance. Both the WRAMC and the Keller Army Community Hospital cost avoidance strategies took place from 1995 through 1997. Of greater significance, however, were its other benefits. Patients enthusiastically endorsed the case management system and reported fewer complications as the intensity of required services plummeted.[57]

A new concept in the 1990s, telenursing was a convenient system that relied on two-way video technology. A personal computer and a camera in the patient's home allowed the nurse to both see and communicate with a patient without the nurse's leaving the health provider's office. Telenursing facilitated greater patient access to health care, with features such as network chat, e-mail capability, and Internet access, as well as the visual/audio visits on 24-hour basis. In Hawaii, community health nurses at TAMC used the technology to decrease the potential for child abuse and neglect in combination with the DoD sponsored program, A Solid Parenting Experience Through Community Teaching and Support (ASPECTS). Telenursing augmented the existing ASPECTS Army Community Health Nurse home visitation program by adding two additional telehealth visits each month. Simultaneously, the program staff implemented a research project to measure the effects of the intervention. The study verified that the one-on-one support and surveillance provided by the ASPECTS and telenursing programs reduced the incidence of child maltreatment within the targeted high-risk population. The intervention also significantly increased new mothers' ego strengths and decreased their feelings of loneliness, rigidity, and unhappiness. It also reduced family problems. Other serendipitous outcomes were an increase in immunization rates, more appropriate access of services, and more patient interest and input into personal health care decisions.[58]

Nurses at Eisenhower Army Medical Center at Fort Gordon, Georgia, established a similar program. They relied on a comparable interactive network to assess patients who were at high risk for post-hospitalization complications and subsequent readmission to the hospital. In its first year, the program made more than 200 telenursing visits to more than two dozen patients. DoD, the Medical College of Georgia, Eisenhower Army Medical Center, and the Georgia Institute of Technology funded the endeavor.[59] Both programs saved a significant amount of staff time and spared health care funding while they notably improved patient outcomes. The use of telenursing technology spread to other MTFs.

Although not totally unprecedented, the joint staffing of a single MTF with multiservice personnel had been a rare event. In the 1990s, however, as military installations closed or realigned and DoD's managed care program, TRICARE, became the prevailing delivery model, the Assistant Secretary of Defense (Health Affairs) Stephen C. Joseph ordered the pooling of personnel resources in settings where two or more military services were closely situated.[60]

DoD previously implemented interservice collaboration in health care facilities at Fort Dix, New Jersey; and Charleston, South Carolina; and, according to Joseph, these first illustrations of joint operations set an example and furnished the services with the chance to grow and interact with other service personnel to improve health care delivery in those locales.[61] By 1995, the shared personnel initiatives had spread to TAMC, where Army, Air Force, and Navy nurses all had staffing responsibilities. TAMC also integrated Veterans Administration (VA) patients into its care network, allocating 10 of its 15 psychiatric beds to VA patients. The VA also built and began operation of an ambulatory care center, administrative offices, a parking garage, and a long-term care facility on the TAMC grounds. In 1997, the VA paid TAMC $9.5 million for space and services rendered. With the partnership, VA patients enjoyed greater access to care, and both TAMC and the VA profited as a result of the greater education and research opportunities.[62]

Certain aspects of military health care in the NCR also became joint efforts.

In 1993, Assistant Secretary of Defense (Health Affairs) Edward Martin issued a memo instructing all MTFs in the NCR to integrate their Graduate Medical Education and specialty services and eliminate duplication of programs. As a result, the National Capital Military Medical Education Consortium formed to make and implement plans. It recommended that the NNMC in Bethesda, Maryland, take on the area's military maternal-child mission with joint Navy and Army staffing. In a complementary move, WRAMC was to employ a joint Army/Navy staff to care for hospitalized adult psychiatric patients, while the Malcolm Grow Medical Center at Andrews Air Force Base was to accept the Alcohol and Drug Abuse Prevention and Control Program mission. The various MTFs implemented these recommendations. For a while, the NNMC operated an adolescent psychiatric unit but it proved to be cost prohibitive and Navy officials closed the program.

There were adjustment issues with the integration, many of which stemmed from the cultural and organizational differences that existed among the services. For instance, when mobilizing, the Navy Medical Department traditionally eliminated peacetime health care services to family members and retirees completely and referred all such patients to civilian sources of care, while the AMEDD continued to carry out both their peacetime and wartime missions with virtually no interruption. Also unlike the Army, the Navy did not have military companies for command and control of military members. The Navy instead decentralized this function in many instances to the head nurses who also had Uniform Code of Military Justice or disciplinary authority over their enlisted corpsmen. Another wrinkle to be ironed out focused on psychiatric practice. Unlike the Army, the Navy allowed nonlicensed providers of psychiatric nursing care to administer medications to psychiatric patients.[63] Further points of dissention had to do with issues such as career progression, leadership roles, rating schemes, staffing ratios and mix, policies, procedures and standard operating procedures, proof of competency, job descriptions, and educational variances.[64]

When it first appeared that the NCR integration actually would go forward, Colonel Janet R. Southby and Captain Carol Carney, the respective chief nurses of WRAMC and NNMC, met with the involved commanders, Major General Ronald Blanck and Rear Admiral Richard Ridenour. After they discussed the prospective merger extensively, Blanck stretched across the conference table and whispered to Southby, "make it happen" and, Southby recalled, "so we did." She confirmed that a cooperative spirit was somewhat lacking initially at the grassroots level among participating Army and Navy nurses. Differences focused on personnel issues such as "creative counting of workload and comments about safe nursing levels." But soon the participants transcended these disagreements and reached consensus about important matters. Southby ascribed the success of the implementation to the fact that she, Carney, and Colonel Joellen de Berg, chief nurse of Malcolm Grow, met regularly and communicated openly. Southby added that a climate of mutual trust prevailed and the triad had "great professional and personal respect for each other." To provide further support for the integration, Southby assigned Colonel Margaret Baird to oversee the exodus of maternal-child AMEDD staff to NNMC and appointed Lieutenant Colonel Victoria Ransom as the interim transi-

Pictured is Colonel Janet R. Southby, who served as chief nurse of Walter Reed Army Medical Center from December 1992 to September 1996.
Photo courtesy of Army Nurse Corps Archives, Office of Medical History, Falls Church, VA.

tion coordinator. She also selected Sergeant First Class Rhonda Broberg, an Army non-commissioned officer, to coordinate and work full-time between all three institutions to facilitate seamless operations. A vanguard of nine Army nurses, of whom five were assigned to the nurseries and four as obstetrical nurses, transferred to NNMC on 5 June 1995.[65] The WRAMC Adolescent Psychiatric Inpatient Unit shifted to the NNMC on 1 August 1995 and simultaneously the NNMC Adult Psychiatric Inpatient Unit moved to WRAMC. Virtually all NCR pediatric services merged at WRAMC on 3 June 1996.[66] On 20 May 1996, six Navy Nurse Corps officers and seven Navy hospital corpsmen reported to WRAMC to support the neurology nursing services and eight reported for duty on the psychiatric units.[67] With time, the tri-service integration spread to other specialty areas until the only Graduate Medical Education and specialty services remaining discrete in both WRAMC and NNMC were general surgery, internal medicine, orthopedics, and the transitional internship.[68]

The assimilation of Air Force Nurse Corps officers into the staff at the U.S. Army Landstuhl Regional Medical Center in Germany in 1993 also was typical of other integrations of staff into the facilities of sister services. Initially, Army nurses resisted the change and expressed feelings of being invaded and overtaken by Air Force nurses. The Air Force nurses also were uncomfortable, feeling unwelcome and confused by the different Army staff positions, customs, terminology, and doctrine. To facilitate the integration, nursing leaders furnished regular familiarization and educational sessions, melded the two services' manning documents, made staff assignments based on qualifications irrespective of service so that each unit soon had a blend of Army and Air Force personnel, and mandated the battle dress uniform as the common duty uniform. With much hard work and a spirit of cooperation, nurses resolved the awkward state of affairs and the two services formed relationships and gained mutual understanding. Both groups recognized that flexibility and acceptance of differences were essential and that despite diversity, clinical nursing was the major commonality and a basic point of agreement. The staff reported learning four important lessons—(1) prior planning was paramount, (2) adaptability and a willingness to learn were essential, (3) full integration at every level was important, and (4) joint staffing can work.[69]

The previously described innovations were but a few of the hundreds of ingenious programs implemented by Army nurses across the AMEDD. Army Nurse Corps officers at fixed installations and those serving in combat or Operations Other Than War conceived, created, and participated in numerous similar programs and countless other unprecedented efforts that saved millions of dollars while maintaining access to quality health care services for soldiers, their families, the retired population, and their eligible family members. Their initiative was a testament to the creativity, professionalism, and dedication of Army nurses serving around the globe.

These same, typical Army Nurse Corps traits of resourcefulness, adaptability, collaboration, fiscal responsibility, and devotion to duty were but a handful of the many attributes that rendered Army nurses as ideal candidates for future unparal-

Colonel Margaret Baird, chief of the Maternal-Child Nursing Section at Walter Reed Army Medical Center, supervised the transition of health care services for obstetrics and pediatrics patients from her institution to the National Naval Medical Center in Bethesda, Maryland, in 1995.
Photo courtesy of Colonel Margaret Baird, Readfield, ME.

leled roles in the AMEDD. For it was at this point in the history of the Army Nurse Corps that formerly closed doors slowly but surely edged open to allow access to new opportunities for Army nurses in command and branch immaterial positions.

# Notes

1. "Analysis of Alternatives," 12 March 1991, Draft Enclosure 2, in "Army Medical Department Realignment Study," n.d.; Thad A. Krupka, "Army Medical Department (AMEDD) Command and Control In Process Review (IPR)," Memorandum for Record, 1 August 1991; Mr. Yaglom, "Army Medical Department (AMEDD) Command and Control Realignment Update," Information Paper, 4 May 1992; and Alcide M. LaNoue, "Revised Concept Plan for Establishment of the US Army Medical Command," Memorandum, 16 July 1993 (all in Army Nurse Corps Collection [ANCC], Office of Medical History [OMH]). L. Martin Kaplan, Department of the Army Historical Summary Fiscal Year 1994 (Washington, DC: Center of Military History, United States Army, 2000), 114–15.

2. Mary Kay Jones, "U.S. Army Medical Department (AMEDD) Center and School (HSW3VZAA), Fort Sam Houston, TX 78234-6100," Permanent Orders 103-1, 15 July 1991; and Bruce T. Miketinac, "Abbreviated Concept Plan for U.S. Army Medical Department (AMEDD) Center and School," n.d. (both in ANCC, OMH).

3. Bettye H. Simmons, "Professional Development and Readiness Guide," 2-2, 7 May 1997, ANCC, OMH.

4. The plan effected a reduction in OTSG in the NCR from a staff of 500 to approximately 100. The former HSC staff was condensed into a MEDCOM organization of 400 staffers. Constance J. Moore, "Input for DA Historical Summary FY 1994," Information Paper, 16 March 1996; Bettye H. Simmons, "Professional Development and Readiness Guide," 2-1, 7 May 1997 (both in ANCC, OMH).

5. Jerry Harben, "Regional HSSAs Manage Health-Care Delivery," *The Mercury* 21 (January 1994): 1. "The MEDCOM," *The Mercury* (Fall 1996): 3. Bettye H. Simmons, "Professional Development and Readiness Guide," 2-1, 7 May 1997; and Terris E. Kennedy, "Minutes of the Regional Chief Nurses Conference," Memorandum, 2, n.d. (both in ANCC, OMH). John T. Greenwood and F. Clifton Berry, *Medics at War, Military Medicine from Colonial Times to the 21st Century* (Annapolis: Naval Institute Press, 2005), 170.

6. Nancy R. Adams, "Message from the Chief," Memo from the Chief, Army Nurse Corps (April 1993): 1; Nancy R. Adams, "Message from the Chief," Memo from the Chief, Army Nurse Corps (August 1993): 1; Constance J. Moore, "Input for DA Historical Summary FY 1994," Information Paper, 16 March 1996; Michael J. Foster, "Minutes of the Army Nurse Corps Staff Meeting on 6 October 1993," Memorandum for Record, 14 October 1993; Raymond T. Burden, "HSSA PAT Storyboard," Memorandum, 27 September

1993; and "Posture Statement by Major General John J. Cuddy, Deputy Surgeon General, United States Army, before the Committee on Appropriations, National Security Subcommittee, U.S. House of Representatives, 2nd Session, 104th Congress, Medical Overview," 24 April 1996 (all in ANCC, OMH). Alcide M. LaNoue, "Army Medicine: 'Caring Beyond the Call of Duty'," *Army* 46 (October 1996): 151–52, 154, 157.

7. Terris E. Kennedy, "Transition Plan for Army Nursing in Support of the AMEDD Reorganization and Restructure," 22 January 1994, Information Paper in Michael J. Foster, "Minutes of the Army Nurse Corps Staff Meeting on 1 February 1994," Memorandum for Record, n.d.; and Terris E. Kennedy, "Minutes of the Regional Chief Nurses Conference," Memorandum, 8, n.d. (both in ANCC, OMH).

8. Raymond T. Burden, "HSSA PAT Storyboard," Memorandum, 27 September 1993; and Alcide M. LaNoue, "Operational Level Guidance," Memorandum for Commanders, Health Service Support Areas (Provisional), 2 December 1993 (both in ANCC, OMH).

9. "The MEDCOM," *The Mercury* (Fall 1996): 5.

10. John T. Greenwood and F. Clifton Berry, *Medics at War, Military Medicine from Colonial Times to the 21st Century* (Annapolis: Naval Institute Press, 2005), 171.

11. Jerry Harben, "Plans for Revised AMEDD Near Completion," *HSC Mercury* 20 (June 1993): 1. Jerry Harben, "Top Leaders Briefed on New AMEDD Structure," *HSC Mercury* 20 (August 1993): 1. Jerry Harben, "New AMEDD Structures Kicks Off This Month," *HSC Mercury* 21 (October 1993): 1, 12. Jerry Harben, "Regional HSSAs Manage Health-Care Delivery," *HSC Mercury* 21 (January 1994): 1. Russ Zajtchuk "Command Name," Memorandum, 15 July 1994; and Alcide M. LaNoue, "Command Name," 8 September 1994 (both in ANCC, OMH). John T. Greenwood and F. Clifton Berry, *Medics at War, Military Medicine from Colonial Times to the 21st Century* (Annapolis: Naval Institute Press, 2005), 171.

12. Originally, TFA was named Project AMEDD Vanguard. Alcide M. LaNoue, "Charter for Project AMEDD Vanguard (Task Force Aesculapius)," Memorandum, 4 February 1993, ANCC, OMH.

13. Alcide LaNoue, "Information 'Wave' Embraced by Army," *U.S. Medicine* 32 (January 1996): 36, 38. "Posture Statement by Lieutenant General Alcide LaNoue, The Surgeon General, United States Army, for the Committee on Appropriations, Defense Subcommittee, United States Senate, 2nd Session, 104th Congress, DOD Medical Overview," 5 June 1996; United States Army, Medical Department, Reorganization, Volume I, Narrative, Task Force Aesculapius, January 1993–June 1995, Official Report; Alcide M. LaNoue, "Charter for Project AMEDD Vanguard (Task Force Aesculapius)," Memorandum, 4 February 1993; Russ Zajtchuk, "Army Medical Department Reorganization, January 1993–June 1995," 16 June 1995; and Bonnie M. Jennings, "Chapter Five Comments," August 2005 (all in ANCC, OMH). Jerry Harben, "Plans for Revised AMEDD Near Completion," *HSC Mercury* 20 (June 1993): 3. Jerry Harben, "New AMEDD Structure Kicks Off This Month," *HSC Mercury* 21 (October 1993): 1, 12. "The MEDCOM," *The Mercury* (Fall 1996): 4. Alcide M. LaNoue, "Army Medicine: 'Caring Beyond the Call of Duty'," *Army* 46 (October 1996): 151–52, 154, 157. Elliott Jacques, *Requisite Organization: A Total System for Effective Managerial Organization and Managerial Leadership for the 21st Century* (Falls Church, VA: Cason Hall & Company, 1998).

14. Bonnie Jennings to Author, E-mail Correspondence, 25 September 2005, ANCC, OMH.

15. Bonnie M. Jennings, "Chapter Five Comments," August 2005; and Terris E. Kennedy, Interview by Constance J. Moore, Transcript, 386–87, 31 October 1996 (both in ANCC, OMH).

16. Bonnie Jennings to Author, E-mail Correspondence, 25 September 2005, ANCC, OMH.

17. Alcide M. LaNoue, "Designation of Deputy Surgeon General and Assistant Surgeon General," Memorandum, 14 December 1992; Nancy R. Adams, "Message from the Chief," Memo from the Chief, Army Nurse Corps (August 1993): 1; and "Posture Statement by Lieutenant General Alcide LaNoue, The Surgeon General, United States Army, for the Committee on Appropriations, Defense Subcommittee, United States Senate, 2nd Session, 104th Congress, DOD Medical Overview," 5 June 1996 (all in ANCC, OMH).

18. Jerry Harben, "Plans for Revised AMEDD Near Completion," *HSC Mercury* 20 (June 1993): 1. Jerry Harben, "Top Leaders Briefed on New AMEDD Structure," *HSC Mercury* 20 (August 1993): 1.

19. Alcide M. LaNoue, "Charter for Project AMEDD Vanguard (Task Force Aesculapius)," Memorandum, 4 February 1993, ANCC, OMH.

20. Nancy R. Adams, "Proposed Reorganization, Our Discussion, July 1992, at Fort Sam Houston, Texas," Memorandum for Major General (P) LaNoue, 8 September 1992, OTSG Collection, OMH. Nancy R. Adams, "Concept Plan for Establishment of the US Army Medical Command (Provisional)," Memorandum, 25 September 1992; and Terris E. Kennedy, Interview by Constance J. Moore, Transcript, 300, 31 October 1996 (both in ANCC, OMH).

21. Alcide M. LaNoue, "Designation of Deputy Surgeon General and Assistant Surgeon General," Memorandum, 14 December 1992; Thomas Frank England, "Designation of Deputy Surgeon General and Assistant Surgeon General," Memorandum, 4 December 1992; Vahan Moushegian, "Designation of Deputy Surgeon General and Assistant Surgeon General," Memorandum, 4 December 1992; Nancy R. Adams, "Message from the Chief," Memo from the Chief, Army Nurse Corps (January 1993): 1; and Nancy R. Adams, "Message from the Chief," Memo from the Chief, Army Nurse Corps (August 1993): 1 (all in ANCC, OMH).

22. "Corps Chiefs," Typewritten Document (TD), n.d., ANCC, OMH.

23. Clara L. Adams-Ender, Handwritten Notes on Draft Manuscript, 28 September 2005, ANCC, OMH.

24. Michael J. Foster, "Minutes of the Army Nurse Corps Staff Meeting of 7 May 1993," Memorandum for Record, 3, 11 May 1993; Nancy R. Adams, "Command of Fitzsimons Health Services Support Region," Memorandum for the Surgeon General, 11 June 1993; Nancy R. Adams to Gordon Sullivan, Draft, Unsent Letter, 1992; and Nancy R. Adams, "Message from the Chief," Memo from the Chief, Army Nurse Corps (December 1993): 1 (all in ANCC, OMH). Harry Noyes, "Nurse to Command Training Company," *The Mercury* 22 (February 1995): 6.

25. Constance J. Moore, "Input for DA Historical Summary FY 1994," Information Paper, 16 March 1996, ANCC, OMH. Jane Gervasoni, "CHPPM Becomes 'Official'," Army Health Connection 2 (Winter 1996): 1–2.

26. Nancy R. Adams, "Message from the Chief," Memo from the Chief, Army Nurse Corps (August 1994): 1; "Posture Statement by Lieutenant General Alcide LaNoue, The Surgeon General, United States Army, for the Committee on Appropriations, Defense Subcommittee, United States Senate, 2nd Session, 104th Congress, DOD Medical Overview," 8–9, 5 June 1996 (both in ANCC, OMH).

27. Nancy R. Adams, Handwritten Notes on Draft Manuscript, 11 July 2005, ANCC, OMH.

28. Terris Kennedy, "Transition of the Office of the Chief Army Nurse Corps and Subsequent Transitioning of Army Nurse Staff Officer Positions within Organizational Elements

of the Office of the Surgeon General," Information Paper, 30 November 1993; Terris Kennedy, "Office of the Chief," Memo from the Chief, Army Nurse Corps (April 1994): 2; Bonnie Jennings, "Nursing Consultant," Memo from the Chief, Army Nurse Corps (April 1994): 4; Terris Kennedy, Untitled Handwritten Note, 28 July 1995; Terris E. Kennedy, Interview by Constance J. Moore, Transcript, 345, 31 October 1996; and Constance J. Moore, "Input for DA Historical Summary, FY 1995," Information Paper, 20 May 1996 (all in ANCC, OMH).

29. "Reorganization ARSTAF and MACOM TDA's," Memorandum, n.d., ANCC, OMH.

30. Terris Kennedy, "Office of the Chief," Memo from the Chief, Army Nurse Corps (April 1994): 2, ANCC, OMH.

31. Nancy McFadin, "Transition of Nursing Division, Health Services Command," Information Paper, 3 January 1994, ANCC, OMH.

32. Carole A. Burke, "Proposed Position Paper on Deputy Chief Nurse," Memorandum, 6 February 1992; "Deputy Commander for Nursing," Position Paper, 25 February 1992; Carole A. Burke, "Proposed Position Paper on Deputy Chief Nurse," Memorandum, 6 February 1992; "Reorganization Department of Nursing, General Leonard Wood Army Community Hospital, Fort Leonard Wood, Missouri," Typewritten Paper, 16 April 1992; J.M. Cook, "Request for Deviation from Standardized Organization Structure of HSC 10-1," 20 April 1993; Thomas I. Clements, "Request for Deviation from Standardized Organization Structure of HSC 10-1," 20 April 1993; Claudia M. Mundy, "Quarterly Report on Test Project for Position of Deputy Commander for Patient Services," Memorandum, 30 June 1994; and "Satisfaction through Caring: More than Words. . . A Philosophy," n.d. (all in ANCC, OMH).

33. This position title at the Fort Knox, Kentucky, MEDDAC was deputy commander for patient services (DCPS). The officer holding the DCPS position was dual-hatted as chief nurse. J.M. Cook, "Request for Deviation from Standardized Organization Structure of HSC 10-1," 20 April 1993; Thomas I. Clements, "Request for Deviation from Standardized Organization Structure of HSC 10-1," 20 April 1993; Claudia M. Mundy, "Quarterly Report on Test Project for Position of Deputy Commander for Patient Services," Memorandum, 30 June 1994; and "Evans Army Community Hospital, Organizational Chart—Carelines," 23 June 1997 (all in ANCC, OMH). Originally, the DCN or DCHS was responsible for the Emergency Medical Service. Later, it added the Nutrition Care Division to its responsibilities. "Satisfaction through Caring: More than Words. . . A Philosophy," n.d., ANCC, OMH. At Evans Army Community Hospital at Fort Carson, Colorado, the DCHS managed nursing services, pharmacy services, nutrition care, the medical library, and the Education and Readiness Division. "Evans Army Community Hospital, Organizational Chart—Carelines," 23 June 1997, ANCC, OMH.

34. Karl S. Snyder, "Organizational Restructure," Memorandum, 17 April 1992; Philip L. Dorsey, "Organizational Restructure," Memorandum, 17 April 1992; Major Allen, "Moncrief Army Community Hospital Reorganization," Executive Summary, 17 April 1992; William P. Allen, "Request for Deviation from Standardized Organization Structure of HSC 10-1," Memorandum, 27 April 1992; Karl S. Snyder, "Reorganization of the Department of Nursing," Memorandum, 24 February 1993; Peggy A. Page, "Revision of the Highlights in the History of the Army Nurse Corps," Memorandum, 1 April 1993; Patricia A.H. Saulsbery, "Trip Report, Ft. Jackson, SC, 30 Aug–2 Sep 93," Memorandum, 2, 24 September 1993; "ANC Input for 1993 AMEDD Stockholders Report," n.d.; and "Moncrief Army Community Hospital, Nursing Reorganization, Information Briefing," Briefing Slides, n.d. (all in ANCC, OMH).

35. "Satisfaction through Caring: More than Words, . . A Philosophy," n.d., ANCC, OMH.
36. Richard D. Cameron, "Medical Treatment Facility (MTF) Reorganization Assessment," Memorandum, 12 September 1994, ANCC, OMH.
37. Tim Porter-O'Grady, "The Real Values of Partnership: Preventing Professional Amorphism," *Journal of Nursing Administration* 24 (February 1994): 11–15.
38. Nancy R. Adams, "Message from the Chief," Memo from the Chief, Army Nurse Corps (April 1994): 1; Nancy R. Adams, "Message from the Chief," Memo from the Chief, Army Nurse Corps (August 1995): 1; Terris E. Kennedy, Interview by Constance J. Moore focusing on "One Moment in Time," Briefing Slides, Transcript, 19–23, 11 February 1997; and Terris E. Kennedy, Interview by Constance J. Moore, Transcript, 371, 31 October 1996 (all in ANCC, OMH).
39. Bettye H. Simmons, Memo from the Chief, "Army Nurse Corps (1 August 1997):1, ANCC, OMH.
40. Nancy R. Adams, Handwritten Notes on Draft Manuscript, 11 July 2005, ANCC, OMH.
41. Carol Reineck, Donna Wright, and Sheila Jones, "Ambulatory Care Registered Nurse Utilization, A Pilot Study," 19 September 1994, ANCC, OMH.
42. "Primary Care Demonstration Project," Memorandum for Col. Terris Kennedy, 12 December 1994; "Primary Care Demonstration Project Overview," TD, n.d.; "Army Nurse Corps Project 'Primary Care'," Briefing Slides, 13 February 1995; Linda J. Stierle, "Report of the Federal Nursing Chiefs to the 1995 ANA House of Delegates," TD, 1, 11 May 1995; and Pew Health Professions Commission, "Health Professions Education for the Future: Schools in Service to the Nation," Printed Report, 30, 83–90, February 1993 (all in ANCC, OMH).
43. Debra Mark, "Primary Care Demonstration Project: Measurement of Provider Practice Styles and Client Outcomes," n.d.; Debra D. Mark, Mary Z. Mays, and Vicki L. Byers, "Primary Care Demonstration Project: Measurement of Provider Practice Style and Client Outcomes," Typewritten Report, 9 April 1997; "Statement by Brigadier General Bettye H. Simmons, Chief, Army Nurse Corps, Army Medical Department, before the Subcommittee on Defense, Committee on Appropriations, United States Senate, 1st Session, 105th Congress, DoD Health Care Programs," 4–5, 23 April 1997; and "Executive Summary," Enclosure 1, 1-2, in James W. Kirkpatrick, Primary Care Demonstration Project—Measurement of Provider Practice Styles and Client Outcomes, 25 November 1997 (all in ANCC, OMH).
44. Nancy R. Adams, Memo from the Chief, Army Nurse Corps (August 1995): 1, ANCC, OMH.
45. Edith Walsh, "Status of Demonstration Project," Information Paper, 19 March 1990; Bonnie Jennings, "Review of the Technical Report on the TAMC Nursing Demonstration Project," Memorandum, 10 February 1991; Lieutenant Colonel Maynard, "Demonstration Project, Nursing Satisfaction Outcomes, First Year—1990," Information Paper, 6 March 1991; Donna L. Patterson, "Status of Tripler Army Medical Center Nursing Demonstration Project," Information Paper, 6 March 1991; Edith Walsh, "Nursing Demonstration Project Funding Requirements for FY 92," Information Paper, 15 March 1991; Lieutenant Colonel Zurcher, "Nursing Shortage," Insert for the Record, Senate Appropriations Committee, 6 May 1991; Healthcare Strategy & Marketing Office, "FY92 Congressional Mark-up," n.d.; Sharon S. DeRuvo, "Status of the Congressional Demonstration Project," Memorandum, 12 January 1992; Linda Kirk and Donna Patterson, "Congressional Demonstration Project, Effects of the Restructuring of Nursing Practice to Effectively Use Ancillary Personnel," Typewritten Report, June 1992; Frederick N. Bussey to Daniel K. Inouye, Typewritten

Letter, 31 July 1992; Terris E. Kennedy, "Congressional Reports," Memorandum, 14 December 1992; Loretta Forlaw, "Nurse Demonstration Project," 3 May 1993; Loretta Forlaw, "Status of the Nurse Test Congressional Demonstration Project," Information Paper, 27 January 1995; and Loretta Forlaw to Iris West, E-mail Correspondence, 17 September 2004 (all in ANCC, OMH).

46. As of 1995, six TAMC nurses staffed a Pain Management Team 24 hours a day, seven days a week. In 1997, as cost-containment efforts expanded, the clinic hours fell to 16-hour days, five days a week, and the nurse staff downsized to three. The staff provided consultation for hospital staff and education and support for patients using patient-controlled analgesic devices and undergoing epidural analgesia. Michele L. Kohl, "Trip Report, Tripler Army Medical Center, Honolulu, Hawaii, 29 July–2 August 1996," Memorandum, 15 August 1996, ANCC, OMH. Diana L. Ruzicka and Don Daniels, "Implementing a Pain Management Service at an Army Medical Center," *Military Medicine* 166 (February 2001): 146–51.

47. Lisa Beckmann, "Tripler's Ambulatory Care Clinic," Information Paper, 9 March 1995; and Lisa Beckman, "Tripler's Specialized Nursing Care Center," Information Paper, 1 April 1996 (both in ANCC, OMH).

48. Barbara S. Stakk, "Pre-Admission Unit," Information Paper, 10 March 1995; and Michele L. Kohl, "Trip Report, Tripler Army Medical Center, Honolulu, Hawaii, 29 July–2 August 1996," Memorandum, 15 August 1996 (both in ANCC, OMH).

49. Alice L. O'K. DeMarais, "Certified Nurse-Midwifery (CNM) Service MEDDAC-AK," Information Paper, 22 May 1995, ANCC, OMH.

50. Laurie Davis, "Women's Health Advanced Practice," *The Army Nursing Newsletter* (December 1997): 13–14, ANCC, OMH.

51. "Landstuhl Regional Medical Center, Nursing Initiatives in Healthcare Delivery," n.d., ANCC, OMH.

52. The Walter Reed Health Care system incorporated a number of health care facilities in the mid-Atlantic region, such as those located at Carlisle Barracks, Pennsylvania, Fort Detrick, Maryland, Fort Meade, Maryland, Aberdeen Proving Ground, Maryland, Fort Belvoir, Virginia, Fort Myer, Virginia, the Pentagon, and Walter Reed Army Medical Center. http://www.wramc.amedd.army.mil/patientinfo/HealthCareSys.htm (accessed 20 September 2005).

53. Margaret M. Baird, "Input for BG Simmons' Congressional Testimony," Memorandum, 20 May 1996; and "Significant Army Nurse Corps UM/Best Practice Initiatives," Typewritten Briefing Outline, July 1997 (both in ANCC, OMH).

54. Bonnie Jennings to Diane Plemenik, E-mail Correspondence, 19 May 1996, ANCC, OMH.

55. Theresa M. Tominey, "General Leonard Wood Army Community Hospital (GLWACH) Health Promotion Center and Clinic," Information Paper, 11 February 1998, ANCC, OMH.

56. Bonnie M. Jennings, "Clinical Case Management in the Army Medical Department," Information Paper, 27 April 1993; Bonnie M. Jennings, "Clinical Case Management in the Army Medical Department," Information Paper, 24 February 1994; Bonnie M. Jennings, "Ideas on Case Management for the Senior Executive Coordinated Care Conference," Information Paper, n.d.; Kathleen Srsic-Stoehr, "Input on Ambulatory Care Initiative/Issues—Summary," Memorandum, 3, 3 March 1996; and Terris E. Kennedy, Interview by Constance J. Moore, Transcript, 347–50, 31 October 1996 (all in ANCC, OMH). Bonnie M. Jennings and Laura R. Brosch, "Clinical Case Management in the Army Medical Department," *Military Medicine* 159 (August 1994): 548–53. Joseph C. Kiser "Critical

Pathways Show Way to Success," *The Mercury* 26 (January 1999): 11.

57. "Significant Army Nurse Corps UM/Best Practice Initiatives," TD, July 1997, ANCC, OMH.

58. "DoD New Parent Support Program, Hawaii," TD, n.d.; Elizabeth Hill, Joann Hollandsworth, JoEllen Cerny, Anthony Ettipio, and Jillian Inouye to Gar Yip, TD, 29 January 1998; "Effects of Telehealth Augmentation of a Home Nursing Care Program for Women with Children at Risk for Child Abuse and Neglect," Typewritten Report, n.d.; and Susie Clark to Wendy Martinson, "Answer to Testimony Questions," E-mail Correspondence, 21 April 1998 (all in ANCC, OMH). Michelle J. Rowan, "Community Health Nurses Take Care Home," *The Mercury* 27 (June 2000): 8.

59. Susie Clark to Wendy Martinson, "Answer to Testimony Questions," E-mail Correspondence, 21 April 1998, ANCC, OMH.

60. Stephen C. Joseph, "Tri-Service Staffing of Tripler Army Medical Center (TAMC)," Memorandum, 1 November 1994, ANCC, OMH.

61. Stephen C. Joseph, "Tri-Service Staffing of Tripler Army Medical Center (TAMC)," Memorandum, 23 February 1995, ANCC, OMH.

62. "Statement by Brigadier General Nancy R. Adams, Chief, Army Nurse Corps, Army Medical Department, before the Defense Subcommittee, Committee on Appropriations, United States Senate, 1st Session, 104th Congress, Health Programs," 10, 13 June 1995; Janet R. Southby, "Walter Reed Army Medical Center, Department of Nursing," Briefing Slides, May 1996; Michele L. Kohl, "Trip Report, Installation Visited: Tripler Army Medical Center, Honolulu, Hawaii, 29 July–2 Aug 1996," Memorandum, 1–2, 15 August 1996; "Statement of Rear Admiral Joan Engel, Nurse Corps, Director, Nurse Corps, United States Navy, June 5, 1996, before the Subcommittee on Defense of the Senate Appropriations Committee," 4; and "Statement by Lieutenant General Ronald R. Blanck, The Army Surgeon General, on Health Care in the United States Army," TD, 23, n.d. (all in ANCC, OMH).

63. Earl Fauver, Interview by Author, 26 August 2005. Claudia Bartz and Gary Sadler, "Recommendation for Training Psychiatric Nurses and Medical Specialists to Practice in Interservice Settings," Memorandum, 1 August 1995, ANCC, OMH.

64. "Tri-Service Transitioning," presented at 4th Annual Leadership Seminar, 17 October 1995, ANCC, OMH.

65. Janet R. Southby to Author, E-mail Correspondence, 30 August 2005; and Janet R. Southby, "66D/66G Assignments to WRAMC," Memorandum, 26 June 1995 (both in ANCC, OMH).

66. Janet R. Southby and Carol A. Carney, "Nurse Staffing Arrangements between WRAMC and NNMC," Memorandum, 1 July 1996, ANCC, OMH.

67. C.A. Carney, "Nursing Service Personnel Transferred to Walter Reed Army Medical Center in Support of Neurology Nursing Services," Memorandum, 13 May 1996; and Ellen Buck to Kathy Tracy, "Staff Detailed to WRAMC," Memorandum, 19 May 1996 (both in ANCC, OMH).

68. Earl Fauver, Interview by Author, 26 August 2005. "Testimony of John R. Pierce, M.D., Colonel, Medical Corps, U.S. Army (Retired), BRAC Commission Hearing," 12, 7 July 2005, ANCC, OMH.

69. Glenn R. Ermer, Brenda J. McEleney, and Iris J. West, "An Oral History of the 'Joint' Nursing Experience at Landstuhl Regional Medical Center," *Military Medicine* 165 (February 2000): 131–34.

*Chapter Sixteen*
# New Frontiers for Army Nurse Corps Officers

Before the 1990s, the notion that Army nurses might advance beyond traditional nursing roles and cross unprecedented command boundaries into areas of new responsibility rarely warranted mention. On the rare occasions that the idea did surface, it was summarily dismissed. For instance in 1972, the surgeon general, Lieutenant General Hal B. Jennings, "erased any doubts" about his "adamant" stance on assigning other than Medical Corps (MC) officers to command Army hospitals. Jennings confidently promised that the physician "would remain the quarterback of the medical team."[1] A few years later, Lieutenant General Charles C. Pixley, surgeon general from 1977 to 1981, reiterated that physicians were the only officers capable of commanding the Army Medical Department (AMEDD) units, submitting:

> . . . that if we had not had Medical Corps officers who were interested in leadership positions and who had not seized the opportunity to be leaders in various roles, such as high level medical staff and command positions over the past 200 years, then many of the great advances of military medicine would never have transpired.[2]

Pixley acknowledged that he had "no quarrel with permitting MSC [Medical Service Corps] officers becoming commanders of TO&E [Table of Organization and Equipment] units where patient care is not being performed. These are training situations."[3]

Lieutenant General Frank F. Ledford, surgeon general from 1987 to 1991, also rejected the notion of command for nurses. During her tenure as chief of the Army Nurse Corps, Brigadier General Clara L. Adams-Ender broached the subject with then Deputy Surgeon General Major General Alcide LaNoue, who "had absolutely no problem with it. His belief was that a leader is a leader, regardless of gender or profession." When LaNoue promised to discuss the question with Ledford, Adams-Ender recalled, "I quietly groaned." She was keenly aware of Ledford's stance on command for nurses. Later, LaNoue related his conversation with the surgeon general on the topic and drolly recalled that after Ledford "broke out all the windows in his office and threw all the books from his bookcase on the floor, I got the feeling he didn't favor nurses being in command."[4] Time proved all of these resolute viewpoints wrong.

For several decades, the Defense Advisory Committee on Women in the Services (DACOWITS) was an important voice advocating for command for Army nurses. Adams-Ender recalled that when she was post commander at Fort Belvoir, Virginia, in 1992, the DACOWITS vice chair visited her to discuss the possibility of Army Nurse Corps officers commanding hospitals. Of course, Adams-Ender endorsed the idea. The vice chair subsequently interviewed the commander and a number of staff at Fort Belvoir's DeWitt Army Community Hospital. Adams-Ender revealed that the vice chair:

> . . . in her outbriefing with me, . . . shared the reactions that she had received to nurses commanding MTFs [military treatment facilities]. I got a real chuckle out of one of them. The vice chair was interviewing a female physician and asked her if nurses should command hospitals. The physician replied, "Absolutely not!" When queried as to why not, the physician responded, "Nurses run everything else in the hospital now. If you give them command, they'll run the whole hospital!"

As an aside, Adams-Ender remarked, "I didn't know that physicians noticed—that was a pretty perceptive comment."[5]

Although the idea of Army Nurse Corps officers holding command positions generally was a taboo subject in certain quarters, there were a few instances where Army nurses commanded hospital units, usually when dictated by expedience. In 1976, Captain Diane Corcoran was chief nurse at the 86th Combat Support Hospital (CSH) at Fort Campbell, Kentucky, when the unit was awaiting the assignment of a new commanding officer. The commander of the 101st Airborne Division intervened and directed Corcoran to assume command of the 86th CSH, stating that he knew she had made many of the decisions in the past while on field maneuvers with the 101st. Corcoran responded that it was traditional for the ranking Medical Service Corps (MSC) officer in the unit to assume command. The 101st commander insisted, overruled the objections of disgruntled MSC officers postwide, cleared his intentions with Brigadier General Madelyn Parks, chief of the Army Nurse Corps, and scheduled a change of command ceremony to take place within two days with 10 battalions participating in the ritual.

With some trepidation but with significant excitement and pride, Corcoran began immediate preparations to lead the pass and review formation. She conferred with the Fort Campbell hospital chief nurse, Colonel John B. Garlick, a former infantry officer, who took Corcoran to the parade grounds and gave her a crash refresher course in drill and ceremonies. Corcoran remembered praying fervently before the ceremony and proceeding through the parade in a "trance mode." During the change of command ceremony, she managed to accept command, passed the reviewing stand under the watchful eyes of Major General James A. Wickham, the post commander, and reached her assigned position on the drill field. She started to relax when several of the infantry commanders in the audience gave

Captain Diane Corcoran, Army Nurse Corps officer and Commander of the 86th Combat Support Hospital at Fort Campbell, Kentucky, confers with officers of the 101st Airborne Division in 1976. The division staff was visiting while the 86th was setting up its hospital during a field exercise.
Photo courtesy of Colonel Diane Corcoran, Durham, NC.

her a thumbs-up signal. Corcoran subsequently received all the accoutrements of command, including official orders and command epaulets for her uniform. For three months she successfully commanded the 86th CSH before leaving Fort Campbell to attend the University of Texas at Austin for her doctorate.[6]

The belief that only male officers could command was so firmly entrenched in the Army's culture that it had been codified into U.S. law and Army regulations. Both 10 USC 3579 and Army Regulation 600-20 specifically prohibited the predominantly female Army Nurse Corps and Army Medical Specialist Corps officers from assuming command positions. In 1980, however, Congress amended §3579 to lift the outdated ban.[7]

Notwithstanding, a decade elapsed before possibility became reality in the AMEDD because segments of the MC, the MSC, and the hierarchy of line officers opposed command for the two mainly female AMEDD branches. In 1990, for example, the MC recommended as a part of the AMEDD Officer Leader Development Action Plan to "not establish a branch immaterial [BI] designator for the AMEDD." The MC "definitely opposed" such an action and "in contradistinction" to the Air Force and the Navy, the AMEDD had many field hospitals that, upon mobilization, male MC officers would have to command. It posed a rhetorical question: "If not afforded the opportunity to be a TDA [Table of Distribution and Allowances] commander, how then to train [MC officers] for a TOE (wartime) command."[8] Other MC officers also firmly believed that only officers of their branch were capable of command or entitled to general officer rank.[9]

Comments emerging from a December 1995 survey directed by Brigadier General Bettye H. Simmons focused on the concerns and ideas of Army Nurse Corps officers also revealed some ill will toward nurses from MSC officers. One Army nurse's response spoke of the "lack of respect from other branches (especially MSC) and the potential threat we pose with the surge of branch immaterial talk" as a current issue affecting the Corps.[10]

General Gordon Sullivan, chief of staff of the Army (CSA), disapproved General Nancy Adams' assignment as commander of the Fitzsimons Health Service Support Area and vetoed the inclusion of nonphysician/nondentist AMEDD officers on select AMEDD General Officer Promotion Boards.[11] The active Army seemingly lagged behind the U.S. Army Reserve (USAR) and Army National Guard (ARNG) and its sister services in implementing the attitudinal change that led to equal command opportunity for all AMEDD branches.

Unlike the Active component, the USAR and ARNG had no prohibitions regarding command for nurses. Brigadier General Dorothy Pocklington, the first female and nurse to be promoted to brigadier general in the USAR, knew this and worked to open command opportunities for USAR and ARNG nurses. The surgeon general, Lieutenant General Frank Ledford, however, did not support her efforts, and numerous MSC officers vehemently opposed her campaign. Both MC and MSC officers likely viewed the potential intrusion of Army nurses into command roles as a threat to their opportunities to achieve such positions. Pocklington still placed the issue on the agenda for the Surgeon General's Reserve Component Medical Advisory Board and challenged the notion that nurses could not command. She testified before other Department of Defense (DoD) policy-making bodies and, in her travels to USAR and ARNG units nationwide, advised nurses to prepare themselves for command and work toward this career goal. She recalled that on one occasion, an Army nurse captain confided that she had commanded a training unit but the unit purposefully kept it "quiet." Pocklington added that she "would not be surprised if there were a few other instances of this happening and no one was supposed to know about it," because the USAR and ARNG in general were laboring under the misapprehension that nurses were banned from command.

Pocklington actively promoted the campaign for command for nurses in the USAR and ARNG. She presented her case across all echelons of the Army from the highest policy-making levels all the way down to the barracks soldiers. Her enthusiasm heightened awareness, and in the late 1980s, her efforts achieved re-

After her change of command ceremony, new commander Colonel Flora Sullivan (right) met with Lieutenant Colonel Dorothy Allbritten (left), who was Sullivan's replacement as chief nurse of the 338th Medical Group.
Photo courtesy of Colonel Flora Sullivan, Glenolden, PA.

sults. Colonel Florence Sullivan, an Army Nurse Corps officer, publicly assumed command of a Pennsylvania USAR hospital unit.[12]

Meantime, the Navy already had selected nurses for command roles, choosing the best-qualified individual for the job regardless of the chosen one's professional discipline or gender. In 1975 a Navy nurse, Captain Harriet A. Simmons, became the officer in charge of the Mayport, Florida, Naval Station Dispensary. Simultaneously, Captain Bernadette A. McKay assumed command responsibilities at the Naval Submarine Medical Center, New London, Connecticut, as director of administrative services. Next, in 1980, Rear Admiral Frances T. Shea accepted command responsibilities at the Naval Health Sciences Education and Training Command.[13] In 1983, Captain Mary F. Hall became the first Navy nurse to command a Naval Hospital, when she took full charge of the facility at Guantanamo Bay, Cuba. There she oversaw health care for 7,000 beneficiaries representing all services, with a staff of 186 officers and enlisted sailors in a 50-bed hospital. Another more challenging assignment two years later furnished testimony to Hall's success in her first command, when she subsequently assumed command at Naval Hospital, Long Beach, California, with its six clinics, 170 beds, and a staff of 1,300.[14]

The Air Force Nurse Corps also had an established history of command. In 1987, the Air Force Medical Service opened the competition for positions as medical group commander to nurses. Most of these command billets were then physician dominated, but the Air Force Nurse Corps had approximately two to three of its officers in command at any one time.[15] During this initial period, the Air Force nurses commanded air evacuation facilities and units only. In 1990, however, an Air Force nurse assumed command of the base clinic at Pope Air Force Base, North Carolina. Colonel Judith Hunt was the first Air Force nurse to assume this level of command at a Medical Treatment Facility. Then Air Force nurse Colonel Gloria K. Kamoureux began her assignment as hospital commander at Loring Air Force Base, Maine, in 1992.[16] As of 1996, many Air Force nurses were commanding at the squadron and group levels. Three officers served as Medical Group commanders while four others served as group commander. Additionally, 39 nurses were squadron commanders within medical groups, and two Air Force Nurse Corps officers were commanders of aeromedical evacuation squadrons.[17]

By 1993, the AMEDD was slowly edging forward with the branch immaterial (BI) concept for command slots, though lagging well behind the Navy and Air Force, which had used a comparable system for some 20 years.[18] In reaction to the inherent problems with the Professional Officer Filler System (PROFIS) commander program, the strong recommendations made by DACOWITS, probing questions posed by members of Congress, and the need for better utilization of general officers within the context of the AMEDD reorganization, the surgeon general, Lieutenant General Alcide LaNoue, announced his support for opening selected opportunities for command for all AMEDD officers.[19] At the behest of General Sullivan, the CSA, LaNoue established a Leader Development Decision Network process in February 1994 to study the issue of BI AMEDD commands. This network ultimately proposed a new policy to select the officer best qualified for command of a unit and retain that officer in command upon mobilization.[20] Secretary of the Army Togo West approved the Leader Development Decision Network process on 14 January 1997.[21] In March 1997, the surgeon general, Lieutenant General Ronald R. Blanck, demonstrated his wholehearted approval by deciding "to open BI fully at the earliest opportunity."[22]

Meanwhile, the AMEDD Command Leader Development Action Plan identified related issues and made corresponding recommendations. It suggested revision of Army regulations and AMEDD policies to facilitate AMEDD Immaterial (AI) commands, designation of selected command positions as AI (thus eliminating the PROFIS command system), identification and utilization of certain AMEDD criteria (i.e., skills, knowledge, and behaviors necessary for officers to qualify for command), reengineering of AMEDD Professional Military Education to support the AI concept, and integration of AI command positions into the Department of Army Command Designated Position List process.[23]

Sullivan supported opening more seats for Army Nurse Corps officers at Command and General Staff College and at the Senior Service Schools and advocated recoding specific AMEDD General Officer positions to BI status.[24] Although no

Army nurses were considered for command at the time, Colonel Doris S. Frazier was the first Army nurse to matriculate at the Army War College in 1973. Immediately after her graduation, only a few Army Nurse Corps officers sporadically participated in the program. By 1986, for instance, only six additional Army nurses had graduated from the Army War College. Despite their lack of command opportunities at the time, the nurse graduates prepared for senior leadership positions by refining their skills in "self-assessment, organizational dynamics, leadership, ethics, and professionalism." The curriculum also provided them with the knowledge and abilities needed to successfully function in diverse staff positions in "major Army commands or at Department of the Army level."[25] Still later, when more seats were allocated, attendance at the Army War College prepared Army Nurse Corps officers for senior-level command.

The Army Nurse Corps leadership worked diligently to justify command positions for Army nurses. They explained how professional leader development advanced within the corps and how it encompassed every phase of the Army Nurse Corps Life Cycle Model, or career plan.[26] Adams asserted:

> The scope of responsibility and accountability of each nursing position increases in every phase of the Army Nurse Corps Life Cycle Model. Each position prepares AN [Army Nurse] officers for more advanced leadership roles. The only difference is that AN leadership positions are not entitled "command." The reality is AN officers have the same military and civilian education and similar leadership experiences as their counterparts/colleagues in other AMEDD Corps who compete for command. Essential and key positions in the AN require the same education that leads to the skills, knowledge, and attitudes that would qualify AN officers for advanced leadership positions as identified in the other AMEDD Corps Life Cycle Models.[27]

As 1995 drew to a close, Army Nurse Corps hopes and efforts were coming to fruition as the Army relaxed policies and opened AI command positions to nurses. After her four-year tenure as chief, Adams assumed command of the Southwest Health Service Support Area located at Fort Bliss, Texas, and in 1997, accepted the flag of command at William Beaumont Army Medical Center. Adams became the first female and first nonphysician to command an Army Medical Center, a watershed event in AMEDD history.[28] Following her command at Beaumont, she was promoted to major general and assumed command of Tripler Army Medical Center in Honolulu, Hawaii. Her additional responsibilities included serving as the U.S. Army, Pacific, surgeon, as commander of the Pacific Regional Medical Command, the TRICARE Pacific lead agent, and the PROFIS commander for Korea's 18th Medical Command. She was the first Army Nurse Corps officer to receive a second star and fulfill these challenging responsibilities.[29] Army Nurse Corps officers also took command of three of five AMEDD Recruiting Detachments at this time, with responsibility for all AMEDD recruiting for every AMEDD enlisted soldier and all AMEDD officer corps.[30] At the AMEDD Center and School (C&S) Brigade, Army Nurse Corps officers assumed new roles as company commanders.[31] The first Army Nurse Corps officer who competed and was selected for an AMEDD C&S training company command was Captain Bethany Alexander. In January 1995, she assumed command of Company D, 232nd Medical Battalion.[32]

In 1995, Colonel William Bester commanded the Advance Party of the 67th CSH in Hungary and Croatia. The next year, the surgeon general requested approval from the secretary of the Army for an interim change to the policy of restricting command of medical treatment facilities to MC officers. The secretary granted the request in January 1997, clearing the way for Colonel Bester to serve as commander of Moncrief Army Community Hospital at Fort Jackson, South Carolina, in 1998.[33] In March of that same year, Colonel Kristine V. Campbell commanded the 396th CSH in Bosnia-Herzegovina, becoming the first female officer and first USAR Army nurse to deploy and command a field hospital overseas in a peacekeeping operation.[34] Campbell led the 450-strong hospital unit and fostered a positive work environment, facilitated a smooth unit operation, and provided resources. She recalled that the command experience was demanding, adding that she managed by focusing on "what I knew I was good at. I knew how to take care of patients"; by concentrating on that strength, she succeeded in her command.[35]

The AMEDD BI Colonel Command Board that convened in January 1998 under the direction of the Army Secretariat represented the first time that Army Nurse Corps colonels were eligible for consideration to command Medical Groups, Scientific/Technical units, Level 1 Medical Treatment Facilities, and Level 1 TO&E hospitals. Army Nurse Corps officers still could not compete for command of larger Level 2 Medical Department Activities or Medical Centers, considered Level 3 commands. After gaining Level 1 TO&E/MTF command experience, these officers would become eligible for consideration in subsequent boards.[36] The AMEDD BI Lieutenant Colonel Command Board that convened in December 1997 selected lieutenant colonels for battalion-level command in BI positions such as TDA Training Commands at the AMEDD C&S, in TDA Scientific/Technical Battalion Equivalents such as at the Center for Health Promotion and Preventive Medicine (CHPPM), and in TO&E Medical Treatment Battalions in Area Support Medical Battalions.[37] The names of those officers selected by the lieutenant colonel and colonel command boards later appeared on a Command Designated Position List, which became the known as the Command Selection List (CSL) in 1998.[38] The AMEDD CSL for fiscal year (FY) 1999 designated four Army nurses for command.[39] By FY 2000, seven Army Nurse Corps colonels appeared on the AMEDD CSL.[40]

Other BI opportunities for command materialized during this time. These non-CSL clinic command opportunities operated under a slightly different format. The MC, MSC, Army Nurse Corps, and Army Medical Specialist Corps each nominated two officers for available clinic commander positions.[41] The regional medical commander then would select the best qualified officer—regardless of branch—for the command position within that region.[42]

By 1998, participants at a chief nurse conference elaborated the Army Nurse Corps philosophy relating to BI command and positions. They believed that company grade BI positions such as company command were simply alternative leader development options analogous to traditional branch-based leadership opportunities such as those found in head nurse positions. Furthermore, they acknowledged that all AMEDD branches could develop leaders comparably within their core disciplines. Finally, they stressed that the discipline of nursing must remain the core competency within the Army Nurse Corps.[43] Brigadier General Bettye Simmons expanded on this philosophy:

> As Branch Immaterial opportunities emerge for us, it will be critical that we never lose focus on our core responsibilities of providing, managing and leading the delivery of nursing care to soldiers and their families. Our real value in all arenas is the perspective of the discipline of nursing. If we lose sight of this or lose sight of our primary responsibility, we have lost the whole point of working to get "to the table."[44]

General Clara Adams-Ender shared her insights on the intermingling of nursing and command roles. She wrote that, "if anything, being in command positions sharpens your skills as a nurse and reinforces the specific skills that nurses bring to the table." Adams-Ender revealed that her unceasing prayer while in command was:

> ... "Thanks, God that you made me a nurse first." Nursing provided me with three unique skills that I used often while in command and in bringing order to my often chaotic life today. [First,] through nursing, I learned about human behavior. Through the behavioral sciences and in the labs, nurses learn that there are some personalities in the world and some real characters—we learn how to cope with them all. [Second,] we learn as nurses how to manage many activities at once on a 24-hour clock. I never thought I'd learned anything of value on the 11-7 shift, but I did learn how to organize activities independently and how to get my staff organized. I would never have learned that as well on the day shift with someone else in charge. [And finally,] nursing taught me a process.[45] Sometimes we don't even value that process much as nurses. However, I've come to realize and value the nursing process because it is just a systematic way of getting things done and it keeps me on the road to successful mission accomplishment.[46]

Adams-Ender recognized that the most important knowledge, values, and skills she contributed to the overall picture were inherent to the discipline of nursing.

Nurses faced other dilemmas in the introduction of command opportunities. After an Army nurse completed a command assignment, the question of a follow-on assignment surfaced. For instance, after commanding a hospital, was it an appropriate career move for an Army Nurse Corps officer to revert to a hospital chief nurse position? Another quandary focused on budgeted end-strength issues. If a hospital had just enough nurses to carry out the existing workload, was it appropriate to pull resources away for command opportunities? In other words, if staffing was tight, was it proper to release a head nurse or a staff nurse to fill a company commander post? The final decision often came down to a choice between offering nurses upward mobility versus providing adequate staff to proffer high quality nursing care.[47] There were no simple answers to these complex questions.

Command positions for Army nurses finally gained sufficient momentum during the 1990s to become a reality. But Army Nurse Corps officers' opportunities to contribute in BI capacities were not only restricted to command roles. They also could participate in a variety of other BI positions.

Early in 1990, the trend of making not only command slots but also other key AMEDD positions into BI billets gained impetus. This movement centered on the idea that certain roles could be efficiently and successfully assumed by any competent officer, irrespective of gender, branch, or specialty. During her tenure as chief of the Army Nurse Corps, Adams-Ender's actions were an expression of this trend. She realized that the AMEDD had to upgrade the position of director of personnel for the surgeon general, elevating it from that of a colonel to the general officer level. This, she believed, would enhance the position's authority and influence when dealing with other elements of the Army and guarantee that AMEDD issues were seriously addressed. Accordingly, Adams-Ender approached Lieutenant General Frank Ledford, the surgeon general, with her idea and he in turn responded, "Clara, if you are crazy enough to volunteer for this position, I am crazy enough to appoint you." Over time, several advantages accrued from the change.

Adams-Ender's personnel staff welcomed their newfound ability to utilize what she called their "referent power." When differences of opinion arose, for example, the personnel officers would announce that the "general said this is the way it is going to be so I would suggest that your general get together with my general and see if they can't work it out." Using some version of this approach made the disagreements by and large disappear. Another beneficial effect of the dual-hatting was the fact that Adams-Ender met often with the deputy chief of staff for personnel (DCSPER) of the Army and the assistant secretary of defense for manpower and reserve affairs (ASD M&RA). At such sessions, she could speak about nursing concerns. She recalled, "General Ono [DCSPER] was always interested in what was happening in nursing and I had convinced Mr. Spurlock [ASD M&RA] that he ought to be interested. It didn't matter, I was going to tell him anyway." Thus, she was able to not only advance the concerns of the AMEDD but also surface matters of interest to the Army Nurse Corps.[48]

As successive chiefs accepted their responsibilities for the Army Nurse Corps, they too assumed other BI roles. As noted, Adams also became the director of AMEDD Personnel and later, commander of CHPPM while serving as chief of the Army Nurse Corps. Simmons commenced her tenure as chief of the Army Nurse Corps in 1996 while simultaneously beginning an assignment as the deputy commandant at the AMEDD C&S.[49] A year later, she moved from the AMEDD C&S to become the Forces Command command surgeon, noting:

> This is a great opportunity for Army Nursing . . . it gives us an opportunity to prove the ability of Army Nurses in nontraditional roles to our line counterparts and to show the value-added of our discipline in working the issues impacting the Army.[50]

In 1999, Simmons relinquished her role at Forces Command and assumed command of the CHPPM.[51] Bester succeeded Simmons as chief of the Army Nurse Corps in 2000 and, like his predecessors, wore two hats. Initially he served as the assistant surgeon general for force projection and subsequently as the CHPPM commander.[52]

In 1993, a small contingent of Army Nurse Corps officers were functioning in a

During this period, Major Mary E.V. Frank was the Army Nurse Corps historian, assigned to the U.S. Army Center of Military History. During her tenure in that assignment, she conducted a number of historical analyses of contemporary issues.
Photo courtesy of Colonel Mary E.V. Frank, St. Michaels, MD.

number of critical positions previously reserved only for other AMEDD officers. In most cases, the respective division/directorate chief specifically requested these Army nurses, whom the Army Nurse Corps then approved to assume these billets (several of which were crucial positions at senior leadership levels).[53] Similar positions held by Army nurses, such as chief, Family Health Clinic, chief, Primary Care, or executive or administrative officer, involved leadership at a local level and existed in various settings.[54] As Army Nurse Corps officers moved into BI command and staff positions in greater numbers, attention turned to expanding horizons even further. Questions emerged about the possibility of opening promotions for Army nurses, indeed for all AMEDD officers, beyond the one-star level.

Since 1967, 10 U.S. Code 3069 limited the tenure of the Army Nurse Corps officer selected to be the chief of the Army Nurse Corps to no more than four years.[55] After the four-year incumbency, chiefs traditionally retired from active duty.[56] The assignment was a terminal position that offered no opportunity to compete for further promotions.[57]

In 1985, Major Mary Frank wrote that the Army Nurse Corps advancement to rank parity paralleled the grueling path nursing took in its quest for professional development and it also echoed the progression of the women's rights movement. She added that advancements came in the guise of "minimally threatening increments" against the backdrop of the AMEDD's, the Army's, and most of the legislators' "gender phobias." Frank also noted that, in the past, progress toward rank parity always required special legislation that, in turn, perpetuated the myth of the Army Nurse Corps as a disparate, atypical branch. This misperception always rendered efforts to move ahead all the more complex, protracted, and costly. Finally, she concluded that every step forward has "been in response to well-documented crises in authority, recruitment and retention and . . . been based on the irrefutable logic of superior performance."[58] The arduous, century-long journey from no rank and little status to relative rank, begrudgingly bestowed on Army nurses in 1920, to the comprehensive opportunities available in 2004 was an epic tale of struggles fought by the senior leadership with the unflagging support of a few enthusiastic benefactors.

Many had long recognized that chiefs of the Army Nurse Corps had the potential to provide further, valuable service to the AMEDD and the Army after their four-year term and Corps-specific responsibilities. In 1991, when Adams became chief of the Army Nurse Corps and the concept of AMEDD BI positions gained more currency, the notion of opening the upper echelons of the AMEDD for all eligible senior officers became a possibility.

Senator Daniel Inouye, long a supporter of the Army Nurse Corps, believed Congress should enact legislation to make the chief of the Corps position a major general billet.[59] Adams privately disagreed with this position and instead favored allowing the chiefs of the Army Nurse Corps to compete for promotion to major general with their AMEDD contemporaries.[60] She believed that fulfilling the Corps chief's responsibilities justified the brigadier general officer position but it also enfranchised the chief of the Army Nurse Corps to compete on equal terms with her contemporaries for other senior leadership positions that no longer were reserved exclusively for the MC. As assistant surgeon general for personnel, she subsequently articulated this option, garnered the surgeon general's support, worked to implement it, and ultimately made this concept the next stage in the evolving process of change.[61]

After her tenure as chief, Army Nurse Corps, Adams had two years remaining on active duty before her mandatory retirement date of 1997 and continued on active duty serving in a BI general officer position. During this time, she became eligible for consideration for promotion to major general by the FY 1998 General Officer Promotion Board that convened in the fall of 1997. The board selected Adams for promotion to major general.[62]

In the interim, however, the campaign waged to open consideration of Army Nurse Corps officers for the AMEDD General Officer Promotion Board turned into another challenging odyssey. In July 1994, Surgeon General LaNoue requested approval from Sullivan, the CSA, to establish a corps immaterial competitive category for promotion to AMEDD brigadier and major general.[63] Sullivan disapproved the request while acknowledging that his decision caused a "disproportionate promotion opportunity for the medical [physician] GOs [General Officers]."[64] Inouye became involved and urged the Chief of Staff of the Army "to reconsider the Army's decision to deny nurses and other qualified AMEDD officers the same opportunities that the physicians and dentists" enjoyed.[65] In April 1995, the surgeon general again sought approval to include all AMEDD branches for consideration in the competitive category for promotion to AMEDD brigadier and major general, this time addressing his request to a new Chief of Staff of the Army, General Dennis J. Reimer.[66] After clarifying several minor details, Reimer approved the surgeon general's proposal and expanded the AMEDD major general promotion competitive category to include all brigadier general officers of the AMEDD regardless of branch in June 1997.[67] That same year the FY 1996 Department of Defense Authorization Act eliminated the legislative restrictions that narrowly limited the three-star position of surgeon general to MC officers only in all three services.[68] These decisions opened the door for Army Nurse Corps officers to compete with their peers in the AMEDD and ensured a relatively level playing field for leadership opportunities for all branches.

While this was taking place, Inouye sponsored legislation to authorize the one-star rank for all three Nurse Corps chiefs and directors (Army, Navy, and Air Force) and the rank of colonel for the assistant chiefs. In practice, this had been the case for decades but had not been previously mandated by law. Inouye explained that he was "concerned that without this official designation, these positions [were] vulnerable to being downgraded or even eliminated." He added:

<small>In recent years, downsizing mandates and new ways of providing health care have led to many reorganization efforts. Unfortunately, reorganization has become a euphemism for eliminating positions—and health care reorganization has too often become an excuse to eliminate nursing positions. . . . Military nurses hit two glass ceilings: one as a nurse in a physician-dominated health care system and one as a woman in a male-dominated military system. The simple fact is that organizations are best served when the leadership is composed of a mix of specialty and gender groups—of equal rank—who bring their unique talents to the corporate table. For military nurses, the general officer chief nurse position is the only way for nurses to get to the corporate executive table.[69]</small>

Pictured is Major General Gale Pollock, who served as the 22nd Chief of the Army Nurse Corps from 2004 to 2008.
Photo courtesy of Army Nurse Corps Archives, Office of Medical History, Falls Church, VA.

Pictured is Major General Patricia Horoho, who served as the 23rd Chief of the Army Nurse Corps from 2008 to 2012.
Photo courtesy of Army Nurse Corps Archives, Office of Medical History, Falls Church, VA.

Congress passed the legislation 30 July 1996 and removed any doubt that henceforth the Army Nurse Corps and the Air Force Corps director positions would be the one-star rank, and their assistants would hold the rank of colonel.[70] The rank of the director of the Navy Nurse Corps had already been guaranteed by Public Law 97-22 in 1981. As a part of Public Law 97-22, the Defense Officer Personnel Management Act, §6, specified that the director of the Navy Nurse Corps would serve in the rank of commodore admiral.[71]

Inouye also continued his efforts to enact legislation to make the chief of the Army Nurse Corps a two-star billet. His justification was based on the fact that the Dental Corps chief position was a two-star billet, while the chief of the Army Nurse Corps wore only a single star. Inouye reasoned that if the two-star Dental Corps chief position carried a scope of responsibility for 1,253 Dental Corps officers, why should the chief of the Army Nurse Corps, who managed 4,207 Army Nurse Corps officers, not carry equal rank?[72] When Sullivan testified before Congress in 1994, Inouye raised the two-star issue:

> Well, I have been talking about this for 20 years now. They [the Nurse Corps] went up to one star, and I think it is about time they went up to two stars. Maybe I am a bit too biased because I spent 21 months of my life in an Army hospital and 95 percent of the time I saw nurses, and maybe 5 percent a physician, including minor surgery.
>
> And so, as far as being autonomous and independent and professional, I have no question about that. And if we want to recruit the best, we better give them opportunities. So I am not doing it just for the Army, I am doing it for the Navy and the Air Force, and hoping that they will come to their senses. And I hope you will seriously consider this matter—not ten years from now.[73]

Sullivan responded, "Can I come back to you on that Senator? . . . I would request you not mandate it yet. . . . we are doing some things for the nurses. And I appreciate personally your views."[74]

It was not until December 2002 that Congress passed Public Law 107-314, which amended Title 10, §3069(b). This legislation authorized the appointment of the chief of the Army Nurse Corps to the rank of major general. In 2004, Colonel Gale S. Pollock was nominated to be the 22nd chief of the Army Nurse Corps. She also was promoted to major general and assumed her assigned duties as chief of the Army Nurse Corps, commander of Tripler Army Medical Center, U.S. Army, Pacific, surgeon, and commander of the Pacific Regional Medical Command.[75]

Over the relatively short period of a decade from 1990 to the birth of the new century, an unprecedented world order evolved and formed a unique context that shaped the Army Nurse Corps. The Cold War ended, the military underwent a stringent retrenchment, and the AMEDD and the Army Nurse Corps reinvented themselves. As this major transformation was coming to pass, the Army and the Army Nurse Corps simultaneously was taking part in a number of large scale, challenging combat operations.

# Notes

1. "Surgeon General Wants MDs to Head Hospitals," *The Stripe* (8 June 1972): n.p., Newspaper Clipping in Army Nurse Corps Collection (ANCC), Office of Medical History (OMH).
2. Charles C. Pixley, Interview by John N. Bogart, Transcript, 65, 1985, Office of Medical History.
3. Ibid.
4. Clara L. Adams-Ender with Blair S. Walker, *My Rise to the Stars, How a Sharecropper's Daughter Became an Army General* (Lake Ridge, VA: Cape Associates, Inc., 2001): 228.
5. Clara L. Adams-Ender, Handwritten Notes on Draft Manuscript, 28 September 2005, ANCC, OMH.
6. Diane Corcoran to Author, E-mail Correspondence, 19 June 2002, ANCC, OMH.
7. "Army Nurses Light 75th Candle, Chief Takes Corps' Pulse," Spotlight, U.S. Army Command Information, No. 142, 2, 29 April 1976; Frank A. Bartimo, "Exercise of Command by Members of the Army Nurse Corps," Memorandum, 16 January 1974; and T.R. Byrne, "Request for Clarification of Definitions and Policies Relating to Assumption of Command by AMEDD Officers," Memorandum, Tab B, Legal References, 29 September 1992 (all in ANCC, OMH).
8. Chief, Medical Corps Affairs, "Do Not Establish a Branch Immaterial Designator for the AMEDD," n.d., Recommendation Number 35, attached to James J. James, "AMEDD Officer Leader Development Action Plan," Memorandum, 12 April 1990; Lieutenant Colonel Christopher, "Command of AMEDD Units," Information Paper, 18 March 1992; AMEDD Center and School, "AMEDD Leader Development," Briefing Slides, n.d.; AMEDD Center and School, "AMEDD Command Leader Development Action Plan," 4, n.d.; and Dorothy B. Pocklington, "My IMA Experiences," E-mail Correspondence, 22 August 2003 (all in ANCC, OMH).
9. Colonel Robert Claypool, M.C., staff officer at OTSG at the time, subscribed to these beliefs. Nancy R. Adams, "Thoughts for MG Tempel," n.d., ANCC, OMH.
10. "Army Nurse Corps Transition Survey," 13, n.d., ANCC, OMH.
11. Nancy R. Adams to Gordon Sullivan, Draft, Unsent Letter, 1992; Nancy R. Adams, "Thoughts for MG Tempel," n.d.; Allan C. Brendsel, "AMEDD Branch Immaterial General Officer Positions," Memorandum, 27 July 1994; and Daniel K. Inouye to General Gordon R. Sullivan, Typewritten Letter (TL), 6 February 1995 (all in ANCC, OMH).

12. Dorothy A. Pocklington, Interview by Joseph Frechette, Transcript, 24–26, 26 May 2000, Army Nurse Corps Oral History Collection. Dorothy A. Pocklington to Author, 7 January 2005; Dorothy A. Pocklington to Author, 12 May 2005 (both E-mail Correspondence, in ANCC, OMH).

13. Susan H. Godson, Serving Proudly, *A History of Women in the U.S. Navy* (Annapolis: Naval Institute Press, 2001), 244. Connie L. Reeves, "Invisible Soldiers, Military Nurses," in *Gender Camouflage, Women and the U.S. Military*, ed. Francine D'Amico and Laurie Weinstein (New York: New York University Press, 1999), 23. Doris M. Sterner, *In and Out of Harm's Way, A History of the Navy Nurse Corps* (Seattle, WA: Peanut Butter Publishing, 1996): 380.

14. J. K. Herman, "A Conversation with RADM Hall," *Navy Medicine* 79 (May–June 1988): 8–11.

15. "Statement of Brigadier General Linda J. Stierle, Director of Medical Readiness and Nursing Services, Office of the Surgeon General," Department of the Air Force, Presentation to the Committee on Appropriations, Subcommittee on Defense, United States Senate, 3, April 1998, ANCC, OMH. Mary C. Smolenski, Donald G. Smith, and James S. Nanney, *A Fit, Fighting Force, The Air Force Nursing Services Chronology* (Washington, DC: Office of the Air Force Surgeon General, 2005), 41.

16. Mary C. Smolenski, Donald G. Smith, and James S. Nanney, *A Fit, Fighting Force, The Air Force Nursing Services Chronology* (Washington, DC: Office of the Air Force Surgeon General, 2005), 45, 47.

17. "Statement of Brigadier General Linda J. Stierle, Director Nursing Services, United States Air Force," Presentation to the Committee on Appropriations, Subcommittee on Defense, United States Senate, 1, June 1996, ANCC, OMH.

18. The terms Branch Immaterial (BI), Corps Immaterial (CI), and AMEDD Immaterial (AI) were used interchangeably. Jerry Harben, "Policy Change Offers All Officers Chance to Command," *The Mercury* 24 (May 1997): 1–2.

19. The existing policy that dictated change of command from the MSC commander in garrison to the PROFIS medical commander upon deployment had a significant potential to "compromise a unit's cohesiveness and mission capability." AMEDD Center and School, "AMEDD Command Leader Development Action Plan," 3, n.d. G.E. Willis, "Policy Changes Open Medical Commands," *Army Times* 38 (14 April 1997): 4. In its Fall 1973 conference, DACOWITS recommended that DoD "prepare a legislative proposal to amend section 3579, title 10, U.S. Code to provide the opportunity for officer [sic] of the Army Nurse Corps and the Army Medical Specialist Corps to exercise command within the Army Medical Department. "DACOWITS 2000 Spring Conference, History of Recommendations, 1951–1999," 74, n.d., ANCC, OMH. G.E. Willis, "Panel Wants Nurses to Command Military Hospitals," *Army Times* 53 (2 November 1992): 11. Evelyn D. Harris, "New DACOWITS Leader Wants Women to Command Hospitals," *The Mercury* 21 (February 1994): 4. Daniel K. Inouye to Gordon R. Sullivan, TL, 6 February 1995, ANCC, OMH. General LaNoue qualified his support, stating that he believed "hospitals should be commanded by physicians, but other commands do not require Medical Corps leadership." Jerry Harben, "Surgeon General Seeks 'Best Qualified' Leaders," *The Mercury* 22 (January 1995): 12. AMEDD Center and School, "AMEDD Command Leader Development Action Plan," 3–7, n.d.

20. "Initiatives, New AMEDD Command Policy," Briefing Slide, in "1993 Army Medical Department Functional Review, Army Medical Department (AMEDD) Overview," TSG Briefing, 25 October 1993; William L. Moore, "Leader Development Decision Network (LDDN) to Study Implementation of Branch Immaterial Army Medical Department

(AMEDD) Commands," Memorandum, 13 December 1993; Daniel K. Inouye to Gordon R. Sullivan, TL, 6 February 1995; and Gordon R. Sullivan to Daniel K. Inouye, TL, 6 March 1995 (all in ANCC, OMH).

21. G.E. Willis, "Policy Changes Open Medical Commands," *Army Times* 38 (14 April 1997): 4. Ronald R. Blanck to Secretary of the Army, "Command of Medical Units— Action Memorandum," 23 October 1996; Colonel Hammerbacher, "Army Medical Department (AMEDD) Corps Immaterial Command Leader Development Decision Network (LDDN)," Information Paper, 19 February 1997; and Alice Demarais, "AMEDD Center & School Personnel Proponent Directorate, Branch Immaterial," Memo from the Chief, Army Nurse Corps (March 1997): 4 (all in ANCC, OMH).

22. Alice Demarais, "AMEDD Personnel Proponent Directorate, Branch Immaterial (BI)," Memo from the Chief, Army Nurse Corps (April 1997): 2, ANCC, OMH.

23. AMEDD Center and School, "AMEDD Command Leader Development Action Plan," 1–13, n.d.

24. Jeffery L. Heslop "Army Nurse Corps (ANC) Leader Development," Typewritten Document, 26 April 1994; Barbara K. Penn, "Army Medical Department (AMEDD) Seats in Command and General Staff College (CGSC) and Senior Service College (SSC)," Executive Summary, 9 May 1994; Roy A. Bryan, "Assignment of Army Nurse Corps (ANC) Officers to ARSTAF Positions, (U) (DASG-PTZ)," Executive Summary, 9 May 1994; and Roy A. Bryan, "AMEDD Branch Immaterial General Officer Positions, (U) (DASG-PTZ)," Executive Summary, 9 May 1994 (all in ANCC, OMH).

25. Clara L. Adams-Ender and Amelia J. Carson, "Capabilities of Army Nurse Corps Officer Graduates of the United Sates Army War College," *Medical Bulletin of the U.S. Army, Europe* 43 (September/October 1986): 27–29.

26. Colonel Kathleen Roehr explained that the ANC Life Cycle Model accurately portrayed "career development opportunities and responsibilities, both institutional and personal." She added that its "three-pronged approach to a successful career clearly identifies the available structured training and the personally designed, developmental opportunities, tied into the appropriate and supportive assignments." Kathleen Roehr, "Taking Command," *The Army Nursing Newsletter* (April 1999): 1, ANCC, OMH.

27. Nancy R. Adams, "The U.S. Army Nurse Corps Professional Leader Development," Printed Document, 16 February 1994, ANCC, OMH.

28. Nancy R. Adams, Memo from the Chief, Army Nurse Corps (November 1995): 1, ANCC, OMH. Jim Conley, "Fort Bliss Welcomes 1st Woman General," *El Paso Times* (29 November 1995): 1A–2A. Leticia Zamarripa, "Woman General a First for Bliss," *El Paso Times* (14 December 1995): 1A–2A. Jerry Harben, "Nurse Takes Command at Medical Center," *The Mercury* 24 (May 1997): 1–2. G.E. Willis, "A Different Kind of First Lady," *Army Times* 38 (14 April 1997): 4.

29. Kathy Titchen, "The General Is a Nurse," *MidWeek* (6 January 1999): 22, 35. Carol Reineck, "Nancy R. Adams," in Dorothy Pocklington, ed., *Heritage of Leadership, Army Nurse Corps Biographies* (Ellicott City, MD: ALDOT, 2004), 115–19.

30. The three were lieutenant colonels Constance Scott, Lenore Enzel, and John Beus, who commanded the newly formed 1st, 2nd, and 6th AMEDD Recruiting Detachments, respectively, and, for the most part, achieved their recruiting missions. Lenore Enzel to Cynthia Brown, E-mail Correspondence, 20 June 1999; and Nancy R. Adams, Memo from the Chief, Army Nurse Corps (August 1995): 2 (both in ANCC, OMH).

31. "Statement by Brigadier General Nancy R. Adams, Chief, Army Nurse Corps, Army Medical Department, before the Defense Subcommittee, Committee on Appropriations, United States Senate, 1st Session, 104th Congress, Health Programs," Record

Version, 11, 13 June 1995, ANCC, OMH.

32. Harry Noyes, "Nurse to Command Training Company," *The Mercury* 22 (February 1995): 6. Carolyn M. Feller and Debora R. Cox, *Highlights in the History of the Army Nurse Corps* (Washington, DC: U.S. Army Center of Military History, 2000), 68.

33. Bettye H. Simmons, "Nurse Progression," n.d., ANCC, OMH. Bettye H. Simmons, "Message from the Chief, Army Nurse Corps," *The Army Nursing Newsletter* (August 1998): 1; and Untitled Chronological List of Command by Army Nurse Corps Officers, n.d. (both in ANCC, OMH).

34. Carolyn M. Feller and Debora R. Cox, *Highlights in the History of the Army Nurse Corps* (Washington, DC: U.S. Army Center of Military History, 2000), 71.

35. Campbell's subsequent promotion to brigadier general was testament to her successful command. Karen Schmidt, "Brig. Gen. Kristine Campbell, On Being an Army Nurse," *NurseWeek* 14 (November 14, 2001): 11–12.

36. Examples of Medical Groups were the 1st Medical Group, Fort Hood, Texas, and the 55th Medical Group at Fort Bragg, North Carolina. Scientific/Technical units suitable for Army nurses' first command experiences were the CHPPMs in Europe and Japan. Level 1 MTFs were installations such as the MEDDACs at Heidelberg, Germany, Fort Sill, Oklahoma, and Fort Drum, New York. A typical TO&E unit that Army nurses were eligible to command was the 21st Combat Support Hospital. Carolyn Bulliner, "PERSCOM Update," *Army Nursing Newsletter* (November 1997): 2; Bettye H. Simmons, "Branch Immaterial," Memo from the Chief, Army Nurse Corps (March 1996): 5; and Alice Demarais, "AMEDD Center & School Personnel Proponent Directorate, Branch Immaterial," Memo from the Chief, Army Nurse Corps (March 1997): 4 (all in ANCC, OMH).

37. Michele Kohl, "PERSCOM Update, LTC AMEDD Command Board," Memo from the Chief, Army Nurse Corps (1 September 1997): 3; and Caroline Bulliner, "PERSCOM Update," Memo from the Chief, Army Nurse Corps (1 October 1997): 3 (both in ANCC, OMH). By mid-1997, the Navy Nurse Corps had 11 nurses in command, with 13 serving as executive officers or chiefs of staffs at Navy MTFs, lead agent staffs, and educational commands. "Statement of Rear Admiral Joan Engel, Nurse Corps, United States Navy, before the Subcommittee on Defense of the Senate Appropriations Committee, April 23, 1997, Concerning Medical Issues," Typewritten Draft, 14, 17 April 1997, ANCC, OMH.

38. Carolyn Bulliner, "PERSCOM Update," *The Army Nursing Newsletter* (August 1998): 3, ANCC, OMH.

39. The four included Colonel William T. Bester, who commanded the MEDDAC at Fort Jackson, South Carolina, Colonel Alice O'K. DeMarais, who commanded the MEDDAC at Fort Sill, Oklahoma, Colonel Patricia A. Saulsbery, who commanded the Heidelberg MEDDAC, and Colonel Patricia B. Wise, who chose to retire from active duty. When Colonel Wise declined the opportunity, Colonel Gale Pollock took her place and commanded the MEDDAC at Fort Drum, New York, in 1999. "FY 99 Colonel Command Principal List, Army Medical Department," n.d.; and Carolyn Bulliner, "PERSCOM Update," *The Army Nursing Newsletter* (June 1998): 3 (both in ANCC, OMH).

40. They included these colonels and their commands: Joan P. Eitzen (Japan CHPPM), Lark A. Ford (Fort Irwin, California, MEDDAC), Jeri I. Graham (Fort Leonard Wood, Missouri, MEDDAC), Deborah A. Gustke (Fort Leavenworth, Kansas, MEDDAC), Eileen B. Malone (Fort Belvoir, Virginia, MEDDAC), Barbara J. Scherb (West Point, New York, MEDDAC), and Arthur P. Wallace (Fort Riley, Kansas, MEDDAC). "FY 00 Colonel Command Principal List, Army Medical Department," n.d.; and Untitled Chronological List of Command by Army Nurse Corps Officers, n.d. (both in ANCC, OMH).

41. The clinic non-CSL command positions available for nominees to fill during the

summer of 1999 included those at Fort Lee, Virginia; Fort Myer, Virginia; Fort Buchanan, Puerto Rico; Fort Huachuca, Arizona; White Sands, New Mexico; Schofield Barracks, Hawaii; Camp Zama, Japan; Schweinfurt, Germany; Stuttgart, Germany; SHAPE, Belgium; and Vicenza, Italy. Carolyn R. Bulliner, "Non-CSL Clinic Commander Positions," 14 October 1998, ANCC, OMH.

42. Carolyn Bulliner, "PERSCOM Update," *The Army Nursing Newsletter* (November 1998): 6, ANCC, OMH.

43. "Army Nurse Corps Issues FY 96–99," 11, n.d., ANCC, OMH.

44. Bettye H. Simmons, Memo from the Chief, Army Nurse Corps (February 1997): 1, ANCC, OMH.

45. The nursing process is the standard method nurses use to diagnose and treat a patient's needs. Its components are fivefold—patient assessment, problem identification, planning a course of action, implementation of care, and evaluation of effectiveness. *Stedman's Medical Dictionary*, 27th ed. (Philadelphia: Williams and Wilkins, 2000), 1245. *Taber's Cyclopedic Medical Dictionary*, 19th ed. (Philadelphia: F.A. Davis, 2001), 1484. *Encyclopedia and Dictionary of Medicine, Nursing, and Allied Health*, 7th ed. (Philadelphia: Saunders, 2003), 1234.

46. Clara L. Adams-Ender, Handwritten Notes on Draft Manuscript, 28 September 2005, ANCC, OMH.

47. Bonnie M. Jennings, "Chapter Five Comments," August 2005, ANCC, OMH.

48. Clara L. Adams-Ender, Interview by Virginia Ruth Cheney, Project 92-3 U. S. Army Military History Institute, Senior Officer Oral History Program, 77–89, 1992, ANCC, OMH.

49. Nancy R. Adams, Memo from the Chief, Army Nurse Corps (November 1995): 1, ANCC, OMH.

50. Jerry Harben, "Simmons to FORSCOM," *The Mercury* 24 (May 1997): 2. Bettye Simmons, "My Reassignment," E-mail Correspondence, 17 February 1997, ANCC, OMH. Bettye H. Simmons, Memo from the Chief, Army Nurse Corps (February 1997): 1, ANCC, OMH.

51. Debora R. Cox, "Army Nurse Corps Annual Historical Report, Calendar Year 1999," Typewritten Report, 2, 9 June 2000, ANCC, OMH.

52. Evelyn B. Riley, "BG William T. Bester Becomes USACHPPM Commander," Press Release, 15 March 2002, ANCC, OMH.

53. The Army nurses filling the BI positions were Colonel Barbara Penn as chief of the AMEDD Education and Training Division, Lieutenant Colonel Rhonda Graves as chief of Program, Policy and Analysis Branch, Major Christie Smith as program analyst in Coordinated Care, Lieutenant Colonel Patricia Buzonas as process action team leader in Procurement, and Lieutenant Colonel Barbara Scherb as combat developments staff officer. Terris Kennedy, "Branch Immaterial Officers/Positions," Information Paper, 2 August 1993, ANCC, OMH.

54. Bettye H. Simmons, "Nurse Progression," n.d., ANCC, OMH.

55. The law directed that the officer be selected by a DA Secretariat Promotion Board, then be appointed by the secretary of the Army on recommendation of the surgeon general. Mary V. Frank, "Historical Review of ANC Efforts to Achieve Rank Parity 1898–1985," Memorandum, 33–37, 1985; Colonel Sierra, "AMEDD General Officer/Corps Chief Authorization," Information Paper, 1 September 1992; and Iris J. West, "Origin of General Officer Billet, Army Nurse Corps," Memorandum, 10 January 1994 (all in ANCC, OMH).

56. Two exceptions to the rule were Colonel Ruby F. Bryant, who reverted to lieutenant colonel and became chief of the Nursing Branch and nursing consultant in Europe, and

Brigadier General Clara L. Adams-Ender, who assumed command of Fort Belvoir, Virginia. These assignments followed Colonel Bryant's and General Adams-Ender's tenures as chiefs of the Army Nurse Corps.

57. Nancy R. Adams, "GO Potential: Chief, Army Nurse Corps," Briefing Slide, n.d., ANCC, OMH.

58. Mary V. Frank, "Historical Review of ANC Efforts to Achieve Rank Parity 1898–1985," 3, 28 February 1985, ANCC, OMH.

59. Patrick DeLeon, Senator Inouye's office chief of staff, also provided significant support and espoused the cause of military nursing.

60. Terris E. Kennedy, Interview by Constance J. Moore, Transcript, 404, 31 October 1996, ANCC, OMH.

61. Nancy R. Adams to Author, E-mail Correspondence, 5 November 2004, ANCC, OMH.

62. Nancy R. Adams, "Thoughts for MG Tempel," n.d.; Nancy R. Adams, "Mandatory Retirement Date (MRD)," Memorandum, 28 January 1994; "Current and Potential Branch Immaterial GO Positions," 4 March 1994; and Nancy R. Adams to Author, E-mail Correspondence, 17 November 2004 (all in ANCC, OMH).

63. Alcide M. LaNoue to Chief of Staff, Army, TL, 8 July 1994, ANCC, OMH.

64. Allan C. Brendsel, "AMEDD Branch Immaterial General Officer Positions," Memorandum, 27 July 1994, ANCC, OMH.

65. Daniel K. Inouye to General Gordon R. Sullivan, TL, 6 February 1995, ANCC, OMH.

66. Alcide M. LaNoue, "Army Medical Department (AMEDD) Branch Immaterial General Officer Positions—Action Memorandum," 20 April 1995, ANCC, OMH.

67. Dennis J. Reimer, "AMEDD General Officer Branch Immaterial Promotion Selections," Memorandum for the Surgeon General of the Army, 20 June 1996; and "CY 96 Zone of Consideration for Promotion to Major General, Army Medical Corps Competitive Category, Promotion Selection Board," MILPER Message NR 97-117, 30 June 1997 (both in ANCC, OMH).

68. Dennis J. Reimer, "AMEDD General Officer Branch Immaterial Promotion Selections," Memorandum for the Surgeon General of the Army, 20 June 1996; Department of the Air Force, "Statement of Brigadier General Linda J. Stierle, Director of Medical Readiness and Nursing Services, Office of the Surgeon General," Presentation to the Committee on Appropriations, Subcommittee on Defense, United States Senate, 4, April 1998; "Promotion Opportunities," n.d., Set of questions with background data posed by Senator Inouye in "SAC DEF 1 April Medical Questions," 7 April 1998; and "CY 96 Zone of Consideration for Promotion to Major General, Army Medical Corps Competitive Category, Promotion Selection Board," MILPER Message NR 97-117, 30 June 1997 (all in ANCC, OMH).

69. Congressional Record—Senate, S6425–S6426, 19 June 1996.

70. Congressional Record—Senate, S6424, 9 June 1996, 104th Congress, 2nd Session, Vol. 142, No. 91, National Defense Authorization Act for 1997, Amendment 4050, Title 10.

71. Iris J. West, "Origin of General Officer Billet, Army Nurse Corps," Memorandum, 10 January 1994, ANCC, OMH.

72. These figures represent FY 1995 officer end strength. "AMEDD General Officer Position Descriptions," n.d. ANCC, OMH. "Army Nurse Corps and Medical Service Corps Rank Structure," Insert for the Record, 15 March 1994, Documenting dialogue between Senator Inouye and General Sullivan; and Nancy R. Adams to Author, E-mail Correspondence, 4 November 2004 (both in ANCC, OMH).

73. "Army Nurse Corps and Medical Service Corps Rank Structure," Insert for the Re-

cord, 15 March 1994, Documenting dialogue between Senator Inouye and General Sullivan, ANCC, OMH.

74. Ibid.

75. Dorothy Pocklington, "Gale S. Pollock," in Dorothy Pocklington, ed., *Heritage of Leadership, Army Nurse Corps Biographies* (Ellicott City, MD: ALDOT, 2004), 133.

## Chapter Seventeen
# The Army and the Army Medical Department in Operation Desert Shield/Operation Desert Storm

The last decade of the 20th century was an active time operationally for the Army, the Army Medical Department (AMEDD), and the Army Nurse Corps as the call came more and more frequently to support a variety of strategic deployments. As the optempo (operations tempo) increased, so too did the perstempo or personnel tempo, the length of time soldiers were deployed to locations away from their garrison or permanent base.[1] Operations in the 1990s included humanitarian, peacekeeping, nation-building, and combat missions. The campaign of Operation Desert Shield/Operation Desert Storm (ODS), a combat mission, opened the decade on an enormous scale.

By the summer of 1990, Saddam Hussein, the president of Iraq, had driven his country into dire financial straits as a consequence of an eight-year war with neighboring Iran. To replenish his coffers, Hussein first attempted to persuade his Organization of Petroleum Exporting Countries partners to simultaneously raise the price and decrease the production of oil. When that tactic failed, he accused Kuwait, another neighboring state on the Persian Gulf, of stealing Iraqi oil. Kuwait refused to submit to Hussein's demands for compensation, and as a result he ordered the Iraqi army to march into and annex the smaller country. The invasion set off alarms in Saudi Arabia, another neighboring state, who feared that Hussein would likewise cross their borders. Consequently, King Fahad of Saudi Arabia asked for military assistance from the United States.[2]

U.S. military leaders designated the first several months, or the buildup of forces for the Persian Gulf War I, as Operation Desert Shield and the subsequent combat phase as Operation Desert Storm.[3] The precombat phase, Operation Desert Shield, referred to all military operations from the initial U.S. response on 6 August 1990 until fighting began on 17 January 1991. The period of combat, Operation Desert Storm, spanned 42 days from 17 January 1991 to 28 February 1991, at which time President George H.W. Bush ordered a provisional ending of hostilities. The temporary truce became a lasting cease-fire on 3 April 1991 with the adoption of the United Nations Security Council Resolution 687. Thereafter, allied forces withdrew from Iraq over several months.[4]

As commander in chief, President Bush had articulated four national security objectives that guided the military campaign: the need to defend American lives, resist the Iraqi offensive, remove Iraqi invaders from Kuwait, and restore that country's legitimate government. These goals remained unchanged during the operations.[5]

The U.S. military functioned with an organization of unified commands, each of which had no permanently assigned troops of its own but was accountable for monitoring the security of large geographical areas that spanned the globe.[6] One of these, the U.S. Central Command (CENTCOM), was responsible for northeast Africa and southwest Asia (SWA) and their adjacent bodies of water. Thus, CENTCOM and its commander, General H. Norman Schwarzkopf, led the U.S. forces during ODS. The Army component of CENTCOM was Army Central (ARCENT), and it drew its troops from Forces Command, which in turn garnered support and assets from other major commands, including Health Services Command (HSC).[7]

The AMEDD mobilization in support of ODS was enormous, complex, and challenging. At that time, two organizational evolutions were occurring—one related to a major equipment conversion and the other related to significant doctrinal transition. The AMEDD was replacing its Vietnam-era Mobile Unit, Surgical, Transportable (MUST) hospital configuration with updated Deployable Medical System (DEPMEDS) equipment. Many of the units deploying to ODS had the MUST equipment. All participants soon discovered that extreme desert conditions severely challenged the efficient operation of those units that went to war with the MUST setup, and this forced an accelerated substitution of DEPMEDS in many of the AMEDD's treatment units. The surgeon general acknowledged that this hurried changeover was a "monumental task."[8]

The 28th Combat Support Hospital (CSH) was the first hospital of the 44th Medical Brigade to provide patient care in the Gulf. It originally used MUST equipment, but its MUST utility packages soon malfunctioned in the extreme heat and blowing sand and abruptly ceased operation. Unexpected power failures plunged operating rooms into darkness and sweltering heat. These and other deficiencies soon became public knowledge, the subject of stateside media attention, and adversely affected morale. Such unfortunate incidents, however, served to spur the implementation of the DEPMEDS modernization program.[9]

The AMEDD was also transitioning to a new doctrine, Medical Force 2000. During ODS, the AMEDD launched two major facets of Medical Force 2000: (1) far forward surgical care and (2) enhanced psychiatric support. It used Forward Surgical Teams (FSTs), highly mobile subunits of the Mobile Army Surgical Hospital (MASH). The FSTs operated separately from their units of origin by moving with the combat troops to provide far forward surgical treatment. The FST usually had a staff of 10 officers and 10 enlisted soldiers. Among the staff of 20 were two nurse anesthetists, an operating room nurse, one medical-surgical nurse, one critical care nurse, three trauma surgeons, an orthopedic surgeon, one field medical officer (Medical Service Corps), four emergency medical technicians, three surgical technologists, and three practical nurses.[10] It also employed Combat Stress Control teams staffed by psychiatric nurses, psychiatrists, psychologists, social workers, chaplains, and Judge Advocate General officers to treat and expeditiously return soldiers with combat stress to the battlefield.[11] A measure of the efficacy of the Combat Stress Control teams was the modest number of psychiatric patients evacuated from the theater, a mere 2.7 per 1,000 patients.[12] The actual number of psychiatric patients evacuated to the U.S. Army Europe for treatment totaled 467, with 313 of those being Army soldiers.[13]

Another long-standing doctrinal concept, echelons of care, was again tested during ODS and proved to be a reliable system, although the need for some minor modifications surfaced.[14] The first of five levels of care, the most approximate to the line of fire, was the attention provided by the combat lifesaver, a fellow line soldier given 30 additional hours of medical training before the war began. The combat lifesaver could apply pressure dressings and initiate field resuscitation for his wounded compatriots. On the same echelon of care, the unit level, the medical aid man provided limited airway management, cardiopulmonary resuscitation, and arranged for evacuation of the casualty.

The second echelon was the battalion aid station usually staffed by a general medical officer or physician assistant. These medical staff members provided care for minor problems or combat stress issues. The clearing station, an element of the forward support brigade, was the third echelon of care. There, several assigned physicians could treat patients and maintain them for about three days in the clearing station's 40 beds. Often at this same third echelon, the FST would provide casualties with their first opportunity for surgical intervention.

The corps hospitals—the MASH with 60 beds, the CSH with 200 beds, and the Evacuation Hospital (EVAC) with 400 beds—represented the fourth echelon. It soon became evident in the Persian Gulf War that these large facilities with numerous beds were unnecessary. However, the acuity of the fewer-than-expected casualties dictated a greater number of staff for a lesser number of beds.

The final echelon of care during ODS was found in the rear area hospitals. In these sizable facilities, often 400 beds or greater, seriously ill or wounded casualties received treatment, were stabilized, and frequently were evacuated out of the theater of operations for more definitive care.

Another crucial challenge that the AMEDD faced before going to war involved the statutory requirement that personnel mobilizing for overseas combat undergo 12 weeks of field preparation and military training. Typically, the Officer Basic Course (OBC) fulfilled this requirement. However, in 1990, thousands of U.S. Army Reserve (USAR) and Army National Guard (ARNG) officers in the AMEDD, primarily nurses, physicians, and dentists, but also veterinarians, Medical Service Corps (MSC), and Army Medical Specialist Corps officers, had not previously attended OBC and thus were considered nondeployable. The Military Science Division chief at the Academy of Health Sciences, Colonel T.R. Byrne, MSC, directed his staff to expeditiously design a two-week course that—when combined with the USAR and ARNG soldiers' prior professional education and background (which gave constructive credit for 10 additional weeks)—would satisfy the requirement. Commonly referred to as the "Shake 'n Bake" OBC, the course had many iterations that met in Blesse Auditorium at the Academy of Health Sciences and on a training area near Salido Creek at Fort Sam Houston, Texas.

Approximately 2,000 AMEDD USAR and ARNG personnel, who were billeted in off-post hotels on the 410 Loop, took part in the program from Labor Day 1990 until February 1991. Byrne expected to have a number of conscientious objectors participating in the program. However, there were none. What did materialize was a group of disgruntled Medical Corps officers, who were irritated because they had been pulled out of their civilian graduate medical education training to mobilize, and another peeved faction composed of various AMEDD branches that had been counting for years on their lack of OBC to keep them from combat. There also were numerous Army nurses and MSC officers who had been trying to get seats in the class for years and were thrilled to have the opportunity to attend. Among the total number of participants were 902 USAR and ARNG Army nurses.

The course curriculum focused on a variety of doctrinal, leadership, and operational subjects and skills. Topics included the military and the AMEDD, the Army division, staff development of subordinates, combat stress, movement under direct and indirect fire, weapons and radio familiarization, Nuclear, Biological, and Chemical protection, the modern medical system, medical regulating and patient evacuation, health care documentation, and the conduct of a Mass Casualty situation. Numerous course participants—many of whom were university faculty from the entire spectrum of academic institutions nationwide—were amazed at the quality of the instruction provided mostly by resident MSC faculty and some MSC officers who then were attending the Officer Advanced Course. Some consideration was given to reinstating the "Shake 'n Bake" OBC during the opening days of Operation Iraqi Freedom; however, that plan was not implemented.[15]

ODS was a massive endeavor that involved participation by the total force—the Active Army, the USAR, the ARNG, civil service personnel, and the retired population.[16] In a mobilization whose speed was unprecedented, the AMEDD deployed approximately 25,000 USAR and ARNG personnel in three months, including 12,000 to SWA, 3,000 to Europe, and 10,000 more within the continental United States (CONUS). The reserve components were approximately 75 percent of the AMEDD's total assets. The AMEDD officer corps, which included all components on active duty, counted approximately 21,800 soldiers worldwide. Of those, 8,500 were Army nurses, 7,300 were physicians, and 6,000 were MSC officers. Several thousand AMEDD retiree and reservist volunteers also responded to an early call to augment the force.[17]

One such retiree was Brigadier General (Ret.) Hazel W. Johnson-Brown, the 18th chief of the Army Nurse Corps. Although Johnson-Brown had not worked in an operating room for 24 years, she volunteered and served as a circulating nurse in the operating rooms at Fort Belvoir, Virginia. She acknowledged that working in the operating room was "just second nature" to her and disclosed that she "was doing this a long time in the Army Nurse Corps, and most of the procedures haven't changed."[18] Johnson-Brown's volunteerism was but one expression of the patriotic support for the war that swept across the nation.

Of all three services, the Army's medical presence in ODS was the largest. The Air Force Medical Service sent 4,868 officers and enlisted airmen to SWA and staffed fifteen 50-bed air transportable hospitals, 33 air transportable clinics, and a 250-bed contingency hospital. A total of 174 Air Force Reserve nurses augmented the 162 active duty Air Force Nurse Corps nurses who served in the Gulf during ODS. The Navy Medical Department deployed 2,277 officers and 8,943 enlisted sailors, who staffed two hospital ships, three fleet hospitals, three host nation facilities, and two Marine Expeditionary Brigades afloat.[19] The Navy Nurse Corps deployed approximately 250 nurses to staff their hospital ships, the Comfort and the Mercy, in the Persian Gulf. They also assigned 21 nurses to their amphibious assault ships, the Guam and Iwo Jima. A total of 31 nurses deployed in support of the 1st Marine Amphibious Brigade and the 1st and 2nd Force Service Support Groups. Finally, a contingent of 152 Navy nurse reservists staffed three fleet hospitals erected in the theater.[20]

ODS was not only a joint operation involving the U.S. Army, Air Force, and Navy but also it was a coalition undertaking that included a vast array of allied forces. Forty countries participated in ODS, including forces from the Americas, the Antipodes, the Pacific, the Far East, the Middle East, Europe, Scandinavia, and Africa.[21]

Projected casualty figures for ODS dictated the need for 18,500 beds in the SWA theater. It also called for a sizable expansion in AMEDD bed resources in other locations. Ultimately, 5,500 hospital beds were available in Europe and provisions were made for more than 10,000 beds in CONUS. In addition, the Veterans Administration provided 25,000 beds for casualties, and the Department of Defense Health Resources Sharing and Emergency Operations Act was prepared for implementation. If needed, the Department of Defense would activate the National Disaster Medical System that involved care in civilian hospitals.[22]

HSC played a significant role in the medical support of ODS within CONUS and also provided additional personnel for SWA and 7th Medical Command in Europe. HSC:

- simultaneously provided its routine health care support for all beneficiaries in CONUS, Hawaii, and Alaska, while fielding a state-of-the-art combat medical service;
- channeled thousands of officers and enlisted soldiers into CENTCOM and the AMEDD facilities in Europe; and
- coordinated the massive deployment of USAR and ARNG hospital units and ensured that they met required set readiness criteria.[23]

The first AMEDD units arrived in SWA in August 1990 including the 44th

Medical Brigade, the 47th Field Hospital, the 28th CSH, and the 5th MASH. Professional Officer Filler System personnel and Forces Command nurses were mobilized with these units and their exodus from HSC units initially created some military treatment facility staffing shortages in CONUS. Soon, however, these facilities used some 800 USAR/ARNG and retiree volunteers, and HSC subsequently activated additional reservists to backfill the CONUS and Europe losses. In a two-phase process, HSC called 24 USAR/ARNG units to active duty. It first activated nine hospitals and two dental units in August 1990 and called the remaining 15 units to active duty in early January 1991.[24]

In theater, the command organized hospitals into three Corps-level hospital clusters: (1) Echelons Above Corps (EAC), (2) XVIII Corps, and (3) VII Corps.

The EAC consisted of four Medical Groups, the XVIII Corps claimed two Medical Groups, and the VII Corps had two Medical Groups and an EVAC task force. There were 13,580 operating beds in 44 hospitals located in four countries (Saudi Arabia, Bahrain, United Arab Emirates, and Oman), which was triple the amount during the height of the Vietnam War. Of the 13,580 beds, 7,300 were in EAC units, 2,980 were in XVIII Corps, and VII Corps operated 3,300. Each Corps had a varied mix of hospital types determined by the Corps mission. Sixteen of the 44 hospitals came from the Active force, while the USAR activated 17 and the ARNG activated 11 facilities. The AMEDD also staffed nine host-nation hospitals, and the Army's 365th EVAC integrated with the Air Force's Contingency Hospital in Oman.[25]

To provide command and control for Army medical assets within SWA, the U.S. Army Forces Central Command Medical Group EAC (Provisional) began operation on 6 December 1990. The CENTCOM Medical Group served as the higher headquarters for four medical groups. The VII Corps and the XVIII Airborne Corps also provided other medical assets within the theater.[26]

The top level of joint leadership in the theater medical command structure consisted of a small cadre of Army and Air Force colonel and Navy captain medical officers, one from each service. Several pundits believed that the rank of these individuals was neither adequate nor commensurate with their responsibilities and advocated general or flag-rank medical officers for the positions. One critic noted the "extraordinary mismatch between the size, diversity and importance of the military medical assets committed in the Gulf and the meager command structure allowed in the theater for its operation and guidance was obvious to everyone from the start." The pre-ODS CENTCOM surgeon was Air Force Colonel Robert P. Belihar, and he remained in that senior position in CENTCOM for the duration of the war, at the direction of General H. Norman Schwarzkopf, who knew and trusted him.[27]

# Notes

1. Phil Gunby, "Military Medicine in the Balkans Now," *Journal of the American Medical Association* 282 (10 November 1999): 1707–09.
2. William Matthews, "Deployment Backs Up Diplomatic Initiatives Designed to Isolate Iraq," Army Times (20 August 1990): 12, 56. Richard L. West and Thomas D. Byrne, *The U.S. Army in Operation Desert Storm, An Overview* (Arlington, VA: Association of the United States Army, 1991), 3–4. Frank N. Schubert and Theresa L. Kraus, eds., *The Whirlwind War, The United States Army in Operations Desert Shield and Desert Storm* (Washington, DC: Center of Military History, United States Army, 1993), 21–23, 49–50. Andrew Leyden, *Gulf War Debriefing Book* (Grants Pass, OR: Hellgate Press, 1997).
3. Both Operation Desert Shield and Operation Desert Storm are abbreviated as ODS. ODS is also referred to as the Persian Gulf War or Gulf War I.
4. Richard L. West and Thomas D. Byrne, *The U.S. Army in Operation Desert Storm, An Overview* (Arlington VA: Association of the United States Army, 1991), 1. Robert H. Scales, *Certain Victory* (Washington, DC: Office of the Chief of Staff, United States Army, 1993). Richard M. Swain, *"Lucky War" Third Army in Desert Storm* (Fort Leavenworth, KS: U.S. Army Command and General Staff College Press, 1994): 1–11.
5. Richard L. West and Thomas D. Byrne, *The U.S. Army in Operation Desert Storm, An Overview* (Arlington VA: Association of the United States Army, 1991), 5. Directorate of Public Affairs, Headquarters, Forces Command, Fort McPherson, GA 30330, "Operation Desert Shield, 'A Line in the Sand'," Bulletin 2-90, 27 August 1990, Smith Collection, U.S. Army Medical Department Museum.
6. Other commands included USEUCOM, USNORTHCOM, USAPACOM, and USSOUTHCOM.
7. Tom Donnelly, "All Eyes on CENTCOM," *Army Times* (20 August 1990): 14. Frank N. Schubert and Theresa L. Kraus, eds., *The Whirlwind War, The United States Army in Operations Desert Shield and Desert Storm* (Washington, DC: Center of Military History, United States Army, 1993), 43–44. Frank Best and Nancy Tomich, *Medicine in the Gulf War* (Washington, DC: U.S. Medicine, 1991), 159–60.
8. Frank F. Ledford, "Army Medicine Balancing Needs with Resources," *Army* 40 (October 1990): 180–83, 185. Frank Best and Nancy Tomich, *Medicine in the Gulf War* (Washington, DC: U.S. Medicine, 1991), 99–100. D.G. Tsoulos, "Command Report, U.S. ARCENT Medical Command, 1 August 1990 to 16 January 1991," Typewritten Report, 2,

1 March 1991, Army Nurse Corps Collection (ANCC), Office of Medical History (OMH). Ronald R. Blanck and William H. Bell, "Special Reports: Medical Aspects of the Persian Gulf War, Medical Support for American Troops in the Persian Gulf," *New England Journal of Medicine* 324 (21 March 1991): 857–59. Frank F. Ledford, "Medical Support for Operation Desert Storm," *The Journal of the US Army Medical Department*, PB8-92-1/2 (January/February 1992): 4. Frank F. Ledford, "Army Overcomes Combat Challenge," *U.S. Medicine* 28 (January 1992): 30–31. Ingeborg Sosa, "The Journal Interviews—LTG Frank F. Ledford, Jr., Surgeon General, United States Army," *The Journal of the US Army Medical Department*, PB8-92-3/4 (March/April 1992): insert between pages 30 and 31. Angel E. Cintron and George D. Magee, "Medical Logistics Support to Desert Storm," *The Journal of the US Army Medical Department*, PB8-92-9/10 (September/October 1992): 35–38. Barbara Jean Smith, "The Nurse Executive in Operation Desert Shield/Desert Storm," *Nursing Management* 24 (January 1993): 68–70.

9. Molly Moore, "Medical Corps Trying to Fill Supply Gap," *Washington Post* (6 January 1991): A21. ABC's Nightline news show highlighted a letter from a 28th CSH physician who complained about "shortages of everything from fluoroscopes and ultrasound equipment to blood, IV fluid and antibiotics." Other interviewed physicians claimed that the "220-bed hospital could . . . handle only 50 seriously wounded patients because of an acute shortage of nurses." James Kitfield, "Combat Medicine," *Government Executive* 23 (January 1991): 26–31. The Army directed that deploying units be filled to their authorized strength before deployment "to the maximum extent possible." Brent H. Fullerton, "Procedure for MACOM Branch Tasking Assignment Branches for Officer Fill in Support of Desert Shield," Information Paper, 14 August 1990, ANCC, OMH. Most of the hospital units in theater had their full complement of Army Nurse Corps officers. Some were even over strength. Marianne Mathewson-Chapman, "Theater Nursing Services," Memorandum, 14 March 1991, ANCC, OMH. However, on 1 April 1991, the 28th CSH had only 39 of its 46 authorized Army nurses. "XVIII Corps Nursing Status," Printed Chart, 1 April 1991, Smith Collection, U.S. Army Medical Department Museum. More letters of complaint surfaced. One concerned relative cited "generalized unsanitary condition[s]" at the 28th CSH, alleging that there was pseudomonas in shower water, filthy, fly-ridden bathrooms, pervasive mold and mildew, a lack of ice, little personal privacy, and a dearth of recreational activities. Concerned Relative to BG Clara Adams-Ender, Printed Letter, 24 August 1990, stapled in diary of Colonel Barbara J. Smith, Smith Collection, U.S. Army Medical Department Museum. Talking points reliably predicted that Persian Gulf operations would "be austere, with long supply and transportation lines." Directorate of Public Affairs, Headquarters, Forces Command, Fort McPherson, GA 30330, "Operation Desert Shield, 'A Line in the Sand'," Bulletin 2-90, 27 August 1990, Smith Collection, U.S. Army Medical Department Museum. "Synopsis of Operation Desert Shield 7 August–10 December 1990," Printed Document, 2, n.d., Smith Collection, U.S. Army Medical Department Museum. Ruth Cheney, "History of the 44th Medical Brigade Chief Nurse, Operations Desert Shield/Desert Storm," Printed Manuscript, 10–11, 7 June 1991, Cheney Collection, U.S. Army Medical Department Museum. James Kitfield, "Combat Medicine," *Government Executive* 23 (January 1991): 26–31. Tim Friend, "Medical Units Plan for Worst, Hope for Best," *USA Today* (20 February 1991): 1A.

10. Harry K. Stinger and Robert M. Rush, "The Forward Surgical Team: The Army's Ultimate Lifesaving Force," *Infantry Magazine* 92 (Winter 2003): 11–13. Brian K. Kondrat, "Battlefield Surgery: Lessons Learned, Present Capabilities, and Future Systems," Research Paper presented to the U.S. Army Command and General Staff College in partial fulfillment of the requirements for A461, Combat Health Support Seminar, 4, 6–8, 2003,

ANCC, OMH. Atul Gawande, "Casualties of War—Military Care for the Wounded from Iraq and Afghanistan," *New England Journal of Medicine* 351 (9 December 2004): 2471–75. "Forward Surgical Teams," http://www.armymedicine.army.mil/about/tl/95-factsfst.htm (accessed 2 September 2005). "801st Forward Surgical Team," http://www.members.aol.com/rotkiv1/fst/ (accessed 2 September 2005).

11. Frank F. Ledford, "War, Peace Roles: Army Measures Up," *U.S. Medicine* 27 (January 1991): 27–28. Frank F. Ledford, "Medical Support for Operation Desert Storm," *The Journal of the US Army Medical Department*, PB8-92-1/2 (January/February 1992): 4–5. Ingeborg Sosa, "The Journal Interviews—LTG Frank F. Ledford, Jr., Surgeon General, United States Army," *The Journal of the US Army Medical Department*, PB8-92-3/4 (March/April 1992): insert between pages 30 and 31. L.S. Holsenback, "'PSYCH-FORCE 90': The OM (Combat Stress) Team in the Gulf," *The Journal of the US Army Medical Department*, PB8-92-3/4 (March/April 1992): 32–36.

12. Office of the Under Secretary of Defense for Acquisition and Technology, *Report of the Defense Science Board Task Force on Persian Gulf War Health Effects* (Washington, DC: Department of Defense, 3 June 1994), 54, 56. Robert J. Ursano and Anne E. Norwood, eds., *Emotional Aftermath of the Persian Gulf War: Veterans, Families, Communities, and Nations* (Washington, DC: American Psychiatric Press, 1996), 18.

13. James A. Martin, Linette R. Sparacino, and Gregory Belenky, *The Gulf War and Mental Health, A Comprehensive Guide* (Westport, CT: Praeger, 1996), 167.

14. "Operation Desert Shield/Storm, Concept of Operations," Typewritten Document, n.d.; and Department of Defense, "Conduct of the Persian Gulf War," Appendix G, 452–53, April 1992 (both in ANCC, OMH).

15. Frank Best and Nancy Tomich, *Medicine in the Gulf War* (Washington, DC: U.S. Medicine, 1991), 8–9. Leigh Page, "Gulf's Medical System Beats Vietnam's, Military Says," *American Medical News* (4 February 1991): 1, 31. Phil Gunby, "Medical Efforts Intensify in Desert Storm's Fourth Week," *Journal of the American Medical Association* 265 (13 February 1991): 692–93, 697. Margaret Roth, "Saving Lives: A New Mission for Combat Troops," *Army Times* 51 (18 February 1991): 4. Joyce Price, "Hospitals Ready for Casualties of Ground War," *Washington Times* (25 February 1991): A10. Ingeborg Sosa, "The Journal Interviews—LTG Frank F. Ledford, Jr., Surgeon General, United States Army," *The Journal of the US Army Medical Department*, PB8-92-3/4 (March/April 1992): insert between pages 30 and 31. Mark Gifford, Interview by Author, 23 August 2005. T.R. Byrne, Telephone Interview with Author, 25 August 2005. Donald Hall, Telephone Interview with Author, 25 August 2005. *Department of Defense, Conduct of the Persian Gulf War, Final Report to Congress* (Washington, DC: Department of Defense, April 1992), Appendix G, Medical Support, 459, 469. John Hudock, "Army Nurse Corps Executive Summary of Desert Shield/Storm," Typewritten Document, n.d., ANCC, OMH. United States General Accounting Office, Report to the Chairman, Subcommittee on Readiness, Committee on Armed Services, House of Representatives, Operation Desert Storm, *War Highlights Need to Address Problem of Nondeployable Personnel*, GAO/NSIAD-92-208 (Washington, DC: GAO, August 1992), 14, 15. United States General Accounting Office, Military Personnel and Compensation, Committee on Armed Services, House of Representatives, Operation Desert Storm, *Full Army Medical Capability Not Achieved*, GAO/NSIAD-92-175 (Washington, DC: GAO, August 1992), 3, 4, 25.

16. William Joe Webb and others, *Department of the Army Historical Summary, Fiscal Years 1990 and 1991* (Washington, DC: Center of Military History, United States Army, 1997), 73. Frank F. Ledford, "War, Peace Roles: Army Measures Up," *U.S. Medicine* 27 (January 1991): 27–28.

17. No retired Army Nurse Corps officers were involuntarily recalled to active duty. However, 40 physicians and 30 physician assistants were so recalled to support ODS. Lieutenant Colonel Smith, "AMEDD Officer Personnel Strength Management," Information Paper, 11 March 1991, ANCC, OMH.

18. "'Desert Shield' Notes," *HSC Mercury* 18 (November 1990): 3.

19. Philip J. Hilts, "Trek across the Desert Thwarts Medical Gains," *New York Times* (1 February 1991): n.p., Newspaper Clipping in ANCC, OMH. Leigh Page, "Gulf's Medical System Beats Vietnam's, Military Says," *American Medical News* (4 February 1991): 1, 31. Marianne Mathewson-Chapman, "Theater Nursing Services," Memorandum, 14 March 1991; and Barbara J. Smith, "Operation Desert Storm Historical Report (17 January–1 April)," Memorandum, 4 April 1991 (both in ANCC, OMH). Frank Best and Nancy Tomich, *Medicine in the Gulf War* (Washington, DC: U.S. Medicine, 1991), 2. Frank F. Ledford, "Medical Support for Operation Desert Storm," *The Journal of the US Army Medical Department*, PB8-92-1/2 (January/February 1992): 3–4. Ben Eiseman, "Observations on the Gulf War by an Alumnus Who Had a Seat on the Fifty-Yard-Line," *The Journal of the US Army Medical Department*, PB8-92-1/2 (January/February 1992): 7–12. Ingeborg Sosa, "The Journal Interviews—LTG Frank F. Ledford, Jr., Surgeon General, United States Army," *The Journal of the US Army Medical Department*, PB8-92-3/4 (March/April 1992): insert between pages 30 and 31. Frank F. Ledford, "Army Overcomes Combat Challenge," *U.S. Medicine* 28 (January 1992): 30–31. Alexander M. Sloan, "Air Force Exhibits 'Global' Prowess," *U.S. Medicine* 28 (January 1992): 28–29. Donald F. Hagen, "Total Quality Highest Concern for Navy," *U.S. Medicine* 28 (January 1992): 40–41. Frank N. Schubert and Theresa L. Kraus, eds., *The Whirlwind War, The United States Army in Operations Desert Shield and Desert Storm* (Washington, DC: Center of Military History, United States Army, 1993), 84. Barbara Jean Smith, "The Nurse Executive in Operation Desert Shield/Desert Storm," *Nursing Management* 24 (January 1993): 68–70. Clara L. Adams-Ender with Blair S. Walker, *My Rise to the Stars, How a Sharecropper's Daughter Became an Army General* (Lake Ridge, VA: Cape Associates, Inc., 2001), 227–28.

20. Susan H. Godson, *Serving Proudly, A History of Women in the U.S. Navy* (Annapolis, MD: Naval Institute Press, 2001), 280. James S. Nanney to Nancy A. Dezell, "Number of AF Nurses Deployed to Gulf," E-mail Correspondence, 3 March 2005, ANCC, OMH.

21. Frank Best and Nancy Tomich, *Medicine in the Gulf War* (Washington, DC: U.S. Medicine, 1991), 115–16, 118–26. Veterans Health Administration, Gulf War (Including Operation Iraqi Freedom) Registry (GWR), *VA Handbook 1303.2* (Washington, DC: Department of Veterans Affairs, 7 March 2005), 1.

22. "VA Readies Its RN Ranks to Care for Critically Wounded Soldiers, *American Journal of Nursing* 91 (March 1991): 108. Virginia C. Stephanakis, "OTSG Input for January 1992 Issue of *U.S. Medicine*," Draft Manuscript, 1, 23 October 1991; and Robert S. Driscoll, "Reconstitution of Seventh Medical Command During Operation Desert Shield/Storm," Typewritten Manuscript, 5–7, 24 February 1993 (both in ANCC, OMH). Frank F. Ledford, "Army Overcomes Combat Challenge," *U.S. Medicine* 28 (January 1992): 30–31. Department of Defense, "Conduct of the Persian Gulf War," Appendix G, 451, 453, 456–57, 469, April 1992.

23. Frank N. Schubert and Theresa L. Kraus, eds., *The Whirlwind War, The United States Army in Operations Desert Shield and Desert Storm* (Washington, DC: Center of Military History, United States Army, 1993), 85–86.

24. Frank N. Schubert and Theresa L. Kraus, eds., *The Whirlwind War, The United States Army in Operations Desert Shield and Desert Storm* (Washington, DC: Center of Military History, United States Army, 1993), 86–87. "U.S. Nurses Mobilize for Operation Desert

Storm," *American Journal of Nursing* 91 (March 1991): 105, 110. United States Department of the Army, 5th Mobile Army Surgical Hospital, "Historical Report, Operations Desert Storm/Desert Shield," Printed Chronology, n.d., ANCC, OMH. Kenneth K. Steinweg, "Mobile Surgical Hospital Design: Lessons from 5th MASH Surgical Packages for Operations Desert Shield/Desert Storm," *Military Medicine* 158 (November 1993): 733–39.

25. Planners calculated required personnel assets and beds using projected numbers of troops and estimated casualties for an offensive operation. Frank F. Ledford, "Medical Support for Operation Desert Storm," *The Journal of the US Army Medical Department*, PB8-92-1/2 (January/February 1992): 3. D.G. Tsoulos, "Command Report, U.S. ARCENT Medical Command, 1 August 1990 to 16 January 1991," Typewritten Report, 2, 1 March 1991; and Barbara J. Smith, "Operation Desert Storm Historical Report (17 January–1 April)," Memorandum, 4 April 1991 (both in ANCC, OMH). Frank F. Ledford, "Army Overcomes Combat Challenge," *U.S. Medicine* 28 (January 1992): 30–31.

26. Frank N. Schubert and Theresa L. Kraus, eds., *The Whirlwind War, The United States Army in Operations Desert Shield and Desert Storm* (Washington, DC: Center of Military History, United States Army, 1993), 89. D.G. Tsoulos, "Command Report, U.S. ARCENT Medical Command, 1 August 1990 to 16 January 1991," Typewritten Report, 3, 1 March 1991, ANCC, OMH.

27. Frank Best and Nancy Tomich, *Medicine in the Gulf War* (Washington, DC: U.S. Medicine, 1991), 55, 71, 77, 80, 82, 96. Ben Eiseman, "Observations on the Gulf War by an Alumnus Who Had a Seat on the Fifty-Yard-Line," *The Journal of the US Army Medical Department*, PB8-92-1/2 (January/February 1992): 8.

*Chapter Eighteen*
# Army Nurse Corps Leadership in Operation Desert Shield/Operation Desert Storm

In the early days of the Persian Gulf war, a select cohort of Army Nurse Corps leaders advanced into the spearhead and provided direction and inspiration for the large, widespread assemblage of nurses. The Office of the Chief of the Army Nurse Corps, however, claimed the ultimate responsibility for oversight and leadership of Army nurses with Brigadier General Clara L. Adams-Ender prepared to meet the challenges.

With the start of Operation Desert Shield (ODS) in August 1990, the Army Nurse Corps faced the first difficult challenge of maintaining peacetime care without degrading quantity or quality while simultaneously supporting its nursing responsibilities for a mobilizing Army. To respond to these dual missions, the Office of the Chief implemented an operational approach that made efficient, rapid responses to the myriad of demands feasible. Adams-Ender and her assistant, Colonel John Hudock, delegated significant decision-making powers to the chief nurses of Health Services Command, Forces Command, and 7th Medical Command in matters related to the mobilization effort and authorized them to communicate directly with major Office of The Surgeon General directorates such as Personnel and Health Care Operations. All parties coordinated and furnished each other feedback, keeping the chief of the Corps office aware of their communications and providing information updates and policy guidance as needed.

In mid-August 1990, the Office of the Chief also formed a Desert Shield Situation Group composed of key Army Nurse Corps officers in the Military District of Washington to facilitate communication and policy formulation. Colonel Barbara J. Smith had been nominated to become the Army Central (ARCENT) chief nurse, and she was able to participate in the Desert Shield Situation Group's planning processes. The team studied several topics, including clinical issues focusing on field nursing documentation, treatment of casualties, and equipment problems. They also sought information about cultural aspects of nursing in the Arab world and disseminated it to the field. They liaised with civilian professional nursing organizations, sharing information and addressing professional concerns. Finally, they focused on educational matters, recommending that virtually all officers participating in Long Term Civilian Health Education and Training curricula remain in their academic programs, that all temporary duty courses be cancelled for the duration of the operation, and that the Academy of Health Sciences convene a two-week mobilization course for activated U.S. Army Reserve (USAR) and Army National Guard (ARNG) personnel. The mobilization course objectives ensured that those activated met minimum deployability standards. A total of 902 USAR and ARNG Army Nurse Corps officers attended the courses held at Fort Sam Houston, Texas.[1]

In mid-summer 1990, the end strength for the Army Nurse Corps was 4,650 officers.[2] By August, the Army Nurse Corps anticipated the need for more nurses and called for USAR/ARNG and retiree volunteers. More than 800 responded, but not all immediately reported for active duty. Based on need, specialty, and rank, the Corps activated a majority of these officers early in the operation. More than 8,000 Army Nurse Corps officers were available to serve worldwide on active duty during ODS. This included the mobilization of approximately 3,450 USAR and ARNG Army nurses.[3] Only 31 Army nurses were released from active duty for reasons of hardship or community essentiality during the period.[4] To prepare for a possible need for even more nurses, the Corps reviewed the records of retired Army nurses in August 1990 in anticipation of an involuntary call-up, but this did not prove necessary because a number of retirees did step forward and returned to active duty.[5]

The Army implemented a stop-loss program on 1 September 1990 that halted voluntary separations for all personnel involved in direct support of ODS.[6] By February 1991, stop-loss had affected 148 Army Nurse Corps officers who were involuntarily extended on active duty. The Army also temporarily discontinued the practice of requiring those officers twice nonselected for promotion to separate from the service, but initially allowed retirements for time in service to proceed as usual.[7] After 5 December 1990, approved voluntary retirements were suspended indefinitely.[8] To stabilize and balance personnel strengths, the Army also involuntarily extended officers serving on overseas tours in foreign countries as well as Hawaii and Alaska.[9]

By 16 January 1991, when the air campaign began, 2,265 Army nurses were serving in the Persian Gulf.[10] At the conclusion of the ground war on 28 February 1991, 2,215 Army Nurse Corps officers were on duty in Southwest Asia.[11] As of April 1991, required strength of the Army Nurse Corps in Southwest Asia was 2,211 and 2,214 Army nurses were assigned there.[12]

The ARCENT surgeon, Colonel Demetrios G. Tsoulous, specifically requested that Colonel Barbara Jean Smith, an Army nurse with extensive field experience, serve as the ARCENT chief nurse during ODS.[13] Although Smith learned of her assignment to this position in late August 1990, she did not depart from the continental United States until 12 November 1990 but was in the country when U.S. Army Forces Central Command Medical Group (Echelons Above Corps) (Provi-

Front row from left to right, Lieutenant Colonel Maureen Combs, chief nurse of the 86th Evacuation Hospital and Colonel Barbara J. Smith, ARCENT chief nurse, pose with a few key officers from the 86th, second row, from left to right, Major Mary Glenn, Major Kathleen Simpson, Lieutenant Colonel Jean Purdom, and Lieutenant Colonel Deborah Castellan during a staff visit in the desert.
Photo courtesy of Colonel Barbara J. Smith, West Columbia, SC.

sional) commenced operation on 6 December 1990. She recalled that the delay was exceedingly difficult, but she studied the annual reports of the chief nurses in Vietnam, read geographical updates of conditions in the Gulf, and collected pertinent nursing care references, hospital/nursing regulations, and other published planning guidance such as relevant field manuals. Smith also asked Adams-Ender for autographed copies of her portrait, which she eventually presented to each hospital chief nurse as she visited their units. Smith carried three duffle bags of predominantly professional/leadership materials with a minimum of personal belongings on her trip overseas.[14]

A crowded office building in Riyadh housed the ARCENT headquarters. There, Tsoulous gave Smith "a lot of latitude" and autonomy to do what—in her judgment—needed to be done.[15] She described her position as predominantly a staff role that stressed support activities and fostered developmental programs. She envisioned another of her responsibilities as promoting collaboration and team building among the nurses as they erected hospitals and cared for casualties.[16]

Smith made it a priority to visit personally the extensive network of U.S. Army hospitals to mitigate the sense of isolation among nurses serving in remote areas. She firmly believed "that her presence and her caring attitude had to be felt by the chief nurses and the nursing staff" who were living and working in extremely

Colonel Barbara J. Smith, ARCENT chief nurse, plots out a route for a journey across the desert accompanied by Colonel Philip Alm, the ARCENT chief of veterinary medicine during Operation Desert Storm. In accordance with Saudi customs, Smith could not drive and did not travel alone.
Photo courtesy of Colonel Barbara J. Smith, West Columbia, SC.

harsh conditions. Thus, about half of Smith's time was spent on the road, often traveling at a snail's pace over lengthy distances on hazardous thoroughfares. The scarcity of military vehicles and the Saudi prohibition banning women from driving or traveling alone complicated her efforts. These circumstances compelled Smith to coordinate her travel plans with other male staffers to make team visits to far-flung hospitals situated across the Saudi Arabia desert. She often spent long hours or even days confined in vehicles with the same individuals, and conditions sometimes called for a generous measure of restraint and a determinedly positive attitude.[17]

One of Smith's first actions was to visit Lieutenant Colonel Ruth Cheney, the chief nurse of the 44th Medical Brigade, in Dhahran. Soon after her arrival, Smith and Cheney conferred with all the 44th Medical Brigade chief nurses, ironing out various nursing issues such as facility problems, standard operating procedure development, the improvement of forms, and other patient care concerns.[18]

While on her rounds, Smith usually prefaced her visits with an informative briefing, updating the nurses about happenings in the continental United States, sharing how citizens in the United States supported their efforts, and bringing greetings from Adams-Ender. During these sessions, Smith was continually impressed with "the enthusiasm and can-do attitude" of the Army Medical Department soldiers. She acknowledged, however, that there usually were one or two

Colonel Barbara J. Smith (left) and Lieutenant Colonel Ruth Cheney, chief nurse of the 44th Medical Brigade in Dhahran (right) meet for an update and discussion of issues.
Photo courtesy of Colonel Barbara J. Smith, West Columbia, SC.

"unhappy campers" in a unit. Nevertheless, most "were wonderful—flexible and ready to help in whatever situation."[19]

Smith attempted to anticipate problems and solve issues before they surfaced. Specifically, she conferred with the nurse consultant, then-colonel Nancy R. Adams, and subsequently adapted peacetime methods of documentation to more appropriate forms suitable for use in combat. She stressed the need for additional in-theater education focusing on handling chemically contaminated casualties and Advanced Trauma Life Support and supported the progress of training teams moving from hospital unit to hospital unit to share information on these topics. Smith noted that participation in the classes and attention to the instruction was extremely high due to the life-or-death nature of the subject matter.[20]

Language and cultural barriers, particularly in host nation hospitals, were problems. Cultural proscriptions banned Saudi women from working as nurses, meaning that virtually all nurses in that nation's hospitals were foreigners. Most spoke English, but communication was still problematic. Some of the foreign nurses were unaccustomed to dealing with advanced technology, which complicated matters. U.S. Army nurses' willingness to share their knowledge—teaching the use of gas masks, the basics of cardiopulmonary resuscitation, and the care of trauma victims, and assisting with the development of Mass Casualty disaster plans—facilitated their integration into these host nation hospitals.

The care of Enemy Prisoners of War and displaced civilians was another challenge met proactively. It required anticipatory guidance and serious attention, and produced ethical dilemmas and diversion of sometimes scarce resources needed for the care of allied forces. Smith fostered a spirit of cohesion and cooperation to overcome these inevitable obstacles.[21] Overall, she functioned as "a supporter, communicator, facilitator, and a consultant."[22]

The echelons of nursing administration below the chief nurse, ARCENT, within Southwest Asia included Lieutenant Colonel Ruth Cheney, the chief nurse of the 44th Medical Brigade of the XVIII Airborne Corps; Lieutenant Colonel Alice Davidson, chief nurse of the 332nd Medical Brigade out of the VII Corps; and the chief nurses in the Echelons Above Corps that fell under the ARCENT chief nurse, Colonel Smith.[23] Serving beneath Cheney were the 1st and 62nd Medical Group chief nurses, Lieutenant Colonel Elizabeth Heil and Colonel Rita Hutcheson.[24] Under Davidson in the 332nd Medical Brigade, Lieutenant Colonel Susan Mallot was chief nurse of the 341st Medical Group, Lieutenant Colonel Jackie Tyler served as chief nurse of the 127th Medical Group, and Major (P) Wendy Bottomley filled the position of chief nurse of the Evacuation Hospital Task Force. In the Echelons Above Corps hospitals, the chief nurses of the 803rd, 202nd, 244th, and 173rd Medical Groups were Colonel Maureen Holland, Lieutenant Colonel Marianne Mathewson-Chapman, Major John Shank, and Lieutenant Colonel Joyce Mezzano, respectively. Each medical group consisted of three to seven hospital units.[25] The medical group chief nurses advised the group commander on nursing matters, established and monitored standards of nursing practice and supervised its performance, established guidelines for the utilization of nursing staff, created and operated educational programs for nurses, coordinated nursing activities among the chief nurses of their subordinate hospitals, and liaised with the medical brigade chief nurse.[26]

Lieutenant Colonel Ruth Cheney's experiences as chief nurse of the 44th Medical Brigade in ODS were illustrative of nursing administration at the corps level. Cheney, a Vietnam veteran like Smith, also had extensive field nursing experience.[27] She signed into the 44th Medical Brigade at Fort Bragg on 19 June 1990 and had only a few weeks to settle into her new role when preparations for ODS began. In the predeployment phase, she immediately confronted several issues. They included concerns about staffing, supplies, nuclear, biological, and chemical protection, quality of patient care, medical regulating, staff health and morale, locations of hospital units, and education, among others.[28]

Cheney arrived at Dhahran Air Base in Saudi Arabia with an advance party on 30 August 1990. Buses transported the group to Dragon Base, XVIII Airborne Corps headquarters. Although forewarned about the differences in the status of women in Saudi Arabia, this bus trip was Cheney's first face-to-face encounter with Saudi cultural beliefs. The bus had a back door labeled "ladies entrance" that allowed women to enter a segregated area in the rear of the bus. Both male and female soldiers loaded into the bus ignoring these signs, but Cheney was surprised by such a flagrant exhibition of gender segregation in spite of the prebriefings she attended focusing on Middle East culture. On the other hand, the Saudis gener-

From left to right, Lieutenant Colonel Marianne Mathewson-Chapman, deputy chief nurse of ARCENT, Lieutenant Colonel Joyce Mezzano, 173rd Medical Group chief nurse, and Colonel Barbara J. Smith, ARCENT chief nurse, departing from a visit to the 300th Field Hospital during Operation Desert Storm.
Photo courtesy of Colonel Barbara J. Smith, West Columbia, SC.

ally treated her with kindness and respect and on one occasion a Saudi military policeman spontaneously presented her with a bouquet of roses. She also was impressed with the various forms of subtle encouragement offered by the Saudi women, many of whom discreetly flashed the American servicewomen a "V for victory" sign, waved, or passed notes expressing support for the servicewomen and their efforts.[29]

Cheney routinely greeted incoming Army nurses and briefed them on the military medical system in Saudi Arabia and Bahrain, warned them about expected Iraqi use of chemical weapons, instructed them on local alcohol prohibitions and uniform policies, and responded to queries. The most frequently posed question by new arrivals was how long they would be in Saudi Arabia. Cheney always replied, "Plan on a year and be pleasantly surprised if it's less." The 44th Medical Brigade also provided arriving Army nurses with a classified tactical briefing.[30] The sessions triggered reality shock and became a moment of truth for the majority of the arrivals once they grasped the seriousness of the combat situation.[31]

This then was the leadership matrix that provided guidance and support to the thousands of Army nurses who deployed to the desert. Its foundations resided in the meticulous pre-combat planning that anticipated the actual event. As a result of this planning, the mission by and large progressed according to plan, apart from the random, irksome, yet inevitable, glitches.

# Notes

1. John Hudock, "Army Nurse Corps Executive Summary of Desert Shield/Storm," Typewritten Document, n.d., Army Nurse Corps Collection (ANCC), Office of Medical History (OMH).

2. Lieutenant Colonel Smith, "AMEDD Officer Personnel Strength Management," Information Paper, 1, 11 March 1991, ANCC, OMH.

3. One source calculated the number of COMPO II and III Army nurses called up at 3,698. "AMEDD Volunteers: Desert Shield," Briefing Slide, n.d., ANCC, OMH.

4. "ANC Desert Shield/Storm," Briefing Slide, n.d.; and John Hudock, "Army Nurse Corps Executive Summary of Desert Shield/Storm," Typewritten Document, n.d. (both in ANCC, OMH). Several sources noted that the Army Nurse Corps ordered 494 volunteers to active duty. Of these, 328 were medical-surgical nurses, 49 were operating room nurses, 27 were nurse anesthetists, 25 were psychiatric nurses, and a few represented the other nurse AOCs (Areas of Concentration). "AMEDD Volunteers: Desert Shield," Briefing Slide, n.d.; and John Hudock, "Operation Desert Shield/Storm," Information Paper, 14 February 1991 (both in ANCC, OMH).

5. John Hudock, "Army Nurse Corps Executive Summary of Desert Shield/Storm," Typewritten Document, n.d.; and HQDA, "Desert Shield Personnel Policy No 7—Recall of Retirees," August 1990 (both in ANCC, OMH).

6. By November 1990, all active Army members became subject to the stop-loss program. Thomas F. Sikora, "Stop Loss Policy Applicability Changes," MILPER Message Nr 91-45, November 1990, ANCC, OMH. "'Stop Loss' Extends Duty for Soldiers," *HSC Mercury* 18 (October 1990): 6.

7. John Hudock, "Operation Desert Shield/Storm," Information Paper, 14 February 1991; Lieutenant Colonel Smith, "AMEDD Officer Personnel Strength Management," Information Paper, 2, 11 March 1991; William H. Reno, "Suspension of Active Component Voluntary Separation of Officers and Enlisted Personnel (Stop Loss) Policy No. 12," 27 August 1990; and "PERSCOM 'Stop Loss Rules'," Printed Document, 4 December 1990 (all in ANCC, OMH).

8. William H. Reno, "Suspension of Active Component Voluntary Separations of Officers and Enlisted Personnel (Stop Loss)," MILPER Message, November 1990, ANCC, OMH.

9. G.L. Brown, "Temporary Worldwide Involuntary Foreign Service Tour Extensions," MILPER Message, November 1990, ANCC, OMH.

10. Lieutenant Colonel Fox, "US Army Medical Department, Operation Desert Shield," Briefing Slides, 16 January 1991, ANCC, OMH.

11. Barbara J. Smith, "Current Status of Army Nurse Corps Activities in the AOR," Memorandum, 1, 10 March 1991, Smith Collection, U.S. Army Medical Department Museum.

12. Marianne Mathewson-Chapman, "Theater Nursing Services," Memorandum, 14 March 1991; and Barbara J. Smith, "Operation Desert Storm Historical Report (17 January–1 April)," Memorandum, 4 April 1991 (both in ANCC, OMH).

13. Smith was a veteran of the Vietnam War, serving in Da Nang in 1970. From 1980 to 1982, she was chief nurse of the 15th CSH at Fort Belvoir, Virginia. Barbara J. Smith, Interview by Constance J. Moore, Transcript, 4–8, 11–12, 17–18, 2 March 1995, Army Nurse Corps Oral History Collection (ANCOHC), OMH. Barbara J. Smith, Interview by Constance J. Moore, Transcript, 18, 19, 2 March 1995, ANCOHC, OMH.

14. Barbara J. Smith, Interview by Constance J. Moore, Transcript, 21, 22, 2 March 1995; and D.G. Tsoulos, "Command Report, U.S. ARCENT Medical Command, 1 August 1990 to 16 January 1991," Typewritten Report, 3, 1 March 1991 (both in ANCOHC, OMH). Frank N. Schubert and Theresa L. Kraus, eds., *The Whirlwind War, The United States Army in Operations Desert Shield and Desert Storm* (Washington, DC: Center of Military History, United States Army, 1993), 89.

15. Barbara J. Smith, Interview by Constance J. Moore, Transcript, 18, 19, 2 March 1995, ANCOHC, OMH.

16. Barbara Jean Smith, "The Nurse Executive in Operation Desert Shield/Desert Storm," *Nursing Management* 24 (January 1993): 68–70. Barbara J. Smith, "Job Description Chief Nurse, U.S. Army Forces Central Command," Printed Document, 4 December 1990, Smith Collection, U.S. Army Medical Department Museum. Barbara J. Smith, "Operation Desert Storm Historical Report (17 January–1 April)," Memorandum, 4 April 1991, ANCC, OMH.

17. Barbara Jean Smith, "The Nurse Executive in Operation Desert Shield/Desert Storm," *Nursing Management* 24 (January 1993): 68–70. Barbara J. Smith, Interview by Constance J. Moore, Transcript, 18, 2 March 1995, ANCOHC, OMH.

18. Barbara J. Smith, Interview by Constance J. Moore, Transcript, 24–25, 2 March 1995, ANCOHC, OMH. Smith helped to develop documentation forms and worked to set up a system for form resupply. The documentation packet designed for the theater included a simplified doctor's order sheet that facilitated transcription of orders, an Emergency Medical Treatment assessment form, and an Intensive Care Unit (ICU) flow sheet. Smith also created a Nursing Monthly Activities Report that tracked nursing workload statistics. Ruth Cheney, "History of the 44th Medical Brigade Chief Nurse, Operations Desert Shield/Desert Storm," Printed Manuscript, 14, 7 June 1991, Cheney Collection, U.S. Army Medical Department Museum. Barbara J. Smith, "Nursing Documentation in the Theater of Operations," Information Paper, 6 December 1990, Smith Collection, U.S. Army Medical Department Museum.

19. Barbara J. Smith, Interview by Constance J. Moore, Transcript, 24–25, 2 March 1995, ANCOHC, OMH.

20. Barbara Jean Smith, "The Nurse Executive in Operation Desert Shield/Desert Storm," *Nursing Management* 24 (January 1993): 68–70. Barbara J. Smith, Interview by Constance J. Moore, Transcript, 30, 2 March 1995, ANCOHC, OMH. Barbara J. Smith, "Nursing Documentation in the Theater of Operations," Information Paper, 6 December

1990, Smith Collection, U.S. Army Medical Department Museum.

21. Barbara Jean Smith, "The Nurse Executive in Operation Desert Shield/Desert Storm," *Nursing Management* 24 (January 1993): 68–70. Barbara J. Smith, "Operation Desert Storm Historical Report (17 January–1 April)," Memorandum, 4 April 1991, ANCC, OMH.

22. Barbara J. Smith, Interview by Constance J. Moore, Transcript, 48, 2 March 1995, ANCOHC, OMH. Barbara J. Smith, "Operation Desert Storm Historical Report (17 January–1 April)," Memorandum, 4 April 1991, ANCC, OMH.

23. Ruth Cheney, "History of the 44th Medical Brigade Chief Nurse, Operations Desert Shield/Desert Storm," Printed Manuscript, 2–3, 7 June 1991, Cheney Collection, U.S. Army Medical Department Museum. Barbara J. Smith, "Guidance for the ARCENT EAC MED GRP Chief Nurses," Memorandum, 27 December 1990, Smith Collection, U.S. Army Medical Department Museum.

24. Ruth Cheney, "History of the 44th Medical Brigade Chief Nurse, Operations Desert Shield/Desert Storm," Printed Manuscript, 14, 7 June 1991, Cheney Collection, U.S. Army Medical Department Museum.

25. Mathewson-Chapman also served as the deputy ARCENT chief nurse under Colonel Barbara J. Smith. Marianne Mathewson-Chapman, "Theater Nursing Services," Memorandum, 14 March 1991, ANCC, OMH. Mathewson-Chapman later was promoted to brigadier general and in 2000 received her second star. She was the first woman in the ARNG to achieve the rank of major general and at that time served in an IMA position as deputy Army surgeon general/National Guard. "First Female," *The Mercury* 27 (July 2000): 3. "EAC Hospitals Nursing Status," 22 February 1991; "VII Corps Nursing Status," 1 April 1991; and "XVIII Corps Nursing Status," 1 April 1991 (Printed Documents, all in Smith Collection, U.S. Army Medical Department Museum).

26. Marianne Mathewson-Chapman, "Job Description, Chief Nurse, Medical Group," Printed Document, 1 June 1991, Smith Collection, U.S. Army Medical Department Museum.

27. Cheney was a Vietnam veteran and had more recently served as chief nurse of the 28th CSH. Ruth Cheney, "History of the 44th Medical Brigade Chief Nurse, Operations Desert Shield/Desert Storm," Printed Manuscript, 2, 7 June 1991, Cheney Collection, U.S. Army Medical Department Museum.

28. Ruth Cheney, "History of the 44th Medical Brigade Chief Nurse, Operations Desert Shield/Desert Storm," Printed Manuscript, 2–3, 7 June 1991, Cheney Collection, U.S. Army Medical Department Museum.

29. Ibid., 4.

30. Tactical briefings, or the "Battle Update Brief," varied from unit to unit depending on the data the commander wanted to be presented. They could provide information about enemy activities/threats, weather conditions, operational orders, and/or readiness status for each section/department of the unit. Red readiness status meant the unit was not mission capable. Amber status denoted the unit was partially mission capable, and Green indicated that the unit was fully mission capable.

31. Ruth Cheney, "History of the 44th Medical Brigade Chief Nurse, Operations Desert Shield/Desert Storm," Printed Manuscript, 7, 7 June 1991, Cheney Collection, U.S. Army Medical Department Museum.

*Chapter Nineteen*
# Army Nurse Corps Activities in Combat Hospitals in Operation Desert Shield/ Operation Desert Storm

A total of 44 hospital units were operational in the Persian Gulf theater. The experiences the six presented here paint a picture of the contributions all Army Nurse Corps officers made during the campaign. Their collective experience can be extrapolated to the aggregate nursing force deployed to the desert.

The 47th Field Hospital (FH) was the first 44th Medical Brigade, XVIII Corps, hospital in the Gulf.[1] The main body of the unit deployed from its home base, Fort Sill, Oklahoma, on 27 August 1990 and settled on the island of Bahrain on "an absolutely barren piece of desert" some distance from the support of brigade headquarters. Daily temperatures topped out at 130° F, and the unit faced an immense task of establishing a field hospital in a primitive environment.[2]

"Setting up" a field hospital in the Gulf included not only erecting outer structures and functionally placing beds, supplies, and equipment, but also building floors to decrease sand encroachment, acquiring latrines and showers, building shelving for a variety of uses, building walkways, establishing living quarters, mess facilities, communications area, TOC [Tactical Operations Center], headquarters, preparing compound security, and other time consuming and labor intensive details. Those with carpentry skills and tools were much in demand. After building the basics, units went on to add personal touches like street signs, tent names, "veranda" chairs and swings.[3]

The hospital became operational on 5 September 1990, just nine days after its departure from its home station. When factoring in travel time, time differences, jet lag, fatigue, and logistical deficiencies, this deployment time was outstanding. The hospital opened with six intensive care unit (ICU) beds and two operating room tables. It was housed in two TEMPERs loaned to the 47th FH by the Air Force, and an Emergency Medical Treatment tent. From the earliest days the sister services helped the 47th FH, which had no organic support. Before the unit's departure from the continental United States, Reynolds Army Community Hospital at Fort Sill lent a variety of equipment to the 47th FH, such as abdominal staple guns, monitors, and other instruments. In the Gulf, the U.S. Marine Corps furnished the unit with fuel for their generators and vehicles. The 47th FH borrowed additional equipment from the local Bahrain Defense Forces hospital, the 82nd Airborne Division, and from the Navy's Fleet Hospital Six. In exchange for the bartered medical equipment, the 47th FH shared various pieces of its non-medical equipment. Reflecting on this arduous scavenger hunt for supplies and equipment, the chief nurse, Colonel Kathryn Deuster, remarked "there is no advantage in getting medical personnel to the theater of operation quickly, if they have nothing to work with when they get there."[4]

The 47th FH's personnel constantly improvised to provide care for their patients, but difficulties plagued the effort. The 44th Medical Brigade commander, Colonel Jerome Foust, was dissatisfied with the unit's level of military discipline and relieved the hospital commander when one member of the unit violated the ban on alcohol. Confusion existed about whether the 47th FH would remain assigned to the 44th Medical Brigade. On 15 December 1990, the 47th FH transferred out of 44th Medical Brigade's control and became assets of Echelons Above Corps, a decision that the 44th Medical Brigade opposed. The hospital then relocated to King Khalid Military City.[5]

Additionally, the 47th FH's issued equipment was Prepositioning of Material Configured to Unit Sets (POMCUS), a tent facility that had been in storage in Bahrain since 1968, but all involved judged the Vietnam-era POMCUS facility and equipment as unfamiliar, inadequate, and antiquated.[6] Packing lists, for instance, did not match the supply containers' contents. The canvas tents and air mattresses had dry rot. Rubber components on equipment had dried up after years in non–air-conditioned storage. Very little in the way of blood pressure cuffs, stethoscopes, medicines, and monitoring equipment was included, but the condition and amount of linens, bedpans, and operating room tables were adequate.[7] On a larger scale, the facility's environmental control units were unequal to dealing with the extremely hot, humid weather. Still, the nursing staff performed well. Cheney observed that they "needed frequent positive feedback from me regarding accomplishments. Because it was earned, it was always a pleasure to give."

The 47th FH nurses helped to establish and man the first Stress Treatment Facility in the Gulf to provide rest and relaxation for soldiers suffering from stress and coping problems so they could expeditiously return to duty.[8] The soldiers, who were not considered to have a psychiatric disease, spent 72 hours in the program attending classes on anger management, stress control, and assertiveness. Group therapy sessions allowed for frustration venting and they built mutual group support. Sporting activities fostered team building and cohesion. Work therapy projects, such as filling sandbags or building bunkers, averted boredom, tested the soldiers' readiness to return to their units, provided anger relief, and furnished the hospital with much-needed protection. Major Dina Sine and Captain Imelda J. Weddington led the facility, which was staffed by the 47th FH nurses, an occupational therapist, and enlisted medics, but was situated nearby at the 28th Combat Support Hospital (CSH) across the causeway in Saudi Arabia.[9] On 1 November 1990, a psychiatric team replaced the 47th FH personnel and praised the original team's efforts.[10] The program was a good example of the successes that nurses could achieve when the creative enthusiasm of junior officers and enlisted medics was coupled with the interest and support of the senior leadership.

Captain Linda Groetken, a 47th FH staff nurse, penned "One Day in the Life of a Staff Nurse," a depiction of an Army nurse's typical day in the Persian Gulf:

0500—Woke up . . . to see dawn emerging over the beach. Quietly I get up off my cot so I won't disturb the twelve other women that share this GP Medium tent. . . . eat some fruit . . . and enjoy the simple vista of white sand, white rock, blue sky and blue sea.

0600—Walked across to Med-Surg Ward #1. . . . Fourteen patients occupy the tent. One is going to surgery for an Open Reduction Internal Fixation of the right arm while two others are recovering from pneumonia. The rest are convalescing from knee surgery, low back pain, hernia repairs or gastroenteritis. . . .

0800—Send those convalescing . . . who can walk to . . . showers while we get basins for bed baths to the few remaining patients. I really appreciate the field surgical sink. Just press a lever and water comes out. . . .

0900—An IV infiltrates and it's time to start another. We've already made up an IV start tray, but, . . . no IV catheters. I find one with a two inch needle—the smallest I could find, but it does the trick. The order calls for a heparin lock, but, . . . we have none. . . We do, however, have a box of extension tubing with no obvious requirement for them. A little innovative adaptation and an extension tube is transformed into a heparin lock. Thus we save a patient from hassle. . . .

1000—Gas alarm drill. We all don protective [gas] masks, . . . and wear them for 15 minutes. My optical inserts make it more difficult for me to see and my movements are as graceful as a gorilla. My nose itches and I scratch the voicemitter in a fruitless attempt to relieve it. I continue to work as usual. . . .

1200—I finish reporting off . . . and walk . . . to the mess hall for lunch.

1300—. . . Time for ADLs [activities of daily living]. First I take a load of laundry down to the showers. In the back are garbage cans where I wash my clothes, darks first, then whites. I jump in and stomp around to Billy Joel, my agitation cycle. Rinse twice, . . . then wring and hang on the clothes line. By this time I'm exhausted and vow I will never take my washer and dryer for granted again.

1430—Polished my boots as I catch a tan on my face and arms. This task is much easier in the heat and the sun as my polish is almost liquid and goes on very smoothly.

1530—Mail call! Great day! . . . I get a real haul: one package of books and two of various snacks. Now where to put it? Resolve some of this problem by promptly eating a package of cookies and sharing a canister of potato chips. The rest I store under my bed with some in the foot locker for those midnight snack attacks.

1600—The wind has died down somewhat. Time to sweep the bed, then the floor. I know it's an endless task, but, I feel better knowing I've rearranged the sand for the present.

1630—Formation and accountability. Yes, I am here. . . .

1700—Time for PT. I dress in the less than flattering PT uniform . . . I feel so light on my feet the miles just fly by. A nice breeze off the beach keeps the sweat from drenching me.

1745—Time to shower. . . . The cool water feels so refreshing as it washes off a long day's sweat.

1900—Back up to supper—a real social occasion. Spaghetti tonight with parmesan cheese on the table.

2030—Back to the tent. Afraid I will have to miss the movie at the MWR [Morale, Welfare, Recreation] tent tonight—up early and will have to go to bed early so I can start another day. I write the day's events in my journal before I sleep—who knows, maybe someday I'll write an article about it or maybe even a book. . . .[11]

Although her day was busy and filled with essential chores, Groetken was working a six-hour shift at this point during Operation Desert Shield/Operation Desert Storm (ODS). Deuster explained that duty schedules were modified according to circumstances, and the nursing staff only worked for as many duty hours as were necessary. At various times, this could be four-, six-, or eight-hour shifts. Every effort was made to give time off equitably. The supervisors routinely worked 12-hour shifts but were not compelled to be within the hospital for the entire shift. The supervisor did have to remain readily available, making frequent rounds, because many of the staff nurses were young and inexperienced and many did not carry medical-surgical nursing as their primary area of concentration.[12]

The 47th CSH was another hospital that deployed early to the desert. The Madigan Army Medical Center, Washington unit, received its alert notification for ODS on 10 August 1990. It deployed to the Persian Gulf in September 1990 and became operational within a few weeks. From October 1990 until January 1991, its 37 Army Nurse Corps officers staffed the 160-bed Medical unit, Self-contained, Transportable; Mobile Unit, Surgical Transportable (MUST) and provided combat service support to the 24th Infantry and the 1st Cavalry Division in Saudi Arabia.

Like many other units, the 47th CSH began its transformation into Deployable Medical System (DEPMEDS) equipment in December 1990 and, while in this state of flux, the unit managed to care for 3,261 ambulatory patients and 509 hospitalized patients, and also carried out 112 surgical cases, predominantly orthopedic and sports injuries, in its MUST facility. The majority of illnesses treated at this time were cases of asthma, dehydration, and diarrhea. The unit also provided care for a number of soldiers with flash burns that resulted from the use of improper fuel to burn latrine cans.

Once the ground war started, the 47th CSH's mission dramatically changed. It became a mobile surgical hospital with 24 intensive care beds, four operating rooms, and support services such as a pharmacy, radiology unit, blood bank, and laboratory. Its staff stabilized casualties, performed life- or limb-saving surgery, and evacuated the wounded to rear-echelon hospitals within the span of a few hours. Ordered to move north into Iraq, the unit endured a "bone-jarring, exhausting, 3-day convoy across the open desert riding and sleeping in the back of 5 ton trucks, through stand [sic] storms, rain, and winds up to 50 mph." On the evening

Standing left to right are Lieutenant Colonel Jeannette Zunino, Colonel Kathryn P. Deuster, Lieutenant Colonel Peggy Garifino, Lieutenant Colonel Carolyn Wier, Lieutenant Colonel Chantal Middleton, Lieutenant Colonel William Mathia, and Lieutenant Colonel Daniel Dolenar. Kneeling left to right are Major Dana Gruber and SFC Atkinson. All were staff of the 47th Field Hospital at Sheikh Isa Air Base in Bahrain.
Photo courtesy of Army Nurse Corps Archives, Office of Medical History, Falls Church, VA.

of 27 February 1991, they expeditiously erected their DEPMEDS equipment under blackout conditions and proceeded to care for Iraqi soldiers, wounded civilians, and a few American casualties. At the time of the cease-fire, the 47th CSH was the most forward deployed hospital, more than 100 miles into enemy territory.

After Desert Storm, the 47th CSH's chief nurse, Lieutenant Colonel Harvey O. Stowe, attributed the Department of Nursing's success to its resolution to assume a positive attitude and to take special pride in their responsibilities from the start. This led them to organize their wards for the highest efficiency and optimal patient care, a complex challenge in the austere environment of combat. Stowe believed that the fact that all the nurses came from the same medical center was important because it promoted cohesion based on established relationships not only among themselves but also with other professional staff. Additionally, the nurses who stayed behind at Madigan offered significant support in the form of letters and care packages that reminded those who had deployed that they remained a part of a home unit that was concerned for their welfare. Stowe also considered the strong emphasis placed on nursing education important. Two Army nurses prepared and organized a selection of classes that was presented throughout the mobilization and in the final analysis enhanced the nurses' combat readiness. Their reaction to a loud explosion while in Iraq demonstrated the value of the instruction. One morning, the hospital shook after a tremendous blast. The nursing staff members automatically threw on their helmets and flak jackets and positioned their patients on the floor. Fortunately, the explosion was not from hostile fire, but it did demonstrate that the nurses had internalized the lessons of combat nursing.

The Department of Nursing philosophy, clearly articulated early in the deployment, also contributed to its positive outcomes. Based on the premise that staff members succeed when they fully understand expectations, the leadership promulgated a set of precepts to guide them and promote an atmosphere conducive to teamwork. These guiding principles stressed that constant, reflexive agreement and accord would likely stifle the group's processes of creative thinking. They warned the staff to say what they mean and mean what they say because rapidly identifying core questions in a combat setting was imperative. The guidance affirmed that the nurses were first and foremost there for the soldiers, who deserved dedicated respect and caring. Another injunction reminded nurses to care for their staff with compassion, concern, and determination. All Army nurses had to have the backbone to make judgments and stand by their decisions. Micromanagement was frowned upon, and leadership by example encouraged. Nurses planned for the worst and remained flexible, finding that this approach allowed them to handle almost constant change with only slight adjustments. The efficient and cohesive 47th CSH Department of Nursing achieved success by assiduously planning, training, and toiling to exceed expectations.[13]

The 85th Evacuation Hospital (EVAC), a Table of Organization and Equipment unit from Fort Lee, Virginia, also prepared to deploy to Saudi Arabia in late summer 1990. The unit predictably faced a series of challenges. Almost immediately, three distinct groups—the non–Fort Lee Professional Officer Filler System (PROFIS) officers who were billeted in an off-post motel, the Fort Lee PROFIS personnel who resided at their homes during the preparatory phase, and the permanently assigned Table of Organization and Equipment unit staff—failed to bond into a cohesive whole but instead remained as separate groups throughout the mobilization.[14]

The Department of Nursing's PROFIS chief nurse assumed leadership and responsibility from the garrison chief nurse, and the transition created some stress and strains. The two worked on a personal level to resolve differences, and the nursing staff adjusted to new leaders. Eventually, the strong nursing leadership and the fact that the Department of Nursing organized itself into its traditional structure—which all recognized, understood, and deemed effective—helped to cement relationships and diminish the group divisions, at least within the ranks of nursing.[15]

The 85th EVAC departed Fort Lee on 22 October 1990 and remained in Southwest Asia (SWA) until July 1991, distinguishing itself by its protracted, dedicated service. At the time of their deployment from Fort Lee, personnel were laden with web gear, canteens, gas masks, rucksacks, and duffle bags. They arrived in Saudi Arabia the next day, settling into Cement City, the site of a concrete factory and staging area 30 miles southwest of Dhahran, where they remained for 28 days. In Cement City, approximately 8,000 to 10,000 troops of all services bunked down while they waited for their equipment to become available and their sites to be prepared. Everyone was billeted in tents spread over 50 acres, and all slept on litters about six inches apart, with male, female, officer, and enlisted mixed throughout the complex. In Cement City, the nurses drank six to 10 liters of water daily to cope with the searing 130° F heat.[16] They learned to adapt and live with "the environment, the unknown, the fears and the uncertainties. After surviving that for a month, the majority of personnel felt like they could handle anything . . . and did."[17]

The 85th EVAC was under the 44th Medical Brigade, and the relationship between the two was strained, or as the official history put it, the relationship was "short lived but stormy."[18] The 85th EVAC believed the 44th Medical Brigade was unreasonably concerned with mundane details such as polished boots and keeping hat strings concealed. The 44th Medical Brigade also needlessly exasperated the 85th, contending it would have "to prove that DEPMEDS were highly mobile despite visual evidence to the contrary," implying that the 85th EVAC would be moving frequently.[19] The situation improved when the 62nd Medical Group arrived in theater, intervened between the command and subordinate unit, and appeared to have more realistic expectations. Nonetheless, a battle raged about who would control the 85th EVAC. The 44th Medical Brigade fell under the XVIII Airborne Corps, which reportedly did not want reserve units serving with them, and so they tried to retain the 85th EVAC, an active component unit. However in mid-December, the 85th EVAC was reassigned to Army Central and became an Echelons Above Corps asset.[20] Overall, the 85th EVAC approved of the realignment, although it believed that there were some drawbacks. From the 85th EVAC's perspective, the change placed them under the command and control of the 173rd Medical Group, an Army reserve component unit, less familiar with Army ways and means and which, in the 85th EVAC's view, seemingly had some bias in favor of reserve units. The 85th EVAC felt the 173rd Medical Group's communications were slow and inadequate, forcing the 85th EVAC to utilize double reporting and develop its own collateral channels of communication, both formal and informal.[21]

A few weeks before the 85th EVAC became an asset of Army Central and the 173rd Medical Group, the unit moved to the King Abdul Aziz Air Base in Dhahran, where it remained.[22] It took eight days to set up and became operational on 4 December 1990. Later that very day the 44th Medical Brigade ordered the 85th EVAC to tear down and move.[23] Morale plummeted. The thought of dismantling the DEPMEDS after so many days of hard labor constructing the facility cast a pall over the staff. One frustrated head nurse coped with the unwelcome news by walking and weeping that evening in the privacy of the desert.[24] Although the unit ultimately did not pull up stakes, the experience demoralized the staff; and repeated indications that a move was imminent, the rapidly changing strategic picture, the constantly circulating rumors, and an almost total lack of stability

This is the site of the 85th Evacuation Hospital's temporary encampment in Cement City southwest of Dhahran, Saudi Arabia in November 1990.
Photo courtesy of Lieutenant Colonel Brenna Aileo, Springville, PA.

further reduced unit esprit de corps and cohesiveness.[25]

Attendance at religious services provided some solace for the nurses. On Christmas day, Major Brenna B. Aileo wrote that she attended midnight Mass and "the priest is very good. . . . His services are very uplifting, though many of us cry our way through them—men and women, it seems to be our real stress release."[26]

However, physical activities and preparations also helped to cope with stress. Colonel Linda Freeman, the unit's chief nurse, told about the nursing staff, both officer and enlisted, filling sand bags to protect themselves, because the hospital was situated 500 meters from a tactical airstrip. One day in early January 1991, her staff filled 21 pallets of sandbags and Freeman said that "my back knows it, my elbow knows it and now you know it." She added that all nurses participated in the effort because they all wanted to create a safety buffer. However, Freeman revealed that she was "catching hell [from the nonnursing elements] but so be it. Only an idiot sits back and does nothing." She revealed:

> Anxiety levels are rising and the physical labor is also therapeutic. Dreams are becoming disturbing. Tempers are shortening. But everyone (nursing is pulling together and supporting each other) reminds each other to take it easy, cut folks some slack and hang together.[27]

In these Desert Shield days, hospital census ran about 150 patients, with six to 10 surgeries per day. Although not normally a responsibility of an EVAC, Level I health care (sick call) saw more than 100 patients daily.[28] Surgical cases included nonemergent appendectomies and the incision and drainage of lesions under anesthesia. One nurse noted that all the surgeons wanted to cut constantly. Doctors, she added, "are the same the world over."[29] Although these routine procedures prepared and tested the system, they also depleted supplies and drained the personnel's strength.[30] Unlike the patients in Vietnam, most of the 85th EVAC's ICU patients were admitted with diagnoses such as chest pain, myocardial infarction, gastrointestinal bleeds, severe depression, seizure disorders, diabetes, and hypertension. The nurses questioned why patients with some of these conditions had not been screened or discovered before deployment.[31] About half of the psychiatric patients were Vietnam veterans who had formerly repressed their combat experiences and were decompensating in the desert.[32] In her study of the Army Medical Department's personnel's adaptation to combat during the Gulf War, Colonel Cynthia Gurney also noted that Vietnam veterans had difficulty adjusting. She attributed this surprising finding to the fact that their prior combat experience was 20 or more years in the past, in a very different type of war, and accompanied by a large measure of "negative baggage."[33]

Once the air campaign commenced on 16 January 1991, the 85th EVAC began taking the prophylaxis pills in the nerve agent blister packs. Numerous alert sirens blared and commanders repeatedly ordered soldiers to don Mission Oriented Protective Postures (MOPP) gear.[34] Nurses attired themselves and equipped and dressed all patients in MOPP. Freeman was proud of the way her staff supported patients and prevented any panic. "Everyone did their jobs beautifully. They were scared but really hung in there. People taking care of people."[35]

With the beginning of the ground war in February 1991, life for the nurses of the 85th EVAC became more dangerous. A prolific correspondent, Aileo shared her thoughts:

> As the news may have told you a Saudi Air Base . . . is taking a lot of SCUD missiles [sic], well it's us! The past week has been hell. Sirens going off mean mask then into full MOPP gear. We've seen the patriots fire from just behind our compound. It is frightening. Then we wait in full MOPP to see if more SCUDs are coming or gas or something else. Last night we had soldiers run into our tent yelling gas as they saw the Patriot fire—we all mask and fell to the ground as the BOOMS started. Since we've had SCUD alerts at all times we never feel safe. Of course it's more often at night. Really awful.

> I was at work @ 7:20 when there was a terrible explosion. We masked—helped pts [patients] mask, grabbed our MOPP and ran into the bunkers as the explosions rocked the tentage. We've taught pts [patients] to pull their EKG leads from the machine, pull their IVs [to remove their tethers and seek cover] and [don their] MOPP. All IV lines are hep [heparin] locked, so lines can be pulled quickly. No real nursing care can go on while in MOPP but reassurance.

> . . . We're working 48 hr weeks. 6–8 hr. shifts.

> DEPMEDS—we have all HP [Hewlett Packard] monitors—they're good—can do a 12 lead [EKG]. Only one pulse ox[imiter] per ICU. No Dynamaps [automatic blood pressure monitors], no IVACs/IMEDs [infusion pumps]. NG [nasogastric] and ET [endotracheal] suction, lighting, air conditioners and heaters are fine.

> I washed used urinals, washbasins, bed pans today. Dried and put back on shelf. We haven't gotten in more so must reuse!

> ... We have no warm water but have asked for 50–100 cup coffee urns to heat bath water, water to warm blood, etc.... We still haven't seen them arrive yet.

> ... Please spread the word—we do not need to hear about the stress WRAMC [Walter Reed Army Medical Center] folks are under. Everyone keeps telling us it's tense there and how awful things are—but at least you're all safe and with your families. We fear for our life 24 hours a day. 30–40% of us are sick from the pyridostigmine tabs [nerve gas antidote enhancer]. Plus we were all sick from the "secret" shot we had. We love everyone's letters—but.

> We have a new diagnosis here. MOPP intolerance. Chest pain or SOB [shortness of breath] while in MOPP4, believe me we've had to AE [air evacuate] a number of folks because of it. Keeps us busy.

> Oh, today we ran out of Rx pads—can you believe it. Yes supply is a problem.[36]

The SCUD attacks continued intermittently and, on 25 February 1991, one of the notoriously inaccurate missiles finally hit a target, a Dhahran warehouse converted into a barracks building and occupied by U.S. reservists from Pennsylvania who were serving with Quartermaster and Transportation units. The explosion killed 28 soldiers and wounded about 260 others. Most of the wounded received treatment in five hospitals, among them the 85th EVAC and 207th EVAC.[37]

Immediately following the lethal attack, the 85th EVAC headquarters activated a Mass Casualty (MASCAL) and the staff responded instantly. The hospital received 25 casualties, four mortally wounded—one who expired en route, two who were in the expectant category upon arrival, and another who died later during surgery in the operating room. Three of the 28 killed were female soldiers. The ICU worked with maximum efficiency, caring for six casualties on ventilators. However, two were weaned within 24 hours and two more were off their ventilators within 36 hours. Every ICU patient had chest tubes and, in one instance, four chest tubes were connected to one suction machine with yards of tubing and Y connectors. The chest injuries resulting from SCUD shrapnel typically were bubbling and sucking wounds. Other casualties had dreadful open bone fractures and some had burns.[38]

After the SCUD attack, all the previous conflicts, personality issues, and power struggles were set aside.[39] The staff worked together to deal with their very serious mission. Freeman wrote:

> You should have seen these kids work—they did it just like they had been taught and even though some of them were paying a really high personal price, they hung in and did beautifully. A specialist from the mess hall took it upon herself to supply [C]okes, coffee and soup to all of the areas—and she kept it coming! She is as much a hero as anyone else—and she stayed until the end. Laundry and bath went ahead and heated up the showers early ... The 47th Medical Supply Command called and wanted to know what we needed—and then they delivered the supplies! ... The docs really came through. No ego's [sic] and no tirades. One of the bad boys kept asking for a specific item and kept being told we didn't have it. Miracle—his response was if he had paid more attention to supplies and had spent less time being an ass then maybe he would have known what was available and what was not. ...[40]

The 85th EVAC finally returned home from the Arabian Peninsula on 26 July 1991. Its nine months in SWA were among the lengthiest of all the units' service.[41]

In January 1991, Major Brenna Aileo and her 85th Evacuation Hospital tentmates wait out an alert in MOPP4 gear in a bunker during Operation Desert Storm.
Photo courtesy of Lieutenant Colonel Brenna Aileo, Springville, PA.

The 21st EVAC staged at Fort Hood, Texas, in June 1991 before deploying to Saudi Arabia to replace the 85th EVAC. At that time, Colonel Pam Burns, a Vietnam veteran, joined the unit as chief nurse from her previous assignment at William Beaumont Army Medical Center. For about a week, the PROFIS officers and Forces Command nurses assigned to the 21st EVAC prepared for their mobilization, picking up TA-50, attending briefings, having health records screened, and undergoing Soldier Readiness Processing.[42] They arrived in Dhahran, Saudi Arabia, on a very hot Fourth of July in 1991.

Originally, the unit bunked down in Khobar Towers but later exchanged places in a piecemeal fashion with assorted elements of the 85th EVAC.[43] Those departing shared lessons learned during their extended stay in the Persian Gulf with the newcomers. For example, they discussed a variety of DEPMEDS idiosyncrasies and the means used to deal with them. As the longest deployed DEPMEDS, the 85th EVAC's facility provided testimony to the wear and tear on the equipment under conditions of heavy use in an extreme environment. Door and window zippers malfunctioned early in the mobilization, and plastic windows deteriorated over time. As the temperature soared to 135° F by mid-morning, large blocks of ice froze around the air conditioners. The fold-up sinks consistently leaked and

As seen here in January 1991, the nursing staff of the 85th Evacuation Hospital clothed patients in protective MOPP4 with every alert. When patients and nurses were in MOPP, patient care was at the very least awkward if not virtually impossible. The nurses wrote out and affixed patients' names with tape on their headgear for purposes of identification.
Photo courtesy of Lieutenant Colonel Brenna Aileo, Springville, PA.

required five-gallon water cans to catch the runoff. Litters with large wheels sooner or later tore gaping holes in the flooring and, when the rains came, streams of water coursed through the middle of the hospital. This presented a special hazard if patients needed to be defibrillated. To prevent rips and tears, the staff placed pallets beneath the flooring and, while this solved the problem, patients on litters endured rough rides, and snakes and other small desert animals found shelter in the subflooring.[44] Despite these circumstances, the experience for the 21st EVAC was generally upbeat. Permanent structures such as air-conditioned Quonset huts and trailers soon replaced the decaying DEPMEDS facilities, and the hospital had abundant supplies and equipment, mostly bequests from hastily departing units.[45]

Captain Teresa Parsons' experience exemplified Army nurses' contributions and illustrated several issues relevant to deployed women. Parsons left her assignment at Fort Riley, Kansas, and she deployed as a PROFIS officer with the 21st EVAC in the summer of 1991. She joined the unit as a Women's Health Nurse Practitioner, although no authorization had previously existed in the Table

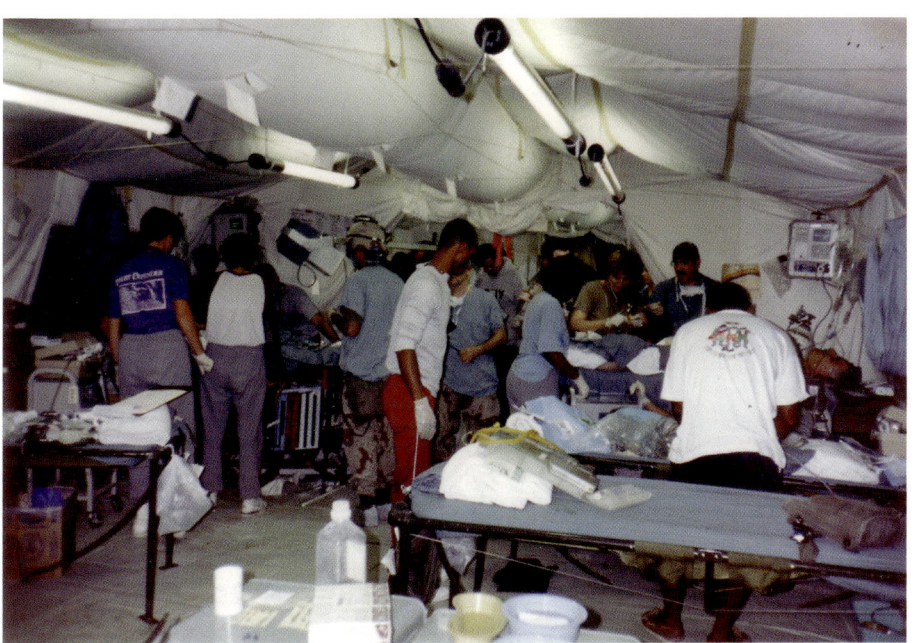

The 85th EVAC nurses respond to a mass casualty situation in February 1991 in the aftermath of the catastrophic SCUD disaster. At the time this photo was taken, the staff already had delivered one patient to the operating room and two others were being prepared for transfer to surgery.
Photo courtesy of Lieutenant Colonel Brenna Aileo, Springville, PA.

of Organization and Equipment for such a specialized health care provider. Nonetheless, her assignment proved to be a wise move in this, the largest mobilization of women in history. Initially, Parsons diagnosed pregnancies and treated vaginitis and sexually transmitted diseases. She subsequently administered numerous repatriation physical examinations for returning reservists and dealt with a multitude of requests to substantiate previously undocumented anthrax immunizations.[46] She also handled myriad issues related to oral contraceptive use, such as breakthrough bleeding, mood changes, weight gain, unavailability of specific oral contraceptives for women whose predeployment supply had run out, and the need for annual Pap smears.[47]

Parsons encountered large numbers of renal calculi (kidney stones) and constipation that developed as a result of chronic dehydration in both men and women soldiers. Women, in particular, did not drink enough water because there was no convenient way for them to use latrines. Taking off their Load Bearing Equipment with all its intricate web gear and suspenders and other accoutrements like their helmets and gas masks led them to conclude that using the latrine was a complicated, time-consuming endeavor to be delayed as long as possible.[48]

As time passed, women appeared at Parsons' clinic requesting treatment for venereal warts, and a number of them presented with abnormal pelvic findings such as possible ectopic pregnancies and abdominal masses. Parsons had access to a computed tomography scanner that interfaced via telemedicine to a Brooke Army Medical Center radiologist who efficiently provided her with diagnostic assistance within hours. Most of these women with life-threatening complaints such as ectopic pregnancies were air-evacuated to Germany for treatment.[49]

Like Army nurses of yesteryear, Parsons used a number of field expedient measures to compensate for equipment inadequacies. She used an inverted bedpan for her first gynecological examinations. Later she delved into an unused operating room CONEX (Container Express, a large corrugated metal shipping container) and found an orthopedic table. She added stirrups and had an improvised gynecological examination table for the balance of her tour in SWA.[50]

After a five-month tour in SWA, the 21st EVAC returned to the continental United States in December 1991. Parsons reported in to her new duty assignment at Fort Sill, Oklahoma, in January 1992.[51]

The 86th EVAC, garrisoned at Fort Campbell, Kentucky, received its alert orders to deploy in support of the 101st Airborne Division (Air Assault) in August 1990. Lieutenant Colonel Maureen Combs served as chief nurse and Major Kathleen Simpson filled the role of chief nurse, days. About 80 percent of the unit's complement of PROFIS nurses came from Blanchfield Army Community Hospital at Fort Campbell. The balance of what the chief nurse referred to as a very cohesive team derived from Eisenhower and Fitzsimons Army Medical Centers.

Almost half the 49 Army nurses who deployed were married and co-located with spouses assigned to the 101st Airborne Division.[52] As the deployment progressed, the married and co-located group experienced constant anxiety. The most frightening concern was the dreadful possibility that their husbands could possibly arrive at their hospital as patients.[53] It was doubtless that these were continual fears, even when the units were in garrison.

In August, the Army nurses alerted for duty with the 86th EVAC implemented their family care plans. Because many of the primary and secondary schools would begin classes early in September, parents sent their children to their specified caregivers immediately. As a result of solid advance planning, no major problems ensued in carrying out the shift of parental authority, and the Fort Campbell families and friends who stayed behind were extremely supportive.[54]

The nurses in the advance party, including Major Kathleen Simpson and Lieutenant Colonel Jean Purdom, departed from Fort Campbell on 21 October and arrived in Dhahran, Saudi Arabia, the next day. They settled in for 11 days in "horrible" Cement City, a staging area situated in a barren spot in the desert. The area was so devoid in resources that a nice piece of cardboard was viewed as a prized possession. The remaining complement, the main body, arrived in early November and settled in at the first of two locations, the King Fahd Airfield, where they were co-located with the 101st Airborne Division. When the main body arrived at this site, they found that Simpson and Purdom had set up their cots

Mail from family and friends at home brings a smile to Major Kathleen Simpson's face while she pauses in her small living space in Cement City in October 1990. The staff of the 86th Evacuation Hospital spent 11 days there before moving to King Fahd Airfield.
Photo courtesy of Colonel Kathleen Simpson, Washington, NC.

The hot, dirty, group of Army nurses were happy to be returning to their compound after a mission to the desert filling sandbags. The women were (front row from left to right) Major Debra Mulhall, AN, Lieutenant Colonel Darla Ebert, AN, Major Cindy Davis, MS, Lieutenant Colonel Deborah Castellan, AN, and Major Carolyn Adams, AN. In the back row, from left to right were Major Mary Glenn, AN, SP4 Stephen McKinney, AKA Skinny McKinney, the truck driver, and Lieutenant Colonel Jean Purdom, AN.
Photo courtesy of Lieutenant Colonel Carolyn Adams, Steilacoom, WA.

and embellished them with a four-star flourish, a mint candy, on the bedcovers.[55] Such attention to detail with a touch of whimsy greatly enhanced adaptation to the new, alien environment. During this time, the hospital ran a census of about 50 to 60 patients and treated about 75 ambulatory patients daily.[56] The hospitalized patients mainly presented with orthopedic conditions (predominantly sports injuries), gastroenteritis, abdominal pain, chest pain, and burns.[57]

The nurses did not limit themselves to caring for patients, however. They helped to erect the hospital, set up beds, inflate air mattresses, and unload the MILVANs (containers for overseas or ground movement of military cargo).[58] They created shelf space, fashioned sharps boxes from taped-together bath basins, and con-

Senior Army nurses did double duty with kitchen responsibilities, Thanksgiving 1990, at the 86th Evacuation Hospital. The cadre of cooks included (left to right) Major Carolyn Adams, Major Mary Glenn, Lieutenant Colonel Deb Castellan, Lieutenant Colonel Jean Purdom, and Major Kathy Simpson. Photo courtesy of Colonel Kathleen Simpson, Washington, NC.

stantly cleaned and dusted in an effort to remove the ubiquitous sand. Two of the Army Nurse Corps officers, captains Michael Jorden and Raymond Bork, operated forklift trucks. The nurses also participated in company details, most notably filling sandbags. The exploits of one group were an expression of the excellent state of morale at that time.

> We found the best sand for making sand bags was located off the compound at the sand dunes. The field grade female officers went together on a 5 ton truck to make sand bags. . . . They had fun making "beach" photos and sliding down the dunes. They became tired after a few minutes of filling, tying and lifting sand bags. LTC Jean Purdom led the group in singing Christmas Carols and the work seemed a lot more fun. A new version of "The Twelve Days of Christmas" was created to include the following "gifts": 1—A hot shower in the morning, 2 near beers, 3 clean latrines, 4 temper tents, 5 MRE's, 6 smiling nurses, 7 Saudis staring, 8 whooa[59] medics, 9 Hueys flying, 10 camels humping, 11 letters from home, 12 thousand filled sand bags. It needs to be noted that these same nurses found fun in doing KP on Thanksgiving Day while their company grade counterparts laughed their way through field sanitation duties. Major Simpson frequently reminded the nurses to never lose their sense of humor.[60]

During off-duty times, the 86th EVAC nurses visited the 101st Airborne's post exchange to shop and enjoy Baskin-Robbins ice cream. Upon occasion they rode in the back of a five-ton truck to Dhahran to shop at a larger Army and Air Force Exchange System and make phone calls back home. The nurses had to lug their

Lieutenant Colonel Jean Purdom (left), operating room nurse, and Major Kathleen Simpson, chief nurse, days, both serving with the 86th Evacuation Hospital in Saudi Arabia, patiently wait in line to use the telephones to call home.
Photo courtesy of Colonel Kathleen Simpson, Washington, NC.

Individual Chemical Equipment bag along on the half-day trip, so they were exhausted but exhilarated by the excursion, especially if their phone calls went through. Some failed to connect with loved ones at home when calls were unanswered or they got a busy signal, and this adversely affected their morale. If, however, the nurses were able to talk with their family within the first few weeks of their arrival in country, they were able "to calm down." Sometimes while waiting in line at the phones at the sports center, an off-limits facility for females, Saudis ordered the Army nurses to leave.[61]

On 5 December 1990, the commander announced that the 86th EVAC would move to another new site, explaining that the change would place the hospital in a better position to care for the combat wounded. The main body thus relocated to King Khalid Military City on 20 December 1990. High winds and rainstorms that flooded the ICUs and a lack of equipment and supplies hampered the efforts to set up the hospital facility. The unit lacked Ambu bags and portable suction machines and had only four ventilators for a 48-bed ICU. The move also brought a new APO postal address and resultant mail difficulties that seriously impacted morale. Although some mail was forwarded and got through, it took up to two months for most letters and packages to reach the new location, and the problem never was satisfactorily

Pictured is Lieutenant Diane Bonnell deploying to Operation Desert Storm/Operation Desert Shield in November 1990.
Photo courtesy of Lieutenant Colonel Carolyn Adams, Steilacoom, WA.

resolved. Also affecting morale were the absence of a truck to clean out the latrine barrels, the lack of A rations, the restrictions placed on women leaving the compound without a male escort, the lack of sites for women to run or work out, and the noise of the Islam prayer call at 0500 hours.[62] To raise spirits, the nursing leaders aggressively addressed the need to constantly nurture one another.

With fighting imminent, the nurses were working 12-hour days six days a week, and the mood was more serious. All were constantly toting their Chemical Protective Overgarments, affectionately called "odor eaters," Individual Chemical Equipment bag, and Kevlar, an enervating but necessary precaution. Frequent SCUD alerts forced all to wear MOPP4 regularly. Staff members in one of the ICUs were caring for a heavy, immobile stroke patient whom the nurses found difficult to get into MOPP and position on the safety of the floor. To simplify matters, they moved him to an air mattress on the floor. First Lieutenant Diane Bonnell, garbed in MOPP2, presented a classic, poignant picture that exemplified the can-do spirit of Army nursing when she knelt on the floor and spoon-fed the patient, also in MOPP2, his breakfast of gelatin dessert. Other patients cared for in January 1991 were those involved in truck accidents and those with stomachaches, backaches, chest pain, and burns. Major Carolyn Adams, the 86th EVAC nurse historian, described January 1991 as a time the nurses "tried to find a healthy balance of caring for our current patients, planning for future MASCAL [Mass Casualty] situations and conserving our strength."[63]

During February 1991 the unit waited patiently for the ground war to begin, responded to SCUD alerts, amassed wartime stockages of supplies, and cared for a few patients. One of the most memorable patients was a British soldier with an arm amputation. Although his American Army nurses gave him state-of-the-art care, his buddies felt obliged to furnish a life-sized plywood "movie star"–type nurse named Nurse Pamela Goodbody to assist in his recovery. They also expressed their appreciation for the care provided by the Americans by treating the staff to a "royal dinner." Another patient at this time was an Enemy Prisoner of War with a severe head injury who was not expected to live. The 86th nurses were touched because he wore a wedding band and mused that he "was somebody's husband and probably somebody's Daddy." They assumed a very "caring attitude about this EPW [Enemy Prisoner of War]." Even though he was the enemy, he was briefly a patient "and someone's loved one in Iraq." To these nurses, a patient was a patient regardless of his past activities or military affiliation. With the cease-fire declared on 28 February, patient numbers dwindled and the unit began preparations for their return home.[64] The majority of the staff of the 86th EVAC had redeployed back to Fort Campbell by the end of April 1991.

In November 1990, the 50th General Hospital (GH), a U.S. Army Reserve unit headquartered at Fort Lawton in Seattle, Washington, with detachments in Tacoma, Bellingham, and Yakima, Washington, received its unit alert notification for ODS. The unit's original 187 Army Nurse Corps officers organized to move from their home stations to the mobilization station, Fort Lewis, Washington, putting their personal, professional, and military lives in order. Simultaneously, a number of PROFIS nurses from across the country reported to the unit upon mobilization along with the chief nurse, Colonel Marcia M. Van Wagner. Van Wagner was new to the unit but blended in well and would prove willing and able to speak out for the nursing perspective and nursing's concerns. The early weeks of mobilization

A handful of senior nursing leaders of the 50th GH pause for an impromptu photo session during their busy duty day in Riyadh, Saudi Arabia. From left to right are Lieutenant Colonel Marjorie Crowl, Chief, Surgical Nursing Section; Sergeant First Class Mary Wilson, Non-commissioned Officer in Charge; Lieutenant Colonel Diane D'Alessandro, assistant chief nurse; Colonel Jan Spane, Chief, Medical Nursing section; and Major Linda Schmidt, Night Supervisor, Medical Nursing Section. Photo courtesy of Colonel Marcia Van Wagner, Lincoln, CA.

were marked by "long tedious days full of anxiety and fear."

The 3/9 Aviation Battalion sponsored the 50th GH at Fort Lewis. The battalion's task was to shift the 50th from its peacetime mission to proper combat readiness.[65] For the unit's predominantly older soldiers, the transition proved arduous and the dawn-to-dark days were filled with a plethora of training activities that eventually led to the unit's validation for deployment.

Physical training was one of the most challenging aspects of the preparations. A diagnostic physical training test, inadvertently scheduled just after soldiers received a panel of deployment immunizations, was administered in inclement weather. The predictable results painted a dismal, inaccurate picture of the participants' level of fitness and produced numerous traumatic injuries. Sporadic aerobic conditioning and strength-building exercises ensued and, in some cases, produced yet more sports injuries.

Following the primary marksmanship training, the activated reservists went to the firing range to qualify with the M16 rifle and the .45 pistol. The miserable weather and the "cold and damp fox holes and firing pits made the process seem to last an eternity BUT EVERYONE QUALIFIED." Nuclear, Biological, and Chemical warfare classes focused on individual survival skills, maintenance and fitting of the protective mask, decontamination, MOPP protection, and the care of chemical casualties. A moment of truth occurred when the unit issued the nurses their decontamination kits with Mark I auto injectors and pyridostigmine tablets.[66] What had previously been a conversation piece with few personal implications

Colonel Marcia Van Wagner, chief nurse of the 50th GH, presided over a special Officers' Call in January 1991 in a hospital auditorium where morning report was held daily. Van Wagner scheduled these sessions when stress levels escalated. She disseminated accurate information and did her utmost to enhance esprit de corps.
Photo courtesy of Colonel Marcia Van Wagner, Lincoln, CA.

became a frightening and dangerous reality. Other educational topics covered in this period were field sanitation, Preparation for Overseas Movement, security measures, and driver's training.

While learning soldier's skills, the nurses simultaneously reviewed and expanded their professional education and in many cases taught classes on subjects such as Advanced Trauma Life Support, Advanced Cardiac Life Support, Basic

Cardiac Life Support, and clinical skills, such as the use of sterile technique, implementation of intravenous therapy, interpretation of arterial blood gases, care of tracheotomies, urinary catheterization, and placement and care of chest tubes. In the final phase of the preparatory process the unit integrated into Madigan Army Medical Center for two weeks to validate their hands-on patient care skills. Although this experience did not replicate the austere, danger-filled conditions they would face in theatre, it did affirm the staff's patient-care skills and bolster their confidence.

The unit's journey to SWA took place in three increments. The advance party departed on 1 January 1991, the main body left two weeks later, and the rear detachment concluded the unit's movement two weeks later. All mobilization assets were in the Persian Gulf by the end of January.

The unit's quarters were in Eskan Village, a walled city constructed for nomadic Bedouin tribes who had refused to accept the complex, judging it too small to house their large, extended families and flocks of goats, sheep, and camels. The village consisted of high-rise apartments with concrete walls, marble floors, high ceilings, and screened windows that offered views of a desolate, empty landscape. The apartments came without furniture, but the unit staff—extremely grateful not to be billeted in tents or foxholes—transformed their space with cardboard boxes and crates as makeshift furniture.[67]

The 50th GH was an element of the 244th Medical Group and was an Echelons Above Corps unit. Its mission was to provide patient care for all allied forces, civilians, and Enemy Prisoners of War within a host nation facility, the 760-bed Riyadh Al Kharj Hospital. The nurses cared mainly for medical patients, those recovering from training and motor vehicle accidents, and some nonelective surgical cases such as appendectomies and hernia repairs. They worked 12-hour shifts and cooperated with their counterparts, local British civilian nurses, who in this situation were not allowed to do venipunctures, initiate intravenous therapy, or manage patients with the same level of autonomy enjoyed by American Army nurses. However, the British nurses' clinical judgment and skills were on a par with those of the American nurses. To upgrade the skills and knowledge of all, the Army nurses offered classes for both civilian and Army nurses on subjects such as epidural analgesia, chemical and warfare casualty care, shock, fracture management, care of head and spinal injuries, burn care, post-trauma response, Acute Respiratory Distress Syndrome, and Arabic language lessons. These presentations enhanced cultural understanding and cemented professional relationships.

The rituals of the Islam religion played a large part in the daily activities of the hospital and required some adjustments on the part of the nurses. A red arrow pointing to Mecca was painted on the ceiling of each hospital room, and the hospital's public address system announced prayer calls five times daily. During prayers, the Arab staff typically knelt in their stocking feet on a small prayer rug in a corner of the room and faced Mecca. They bowed, kissed the ground, and recited their prayers for a short interval. When prayers were said, staff returned to business as usual.

The firing of Patriot missiles and SCUD alerts also changed the nurses' daily lives. A Patriot missile battery and an airfield were located adjacent to the hospital and every day numerous aircraft took off or landed and missile launchings were frequent. The cacophonous roar of jet engines seemed a constant assault on the ears, and the fog of JP5, jet fuel, lingered persistently in the atmosphere, irritating eyes, making breathing difficult, and layering skin and clothing with a fine black soot. After the air war began, SCUD alerts were regular nightly occurrences between 0200 and 0400 hours. Nurses donned their MOPP gear, and fear, anxiety, hyperventilation, and panic were commonplace reactions. Soon, however, the alerts became routine, accepted events and often the nurses would retire to their beds for the night fully clad in MOPP4 to avoid the necessity to fully awaken and don the protective gear when the sirens blared.

With the onset of the ground war, everyone anticipated a rush of casualties, but patients failed to appear. Then, the 50th GH expected to be ordered to Kuwait but no such orders materialized. Instead, on 8 March 1991, Army authorities abruptly directed the unit to prepare to redeploy from SWA within 90 hours. After receiving departure orders, the nurses packed their gear, turned over their patients, and boarded an aircraft and flew home. Upon arrival at McChord Air Force Base, family, friends, and dignitaries greeted the unit with flowers, balloons, and welcome home signs. State troopers escorted the unit's buses the short distance down Interstate 5 to Fort Lewis with sirens blowing and lights flashing. Passing cars honked their horns. Demobilization processing took place at Fort Lewis and the soldiers rejoined their families and began to reacquaint themselves with the civilian reality they had left behind.[68]

Those who were left behind also felt the effects of the war. Although they were safe from SCUDs and other hostile threats, they struggled with enemies of their own. Lieutenant Colonel Judy Nupen of Port Orchard, Washington, was a U.S. Army Reserve nurse and a wife and mother who activated with the 50th. At the time of her mobilization, Nupen had three young children—two daughters, five and three years old, and a four-month-old son. With her husband, a physicist employed by the Navy in Bremerton, Washington, she hastily arranged for a daytime nanny and began her stressful transition from civilian to military life. Nupen took several steps to mitigate the effects of the separation on her children. She recorded their favorite books on tape so the children could hear her voice while she was away. She created a calendar and noted certain days that the children would receive previously purchased mementos and toys from their mother. Nupen sent regular letters and gifts while in Saudi Arabia and telephoned at intervals. The phone calls, however, were a mixed blessing. On the one hand they were a comfort, yet on the other hand they exposed the children to the parents' troubles and travails.

Nupen's husband also made huge sacrifices. He stayed behind, working for an unsympathetic boss, losing sleep while caring for the baby at night, and worrying about his wife's safety in the line of fire. Despite having the best of child care, the children suffered too. One daughter, in particular, developed a stress-related dermatitis and her speech regressed while Nupen was away.

While mulling over the apparent incongruities between her allegiance to family versus country, Nupen asserted that she had "signed on the dotted line all those years ago" and gave a promise to her country that she could not ignore, adding that as hard as leaving was, reneging on her word would have proved even more difficult. With her safe return and the healing passage of time, Nupen and her family recovered from the trauma and once again enjoyed a normal family life.[69]

Family separations—an inherent part of military life—always carry serious personal repercussions. ODS, however, saw a large number of women participants and unprecedented numbers of mothers separated from their children.[70] About 35,000 military women served in the Persian Gulf and made up approximately 7 percent of the U.S. forces there.[71] Air Force Colonel Penny Pierce's study investigating the emotional and physical health of U.S. Air Force women who served in ODS found that 45 percent of the women were parents. Her research revealed that those women who served in SWA more than 120 days suffered a significant decrease in self-esteem that perhaps, Pierce suggested, related in part to the participants' parental roles and the effects of their separation from their children.[72] Elisabetta Addis, an international researcher, posited that the military role is a greater challenge to women than to men because the female relationship to their children is unique.[73] This debate will no doubt continue as gender roles evolve.

The experiences of Army Nurse Corps officers who served in the Persian Gulf during ODS included some unique features and a number of familiar old refrains. The unprecedented components included the inhospitable desert milieu; the constant threat of chemical, biological, and/or radiological weapons with its attendant prevention and treatment implications; the introduction of complex technology and advanced equipment into the field setting; the ban on alcoholic beverages; the noteworthy numbers of wives and mothers on active service with all its familial repercussions; and the gender restrictions imposed on women soldiers by the indigenous Muslim culture. Predictable, expected combat circumstances involved the time-honored need for improvisation dictated by the dearth of supplies and equipment; the hurry up and wait framework; the significance of mail and communications from home; the spirit of camaraderie and teamwork during intense casualty situations; the longer, more extensive duty days; the effect exerted on morale by food and drink and living conditions; and the prevalence of more autonomous nursing practices. A blend of similar themes combining both the status quo of prior combat operations and the unique, unparalleled conditions of contemporary combat also manifested themselves in Europe, that—in ODS—represented the communications zone.

# Notes

1. Ruth Cheney, "History of the 44th Medical Brigade Chief Nurse, Operations Desert Shield/Desert Storm," Printed Manuscript, 9, 7 June 1991, Cheney Collection, U.S. Army Medical Department Museum.
2. Kathryn P. Deuster, "Desert Shield/Desert Storm, 1990–1991, Afteraction Report," 4, 29 July 1991, Army Nurse Corps Collection (ANCC), Office of Medical History (OMH).
3. Ruth Cheney, "History of the 44th Medical Brigade Chief Nurse, Operations Desert Shield/Desert Storm," Printed Manuscript, 9, 7 June 1991, Cheney Collection, U.S. Army Medical Department Museum.
4. Kathryn P. Deuster, "Desert Shield/Desert Storm, 1990–1991, Afteraction Report," 4–6, 29 July 1991, ANCC, OMH.
5. Ruth Cheney, "History of the 44th Medical Brigade Chief Nurse, Operations Desert Shield/Desert Storm," Printed Manuscript, 12, 19, 7 June 1991, Cheney Collection, U.S. Army Medical Department Museum.
6. Ibid., 9–10.
7. Kathryn P. Deuster, "Desert Shield/Desert Storm, 1990–1991, Afteraction Report," 5, 29 July 1991, ANCC, OMH. Logistical support was a problem for many units. United States General Accounting Office, "Operation Desert Storm, Full Army Medical Capability Not Achieved," GAO/NSAID-92-175, 2, 4, 30–39, August 1992.
8. Ruth Cheney, "History of the 44th Medical Brigade Chief Nurse, Operations Desert Shield/Desert Storm," Printed Manuscript, 9–10, 7 June 1991, Cheney Collection, U.S. Army Medical Department Museum. Kathryn P. Deuster, "Desert Shield/Desert Storm, 1990–1991, Afteraction Report," 8, 29 July 1991, ANCC, OMH.
9. First Lieutenant Frank Pascarelli was the occupational therapist. Army nurses involved in the program were Captain John Reynolds and first lieutenants Joe Reis and Lynette Van Beest. The enlisted staff included Staff Sergeant Stephen Henderson, sergeants Myrna Matos and Ruby Brown, and specialist Erick Laine. Imelda J. Weddington, "Stress Management Team Serves in Saudi," Flash from Nursing, 47th Field Hospital, Operation Desert Shield 1 (November 1990): 1, ANCC, OMH.
10. Imelda J. Weddington, "Stress Management Team Serves in Saudi," Flash from Nursing, 47th Field Hospital, Operation Desert Shield 1 (November 1990): 1, ANCC, OMH. Kathryn P. Deuster, "Nursing Historical Report/Afteraction Report on Operation Desert Shield/Storm," Memorandum for ARCENT Chief Nurse, 8, 17 July 1991, Smith

Collection, U.S. Army Medical Department Museum.

11. Linda Groetken, "One Day in the Life of a Staff Nurse," Flash from Nursing, 47th Field Hospital 1 (November 1990): 2–4, Smith Collection, U.S. Army Medical Department Museum.

12. Presumably their primary AOC preparation was as pediatric, obstetrics, psychiatric, or community health nurses. Kathryn P. Deuster, "Desert Shield/Desert Storm, 1990–1991, Afteraction Report," 7, 29 July 1991, ANCC, OMH.

13. Harvey O. Stowe, "Into Iraq, Nursing Organization in a Combat Support Hospital," *Journal of Nursing Administration* 22 (February 1992): 49–53.

14. "Memories of an 85th Evacuation Hospital Chief Nurse during the Persian Gulf War, Dhahran, Saudi Arabia, Letters from COL Linda Freeman," Appendix 2000, in Sharon Forman Bystran, 85th Evacuation Hospital, Phu Tanh Valley & Qui Nhon, South Vietnam, 1965–1966 (Crofton, MD: 1575 Eton Way, 1993), E-5. Linda Freeman, Interview by Patricia Wise, Transcript, 7, 29 March 1991, Army Nurse Corps Oral History Collection (ANCOHC), OMH.

15. "Memories of an 85th Evacuation Hospital Chief Nurse During the Persian Gulf War, Dhahran, Saudi Arabia, Letters from COL Linda Freeman," Appendix 2000, in Sharon Forman Bystran, 85th Evacuation Hospital, Phu Tanh Valley & Qui Nhon, South Vietnam, 1965–1966 (Crofton, MD: 1575 Eton Way, 1993), E-5. Linda Freeman to Sharon Bystran, Handwritten Letter, 28 October 1990; and Linda Freeman to Sharon Bystran, Printed Letter, 7 March 1991 (both in ANCC, OMH). Linda Freeman, Interview by Patricia Wise, Transcript, 7–8, 29 March 1991, ANCOHC, OMH.

16. Brenna Aileo to Sharon Bystran, Handwritten Letter, 25 October 1990; Linda Freeman to Sharon Bystran, Handwritten Letter, 28 October 1990; and Linda Freeman to Sharon Bystran, Printed Letter, 19 January 1991 (all in ANCC, OMH). Linda Freeman, Interview by Patricia Wise, Transcript, 11–13, 29 March 1991, ANCOHC, OMH.

17. "Memories of an 85th Evacuation Hospital Chief Nurse During the Persian Gulf War, Dhahran, Saudi Arabia, Letters from COL Linda Freeman," Appendix 2000, in Sharon Forman Bystran, 85th Evacuation Hospital, Phu Tanh Valley & Qui Nhon, South Vietnam, 1965–1966 (Crofton, MD: 1575 Eton Way, 1993), E-5, E-6.

18. 85th Evacuation Hospital, "Gone with the 85th, Deployment Historical Report," Printed Report, 10, ANCC, OMH.

19. It soon became obvious that all types of hospitals, whether CSHs, MASHs, or EVACs, were much too heavy to easily move with the few transportation assets the medical units had available, and they could not keep pace with the fast-moving operations. United States General Accounting Office, "Operation Desert Storm, Full Army Medical Capability Not Achieved," GAO/NSAID-92-175, 40–44, August 1992.

20. "Memories of an 85th Evacuation Hospital Chief Nurse During the Persian Gulf War, Dhahran, Saudi Arabia, Letters from COL Linda Freeman," Appendix 2000, in Sharon Forman Bystran, 85th Evacuation Hospital, Phu Tanh Valley & Qui Nhon, South Vietnam, 1965–1966 (Crofton, MD: 1575 Eton Way, 1993), E-5, E-6. Linda Freeman to Sharon Bystran, Handwritten Letter, 14 November 1990; and Linda Freeman to Sharon Bystran, Printed Letter, 20 April 1991 (both in ANCC, OMH). Frank Best and Nancy Tomich, Medicine in the Gulf War (Washington, DC: U.S. Medicine, 1991), 40.

21. Linda Freeman to Sharon Bystran, Printed Letter, 19 January 1991, ANCC, OMH. Linda Freeman, Interview by Patricia Wise, Transcript, 31–34, 29 March 1991, ANCOHC, OMH.

22. Brenna Aileo to Sharon Bystran, Handwritten Letter, 11 November 1990, ANCC, OMH.

23. "Memories of an 85th Evacuation Hospital Chief Nurse During the Persian Gulf War, Dhahran, Saudi Arabia, Letters from COL Linda Freeman," Appendix 2000, in Sharon Forman Bystran, 85th Evacuation Hospital, Phu Tanh Valley & Qui Nhon, South Vietnam, 1965–1966 (Crofton, MD: 1575 Eton Way, 1993), E-3, E-6. Linda Freeman to Sharon Bystran, Handwritten Letter, 7 December 1990, ANCC, OMH.

24. Brenna Aileo to Sharon Bystran, Handwritten Letter, 9 December 1990, ANCC, OMH.

25. Linda Freeman to Sharon Bystran, Handwritten Letter, 23 December 1990, ANCC, OMH.

26. Brenna Aileo to Sharon Bystran, Handwritten Letter, 25 December 1990, ANCC, OMH.

27. Linda Freeman to Sharon Bystran, Handwritten Letter, 3 January 1991, ANCC, OMH.

28. Linda Freeman to Sharon Bystran, Handwritten Letter, 28 October 1990, ANCC, OMH. Frank Best and Nancy Tomich, *Medicine in the Gulf War* (Washington, DC: U.S. Medicine, 1991), 40. 85th Evacuation Hospital, "Gone with the 85th, Deployment Historical Report," Printed Report, 10, ANCC, OMH.

29. Brenna Aileo to Sharon Bystran, Handwritten Letter, 31 December 1990, ANCC, OMH.

30. Linda Freeman to Sharon Bystran, Handwritten Letter, 3 January 1991, ANCC, OMH.

31. Brenna Aileo to Sharon Bystran, Handwritten Letter, 9 December 1990; and Brenna Aileo to Sharon Bystran, Handwritten Letter, 25 December 1990 (both in ANCC, OMH). After ODS, the General Accounting Office (GAO) found many soldiers deployed with preexisting conditions that adversely affected their ability to contribute to the mission. One of the most frequently occurring issues was dental problems. Other questionable cases involved a disabled surgeon who could remain standing for only 30 minutes and another with Parkinson's disease. Both mobilized and deployed with the reserves. United States General Accounting Office, Report to the Chairman, Subcommittee on Readiness, Committee on Armed Services, House of Representatives, Operation Desert Storm, *War Highlights Need to Address Problem of Nondeployable Personnel*, GAO/NSIAD-92-208 (Washington, DC: GAO, August 1992), 1, 5, 14, Appendix IV, 33. United States General Accounting Office, Military Personnel and Compensation, Committee on Armed Services, House of Representatives, Operation Desert Storm, *Full Army Medical Capability Not Achieved*, GAO/NSIAD-92-175 (Washington, DC: GAO, August 1992), 3, 24. One area of significant concern was predeployment physicals. Some concluded that the GI bleeds and myocardial infarctions that occurred in the Persian Gulf could have been averted by better implementation of predeployment physicals. A Presidential Advisory Committee found in general that predeployment physicals were poorly done, not done at all, or were merely screenings. "United States of America Presidential Advisory Committee on Gulf War Veterans' Illnesses," Transcript, 72, 15 August 1995, http://www.gulflink.osd.mil/gwvi/0815gulf.html (accessed 12 September 2005). "United States of America Presidential Advisory Committee on Gulf War Veterans' Illnesses," Volume 2, Transcript, 283, 286, 294, 297, 5 December 1995, http://www.gulflink.osd.mil/gwvi/1205gulf.html (accessed 12 September 2005).

32. Linda Freeman to Sharon Bystran, Handwritten Letter, 23 December 1990, ANCC, OMH. Cynthia A. Gurney, "Adaptation of Medical Personnel to Combat," *Army Medical Department Journal*, PB 8-01-10/11/12 (October/November/December 2001): 6–15.

33. Cynthia A. Gurney, "Adaptation of Medical Personnel to Combat," *Army Medical Department Journal*, PB 8-01-10/11/12 (October/November/December 2001): 6–15.

34. MOPP (Mission Oriented Protective Posture) is a series of four levels of protection from a nuclear, biological, or chemical hazard. MOPP consists of a two-piece overgarment that covered the uniform. It is constructed from an outer layer of nylon and cotton and an inner layer of charcoal-impregnated polyurethane foam. MOPP also includes a mask/hood, footwear covers, and cotton gloves worn under rubber gloves. MOPP4 involves wearing all four components. The equipment has a short shelf life once the packaging is opened. J. Paul Scicchitano, "Pentagon Says Iraqi Chemical Threat Is Real," *Army Times* (20 August 1990): 16.

35. Linda Freeman to Sharon Bystran, Handwritten Letter, 17 January 1991, ANCC, OMH.

36. Brenna Aileo to Sharon Bystran, Handwritten Letter, 23 January 1991, ANCC, OMH.

37. While usually intercepted by the Patriot antimissile system, this time the SCUD disintegrated in air and the Patriot targeted the largest fragment rather than the warhead itself. Joyce C. Humphrey, "Casualty Management: Scud Missile Attack, Dhahran, Saudi Arabia," *Military Medicine* 164 (May 1999): 322–26. Frank N. Schubert and Theresa L. Kraus, eds., *The Whirlwind War, The United States Army in Operations Desert Shield and Desert Storm* (Washington, DC: Center of Military History, United States Army, 1993), 155. "A False Sense of Security," Newspaper Clipping, n.d., in Mary L. Messerschmidt, Desert Shield/Storm Records, Volume 1, Department of Nursing, ANCC, OMH.

38. Linda Freeman to Sharon Bystran, Printed Letter, 26 January 1991; and Brenna Aileo to Sharon Bystran, Handwritten Letter, 27 February 1991 (both in ANCC, OMH). Linda Freeman, Interview by Patricia Wise, Transcript, 22–24, 29 March 1991, ANCOHC, OMH. Frank N. Schubert and Theresa L. Kraus, eds., *The Whirlwind War, The United States Army in Operations Desert Shield and Desert Storm* (Washington, DC: Center of Military History, United States Army, 1993), 211. 85th Evacuation Hospital, "Gone with the 85th, Deployment Historical Report," Printed Report, 12, ANCC, OMH.

39. Linda Freeman to Sharon Bystran, Printed Letter, 19 January 1991; and Linda Freeman to Sharon Bystran, Handwritten Letter, 23 January 1991 (both in ANCC, OMH). Confrontations and conflicts were not rare occurrences. Peter A. Cardinal, "Health Service Support in Operations Desert Shield and Desert Storm," *Military Medicine* 157 (April 1992): 175–79.

40. Linda Freeman to Sharon Bystran, Printed Letter, 26 January 1991, ANCC, OMH.

41. 85th Evacuation Hospital, "Gone with the 85th, Deployment Historical Report," Printed Report, ii, 16, ANCC, OMH.

42. SRP, Soldier Readiness Processing, involved completing and checking wills, powers of attorney, immunizations, family care plans, dog tags, and Geneva Convention cards. Teresa Parsons, Interview by Mary T. Sarnecky, Transcript, Tape 1, 13–14, 11 January 2001; and Teresa Parsons, Interview by Mary T. Sarnecky, Transcript, Tape 2, 23, 27 June 2001 (both in ANCOHC, OMH).

43. Hezbollah terrorists bombed the Khobar Towers several years later, on 25 June 1996. The massive explosion killed 19 American servicemen and injured 372. http://www.fbi.gov/pressrel/pressrel01/khobar.htm (accessed 27 August 2009).

44. Teresa Parsons, Interview by Mary T. Sarnecky, Transcript, Tape 1, 15–18, 11 January 2001, ANCOHC, OMH.

45. Teresa Parsons, Interview by Mary T. Sarnecky, Transcript, Tape 1, 18, 11 January 2001, ANCOHC, OMH.

46. According to Parsons, these had not been recorded at the time of administration, and returning soldiers, many of them irate, demanded some evidence of these immunizations

for future potential VA claims. The theater surgeon consulted with higher authorities in CONUS and an ensuing policy dictated that a printed notation be included in the soldier's shot record attesting to the fact that this individual may have received from one to four doses of anthrax injections. No drug lot numbers or any more specific information was included in the statement. Teresa Parsons, Interview by Mary T. Sarnecky, Transcript, Tape 2, 1–8, 27 June 2001, ANCOHC, OMH. Within a few years, DoD incorporated the immunizations into the SRP. It also was recording anthrax immunizations both in a computerized database and on the yellow immunization record booklets. "Anthrax Vaccinations Will Protect Troops," *The Mercury* 25 (February 1998): 1, 12. Jim Garamone, "Anthrax Immunizations Begin in Gulf Area," *The Mercury* 25 (April 1998): 12.

47. Research on gynecological care provided by the 8th EVAC revealed similar conditions encountered in women patients. The first most common cause for women seeking care was pregnancy. The second and third most common reasons were pelvic pain and the need for a refill prescription of birth control pills. Glenn Markenson, Eduardo Raez, and Mauro Colavita, "Female Health Care During Operation Desert Storm: The Eighth Evacuation Hospital Experience," *Military Medicine* 157 (November 1992): 610–13.

48. Teresa Parsons, Interview by Mary T. Sarnecky, Transcript, Tape 2, 6–12, 27 June 2001, ANCOHC, OMH.

49. Ibid., Tape 2, 16–19.

50. Ibid., Tape 2, 15–16.

51. Ibid., Tape 2, 30.

52. Congress examined the issue of co-deploying spouses. It considered a bill that would exempt one spouse in the family dyad, a move that would potentially excuse about 17,000 military members. However, the bill ultimately died under pressure from the White House and DoD. Andrew Leyden, *Gulf War Debriefing Book* (Grants Pass, OR: Hellgate Press, 1997), 36.

53. To ease the stress, two of the 86th EVAC's nurses who were Vietnam veterans conducted group therapy sessions for the nurses with co-deployed family members. Maureen Combs, Interview by Patricia Wise, Transcript, 3–5, 7–8, 15, 19–20, 11 March 1991, ANCOHC, OMH.

54. Maureen Combs, Interview by Patricia Wise, Transcript, 3–5, 11 March 1991, ANCOHC, OMH.

55. Carolyn Adams, e-mail correspondence, 9 March 2009, ANCC, OMH.

56. Maureen Combs, Interview by Patricia Wise, Transcript, 5–7, 11 March 1991, ANCOHC, OMH. "86th EVAC Hospital Briefing for Colonel Smith," Memorandum, November 1990; and Carolyn H. Adams, "Historical Record December 1990," Memorandum, 2, 2 January 1991 (both in Smith Collection, U.S. Army Medical Department Museum).

57. Carolyn H. Adams, "Historical Record December 1990," Memorandum, 1, 2 January 1991, Smith Collection, U.S. Army Medical Department Museum.

58. The milvan, or military van (container), was a "(DOD) Military-owned, demountable container, conforming to US and international standards, operated in a centrally controlled fleet for movement of military cargo." http://www.dtic.mil/doctrine/jel/doddict/data/m/03378.html (accessed 22 February 2005).

59. Frequently, this is written "hooah." The real acronym is HUA, which stands for "Heard, Understood, Acknowledged."

60. Carolyn H. Adams, "Historical Record December 1990," Memorandum, 1, 2 January 1991, Smith Collection, U.S. Army Medical Department Museum.

61. Carolyn H. Adams, "Historical Record December 1990," Memorandum, 1–2, 2 January 1991, Smith Collection, U.S. Army Medical Department Museum.

62. Field Ration A is the most desirable food available in a nongarrison environment. It includes fresh meat, fruits, vegetables, and dairy products. These perishables usually require local refrigeration in the field setting.

63. Carolyn H. Adams, "Historical Record December 1990," Memorandum, 1–2, 2 January 1991; and Carolyn H. Adams, "Historical Record January 1991," Memorandum, 1, n.d. (both in Smith Collection, U.S. Army Medical Department Museum). Maureen Combs, Interview by Patricia Wise, Transcript, 8–13, 11 March 1991, ANCOHC, OMH.

64. Carolyn H. Adams, "Historical Record February 1991," Memorandum, 1–3, n.d., Smith Collection, U.S. Army Medical Department Museum.

65. It is likely that this was a local effort, similar to the "Shake 'n Bake" OBC provided at Fort Sam Houston, to furnish the deploying reservists with the mandated two weeks of field training.

66. Linda A. Schmidt, "Nursing History for Operation Desert Shield/Storm," 26 July 1991, Smith Collection, U.S. Army Medical Department Museum. Judy Nupen, Interview by Mary T. Sarnecky, Transcript, 22, 12 January 2001, ANCOHC, OMH. Marcia M. Van Wagner, "War in the Persian Gulf, A Study in Contrasts," Unpublished Manuscript, 1–2, January 1991, ANCC, OMH. The Army issued every soldier deployed to SWA with four types of pharmaceutical protection against chemical warfare agents. The first was pyridostigmine bromide (PB), a pretreatment taken to prevent the effects of exposure to nerve agents. The second agents were included in the Mark I nerve agent antidote kit. It contained two auto-injectors, one with atropine (which interrupts the activity of chemical nerve agents) and the other with pralidoxime chloride (which restores normal nerve function). The third agent was diazepam, or Valium, used to treat nerve agent–related convulsions. The fourth element of chemical defense was a skin decontamination kit that contained a topical compound of nontoxic ion exchange and charcoal-based resins. Chuck Dasey, "Medical R&D Command Contributions to Operation Desert Storm," *Army Research, Development Acquisition Bulletin*, PB-70-91-3 (May–June 1991): 10–14. Jill R. Keeler, Charles G. Hurst, and Michael A. Dunn, "Pyridostigmine Used as a Nerve Agent Pretreatment under Wartime Conditions," *Journal of the American Medical Association* 266 (7 August 1991): 693–95. James E. Cook, Margaret A. Kolka, and C. Bruce Wenger, "Chronic Pyridostigmine Bromide Administration: Side Effects among Soldiers Working in a Desert Environment," *Military Medicine* 157 (May 1992): 250–54.

67. Linda A. Schmidt, "Nursing History for Operation Desert Shield/Storm," 26 July 1991, Smith Collection, U.S. Army Medical Department Museum. Judy Nupen, Interview by Mary T. Sarnecky, Transcript, 22, 12 January 2001, ANCOHC, OMH. Marcia M. Van Wagner, "War in the Persian Gulf, A Study in Contrasts," Unpublished Manuscript, 1–2, January 1991, ANCC, OMH.

68. Linda A. Schmidt, "Nursing History for Operation Desert Shield/Storm," 26 July 1991, Smith Collection, U.S. Army Medical Department Museum. Judy Nupen, Interview by Mary T. Sarnecky, Transcript, 22, 12 January 2001, ANCOHC, OMH.

69. Judy Nupen, Interview by Mary T. Sarnecky, Transcript, 18–21, 24–34, 36, 44, 48–50, 12 January 2001, ANCOHC, OMH.

70. Melinda Beck and others, "Our Women in the Desert," *Newsweek* (10 September 1990): 22. Sunnie Scarlett, "Honest Info Helps Children Cope," *HSC Mercury* 18 (December 1990): 6.

71. Rosemarie Skaine, Women at War, *Gender Issues of Americans in Combat* (Jefferson, NC: McFarland & Company, 1999), 64. Veterans Health Administration, Gulf War (Including Operation Iraqi Freedom) Registry (GWR), *VA Handbook 1303.2* (Washington, DC: Department of Veterans Affairs, 7 March 2005), 1. Andrew Leyden, *Gulf War Debrief-*

*ing Book* (Grants Pass, OR: Hellgate Press, 1997), 35. The Army tabulated female participation in SWA at 8.6 percent of all soldiers. William Joe Webb and others, *Department of the Army Historical Summary, Fiscal Years 1990 and 1991* (Washington, DC: Center of Military History, United States Army, 1997), 42.

72. Penny F. Pierce, "Physical and Emotional Health of Gulf War Veteran Women," *Aviation, Space, and Environmental Medicine* 68 (April 1997): 317–21.

73. Rosemarie Skaine, *Women at War, Gender Issues of Americans in Combat* (Jefferson, NC: McFarland & Company, 1999), 138.

*Chapter Twenty*
# Army Nurse Corps Activities in Europe and the Continental United States in Operation Desert Shield/Operation Desert Storm and in the Aftermath

U.S. Army European Command, the communications zone, provided the key link between the Arabian Peninsula and the continental United States (CONUS) during Operation Desert Shield/Operation Desert Storm (ODS).[1] Numerous Army Nurse Corps officers permanently assigned in Europe served there, providing essential care to casualties moving along the evacuation chain as well as to their normal beneficiaries. Others in Europe deployed as Professional Officer Filler System (PROFIS) personnel to Southwest Asia (SWA) with Table of Organization and Equipment (TO&E) units based in Europe. Still others arrived from various worldwide locations and backfilled the facilities in 7th Medical Command (MEDCOM) to replace staff who had deployed into the combat zone.[2]

During the early days of ODS, the 7th MEDCOM began planning to deal with the expected influx of battle casualties. It selected three major units in 7th MEDCOM to care for the 1,760 expected combat casualties: the 2nd and 97th General Hospitals at Landstuhl and Frankfurt, respectively, and the 98th General Hospital at Nürnberg. To augment the staff of these three casualty centers, all 11 hospitals in 7th MEDCOM shared personnel. The in-house and satellite clinics of the 11 hospitals at first remained open to provide care for the usual population of military personnel and family members assigned to Europe. Over time, however, some clinics and offices relocated away from hospital facilities to allow space for more beds. When ODS' air campaign launched on 16 January 1991, the facilities reduced selected health care services for some of their usual patients. Frankfurt Army Regional Medical Center, for example, referred its obstetrical patients to the German Krankenhausen, local civilian hospitals, for deliveries and either postponed or similarly referred elective surgeries to local host nation institutions.[3] Supplementing the three Casualty Care Centers were five other supporting hospitals. Based on two criteria—accessibility to an airport to facilitate reception of incoming casualties and sufficient space to expand—the five selected were the Community Hospitals at Heidelberg, Würzburg, Bad Cannstatt, Augsburg, and Bremerhaven, Germany. They added 753 operating beds to 7th MEDCOM's capacity.[4]

In November 1990, Forces Command tasked three TO&E hospitals from 7th MEDCOM, the 12th Evacuation Hospital, the 128th Combat Support Hospital, and the 31st Combat Support Hospital, to deploy from Europe to SWA in support of ODS. The 7th MEDCOM ordered 123 Army Nurse Corps officers from their 11 in-country fixed facilities to accompany the deployment. Of the 123 deployed with the three TO&E hospitals, 90 were medical-surgical nurses, 19 operating room nurses, and 14 nurse anesthetists. The original plan was to backfill the 123 vacancies with U.S. Army Reserve (USAR) personnel, but by December 1990 it was clear that the three hospitals would have to deploy before the arrival of reserve units from the United States. To bridge the gap and provide a modicum of relief, 7th MEDCOM requested Health Services Command (HSC) to send 11 Army nurses from CONUS to augment operating room and anesthesia services in Europe. These officers provided professional services for about three weeks. The three TO&E units that deployed to SWA returned to their home stations in Europe four months later in April 1991.

Meantime, 7th MEDCOM dispatched a team with an Army Nurse Corps representative, Lieutenant Colonel Betty Gruner, back to CONUS to consult with the first six reserve hospitals destined for Europe.[5] The team's mission was to facilitate the integration of the units into the European theater hospitals and clinics and to acquaint the unit personnel with the U.S. Army European Command's requirements. The team also was charged to identify shortfalls or deficiencies in the units' staff.[6]

Another 7th MEDCOM team met the incoming reservists at Rhein-Main Air Base in Germany, made on-the-spot assignments, and immediately transported the individuals to their destinations via car, train, or bus. Since all 11 hospitals in 7th MEDCOM had deployed at least some of its active duty staff to SWA, sending an entire unit to one hospital was not an option. Thus, specially selected members from backfill units went to different locations and the units were separated, a distressing moment for many of the USAR and Army National Guard (ARNG) soldiers.[7]

Lieutenant Colonel Kathy Rockwell was one such reservist who mobilized with her USAR unit, the 94th General Hospital (GH), at Mesquite, Texas, in early January 1991. After processing for overseas rotation at Camp Bullis, Texas, the unit departed on a commercial flight to Frankfurt, Germany. It was a poignant experience both for Rockwell and some of the flight attendants because they had flown similar flights into Vietnam three decades earlier. On arrival, Rockwell learned that the unit's expectation that they would remain together "was a dream," because there was no need for a whole unit to set up in its entirety. Most found the reality of being divided into groups of 15 to 20 "very disappointing and very scary." Soon, however, the contingent was rolling down the autobahn toward Augsburg and the 34th GH in a bus with a German bus driver who spoke no English. In the dark of night, the bus abruptly stopped and the only understandable communication between driver and soldiers was the word "kaput!" An hour later, another bus picked up the weary soldiers, but now the driver went astray, arriving at the wrong location in Augsburg. The nurses finally arrived at the hospital "and were warmly welcomed" to their new home.

The newcomers immediately enhanced the Augsburg hospital's medical readiness and initiated preparations to expand the hospital from 125 to 1,000 beds. Members of the 328th GH from Fort Douglas, Utah, who had arrived before Christmas, were also assigned to the 34th GH. Rockwell recalled that a sense of camaraderie developed between the two USAR units was mutually beneficial because the Utah cohort went through emotional peaks and valleys similar to those experienced by the Texas unit. One lieutenant colonel from the 328th GH had left five children younger than the age of three (two sets of twins and a baby). One 94th GH physician was away from his wife and four children. Rockwell likewise had said goodbye to her husband and four children. An informal support system developed among those who shared the hardships of mobilization.

The ground war began and ended so quickly that the 34th GH received only a few orthopedic casualties and most of their patients were not battle casualties. Although in retrospect all the preparations seemed unnecessary, the medical build-up was an essential component of prudent planning. In May 1991, the 94th GH redeployed to Texas. Rockwell reflected that her "homecoming was wonderful. What a difference from Viet Nam! There were balloons, flowers and a cheering group" hailing their return.[8]

Across Europe, reservists filled vacancies in all 11 depleted facilities. While in their assigned locations, the local military communities provided moral support for the reservists, taking them on tours of the surrounding sights, offering language classes, and housing them in living quarters that in some instances were reputedly superior to the billets inhabited by the permanent party. In Germany, the local nationals also hosted the reservists at concerts, volksmarches, dinners, shooting contests, and china factory visits.

Almost 541 USAR and ARNG Army nurses, whose number included 85 operating room nurses and 47 nurse anesthetists, reinforced the hospitals in Europe. The greatest area of need was for staff-level nurses capable of providing hands-on clinical care. The supply of backfill USAR and ARNG staff nurses did not precisely fit the demand. Many nurse administrators belonged to reserve units but the Table of Distribution and Allowances hospital chief nurses were able to make good use of all these officers who likewise were willing and able to fulfill virtually any role.

Although the entire assimilation was predominantly trouble free, a few difficulties arose. Commanders who attempted to retain control of their personnel complicated the integration of the USAR/ARNG personnel into units. Confusion ensued when the integrated Army nurses and enlisted nursing personnel were compelled to respond to two chains of command. Many of the reservists also felt underutilized, probably as a consequence of the short, rapid war that resulted in few U.S. casualties.[9] Pay problems, billeting difficulties, and the loss of USAR and ARNG units' integrity that occurred when 7th MEDCOM dispatched various unit members to separate hospitals were all distractions.[10] Most, however, regarded the mobilization as a meaningful experience. Captain Linda Fortmeier, a reservist hailing from San Antonio, Texas, who served as an operating room nurse at the 97th General Hospital in Frankfurt, remarked:

> I knew what to expect. Our role is to take care of military members, and that's important to me.... I'm patriotic, so it's my way of committing myself to that feeling. When I signed up with the military, I was single. But now I'm married and have a small son, so there are other things pulling at me.... I'm still committed to the reserves—it's just more difficult now.[11]

Fortmeier's comments reflected the reality of many Army Nurse Corps officers, other female soldiers, and male parents—irrespective of component—who had to leave their young children. With many more women making up the total force, ODS was the first major operation where this became a significant issue. Nonetheless, female parents competently carried out their combat responsibilities during the Persian Gulf War, albeit with high levels of anxiety for their children and loved ones left behind.[12]

The redeployment of USAR and ARNG personnel to CONUS started in mid-March 1991. The command timed individual departures to coincide with the return of VII Corps forces to Europe. Almost all COMPO II and III soldiers assigned to Europe had returned home to CONUS and were inactivated by June 1991.[13]

ODS likewise affected daily operations in Army hospitals within the United States. While responding to the collective mandate to continue providing care for their usual patients, virtually all military treatment facilities had to deploy a significant number of their staff as PROFIS or Forces Command personnel for mobilizing TO&E units. Moreover, they transferred or cross-leveled certain staff to other CONUS Table of Distribution and Allowances hospitals.[14] HSC facilities also billeted and validated the credentials and skills of backfill USAR and ARNG personnel. HSC tasked six installations as Army Primary Casualty Receiving Centers for the SWA theater, requiring these hospitals to expand their operating beds and bring their staff and supply levels up to required numbers to accommodate the expected increased casualty workload.[15] The following narratives offer a brief glimpse into the wartime activities in the Primary Casualty Receiving Centers.

During ODS, Fitzsimons Army Medical Center in Aurora, Colorado, expanded its capacity to 750 operational beds, but fortunately it received only 127 Desert Storm casualties. Fitzsimons Army Medical Center deployed 195 of its staff to Saudi Arabia and furnished 56 additional service members as backfill at other CONUS facilities. To compensate, it relied on the services of 444 additional personnel, among them the 5502nd U.S. Army Hospital (USAH), Individual Mobilization Augmentees, those from Troop Program Units, Individual Ready Reserve reservists, and voluntarily recalled retirees. Fitzsimons Army Medical Center provided personal affairs assistance and moral support to 215 family members of deployed staff and the casualties hospitalized at the installation. It made every effort to fill all requests for Class VIII (medical) supplies for deploying units. Similar activities occurred at Brooke Army Medical Center (BAMC) at Fort Sam Houston, Texas.

Before ODS, BAMC counted 346 operational beds. To prepare for expected casualties, HSC directed BAMC to implement a phased expansion that would make 1,406 beds available. BAMC located the additional beds in the Main Hospital, Beach Pavilion, and eight nearby buildings in an outlying area that would accommodate wards, with a total of 480 minimal care beds. Planners considered using beds in Chambers Pavilion, a closed facility formerly used for psychiatric patients, but rejected that option. Extensive building repairs, alterations, and improvements were required to transform the existing structures into acceptable facilities. From August 1990 to March 1991, BAMC cared for 214 military casualties from SWA. Of those, 26 involved combat-related injuries.

BAMC sent 69 PROFIS officers to Saudi Arabia and cross-leveled 153 to other CONUS health care facilities. To offset these losses, BAMC received 850 officers and enlisted soldiers from its augmentation unit, the 5501st USAH, and approximately 600 reservists from Troop Program Units, predominantly nurses, 91Cs (practical nurses), and physicians.[16]

Walter Reed Army Medical Center (WRAMC) also transformed itself in preparation for ODS. Like other major Army hospitals, WRAMC's assigned mission was to deploy its PROFIS personnel; support backfill taskings to other CONUS and European facilities; continue to provide health care for all categories of patients and SWA casualties; and to receive, integrate, and support incoming USAR and ARNG personnel and recalled military retirees. It initially planned to expand from 851 to 1,000 operational beds, with a capacity to add another 300 beds if so ordered.[17]

WRAMC began early in January 1991 to dismantle and recapture patient rooms being used as offices, sleep rooms, clinics, and other areas not being designated for actual patient occupation on active wards in the new hospital, the Heaton Pavilion, Building Two. Working floor by floor, a commercial moving company packed the contents of each room and stored them off post. Maintenance crews then reconnected medical gas, electrical, plumbing, ventilation, and communication systems. Housekeeping cleaned the rooms, and then the director of logistics moved in hospital beds and patient equipment.[18] A similar sequence occurred as the Department of Nursing orchestrated the opening of Ward 9 and Ward 21/22 in the old hospital, Building One, that were designated as minimal care wards.[19] The Property Management Division furnished these wards with beds, overbed tables, and bedside cabinets purchased in 1951 and 1952 during the Korean War (1950–1953) for that war's casualties and stored for half a century in Edgewood, Maryland, near Aberdeen Proving Ground.[20]

From 23 January to 15 February 1991, more than 1,200 USAR and ARNG personnel in-processed at WRAMC's Delano Hall. "They came by convoys from New England, by train from Ohio, by POV [privately owned vehicle] from New York and New Jersey. They came and they came." By mid-January the assemblage included members of nine reserve groups, with the largest being a contingent from Rockville, Maryland: the 2290th USAH.[21] Forces Command initially disapproved HSC's request to activate the entire 2290th USAH, WRAMC's primary augmentation reserve unit.[22] Instead, certain elements of the 2290th USAH were activated with a nursing component of 10 operating room nurses, three nurse anesthetists, and 31 practical nurses.[23] Plans called for the rest of the unit to be mobilized once hostilities commenced.[24] As a consequence, 200 reservists of the total officer and enlisted complement of the 2290th USAH arrived in January 1991, and an additional 500 signed in during February 1991. To prepare the influx of USAR and ARNG staff for their assignments at WRAMC, the Department of Nursing implemented several programs. It presented an orientation program, developed several educational offerings that focused on the care of combat casualties, created a Skills Lab where instructors assessed basic nursing proficiencies and provided remedial training in a controlled environment, and offered an intravenous proficiency class for all incoming nursing staff.[25] All told, 206 Army Nurse Corps USAR and ARNG officers served at WRAMC during ODS.[26]

In January 1991, Dr. Phyllis Collins, an associate professor of nursing at the City of New York College of Staten Island, transitioned into her citizen-soldier role as Captain Collins of the 1208th USAH. The first alert for the 1208th came at a propitious time in late December 1990, fitting into the college's semester break and allowing another faculty member to assume Collins' academic duties. Collins mobilized at Fort Monmouth, New Jersey; reported in to WRAMC; and began work as a staff nurse on the hospital's head and neck surgical reconstruction unit. She credited the unit's head nurse, Major Elaine Walizer, as "having an excellent orientation for the reservists assigned to her unit" as well as outstanding leadership skills. Collins marveled at the ward's system of tracking discharged patients, its use of the Workload Management System for Nurses (the military's patient classification system), and the Army-wide universal system of documentation that facilitated the care of patients who transferred from one Army facility to another.[27]

Collins noted that there were obvious divisions between reservists and active duty staff at WRAMC, but many of the permanent party were hospitable and friendly.[28] She recalled a chance meeting with Lieutenant Colonel Jean Reeder that opened up doors to collegial relationships that spanned both professional and social worlds. After introducing herself to Collins in the WRAMC dining facility, Reeder invited her to visit the Nursing Research Service offices and meet the unit's staff.[29] A cohesive group of nurses holding doctorates subsequently came together, and scholarly discussions and social gatherings ensued. Many took advantage of the Washington area's cultural and historical resources. After the conclusion of the ground war, Collins and other reservists with research or academic backgrounds were assigned to the Nursing Research Service to implement a major research project focusing on the activated reservists.[30]

Collins' experiences taught her that "active duty Army is a family of one," where all participants look out for one another. Nurses celebrated festive holidays

Reservist and Army Nurse Corps officer, Captain Phyllis B. Collins, served at Walter Reed Army Medical Center during Operation Desert Storm from January to September 1991.
Photo courtesy of Lieutenant Colonel Phyllis Collins, Staten Island, NY.

Four Army Nurse Corps officers serving at Walter Reed's Nursing Research Service during ODS gather around boxes of surveys sent to 6,000 Army Medical Department officer and enlisted personnel. The instruments provided the data to study the determinants of adaptation of medical department personnel during combat. The project investigator was Lieutenant Colonel Cindy Gurney. From left to right are Lieutenant Colonel Jean M. Reeder, Gurney, Lieutenant Colonel Mary T. Sarnecky, and Colonel Valerie E. Biskey, chief of the unit.
Photo courtesy of Colonel Cindy Gurney, Clifton Park, NY.

together, worked as a unified team, and were committed to their country. The deployment was the highlight of Collins' military career. After the deactivation of most of her fellow unit members, Collins remained on active duty until September 1991 to compile and analyze the data gathered in the course of the reservists' special study.[31]

The Department of Nursing at WRAMC created a number of contingency plans, including one to deal with a local terrorist attack. Anticipating large numbers of seriously ill patients in such an event, personnel in the Nursing Education and Staff Development Service proposed a short-term, three-week intensive care unit course to upgrade the skills of existing and incoming staff.[32] Colonel Sharon Bystran, a Vietnam veteran with two previous assignments at WRAMC, was chief, Clinical Nursing Service. She competently updated the department's Mass Casualty Plan.[33]

Colonel Diane Butke, WRAMC's assistant chief nurse, took on the task of assigning incoming nurses to clinical units. She contacted chief nurses at mobilization sites and requested that they interview the nurses, summarize the deploy-

Pictured here is Colonel Sharon Bystran, who served as Chief, Clinical Nursing Service at Walter Reed Army Medical Center in 1991.
Photo courtesy of Colonel Sharon Bystran, Aptos, CA.

ing nurses' clinical experience and background, and forward that information to WRAMC. Cooperation at every level made for efficiency. Butke then matched the incoming nurses' proficiencies to areas of need, methodically placed them on specific nursing units, and coordinated these assignments with the chiefs of the clinical nursing sections. She became renowned as the "keeper of the lists." WRAMC's chief nurse, Colonel Mary Messerschmidt, remarked that the "credit for the successful intergration [sic] of the reservists in the DON [Department of Nursing] belongs largely to her [Butke]. . . . She set the tone."[34]

To prepare for staffing the minimal care wards in Building One, the units' head nurse, Major Maudie Jones, and the project director, Colonel Brooke Serpe-Ingold, drafted staffing requirements. Both revised plans, coordinated with work crews, and wrote protocols for the wards. The units never had to be opened because the average daily hospital census never exceeded 700 patients. The Department of Nursing dismantled the wards in April 1991 and the beds and equipment were again retired to storage.[35]

In retrospect, Messerschmidt wrote that the WRAMC nurses who served during this period of war wanted their successors to capitalize on "the momentum and dedication of [WRAMC's] Department of Nursing during Operation Desert Shield/Storm." Overall conditions reflected a "high degree of cooperation and sense of pride that everyone shared. It was one of the finest hours in the history of WRAMC's Department of Nursing." Finally, Messerschmidt formally thanked and recognized "all of the nursing staff at WRAMC: . . . to those who stayed, and to those who went, and to those who came to take their place."[36]

These vignettes exemplify the story of Army nurses' experiences, issues, and contributions during ODS. They document aspects of Army Nurse Corps participation, including some unprecedented, some familiar, and many that were minor variations on historical themes. They underscore the fact that representatives of all elements (active, USAR, ARNG, or retiree and the civil service nurses)—the vast, diverse, official and unofficial aggregate of the Army Nurse Corps serving worldwide—once again made many significant sacrifices and huge contributions to the war effort.

During ODS, the U.S. Army Nurse Corps demonstrated a high standard of readiness and fitness far superior to that of early days in previous operations. Their high levels of physical fitness provided them with the wherewithal to work harder and longer in situations where staffing levels were less than ideal. The realization of the "one Army" doctrine was a prominent feature of Army Nurse Corps involvement. The USAR and ARNG nurses successfully activated and integrated into the force. While stresses and strains were inevitable, by and large the concept worked.

In ODS, female Army nurses faced gender discrimination. They experienced intolerance not so much from their male counterparts in the U.S. military, but rather from the Muslim culture that the women were serving to protect. Cultural norms dictated that U.S. servicewomen wear uncomfortably hot clothing, prohibited them from driving, and relegated women to a separate, subservient class.

Additional hassles and tensions resulted from such treatment.

Army Nurse Corps officers traditionally have endured family separations in wartime, but during ODS the nature of the relationships and the identity of those involved in the separation changed radically. Approximately half the female Army nurses deployed to SWA were parents with one or more children. The resultant separation between parent and child provoked worries and concerns and was generally difficult for all involved. Doubtless, male nurses in similarly difficult circumstances suffered equally.

Army nurses used social support, spirituality, humor, physical activity, and correspondence with friends and family to adapt to the rigors and deprivations of serving in a field army. The use of alcohol to mitigate stress—not uncommon in previous wars—was prohibited in SWA because of the Muslim ban of such substances. This prohibition undoubtedly generated many positive consequences such as less violence, fewer accidents, and healthier lifestyles.

The need to function in a hostile milieu while hamstrung with logistical constraints was nothing new for Army nurses. Only the details changed. Army nurses improvised and used creativity and ingenuity to make the most of their circumstances. The desert environment with its climatic extremes; the ubiquitous threat of nuclear, biological, and chemical warfare; and shortages of supplies and equipment, such as high-tech items perceived as necessities, constantly demanded endurance, adaptability, and innovation.

Like their predecessors, Army nurses who served during ODS were much more than nurses. They were soldiers as well. They unpacked MILVANs (containers for overseas or ground movement of military cargo) and inflated air mattresses, served on company details, dug seepage pits, and removed rocks from proposed hospital sites. They performed guard duty, filled sandbags, participated in water details, pitched in with mess duties, and assisted with field sanitation chores. Their flexibility in the exceptionally austere conditions of ODS epitomized the strengths of Army nurses. Colonel B.J. Smith noted that countless commanders acknowledged that the mission could not have been accomplished without the dedication of Army nurses who contributed to the war effort with a team spirit, a sense of humor, and an attitude of infectious enthusiasm.[37]

As many as 100,000 of the 697,000 military members, who served in SWA during ODS, reported significant health problems after leaving the Persian Gulf. They exhibited various combinations of symptoms such as bronchitis, emphysema, asthma, exhaustion, loss of memory, difficulty in concentrating, excruciating headaches, disturbed sleep, stomach disorders, lingering skin rashes, muscular/joint pain, and hearing ailments. Exhaustive studies and research have failed to reveal a single, definite cause for the so-called Gulf War Syndrome. It has been variously attributed to combat stress, contamination with poison gas, side effects of prescribed prophylaxis, leishmaniasis, exposure to sand and dust, depleted uranium, pesticides, chemical agent–resistant coatings, and/or exposure to petroleum products.[38]

No statistics exist documenting the numbers of Army Nurse Corps officers—

if any—affected by this illness.[39] However, the Department of Veterans Affairs examination of the case records of 5,483 women who served in the Gulf War demonstrated that women in their sample experienced fatigue and headaches slightly more often than male veterans but reported having less muscle and joint pain than their male counterparts. The small differences were not statistically significant.[40]

No Army Nurse Corps officers lost their lives in ODS. However, several enlisted medics were killed in action or died from nonbattle injuries.[41] The U.S. Army suffered 354 wounded in action and 98 killed in action, with 128 other soldiers dying from noncombat causes.[42]

# Notes

1. "Operation Desert Shield/Storm, Concept of Operations," Typewritten Document, n.d., Army Nurse Corps Collection (ANCC), Office of Medical History (OMH).

2. Michael J. Scotti, "Team Concept Contributed to Success," *MEDCOM Examiner* 20 (April 1991): 2. Nancy N. Nooney, "Hq, 7th MEDCOM Nursing Support to SWA," Memorandum, n.d.; and Robert S. Driscoll, "Reconstitution of Seventh Medical Command during Operation Desert Shield/Storm," Typewritten Manuscript (TM), 2, 24 February 1993 (both in ANCC, OMH). William J. Vogt, "USAR Medical Professionals Earn Their 'Spurs' During Desert Storm," *Army Reserve Magazine* (Fourth Issue of 1991): 17, 25.

3. Nancy N. Nooney, "Hq, 7th MEDCOM Nursing Support to SWA," Memorandum, n.d., ANCC, OMH. Paul R. McGinn, "Army Hospital in Germany Poised to Receive Casualties," *American Medical News* (4 February 1991): 2. Susan Okie, "Plan for Stateside Care of Casualties Criticized," *Washington Post* (7 February 1991): A26. Joyce Price, "Hospitals Ready for Casualties of Ground War," *Washington Times* (25 February 1991): A10. "Reservists Key to Successful Expansion," *MEDCOM Examiner* 20 (April 1991): 4, 7.

4. Robert S. Driscoll, "Reconstitution of Seventh Medical Command During Operation Desert Shield/Storm," TM, 5–6, 24 February 1993, ANCC, OMH.

5. The first six units deployed to Europe were the 300th MASH (an ARNG unit) from Smyrna, TN, the 45th Station Hospital from Vancouver, WA, the 56th Station Hospital from Richmond, VA, the 44th General Hospital from Madison WI, the 94th General Hospital from Mesquite, TX, and the 328th General Hospital from Fort Douglas, UT. The latter five were USAR units. "Operation Desert Shield/Storm, A FORSCOM Perspective," Briefing Slides, n.d., ANCC, OMH. Ultimately, 18 USAR or ARNG hospital units had soldiers in five countries in 7th MEDCOM—Germany, Italy, Belgium, Turkey, and England. "Reserve Members Contributions Are Recognized," *MEDCOM Examiner* 20 (April 1991): 1. "Medical Reservists Served in Five Countries," *MEDCOM Examiner* 20 (April 1991): 3. Robert S. Driscoll, "Reconstitution of Seventh Medical Command During Operation Desert Shield/Storm," TM, 8, 24 February 1993, ANCC, OMH.

6. Robert S. Driscoll, "Reconstitution of Seventh Medical Command During Operation Desert Shield/Storm," TM, 8, 24 February 1993, ANCC, OMH.

7. Nancy N. Nooney, "Hq, 7th MEDCOM Nursing Support to SWA," Memorandum, n.d., ANCC, OMH. Paul R. McGinn, "Army Hospital in Germany Poised to Receive Casualties," *American Medical News* (4 February 1991): 2. "Local Hospitality a Hit," *MEDCOM*

*Examiner* 20 (April 1991): 7. Robert S. Driscoll, "Reconstitution of Seventh Medical Command During Operation Desert Shield/Storm," TM, 8–9, 24 February 1993, ANCC, OMH.

8. Kathy Rockwell, "Documentation of Events During Support of Operation Desert Shield/Storm, Some References to My Other War, Viet Nam," Printed Document, 5 May 2005, ANCC, OMH.

9. Nancy N. Nooney, "Hq, 7th MEDCOM Nursing Support to SWA," Memorandum, n.d., ANCC, OMH. Paul R. McGinn, "Army Hospital in Germany Poised to Receive Casualties," *American Medical News* (4 February 1991): 2. "Local Hospitality a Hit," MEDCOM Examiner 20 (April 1991): 7. Robert S. Driscoll, "Reconstitution of Seventh Medical Command During Operation Desert Shield/Storm," TM, 8–9, 24 February 1993, ANCC, OMH.

10. "Has Your Activation to Duty for Operation Desert Storm Affected Your Commitment to the Army Reserves?" *MEDCOM Examiner* 20 (April 1991): 2. William J. Vogt, "USAR Medical Professionals Earn Their 'Spurs' During Desert Storm," *Army Reserve Magazine* (Fourth Issue of 1991): 17, 25.

11. Has Your Activation to Duty for Operation Desert Storm Affected Your Commitment to the Army Reserves?" *MEDCOM Examiner* 20 (April 1991): 2.

12. Rosemarie Skaine, *Women at War, Gender Issues of Americans in Combat* (Jefferson, NC: McFarland & Company, 1999), 139.

13. Nancy N. Nooney, "Hq, 7th MEDCOM Nursing Support to SWA," Memorandum, n.d., ANCC, OMH. Paul R. McGinn, "Army Hospital in Germany Poised to Receive Casualties," *American Medical News* (4 February 1991): 2. Robert S. Driscoll, "Reconstitution of Seventh Medical Command During Operation Desert Shield/Storm," TM, 10, 24 February 1993, ANCC, OMH. William J. Vogt, "USAR Medical Professionals Earn Their 'Spurs' During Desert Storm," *Army Reserve Magazine* (Fourth Issue of 1991): 17, 25.

14. Cross-leveling involved sharing personnel between one facility and another on a temporary basis or for the duration of a war.

15. Ronald R. Blanck and William H. Bell, "Special Reports: Medical Aspects of the Persian Gulf War, Medical Support for American Troops in the Persian Gulf," *New England Journal of Medicine* 324 (21 March 1991): 857–59. William A. Matheson, "After Action Reports—Operation DESERT SHIELD/DESERT STORM," 24 May 1991, ANCC, OMH. The six Army PCRCs were Walter Reed, Eisenhower, Brooke, Fitzsimons, William Beaumont, and Madigan Army Medical Centers. Handwritten note and map, n.d., in Mary L. Messerschmidt, Desert Shield/Storm Records, Volume 1, Department of Nursing, ANCC, OMH.

16. Donald A. Donahue, "After Action Report, Operation DESERT SHIELD/DESERT STORM," 24 May 1991, ANCC, OMH.

17. "Walter Reed Army Medical Center DESERT SHIELD Support Plan," Printed Document, 2, A-1, 4 January 1991, ANCC, OMH.

18. Peter Dougherty, "Desert Shield Update #6," 1, 3 January 1991; and Llewellyn E. Piper, "Mobilization Bed Expansion, Memorandum, n.d. (both in ANCC, OMH).

19. Note attached to June Sekiguchi, "Phase I Mobilization Expansion Maintenance Date (3 January 1991)—Progress Report," Memorandum, 3 January 1991; and Richard W. Salgueiro, "Minimal Care Conversion Milestones," Memorandum, 15 January 1991 (both in Mary L. Messerschmidt, Desert Shield/Storm Records, Volume 1, Department of Nursing, ANCC, OMH).

20. Bonnie S. Heater, "Post Gears Up for Desert Storm," Newspaper Clipping from the Stripe, in Mary L. Messerschmidt, Desert Shield/Storm Records, Volume 1, Department of Nursing, ANCC, OMH.

21. Larry Lane, "Active Duty, Reservists Unite," Stripe (11 January 1991): 1, 4, with note attached, in Mary L. Messerschmidt, Desert Shield/Storm Records, Volume 1, Department of Nursing, ANCC, OMH.

22. The activation of reserve component units in support of HSC actually took place in three phases. The initial call-up occurred during August 1990 and was in support of installations with large troop deployments. The second phase consisted of selected personnel of units who reported from 11 to 15 January 1991. The final phase involved those who activated as whole units, and they reported for duty on 4 February 1991. "RC Unit Activations in Support of HSC," n.d., ANCC, OMH

23. Peter Dougherty, "Desert Shield Update #6," 2, 3 January 1991; and Mary L. Messerschmidt, Handwritten Note attached to "Desert Shield Update #6," 7 January 1991 (both in Mary L. Messerschmidt, Desert Shield/Storm Records, Volume 1, Department of Nursing, ANCC, OMH).

24. "Walter Reed Army Medical Center DESERT SHIELD Support Plan," Printed Document, 2, 4 January 1991, ANCC, OMH.

25. Sandra L. Venegoni and others, "Operation Desert Shield/Storm, 'Lessons Learned,'" Walter Reed Army Medical Department, Department of Nursing," 3–4, July 1991, ANCC, OMH.

26. Mary E. Keaveny, "Nurse Reservists Answer the Call," Unidentified Article, n.d., in Mary L. Messerschmidt, Desert Shield/Storm Records, Volume 1, Department of Nursing, ANCC, OMH.

27. Phyllis Collins to Author, E-mail Correspondence, 10 March 2005, ANCC, OMH.

28. Collins noted that at the point when the reservist felt respect and approval finally developing in the relationship between the two individuals (USAR and active duty), "there would be a glance down at your ID which was a different color (blue?) versus the AD (green?)" and the whole tone of the interaction reverted into nuances of distrust and distance. Phyllis Collins to Author, E-mail Correspondence, 10 March 2005, ANCC, OMH.

29. At that time, Colonel Valerie Biskey was chief of NRS, with a staff of nurse researchers that included lieutenant colonels Mary T. Sarnecky, Jean Reeder, and Cynthia A. Gurney and Captain Elizabeth Cook Greenwell.

30. Other researchers who collaborated on the study, "Together We Serve," were Colonel Mamie Montague and Captain Esther Brill. In civilian life, Montague was on faculty at Howard University and Brill at Long Island University. Phyllis Collins to Author, E-mail Correspondence, 10 April 2005, ANCC, OMH.

31. Phyllis Collins to Author, E-mail Correspondence, 10 March 2005, ANCC, OMH.

32. "Proposed ICU Orientation Program," Handwritten Draft Course Outline, January 1991, ANCC, OMH.

33. Notes attached to "Mass Casualty/Terrorist Attack/ Operation Desert Storm, Walter Reed Army Medical Center, Patient Flow Plan," n.d., ANCC, OMH.

34. Elizabeth A. Sullivan, "Reserve ANC's Assigned to WRAMC," Memorandum, 18 January 1991; Patricia L. Curry, "1125th Nurses to be Assigned to WRAMC," Memorandum, 18 January 1991 (Notes attached to the two memorandums, all in Mary L. Messerschmidt, Desert Shield/Storm Records, Volume 1, Department of Nursing, ANCC, OMH).

35. "Personnel Staffing Assessment," Printed Document, n.d.; and "These Would Be the Minimal Care Wards," Note, n.d. (both in Mary L. Messerschmidt, Desert Shield/Storm Records, Volume 1, Department of Nursing, ANCC, OMH).

36. Mary L. Messerschmidt, Typewritten Foreword, in Mary L. Messerschmidt, Desert Shield/Storm Records, Volume 1, Department of Nursing, ANCC, OMH.

37. Barbara J. Smith, "Operation Desert Storm Historical Report (17 January–1 April)," Memorandum, 4 April 1991, ANCC, OMH.

38. NIH Technology Assessment Workshop Panel, "The Persian Gulf Experience and Health, *Journal of the American Medical Association* 272 (3 August 1994): 391–96. "Report on Possible Effects of Organophosphate 'Low-Level' Nerve Agent Exposure," http://www.dtic.dla.mil/gulflink/finalagt.html (accessed 2 October 1996). Jim Schnabel, "The Real Causes of 'Gulf War Syndrome'," *Washington Post* (15 November 1996): A31. Presidential Advisory Committee of Gulf War Veteran's Illnesses Final Report (Washington, DC: Government Printing Office, 1996). Institute of Medicine, Committee on the DoD Persian Gulf Syndrome Comprehensive Clinical Evaluation Program, *Evaluation of the U.S. DoD Persian Gulf Syndrome Comprehensive Clinical Evaluation Program, Committee on the DOD Persian Gulf Comprehensive Clinical Evaluation* (Washington, DC: National Academy Press, 1996). Stephen C. Joseph, "Bosnia Deployment Tests DoD Training," *U.S. Medicine* 32 (January 1996): 8–10. United States General Accounting Office, *Defense Health Care, Medical Surveillance Improved since Gulf War, but Mixed Results in Bosnia* (Washington, DC: USGAOO/NSIAD, 1997). Thomas E. Ricks, "Is Gulf War Syndrome Linked to Stresses of Combat," *Wall Street Journal* (6 January 1997): 1, 14. Stephen C. Joseph, "A Comprehensive Clinical Evaluation of 20,000 Persian Gulf War Veterans," *Military Medicine* 162 (March 1997): 149–55. "Investigators Issue Report on Ill Gulf War Veterans," *The Mercury* 25 (February 1998): 7. Janet A. McDonnell, *After Desert Storm, The U.S. Army and the Reconstruction of Kuwait* (Washington, DC: Department of the Army, 1999), 183–90. Coleen Baird Weese, "Population Health and Deployed Forces," *Army Medical Department Journal*, PB 8-01-10/11/12 (October/November/December 2001): 24–30. Lois M. Joellenbeck, "The Institute of Medicine's Independent Scientific Assessment of Gulf War Health Issues," *Military Medicine* 167 (March 2002): 186–90. "Combined Analysis of the VA and DOD Gulf War Clinical Evaluation Programs, A Study of the Clinical Findings of 100,339 U.S. Gulf War Veterans," September 2002, http://www.gulflink.osd.mil/combined_analysis/index.htm (accessed 28 February 2005).

39. Clara Adams-Ender to Author, E-mail Correspondence, 7 March 2005; Nancy Adams to Author, E-mail Correspondence, 14 March 2005; and Terris Kennedy to Author, E-mail Correspondence, 20 March 2005 (all in ANCC, OMH). Barbara J. Smith, Telephone Conversation 17 April 2005.

40. Frances M. Murphy and others, "The Health Status of Gulf War Veterans: Lessons Learned from the Department of Veterans Affairs Health Registry," *Military Medicine* 164 (May 1999): 327–31. Veterans Health Administration, Gulf War (Including Operation Iraqi Freedom) Registry (GWR), *VA Handbook 1303.2* (Washington, DC: Department of Veterans Affairs, 7 March 2005), 2.

41. Clara L. Adams-Ender with Blair S. Walker, My Rise to the Stars, *How a Sharecropper's Daughter Became an Army General* (Lake Ridge, VA: Cape Associates, Inc., 2001), 228. "AMEDD Losses—Operation Desert Storm," Typewritten List, n.d., ANCC, OMH.

42. "Taking the Gulf Medicine," *Jane's Defense Weekly* (16 May 1992): 5–6.

*Chapter Twenty-one*
# Operation Restore Hope in Somalia

Operation Restore Hope began as an Operation Other Than War, with humanitarian aspects and nation-building overtones. It rapidly became a straightforward combat mission that took place in Somalia, a nation situated on the Gulf of Aden and the Indian Ocean on the horn of Africa. Conditions had deteriorated in Somalia after the toppling of Siad Barre's government in January 1991. Numerous tribal clans and subclans began fiercely vying for supremacy. Civil unrest, anarchy, and lawlessness ensued, with marauding hoodlums in "technicals," vehicles with mounted heavy automatic weapons, ruling the streets and terrorizing the citizenry. As months of unrest turned into two years of civil war, the nation's infrastructure crumbled. The overwhelming chaos prevented farmers from growing crops, and feuding warlords then used scarce food as one of their weapons to gain power. Widespread starvation followed and ultimately the United Nations and the U.S. government intervened with famine relief efforts. Equitable distribution of food proved next to impossible because bandits who used the provisions to reward their followers forced international aid organizations to pay protection money to the warlords or hire armed guards to protect the food supplies.[1]

The United Nations Operation in Somalia launched in April 1992. After frustrating months of looting, extortion, and running street battles, U.S. forces implemented what eventually became a four-phased operation known as Operation Restore Hope. During the operation, Major General Steven Lloyd Arnold, the commander of Army Forces, Somalia, established a "Four No's" policy—no bandits, no checkpoints to extort fees from relief convoys, no technicals, and no visible weapons would be tolerated. Phase I of Operation Restore Hope ran from 9 to 16 December 1992 and involved an unopposed Marine amphibious landing at the capital city of Mogadishu to secure the port and nearby airfields.[2] Phase II, from 17 to 28 December 1992, expanded security operations out to humanitarian relief distribution sites. Phase III, from 29 December 1992 to 17 February 1993, further expanded security operations and sought to uncover and seize weapon caches. Phase IV, 18 February 1992 to 4 May 1992, entailed a handover of authority to the United Nations and signaled the conclusion of Operation Restore Hope. A United Nations peacekeeping mission, the United Nations Operation in Somalia II, remained in Somalia with a contingent of U.S. military who provided stability under the mantle of Operation Continue Hope.[3] Hostilities persisted. In one outbreak, Somalia warlord and major clan leader General Mohamed Farrah Aidid probably was responsible for the deaths of 24 Pakistani soldiers on 5 June 1993. Aidid's followers also killed four U.S. Army soldiers in a land mine attack on 8 August 1993. Additionally, his militia shot down a UH-60 Black Hawk helicopter on a surveillance mission over southern Mogadishu on 26 September 1993. Three soldiers perished in the crash. A week later, a firefight between Aidid's militants and U.S. Army Rangers left 18 American dead and about 100 wounded. All U.S. troops finally left Somalia by September 1994.[4]

In the early days of Operation Restore Hope, the U.S. Navy provided limited medical support for theater forces. Beginning on 9 December 1992, a Marine Collecting and Clearing Company, which operated 20 beds and an operating room (OR), provided basic Level II care on land. At the same time the Navy provided Echelon III, more specialized care, aboard its Task Force 156 vessels, the USS *Tripoli*, the USS *Juneau*, and the USS *Mount Rushmore*. Also on 9 December 1992, the USS *Tripoli* assumed responsibility for interim medical evacuation activities with a helicopter on standby and dedicated to pick up casualties. When the 10th Mountain Division's organic medical assets arrived in the country on 18 December 1992, it also provided care. On 8 January 1993, the 86th Evacuation Hospital (EVAC) became operational and subsequently provided all Level III health service support in theater. The U.S. Air Force (USAF) set up an Air Transportable Hospital in Egypt at Cairo West Air Base on 12 January 1993. It served as a link in the air evacuation chain, transporting patients back to the 2nd General Hospital in Landstuhl and the 97th General Hospital in Frankfurt, Germany. The U.S. Army's 62nd Medical Group assumed overall responsibility for all theater health service support on 1 February 1993. The Swedish military also set up a hospital and cared for coalition forces.[5]

The U.S. Army originally planned to deploy a Combat Support Hospital (CSH) to provide health service support using Deployable Medical System equipment prepositioned aboard a Navy ship in Diego Garcia. The equipment required 62 containers and could not be loaded off the ship, the USS *Green Valley*, because of the shallow Mogadishu harbor, high waves, and cyclonic winds. Central Command then instructed Forces Command (FORSCOM) to deploy a 100-bed element of the 86th EVAC by air from Fort Campbell, Kentucky, to Somalia. The *Green Valley* never unloaded its cargo in Somalia, returning after a month to Diego Garcia.[6]

During the entire mission, three rotations of Army medical units provided health service support. The first rotation spanned from 9 December 1992 until 1 May 1993. The 62nd Medical Group out of Fort Lewis, Washington, had overall responsibility for theater medical services, while the 86th EVAC from Fort Campbell, Kentucky, served as the primary source of care. The 42nd Field Hospital,

Lieutenant Colonel John Pawley, chief nurse of the 62nd Medical Group, works in his improvised office in Somalia during Operation Restore Hope.
Photo courtesy of Army Nurse Corps Archives, Office of Medical History, Falls Church, VA.

garrisoned at Fort Knox, Kentucky, assumed health service support responsibilities during the second rotation, from 1 May 1993 to 15 August 1993. The 46th CSH from Fort Devens, Massachusetts, deployed for the third and final rotation from 15 August 1993 until 31 March 1994. Its seven-month tour was the longest of the three rotations.[7]

Health Services Command placed the 86th EVAC, garrisoned at Fort Campbell, Kentucky, on alert for deployment to Somalia early in December 1992. The timing of the operation's launch, which coincided with the December holiday period, had a depressing effect on all involved. Nonetheless, the men and women of Fort Campbell's Blanchfield Army Community Hospital (BACH) faced the challenge with determination and confidence in their ability to accept and complete the mission in spite of personal cost.[8]

Over half of the Army nurses serving at BACH, 31 of 52, were either FORSCOM or Professional Officer Filler System (PROFIS) assigned to the 86th EVAC, and Colonel JoEllen Vanatta, BACH's chief nurse, immediately began planning for their imminent deployment. She evaluated the impact their departure would make on the hospital and made sure that all were ready to deploy. Vanatta understood

Pictured is Colonel JoEllen Vanatta, chief nurse of Blanchfield Army Community Hospital from 1992 to 1993.
Photo courtesy of Colonel JoEllen Vanatta, Lakewood, WA.

the mobilization would deplete her operation room and anesthesia staff and the number of nurses in the emergency room, intensive care units, and medical/surgical wards. It also would reduce the numbers of nurse practitioners in the clinics. In a spirited show of support following the alert, the assigned civilian nurses stepped forward without hesitation to maintain the hospital and "immediately came on line and said they would work extra shifts." The BACH civilian staff had always been known for its caring, cooperative, team approach, and their actions in the early days of Operation Restore Hope were typical of their attitude. The civilians intoned that "we have patients to take care of and we will stay."

Health Services Command also responded expeditiously. Groups of cross-leveled active duty personnel and Individual Mobilization Augmentees, purposely requested by Vanatta to report after the holidays, arrived at BACH. On 3 January 1993, 28 active Army Nurse Corps officers arrived and two days later the Department of Nursing at the hospital received a list of 12 more reservist Army nurses who would serve as Individual Mobilization Augmentees and whose presence would allow for the return of the active duty backfill to their home hospitals. Almost all the reservists were "absolutely superb," sound from a clinical standpoint, and had a positive frame of mind. Vanatta also initiated an emergency purchase request for contract nurses from a staffing agency in Nashville, Tennessee, although a need for their services never materialized.[9]

Vanatta made certain that all departing nurses underwent Preparation for Overseas Movement and made sure that no one—for any reason—would have to be dropped from the final PROFIS list. There were a few substitutions for extenuating circumstances, but other Army nurses at BACH volunteered to replace those unable to deploy.[10] Vanatta released the mobilizing nurses from duty, and so they had some limited time to tend to family and personal concerns, process into the mobilizing unit, and attend predeployment briefings. These sessions focused on staying healthy in a developing country rife with unfamiliar endemic diseases, highlighting the care of patients suffering with these ailments, and briefed the deploying nurses on family support issues. The deploying nurses were issued flak vests, desert boots, large rucksacks, and goggles. Many of the nurses began taking Mefloquine malarial prophylaxis during this preparatory period.[11]

When the operational alert occurred, the unit's chief nurse, Major Carolyn Adams, was participating in C4 (Combat Casualty Care Course) at Fort Sam Houston, Texas, but she soon completed the program and returned to Fort Campbell, Kentucky. In the meantime, some confusion and frustration surfaced regarding whether Adams, the garrison chief nurse, or Colonel Elise Gates Roy, the PROFIS chief nurse, would deploy with the 86th EVAC.[12] FORSCOM ruled that Adams would serve in this role, and she then was frocked to lieutenant colonel.[13] The rationale for her frocking was that she was on the promotion list, all the Table of Organization and Equipment chief nurse positions were being upgraded to lieutenant colonel, and several PROFIS lieutenant colonels would join the unit and be staffed in positions subordinate to Adams.[14]

Adams deployed with a handful of nurses on 30 December 1992 and arrived in

A smiling Major Carolyn Adams has silver oak leaves pinned on her uniform during her promotion ceremony. From left to right are Lieutenant Colonel Frank Blakely, Medical Service Corps, 86th EVAC commander, the newly frocked Lieutenant Colonel Carolyn Adams, and her husband, Colonel Bert Adams, DC.
Photo courtesy of Lieutenant Colonel Carolyn Adams, Steilacoom, WA.

Somalia one day later. Three chalks of nursing personnel, each aboard a USAF C-5 aircraft, followed a few days later, with a total of 31 Army Nurse Corps officers deployed.[15] Vanatta attended every departure—whether during the day or at night—dispensing cookies and hugs to the departees to make it "a very good send off, under the circumstances." Several USAF KC-10 planes transported the hospital's supplies and equipment to Somalia.[16]

Because of their relatively late arrival, the 86th EVAC had to set up in a less-

Operation Restore Hope in Somalia 489

Lieutenant Colonel Carolyn Adams, decked out in her TA-50, is pictured here as she deployed with soldiers from the 86th EVAC who were gathering in the background. Adams recalled that almost all in her chalk were in high spirits. She added that deploying on a mission to care for troops and to help other unfortunate people was an awesome responsibility and the ultimate experience for an Army nurse.
Photo courtesy of Lieutenant Colonel Carolyn Adams, Steilacoom, WA.

During a rare moment of calm in 1992, 86th EVAC Army nurse Captain Richard M. Prior visited with Somali children at a refugee center and distributed small tokens of friendship during Operation Restore Hope.
Photo courtesy of Lieutenant Colonel Richard M. Prior, Alexandria, VA.

than-ideal spot because other coalition units had secured the prime real estate. The 86th EVAC had to locate at the end of the somewhat secure airport's departure runway, with high noise levels, blowing dust and sand as aircraft arrived and departed, and significant hazards from the advanced state of disrepair on the runway.[17]

Immediately after their arrival, the staff constructed their Deployable Medical System equipment, and the hospital was thereafter affectionately referred to as Somalia Army Medical Center.[18] One nurse observed, "Everybody from colonel down to private was out there slinging tents, putting up Temper, and doing manual labor."[19] The nurses helped to erect the facility and also filled sandbags. "Most . . . decided that it was sort of fun to take time for mindless jobs."[20]

On 8 January 1992, the hospital began seeing patients on a limited basis. Its first patient was a three-year-old Somali with a foreign body lodged in his trachea. Many other pediatric cases, victims of vehicular accidents or random gunfire, later followed this child as patients of the 86th EVAC. From the outset, the hospital had no pediatric nurses and no pediatric supplies or equipment. At first they improvised, but eventually the hospital received pediatric items after requisitioning them through normal supply channels or acquiring them on loan from hospitals in Europe.[21]

Within a matter of weeks, the 86th EVAC had erected two operating rooms (ORs) and had expanded its bed capacity from 24 to 104 beds, with two 12-bed Intensive Care Units and four 20-bed Intermediate Care Wards in full operation.[22] The EVAC was caring for 40 to 50 patients in its emergency room daily and supported an inpatient census of about 50 patients every day. Patients included soldiers and marines with malaria, dengue fever, diarrheal diseases, chicken pox, asthma, acute febrile illnesses, gunshot wounds, motor vehicle accidents, amputations, and sports injuries. To care for these patients, the nurses worked six 12-hour shifts a week, and such long hours were tiring. Adams wrote, "Between working, eating, laundry and showers there is little time for anything else except sleeping." She added that the nurses "learned to sleep through gunfire and very loud airplanes."[23]

In March of 1993, fighting tapered off significantly in Somalia, and a deceptive atmosphere of relative calm settled over the area. The 86th EVAC received the welcome news that it would be relinquishing its responsibilities to another Army Table of Organization and Equipment hospital unit and would be returning home in the near future. Before its departure, however, plans to move the hospital to a better site had to be implemented. The monsoon season was approaching, and prevailing winds and weather conditions forced arriving planes to alter their previously fixed flight patterns. Because of the winds, arriving flights would be passing directly over the hospital during landings, an unacceptable state of affairs. Furthermore, the existing site was too small to accommodate the hospital. The 86th EVAC staff began their move to the golf course on the U.S. Embassy compound on 26 March 1993. During the 15-day odyssey, the USS *Wasp*, the 423rd Clearing Company, and a Swedish military hospital provided health care; and those members of the 86th EVAC not involved in the actual move augmented the Swedish hospital staff. The new location had security drawbacks, communication problems, and patient transport and aeromedical evacuation difficulties, but overall it was an improvement. It gave the unit additional physical space and a more level site and allowed for floors and connecting ramps in and among the various structures of the facility.[24]

The main body of the 86th EVAC left Somalia on 6 May 1993, and most of the first rotation health service support staff departed by the end of May 1993. Their replacements, the officers and enlisted of the 42nd Field Hospital, arrived in the country on 24 April 1993 and took charge of patient care by the end of April.[25]

Hurried preparations marked the 42nd Field Hospital's deployment from Fort Knox, Kentucky, in late April 1993. Captain Sharon Pryor, for instance, closed her on-post house, packed her household goods in a truck, and drove her four sons home to Chicago, all within a two-week period. She participated in threat briefs and health briefs. With packing lists furnished, she organized her belongings and filled the two duffle bags allowed her with three issued desert camouflage uniforms, head gear, TA-50, chemical equipment, and an air mattress. Pryor packed batches of personal supplies and gave them to her mother so she could incremen-

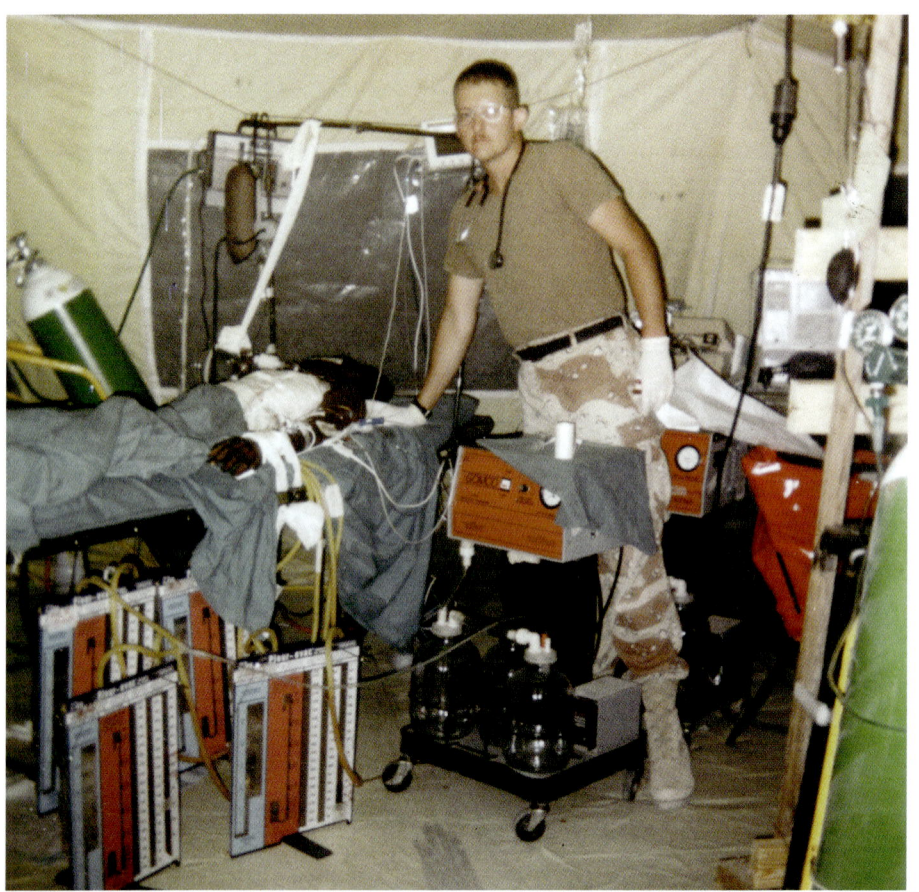

First Lieutenant Lyle Keplinger, a staff nurse in the intensive care unit at the 86th EVAC in Somalia, tends to a patient with multiple chest tubes early in 1993.
Photo courtesy of Army Nurse Corps Archives, Office of Medical History, Falls Church, VA.

tally mail them to her in Somalia.[26]

The 42nd Field Hospital deployed as a unit on a commercial flight, leaving Fort Knox in the early morning on 23 April 1993 and arriving in Mogadishu on 24 April. Stepping off the plane, the staff encountered a blast of intense heat and mixed greetings from the Somalis, some of whom "yelled 'Americans' joyfully and others [who] waved foul hand gestures." The 42nd Field staff had expected to be viewed as heroes, "but obviously not to all."[27]

The 86th EVAC's welcome for the 42nd Field was "warm, friendly, and helpful." The incoming unit fell into the 86th EVAC's Deployable Medical System equipment and tent billets and assumed responsibility for nursing care on the third day after their arrival. Nine days later, the 86th departed, but in the interim

The 62nd Medical Group's Lieutenant Suzanne Richardson was on duty on the Medical Ward at the 86th EVAC in Somalia in spring 1993. Note the calendar on the upper right with the days crossed off, counting down to redeployment day. This was a time-honored tradition in the combat theater and was one method used to cope with the stress of being away from home.
Photo courtesy of Army Nurse Corps Archives, Office of Medical History, Falls Church, VA.

relations between the two units became progressively strained. The 42nd Field nurses believed that their 86th EVAC counterparts were reluctant to "hand over the reins" and "felt lost in losing control." However, the 86th EVAC nurses were anxious to redeploy. Adding to the frustration over the 86th EVAC's ambivalence was the resentment that the 42nd Field nurses were "walking into better living and working conditions" than those originally experienced by the 86th EVAC nurses. Crowded conditions resulting from two units occupying a small space added to the dissonance. In retrospect, the 42nd Field nurses believed that 12 days of overlap was excessive and recommended facilitating a rapid departure for the outgoing unit in future changeovers.[28]

The 42nd Field Hospital began its service in a period of relative calm, but things soon changed. Peace talks that had begun in March stalled and tensions rose. As coalition military personnel and equipment redeployed out of the country and the United Nations took over, patrols decreased. Aidid took advantage of this laxity and once again infiltrated his militia into Mogadishu. The sounds of gunfire returned. American battle casualties correspondingly rose from one case in May 1993 to 11 in June, 12 in July, 19 in August, 21 in September, and 165 in October with the Black Hawk Down incident.[29]

The unit's first of many mass casualties (MASCALs)—this one involving injuries to two American and an additional number of Pakistani soldiers—occurred in the first week of June. The nurses' emotions ran high because most had never before encountered such traumatic battlefield injuries. Furthermore, the nurses heard the sounds of nightly gunfire, and the commander restricted all staff to the compound and ordered additional coils of concertina wire to be strung around the unit's perimeter. Twelve days later another MASCAL occurred, with numerous Pakistani and Moroccan casualties. A third MASCAL during the last week of June involved wounded Italian soldiers, and in mid-July all were saddened by the beating death of a young Cable News Network reporter, who was well known to the hospital staff. By this time, the mood on the compound mirrored the dismal, rainy weather, although spirits occasionally received a boost from periodic A rations, participation in morale-raising activities such as a Fourth of July party, rest and recreation trips to Mombassa and Nairobi, watergun fights, pinochle, music, books, and thoughts of the future redeployment home scheduled for mid-August.[30]

The 42nd Field Hospital staff departed the United States Embassy compound on 16 August 1993. M-17 and UH-60 helicopters shuttled them to the Mogadishu airport for their flight home. Their replacements, the 46th CSH, based in Fort Devens, Massachusetts, had arrived only a few days earlier.[31]

Like its predecessors, the incoming unit, the 46th CSH, enjoyed its first few days in country in relative calm before Aidid ordered an upsurge in the attacks on Americans. With the crescendo of hostilities, a siege mentality quickly developed on the embassy compound, and the Medical Task Force 46 commander directed that MILVANs (containers for overseas or ground movement of military cargo) be placed around the compound's perimeter to augment existing defenses and serve as an enhanced shield from small arms fire.[32]

During the last two weeks of August and throughout September 1993, the 46th CSH received sporadic casualties. A land mine explosion injured four soldiers on 19 August. Another detonated land mine likewise wounded six more soldiers three days later. A helicopter door-gunner sustained fragment wounds on 2 September 1993, and a helicopter pilot suffered a similar fate on 6 September 1993. As days passed, a number of U.S. soldiers fell victim to gunshot wounds and shrapnel injuries, fractures, eye trauma, and stress-related illnesses. On 25 September, hostile fire downed a UH-60 helicopter. Three U.S. soldiers perished and three others were seriously wounded. One required a below-the-knee and a below-the-elbow amputation and had burns to the eyes. The second soldier had a bullet wound to the neck with involvement of the cervical spine and a fractured hand, and a third soldier sustained a gunshot wound to the thigh. All of these incidents plus a fatal shark attack failed to prepare the 46th CSH for what was soon to come.[33]

Attacks and casualties peaked on 3 October with a 15-hour-long battle, later chronicled by Mark Bowden's book *Black Hawk Down*. Task Force Ranger, a Special Operations task force, attempted to capture Aidid. During the firefight, the warlord's militia succeeded in bringing down two Task Force Ranger helicopters with Rocket Propelled Grenades. Heavy street fighting left 18 Rangers dead and approximately 100 wounded in action.[34]

The 46th CSH had four OR tables and 52 beds, of which 12 were intensive care and 40 intermediate care beds. The facility was only staffed to support 32 beds. Nonetheless, the staff efficiently responded to the MASCAL. It helped that the casualties arrived in well-spaced increments, with a few trickling in between pushes. The first wave of 24 casualties arrived at 1730 hours on 3 October, two hours after the operation began. The second wave of 36 wounded arrived on a helicopter a little more than 12 hours later. The Swedish hospital cared for a number of those with orthopedic injuries, and a contingent of German physicians augmented hospital personnel of the 46th CSH. Over the MASCAL's two days, 56 operative procedures took place on the four OR tables. Two USAF C-141 aircraft evacuated 55 casualties to Landstuhl Army Medical Center in Germany in the immediate aftermath of the MASCAL.[35]

Army nurses were ready to care for the battle casualties from the outset of the operation. Their actual participation began when one of the Army Nurse Corps officers assigned to the 46th CSH spotted a landing Black Hawk helicopter rather than the usual Medical Evacuation Huey and knew it was an ominous sign. Then the first wounded descended on the hospital. The Emergency Medical Treatment area soon had all its tables occupied with incoming casualties, and the "wounds were just incredible." The hospital staff rose to the occasion.

> We utilized every person on the compound. Everyone pitched in and contributed in one way or another. We were familiar with how the system worked and were able to make it all come together. People were scared, but everyone did a wonderful job. Staff felt very proud of themselves to know that when the rubber met the road they could do it.[36]

No one could remain unaffected by those days' events and all experienced some degree of emotional reaction. To ameliorate the effects of the MASCAL and the stressful environment in general, the Army Medical Department had a combat stress team. This group conducted interviews and debriefings that served as a catharsis and helped the 46th CSH staff cope with the event.[37]

Original plans were to relieve the 46th CSH with the 115th Field Hospital from Fort Polk, Louisiana, in late December 1993 or early January 1994. With shifting political winds, however, plans changed. The commander in chief, Central Command, and the FORSCOM commander directed the 46th CSH to stay and gradually phase down in accordance with the overall reduction of U.S. presence in Somalia. In January 1994, 115 Army Medical Department personnel redeployed to their home stations. Other soldiers followed them, returning home individually through mid-February 1994. From 64 beds and 350 personnel in November 1993, the 46th CSH was down to 14 beds and 175 staff in February 1994. The Army transferred responsibility for health service support to the Navy in March 1994. This concluded Army Medical Department involvement in Somalia. Thereafter, a Marine Corps Collecting and Clearing Company situated at the Mogadishu air-

A number of celebrities joined forces with the USO to visit the troops, the hospital, and its patients during Operation Restore Hope in Somalia. Here, in 1993, Charlton Heston (left) paused for a moment with First Lieutenant Patricia Hall (right) of the 86th EVAC. Hall was caring for a child (center) pushed in front of a truck by his mother who erroneously assumed her son's injuries would ensure his speedy passage to America.
Photo courtesy of Army Nurse Corps Archives, Office of Medical History, Falls Church, VA.

Colonel Iris J. West (right) did extensive historical research focusing on Operation Restore Hope. Here she accepts a meritorious service medal for her many contributions while Army Nurse Corps historian, assigned to the U.S. Center of Military History. Presenting the award in October 1994 was Colonel John W. Mountcastle, Chief of Military History (left).
Photo courtesy of Colonel Iris West, Dexter, NY.

field held sick call and offered limited holding and emergency care.[38]

Stress was an unavoidable feature of service in Somalia. Numerous mass casualty situations, horrific wounds, frequent sudden deaths among a population of young adults, insufficient or inappropriate supplies, and caring for the enemy plagued the nurses. Cycles of inactivity and boredom followed by periods of frenetic action, few rest and recreation opportunities, rare to nonexistent mail deliveries, and a dearth of telephones added to the sense of isolation. Those who had served in Operation Desert Storm said that they saw far more trauma in Somalia than they had encountered in the previous war. When a young Irish nurse riddled with bullet wounds died on the operating table, the OR nurse confided, "It was that day that it really sunk into everyone's mind that we were in a very unsafe environment. It opened a lot of eyes." Church services, discussions, physical activities, and sleep boosted morale, as did the country and western band formed by a group of 86th medics and the USO tours featuring Charlton Heston, Clint Black, Gerald McRainey, and Lisa Hartman.[39]

The art of field expediency—one of Army nurses' unsung talents—manifested itself as well in Operation Restore Hope. Hampered by too few urinals and measuring devices, Army Nurse Corps officers fashioned empty water bottles into vessels to accurately gauge intake and output. They filled empty saline bottles with sand to serve as traction weights. They improvised a Stryker frame with anchoring wood blocks to mimic a modern-day rocking bed and thus prevented pulmonary congestion by regularly changing the patient's position. Lieutenant Colonel Larry Grant, the 86th EVAC's OR head nurse, rearranged the Operating Room/Central Materiel Supply suite into a one-way loop for supplies to flow and thus fostered asepsis and prevented cross-contamination. This became known as "Grant's Loop."[40]

Colonel Iris West studied the Army Nurse Corps participation in Operation Restore Hope and her observations provide a fitting conclusion to this chapter:

> What were the lessons learned. . . ? What do we need to draw from this at times painful period. . . ? The first lesson is that despite of all the difficulties, the lack of supplies, discomfort, and danger, the Army Nurse Corps was always there providing quality patient care. Operation Restore Hope was different than anything else the corps had done in recent history. However, with the end of the Cold War, this type of operation may well be a template for the future. Can an Army designed for a Cold War environment perform in "operations other than war"? The answer is yes, but the solution as well as the second lesson is that the old methods of operation do not always work. Army nurses must continue to be flexible and innovative. . . . Do not expect that everything one has in a peacetime hospital will be there in an austere theater of operation. Do be prepared to find field expedients to make things work. The third lesson is one that the corps has always had to grapple with. Army nurses are more than nurses; we are also soldiers. To be the greatest asset, an Army nurse who deploys to the field must know basic soldier skills such as use of weapons, personal defense, and fieldcraft. Finally, providing medical/nursing care to people of a different culture with different values presents unique and challenging ethical quandarys [sic].
>
> All in all, the deployment to Somalia furnished Army nurses with unique opportunities to grow, a greater knowledge of diverse cultures, and for most an enhanced sense of personal strength. There was also a renewed sense of gratitude, pride, and appreciation for what our country means to us. And for most a reaffirmation of why we chose to wear the uniform.[41]

# Notes

1. Patrick Gilkes, "From Peace-Keeping to Peace Enforcement: The Somalia Precedent," Middle East Report (November–December 1993): 21–24. Center for Army Lessons Learned (CALL), U.S. Army Combined Arms Command (CAC), Fort Leavenworth, Kansas, "Operation Restore Hope," Draft Report, 1993, Army Nurse Corps Collection (ANCC), Office of Medical History (OMH). Stephen E. Everett and L. Martin Kaplan, *Department of the Army Historical Summary, Fiscal Year 1993* (Washington, DC: Center of Military History, United States Army, 2002), 57–58. Lois M. Davis and others, "Army Medical Support for Peace Operations and Humanitarian Assistance," 1996, http://www.rand.org/publications/MR/MR773/ (accessed 6 July 2004). Sarah A. Ingram, *Somalia Medical Operations* (Arlington, VA: Camber Corporation, n.d.), 1–4.

2. A swarm of media cameras with bright lights documented this invasion, sparking questions about OPSEC (Operational Security) and a debate about the role of the media in military operations. "Plunging Ashore into Blazing—TV Lights?" *Time* (21 December 1992): 16–17. Jill Smolowe, "Great Expectations," *Time* (21 December 1992): 32–35.

3. Center for Army Lessons Learned (CALL), U.S. Army Combined Arms Command (CAC), Fort Leavenworth, Kansas, "Operation Restore Hope," Draft Report, 2–3, 1993, ANCC, OMH. "Jerry Harben, "Restore Hope Troops Must Deal with Heat, Diseases in Somalia," *HSC Mercury* 20 (January 1993): 1. Stephen E. Everett and L. Martin Kaplan, *Department of the Army Historical Summary, Fiscal Year 1993* (Washington, DC: Center of Military History, United States Army, 2002), 57–58. L. Martin Kaplan, *Department of the Army Historical Summary, Fiscal Year 1994* (Washington, DC: Center of Military History, United States Army, 2000), 63.

4. Stephen E. Everett and L. Martin Kaplan, *Department of the Army Historical Summary, Fiscal Year 1993* (Washington, DC: Center of Military History, United States Army, 2002), 57–58. L. Martin Kaplan, *Department of the Army Historical Summary, Fiscal Year 1994* (Washington, DC: Center of Military History, United States Army, 2000), 63. Katherine McIntire, "Deaths Heighten Debate about Mission," *Army Times* (11 October 1993): 12. Paul Quinn-Judge, "Film of Somalia Gunfight Shows It Was Not a Rout, US Says," *Boston Globe* (3 November 1993): 2. Keith B. Richburg, "U.S. Envoy to Somalia Urged Policy Shift before 18 GIs Died," *Washington Post* (11 November 1993): 39. Keith B. Richburg, "Some Detained Somalis Said to Have Killed American Soldiers," *Washington*

*Post* (12 November 1993): 47. Mark Bowden, *Black Hawk Down, A Story of Modern War* (New York: Penguin Books, 1999). Sarah A. Ingram, *Somalia Medical Operations* (Arlington, VA: Camber Corporation, n.d.), 100, 102, 105–06.

    5. Center for Army Lessons Learned (CALL), U.S. Army Combined Arms Command (CAC), Fort Leavenworth, Kansas, "Operation Restore Hope," Draft Report, XI-11, 1993, ANCC, OMH. Lois M. Davis and others, "Army Medical Support for Peace Operations and Humanitarian Assistance," 1996, http://www.rand.org/publications/MR/MR773/ (accessed 6 July 2004). Sarah A. Ingram, *Somalia Medical Operations* (Arlington, VA: Camber Corporation, n.d.), 10–11.

    6. Center for Army Lessons Learned (CALL), U.S. Army Combined Arms Command (CAC), Fort Leavenworth, Kansas, "Operation Restore Hope," Draft Report, 7, X-3, XI-11, 1993; Richard D. Cameron, "Impact of Operation Restore Hope Notification, Preparation, and Deployment," 1st Endorsement, Printed Letter, 5–6, 29 April 1993; and Carolyn A. Adams, "Operation Restore Hope," Printed Chronology, 21 August 1993 (all in ANCC, OMH). Iris J. West and Christopher Clark, "The Army Nurse Corps and Operation Restore Hope," *Military Medicine* 160 (April 1995): 179–83. Robert L. Mabry and others, "United States Army Rangers in Somalia: An Analysis of Combat Casualties on an Urban Battlefield," *Journal of Trauma, Injury, Infection, and Critical Care* 49 (September 2000): 515–28. Sarah A. Ingram, *Somalia Medical Operations* (Arlington, VA: Camber Corporation, n.d.), 17–19, 27.

    7. Lois M. Davis and others, "Army Medical Support for Peace Operations and Humanitarian Assistance," 1996, http://www.rand.org/publications/MR/MR773/ (accessed 6 July 2004). Iris J. West and Christopher Clark, "The Army Nurse Corps and Operation Restore Hope," *Military Medicine* 160 (April 1995): 179–83.

    8. George J. Brown, "Impact of Operation Restore Hope Notification, Preparation, and Deployment," Memorandum, 22 March 1993, ANCC, OMH. JoEllen Vanatta, Interview by Iris J. West and Chris Clark, Transcript, 2–3, 15 July 1994, Army Nurse Corps Oral History Collection (ANCOHC), OMH. Sarah A. Ingram, *Somalia Medical Operations* (Arlington, VA: Camber Corporation, n.d.), 29–30.

    9. JoEllen Vanatta, Interview by Iris J. West and Chris Clark, Transcript, 3–6, 9–11, 13, 18, 15 July 1994, ANCOHC, OMH. JoEllen N. Vanatta, "Operation Restore Hope," Printed Chronology, 4, 9 February 1993, ANCC, OMH. Sarah A. Ingram, *Somalia Medical Operations* (Arlington, VA: Camber Corporation, n.d.), 31.

    10. Four Army nurses at BACH were found nondeployable. One had an impending ETS (expiration of term of service), another was pregnant, and two others had extenuating family situations. Sarah A. Ingram, *Somalia Medical Operations* (Arlington, VA: Camber Corporation, n.d.), 37.

    11. JoEllen Vanatta, Interview by Iris J. West and Chris Clark, Transcript, 7, 15 July 1994, ANCOHC, OMH. George J. Brown, "Impact of Operation Restore Hope Notification, Preparation, and Deployment," Memorandum, 2, 22 March 1993; JoEllen N. Vanatta, "Operation Restore Hope," Printed Chronology, 5, 9 February 1993; Department of Nursing, 86th Evacuation Hospital, Mogadishu, Somalia, Africa, "Historical Notes: December 1992–January 1993," Printed Document, n.d.; Major Gunn, "Medical Evaluation—Potential Somalia Deployment," Information Paper, 2 December 1992; "Historical Data," Handwritten Chronology, n.d. (all in ANCC, OMH).

    12. During Operation Restore Hope, the policy on TO&E chief nurses was in transition. FORSCOM was in the process of deleting the PROFIS chief nurse position that usually was vested in the nearby TDA hospital assistant chief nurse position. With this change, the garrison chief nurse would remain in that role upon mobilization. By 1994, this change was

completely realized. JoEllen Vanatta, Interview by Iris J. West and Chris Clark, Transcript, 15–16, 23, 15 July 1994, ANCOHC, OMH.

13. Frocking involved an early, out-of-sequence promotion from the list of those selected for promotion.

14. JoEllen Vanatta, Interview by Iris J. West and Chris Clark, Transcript, 7, 15–16, 15 July 1994, ANCOHC, OMH. Carolyn A. Adams, "Operation Restore Hope," Printed Chronology, 1, 21 August 1993; JoEllen N. Vanatta, "Operation Restore Hope," Printed Chronology, 5, 9 February 1993; and Department of Nursing, 86th Evacuation Hospital, Mogadishu, Somalia, Africa, "Historical Notes: December 1992–January 1993," Printed Document, n.d. (all in ANCC, OMH).

15. A chalk is an increment or group of personnel manifested for transport on an Air Force plane.

16. Department of Nursing, 86th Evacuation Hospital, Mogadishu, Somalia, Africa, "Historical Notes: December 1992–January 1993," Printed Document, n.d.; and "Historical Data," Handwritten Chronology, n.d. (both in ANCC, OMH). JoEllen Vanatta, Interview by Iris J. West and Chris Clark, Transcript, 7, 8, 15 July 1994, ANCOHC, OMH.

17. Sarah A. Ingram, *Somalia Medical Operations* (Arlington, VA: Camber Corporation, n.d.), 19–20. Iris J. West and Christopher Clark, "The Army Nurse Corps and Operation Restore Hope," *Military Medicine* 160 (April 1995): 180. Carolyn A. Adams, "Greetings from Somalia," Handwritten Letter, 23 January 1993, ANCC, OMH.

18. "Historical Data," Handwritten Chronology, notations under dates of 2 and 4 January 1994, ANCC, OMH.

19. Iris J. West and Christopher Clark, "The Army Nurse Corps and Operation Restore Hope," *Military Medicine* 160 (April 1995): 180.

20. "Historical Data," Handwritten Chronology, notation under date of 2 January 1994, ANCC, OMH.

21. Iris J. West and Christopher Clark, "The Army Nurse Corps and Operation Restore Hope," *Military Medicine* 160 (April 1995): 180. "Historical Data," Handwritten Chronology, notation under date of 8 January 1994, ANCC, OMH.

22. Sarah A. Ingram, *Somalia Medical Operations* (Arlington, VA: Camber Corporation, n.d.), 26. Iris J. West and Christopher Clark, "The Army Nurse Corps and Operation Restore Hope," *Military Medicine* 160 (April 1995): 180.

23. Carolyn A. Adams, "Greetings from Somalia," Handwritten Letter, 23 January 1993; Unidentified Handwritten Chronology, 15 January 1993 to 22 January 1993; "EMT Historical," Handwritten Chronology, 5 January 1993 to 20 January 1993 (all in ANCC, OMH). Iris J. West and Christopher Clark, "The Army Nurse Corps and Operation Restore Hope," *Military Medicine* 160 (April 1995): 181.

24. Sarah A. Ingram, *Somalia Medical Operations* (Arlington, VA: Camber Corporation, n.d.), 65–67. Iris J. West and Christopher Clark, "The Army Nurse Corps and Operation Restore Hope," *Military Medicine* 160 (April 1995): 180. Sharon Pryor, Interview by Mary T. Sarnecky, Transcript, 11, 10 January 2001, ANCOHC, OMH.

25. Sarah A. Ingram, *Somalia Medical Operations* (Arlington, VA: Camber Corporation, n.d.), 67. Iris J. West and Christopher Clark, "The Army Nurse Corps and Operation Restore Hope," *Military Medicine* 160 (April 1995): 180. "New Hospital Begins Support in Somalia," *HSC Mercury* 20 (June 1993): 1.

26. Sharon Pryor, Interview by Mary T. Sarnecky, Transcript, 5–10, 10 January 2001, ANCOHC, OMH. Sharon Pryor, Jill Mierau, and Ellen Rogers, "Operation 'Continue Hope' Department of Nursing, Nursing Log," 1, 18 April 1993 to 17 August 1993, ANCC, OMH.

27. Sharon Pryor, Jill Mierau, and Ellen Rogers, "Operation 'Continue Hope' Department of Nursing, Nursing Log," 1, 18 April 1993 to 17 August 1993, ANCC, OMH.

28. Sharon Pryor, Jill Mierau, and Ellen Rogers, "Operation 'Continue Hope' Department of Nursing, Nursing Log," 2–5, 18 April 1993 to 17 August 1993, ANCC, OMH.

29. Sarah A. Ingram, *Somalia Medical Operations* (Arlington, VA: Camber Corporation, n.d.), 99–111.

30. Sharon Pryor, Jill Mierau, and Ellen Rogers, "Operation 'Continue Hope' Department of Nursing, Nursing Log," 8–15, 18 April 1993 to 17 August 1993, ANCC, OMH. Sharon Pryor, Interview by Mary T. Sarnecky, Transcript, 14–17, 10 January 2001, ANCOHC, OMH. Lois M. Davis and others, "Army Medical Support for Peace Operations and Humanitarian Assistance," 1996, http://www.rand.org/publications/MR/MR773/ (accessed 6 July 2004).

31. Sarah A. Ingram, *Somalia Medical Operations* (Arlington, VA: Camber Corporation, n.d.), 102. Sharon Pryor, Interview by Mary T. Sarnecky, Transcript, 22, 10 January 2001, ANCOHC, OMH. Lieutenant Colonel Lemon, "Situational Update—Somalia," Executive Summary, 16 August 1993, ANCC, OMH.

32. Sarah A. Ingram, *Somalia Medical Operations* (Arlington, VA: Camber Corporation, n.d.), 102–03.

33. Ibid., 102–05. Iris J. West and Christopher Clark, "The Army Nurse Corps and Operation Restore Hope," *Military Medicine* 160 (April 1995): 181.

34. Robert L. Mabry and others, "United States Army Rangers in Somalia: An Analysis of Combat Casualties on an Urban Battlefield," *Journal of Trauma, Injury, Infection, and Critical Care* 49 (September 2000): 516. Mark Bowden, *Black Hawk Down, A Story of Modern War* (New York: Penguin Books, 1999). Kevin Fedarko, "Somalia: Amid Disaster, Amazing Valor," *Time* 143 (18 February 1994): 46–48.

35. Robert L. Mabry and others, "United States Army Rangers in Somalia: An Analysis of Combat Casualties on an Urban Battlefield," *Journal of Trauma, Injury, Infection, and Critical Care* 49 (September 2000): 516–17. John Lancaster, "Combat in Mogadishu Posed a Challenge for Small U.S. Army Hospital," *Washington Post* (20 October 1993), A36.

36. Iris J. West and Christopher Clark, "The Army Nurse Corps and Operation Restore Hope," *Military Medicine* 160 (April 1995): 181.

37. Ibid. Major Gunn, "Deployment of Mental Health Assessment Team to Somalia," Executive Summary, 5 August 1993, ANCC, OMH.

38. Sarah A. Ingram, *Somalia Medical Operations* (Arlington, VA: Camber Corporation, n.d.), 130–31.

39. Iris J. West and Christopher Clark, "The Army Nurse Corps and Operation Restore Hope," *Military Medicine* 160 (April 1995): 181. Chris Hober, "Medical Commanders Reflect on Somalia," *Northwest Guardian* (8 July 1993): 8. "Historical Data," Handwritten Chronology, notations under dates of 12, 13, 15, 17, and 18 January 1994; and Nancy R. Adams, "Trip Report to USAREC Fort Knox, Kentucky and to 86th Evacuation Hospital Fort Campbell, Kentucky, 23 and 24 August 1993" (both in ANCC, OMH). "Medics Overcome Danger, Boredom in Somalia," *HSC Mercury* 20 (August 1993): 8.

40. Iris J. West and Christopher Clark, "The Army Nurse Corps and Operation Restore Hope," *Military Medicine* 160 (April 1995): 181. Chris Hober, "Medical Commanders Reflect on Somalia," *Northwest Guardian* (8 July 1993): 8. "Medics Overcome Danger, Boredom in Somalia," *HSC Mercury* 20 (August 1993): 8.

41. Iris J. West and Christopher Clark, "The Army Nurse Corps and Operation Restore Hope," *Military Medicine* 160 (April 1995): 183.

*Chapter Twenty-two*
# Operations in the Former Republic of Yugoslavia

The complex affairs in the former republic of Yugoslavia in the late 20th century were a tangled web woven by centuries of subjugation under various foreign conquerors. These "conflicting imperialisms" as well as "arbitrary boundaries, and substantially different political cultures" contributed to the area's instability.[1] Yugoslav dictator Josip Broz—Marshal Tito—held together a relatively stable communist federation after World War II, but 10 years after Tito's death in 1980, the country had fragmented into six republics and two provinces marked by political, economic, religious upheavals, and cultural diversity and strife.[2]

In the early 1990s, tensions among the various ethnic groups sowed the seeds of civil war. The bloodiest European conflict since World War II followed. What came to be euphemistically known as "ethnic cleansing," viewed by the global community as mass murder, resulted in approximately 10,000 deaths—mostly among Croatians—during the final four months of 1991. By then there were also an estimated 600,000 Yugoslav refugees.[3]

The European Union imposed a set of economic sanctions on the Balkan states in November 1991, but this had no effect on the ongoing internal struggles. The United Nations took action on 21 February 1992, passing Security Council Resolution 743 that called for the creation of the U.N. Protection Force referred to as UNPROFOR. This was followed by Security Force Resolution 749, which authorized the deployment of U.N. forces to Croatia and Bosnia-Herzegovina.[4]

To provide health service support for UNPROFOR, the commander-in-chief of U.S. Army, Europe tasked V Corps to move a 60-bed hospital to Croatia and to augment the hospital with staff and equipment from 7th Medical Command.[5] The implementation of this deployment reduced the ability to deliver health care within the 7th Medical Command at a time when U.S. forces in Europe were undergoing a sizeable drawdown of personnel. Several months later in Operation Provide Promise, when the 502nd Mobile Army Surgical Hospital (MASH) became the second hospital to deploy from Europe, it drew significant staff from the 3rd Combat Support Hospital (CSH) at Nürnberg. Colonel Charles F. Miller observed that there was "no more wiggle room to take care of retirees" and warned that there likewise might "not be enough wiggle room in the next year to take care of dependents if the draw down continues." Only the closure of the Nürnberg and Erlangen military communities prevented the realization of this dire prediction.[6] The first Table of Organization and Equipment hospital chosen to deploy to Zagreb, Croatia, was the 212th MASH.

The 212th MASH was subordinate to the 68th Medical Group, garrisoned at Wiesbaden Air Force Base in Germany.[7] Most of the unit's Professional Officer Filler System staff learned "off the record" about their future deployment while on REFORGER 92, an annual field exercise that the U.S. Army, Europe curtailed to permit the Table of Organization and Equipment personnel and their Deployable Medical System (DEPMEDS) equipment time to prepare for the deployment. The unit received its warning orders in October 1992, and the unit staged in Wiesbaden. All deploying soldiers qualified on their weapons and all attended refresher courses on nuclear, biological, and chemical protection. They also participated in briefings on safety measures, cold weather hazards, the articles of the Geneva Convention, the Code of Conduct, management of stress, the current threat situation, and the avoidance of land mines, and heard a historical précis on their destination country, Yugoslavia.[8]

The main body of the 212th MASH flew via charter aircraft to Zagreb in mid-November 1992. The vehicles, supplies, and DEPMEDS equipment came by rail. Upon arrival, the staff of the hospital under the command of Lieutenant Colonel Everett Newcomb immediately erected their 11 tents and readied their perimeter protection of five MILVANs (containers for overseas or ground movement of military cargo) on a plot of land called Camp Pleso, adjacent to a hangar riddled with bullet holes that bore silent testimony to a violent past. Their allotted space was about a mile and a half from the Zagreb Airport's passenger terminal. Parts of the MASH, the inpatient wards, were erected in the hangar, while another section housing other components extended out from the building. The 60-bed MASH included one 12-bed Intensive Care Unit, two 20-bed Intermediate Care Wards, an eight-bed Mental Health Section, and an Emergency Medical Treatment (EMT) area. Two operating room suites accommodated two operating room tables each. The 212th MASH staff billets were General Purpose Large tents.

Living conditions were primitive. Twelve soldiers shared each tent. Each soldier's personal space was about six by eight feet and it took great ingenuity to create a semblance of privacy. The tents' inhabitants strung lashing rope or wire to support improvised room dividers fashioned from ponchos, sheets, draperies, or locally purchased fabric. A friendly contingent from the Netherlands helped the 212th MASH soldiers set up their billeting tents. The soldiers from Holland were living in 1940s-era tents that were very rudimentary. The 212th MASH had several excess General Purpose Large tents, so they lent them to the Dutch soldiers in appreciation for their assistance.

The unit's stated mission was to provide health care and a 30-day patient holding capability for the more-than-20,000-strong U.N. forces, including U.N. civilians serving in the area. They treated their first patient, a civilian injured by a land mine that detonated while he was clearing an area for the hospital, on 13 November 1992. The next day the hospital formally opened with a ribbon-cutting ceremony attended by two members of Congress, Arizona Senator Dennis DeConcini and Indiana Representative Frank McCloskey.[9]

The 212th MASH's nursing staff consisted of 41 Army Nurse Corps officers and 81 enlisted medics. Approximately one-third of the latter were 91Cs, licensed practical nurses. Nursing personnel came from various units in Europe, including the SHAPE Medical Department Activity in Belgium, the Berlin Medical Department Activity, the 2nd General Hospital, the 97th General Hospital, and the 130th Station Hospital, all of the latter four in Germany. Major Paul Erlich, the hospital's chief nurse, used the newly formulated (December 1990) "Standards for Nursing in Mobilization" to organize the Department of Nursing. He promptly set up procedures to ensure quality of care and established a Nursing Education and Staff Development Program that was administered by Captain Jenevie Llanes. Among the educational presentations offered were a Journal Club, a course on trauma nursing, and Advanced Cardiac Life Support programs. Captain Elizabeth Bowie chaired the Infection Control Committee that monitored the hospital's four nosocomial infections, three of which were in patients with penetrating combat wounds. Every day at 1000 hours Erlich held head nurse meetings. Typical agenda topics included information disseminated from the task force commanders, new nursing policy instructions, and security concerns. Head nurses recorded the shared information in their ward's commobook (communications book), which all unit staff read and initialed daily. Captain Jimmy Johnson, the Army Community Health Nurse, served as chief of preventive medicine and immediately implemented initiatives, such as programs for pest control, sanitation, water purification, and prevention of sexually transmitted diseases.

Language barriers were perplexing. With a multinational clientele from approximately 33 countries who spoke numerous languages, communication was often difficult.[10] To circumvent these barriers, the nurses used flash cards, pointing to body parts, hand signals, translators, and—if all else failed—charades to communicate with patients. Other issues included finding a place to accommodate respiratory isolation patients and relearning the field expedient mindset to adapt available supplies and equipment to meet unanticipated needs.[11] With the extremely cold weather in January 1993, further improvisations became necessary. The −30° F weather caused everything—medications, intravenous fluids, K-thermia pads, and even lubricant jelly—to freeze. In the operating room, the nurses thawed medication vials by placing them in their clothing, close to their bodies. They put frozen water tubing in the overhead heating vents to obtain water. They shined high-intensity spotlights on intravenous bags to heat them. Captain Nelda Barnhill thought that this was "probably one of the most unusual things that has ever happened in operating room nursing." She added that the attempts to deal with the subzero cold were "a group effort." All were creatively thinking of ways to deal with the extraordinary circumstances and improve patient care.[12]

Despite wearing ungainly thermal underwear, all the nurses remained bitterly cold and uncomfortable. When they donned their issued bulky cold-weather garb, they felt like the "Michelin man" or the "Pillsbury doughboy." The French soldiers, however, looked toasty warm, "slim, trim, and ready to move." After talking to the French troops, the nurses discovered that they wore silk underwear. Soon most of the Army nurses ordered their own silk undergarments from catalogues and were much warmer and more comfortable. The women's spirits skyrocketed as well, feeling their appearance and military bearing had been restored as they shed the cumbersome clothing.[13]

The hospital was much less busy than the staff originally expected. The EMT area, for example, treated from five to 20 patients on a typical day, and the patients were much less critical than those usually seen in an emergency room. The EMT, in effect, served as a sick call, predominantly caring for those with minor complaints such as colds and backaches. A few exceptions occurred when victims of motor vehicle accidents, land mine accidents, or patients with chest pain also were admitted.[14]

Although the operating room had four tables, it rarely used more than two tables at any one time, and the average number of surgeries was 1 case per day. Surgical procedures involved dental work for abscessed teeth or fractured jaws, treatment of orthopedic wounds resulting from land mines or missile injuries, abdominal cases from gunshot wounds, and vascular surgery required for wounds caused by detonated land mines.[15]

The normal daily census in the inpatient units, the Intensive Care Unit and the Intermediate Care Wards, ranged from 10 to 30 patients.[16] Because the workload was significantly lighter than expected, the commander sent 46 of the 212th MASH staff back to Germany two months before the unit's scheduled redeployment.[17] He instructed them about being subject to recall within a 48-hour notice.[18]

After settling in Zagreb, the cohesive unit bonded with other U.N. forces in their surrounding area. Their activities and interactions helped to cope with the difficult circumstances of living and working in the frigidly cold, war-torn Balkans. These friendly, collaborative associations also were textbook examples of international diplomacy.

The congenial interactions took many forms in a number of venues. Several activities highlighting each nationality supplied a cultural awareness. Music also served as a means of communication and social support. Colonel Greg Stevens, the commander of the 68th Medical Group and Task Force 212, had packed amplifiers, speakers, keyboards, drums, and other musical instruments and formed a band whose specialty was 1960s and country music. The amateur musicians provided concerts on the tarmac that lightened the mood and provided a distraction for all.[19] All nationalities attended the sessions. At the final concert, more than 2,000 U.N. forces participated in the merriment. "There was a lot of people-to-people diplomacy going on" and many wide-reaching friendships formed.[20] Other activities appealed to the nurses' aesthetic sense and cultural interests. One of the physicians was able to get blocks of tickets for concerts and ballets in Zagreb, and groups of the 212th MASH attended these performances.[21]

The 212th MASH also sponsored an untraditional triathlon with events including a five-mile run, three basketball free throws, carrying an egg in a spoon for 50 meters, and a bicycle ride. For those who could not ride a bicycle, pushing someone in a wheelchair for a mile was offered as a substitute. Those who could not participate in the race lined the course and either yelled encouraging words or shouted harassment, as they felt so inclined.[22]

The "Men of Anesthesia" also provided comic relief. On one occasion, the commander facetiously ordered them into his office, jokingly threatening them with disciplinary action. In mock retaliation, the "Men of Anesthesia" reversed the bills of their blue U.N. baseball caps, donned Blues Brothers sunglasses, and sauntered into Newcomb's office swinging their dog tag chains around their necks. All the hospital staff was consumed with mirth. To everyone's glee—including the commander's—the practical joke turned out to be a trick that backfired on him.[23]

Originally, the U.S. contingent was the only force to include female soldiers. Over time and successive rotations of personnel, other national groups also included female soldiers in their units. Some thought that the Americans demonstrated to all that women could function as well as men in tough environments. At least 60 percent of the Swiss group that subsequently rotated into Camp Pleso was female. Soon the women of many nations, including the Norwegian contingent and the female nurses and physicians from the U.S. Army, formed an international girls' club. Friendships developed. Barnhill recalled that it was "an educational experience; you couldn't match it anywhere else."[24]

In April 1993, just before their redeployment back to Germany, the 212th MASH sponsored a health fair. Organizers expected just a few hundred attendees, but more than 5,000 people representing all nations—military and civilian—participated. The fair's promoters offered many services, such as cholesterol screening and cardiovascular tests. They gave aerobic exercise demonstrations and served a nutritious lunch. But before eating, all had to attend and participate in a hand-washing demonstration.[25] The effects of the health fair likely exceeded the health benefits accrued.

The staff remained upbeat thanks to both the unit leadership and the attitude of the 212th MASH's rank and file. Their positive outlook and collaborative spirit have served as an example for humanitarian relief missions that increasingly have been conducted in an atmosphere of potential and sometimes actual hostility.

One month before the 212th MASH's deployment in Zagreb was to end, it had cared for more than 3,070 patients—both ambulatory and hospitalized—from more than 30 countries. Of these, 382 were wounded in the line of fire. The remainder represented disease or nonbattle injuries. Those killed from hostile action numbered 32.[26] At the conclusion of the mission on 27 April 1993, the 212th MASH counted 333 patient admissions and cared for an additional 3,666 as outpatients.[27]

A crane lifts a CONEX into place as part of the heightened security measures implemented during September 1993 by the 502nd MASH in Zagreb, Croatia.
Photo courtesy of Army Nurse Corps Archives, Office of Medical History, Falls Church, VA.

The 212th MASH redeployed to Germany on 28 April 1993. It handed over its mission responsibilities to the 502nd MASH with Major (P) Paul Chadek assuming the chief nurse role.[28]

The 185-strong staff of the 502nd MASH arrived in Zagreb, Croatia in three increments, from 26 to 28 April 1993, and remained in the country until 8 October that year, just shy of the 179 days that defined a temporary tour of duty.[29] The U.S. Air Force planes that delivered the incoming 502nd MASH from Nürnberg returned with 212th MASH personnel to Wiesbaden, limiting the lengthy overlap of personnel.[30] Upon arrival, the 502nd MASH fell in on the 212th MASH's hospital, equipment, and billeting tents.[31] The majority (165) of the 502nd MASH staff deployed from the 3rd CSH garrisoned at Nürnberg.[32]

Many of the experiences of the 212th MASH were replicated by the 502nd. Some things changed. During the 502nd MASH's deployment, the hospital gradually reduced from 60 beds to approximately 20 beds. The average daily hospital census at that time ranged from eight to 12 patients, and the staff created an isolation ward that later was converted into a children's ward.[33] Another improvement was the installation of the Remote Clinical Communications System at the 502nd MASH. This system allowed caregivers in Zagreb to send a voice message, a written consultation, and a digital color image by telephone line or satellite from the 502nd MASH to consultants at the 2nd General Hospital in Landstuhl, Ger-

After placement, the CONEX served as an underground area for patient treatment adjacent to the 502nd MASH in Zagreb, Croatia.
Photo courtesy of Army Nurse Corps Archives, Office of Medical History, Falls Church, VA.

many, or to Walter Reed Army Medical Center in Washington, D.C.[34]

Other changes involved the hostile threat and the level of security. In September 1993, the Serbs threatened to shell the Zagreb airport, and the hospital feared it would be caught in the crossfire.[35] Some mortar rounds actually passed over the hospital. To improve security, everyone began filling sandbags. The commander ordered the sandbags to be placed on the insides of tents to avoid looking "militaristic" as opposed to humanitarian. The hospital staff also dug trenches, hollowed out tunnels, and buried CONEXs (large, corrugated metal shipping containers) as underground bunkers. One of the bunkers unexpectedly caved in two days after it was built. Fortunately, no one was injured in the collapse, and no 502nd MASH member was hit by hostile fire.[36]

The mission, previously limited to caring for UNPROFOR participants, also underwent a metamorphosis. The 212th MASH was only allowed to care for non-UNPROFOR forces or local civilians "in emergency situations to save life, limb, or eyesight."[37] The 502nd MASH, however, began to accept a wider variety of patients. Captain Kevin Galloway stated that whenever patients made it into the EMT, they were accepted automatically into the hospital. Virtually anyone who showed up received care, as the acceptance policy expanded to include children.

Lieutenant B. Baker makes her way to a shower with a smile on her face after a dirty day of sandbagging to reinforce and secure the 502nd MASH hospital tents in Zagreb, Croatia.
Photo courtesy of Army Nurse Corps Archives, Office of Medical History, Falls Church, VA.

This was a difficult challenge because the hospital had no pediatric supplies or equipment and the nurses had limited experience with pediatric patients. Galloway recalled two children as his most memorable patients. A young brother and his sister came from the village of Mostar. The siblings, both Muslim, were victims of sniper fire who first received care in their local hospital where conditions were "bad—minimal drugs, minimal staff, minimal equipment." The hospital in Mostar had amputated the sister's arm without benefit of general anesthesia. The boy had part of his foot amputated as a result of infection. Initially, both children—who spoke hardly any English—were petrified whenever the 502nd

Captain Jacqueline Schulz (left), an unidentified Air Force nurse (center), and Captain Genevieve Grossnickle (right), share information about the hospital and its operation in Zagreb, Croatia, during the week-long staff transfer from the Army's 502nd MASH to the Air Force's 48th Air Transportable Hospital in October 1993.
Photo courtesy of Army Nurse Corps Archives, Office of Medical History, Falls Church, VA.

MASH nurses carried out a simple procedure such as a dressing change. Eventually, however, both adjusted to the Americans, recovered, and returned to their home in Mostar.[38] Captain Jacqueline Schulz recalled a pediatric patient who had memories of having an endotracheal tube placed while fully conscious at her local Yugoslavian hospital. The mere thought evoked painful images. Later, Schulz pondered the brutal, senseless discord in Yugoslavia:

> I just think it's a waste of life. I just see that the cruelty that they inflict upon each other is just unbelievable.... To see the injuries that they [the children] had to suffer for no reason. They were innocent.... And to have them come in with pieces of their body missing, an arm, and shrapnel in their face and scarred for life.... Men should be able to sit down and talk things out.... but I'm here to take care of the injured and the sick. So that's the best I can do.[39]

Schulz' thoughts echoed sentiments expressed by Army nurses in all previous conflicts.

The 502nd MASH redeployed to Germany on 8 October 1993. The Air Force's 48th Air Transportable Hospital, the 48th Medical Group, from Lakenheath, England, took charge of the existing facilities.[40] The two units had a weeklong handover. Lieutenant Scott McDannold recalled that the Air Force nurses spoke of things to change and improvements to make, adding that he "thought it was great, because that's how the process works." McDannold felt that the incoming Air Force nurses "were super, and real impressed" with the set-up. In summary, he "was kind of sad to leave, because it was an interesting mission." The Navy's Fleet Hospital replaced the 48th Air Transportable in March 1994. Fleet Hospital 5 then took over the facility in August 1994, followed by the 60th Medical Group from Travis Air Force Base, California, and later the 74th Medical Group.[41]

Overall, these early deployments illustrated the concept of mission creep. At the outset, the Army narrowly defined the clientele to be supported. As time passed, the parameters of the patient population expanded to include any and all sick or injured persons. The single criterion was that the patient needed medical care. The character of the deployment also evolved. What began ostensibly as a secure, nonhostile mission over time degenerated into service in the line of fire.

Following the redeployment of the 502nd MASH from Zagreb, Croatia, civil unrest smoldered and flared for years in the Balkans. In 1993, a series of protracted peace talks began that culminated in the Dayton Peace Accords, or the General Framework Agreement for Peace, negotiated in Dayton, Ohio, and signed in Paris on 14 December 1995. As 1995 came to a close, Operation Joint Endeavor monitored and enforced the General Framework Agreement for Peace to establish peace and stability in the region.[42] Simultaneously, the North Atlantic Treaty Organization (NATO) imposed a cease-fire and the four-year conflict slowed. The U.N. coalition adopted the Implementation Force and, later, the Stabilization Force as peacekeeping apparatus. The U.S. element of the Implementation Force took the name of Task Force Eagle. Its mission was to enforce the withdrawal of various warring factions to specified locations and to provide a safe and secure setting to ensure peace in the breakaway republics of Yugoslavia and surrounding countries.[43]

Several U.S. Army units provided health service support for Task Force Eagle during its tenure in the former republic of Yugoslavia. Among them were elements of the V Corps' 30th Medical Brigade, the 212th MASH, the 67th CSH, and the 84th Medical Detachment (Combat Stress Control) from Fort Carson, Colorado.[44]

Many of the troops, predominantly 1st Armored Division soldiers bound for Task Force Eagle, staged in Hungary before crossing the border into Bosnia to implement their peacekeeping mission. Task Force Eagle's combat service support elements also deployed to Hungary and set up at Taszar Air Base, an abandoned Russian MIG installation.[45] The 67th CSH from Würzberg was one of the units at Taszar.

Hints of the 67th CSH's imminent mobilization to the Balkans circulated through the corridors of the Würzberg hospital as early as the summer of 1995. The rumors became more plausible when the unit participated in two-week multinational field exercises in September and November 1995. Colonel William T. Bester, chief nurse of both the 67th CSH and the Würzberg hospital, received the

Chief nurse Colonel William Bester (far right) confers with (from left to right) Colonel Homer Wright, commander of the 67th Combat Support Hospital, Command Sergeant Major Craig Dunbar, Command Sergeant Major of the 67th Combat Support Hospital, Lieutenant General John Abrams, the V Corps commander and commander of the deployment, and Major General Jim Wright, commander of the logistical component of the deployment. The group met inside the 67th Combat Support Hospital compound.
Photo courtesy of Brigadier General William Bester, Silver Spring, MD.

unit's alert notification on 11 December 1995, informing him that a contingent from the 67th CSH would deploy the next afternoon. The hospital commander informed Bester that he would serve as the interim hospital and medical task force commander, pending the arrival of the permanently designated commander, Colonel Homer J. Wright.[46] Despite the extremely short notice and the timing of the deployment just before the holiday season, the nurses' response was "nothing short of spectacular."[47]

To maintain quality health services in Würzberg, Heidelberg, and Landstuhl after the 67th CSH left, Health Services Command initially backfilled the institutions with 135 U.S. Army Reserve (USAR) Army Medical Department reservists from the 4005th U.S. Army Hospital based in Houston and Lubbock, Texas; 134 members of the 5502nd U.S. Army Hospital, a USAR hospital unit stationed in Aurora, Colorado; and a smaller number of soldiers from several other USAR units. Their tour of duty extended to 140 days. Several from the first rotation of reservists volunteered to remain in Europe to augment a second 140-day cohort staffed by reservists predominantly from the 88th and 89th Regional Support

Commands variously home-located in the Midwest—Ohio, Michigan, Indiana, Illinois, Wisconsin, Minnesota, and Kansas.[48] A third group of 340 reservists replaced the second cohort, and 81 of the third group subsequently volunteered to extend and serve with the fourth team. The fourth team was 258 soldiers strong. Most of the latest team came from units of the 8th Medical Brigade stationed in New York and New Jersey.[49]

The deploying 67th CSH contingent included 44 Army Nurse Corps officers and 116 enlisted nursing personnel. After their arrival in the Balkans, one Army nurse and four enlisted medics were detailed from the 67th CSH to the Sava River area in early January 1996 to support the 212th MASH Forward Surgical Element operating there.[50]

From Würzberg, the 67th CSH troop began its 42-hour train ride that ended in Taszar on 14 December 1995. They immediately offloaded their equipment and billeted themselves in a derelict Russian barracks that had remained empty for five years. At first, no running water was available, but within a few days, the pipes produced cold water. After a week, hot water was available and the appreciative nurses all had their first showers in two weeks. Bester was billeted on a top bunk in a 12-foot-square room with seven other male soldiers. All meals consisted of T rations and ready-to-eat meals and no alcohol was allowed.[51]

The ban on alcohol was announced in Task Force Eagle General Order No. 1. Most acknowledged that the ban was a wise move that prevented unfavorable incidents, ultimately garnered the respect of other coalition forces, and made the American soldiers "stand taller" than their counterparts from other nations. Regulations that stipulated that the U.S. Army always wear "battle rattle" (Battle Dress Uniforms: waterproof pants and parka, rifle or pistol and ammunition, load-bearing suspenders and belt, two canteens and cup, first aid kit, helmet, boots, wool sweater and gloves in cold weather, and a body armor vest) outside the compound also made the U.S. contingent "stand out as more soldierly." These precautions likely contributed to the low levels of accidents and illness.[52]

Bester joked that the primitive living arrangements were by no means the way he had envisioned his life would be at age 45. The prevailing esprit de corps counterbalanced the primitive conditions. All the nursing personnel pitched in and helped to erect the DEPMEDS. Bester thought that "their morale [was] extremely high & they have provided very strong support systems for each other." He concluded, the "future of the Corps is in very good hands if these folks are an indicator of our young officers & enlisted nursing personnel."

A small helicopter pad was the site of the rudimentary hospital that included one operating room and central material supply, four inpatient beds, and an emergency room. As time passed, the Area Support Group made more land available, and the 67th CSH enlarged its facility to include 52 operating beds, two operating rooms, and various support services such as clinics, pharmacy, labs, and administrative activities.

The patient load was light. The hospital census on the wards ran about 10 to 15 patients daily. The emergency room and clinics combined treated about 50

Major Dan Zimmerman, Family Nurse Practitioner (left), and Colonel William Bester (right) pause for a moment between the front entrance of the 67th Combat Support Hospital and the flightline located in Taszar, Hungary.
Photo courtesy of Brigadier General William Bester, Silver Spring, MD.

patients each day.[53] By July 1996, little had changed. The staff's spirits and their work ethic remained high, while patient activity was low. By then, the 67th CSH had hospitalized a cumulative total of about 450 active duty soldiers. They tallied 8,500 outpatient visits and performed approximately 40 surgical cases.[54] The first rotation from the 67th CSH redeployed to Germany in the summer of 1996.[55]

Elements of the 212th MASH also deployed to the Balkans in 1995 and remained through 1996. As the last standing MASH in the active Army, it supported V Corps in Europe.[56] The unit conducted a number of split base operations in the former Yugoslavia during 1996, including a parachute jump into Slavonski Brod, Croatia. The 212th MASH's final move in 1996 was to set up at Blue Factory situated adjacent to Guardian Base in Tuzla, Bosnia-Herzegovina. Named because of the buildings' blue color, the Blue Factory was formerly a truck stop, and personnel adapted its various rooms for a medical mission. It served as the central location for health service support in Bosnia.[57]

After several months, other hospital units rotated into Guardian Base and operated the facility at Blue Factory. The 21st CSH deployed from Fort Hood, Texas, in November 1996. During its deployment, the unit's deputy commander for nursing, Lieutenant Colonel Gail Ford, made it a personal goal to further develop her

This is the exterior view of the 67th Combat Support Hospital, Taszar Airfield in Hungary in February 1996. The 52-bed hospital performed all the functions of a typical stateside hospital during Operation Joint Endeavor.
Photo by Sargeant Larry Aaron, 55th Signal Company (Combat Camera). Courtesy of Army Nurse Corps Archives, Office of Medical History, Falls Church, VA.

already proficient staff and advance their nursing and soldier skills. She strongly encouraged fitness activities and supported the enhancement of professional knowledge. To boost their versatility, Army nurses cross-trained in various specialties. For instance, one obstetrics/gynecology nurse worked in the emergency room where Major Richard Ricciardi, the unit's head nurse, helped her add valuable new knowledge and skills to her repertoire. Assigned to the intensive care unit, a pediatric nurse acquired critical care nursing expertise under the mentoring of Major Linda Hundley, the unit's head nurse.

The patients cared for at the 21st CSH were a mix of battle wounds such as land mine accidents, shrapnel injuries, or chest wounds, and diseases such as common colds and appendicitis. The average number seen at daily sick call ran between 25 and 30 soldiers. Although the hospital operated 19 beds, only about four or five were filled at any one time. When the unit redeployed to Fort Hood in April 1997, Ricciardi expressed his hope that "we've done something to assist the different factions here to get over their problems and be better off when we leave." Two reserve units, the 405th CSH from West Hartford, Connecticut, and the 324th CSH from Perrine, Florida, assumed the mission after the departure of the 21st CSH.[58]

In October 1997, the 396th CSH, a USAR unit out of Vancouver, Washington,

Major Charles Lutz (left) and Major Richard Ricciardi (right) pause for a moment at the perimeter of the 21st Combat Support Hospital compound. Lutz served as head nurse of the hospital's operating room, while Ricciardi was head nurse of the unit's Emergency Medical Treatment section from November 1996 to April 1997.
Photo courtesy of Colonel Richard Ricciardi, Rockville, MD.

Lieutenant Colonel Gail Ford, chief nurse of the 21st Combat Support Hospital, stretched her legs at a roadside rest stop with part of a convoy that was traveling the road from Tuzla to Sarajevo. A few key personnel made the trip there to coordinate with British Forces who had responsibility for that sector and were headquartered in Sarajevo. Land mines frequently were embedded on the shoulders of the roads making the trip a dangerous endeavor.
Photo courtesy of Colonel Gail Ford, Atlanta, GA.

Lieutenant Colonel Gail Ford, chief nurse of the 21st Combat Support Hospital, poses with a friendly Norwegian Army Medical Major whose unit was co-located on the compound at the Blue Factory just outside Tuzla, Boznia-Herzegovina.
Photo courtesy of Colonel Gail Ford, Atlanta, GA.

Pictured is Colonel Kristine K. Campbell (center) with Brigadier General Pat Anderson (left), Individual Mobilization Augmentee to the chief, Army Nurse Corps, and Brigadier General Donna Barbisch (right), Chief Nurse, 3rd MEDCOM. Anderson and Barbisch met the 396th when it arrived in Atlanta on the way home from its deployment.
Photo courtesy of Brigadier General Kristine K. Campbell, Longview, WA.

took over the mission at the Blue Factory.[59] Colonel Kristine K. Campbell, the 396th CSH's former chief nurse, assumed command of the hospital, becoming the first USAR nurse to command a field hospital overseas in a hazardous duty area. Colonel Sarah Nordquist served as the 396th CSH's chief nurse in this time frame. The unit brought together soldiers from many different locations and institutions in the northwestern United States. The 396th CSH claimed a number of distinctions and strengths such as "a lot of different ideas and ways of doing things," including many soldiers "with relatively low rank [who had] 20–25 years of experience in their field" and contributed "a richness of experience and knowledge base" to the Bosnia mission.[60] From April to October 1998, elements of the 67th CSH again deployed to Bosnia to support Task Force Eagle. With Lieutenant Colonel Barbara Bruno as chief nurse, it too set up operations in Blue Factory.[61]

Other hospital units rotated through Tuzla, including the 41st CSH based at Fort Sam Houston, Texas, and the 10th CSH garrisoned at Fort Carson, Colorado. All functioned in a semipermanent wooden-framed structure surrounded by TEMPERs (soft-sided DEPMEDS structures), MILVANs (containers for overseas or ground movement of military cargo), and ISOs (hard-walled DEPMEDS structures). This camp was located 20 minutes from downtown Tuzla, tucked between

Pictured is Colonel Kristine K. Campbell (left) with Captain Shawnda Zuegner (right), Company Commander with 261st Medical Battalion in Bosnia.
Photo courtesy of Brigadier General Kristine K. Campbell, Longview, WA.

the air base and helipad and the main thoroughfare into Eagle Base.[62]

A contingent of the 21st CSH deployed again from Fort Hood, Texas, to Bosnia and staffed the hospital facility during the first months of 2000. The 21st CSH staff thought their interactions with military nurses from coalition countries were some of their most memorable experiences in Bosnia. Five U.S. Army nurses spent time at Camp Oden, the Swedish camp, where they discovered that the military nurses from Sweden had significant autonomy in their practice. For example, in emergency situations these professionals were authorized to administer drugs such as atropine, valium, and morphine without physician oversight. The Swedish nurses also ran their soldiers' sick call. They were members of a rescue-evacuation team that operated out of a Finnish Armored Personnel Carrier transformed into an ambulance and also served with an Explosive Ordnance Disposal team, available to provide emergency care when team members were injured. The Army Nurse Corps officers of the 21st CSH also visited the Russian hospital situated nearby in Uglivik and the local Bosnian hospital, the Univerzitetski Klinicki Centar, in Tuzla. They benefited professionally and personally "from many of the unique learning experiences available" and concluded that their part of the multinational involvement contributed to the country's evolution and stability.[63]

Likewise in 2000, the 115th Field Hospital (FH) deployed from Fort Polk, Louisiana, and operated its 20-bed (expandable to 40) hospital on Eagle Base in support of a National Guard division from Texas, the 49th Armored Division. Major (P) James Larabee led the hospital's staff of 10 Army Nurse Corps officers.[64] The nurses' goals were to provide patient care and to develop and sustain a sound educational system. To develop the staff's field nursing skills, classes convened on a variety of subjects from Combat Life Saver to trauma nursing courses. Military training involved collaborating with NATO counterparts using their equipment—for example, a Danish armored ambulance and a British CH-47 Chinook helicopter. Several Army nurses became members of the Forward Area Medical Team and helped to extricate patients with air ambulance assets using a Sked litter and a jungle penetrator after being lowered from a hovering UH-60 Black Hawk helicopter on an extraction hoist.[65] Lieutenant B. Eli Seeley found that "during daylight, this task is educational," but at night using night vision goggles, "the word extraction takes on a whole new meaning." The 115th FH nurses also availed themselves of educational ventures and recreational excursions that provided a window into the surrounding ancient eastern European culture. They visited other U.S. camps, NATO installations, centuries-old castles, local hospitals, and schools.

Having pondered his deployment to the Balkans, Seeley wrote about his experience:

> Deploying with the United States Army is challenging and rewarding at the same time. It represents what makes an Army Nurse Corps officer's job different and unique from their civilian counterparts. Besides having to leave loved ones stateside, this deployment represents the times that these officers will remember most fondly about their career with the military.[66]

As 2000 came to a close, the 44th Medical Brigade, headquartered at Fort Bragg, North Carolina, assumed responsibility for five sequential six-month deployments in support of Task Force Med Eagle in Bosnia-Herzegovina. These rotations covered the mission from September 2000 through March 2003. The first 44th Medical Brigade unit to fulfill this requirement was the 249th General Hospital (GH) from Fort Gordon, Georgia.

Extensive preparations preceded the 249th GH's deployment and focused on the U.S. Army Europe, NATO, and U.S. Army predeployment requirements. Personnel, including 10 nurses, began their training in July and August 2000 with three days of instruction focused on Common Task Training, equipment issue, and mission briefs; and sessions on MEDEVAC procedures, the Law of Land Warfare, antiterrorism measures, and security. Individual Readiness Training then followed during the hot summer Georgia days.[67] Lectures and briefings highlighted the Balkans' culture and turbulent history, Rules of Engagement, force protection, land mine awareness, convoy operations, environmental hazards, and media interactions. The second day of training involved practical field exercises in full "battle rattle." Next came a Mission Rehearsal Exercise at Fort Polk, Louisiana where briefings informed the deploying soldiers about the multinational chain of command, quality of life, personnel and finance subjects, geography, and the meteorological and political climate.

Once the 249th GH arrived in Bosnia, the turnover from the 115th FH to the

249th GH commenced. The Balkan Theater of Operations policy was to implement "an intentional, two-week overlap, . . . the 'Right Seat/Left Seat Ride'," as it was called. At first, the incoming unit occupied the right seat of the car, observing their predecessors in action and receiving an orientation to their new environment. A mass casualty exercise demonstration occurred during the right seat ride portion of the changeover. During the subsequent left seat ride, the 249th GH, the incoming unit, sat in the driver's seat and took control of the facility with the 115th FH, the departing unit, watching and advising.[68] After the transfer of authority, the 115th Field Hospital then redeployed to its home station.

In December 1995 Major Kathryn Gaylord, a psychiatric clinical nurse specialist, deployed from Fort Carson, Colorado, to Bosnia-Herzegovina. Her unit, the 84th Medical Detachment (Combat Stress Control), was a combat stress control detachment. As Officer in Charge of the Combat Stress Control's Restoration Unit, Gaylord operated out of an abandoned oil refinery at Kukavac, Bosnia. The Restoration Unit's mission was to treat combat stress according to the "four Rs"—rest, restore physiologic status, reassurance of normalcy, and expect a return to duty.

The Restoration Unit team consisted of the Officer in Charge, an occupational therapist, a wardmaster, a ward clerk, and five behavioral science specialists, psychiatric technicians, or occupational therapy aides. As Officer in Charge, Gaylord oversaw general operations, staffed the unit, scheduled its personnel, and provided direct clinical services for soldiers in her caseload. She also collaborated with psychiatrists to ensure that soldiers admitted to the unit received the best care.[69] The occupational therapist developed and administered the stress program. The wardmaster and ward clerk dealt with day-to-day details to ensure that the unit ran smoothly. The five enlisted staff provided direct one-on-one clinical support to soldiers participating in the program.

The Restoration Unit admitted most soldiers for three to seven days, with the average stay being six days. Over its yearlong deployment, the unit treated 123 soldiers with battle fatigue, and 105 (85 percent) soldiers successfully returned to duty.[70] In fostering adaptation to combat stress, the services offered by the Restoration Unit made a major contribution to the success of the Task Force Eagle mission.

The deployment to the Balkans was not a benign process for those who participated. All the phases—predeployment, deployment, sustainment, redeployment, and postdeployment—were highly stressful. Every day traumatic experiences in the combat zone confirmed the long-ago learned lesson on the importance of stress management.[71]

After the successful September 1996 elections in Bosnia and the completion of the Implementation Force mission, the United Nations reduced its military presence to consolidate and stabilize the peace.[72] This signaled the conclusion of Operation Joint Endeavor and the beginning of Operation Joint Guard, a Support and Stability Operation.

With the new U.N. mission, peace still proved to be an elusive goal in the Balkans. The 1st Infantry Division, the Big Red One, which relieved the 1st Armored Division, was called on frequently to intervene and control altercations between the still warring factions.⁷³ Conditions deteriorated into 1999. Military forces from the Federal Republic of Yugoslavia and the Kosovo Liberation Army constantly clashed as ethnic tensions claimed many lives and created about a million civilian refugees. U.N. Security Council Resolution 1244 then authorized the formation of the Kosovo Force, which entered the former republic of Yugoslavia on 12 June 1999 in yet another effort to establish and maintain peace in Kosovo, but the U.N. effort proved largely unsuccessful.⁷⁴ In the interim, however, Task Force Hawk and Task Force Falcon were implemented to bring stability to the Balkans.

In April 1999, a Contingency Medical Force (CMF) drawn from the 212th MASH deployed to support Task Force Hawk at Tirana-Rinas Airport in Albania.⁷⁵ With a 72-hour evacuation policy, this MASH slice provided surgical resuscitation and hospitalization for approximately 5,000 U.S. forces that had deployed to Albania to stage 24 AH-64 Apache helicopters and operate several Multiple Launch Rocket System batteries for deep strike operations into Kosovo.⁷⁶ Lieutenant Colonel Suzan Denny served as chief nurse and executive officer of this mission with a staff of three operating room nurses, three anesthetists, and four critical care nurses.⁷⁷ The 212th CMF remained in Albania until June 1999.⁷⁸ During their 67 days in country, the unit was extremely busy and had many "wild adventures":

> We met the challenges of a base camp [erected on an unstable foundation of mud and sand dunes], found ways to make a home wherever the Kevlar went, and found new friends in an austere, humble but comfortable environment. We had some incredible trauma patients . . . had the "Appy" of the week club, and performed some awesome repairs for lacerations and fractures. We responded magnificently to a mass casualty situation—12 patients from a C130 crash. . . . We didn't have a single death at Task Force Hawk, an amazing feat considering two forklift rollovers down a ravine and heavy equipment moving around soldiers on the ground in the dark. We learned a lot about ourselves, our capabilities, our training requirements and the military, and we got to watch great leaders and great people make things happen all around.⁷⁹

In June 1999, the 212th CMF moved to Camp Able Sentry in Macedonia in support of another mission, Task Force Falcon.⁸⁰

On 3 April 1999, the 67th Forward Surgical Team (FST), an element of the 67th CSH, deployed from Würzburg into Camp Able Sentry, Macedonia, along the Serbian border to support Task Force Falcon. The FST later moved 30 miles forward to Camp Bondsteel near Urosevac, Kosovo, on 16 June 1999, and set up its facility in eight hours. The staff accepted their first patient, a mine blast casualty, only 24 hours later. The 67th FST was the only unit providing resuscitative surgery for the entire month and served as interim medical support until the 67th CSH (Forward) arrived in the country in July 1999. The 67th FST redeployed in July 1999.⁸¹

On 10 July 1999, the 67th CMF deployed from Germany to Kosovo to support Task Force Falcon. With Colonel Russell Taylor, an Army Nurse Corps officer, as commander and Major Jimmie O. Keenan as chief nurse, the unit set up on a wheat field at Camp Bondsteel, in Kosovo.⁸² One day after their arrival, the staff erected their 32-bed (expandable to 52 beds) hospital and on 14 July 1999, just a few hours after opening, admitted its first two patients, both victims of gunshot wounds. The 67th CSH initially resuscitated both, who also received interim treatment from the 212th MASH before being transferred to the 67th CMF.

From the outset, the 11-strong nursing staff of the 67th CMF was unexpectedly inundated with victims of trauma.[83] On their second day of operations, for instance, a visit by the chairman of the Joint Chiefs of Staff, General Henry Shelton, coincided with the arrival of five casualties from a grenade blast. Keenan explained, "General Shelton got to see us in action! He even offered to start an IV!" The majority of patients treated were local nationals and most involved complex trauma cases whose wounds resulted from high- and low-velocity weapons, artillery, mortars, grenades, unexploded ordnance, beatings, or stabbings. The 67th CMF treated 56 trauma patients during its first month of operation.[84] After several months of an almost constant surgical workload, however, the small operating room staff was nearing total exhaustion, often operating for 20 hours a day. With grave concern for their welfare, Taylor planned the rotation of an entire surgical team (surgeons, anesthetists, operating room nurses, and technicians) in from Europe for a week to give those in Kosovo some respite. The plan never came to fruition, however, because after about 45 days, the volume of trauma and likewise the volume of surgical procedures gradually decreased.[85]

The staff of the 67th CMF developed an exit strategy consisting of two goals to ease their departure from Kosovo. The first goal was to assist two civilian hospitals in the area to rebuild and eventually assume the health care responsibilities formerly carried out by the 67th CMF. The second goal, a humanitarian mission, was to adopt a local school. All the nearby institutions were in ruins. Most had no electricity, running water, windows, sewer systems, or furniture. Graffiti and filth abounded. To correct these deficiencies, the staff partnered with nongovernmental organizations, the hospitals' staff, and the school's teachers, parents, and pupils to fix the facilities.[86]

At the Ferizaj Hospital in Kosovo, for instance, the mission was to return the hospital "to pre-war standards, so they can eventually assume the health care of their own population." Teams from the 67th CMF rewired the hospital's electrical system and renovated the emergency room. They installed two washing machines in the hospital basement. In the operating suite, they mounted lighting and accessories and set up anesthesia apparatus, EKG machines, a portable x-ray, a sterilizer, and three infusion pumps.[87]

In the sponsored school, the soldiers and students, teachers, and parents painted, cleaned, swept, repaired, and fabricated. The teams' efforts contributed to reopening the building and regenerating its equipment, and soon students were able to return to their lessons. Soldiers and locals with carpentry skills also built swing sets on the school grounds, a first in the memories of Kosovars. The swings were suspended with nylon ropes but were so popular and so heavily used that chains had to be installed to replace the worn nylon ropes. It was not unusual for 60 to 70 children to form a line to wait to use the playground equipment. The idea was so successful that the nongovernmental organization installed nine swing sets on the grounds of various Kosovar schools. The task force also set up a basketball hoop, and the soldiers taught the children the basics of the game.[88]

The involvement with local nationals generated many positive effects. The example of the racial and ethnic blending of a diversity of U.S. soldiers—blacks, whites, Hispanics, Asians, Hindus, and Muslims—all working peacefully together toward a common goal served as a model of nonviolent collaboration for the Serbs and Albanians. The volunteer efforts also affected the soldiers. Although most worked 80-hour weeks at their 67th CMF workstation, the majority spent all their free time striving to improve the lot of local nationals. The involvement provided them with a distraction and gave them an enhanced sense of accomplishment.[89] It also kept them upbeat and vigilant. Taylor acknowledged the reality:

> The biggest challenge that any leader has in this kind of environment is fighting complacency. Even when the soldiers are busy, injuries and deaths . . . happen when a soldier loses his focus. . . . And it's dangerous when the mind drifts, when you start taking shortcuts, when you start thinking about home. . . . Most of the injuries and some of the deaths that we had were caused because soldiers lost their focus, sometimes for just a moment. . . . And my biggest challenge was not having my soldiers hurt for that reason.[90]

During their deployment, the 67th CMF became convinced that honing combat nursing skills was imperative. Keenan encouraged all nurses to participate in the Combat Trauma Nurse, Advanced Cardiac Life Support, Basic Cardiac Life Support, and Pediatric Advanced Life Support courses before future deployments. Similarly, the nurses ascertained the importance of teamwork and cross-training so that all nursing staff were capable of working in any section of the hospital whenever circumstances dictated. The attribute of adaptability—so imperative in field nursing—stood in sharp contrast to the emphasis on specialization so prevalent in peacetime settings. To shift from being a specialist to a generalist and learn new skills required flexibility, energy, focus, and a sense of commitment.

The staff also understood the necessity of dealing appropriately with the media and other official delegations, discovering quickly "that anything you say can later be quoted out of context!" To prevent embarrassment, they printed PowerPoint slides to highlight their capabilities and prominently displayed the information by the entrance to every section. They encouraged all staff to improve their public speaking skills and better interact with the media. The first iteration of the 67th CMF redeployed completely to Germany by December 1999 but before their departure they provided a right seat ride for their replacements, the second rotation of the 67th CSH.[91]

The second element to man the facility at Camp Bondsteel, Kosovo, Task Force Med Falcon 1B, consisted of 12 Army Nurse Corps officers who staffed a new CMF from the 67th CSH in Würzburg from December 1999 to March 2000. Major Shelley A. Rice served as chief nurse.[92] The 160th FST and later the 250th FST augmented the task force.

In September 1999, the 160th FST activated at Landstuhl, Germany, as an element of the 212th MASH. With Major Rebecca Yurek as chief nurse, the team participated in the Combined Maneuver Training Center exercise Maroon Forge in October 1999. This exercise identified equipment and supply deficiencies that

In the summer of 1999, all soldiers of the 212th MASH pitched in to erect their TEMPER tents after their move from Albania to Macedonia.
Photo courtesy of Major Teresa Duquette-Frame, Bowie, MD.

were subsequently corrected.

In December 1999, the unit deployed to Camp Able Sentry, Macedonia. Throughout the winter, the 160th FST provided a surgical capability for the staging base located there and fielded a DEPMEDS slice or section that included an ISO (hard-walled DEPMEDS structure) operating room suite and a four-section TEMPER for immediate pre- and post-operative care. The 250th FST, a Forces Command unit, replaced the 160th FST in February 2000 and remained in Macedonia until 1 August 2000.[93] At that time, the U.S. Army, Europe commander agreed that an immediate replacement FST need not be waiting in the wings because all concurred that the FST's participation was only imperative from October through March when the winter weather precluded easy evacuation.[94]

The 160th FST handled surgical cases in Macedonia, and the second iteration of the 67th CMF treated similar cases in Kosovo.[95] During their rotation, the latter dealt with approximately 24 to 35 trauma cases per month. The 67th CMF also began a Gnjilane Hospital support program, offering training and assistance in nursing topics and general and orthopedic surgery and staffing Medical Civilian Assistant Program outreach operations. It concluded its tour of duty with an eight-day Right Seat/Left Seat Ride program. The second iteration of the 67th CMF redeployment to Germany was completed by 2 April 2000.[96]

Captain Teresa Duquette (left) and Lieutenant Amy Weston (right), 212th MASH operations officers, rest after their strenuous efforts setting up the unit in Macedonia.
Photo courtesy of Major Teresa Duquette-Frame, Bowie, MD.

During the summer of 1999, the element of the 212th MASH supporting Task Force Hawk in Tirana, Albania, shifted its mission and moved to Camp Able Sentry in Skopje, Macedonia, to support Task Force Falcon. Within 48 hours, Captain Carla Buckles wrote, the 212th MASH was "locked and loaded for movement." The journey from Albania, to Macedonia, however, turned into quite an adventure. Originally projected to take 15 hours, the lengthy convoy of military vehicles and civilian buses took almost 24 hours, traveling an average speed of five miles per hour to its destination. In Albania a five-ton truck "failed to make it up a last hill," so in the Albanian mountains overlooking Lake Ohrid, the troops spent the night camping out and yes, as Captain Kimberly Crossland shared, it rained. Three more vehicle breakdowns ensued, involving an overheated truck, a broken bus axle, and a flat tire on another bus. According to Captain Terry Duquette, "perseverance prevailed, the obstacles were overcome and we rolled into Camp Able Sentry 23 hours later." Captain Javier Altamirano was "proud to have been part of this convoy . . . and will always cherish these memories."[97]

Within six hours after the pallets were offloaded, the unit had set up its facility.

Captain Teresa Duquette, head nurse of the Emergency Medical Treatment section of the 212th MASH's Crisis Medical Force, halts briefly in front of her duty section.
Photo courtesy of Major Teresa Duquette-Frame, Bowie, MD.

Major Karen Morris saw that "practice makes perfect . . . that was truly evident as we set up the hospital the second time around." Everyone was "now an expert on TEMPER and we are experimenting with new and innovative ways to internalize and operate in our sections." Anesthetist Captain Paul Barras also was experimenting with new equipment, an anesthesia machine, the Narkomed M supplied courtesy of the 30th Medical Brigade in Germany. The state-of-the-art equipment soon found good use, as Captain Sarah J. Krajnik wrote, because two trauma patients with gunshot wounds arrived at the MASH facility within 12 hours of its arrival in Macedonia. The whole deployment was challenging but the nurses coped. Captain Mike Rizzo recounted the lessons learned from the 212th MASH CMF deployment. He advised, "Laugh . . . it is better than the alternative," and warned, "Take little (if nothing) for granted, it can only add to your happiness."[98]

A right seat ride with the 67th CMF 1B team took place almost immediately. Then the 212th MASH CMF was ready to assume the mission.[99] The unit's workload remained challenging, and in the unit's first 30 days of operation, it treated 46 cases of trauma and 19 major medical patients.[100] When not caring for these complex cases, however, the Army nurses upgraded the skills of the nurses at the local Gnjilane Hospital. Denny worked with local officials to identify deficiencies and coordinated with her staff to create and present appropriate instruction. Captain Diana Deschamps, the CMF's Intermediate Care Ward head nurse, collaborated with the local nurses to devise a curriculum, brief the interpreters, and prepare the Army nurses who would teach the courses. They taught classes on life support, trauma care, basic nursing skills, and aseptic technique to about 30 local nursing staff. The American nurses also taught local national patients a variety of skills such as wound care and home nursing techniques. All these efforts contributed to the rehabilitation of the country's medical infrastructure.[101]

The 212th CMF staff also found time to improve and refine the DEPMEDS set-up. Changes included the addition of "isolation rooms and private ER exam rooms (plywood cubicles with air vents [for] proper air movement), and flush toilets!" Denny recalled:

> There were a lot of great patient care stories/challenges, from newborns left to die in the cold and successfully resuscitated and later adopted despite few of the facilities being prepared to deal with infants and pediatric cases. [The hospital admitted] a 2 yr old with necrotizing fasciitis [that involved] ICU care, daily debridement, starting TPN [total parenteral nutrition] that was urgently obtained thru the evac system in Germany, . . . [They also treated] an 8 yr old with several GSW (most severe shot blew out her humerous [sic]), requiring bone grafts and internal fixators that [were] obtained from a Germany field hospital. . . . Her arm maintained almost full return of function. The challenges of nursing in an austere field environment [were] amazing.

Denny added that during this rotation, the 212th CMF utilized the cutting-edge Life Support for Trauma and Transport system, an Intensive Care Unit litter that allowed for safer patient movement, for the first time.[102]

On 28 April 2000, replacements, also from the 212th MASH, incrementally took over while the original 212th staff members returned to Germany. Although the staff changed and equipment was upgraded, the daily quota of trauma patients remained constant. Between 28 April and 28 September 2000, the new staff cared for more than 339 trauma and major medical patients at their new location at Camp Bondsteel. Patients included mostly local nationals critically wounded by bullets, grenades, cluster bombs, knives, or motor vehicle accidents. Denny explained the excessive numbers of automobile accidents resulted because the "local nationals . . . pile as many people as will fit into tiny, old cars without seatbelts," then, "drive fast down crater-filled roads without shoulders." Head-on collisions and rollovers resulted.[103]

A major change occurred at Camp Bondsteel when the 212th CMF transferred its authority on 25 September 2000 and both USAR personnel from the continental United States and active component soldiers from 30th Medical Brigade in Europe took over. The largest element of this rotation was 85 soldiers from the 313th Hospital Unit Surgical who deployed from Springfield, Missouri.[104] The total numbers deployed varied but they included about 160 USAR and 75 active soldiers at the time of final redeployment on 2 April 2001. Most of the USAR personnel served for a three-month period during one of three 90-day iterations.[105]

During its tenure in Camp Bondsteel, this rotation operated 26 beds (expandable to 52) and treated more than 310 patients. It performed 120 emergency surgeries and managed 104 trauma patients. The staff continued to develop and assist the local health care system, offering education, consultation, and surgical assistance to the hospital in Gnjilane, and nurses actively participated in these outreach activities.[106] Major Stella Demster, a medical-surgical nurse from the Intermediate Care Ward, taught maternal child nursing classes at the Gnjilane hospital along with the Finnish Red Cross nurses. She was impressed by the staff's spirited enthusiasm in spite of the facility's lack of equipment and abysmal state of repair.[107]

The experiences of Army Nurse Corps officers who served in the Balkans bore predictable similarities to previous operations. Those who deployed to the former republic of Yugoslavia, particularly during the early rotations, lived and worked in exacting conditions and provided high-quality care for significant numbers of casualties suffering massive trauma. The operational setting in the Balkans was very demanding and rife with danger, threats, multinational bureaucratic snarls, and bitter weather. The traditional implementation of field expediency skills and the willingness to make substantial personal sacrifices to provide health care for the deployed U.S. soldiers typified the nurses' contributions.

Participation in the Balkan operations enabled Army Nurse Corps officers to excel in new branch immaterial roles and command slots. They played an active part in personnel, equipment, and doctrinal planning and development for deployments, and their impact exceeded the traditional boundaries of nursing. Their multinational patient population presented communication and cultural challenges on a daily basis. The operations in the Balkans were a blend of war and Operations Other Than War, with components of nation building, humanitarian assistance, and Support and Stability Operations. Through it all, the old and the new, the good and the bad, the easy and the difficult, the Army Nurse Corps officers' esprit de corps remained high and their contributions significant.

# Notes

1. Robin Alison Remington, "Bosnia: The Tangled Web," *Current History* 92 (November 1993): 364–69. "Ethnic Conflicts Produce Tragedy in Bosnia," *HSC Mercury* (May 1993): 6. "Morass of Ethnic Conflict Haunts Balkans," *The Mercury* 23 (December 1995): 7. "History of BiH," 4 April 2003, http://www.tfeagle.army.mil/TFE/bosnia_history.htm (accessed 22 April 2005).

2. The six republics were Bosnia and Herzegovina, Croatia, Macedonia, Montenegro, Serbia, and Slovenia, while the two provinces were Kosovo and Vojvodina. Glenn E. Curtis, *Yugoslavia: A Country Study*, DA Pamphlet 550-99 (Washington, DC: Department of the Army, 1992), iii.

3. Glenn E. Curtis, *Yugoslavia: A Country Study*, DA Pamphlet 550-99 (Washington, DC: Department of the Army, 1992). Charles Krauthammer, "Drawing the Line at Genocide," *Washington Post* (11 December 1992): 9–10. "Morass of Ethnic Conflict Haunts Balkans," *The Mercury* 23 (December 1995): 7.

4. Charles Kirkpatrick, "Operation PROVIDE PROMISE," Printed Manuscript, 1–3, n.d., Army Nurse Corps Collection (ANCC), Office of Medical History (OMH). Stephen L.Y. Gammons and William M. Donnelly, *Department of the Army Historical Summary, Fiscal Year 1995* (Washington, DC: Center of Military History, United States Army, 2004), 48.

5. At the time, V Corps headquarters was located in the C.W. Abrams building (formerly the I.G. Farben building) in Frankfurt am Main. In 1994, V Corps moved to Campbell Barracks, Heidelberg. http://www.vcorps.army.mil/ (accessed 22 September 2005).

6. When local units closed, the active duty and family member patient base disappeared. Charles Kirkpatrick, "Operation PROVIDE PROMISE," Printed Manuscript, 3, 13, 27, 29, n.d., OMH. Retirees living in the communities presumably then obtained care from local German providers or traveled to the nearest U.S. health care facility.

7. When the 68th Medical Group commander, Colonel Greg Stevens, deployed to Zagreb, Croatia, in November 1992, Lieutenant Colonel Holly Buchanan, an Army Nurse Corps officer, assumed command of the unit in garrison at Wiesbaden AFB. Holly K. Buchanan, "Annual Historical Report," 25 October 1993, ANCC, OMH. Buchanan "ran a hard-working family-support group." Harry Noyes, "U.S. Medics Serve U.N. in Croatia," *HSC Mercury* (August 1993): 9.

8. Charles Kirkpatrick, "Operation PROVIDE PROMISE," Printed Manuscript, 3, 12,

n.d., OMH. Bobbie H. Henley, Interview by Iris J. West, Transcript, 2, 11 February 1994; Nelda Barnhill, Interview by Iris J. West, Transcript, 2–4, 5–6, 11 February 1994; and Jerry L. Green, Interview by Iris J. West, Transcript, 3, 8 February 1994 (all in Army Nurse Corps Oral History Collection [ANCOHC], OMH).

9. Charles Kirkpatrick, "Operation PROVIDE PROMISE," Printed Manuscript, 18, 24, n.d., OMH. Terris E. Kennedy, "After Action Report Staff Visit 212th MASH," Printed Document, 21 December 1992, ANCC, OMH. Chuck Sudetic, "A MASH with a Difference Is Set Up in Croatia," *New York Times* (16 November 1992): 5. "U.S. Hospital in Croatia Treats U.N. Soldiers," *Stars and Stripes* (18 November 1992): 2. Nelda Barnhill, Interview by Iris J. West, Transcript, 3–5, 11 February 1994; and Jerry L. Green, Interview by Iris J. West, Transcript, 5, 7, 8, 15, 19, 25, 8 February 1994 (both in ANCOHC, OMH). "U.S. Army Opening Tent Hospital in Croatia," *Washington Post* (14 November 1992): A19. Paul R. Erlich, "212th MASH After Action Review—Operation Provide Promise, Zagreb, Croatia," Memorandum, 2 June 1993, ANCC, OMH. Harry Noyes, "U.S. Medics Serve U.N. in Croatia," *HSC Mercury* (August 1993): 9.

10. Some of the United Nations countries participating in the operation were the Netherlands, Finland, Sweden, Norway, Canada, Australia, France, Britain, Argentina, Egypt, Jordan, Nepal, Pakistan, Kenya, Poland, Russia, Ukraine, and Slovak Republic, all with diverse cultures and/or languages. Lois M. Davis and others, "Army Medical Support for Peace Operations and Humanitarian Assistance," 1996, http://www.rand.org/publications/MR/MR773/ (accessed 6 July 2004).

11. Terris E. Kennedy, "After Action Report Staff Visit 212th MASH," Printed Document, 21 December 1992, ANCC, OMH. Bobbie H. Henley, Interview by Iris J. West, Transcript, 8, 11, 11 February 1994; Nelda Barnhill, Interview by Iris J. West, Transcript, 23, 11 February 1994; and Jerry L. Green, Interview by Iris J. West, Transcript, 26, 58–59, 8 February 1994 (all in ANCOHC, OMH). Paul R. Erlich, "212th MASH After Action Review—Operation Provide Promise, Zagreb, Croatia," Memorandum, 2 June 1993, ANCC, OMH.

12. Nelda Barnhill, Interview by Iris J. West, Transcript, 24–25, 11 February 1994, ANCOHC, OMH.

13. Ibid., 69–70.

14. Bobbie H. Henley, Interview by Iris J. West, Transcript, 4, 11 February 1994, ANCOHC, OMH.

15. Nelda Barnhill, Interview by Iris J. West, Transcript, 6, 11 February 1994; and Jerry L. Green, Interview by Iris J. West, Transcript, 35–36, 8 February 1994 (both in ANCOHC, OMH). Barbara F. Eller, "Trip Report: Visit to 212th MASH, Zagreb, Croatia, 27 March–3 April 1993," 1, 5 April 1993, ANCC, OMH.

16. Jerry L. Green, Interview by Iris J. West, Transcript, 29, 59–60, 8 February 1994, ANCOHC, OMH. Barbara F. Eller, "Trip Report: Visit to 212th MASH, Zagrev, Croatia, 27 March–3 April 1993," 1, 5 April 1993, ANCC, OMH.

17. Some of the Army nurses volunteered to remain for the full 179-day tour so that new mothers with infants, recently married soldiers, or those with very young children could return home. Second Lieutenant Jerry Green was one such selfless volunteer. Jerry L. Green, Interview by Iris J. West, Transcript, 73–74, 8 February 1994, ANCOHC, OMH.

18. Lois M. Davis and others, "Army Medical Support for Peace Operations and Humanitarian Assistance," 1996, http://www.rand.org/publications/MR/MR773/ (accessed 6 July 2004). Paul R. Erlich, "212th MASH After Action Review—Operation Provide Promise, Zagreb, Croatia," Memorandum, 2 June 1993, ANCC, OMH. Harry Noyes, "U.S. Medics Serve U.N. in Croatia," *HSC Mercury* (August 1993): 9.

19. Nelda Barnhill, Interview by Iris J. West, Transcript, 19, 11 February 1994; and Jerry L. Green, Interview by Iris J. West, Transcript, 54, 8 February 1994 (both in ANCOHC, OMH).

20. Nelda Barnhill, Interview by Iris J. West, Transcript, 20–21, 11 February 1994, ANCOHC, OMH.

21. Ibid., 19.

22. Ibid., 52.

23. Ibid., 56–57.

24. Ibid., 20.

25. Ibid., 22.

26. Charles Kirkpatrick, "Operation PROVIDE PROMISE," Printed Manuscript, 28–29, n.d., OMH. Jerry L. Green, Interview by Iris J. West, Transcript, 73, 8 February 1994, ANCOHC, OMH.

27. Lois M. Davis and others, "Army Medical Support for Peace Operations and Humanitarian Assistance," 1996, http://www.rand.org/publications/MR/MR773/ (accessed 6 July 2004). Paul R. Erlich, "212th MASH After Action Review—Operation Provide Promise, Zagreb, Croatia," Memorandum, 2 June 1993, ANCC, OMH. Harry Noyes, "U.S. Medics Serve U.N. in Croatia," *HSC Mercury* (August 1993): 9.

28. Paul R. Erlich, "212th MASH After Action Review—Operation Provide Promise, Zagreb, Croatia," Memorandum, 2 June 1993, ANCC, OMH.

29. Lois M. Davis and others, "Army Medical Support for Peace Operations and Humanitarian Assistance," 1996, http://www.rand.org/publications/MR/MR773/ (accessed 6 July 2004). Jacqueline J. Schulz, Interview by Iris J. West, Transcript, 3, 11 February 1994, ANCOHC, OMH. Major Stroud and Major Vance, "Replacement of the 502d MASH at Zagreb," Operations Support Directorate, April 1993; and Major Heintz, "Medical Support to Operation Provide Promise and Able Sentry," Information Paper, 24 August 1993 (both in ANCC, OMH).

30. Charles Kirkpatrick, "Operation PROVIDE PROMISE," Printed Manuscript, 30, n.d., ANCC, OMH. Lois M. Davis and others, "Army Medical Support for Peace Operations and Humanitarian Assistance," 1996, http://www.rand.org/publications/MR/MR773/ (accessed 6 July 2004).

31. Lois M. Davis and others, "Army Medical Support for Peace Operations and Humanitarian Assistance," 1996, http://www.rand.org/publications/MR/MR773/ (accessed 6 July 2004). Jacqueline J. Schulz, Interview by Iris J. West, Transcript, 5–6, 11 February 1994, ANCOHC, OMH.

32. Charles Kirkpatrick, "Operation PROVIDE PROMISE," Printed Manuscript, 29–30, n.d., ANCC, OMH.

33. Kevin T. Galloway and Scott McDannold, Interview by Iris J. West, Transcript, 14, 15, 9 February 1994; and Jacqueline J. Schulz, Interview by Iris J. West, Transcript, 8, 11 February 1994 (both in ANCOHC, OMH).

34. Marybeth Arenz, "High-tech System Helps MASH Doctors in Croatia," *MEDCOM Examiner* 22 (July 1993): 1, 8. Kevin T. Galloway and Scott McDannold, Interview by Iris J. West, Transcript, 75–76, 9 February 1994, ANCOHC, OMH. The Army passed the RCCS on to the Air Force when the 502nd MASH redeployed to Germany. Colonel Jones, "Remote Clinical Consultation [["Communications" above]] System (RCCS)," Operations Support Directorate, September 1993, ANCC, OMH.

35. Steve Vogel, "U.S. Forces Ready for Possible Shelling of Zagreb Airport," *Army Times* (11 October 1993): 12.

36. Kevin T. Galloway and Scott McDannold, Interview by Iris J. West, Transcript, 51–

52, 57–58, 9 February 1994; and Jacqueline J. Schulz, Interview by Iris J. West, Transcript, 23, 11 February 1994 (both in ANCOHC, OMH).

37. Charles Kirkpatrick, "Operation PROVIDE PROMISE," Printed Manuscript, 104, n.d., ANCC, OMH.

38. Kevin T. Galloway and Scott McDannold, Interview by Iris J. West, Transcript, 8–9, 18–23, 9 February 1994, ANCOHC, OMH. Todd Gavin, "Injured Bosnian Children Find Refuge at MASH," *HSC Mercury* 21 (December 1993): 1.

39. Jacqueline J. Schulz, Interview by Iris J. West, Transcript, 24–25, 32–33, 11 February 1994, ANCOHC, OMH.

40. Major Heintz, "Provide Promise," Executive Summary, 10 September 1993; Major Heintz, "Provide Promise," Executive Summary, 13 September 1993; and Major Heintz, "Medical Support to Operation Provide Promise and Able Sentry," Information Paper, 24 August 1993 (all in ANCC, OMH). Mary C. Smolenski, Donald G. Smith, and James S. Nanney, *A Fit, Fighting Force, The Air Force Nursing Services Chronology* (Washington, DC: Office of the Air Force Surgeon General, 2005), 48.

41. Lois M. Davis and others, "Army Medical Support for Peace Operations and Humanitarian Assistance," 1996, http://www.rand.org/publications/MR/MR773/ (accessed 6 July 2004). Jacqueline J. Schulz, Interview by Iris J. West, Transcript, 39–40, 11 February 1994; and Kevin T. Galloway and Scott McDannold, Interview by Iris J. West, Transcript, 78–79, 9 February 1994 (both in ANCOHC, OMH). Marian Hamilton, "New Navy Hospital Workers Take Over Facility in Zagreb," *Stars and Stripes* (1 September 1994): 3. Carolyn M. Feller and Debora R. Cox, *Highlights in the History of the Army Nurse Corps*, 100th Anniversary Edition (Washington, DC: U.S. Army Center of Military History, 2000), 65. Alana M. Benton, "Navy Nurse Mission," *Nursing Spectrum* (DC/Baltimore Metro Edition) 6 (20 May 1996): 9. Carolyn D. Zdrodowski, Elaine Dekker, and Cylysce C. Vogelsang-Watson, "Medical Deployment to Croatia: Operation Provide Promise," *Today's Surgical Nurse* 18 (May/June 1996): 28–34.

42. Connie L. Reeves, *Department of the Army Historical Summary, Fiscal Year 1996* (Washington, DC: United States Army Center of Military History, 2002), 72–74. Kimberly Green, "U.S. Troops Land, Set Up in Hungary," *American Endeavor* 1 (29 December 1995): 1. Charles Moskos and Laura Miller, "Task Force Eagle," *Army* 49 (February 1999): 40–46. "History of BiH," 4 April 2003, http://www.tfeagle.army.mil/TFE/bosnia_history.htm (accessed 22 April 2005). "History of the NATO-led Stabilisation Force (SFOR) in Bosnia and Herzegovina," http://www.nato.int/sfor/docu/d981116a.htm (accessed 24 April 2005).

43. Markus Novosel and Nedima Hadziibrisevic, "The End of an Era—Looking Back at a Decade of American Involvement in Bosnia," *Talon* 15 (12 November 2004): 6. Constance J. Moore, "Recent 'Operations Other Than War'," Information Paper, 14 June 1996, ANCC, OMH. Charles Moskos and Laura Miller, "Task Force Eagle," *Army* 49 (February 1999): 40–46. Stanley F. Cherrie, "Task Force Eagle, Bosnia, Lessons Learned," *Military Review* 77 (July–August 1997): 62–72.

44. Constance J. Moore, "Recent 'Operations Other Than War'," Information Paper, 14 June 1996, ANCC, OMH. Kathryn M. Gaylord, "Psychiatric Nursing: A Critical Role in Deployment," *Army Medical Department Journal*, PB8-98-34 (March/April 1998): 28–31.

45. Kimberly Green, "U.S. Troops Land, Set Up in Hungary," *American Endeavor* 1 (29 December 1995): 1.

46. Later, in the waning days of the deployment, Bester once again assumed command of the task force and was responsible for all medical assets in Hungary and Croatia during

the unit's final 60 days in the Balkans. "Brigadier General William T. Bester, Chief, Army Nurse Corps," *Army Nurse Corps Newsletter* 99 (May–June 2000): 1, ANCC, OMH.

47. William Bester to Bettye Simmons and Susan McCall, Handwritten Letter, n.d.; and William Bester to AN Branchettes, Printed Letter, 29 February 1996 (both in ANCC, OMH).

48. Jerry Harben, "Medical Support Ready for Bosnia Operations," *The Mercury* 23 (February 1996): 1. Harry Noyes, "New Reservists Go to Germany for Backfill," *The Mercury* 23 (November 1996): 1. John Rodgers, Interview by Mary T. Sarnecky, Transcript, 57–58, 28 June 2001, ANCOHC, OMH.

49. Harry Noyes, "New Troops to Replace Bosnia Force," *The Mercury* 24 (December 1996): 1. Burton L. Masters, "Reservists in Europe Fill Gaps While Hospital Staffers Deploy," *The Mercury* 24 (December 1996): 1.

50. William Bester to Bettye Simmons and Susan McCall, Handwritten Letter, n.d., ANCC, OMH. Jerry Harben, "Medical Support Ready for Bosnia Operations," *The Mercury* 23 (February 1996): 1.

51. Charles Moskos and Laura Miller, "Task Force Eagle," *Army* 49 (February 1999): 40–46. Phil Gunby, "Military Medicine in the Balkans Now," *Journal of the American Medical Association* 282 (10 November 1999): 1707–09.

52. Charles Moskos and Laura Miller, "Task Force Eagle," *Army* 49 (February 1999): 40–46. Phil Gunby, "Military Medicine in the Balkans Now," *Journal of the American Medical Association* 282 (10 November 1999): 1707–09.

53. William Bester to Bettye Simmons and Susan McCall, Handwritten Letter, n.d.; and William Bester to AN Branchettes, Printed Letter, 29 February 1996 (both in ANCC, OMH). Karen S. Morarie, "67th CSH Sets Up High-Tech Tents," *American Endeavor* 1 (29 December 1995): 3.

54. William T. Bester to Susan McCall, Printed Letter, 15 July 1996, ANCC, OMH.

55. John Rodgers, Interview by Mary T. Sarnecky, Transcript, 58–59, 28 June 2001, ANCOHC, OMH.

56. "The 212th Mobile Army Surgical Hospital (MASH), 'The Last MASH Standing!'" Briefing Slides, n.d., ANCC, OMH.

57. The 212th MASH chief nurses during these rotations were lieutenant colonels Elijah Gilreath and Mark Bither. Suzan Denny, "AN Highlights, 30th MED BDE Significant Developments and Events since 1995," Printed Document, n.d., ANCC, OMH. Eric C. Barker, "Army Reserve Hospitals Keep Troops Healthy in Bosnia," *The Mercury* (March 1998): 6. A. Stamides, "After Action Report—Replacement Facility for the Blue Factory, Planning and Construction for Eagle Base Hospital, Tuzla, Bosnia, Medical Task Force Eagle," 23 October 1998, Box 126 C, OMH.

58. Steven S. Collins, "Nurses Gain Valuable Experience in Bosnia," *The Mercury* 24 (June 1997): 2.

59. Jerry Harben, "New Troops Head for Bosnia," *The Mercury* 25 (October 1997): 12.

60. Eric C. Barker, "Army Reserve Hospitals Keep Troops Healthy in Bosnia," *The Mercury* (March 1998): 6.

61. Suzan Denny, "AN Highlights, 30th MED BDE Significant Developments and Events since 1995," Printed Document, n.d., ANCC, OMH.

62. Benjamin Eli Seeley, "Task Force Med Eagle," *Army Nurse Corps Newsletter* (May–June 2000): 11–13.

63. Roddex Barlow and Theresa Mack, "Update from the Army Nurses of Task Force Med Eagle," *Army Nursing Newsletter* (March 2000): 8–9, ANCC, OMH.

64. Besides Larabee, the nursing staff consisted of majors Theresa Taylor, Patricia Fort-

ner, and Elizabeth Mills, captains Nelson Burgos and Vina Rajski, and first lieutenants Kelli Deacon, Thurman Saunders, Jeromy Jones, and B. Eli Seeley. Benjamin Eli Seeley, "Task Force Med Eagle," *Army Nurse Corps Newsletter* (May–June 2000): 11–13.

65. The Sked stretcher is a litter designed for "confined space, high angle or technical rescue, and traditional land based applications." Its design provides for patient protection and security. The Sked "comes equipped for horizontal hoisting by helicopter or vertical hoisting in caves or industrial confined spaces." http://www.skedco.com/sk200.htm (accessed 21 July 2005).

66. Benjamin Eli Seeley, "Task Force Med Eagle," *Army Nurse Corps Newsletter* (May–June 2000): 11–13.

67. The nursing staff included majors Graham and Hinton, captains Cartwright, Glenn, MacDougall, Milam, and Shackleford, and first lieutenants Dudley, Hall, and Kobiela. Walt Hinton, "Task Force Med Eagle, Eagle Base, Bosnia-Herzegovina, The Nurses of the 249th General Hospital (FWD)," *Army Nurse Corps Newsletter* (November 2000): 16–18.

68. Walt Hinton, "Task Force Med Eagle, Eagle Base, Bosnia-Herzegovina, The Nurses of the 249th General Hospital (FWD)," *Army Nurse Corps Newsletter* (November 2000): 16–18. "Task Force Med Eagle, Life in the Balkans by the Nurses of Task Force Med Eagle (TFME), 249th General Hospital (FWD), Eagle Base, Bosnia-Herzegovina," *Army Nurse Corps Newsletter* (December 2000): 11–13.

69. The unit included three psychiatrists. Two served down range with Prevention Teams. The third, the commander, provided services at the Restoration Unit but also traveled to provide support to the Prevention Teams. Kathryn Gaylord to Author, E-mail Correspondence, 22 September 2005, ANCC, OMH. Kathryn M. Gaylord, "Psychiatric Nursing: A Critical Role in Deployment," *Army Medical Department Journal*, PB8-98-34 (March/April 1998): 28–31.

70. Kathryn M. Gaylord, "Psychiatric Nursing: A Critical Role in Deployment," *Army Medical Department Journal*, PB8-98-34, (March/April 1998): 28–31.

71. Simon H. Pincus and Theodore S. Nam, "Psychological Aspects of Deployment: The Bosnian Experience," *Army Medical Department Journal*, PB8-99-1/2/3 (January/February/March 1999): 38–44. Nancy Tomich, "Peacekeeping Lesson: Expect Trauma," *U.S. Medicine* (November 1999): 11.

72. "History of the NATO-led Stabilization Force (SFOR) in Bosnia and Herzegovina," http://www.nato.int/sfor/docu/d981116a.htm (accessed 24 April 2005).

73. "History of SFOR," n.d., http://www.tfeagle.army.mil/TFE/SFOR_History.htm (accessed 22 April 2005).

74. George Robertson, "What's Going Right in Kosovo," *Washington Post* (7 December 1999): A31. Russell Taylor, Interview by John Greenwood, Transcript, 9–11, 24 May 2000, OMH. http://www.answers.com/KFOR (accessed 18 April 2005).

75. The CMF was a rapid deployment element carved from the MASH. With a very small footprint, the CMF provided combat service support for the austere, ambiguous contingency missions of that era. The CMF base had four Advanced Trauma Life Support trauma tables in the emergency room, four Intensive Care Unit beds, 10 holding beds, and two operating room tables and sterilizers. Designed by lieutenant colonels Alan Moloff, MC, and Suzan Denny, ANC, the CMF could carry out 24 major surgeries within 72 hours without resupply. The unit could be transported on two C-130 aircraft. "Interview with LTC Suzan Denny, Chief Nurse, 212th MASH," n.d.; "Interview—LTC Alan Moloff, Commander, 212th CMF, TF Hawk," 17 May 1999; and Bob Glesson, Unidentified Presentation, Script, 1 October 1999 (all in Box 126D, OMH). Steven M. Astriab, *Vendetta: Military Medical Peace Operations in Kosovo* (Atlanta, GA: Eagle Group International, n.d.), 2-8 to 2-14.

76. A "slice" is an element of a unit. A slice is used for a contingency operation when the full complement of the unit is not needed. "TF Hawk," Briefing Slides, n.d., Box 126 D, OTSG Files, OMH. Matthew Cox, "Troops and Tanks Beef Up Task Force Hawk," *Army Times* (14 June 1999): 16. Sean D. Naylor, "Task Force Proves Its Worth to Air War Planners," *Army Times* (14 June 1999): 16–17. Steven M. Astriab, *Vendetta: Military Medical Peace Operations in Kosovo* (Atlanta, GA: Eagle Group International, n.d.), 2-3, 2-7.

77. The three operating room nurses were majors Karen Morris and Javier Altamirano and Captain Carla Buckles. The three anesthetists were majors Dave Joss and Kim Blackburn and Captain Paul Barras. The critical care nurses were captains Teresa Duquette, Michael Rizzo, and Sarah Krajnik and First Lieutenant Sean Magnuson. Suzan Denny, "AN Highlights, 30th MED BDE Significant Developments and Events since 1995," Printed Document, n.d., ANCC, OMH. John Gordon IV, Bruce Nardulli, and Walter L. Perry, "The Operational Challenges of Task Force Hawk," *Joint Force Quarterly* 29 (Autumn/Winter 2001–2002): 52–57. Bob Glesson, Unidentified Presentation, Script, 1 October 1999, Box 126D, OMH.

78. Steven M. Astriab, *Vendetta: Military Medical Peace Operations in Kosovo* (Atlanta, GA: Eagle Group International, n.d.), 2-3, 2-29 to 2-30.

79. The CMF performed one appendectomy per week for the first six weeks. "TF Hawk," Briefing Slides, n.d., Box 126 D, OMH. Suzan Denny, "212th MASH: The Next Mission," *Army Nursing Newsletter* 99 (July 1999): 11–12, ANCC, OMH.

80. Jimmie O. Keenan, "Task Force Med Falcon, Kosovo Report," *Army Nursing Newsletter* (September 1999): 10–11, ANCC, OMH. Jim Garamone, "Medics Prepare for Hazards of Kosovo," *The Mercury* 26 (August 1999): 1. "TF Hawk," Briefing Slides, n.d., Box 126 D, OMH. Stephen L.Y. Gammons and William M. Donnelly, *Department of the Army Historical Summary, Fiscal Year 1995* (Washington, DC: Center of Military History, United States Army, 2004), 48. Steven M. Astriab, *Vendetta: Military Medical Peace Operations in Kosovo* (Atlanta, GA: Eagle Group International, n.d.), 2-31.

81. Steven M. Astriab, *Vendetta: Military Medical Peace Operations in Kosovo* (Atlanta, GA: Eagle Group International, n.d.), 2-31, 3-3, 3-36. Jimmie O. Keenan, "Task Force Med Falcon, Kosovo Report," *Army Nursing Newsletter* (September 1999): 10–11, ANCC, OMH.

82. The detachment commander, First Lieutenant April Byrd, also was an Army nurse. Jimmie O. Keenan, "Task Force Med Falcon, Kosovo Report," *Army Nursing Newsletter* (September 1999): 10–11, ANCC, OMH. Keenan was part of the Advance Party and also served as the unit engineer, overseeing site preparations for the hospital. In a previous assignment she was a Nurse Methods Analyst with significant health facility planning experience. Her background stood her in good stead. Steven M. Astriab, *Vendetta: Military Medical Peace Operations in Kosovo* (Atlanta, GA: Eagle Group International, n.d.), 3-15 to 3-16, 3-33.

83. The 11 Army Nurse Corps officers were majors Charlotte Scott and Karalee Sutterlin, captains (P) David Kendrick and Joe O'Sullivan, captains Tammy Crawford, Julie Benson, and Karlo Tutt, and first lieutenants Jeff Borders, Bill Needham, Nicole Bowns, and Nighat Kahn. An Air Force nurse, First Lieutenant Gayle Randall served on the 67th CSH Aeromedical Evacuation Liaison Team. Jimmie O. Keenan, "Task Force Med Falcon, Kosovo Report," *Army Nursing Newsletter* (September 1999): 10–11, ANCC, OMH. Russell Taylor, Interview by John Greenwood, Transcript, 12, 24 May 2000, OMH.

84. Jimmie O. Keenan, "Task Force Med Falcon, Kosovo Report," *Army Nursing Newsletter* (September 1999): 10–11, ANCC, OMH. Russell Taylor, Interview by John Greenwood, Transcript, 12, 24 May 2000, OMH. Christopher DeHart, "67th CSH Answers Call

in Kosovo," *The Mercury* 27 (October 1999): 1. Phil Gunby, "Military Medicine in the Balkans Now," *Journal of the American Medical Association* 282 (10 November 1999): 1707–09. Steven M. Astriab, *Vendetta: Military Medical Peace Operations in Kosovo* (Atlanta, GA: Eagle Group International, n.d.), 3-34, 3-36.

85. Russell Taylor, Interview by John Greenwood, Transcript, 29–31, 24 May 2000, OMH.

86. Ibid., 36–40.

87. Chris DeHart, "Medics Upgrade Hospital to Care For Kosovars," *The Mercury* 27 (February 2000): 2.

88. Russell Taylor, Interview by John Greenwood, Transcript, 36–40, 24 May 2000, OMH. Steven M. Astriab, *Vendetta: Military Medical Peace Operations in Kosovo* (Atlanta, GA: Eagle Group International, n.d.), 3-21, 3-43 to 3-44.

89. Russell Taylor, Interview by John Greenwood, Transcript, 36–40, 24 May 2000, OMH.

90. Ibid., 40–41. Phil Gunby, "Military Medicine in the Balkans Now," *Journal of the American Medical Association* 282 (10 November 1999): 1707–09.

91. Jimmie O. Keenan, "Goodbye to Kosovo," *Army Nursing Newsletter* (November 1999): 13, ANCC, OMH. Steven M. Astriab, *Vendetta: Military Medical Peace Operations in Kosovo* (Atlanta, GA: Eagle Group International, n.d.), 3-5, 3-46 to 3-47.

92. The 12 included the chief nurse, Major Shelley Rice, Lieutenant Colonel MaryEllen Wygant, Captain (P) Patricia Hembree, captains Diane Paulson, Carla Crouch, and Cynthia Nielsen-McArdle, First Lieutenant (P) Michael Nagra, first lieutenants Karen Ramey, Dianne Paraoan, and Markus Lee, and second lieutenants Jessica Lussier and Sean Elliot. All deployed from the 67th CSH in Würzburg except for Wygant, who deployed from Landstuhl Regional Medical Center. "Army Nurse Corps 99th Anniversary Celebration," *Army Nursing Newsletter* (March 2000): 11, ANCC, OMH. Steven M. Astriab, *Vendetta: Military Medical Peace Operations in Kosovo* (Atlanta, GA: Eagle Group International, n.d.), 4-10, 4-30.

93. Suzan Denny, "AN Highlights, 30th MED BDE Significant Developments and Events since 1995," Printed Document, n.d., ANCC, OMH.

94. Steven M. Astriab, *Vendetta: Military Medical Peace Operations in Kosovo* (Atlanta, GA: Eagle Group International, n.d.), 5-65.

95. Ibid., 4-11.

96. Ibid., 4-54.

97. Suzan Denny, "AN Highlights, 30th MED BDE Significant Developments and Events since 1995," Printed Document, n.d., ANCC, OMH. Suzan Denny, "212th MASH: The Next Mission," *Army Nursing Newsletter* 99 (July 1999): 11–12, ANCC, OMH.

98. Ibid.

99. Suzan Denny to Author, E-mail Correspondence, 16 June 2005, ANCC, OMH.

100. Steven M. Astriab, *Vendetta: Military Medical Peace Operations in Kosovo* (Atlanta, GA: Eagle Group International, n.d.), 5-7.

101. Ibid., 5-24.

102. Suzan Denny to Author, E-mail Correspondence, 16 June 2005, ANCC, OMH.

103. Suzan Denny, "Task Force Med Falcon," *Army Nurse Corps Newsletter* (July 2000): 18–19; and Elizabeth Vinson, "Task Force Med-Falcon," *Army Nurse Corps Newsletter* (October 2000): 13–14 (both in ANCC, OMH).

104. Steven M. Astriab, *Vendetta: Military Medical Peace Operations in Kosovo* (Atlanta, GA: Eagle Group International, n.d.), 6-4.

105. Ibid., 6-17.

106. Ibid., 6-13.

107. Ibid., 6-24.

*Chapter Twenty-three*
# Operation Uphold Democracy in Haiti

Operation Uphold Democracy, an Operation Other Than War, took place in Haiti. On 15 September 1994, elements of the XVIII Airborne Corps, the 82nd Airborne Division from Fort Bragg, North Carolina, and the 10th Mountain Division (Light) from Fort Drum, New York, deployed to the Caribbean island of Haiti as part of a Multinational Force under the banner of Operation Uphold Democracy. The operational mission was to provide protection for U.S. citizens and interests, certain Haitians, and other third-country nationals while reestablishing civil order, reorganizing the Haitian military, and assisting in the establishment of a democratic government. An immediate goal was to remove the military junta that had toppled the democratically elected president, a former Roman Catholic priest, Jean Bertrand Aristide, and return him to office.[1] A complex series of events and circumstances preceded the deployment.

Haiti, a French Creole–speaking country, was a developing nation whose history involved almost two centuries of instability, poverty, disease, civil wars, partitions, rebellions, coups, revolutions, reunions, power struggles, and uprisings. Periodic U.S. intervention in the struggling country first began in 1914 when a group of U.S. Marines came ashore at Port-au-Prince to secure the Haitian National Bank and preserve the Haitian economy. Several U.S. interventions followed during the first half of the 20th century.[2] Further involvement with Haitians then transpired in the 1990s.

Several years before Operation Uphold Democracy, a number of Army Nurse Corps officers had contact with Haitians at Guantanamo Bay, Cuba. Approximately 15,000 Haitians had fled their country in the autumn of 1991 after the overthrow of the Aristide democratic government. Most did not qualify for asylum in the United States, so they were sequestered on Guantanamo Bay before being returned to Haiti.[3]

To care for the Haitians, a group of Army Medical Department personnel attached to the Alpha Collecting and Clearing Company of the U.S. Joint Tactical

Force set up a field hospital in Guantanamo Bay in December 1991. It cared for about 150 to 300 Haitians daily. Its tentage housed a sick call component, a ward, an intensive care unit, operating and recovery rooms, and an isolation unit for patients with communicable diseases such as chicken pox and tuberculosis.

Since there were approximately 340 pregnant Haitians among the detainees, an Army obstetrician and two obstetrics/gynecology nurses also deployed to Guantanamo Bay. With only a few days warning, Lieutenant Edythe Robinson, an obstetrical nurse from Walter Reed Army Medical Center, deployed to Guantanamo Bay, where she worked 12 to 14 hours a day assisting patients in labor and delivery. She provided others with prenatal and postpartum care.[4]

Army nurses served for several years in Guantanamo Bay and also in Panama City, Panama, and Paramaribo, Suriname, and gave assistance to both Cuban and Haitian refugees.[5] In December 1994, Captain Kathryn Gaylord deployed to the Navy/Marine base at Guantanamo Bay with elements of the 85th Medical Detachment's Combat Stress Control unit and a psychiatric slice of the 21st Combat Support Hospital (CSH) from Fort Hood, Texas, to provide inpatient and outpatient mental health services for the Cuban and Haitian refugees. Gaylord's assignment was as Officer-in-Charge of the inpatient psychiatric unit, whose usual daily census was about 14 psychiatric cases. Many of these refugees had endured harrowing events such as family separations and witnessing family members drown or be killed by sharks, and most suffered from stress as a result of their internment that involved overcrowding, little to no privacy, and limited lifestyle choices. Once stabilized by the psychiatric inpatient unit, the patients returned to their assigned camp, and later, most were repatriated to their home country.

Originally, the psychiatric facilities conducted business in double hardback tents. When these proved woefully inadequate, Gaylord acquired a condemned Navy brig that offered running water, toilets, office space, and an enclosed ward. This energetic Army nurse went one step further. She organized a work detail of Cuban refugees and directed them to construct partitions, safety doors, and ramps from plywood. She had them screen windows to exclude mosquitoes, other vectors, and vermin and build a nurse observation desk to maintain patient surveillance. She obtained wooden cabinets from condemned housing and had them installed and requisitioned paint from salvage and had the Cubans do interior painting. They remodeled a guard observation room into a locked medication room. The patients and the occupational therapy and nursing staffs planted flowers and changed the neglected yard into a picturesque garden. Gaylord was thrilled with the transformation of the barbwire-enclosed compound, seeing it as "an opportunity to provide a better standard of care" for the refugees.[6]

Lieutenant Colonel Gemryl Samuels was one of three Army Community Health Nurses who served with JTF 160 (Operation Sea Signal) in Guantanamo Bay in the mid-1990s. Her tour of duty lasted four and a half months. Samuels' initial charge was to interface with villagers and migrants, identify their health needs, and conduct health education classes. She soon assumed additional responsibilities such as communicable disease surveillance, discharge planning, public health education, maternal and child health, and family safety. Samuels also had an opportunity to advance the cause of community health nursing with Navy nursing personnel. The Army was the only Department of Defense branch to utilize the specialty services of community health nurses. During this period, however, the Navy nurses assigned to Guantanamo Bay also became interested in providing community outreach. The incumbent senior Navy Nurse Corps officer assigned three Navy nurses and a Navy corpsman with Spanish language skills to work in clinical preceptorships under Samuels' supervision. Their joint efforts expanded and improved the existing services to the migrant population and added a new dimension to Navy nursing.

Samuels reflected on the lessons she learned and subsequently formulated recommendations for future humanitarian missions. She noted that highly skilled Cuban migrant health professionals often were poorly utilized, treated with a lack of respect, and assigned menial tasks. She recommended that, in the future, an effort be made to promote their "acceptance, expand their use, and better integrate them into the health care delivery system." Samuels also observed that a climate of mistrust existed between the military and the migrants. She attributed this unease to the migrants' past exposure to a rigid, uniformed military that often was tyrannical. Samuels advised that, in future humanitarian mobilizations, the military attempt to be more low key, flexible, and cognizant of the internees' history and background. Samuels acknowledged the importance of being aware of cultural beliefs and emphasized how a lack of such knowledge could impact professional practice. In one instance, her team planned a day on the beach to focus on women's issues with a group of Haitian women. Not one woman participated in the program. Samuels later learned that the Haitian culture frowned on independent activities for women without the approval and cooperation of their male partners. The men simply had vetoed the women's attendance.

Samuels concluded that Army Community Health Nurses:

> . . . played key roles in Operation Sea Signal. Thousands of immigrants benefited from their creativity, energies, and enterprising activities. What remained constant [was] the extreme importance of dealing with the human factor: to appropriately assess people's needs, identify resources to cope with them, support the strengths, and find appropriate ways of meeting the deficits.[7]

While Gaylord and Samuels were carrying out their missions in Guantanamo Bay, Operation Uphold Democracy was underway in nearby Haiti.

Elements from several Table of Organization and Equipment hospital units served sequentially in Haiti and provided medical support and humanitarian assistance during Operation Uphold Democracy. The first unit to deploy was the 274th Surgical Detachment from Fort Bragg, North Carolina. It arrived in Haiti on D+1 in the early morning and within hours a surgical capability was operational. The 28th CSH, also a unit of the 44th Medical Brigade at Fort Bragg, sent a 52-bed package that entered the country on D+2 while its personnel arrived on D+6. The 47th Field Hospital from Fort Sill, Oklahoma, followed. The 86th CSH out of Fort Campbell, Kentucky, and the 131st Field Hospital from Fort Bliss, Texas, each manned one of the final two rotations of the operation.[8]

The Medical Rules of Engagement for this mission stipulated that no host nation health facilities would be used by U.N. forces because the few local hospitals that did exist were in a lamentable state. Major Patty Horoho, a Nurse Methods Analyst, belonged to one of two Health Facility Assessment Teams deployed in Haiti at the direction of Brigadier General James Peake, the JTF 180 surgeon and commander of the 44th Medical Brigade.[9] Horoho immediately recognized the impossibility of using the host nation facilities during her first inspection visit to the Hotel Simbie, a makeshift hospital in Port-au-Prince:

> When we arrived we found 200 families living in the abandoned hotel. The hotel was dilapidated and filthy. There were waste products all over and dripping off some of the balconies. A few dirty needles were lying on the ground in some areas, and a few elderly males were lying curled up in a corner dying of starvation. There was no electricity or running water. Children ran around without any clothes and urinated wherever. Initially the occupants were guarded because they felt that we were going to take away their home. Sargeant Jacques [the linguist] and I were cornered on the second floor by approximately 25 hostile occupants. We both remained calm and Sargeant Jacques did an excellent job of talking to them in Creole and was able to calm them down . . . . The initial assessment was that the hotel could be renovated but this would require a lot of work.

Most of the facilities' equipment and supplies were nonfunctional, 40 to 50 years old, and quite obsolete. Few medications were available. Nonetheless, Horoho was amazed by the "irrepressible good humor of most of the population."[10]

Another Medical Rule of Engagement directed U.S. medical forces not to treat Haitians. Exceptions to the rule involved detainees and those Haitians who required emergency care for injuries incurred as a result of U.S./U.N. activities. Emergency care, however, would be limited to measures implemented to prevent loss of life or limb.[11]

The implementation of the Medical Rules of Engagement involved some strange situations. When Lieutenant Diane Diehl deployed to Haiti with the 47th Field Hospital in January 1995, the hospital admitted a Haitian male for treatment. The man had doused his wife with gasoline and was preparing to set her aflame. A multinational force trooper intervened and shot the man, who then received care for his wounds at the 47th Field Hospital.[12] In another case, a 13-year-old boy flung himself under the wheels of a multinational force water buffalo truck, mistakenly believing that his injuries represented a ticket to the United States. The 47th Field Hospital treated the youth for a fractured pelvis. Diehl explained that the locals failed to comprehend that even if they were evacuated to the United States for treatment, they would be returned to Haiti.[13] The 47th Field Hospital also provided care for Brown and Root employees, contract workers who maintained the showers and toilets and provided laundry services.[14]

Captain Susan M. Raymond, who deployed with the 86th CSH, the unit that replaced the 47th Field Hospital in Haiti, confirmed Diehl's observations. Raymond cared for many local nationals, some of whom stepped in front of buses or Humvees to obtain health care from the 86th CSH. During her tour in Haiti, the opera-

Major Patricia Horoho (right) and two fellow soldiers pause for a spontaneous meal in the midst of their duty day with a Health Facility Assessment Team in Haiti during Operation Uphold Democracy in the autumn of 1994.
Photo courtesy of Colonel Patricia Horoho, Tacoma, WA.

tion changed from a multinational force to the United Nations Mission in Haiti. Thereafter, many of the patients who received care were U.N. peacekeepers.[15]

The 47th Field Hospital ran an average census of 30 hospital patients daily, several with dengue fever and others with more common maladies such as heart attacks.[16] Other typical diagnoses were fevers of unknown origin and diarrhea, and most patients treated were nonbattle casualties.[17]

On 11 September 1994, Major Ellen Forster received mobilization orders instructing her to report to Fort Bragg, North Carolina. Her educated guess that she would be deploying to Haiti proved correct. The notification directed her to mobilize with the 28th CSH in support of Operation Uphold Democracy. During the 10 days before her actual deployment, Forster attended briefings on the cultural, historical, and political context and the French Creole dialect of her destination, on threats to health and safety, and on universal precautions. Universal infection control precautions were especially important in Haiti, where the incidence of HIV/AIDS was exceptionally high. One source noted that "at least 70 percent of prostitutes and 8 percent of young adults in Haiti are HIV-positive."[18] Forster was issued a Kevlar helmet and flak jacket. Those deploying nurses who chose to bear arms also were issued a 9-mm. pistol.[19] Forster preferred not to carry the issued weapon.[20]

Lieutenant Colonel Nancy Allmon, chief nurse of the 86th Combat Support Hospital during that unit's Operation Uphold Democracy deployment in Haiti in August 1995, cuddles a smiling Haitian child. Photo courtesy of Army Nurse Corps Archives, Office of Medical History, Falls Church, VA.

Upon their arrival in Port-au-Prince, the local Haitians either cheered or jeered as the 28th CSH nurses loaded onto a military truck for the three-mile trip to their final destination. Because of the surging crowds, it took over an hour for the nurses to reach two enormous vacant warehouses in an industrial area of Port-au-Prince.[21] Obviously used as dumps in the past, both were littered with detritus and excreta.[22] The nurses first policed the two buildings, one of which was designated as billets and the other as a shelter for the Deployable Medical System. Then everyone—physicians, nurses, and medics—collectively helped to erect the facility, a formidable effort in the 100° F temperatures. Their successful accomplishment of this chore affirmed the wisdom of the Army's insistence on high levels of physical fitness. The 52-bed package that housed the 28th CSH included 20 minimal care and 20 intermediate care beds and a 12-bed intensive care unit.[23]

Within a few days the hospital's first test occurred. A Mass Casualty was called when a grenade detonated in a crowd of Haitians at a demonstration. Most of the 63 patients triaged and treated within two hours at the 28th CSH presented with minor injuries.[24] As head nurse of Emergency Medical Treatment, Forster and the Emergency Medical Treatment area chief organized four trauma teams consisting of a physician, a nurse, and two medics and furnished them with supplies and equipment required to treat blast wounds, such as chest tubes, nasogastric tubes, Foley catheters, and large-bore intravenous equipment. Before this incident, Forster was concerned about supporting an adequate level of care with the available staff and facilities. Afterward, she was reassured about the 28th CSH's "ability to provide quality trauma care." Nonetheless, no one was complacent and Forster instructed her staff to fine-tune their trauma sets, intensively train on their field equipment, and develop treatment protocols.

Another of Forster's responsibilities was to conduct sick call. Since the 28th CSH was the most sophisticated health care facility on the island, the diverse patient base included not only multinational force personnel but also VIPs, the media, and foreign service personnel. Presenting medical complaints involved acute minor illnesses, gastrointestinal maladies, and orthopedic conditions.

All were conscious of the threat of malaria and most took chloroquine weekly, used insect repellent religiously, and slept under nets as prophylaxis. Still, insect bites were common.[25] The unit only treated two malaria cases, both of whom were previously afflicted missionaries.

An immediate concern was the lack of hygiene facilities. There were no toilets available initially, and the 28th CSH staff improvised with empty milk cartons. Soon lumber arrived and outhouses were built. Then portable toilets finally materialized. The nurses became proficient in using "Australian showers." This basic apparatus comprised several suspended water blivets whose "challenge lay in filling the bags with water from 5-gallon tanks and hoisting them up with a rope and pulley. This required a good friend, brute strength, and great skill in water conservation." To use the shower, the bather released a flow of water from above, hastily wet themselves, lathered, and rinsed.

The nurses mused about where their "responsibilities began and ended":

We cared for many indigents, many of whom had never had even the rudiments of medical care. How much could we do for them in the time we would be in Haiti? How could we help a severely malnourished baby? So many people needed so much help, and our resources were limited. The Haitian-on-Haitian violence was frequently out of control. It was not uncommon for us to treat several patients with gunshot wounds, machete injuries, and stab wounds per day. When supplies ran short, as they sometimes did, we wondered how we would react if we had to make a choice between treating an injured American soldier or a Haitian soldier. We . . . tried to provide the best nursing care we could.[26]

Four American holidays—Halloween, Thanksgiving, Christmas, and New Year's Day—passed. When the nurses were separated from loved ones, these occasions had the potential to be very depressing times. To counteract melancholy, the nurses held parties, staged talent shows, listened to concerts, and derived solace from their patriotic service and the knowledge that in the next year, the holiday season would be even more special.

Forster thought the deployment was a good and meaningful experience. The 28th CSH "provided a high level of quality care in a third world country" and "we made a difference, and I am proud to have been part of this team."[27]

Small support groups remained in Haiti from 1996 until 2000 as a part of the U.N. Mission in Haiti. Medical personnel from the sister services as well as the Army successively aligned with those groups and provided care to indigent Haitians at a base camp field hospital near the international airport.[28] In February 1998, Medical Treatment Facility (MTF) 555—the 555th Forward Surgical Team and the 61st Area Support Medical Battalion from Fort Hood, Texas—relieved the Air Force 28th Air Transportable Hospital. MTF 555's mission was to care for U.S. military forces and contract employees and provide humanitarian assistance to Haitians. The latter consumed most of MTF 555's attention and energy. By the time Haitians appeared for treatment, their ailments were well advanced. Untreated infections and unset fractures that resulted in misaligned bones were common presentations. One man whose foot was run over by a "tap-tap" (a taxi) languished in the local hospital and received no treatment. When he arrived at MTF 555, his foot was gone and maggots crept out of the wound.

Beyond the unit's walls, various staff members conducted Medical Civilian Assistant Programs. One Army nurse, Lieutenant Colonel Toni Massenbury, visited St. Theresa's Orphanage in Port-au-Prince and cared for malnourished babies. Despite the hardships, most considered the deployment an invaluable experience. Most had never seen such extreme cases of long-neglected yet common maladies, while others cited the opportunities afforded to assist those so desperately in need. Some expressed the idea that the deployment had enhanced their appreciation for all they enjoyed as U.S. citizens.[29] All U.S. troops left Haiti by January 2000.[30]

The Army Nurse Corps began the decade with a deployment in the Arabian desert and the expectation of heavy battle casualties. Fortunately, the war was short-lived, with more deaths due to injuries than combat. Nonetheless, the Army Medical Department and the Army Nurse Corps were prepared, functioned well, and were ready to provide care for the expected numbers of casualties. The differences with the Muslim culture and its views on the place and lifestyles of women were dealt with gracefully.

A series of humanitarian postings in Bosnia, Kosovo, and Macedonia presented a new generation of Army nurses with the traditional challenges and satisfactions of field nursing and medical civic action. Even when carrying heavy operational workloads, they found the time and energy to rehabilitate local hospitals and schools. In the Balkans, nurses commanded Table of Organization and Equipment hospitals for the first time.

In Somalia, the work of Army nurses fluctuated between routine everyday care and the unexpected mass casualty care of battle-wounded soldiers. The lessons of past wars had not been forgotten and the Army Nurse Corps moved into triage and surge responses quickly and smoothly.

A geopolitically awkward assistance mission to the government of Haiti exposed Army nurses to the degrading and hopeless poverty of the people living on this Caribbean island. Operating under restrictive Rules of Engagement for a providentially brief operation prevented the nurses from doing large-scale humanitarian work.

In all these various deployed assignments, in medical units from Forward Surgical Teams to Mobile Army Surgical Hospitals and CSHs, Army nurses efficiently and automatically applied the principles and practices of "nursing the Army way."

The successful operations of the 1990s allowed the executive branch to concentrate on domestic policy and focus attention on decreasing the size and changing the structure of the armed forces. The resultant reorientation and reductions had inevitable effects on the Army Nurse Corps.

# Notes

1. Paulette V. Walker, "Who's There? 47 Units Deploy to Haiti," *Army Times* 55 (3 October 1994): 14. Donna Miles, "One Army, Two Fronts," http://www.army.mil/soldiers/dec94/pr.html (accessed 9 May 2005). Donna Miles, "Upholding Democracy in Haiti," *Soldiers* 49 (November 1994): 4–5. L. Martin Kaplan, *Department of the Army Historical Summary, Fiscal Year 1994* (Washington, DC: Center of Military History, United States Army, 2000), 63. Stephen L.Y. Gammons and William M. Donnelly, *Department of the Army Historical Summary, Fiscal Year 1995* (Washington, DC: Center of Military History, United States Army, 2004), 46. Connie L. Reeves, *Department of the Army Historical Summary, Fiscal Year 1996* (Washington, DC: United States Army Center of Military History, 2002), 74–75. "Medical Units Support U.S. Troops in Haiti," *The Mercury* 22 (November 1994): 1. Thomas K. Adams, "Intervention in Haiti: Lessons Relearned," *Military Review* 76 (September–October 1996): 45–56. John T. Fishel, "Operation Uphold Democracy: Old Principles, New Realities," *Military Review* 77 (July–August 1997): 22–30. Bob Shacochis, *The Immaculate Invasion* (New York: Penguin Books, 1999).

2. Paulette V. Walker, "Who's There? 47 Units Deploy to Haiti," *Army Times* 55 (3 October 1994): 14. Donna Miles, "One Army, Two Fronts," http://www.army.mil/soldiers/dec94/pr.html (accessed 9 May 2005). Donna Miles, "Upholding Democracy in Haiti," *Soldiers* 49 (November 1994): 4–5. L. Martin Kaplan, *Department of the Army Historical Summary, Fiscal Year 1994* (Washington, DC: Center of Military History, United States Army, 2000), 63. Stephen L.Y. Gammons and William M. Donnelly, *Department of the Army Historical Summary, Fiscal Year 1995* (Washington, DC: Center of Military History, United States Army, 2004), 46. Connie L. Reeves, *Department of the Army Historical Summary, Fiscal Year 1996* (Washington, DC: United States Army Center of Military History, 2002), 74–75. "Medical Units Support U.S. Troops in Haiti," *The Mercury* 22 (November 1994): 1. Thomas K. Adams, "Intervention in Haiti: Lessons Relearned," *Military Review* 76 (September–October 1996): 45–56. John T. Fishel, "Operation Uphold Democracy: Old Principles, New Realities," *Military Review* 77 (July–August 1997): 22–30. Bob Shacochis, *The Immaculate Invasion* (New York: Penguin Books, 1999).

3. Henry H. Shelton, "Contingency Operations in an Uncertain World: The Case of Haiti," *Strategic Review* 26 (Fall 1998): 37–41. Bernard S. Little, "Nurse Helps Haitians in Cuba," *HSC Mercury* 19 (July 1992): 6.

4. Bernard S. Little, "Nurse Helps Haitians in Cuba," *HSC Mercury* 19 (July 1992): 6.

5. Carolyn M. Feller and Debora R. Cox, *Highlights in the History of the Army Nurse Corps, 100th Anniversary Edition* (Washington, DC: U.S. Army Center of Military History, 2000), 68.

6. Kathryn M. Gaylord, "Psychiatric Nursing: A Critical Role in Deployment," *Army Medical Department Journal*, PB8-98-34, (March/April 1998): 28–31.

7. Gemryl Louisa Samuels, "Army Community Health Nurses' Role in Humanitarian Relief Effort, Operation Sea Signal, Guantanamo Bay, Cuba," *Military Medicine* 162 (March 1997): 190–93. Gemryl L. Samuels and Mathew D. Sommer, "The Role of the Community Health Nurse in Military Humanitarian Operations: Lessons from Operation Sea Signal—Guantanamo Bay, Cuba," *Journal of Community Health Nursing* 14 (February 1997): 73–79.

8. James B. Peake, Interview by Christopher Clark, Transcript, 338–39, 343, 16 October 1994, in "JTF–180 Uphold Democracy Oral History Interviews," n.d., Excerpt in Office of Medical History (OMH). Gerald A. Palmer, Interview by Christopher Clark, Transcript, 270–71, 10 October 1994; and Virgil T. Deal, Interview by Christopher Clark, Transcript, 279, 11 October 1994 (both in Cynthia L. Hayden, ed., "Oral History Interviews, Operation Uphold Democracy," n.d., Excerpt in OMH). "Operation Uphold Democracy, U.S. Army Order of Battle," 19 September 1994, http://www.globalsecurity.org/military/ops/uphold_democracy-orbat.htm (accessed 9 May 2005). Carolyn M. Feller and Debora R. Cox, *Highlights in the History of the Army Nurse Corps, 100th Anniversary Edition* (Washington, DC: U.S. Army Center of Military History, 2000), 67.

9. Other team members were a health facility planning officer, a biomedical equipment technician, an environmental engineer, and a Haitian linguist. Walter E. Kretchik, Robert F. Bauman, and John T. Fishel, *A Concise History of the U.S. Army in Operation Uphold Democracy* (Fort Leavenworth, KS: U.S. Army Command and General Staff College Press, 1998), Transcript, 341, 16 October 1994, in "JTF–180 Uphold Democracy Oral History Interviews," n.d., Excerpt in OMH.

10. Walter E. Kretchik, Robert F. Bauman, and John T. Fishel, *A Concise History of the U.S. Army in Operation Uphold Democracy* (Fort Leavenworth, KS: U.S. Army Command and General Staff College Press, 1998), http://www.globalsecurity.org/military/library/report/1998/kretchik-chapter3.htm (accessed 10 May 2005).

11. Gerald A. Palmer, Interview by Christopher Clark, Transcript, 269, 10 October 1994, in Cynthia L. Hayden, ed., "Oral History Interviews, Operation Uphold Democracy," n.d., Excerpt in OMH. Walter E. Kretchik, Robert F. Bauman, and John T. Fishel, *A Concise History of the U.S. Army in Operation Uphold Democracy* (Fort Leavenworth, KS: U.S. Army Command and General Staff College Press, 1998), http://www.globalsecurity.org/military/library/report/1998/kretchik-chapter3.htm (accessed 10 May 2005).

12. Reportedly, after taking all the man's money, the wife was getting a divorce. The enraged husband was seeking revenge. Diane Diehl, Interview by Mary T. Sarnecky, Transcript, 17–18, 9 January 2001, Army Nurse Corps Oral History Collection, OMH.

13. Diane Diehl, Interview by Mary T. Sarnecky, Transcript, 38, 9 January 2001, Army Nurse Corps Oral History Collection, OMH.

14. Ibid., 35, 39–40.

15. Susan M. Raymond, Interview by Debora Cox, Transcript, 7, 8, 23, 15 February 2001, Army Nurse Corps Oral History Collection, OMH.

16. Gerald A. Palmer, Interview by Christopher Clark, Transcript, 271, 10 October 1994; and Virgil T. Deal, Interview by Christopher Clark, Transcript, 284, 11 October 1994 (both in Cynthia L. Hayden, ed., "Oral History Interviews, Operation Uphold Democracy," n.d., Excerpt in OMH).

17. James B. Peake, Interview by Christopher Clark, Transcript, 342, 16 October 1994, in "JTF—180 Uphold Democracy Oral History Interviews," n.d., Excerpt in OMH. Virgil T. Deal, Interview by Christopher Clark, Transcript, 283, 11 October 1994, in Cynthia L. Hayden, ed., "Oral History Interviews, Operation Uphold Democracy," n.d., Excerpt in OMH.

18. "Haiti Facts and Figures," *The Mercury* 22 (November 1994): 1.

19. Ellen Forster, "Deployment to Haiti: An Emergency Nurse's Story," *Journal of Emergency Nursing* 22 (April 1996): 160–62.

20. Ellen Forster, Telephone Interview with Mary T. Sarnecky, 25 August 2005.

21. Ellen Forster, "Deployment to Haiti: An Emergency Nurse's Story," *Journal of Emergency Nursing* 22 (April 1996): 160–62.

22. Gerald A. Palmer, Interview by Christopher Clark, Transcript, 276, 10 October 1994; and Virgil T. Deal, Interview by Christopher Clark, Transcript, 281–92, 11 October 1994 (both in Cynthia L. Hayden, ed., "Oral History Interviews, Operation Uphold Democracy," n.d., Excerpt in OMH). Ellen Forster, "Deployment to Haiti: An Emergency Nurse's Story," *Journal of Emergency Nursing* 22 (April 1996): 160–62.

23. Ellen Forster, "Deployment to Haiti: An Emergency Nurse's Story," *Journal of Emergency Nursing* 22 (April 1996): 160–62.

24. Gerald A. Palmer, Interview by Christopher Clark, Transcript, 273, 10 October 1994, in Cynthia L. Hayden, ed., "Oral History Interviews, Operation Uphold Democracy," n.d., Excerpt in OMH. Ellen Forster, "Deployment to Haiti: An Emergency Nurse's Story," *Journal of Emergency Nursing* 22 (April 1996): 160–62.

25. Gerald A. Palmer, Interview by Christopher Clark, Transcript, 275, 10 October 1994, in Cynthia L. Hayden, ed., "Oral History Interviews, Operation Uphold Democracy," n.d., Excerpt in OMH. Ellen Forster, "Deployment to Haiti: An Emergency Nurse's Story," *Journal of Emergency Nursing* 22 (April 1996): 160–62.

26. Ellen Forster, "Deployment to Haiti: An Emergency Nurse's Story," *Journal of Emergency Nursing* 22 (April 1996): 160–62.

27. Ibid., 160–62.

28. Seth M. McMullen, "New Task Force Assumes Duties in Haiti," *The Mercury* 25 (April 1998): 1. Michael Norton, "Haitian Mission Quietly Draws to a Close," *Army Times* 60 (7 February 2000): 12. Henry H. Shelton, "Contingency Operations in an Uncertain World: The Case of Haiti," *Strategic Review* 26 (Fall 1998): 37–41.

29. Seth M. McMullen, "New Task Force Assumes Duties in Haiti," *The Mercury* 25 (April 1998): 1.

30. Michael Norton, "Haitian Mission Quietly Draws to a Close," *Army Times* 60 (7 February 2000): 12.

*Chapter Twenty-four*
# The Final Word
# Epilogue

Within the relatively short span of three decades, the Army and the Army Medical Department underwent a reformation. So too did the Army Nurse Corps. From the nadir of the immediate post–Vietnam War era to the bright hopes of the new millennium, the Army Nurse Corps renewed itself by expanding its roles and functioning at higher levels. The Army Nurse Corps improved professional performance and credibility by requiring a baccalaureate degree for all active component officers and by augmenting their skills and acumen in many spheres. The Army Nurse Corps upgraded its levels of fitness and readiness. It became a master in the art and science of enhancing quality, expanding access, and reducing costs. As numbers diminished and the workload remained the same or even increased, Army nurses honed talents of proficiency and efficiency. The U.S. Army Reserve and the Army National Guard surpassed themselves as all components worked together to overcome old limitations and to embrace the concept of an "Army of One." Finally, Army nurses crossed over old boundaries that had defined Army nursing and moved into unprecedented realms and roles in staff and command assignments. There were some problems, but these were minor in light of the vast array of worthwhile endeavors and positive accomplishments.

On 2 February 2001, the Army Nurse Corps marked its centennial. Army nurses, their friends, and supporters participated in celebrations all around the globe. But the roots of the heritage of the Army Nurse Corps originated long before the celebration of its first centennial. Today's Army nurses trace their lineage back several centuries, embracing the men and women who provided nursing care during the Revolutionary War and the Civil War, the wives and laundresses who cared for the Frontier Army in America's West, the contract nurses of the Spanish–American War, and the members of the Army Nurse Corps (female) of World War I. Also incorporated in the family tree are the Army nurses of World War II who progressed from relative rank to commissioned rank. The Army Nurse Corps heritage also

Major Debora R. Cox, the Army Nurse Corps historian, was one of a number of active and retired Army Nurse Corps officers who organized the Army Nurse Corps 100th anniversary celebration in Washington, D.C., in 2001.
Photo courtesy of Lieutenant Colonel Debora R. Cox, Bethesda, MD.

Three decades of seasoned leadership gather around Brigadier General William T. Bester at the Army Nurse Corps 100th anniversary celebration on 2 February 2001 in Washington, D.C. From left to right are Major General Nancy R. Adams, Brigadier Generals Lillian Dunlap, Hazel W. Johnson, Bester, Anna Mae V. Hays, Connie L. Slewitzke, and Clara L. Adams-Ender.
Photo courtesy of Lieutenant Colonel Debora R. Cox, Bethesda, MD.

Colonel Betty J. Antilla (right), U.S. Army retired, was another collaborator in planning the week-long festivities convened to honor the Army Nurse Corps 100th anniversary. On the left is Major Debora R. Cox.
Photo courtesy of Lieutenant Colonel Debora R. Cox, Bethesda, MD.

counts the contributions of those who served in the Korean War as well as the male and female Army Nurse Corps officers who served in Vietnam, Grenada, Panama, the Persian Gulf, Somalia, the Balkans, and Haiti. Equally important on the homefront, it includes the Army Nurse Corps officers and civil service nurses based in the continental United States and other zones remote from the battlefield who had the herculean task of follow-on and long-term care of the sick and the wounded, as well as retirees and family members.

Predictably and invariably, even newer threats appeared. On 11 September

2001, terrorists commandeered four commercial airliners to strike at the heart of America—the Twin Towers of New York City, the Pentagon, and the nation's Capitol. Valiant passengers and crew foiled the latter attempt causing the last aircraft to crash into a field near Shanksville, Pennsylvania. Operation Iraqi Freedom and Operation Enduring Freedom followed. Once again, Army Nurse Corps officers answered their country's clarion call to duty and delivered the unique care they alone could administer to American soldiers in combat.

Given its storied history of achievements, patriotism, and selfless dedication, the Army Nurse Corps expects to carry on its unbroken line of professional service and shall adapt its knowledge and skills to meet the challenges of the future. Although its ranks will inevitably age, retire, and fade away, the Corps shall rise like a phoenix and renew itself with each passing generation marching in review.

# Acronyms and Abbreviations

| | |
|---|---|
| ACHN | Army Community Health Nurse |
| ACLS | Advanced Cardiac Life Support |
| AECP | AMEDD Enlisted Commissioning Program |
| AFNC | Air Force Nurse Corps |
| AHS | Academy of Health Sciences |
| AI | AMEDD Immaterial |
| AMEDD | Army Medical Department |
| AMEDD C&S | AMEDD Center and School |
| AMEDDPERSA | Army Medical Department Personnel Support Agency |
| AMOSIST | Automated Military Outpatient System Specialist |
| ANA | American Nurses Association |
| ANC | Army Nurse Corps |
| ANCA | Army Nurse Corps Association |
| ANC-CHEP | Army Nurse Corps Continuing Health Education Program |
| ANCCPP | Army Nurse Corps Contemporary Practice Program |
| AN-CP | Army Nurse Clinician Program |
| APPD | AMEDD Personnel Proponency Division |
| ARCENT | Army Central |
| ARNG | Army National Guard |
| ASC | Ambulatory Surgery Center |
| ASD(HA) | Assistant Secretary of Defense (Health Affairs) |
| ASD M&RA | Assistant Secretary of Defense for Manpower and Reserve Affairs |
| ASPECTS | A Solid Parenting Experience Through Community Teaching and Support |
| ATLS | Advanced Trauma Life Support |
| BACH | Bassett Army Community Hospital; Blanchfield Army Community Hospital |
| BAMC | Brooke Army Medical Center |
| BCP | Board Certification Pay |

| | |
|---|---|
| BI | Branch Immaterial |
| BRAC | Base Realignment and Closure |
| BSN | Bachelor of Science in Nursing |
| C4 | Combat Casualty Care Course |
| CAO | Career Activities Office |
| CCP | Coordinated Care Program |
| CENTCOM | Central Command |
| CHCS | Composite Health Care System |
| CHPPM | Center for Health Promotion and Preventive Medicine |
| CMF | Career Management Field; Contingency Medical Force |
| CNMW | Certified Nurse Midwife |
| CNS | Clinical Nurse Specialist |
| CONEX | Container Express (large, corrugated metal shipping container) |
| CONUS | Continental United States |
| CRNA | Certified Registered Nurse Anesthetist |
| CSH | Combat Support Hospital |
| CSL | Command Selection List |
| CSRN | Civil Service Registered Nurse |
| CVI | Conditional Voluntary Indefinite |
| DACOWITS | Defense Advisory Committee on Women in the Services |
| DCSPER | Deputy Chief of Staff for Personnel |
| DEPMEDS | Deployable Medical System |
| DMSB | Defense Medical Standardization Board |
| DoD | Department of Defense |
| DON | Department of Nursing |
| DOPMA | Defense Officer Personnel Management Act |
| EAC | Echelons Above Corps |
| EMT | Emergency Medical Treatment; Emergency Medical Technician |
| EPW | Enemy Prisoner of War |
| EVAC | Evacuation Hospital |
| FAMC | Fitzsimons Army Medical Center |
| FH | Field Hospital |
| FORSCOM | Forces Command |
| FST | Forward Surgical Team |
| FY | Fiscal Year |
| GH | General Hospital |
| GS | General Schedule |
| GSN | Graduate School of Nursing |
| GTC | Gateway to Care |
| HSC | Health Services Command |
| HSSA | Health Service Support Area |
| HUDS | Hospital Unit Dose Drug Distribution System |

| | | |
|---|---|---|
| ICU | Intensive Care Unit | |
| IMA | Individual Mobilization Augmentee | |
| ISO | International Standardization Organization (hard-walled DEPMEDS structures) | |
| ISR | Institute of Surgical Research; In-Service Recruiter | |
| JCCP | Joint Casualty Collection Point; Joint Casualty Control Point | |
| JTF | Joint Task Force | |
| MACH | Moncrief Army Community Hospital | |
| MACOM | Major Command | |
| MAMC | Madigan Army Medical Center | |
| MASCAL | Mass Casualty | |
| MASH | Mobile Army Surgical Hospital | |
| MC | Medical Corps | |
| MEDCOM | Medical Command | |
| MEDDAC | Medical Department Activity | |
| MEDEL | Medical Element | |
| MILVAN | Container for overseas or ground movement of military cargo | |
| MOPP | Mission Oriented Protective Postures | |
| MOS | Military Occupational Specialty | |
| MOU | Memorandum of Understanding | |
| MSC | Medical Service Corps | |
| MTF | Military Treatment Facility/Medical Treatment Facility | |
| MTO&E | Modified Table of Organization and Equipment | |
| MTT | Military Training Team | |
| MUST | Medical Unit, Self-contained, Transportable; Mobile Unit, Surgical, Transportable | |
| NATO | North Atlantic Treaty Organization | |
| NCLEX | National Council of State Boards of Nursing Licensure Examination | |
| NCR | National Capital Region | |
| NETS | Nursing Education and Training Service | |
| NMA | Nurse Methods Analyst | |
| NNC | Navy Nurse Corps | |
| NNMC | National Naval Medical Center | |
| NP | Nurse Practitioner | |
| NRAB | Nursing Research Advisory Board | |
| OBC | Officer Basic Course | |
| ODS | Operation Desert Shield/Operation Desert Storm | |
| OER | Officer Efficiency Report | |
| OR | Operating Room | |
| OTSG | Office of the Surgeon General | |
| PA | Physician Assistant | |

| | |
|---|---|
| PAU | Pre-Admission Unit |
| PBG | Program Budget Guidance |
| PIC | Physician-in-Charge |
| PNP | Pediatric Nurse Practitioner |
| POMCUS | Pre-positioning of Material Configured to Unit Sets |
| PROFIS | Professional Officer Filler System |
| RANCA | Retired Army Nurse Corps Association |
| RC | Reserve Component |
| RMC | Regional Medical Commander |
| ROTC | Reserve Officers' Training Corps |
| ROTCNAC | Reserve Officers' Training Corps Nursing Advanced Camp |
| SERB | Selective Early Retirement Board |
| SMART | Systematic Modular Approach to Realistic Training |
| SWA | Southwest Asia |
| TAMC | Tripler Army Medical Center |
| TDA | Table of Distribution and Allowances |
| TEMPER | Tent, Extendable, Modular, Personnel (soft-sided DEPMEDS structures) |
| TFA | Task Force Aesculapius |
| TO&E | Table of Organization and Equipment |
| TPU | Troop Program Unit |
| TRIMIS | Tri-Service Medical Information System |
| TSG | The Surgeon General |
| TSNR | TriService Nursing Research |
| TSNRP | TriService Nursing Research Program |
| UNPROFOR | United Nations Protection Force |
| USAH | United States Army Hospital |
| USAR | United States Army Reserve |
| USAREC | United States Army Recruiting Command |
| USAREUR | United States Army, Europe |
| USPHS | United States Public Health Service |
| USUHS | Uniformed Services University of the Health Sciences |
| VA | Veterans' Administration (Department of Veterans Affairs) |
| VI | Voluntary Indefinite |
| WHNP | Women's Health Nurse Practitioner |
| WMSN | Workload Management System for Nurses |
| WRAIN | Walter Reed Army Institute of Nursing |
| WRAIR | Walter Reed Army Institute of Research |
| WRAMC | Walter Reed Army Medical Center |

# Index

*Numbers with "n" preceding them indicate these items appear in the Notes section at the end of the chapter.*

## A

Abdellah, Rear Adm. Faye G., 229
Abrams, Lt. Gen. John, photo, 513
Academy of Health Sciences
    Community Health and Environmental Science Course Program of Instruction, 109
    establishment of, 8
    expansion of training opportunities for reservists, 66
    Field Nursing Course, 265
    mobilization course for activated USAR and ARNG personnel, 426
    name change to Army Medical Department Center and School, 363
    nurse practitioner courses, 106
ACHNs. *See* Army Community Health Nurses
Acord, Dr. Lea, 70
Adams, Col. Bert, photo, 488
Adams, Lt. Col. Carolyn
    frocking of, 487, 501 n13
    Operation Desert Shield/Operation Desert Storm and, 454
    Operation Restore Hope and, 487, 489, 491
    photos, 450, 451, 488, 489
Adams, Maj. Gen. Nancy
    AMEDD C&S and, 366
    budget cuts during the 1990s and, 337
    career and achievements, 347, 349
    command position, 395
    Conceptual Model of Army Nursing Practice and, 203
    Gen. Sullivan's disapproval of her command position assignment, 392
    Graduate School of Nursing and, 230–232
    medical model views, 370
    opening promotions for ANC officers beyond the one-star level and, 400–401
    photos, 348, 554
    Standards of Nursing Practice and, 211 n21
    triple roles of, 366
    views on the survival of nursing, 370
    Workload Management System for Nurses and, 262–263
Adams-Ender, Brig. Gen. Clara
    Army Nurse Corps leadership role, 34, 171, 173, 175–176
    Army Nurse Corps officers' service on the House Armed Services Committee and, 177
    assignment of nurses to command positions and, 389–390
    baccalaureate degree requirement for nurses and, 209
    Civil Service Registered Nurses and, 222, 224
    command of Fort Belvoir, Virginia, 409 n56
    contract nurses views, 240
    Individual Mobilization Augmentee program and, 272
    integration movement and, 36
    nurse recruitment and retention efforts, 227–228, 246 n57, 246 n61, 246 n63
    nurse recruitment efforts, 173
    Operation Desert Shield/Operation Desert Storm role, 425–426, 428
    photos, 172, 225, 554
    prototype HSSA at Fitzsimmons Army Medical Center and, 366–367
    ROCKS volunteer program and, 34
    upgrading of the position of director of personnel for the surgeon general and, 398
    U.S. Army Center for Health Promotion and Preventive Medicine and, 367

views on intermingling of nursing and command roles, 397
Addis, Elisabetta, 459
Administrative questions
  changes in uniforms, 90–95, 101 n79
  compliance with military downsizing, 79–84
  Hospital Unit Dose Drug Distribution System, 87
  nursing shortage, 79–86
  nursing standards, 88
  Physician-in-Charge Program, 88–90
  Pri-Team concept for nursing care, 86–87
Advanced practice. *See also* Army Nurse Corps Contemporary Practice Program; Nurse practitioners
  National Council of State Boards of Nursing definition, 19 n5
  views of the professional nursing community on, 103–104
AECP. *See* AMEDD Enlisted Commissioning Program
AFNC. *See* Air Force Nurse Corps
African-Americans. *See* Racial and ethnic issues; *specific persons*
AHS. *See* Academy of Health Sciences
Aidid, Gen. Mohamed Farrah, 484, 493–494
Aileo, Maj. Brenna B., 442, 443–444
Aileo, Maj. Brenna B., photo, 445
Air Force Aeromedical Staging Facility, 312
Air Force Medical Service, Operation Desert Shield/Operation Desert Storm, 417
Air Force Nurse Corps. *See also* U.S. Air Force
  anesthesia nurse graduate course, 214 n75
  assimilation of officers into the staff at Landstuhl Regional Medical Center and, 380
  baccalaureate degree requirement and, 209, 217 n98
  Battlefield Nursing Course, 265
  command positions and, 394
  Graduate School of Nursing and, 230
  Nurse Internship Program, 205–206
  nurse practitioners and, 105
  nursing shortage and, 220–221, 227
  Operation Desert Shield/Operation Desert Storm role, 417
  recruitment and retention challenges, 221, 338–339
  recruitment goals, 240
  Registered Care Technician proposal opposition, 336–337
  Tri-Service Medical Information System and, 213 n46
  Workload Management System for Nurses and, 199
Air Force Tactical Hospital, 141–143

Airborne training, ROTC nurses and, 71–73
Aitcheson, Maj. Annette
  educational mission to Jordan, 158–159
  Jordanian Army Burn Treatment Centre mission, 157–158
Albania, Task Force Hawk and, 524
Aleman-Guzman, Capt. Nelly
  El Salvador relief effort and, 297–298
  military exercises in Honduras role, 294
Alexander, Capt. Bethany, 395
Alexander, Lt. Col. (P) Gus N., 53
Alire, Lt. Col. Marie P., 284 n92
Allbritten, Lt. Col. Dorothy, photo, 393
Allen, Capt. Steve, 327 n67
Allen, Lt. Col. Susanne, 279 n12
Allmon, Lt. Col. Nancy, photo, 546
Alm, Col. Philip, photo, 428
Altamirano, Capt. Javier, 528, 538 n77
AMEDD. *See* Army Medical Department
AMEDD C&S. *See* Army Medical Department Center and School
AMEDD Enlisted Commissioning Program
  description, 234–235
  long-term career consequences for participants, 235–236, 250 n103
  name changed from Medic to RN Program, 234
  service obligation, 235, 338
AMEDD Personnel Proponency Division, 179–180
American Association of Nurse Anesthetists, 112
American Hospital Association
  Advisory Committee on Infections recommendations on nosocomial infections, 113
  nationwide nurse vacancy rates, 220
American Medical Association, Registered Care Technician proposal, 336–337, 355 n18
American Nurses Association
  Army Nurse Corps Continuing Health Education Program, 46
  leak about Physician-in-Charge Program and, 89–90
  physician assistants and, 118–119
  Registered Care Technician proposal and, 336–337
  Standards of Nursing Practice and, 190, 194
  support for the baccalaureate degree requirement for nurses, 43
AMOSISTs. *See* Automated Military Outpatient System Specialists
ANA. *See* American Nurses Association
ANC-CHEP. *See* Army Nurse Corps Continuing Health Education Program
ANCCPP. *See* Army Nurse Corps Contemporary Practice Program

Anderson, Alma B., 186 n46
Anderson, Brig. Gen. Pat, photo, 520
Anderson, Capt. Robena, 135 n72
Andrews, 1st Lt. Mary, 236
Anesthesia nursing, 111–112
Antilla, Col. Betty J., photo, 555
Apache helicopters, Task Force Hawk and, 524
APPD. *See* AMEDD Personnel Proponency Division
ARCENT. *See* Army Central
Army Central
   Col. Smith's leadership, 425–431
   headquarters for, 427
   Operation Desert Shield/Operation Desert Storm and, 425–431
Army Community Health Nurses
   Armed Forces Network radio for dissemination of health information, 110–111
   Guatemalan earthquake mission, 152
   medication prescribing responsibilities, 109
   Operation New Life and Operation New Arrivals role, 147–149
   practice scope, 109
   vans for care delivery, 109–110
   work with Haitian refugees at Guantanamo Bay, 541–543
Army Education Review Board, 47
Army Emergency Medicine, residency programs, 118
Army Medical Department. *See also specific units*
   ANC officers functioning in critical positions in, 398, 400
   Army Nurse Corps Professional Development Funding Package, 236
   Berry plan deferment for physicians and, 4
   board to consider applicants for nurse practitioner courses, 106–107
   clinic non-CSL command positions, 408 n41
   continuing education program proposal, 46
   conversion of Evacuation Hospitals and Mobile Army Surgical Hospitals to Medical Unit, Self-contained, Transportable (MUST) facilities, 59
   core mission, 333
   cost of Operation New Life and Operation New Arrivals, 150
   cost-reduction projects, 169
   Cuban Refugee Operation and, 287–291
   cuts in nursing education programs, 4
   Deployable Medical System and, 59–60
   downsizing of the 1990s and, 333–352
   Enlisted Commissioning Program, 234–236, 338
   evolution of during the 1980s, 169
   Gateway to Care delivery approach, 334–335, 354 n9
   Graduate School of Nursing and, 230
   Haitian refugees at Guantanamo Bay and, 541–543
   Hospital Unit Dose Drug Distribution System and, 87
   Medical Force 2000 doctrine, 414–415
   military courses for nurses, 205
   Mobilization Designee program expansion, 67
   Nicaraguan earthquake of December 1972 and, 143
   Officer Leader Development Action Plan, 392
   Officer Structure Study, 237–238, 251 n113
   Operation Desert Shield/Operation Desert Storm role, 413–418
   personnel and budget cuts, 86
   Personnel Proponency Division, 179–180
   Personnel Support Agency, 65, 106
   physician assistant education, 118
   postgraduate short courses for nurses, 46–47
   Quicksilver downsizing initiative, 363
   "readiness" definition, 259
   reasons for the nursing shortage, 220
   Research Analysis Corporation study of readiness and, 65–66
   revamping of organizational structure, 334, 363–368
   U.S. Army Health Facility Planning Agency, 113–114
Army Medical Department Center and School
   activities of, 363
   ANC officers in command positions and, 395
   establishment of, 363
   staff and faculty for, 363
Army Medical Department Museum, 14
Army Medical Specialist Corps
   decline in authorizations, 338
   expanded responsibilities, 118
Army Natick Research and Development Command, uniform options for women, 91
Army National Guard. *See also* U.S. Army Reserve
   Active, Guard, Reserve (AGR) recruiters, 252 n121
   adequacy of numbers and, 9
   assignment of retired Army Nurse Corps officers to, 271–273
   challenges in the post-Vietnam War era, 64–67
   Combat Nursing Course, 266
   direct mail campaign for nursing opportunities, 222, 238
   extension of maximum age for initial appointment to the ARNG and USAR, 238

Former Republic of Yugoslavia operations and, 521–522
Individual Mobilization Augmentee program and, 271–273
integration into regular Army units and, 469–470, 472, 474, 481 n28
more active and inclusive role for, 9
nursing shortage and, 222, 238
Operation Desert Shield/Operation Desert Storm and, 415–416, 418, 426, 468–470, 471–476, 481 n22
readiness improvements and, 65–67
readiness issues, 271
"Shake 'n Bake" Officer Basic Course for Operation Desert Shield/Operation Desert Storm and, 415–416
Slewitzke's role, 171
source of nurses, 84
women in command positions and, 392
Army Nurse Candidate Program
accession bonus and monthly stipend, 228
service obligation, 338
Army Nurse Clinician Program. *See also* Army Nurse Corps Clinician Program
Army Nurse Corps Contemporary Practice Program name changed to, 120
cuts in personnel and, 80
name change to Army Nurse Practitioner Program, 120
nurse practitioner movement and, 104
Army Nurse Corps. *See also specific leaders*
assignment of ROTC chief nurses to the four ROTC regions, 70
Automated Military Outpatient System Specialists, 117–118
background of, 553–555
budget cuts during the 1990s, 337
centennial celebration, 553–555
chief, nursing education and staff development service responsibilities, 46–47
civilian nurses and, 224, 341
command positions for officers, 389–404
Defense Officer Personnel Management Act and, 51–53, 237–238
Desert Shield Situation Group, 425
downsizing of the 1990s and, 333–352
Field Nursing Course, 265
foreign nurse graduates and, 236–237
Former Republic of Yugoslavia operations and, 505–531
four pillars of professional nursing, 333
increase in the number of ROTC scholarships offered to collegiate nursing students, 233–234
increase in the number of women in the military and, 63, 167–168

Life Cycle Model, 395
National Council of State Boards of Nursing Licensure Examination and, 201
1980 Professional Development Workshop, 268
nursing process, 397, 409 n45
Office of the Chief of the Army Nurse Corps reorganization, 367–368
Operation Desert Shield/Operation Desert Storm combat hospital activities, 435–459
Operation Desert Shield/Operation Desert Storm leadership, 425–431
Pri-Team concept, 86–87
Primary Care Demonstration Project, 371
Professional Development Funding Package, 236
rank restructuring and, 237–238
recruitment and retention challenges and strategies, 221, 236–237, 240, 250 n107, 338–339
Registered Care Technician proposal opposition, 336–337, 355 n18
revamping of the organizational structure, 366–381
Selective Early Retirement Boards for senior officers, 338, 339–340
"Standards for Nursing in Mobilization," 505
tenure limitation, 400, 409 n55
Voluntary Indefinite (VI) or Conditional Voluntary Indefinite (CVI) status and, 338, 339, 341, 357 n33
Army Nurse Corps Accession Bonus Program, 228
Army Nurse Corps Association
biennial conventions, 180–181
Col. Florence A. Blanchfield Community Hospital naming and, 181–182
Retired Army Nurse Corps Association name changed to, 180
Army Nurse Corps Branch, name change to Career Activities Office, 9, 51
Army Nurse Corps Clinician Program, 4
Army Nurse Corps Contemporary Practice Program. *See also* Army Community Health Nurses; Nurse practitioners
Academy of Health Sciences and, 106
advanced practice roles, 4, 19 n5
Army physician resistance to, 119
circumstances favoring, 103
civilianization of nursing jobs and, 106
Clinical Nurse Specialist role, 121
concept of, 4, 19 n5
decline in authorizations for the Department of Defense and, 106
expansion of courses for, 104–105

implementation of, 103
medication prescribing responsibilities, 109, 133 n44
military treatment facilities and, 106
name change to Army Nurse Clinician Program, 120
"Nurse Practitioner" designation, 120–121
original vision for, 104
specialities, 104–105, 107
workload and productivity issues, 107–108
"zero-procurement objective" and, 80–81
Army Nurse Corps Continuing Health Education Program, description, 46
Army Nurse Corps Fellows Program
description and participants, 206–208
expansion of the program, 208
Army Nurse Corps Strategic Planning Conference, nursing shortage and, 228
Army Nurse Practitioner Program, name change, 120
Army of Excellence
adoption of, 169
quality of care and, 189
Army Pamphlet 40-5, Standards of Nursing Practice, 192, 194
Army Physical Fitness Test
components of, 278 n4
need for twice-yearly completion of, 255
nurses' attendance at educational courses and, 255–256
Army Registered Nurse Program, shift of assets, 4
Army Regulation 600-9, weight control and physical fitness, 62
Army Regulation 600-20, assignment of women to command positions, 391
Army Student Nurse Program
discontinuation, 84
shift of assets away from, 4
Army Student Nurse Program, baccalaureate degree requirement, 42
*Army Times*
article on military medicine's problems, 55 n21
article on the quality of care in the Army health care system, 44
ARNG. *See* Army National Guard
Arnold, Maj. Gen. Steven Lloyd, 483
ASPECTS program. *See* A Solid Parenting Experience Through Community Teaching and Support program and
Association of the United States Army, nursing shortage report, 227
Atkinson, SFC, photo, 439
Atwood, 1st Lt. Rebecca, 161 n10
Automated information systems

quality of care and, 199–201
Tri-Service Medical Information System, 199–201
Automated Military Outpatient System Specialists
algorithm approach and, 117–118
Army Nurse Corps support for, 117–118
autonomy and scope of practice and, 117, 136 n85
description, 117
educational requirements, 117
Triage and Acute Minor Illness clinics and, 117
Triage Manual use and, 117
Troop Medical Clinics and, 118

# B

Baccalaureate degrees
Army Nurse Corps task force and, 41–42
Army nurses' views on requirement for, 43–44
commissioning as first lieutenant and, 41
opposition to the requirement for, 42–43
"reality shock" of recent graduates moving into clinical practice, 204–205
requirement for, 41–44, 85, 201–202, 204–205, 208–209
support for the requirement for, 43
BACH. *See* Bassett Army Community Hospital, Fort Wainwright, Alaska
Bailey, Brig. Gen. Inez, 91
Bailey, Brig. Gen. Mildred, 10–11
Bailey, Col. Margaret
integration movement and, 34, 36
photo, 35
Baird, Col. Margaret
photo, 381
WRAMC and Malcolm Grow program integration and, 378
Baker, Lt. B., photo, 510
The Balkan states. *See* Former Republic of Yugoslavia
Balkema, Lt. Col. Sarah, 108
Balliram, Maj. Niranjan, 239
BAMC. *See* Brooke Army Medical Center
Baptist Medical Center, Columbia, South Carolina, 220
Barbieri, Col. Marian C.
letters to Parks, 164 n62
Military Training Team mission to Jordan and, 155–157
Barbisch, Brig. Gen. Donna, photo, 520
Barkley, Lt. Col. Velma, 146–148
Barnhill, Capt. Nelda, 505–506
Barras, Capt. Paul, 530, 538 n77
Barre, Siad, 483
Bartz, Col. Claudia

accession of foreign nurse graduates and, 236–237
Standards of Nursing Practice and, 211 n21
Base Realignment and Closure Commission
closure of hospitals, 342–347
lost positions and, 337
personnel drawdown and, 342–347
restructuring of AMEDD and, 363–368
Bassett Army Community Hospital, Fort Wainwright, Alaska
Certified Nurse Midwives Service, 373
well-woman clinic, 373
Beary, Assistant Secretary of Defense (Health Affairs) John, medical readiness views, 259, 260
Bechtold, Col. Dianne, 211 n21
Becker, Surgeon General, Lt. Gen. Quinn, 259, 260, 284 n84
Belgium, closure of bases and hospitals, 343
Belihar, Col. Robert P., 418
Benson, Capt. Julie, 538 n83
Bernheim, Maj. Carolyn, 279 n12
Berry plan, deferment for physicians, 3–4
Bester, Brig. Gen. William T.
career and achievements, 352
command position, 396, 408 n39
Cuban Refugee Operation and, 300 n11
Former Republic of Yugoslavia operations and, 512–513, 514, 535 n46
photos, 351, 513, 515, 554
role in Hungary and Croatia, 396
Beus, Lt. Col. John, 407 n30
BI. *See* Branch immaterial concept
Big Pine II. *See* Honduras
Biskey, Col. Valerie
Operation Desert Shield/Operation Desert Storm and, 481 n29
photo, 474
Bither, Lt. Col. Mark, 536 n57
Black, Clint, 498
*Black Hawk Down* (Bowden), 494–495
Black Hawk helicopters
Former Republic of Yugoslavia operations and, 522
Operation Restore Hope in Somalia and, 484, 493–494
Blackburn, Maj. Kim, 538 n77
Blakely, Lt. Col. Frank, photo, 488
Blanchfield, Col. Florence A., 181–182
Blanchfield Army Community Hospital, Fort Campbell, Kentucky
Certified Nurse Midwives Service, 373–374
Operation Restore Hope and, 485, 487, 500 n10
strategies to relieve the nursing shortage, 239

Women's Health Nurse Practitioners, 373–374
Blanck, Surgeon General, Lt. Gen. Ronald R.
Leader Development Decision Network process and, 394
WRAMC and Malcolm Grow program integration and, 378
Bombard, Lt. Col. Charles
assistance mission to Saudi Arabia, 317
Operation Just Cause and, 316
Bonnell, 1st Lt. Diane
Operation Desert Shield/Operation Desert Storm and, 454
photo, 453
Bonnet, Col. Edith J.
Army Nurse Corps leadership role, 14
photo, 49
Borders, 1st Lt. Jeff, 538 n83
Bork, Capt. Raymond, 451
Bosnia. *See* Former Republic of Yugoslavia
Bottomley, Maj. (P) Wendy, 430
Bowden, Mark, *Black Hawk Down*, 494–495
Bowie, Capt. Elizabeth, 505
Bowns, 1st Lt. Nicole, 538 n83
Branch immaterial concept
ANC philosophy relating to, 396–397
budgeted end-strength issues and, 397
Colonel Command Board, 396
command positions and, 394–401
Command Selection List and, 396
follow-on assignments and, 397
key AMEDD positions and, 398
opening promotions for ANC officers beyond the one-star level, 400–401, 404
recoding of specific AMEDD General Officer positions to BI status, 394–395
recommendation not to establish a BI for the AMEDD, 392
terminology, 406 n18
Brice, Lt. Col. Betty, 63
Brill, Capt. Esther, 481 n30
Broberg, Sgt. 1st Class Rhonda, 380
Brooke Army Medical Center
designation as an Army Primary Casualty Receiving Center during Operation Desert Shield/Operation Desert Storm, 470–471
Operation Just Cause and, 314–316, 328 n88
Physician-in-Charge Program and, 88
Brousseau, Capt. Leslie
health fitness consultant role, 256
physical fitness program and, 279 n12
Brown, Col. Virginia L.
Army Nurse Corps leadership role, 14
Nursing Division chief, 6
photo, 7

Index   xxix

retirement of, 17
Brown, Sgt. Ruby, 460 n9
Bruno, Lt. Col. Barbara, 520
Bryant, Col. Ruby F., 409 n56
Buchanan, Lt. Col. Holly, 532 n7
Buckles, Capt. Carla, 538 n77
Buescher, Col. Ed, 125
Burns, Col. Pam, 445
Burt, Lt. Col. Margie O., 67
Bush, Pres. George H.W., 413–414
Butke, Col. Diane, 474, 476
Buzonas, Lt. Col. Patricia, 409 n53
Byrd, 1st Lt. April, 538 n82
Byrne, Col. T.R., 415–416
Bystran, Col. Sharon
  nurses' readiness and, 269
  photos, 270, 475
  WRAMC Mass Casualty Plan and, 474

## C

Camacho, Macho, 313–314
Cameron, Maj. Gen. Richard, 369
Camp Pendleton, California, Operation New Life and Operation New Arrivals, 144
Campbell, Col. Kristine V.
  command position, 396
  Former Republic of Yugoslavia operations and, 520
  photos, 520, 521
CAO. *See* Career Activities Office
Capps, Maj. Dianne, 185 n25
Career Activities Office
  Army Nurse Corps Branch name changed to, 9, 51
  career planning responsibilities, 48, 51
  components of, 48
  relocation of, 51
Career advancement. *See* Educational concerns and career advancement
Carney, Capt. Carol, 378
Carns, Lt. Col. Edwin H., 289
Carson, Col. Amelia J.
  Army National Guard's Combat Nursing Course role, 266
  Individual Mobilization Augmentee program and, 271
  photo, 267
Carter, Pres. Jimmy
  Cuban Refugee Operation and, 287
  Nurse Training Act veto, 19 n8
  photo, 174
Carter administration, social tone, 174–175
Cartwright, Capt., 537 n67
Cartwright, Gen. Roscoe (Rock) C., 33–34
Castellan, Lt. Col. Deborah
  photo, 427, 450, 451

Castro, Fidel, Cuban Refugee Operation and, 287
CCP. *See* Coordinated Care Program
CENTCOM. *See* U.S. Central Command
Centers for Disease Control and Prevention
  National Nosocomial Infections Surveillance, 113
  Study on the Efficacy of Nosocomial Infection Control, 113
Certified Registered Nurse Anesthetists
  Board Certification Pay and, 231–232
  incentive pay for, 232–233, 248 n84
  "Proud to Care" survey and, 232
CHAMPUS. *See* Civilian Health and Medical Program of the Uniformed Services
CHCS. *See* Composite Health Care System
Cheney, Lt. Col. Ruth
  field experience, 430, 434 n27
  Operation Desert Shield/Operation Desert Storm role, 428, 430–431, 436
  photo, 429
  tactical briefings, 431, 434 n30
Christman, Luther, 26
Christoph (Shipley), Col. Susan, 240
Civil Rights Act, provisions, 10
Civil Service Registered Nurses
  career development opportunities and, 223–224
  career ladders and, 244 n35
  contract nurses and, 240
  hourly wages for, 253 n135
  legislation to attract, 224, 244 n38
  nursing shortage and, 222–226
  pay issues, 224
  satisfaction and dissatisfaction factors, 222
Civil Service Task Force, career advancement for CSRNs, 224
Civilian Health and Medical Program of the Uniformed Services
  Gateway to Care delivery approach and, 335
  patient cost surveillance and, 169
Clark, Lt. Col. Dorothy, 318
Clarke, Brig. Gen. Mary E., 12
Clarke, Capt. Sheila, 300 n11
Clinical Nurse Specialists
  nonmilitary model compared with the military model, 121
  role of, 121
Clinical Nursing Records Study, 189–190
Clinton, Gov. William, Cuban Refugee Operation "refugee discontent," 288
Clinton, Pres. William, U.S. Department of Defense budget cuts, 333–334
CMFs. *See* Contingent Medical Forces
Cobb, Doris M., 186 n46
Cobb, Maj. Christine, 268

Coenen, Capt. Andrea, 320
Collins, Capt. Phyllis
　Operation Desert Shield/Operation Desert Storm and, 472, 474, 481 n28
　photo, 473
Combat Casualty Care Course
　readiness and, 265–266, 268
　Uniformed Services University of the Health Sciences and, 118
Combat Stress Control teams
　Haitian refugees at Guantanamo Bay and, 541
　Operation Desert Shield/Operation Desert Storm and, 415
　Restoration Unit, 523, 537 n69
Combat Support Hospitals. *See also specific hospitals*
　conversion to, 59
　transition of European Army hospitals to, 343
Combs, Lt. Col. Maureen, photo, 427
Command and General Staff College
　opening of more seats for ANC officers at, 394–395
　Slewitzke's attendance and leadership, 47, 48, 120
Composite Health Care System
　concept of, 200
　flaws in, 201
　outside sources for processing, 200–201
　rationale for, 214 n50
Conceptual Model of Army Nursing Practice, 203
Condit, Lt. Col. Mary, 104
Congressional Fellowship Program for Army Nurse Corps officers, 173, 175–179
*The Connection,* Army Nurse Corps Association newsletter, 181
Conneen, Maj. Robert, 327 n67
Connelly, Maj. Lynne
　Field Nursing Course and, 265
　photo, 266
Connor, Maj. Susan, 176–177
Constantine, Staff Sgt. Joe, 158–159
Continental United States
　ANC activities in during Operation Desert Shield/Operation Desert Storm, 470–478
　closure of bases and hospitals, 345–346
Contingent Medical Forces. *See also specific units*
　description, 537 n75
Continuing education
　Army regulations for licensing and, 44, 46
　contract hours or continuing education units, 56 n25
　state requirements for license renewals, 44

Contract nurses
　advantages and disadvantages of, 239
　Civil Service Registered Nurses and, 240
　nursing shortage and, 226, 239–240
CONUS. *See* Continental United States
Coordinated Care Program
　features of, 335
　transformation into TRICARE, 335
Corcoran, Lt. Col. Diane
　command position, 390–391
　DEPMEDS role, 264
　photo, 391
　Systematic Modular Approach to Realistic Training program and, 273, 276
Corps Specific Branch Proponency Officers, 179–180
Cost, Ann B., 186 n46
Costello, Lt. Col. Barbara R., 20 n23
Cox, Maj. Debora R., photo, 554, 555
Crawford, Capt. Tammy, 538 n83
Criswell, Capt. Mary L., 161 n10
CRNAs. *See* Certified Registered Nurse Anesthetists
Croatia. *see* Former Republic of Yugoslavia
Crossland, Capt. Kimberly, 528
Crouch, Capt. Carla, 539 n92
Crowl, Lt. Col. Marjorie, photo, 455
CSHs. *See* Combat Support Hospitals
CSRNs. *See* Civil Service Registered Nurses
Cuba
　Cuban Refugee Operation, 287–293
　Haitian refugees at Guantanamo Bay, 541–543
Cuban Refugee Operation
　After Action Report on, 292–293
　babies born during, 288, 300 n7
　control of displaced persons and, 289–290
　duty shifts for nurses, 289
　Federal Emergency Management Agency and, 287, 291
　field hospital role, 293
　need to upgrade the MTO&E system and, 290
　number of refugees processed, 299 n1
　overall health of the immigrants, 291
　"refugee discontent" and, 288
　supply issues, 289
　transportation issues, 290
　types of medical problems, 288
　U.S. Public Health Service and, 287, 288, 289
Cuban Relief Mission, Army Nurse Corps role, 167
Cudnohufsky, Capt. Eugene, 92–93
Cultural issues
　Guatemalan earthquake relief effort, 154

Jordan missions, 156, 157
Operation Brightstar, 318
Operation Desert Shield/Operation Desert Storm and, 429, 430, 457, 459, 476–477, 548

# D

DACOWITS. *See* Defense Advisory Committee on Women in the Services
D'Alessandro, Lt. Col. Diane, photo, 455
Daniels, Capt. Delois, 317
Davidson, Lt. Col. Alice, 430
Davis, Maj. Cindy, photo, 450
Davis, Maj. Mary C., 279 n12
Davis, Maj. Shirley A., 307, 310
Dayton, Maj. Loraine, 300 n11
de Berg, Col. Joellen, 378
Deal, Capt. Dora, 300 n11
DeConcini, Sen. Dennis, 212th Mobile Army Surgical Hospital ribbon-cutting ceremony and, 505
Defense Advisory Committee on Women in the Services
  assignment of nurses to command positions and, 390, 394
  nursing shortage and, 228
  objectives, 10
Defense Authorization Act
  financial support for TriService Nursing Research Group, 130
  surgeon general's three-star position and, 401
Defense Officer Personnel Management Act
  authorization of the one-star rank for ANC chiefs and directors and the rank of colonel for the assistant chiefs, 404
  basis for, 52
  due-course officers and, 52, 251 n111
  implications for the Army Nurse Corps, 51–53, 237–238
  Medical and Dental Corps officers and, 58 n53
  non-due-course officers and, 52
  promotion guidelines, 51–53, 237–238, 251 n111
  rank restructuring and, 237–238
  Sen. Nunn's role, 57 n47, 57 n48
  slow rate of promotions for upcoming officers and, 52–53
  year groups and, 237, 251 n110, 358 n40
Deffer, Brig. Gen. Philip A., 88
DeMarais, Col. Alice O'K., 408 n39
Demster, Maj. Stella, 531
Denny, Lt. Col. Suzan, 524, 530
Dental Corps
  decline in authorizations, 338, 356 n22

Defense Officer Personnel Management Act and, 58 n53
  fellowship program, 206
*Department of Army Historical Summary,* negative view of U.S. medical readiness, 260
Department of Defense Health Resources Sharing and Emergency Operations Act, 417
Department of Nursing Organizational Model
  "Deputy Commander Patient Care Services" designation, 214 n65
  quality of care and, 202
Department of the Army, women's uniforms, 91
Department of Veterans Affairs
  Gulf War Syndrome and, 478
Deployable Medical System
  advantages and disadvantages of, 261
  computerization of supply lists, 264
  Contingency Medical Force and, 261
  Defense Medical Standardization Board and, 261
  Fuertes Caminos 89 in Honduras and, 260–261, 280 n33
  Joint Services Nursing Advisory Group and, 261–262
  Military Field Medical Systems Standardization Steering Group and, 260
  mini-MASH units and, 261
  module configurations, 261
  nurse staffing requirements and, 263–264
  Operation Brightstar and, 317–318
  Operation Desert Shield/Operation Desert Storm and, 414, 438–439, 445–446
  Operation Restore Hope and, 490, 492
  organic vehicles and, 261, 281 n40
  TEMPER tent fabric and, 260, 261, 317
  U.S. Congress funding for, 260
  Workload Management System for Nurses and, 262–264
DEPMEDS. *See* Deployable Medical System
Deschamps, Capt. Diana, 530
Deuster, Col. Kathryn P.
  Cuban Refugee Operation and, 300 n11
  duty schedules during Operation Desert Shield/Operation Desert Storm, 438
  photo, 439
Dewan, Lt. Col. Mary, 148–149
Diehl, Lt. Diane, 544
DiGirol, Col. Marilyn, 239
Direct Combat Probability Coding System
  Army Nurse Corps and, 168, 307
  "direct combat" definition, 183 n8
  Operation Urgent Fury and, 307
Discrimination
  gender discrimination during Operation Desert Shield/Operation Desert Storm, 476–477

gender discrimination during Operation Urgent Fury, 308–309, 310
male nurses and, 26–27
racial, 33–36
Diskin, Lt. Col. Patricia A., Operation Urgent Fury, 306–307, 309, 323 n12, 325 n34
Dolenar, Lt. Col. Daniel, photo, 439
Donohue, Capt. Maureen, 185 n25
DOPMA. *See* Defense Officer Personnel Management Act
Driscoll, Capt. Dennis, 320
Dudley, 1st Lt., 537 n67
Duerk, Adm. Alene, 92
Duley, Maj. Clara, 123
Dunbar, Command Sgt. Maj. Craig, photo, 513
Dunlap, Brig. Gen. Lillian
  Army Nurse Corps chief, 6
  biographical information, 14
  black beret views, 91
  briefing to the Surgeon General on the implications of downsizing on the Army Nurse Corps, 81
  Career Activities Office role, 57 n42
  career advancement views, 51
  DOPMA views, 53
  duty pantsuit views, 92
  photos, 13, 49, 116, 554
  Physician-in-Charge Program and, 89–90
  views on physician assistants, 119
  views on the baccalaureate degree requirement for nurses, 42
  views on the issue of the pregnancy of officers, 30
Duquette, Capt. Teresa
  photos, 528, 529
  Task Force Hawk and, 528, 538 n77
Dwight David Eisenhower Army Medical Center, 87

# E

Ebert, Lt. Col. Darla, photo, 450
Echelons Above Corps, 418, 430, 436
Educational concerns and career advancement
  advanced study courses, 203–204
  anesthesia nursing, 111–112
  Army Medical Department's cuts in nursing education programs, 4
  Army-sponsored graduate education in civilian institutions, 204
  Automated Military Outpatient System Specialists, 117
  baccalaureate degree as a prerequisite for entry into the Army Nurse Corps, 41–44
  Career Activities Office and, 48, 51
  Combat Casualty Care Course, 265–266, 268
  concept of career planning for Army Nurse Corps officers, 48, 51
  continuing education, 44, 46
  Defense Officer Personnel Management Act and, 51–53
  Field Nursing Course, 265
  intent of career planning, 48
  Long Term Civilian Training Program, 204
  military courses, 204
  military education level and, 47–48
  Military Training Team mission to Jordan, 154–157
  nurse practitioner training, 104–105, 121, 123
  "nursing instructor" role, 56 n29
  nursing shortage and, 222, 224, 228–234
  officer professionalism courses, 203
  physician assistants, 118
  postgraduate short courses, 46–47
  Preceptor Program, 205
  "reality shock" of recent graduates moving into clinical practice, 204–205
  specialty courses, 203
Eglin Air Force Base, Florida, 144
Egypt
  Operation Brightstar, 317–318
  Project Hope, 317
XVIII Corps
  Operation Desert Shield/Operation Desert Storm and, 418
8th Evacuation Hospital
  Fuertes Caminos 89 in Honduras and, 260–261, 280 n33
86th Combat Support Hospital
  Corcoran's command position, 390–391
  Cuban Refugee Operation and, 291–292
  Operation Uphold Democracy and, 543–544
85th Evacuation Hospital
  Department of Nursing PROFIS chief nurse leadership, 440
  Mission Oriented Protective Postures gear and, 443
  Operation Desert Shield/Operation Desert Storm and, 440–445
  physical activities and, 442
  relationship with the 44th Medical Brigade, 441
  religious service attendance and, 442
  relocation challenges, 441–442
  SCUD missile attacks and, 444
86th Evacuation Hospital
  Enemy Prisoner of War and, 454
  family care plans and, 448
  lack of A rations, 453, 465 n62
  married and co-located spouses and, 448–454

MILVANs and, 450, 464 n58
MOPP gear and, 454
off-duty activities, 451–452
Operation Desert Shield/Operation Desert
  Storm and, 448–454
Operation Restore Hope and, 484, 485–491,
  492–493
relationship with the 42nd Field Hospital,
  492–493
relocation to King Khalid City, 452–453
SCUD missile attacks and, 454
84th Medical Detachment
  Combat Stress Control's Restoration Unit,
    523, 537 n69
85th Medical Detachment
  Combat Stress Control unit's work with Haitian refugees at Guantanamo Bay, 541
Eisenhower Army Medical Center, Fort Gordon,
  Georgia
  strategies to relieve the nursing shortage, 239
  telenursing and, 377
Eitzen, Col. Joan P., 408 n40
El Salvador
  Army Nurse Corps role in humanitarian
    efforts, 296–298
  civil war in, 296
  dangers of serving in, 297–298
Eller, Maj. Barbara, 185 n25
Elliot, 2d Lt. Sean, 539 n92
Enzel, Lt. Col. Lenore, 407 n30
Equal Employment Opportunity Commission, 10
Equal Pay Act, 10
Equal Rights Amendment, ratification efforts,
  10, 22 n46
ERA. *See* Equal Rights Amendment
Erlich, Maj. Paul, 505
Escott, 2d Lt. Paul, 317
Europe. *See also specific countries*
  ANC activities in during Operation Desert
    Shield/Operation Desert Storm, 467–470
  closure of bases and hospitals, 343–344, 503
  units deployed to during Operation Desert
    Shield/Operation Desert Storm, 479 n5
European Union, economic sanctions on the
  Balkan states, 503
Evolution and reorganization
  Academy of Health Sciences opening, 3, 8
  Army Reserve and National Guard improvements, 3, 9–10
  Health Services Command launch, 3, 4–8
  Nurse Corps leadership in the late- and post-
    Vietnam era, 12–17
  Office of the Army Surgeon General
    changes, 3, 8–9
  Selective Service System dismantling, 3–4
  women's movement, 3, 10–12

## F

F. Edward Hébert Medical School, 4
Fahad, King (Saudi Arabia), Saddam Hussein's
  invasion of Kuwait, 413
Fairman, Julie, 103, 111
FAMC. *See* Fitzsimmons Army Medical Center,
  Aurora, Colorado
Farineau, Maj. Paul, 317
Faupel, Capt. Mary F., 161 n10
Federal Emergency Management Agency, Cuban Refugee Operation and, 287, 291
Federal Nursing Research Interest Group
  formation and activities of, 130
  name change to TriService Nursing Research Group, 130
Feingold, Sen. Russell, proposed closure of
  USUHS and, 232
FEMA. *See* Federal Emergency Management
  Agency
Ferguson, Lt. Debra L., 329 n102
Ferington, Fay, 100 n59
Ferry, Capt. Patrick J., 71
Field units, evolution of, 59–61
15th Combat Support Hospital, 149–150
50th General Hospital
  combat readiness activities, 455–457, 465
    n65
  Islamic rituals and, 457
  mission of, 457
  Operation Desert Shield/Operation Desert
    Storm and, 454–459
  SCUD alerts and Patriot missile firings, 458
Filer, Col. Iladine, 21 n41
Fitzsimmons Army Medical Center, Aurora,
  Colorado
  closure of, 346
  designation as an Army Primary Casualty Receiving Center during Operation
    Desert Shield/Operation Desert Storm,
    470–471
  nursing shortage and, 226
  prototype HSSA at, 366–367
502nd Mobile Army Surgical Hospital
  experiences compared with those of the
    212th MASH, 508–509
  Former Republic of Yugoslavia operations
    and, 508–512
  lack of pediatric supplies, 510–511
  mission of, 509–510
  redeployment to Germany, 511–512
  Remote Clinical Communications System
    and, 508–509
5th Forward Surgical Team
  Operation Just Cause and, 312, 314–317,
    327 n61
555th Forward Surgical Team

Operation Uphold Democracy and, 548
5th Mobile Army Surgical Hospital
  Operation Brightstar and, 317–318
  Operation Urgent Fury and, 305–310, 311
V Corps
  Former Republic of Yugoslavia operations and, 503, 515
  relocation to Germany, 532 n5
Flecha, Lt. Col. Maria L., 291, 292–293
Foley, Lt. Col. Mary A., 20 n25
Foody, Capt. Naomi, 300 n11
Forces Command
  assignment of authorized nurse officers to with a Memorandum of Understanding, 269–271
  Cuban Refugee Operation and, 288, 292
  Operation Desert Shield/Operation Desert Storm role, 42, 414, 418
Ford, Col. Lark A., 408 n40
Ford, Loretta C., 103–104
Ford, Lt. Col. Gail
  Former Republic of Yugoslavia operations and, 515–516
  photos, 518, 519
Ford administration, social tone, 174
Forlaw, Lt. Col. Loretta, 177
Former Republic of Yugoslavia
  ban on alcohol and, 514
  civil war in, 503–532
  Dayton Peace Accords, 512
  "ethnic cleansing" and, 503
  European Union economic sanctions on, 503
  fragmentation into six republics and two provinces, 503, 532 n2
  language barriers and, 505–506
  Operation Joint Endeavor and, 512, 523
  Operation Joint Guard and, 523
  operational setting, 531
  primitive living conditions, 504, 506, 514
  Right Seat/Left Seat Ride policy for turnover, 523, 526, 527
  Sked stretchers and, 537 n65
  "slices" and, 538 n76
  "Standards for Nursing in Mobilization" and, 505
  Task Force Eagle and, 512, 520, 522, 523
  Task Force Falcon and, 524–528, 530
  Task Force Hawk and, 524, 530, 538 n77
  United Nations countries participating in operations in, 505, 533 n10
  U.S. Army medical units involved in operations in, 504–531, 549
  U.S. Army Reserve units serving in, 513–515, 516, 520
FORSCOM. *See* Forces Command

Forster, Maj. Ellen, 545, 547–548
Fort Bragg, North Carolina, 305
Fort Chaffee, Arkansas
  Cuban Refugee Operation and, 287–290
  Operation New Life and Operation New Arrivals and, 146–148
Fort Hood, Texas, 110
Fort Indiantown Gap, Pennsylvania
  Cuban Refugee Operation and, 290–291
  Operation New Life and Operation New Arrivals and, 148–150
Fort Leonard Wood, Missouri, 239
Fort McCoy, Wisconsin, 291–293
Fortmeier, Capt. Linda, 470
42nd Field Hospital
  Cuban Refugee Operation and, 290–291
  Medical Mobile Training Team mission in Liberia and, 318
  Operation New Life and Operation New Arrivals and, 148–149
  Operation Restore Hope and, 484–485, 491–494
  relationship with the 86th Evacuation Hospital, 492–493
46th Combat Support Hospital
  Operation Restore Hope and, 494–495
47th Combat Support Hospital
  Department of Nursing precepts and, 440
  Operation Desert Shield/Operation Desert Storm and, 438–440
47th Field Hospital
  Cuban Refugee Operation and, 287–289
  Guatemalan earthquake mission, 151–154
  military exercises in Honduras and, 293–296
  Operation Desert Shield/Operation Desert Storm and, 435–438
  Operation Uphold Democracy and, 543–545, 544–545
44th Medical Brigade. *See also* 47th Field Hospital
  Former Republic of Yugoslavia operations and, 522
  Forward Surgical Team concept and, 311
  Operation Desert Shield/Operation Desert Storm and, 428, 430–431
  Prepositioning of Material Configured to Unit Sets (POMCUS) and, 436
  relocation to King Khalid Military City, 436
  Stress Treatment Facility, 436–437
Forward Surgical Teams
  air-dropping of equipment and, 311–312, 326 n50
  concept of, 311, 325 n45
  description, 311
  Operation Desert Shield/Operation Desert Storm and, 414–415

Operation Desert Storm and, 312
Operation Just Cause and, 311–317
staffing, 361 n79
Foster, Col. Catherine, 272
Foster, Gaines M., 154
Foust, Col. Jerome
    Deployable Medical System and, 261
    44th Medical Brigade role in Operation Desert Shield/Operation Desert Storm and, 436
Fox-Johnson, Maj. Leana, 185 n25
Frank, Maj. Mary E.V., photo, 399
Frazier, Col. Doris S.
    Army War College attendance, 395
    Command and General Staff College attendance, 47–48
    photo, 49
    Physician-in-Charge Program and, 89–90, 101 n77
    Pri-Team testing and, 100 n59
Frederico, Lt. Col. Anna, 161 n10
Freedom Flotilla. *See* Cuban Refugee Operation
Freeman, Col. Linda, 442, 444
Frocking issue
    AUS promotion and, 57 n50
    description, 58 n57
    examples, 53
    Lt. Col. Carolyn Adams and, 487, 501 n13
*Frontiero v. Richardson,* spousal rights for military wives, 11
FSTs. *See* Forward Surgical Teams

# G

Gahol, Capt. Pablito, 321
Galante, Maj. Christine, 177
Galloway, Capt. Kevin, 509–510
Galloway, Col. Katherine
    Career Activities Office role, 57 n42
    Nursing Research Service role, 127
    photo, 126
Gardiner, 2d Lt. Ruth M., 187 n54
Garifino, Lt. Col. Peggy, photo, 439
Garlick, Col. John B., 390
Gaylord, Maj. Kathryn
    Former Republic of Yugoslavia operations and, 523
    Haitian refugees at Guantanamo Bay and, 541, 543
Geis, Lt. Col. Rita, photo, 94
Gender and minority issues
    gender discrimination during Operation Urgent Fury, 308–309, 310
    male nurses, 25–27
    marital status of officers, 27–29
    Operation Desert Shield/Operation Desert Storm and, 476–477
    racial issues, 33–36
    servicemembers' pregnancies, 29–32
    sexual harassment, 32–33
General Leonard Wood Army Community Hospital, Fort Leonard Wood, Missouri, 375–376
Germany
    closure of bases and hospitals, 343–344
    hospitals used for Operation Desert Shield/Operation Desert Storm casualties, 467–470
Gilmore-Lee, Lt. Col. Nancy, 177, 179
Gilreath, Lt. Col. Elijah, 536 n57
Ginsberg, Capt. Miriam, 123, 124
Glenn, Capt., 537 n67
Glenn, Maj. Mary, photo, 427, 450, 451
Glenn, Sen. John
    Maj. Susan Connor's service in the office of, 176–177
Glor, Col. Beverly
    patient classification system, 195
    Pri-Team testing and, 100 n59
Godwin, Capt. Marty, 327 n67
Gordon, Capt. Vinette, 185 n25
Gore, Vice Pres. Albert, Jr., proposed closure of USUHS and, 232
Gorgas Army Community Hospital, Panama
    closure, 345
    Operation Just Cause and, 312, 326 n54
    strategies to relieve the nursing shortage, 239
Gorman, Col. Eily P.
    Army Nurse Corps leadership role, 171
    Civil Service Registered Nurses and, 222–224
    DEPMEDS role, 264
    mentorship program and, 206, 207
    photo, 223
Graduate Medical Education, integration of with specialty services, 378, 380
Graham, Col. Jeri I., 408 n40
Graham, Maj., 537 n67
Granada, Operation Urgent Fury, 305–310
Grant, Lt. Col. Larry, 498
Graves, Lt. Col. Rhonda, 409 n53
Gray, 1st Lt. Ollie B., 161 n10
Green, 2d Lt. Jerry, 533 n17
Green to Gold program
    description, 233–234
    requirements for, 234
Greene, Lt. Col. Patricia A., 20 n23
Greenfield, Col. Elizabeth, 128
Greenfield, Maj. Ruth, 123
Groetken, Capt. Linda, 437–438
Grossnickle, Capt. Genevieve, photo, 511
Gruber, Maj. Dana, photo, 439
Gruner, Lt. Col. Betty, 468

Guam, Operation New Life and Operation New Arrivals and, 144–146
Guatemalan earthquake
  Army Community Health Nurses and, 152
  Army Nurse Corps mission, 151–154
  cultural issues, 154
  operational snags, 153
  public relations issues, 153–154
  weather issues, 153
Gullet, Maj. Flint
  Operation Urgent Fury and, 308, 325 n34
Gunn, Lt. Col. Ira P., 112
Gurney, Col. Cynthia
  military exercises in Honduras role, 294–295
  Operation Desert Shield/Operation Desert Storm and, 443
  photo, 295, 474
  TriService Nursing Research Group role, 130
Gustke, Col. Deborah A.
  AMEDD CSL and, 408 n40
  AMEDD Personnel Proponency Division role, 186 n42

# H

Hagey, Lt. Col. Antoinette
  health risk assessment component of the Army Health Promotion Program role, 259
  physical fitness program and, 279 n12
Haiti
  geographic location, 541
  Haitian refugees at Guantanamo Bay, 541–543
  Operation Uphold Democracy, 541–549
Hall, Capt. Mary F., 393
Hall, 1st Lt. Patricia
  photo, 496
  Task Force Eagle and, 537 n67
Halliburton, Col. Sarah, 129
Harbin, Capt. Richard
  nurse practitioner role, 119
Harris, Maj. Sheila, 226
Hartman, Lisa, 498
Hays, Brig. Gen. Anna Mae V.
  Army Nurse Corps chief, 14
  photos, 116, 554
Health Care Studies and Clinical Investigation Activity, survey of retired Army nurses, 271
Health facility planning, Nurse Methods Analysts and, 114–117
Health maintenance organizations
  downsized nursing staffs and, 337
  proliferation of, 337
Health Professions Scholarship Program, physician shortfalls and, 4
Health Service Support
  Air Land Battle doctrine, 255, 271, 277 n2
  Operation Just Cause and, 313
Health Services Command
  Academy of Health Sciences launch, 8
  advertisements in national publications for civilian nurses, 224
  Area of Concentration nurses, 224, 245 n41, 360 n73
  Army Medical Department cuts in nursing education programs and, 4
  Army Nurse Corps officers originally assigned to, 6
  Army Primary Casualty Receiving Centers, 470–476
  Budget Manpower Guidance, 81
  creation of, 5
  evaluation of, 8
  Guatemalan earthquake and, 151
  Medical Major Command replacement of, 363
  missions of, 5, 8
  movement of some Army Nurse Corps operations to, 6
  nurse practitioners and, 107
  Operation Desert Shield/Operation Desert Storm and, 414, 417, 425, 468, 470
  Operation New Life and Operation New Arrivals and, 144–151
  "single manager approach" for health care service delivery, 5
  transition from using the HSC manpower survey to using the Workload Management System for Nurses, 221
  weight control and physical fitness regulations, 62
Health Services Command Inspector General Team
  survey of grassroots attitudes toward the Army's pregnancy policy, 31
Health Services Support Areas
  Army Nurse Corps officers and, 364
  name change to Regional Medical Commands, 364
Heil, Lt. Col. Elizabeth, 430
Hembree, Capt. (P) Patricia, 539 n92
Hemme, 1st Lt. Anne, 120
Henderson, Staff Sgt. Stephen, 460 n9
Hendrix, Capt. Steve, 327 n66
Henson, Maj. Linda, 318
Heston, Charlton
  photo, 496
  visit to Somalia, 498
Hill, Lt. Col. Maurine, 146–148
Hill, Maj. Elizabeth

Conceptual Model of Army Nursing Practice and, 203
mission to Sweden, 320
Hills, Command Sgt. Maj., photo, 235
Hinton, Maj. Walt, 537 n67
Hix, Maj. Gary D., 329 n102
Hoisington, Brig. Gen. Elizabeth, 12
Holland, Col. Maureen, 430
Honduras
children's health problems, 295
Fuertes Caminos 89 and, 260–261, 280 n33
Medical Element role, 293–296
military exercises, 293–296, 301 n31
pregnancy rate, 301 n33
Hopkins, Lt. Col. Roger, 264
Hoppe, Lt. Col. Jeanne
HSC leadership, 20 n25
Operation New Life and Operation New Arrivals and, 145–146
photo, 146
Horoho, Maj. Gen. Patricia
Operation Uphold Democracy and, 544
photo, 403
Hospital Unit Dose Drug Distribution System, description and implementation, 87
Houghton, Lt. Col. Jean M., 119
House Armed Services Committee
baccalaureate degree for nurses and, 208–209
Congressional Liaison Office request for Army Nurse Corps to work with, 177
HSC. *See* Health Services Command
HSSAs. *See* Health Services Support Areas
Hudak, Col. Jane L., photo, 270
Hudock, Col. John M.
Army Nurse Corps leadership role, 171
DOPMA promotion guidelines and, 237
Officer Structure Study and, 251 n113
Operation Desert Shield/Operation Desert Storm role, 425
photo, 225
views on Civil Service Registered Nurses, 224, 226
HUDS. *See* Hospital Unit Dose Drug Distribution System
Humanitarian relief and assistance missions. *See also* Operation Desert Shield/Operation Desert Storm; Operation Restore Hope; Operation Uphold Democracy
civil war in El Salvador, 296–298
Cuban Refugee Operation, 287–293
educational missions to Jordan, 154–159
eruption of Mount Pinatubo, 320–321
Guatemalan earthquake, 151–154
military exercises in Honduras, 293–296
missions to the Georgian Republic, Kirghizstan, and Ukraine, 321
Nicaraguan earthquake, 141–143
Operation Babylift, 151
Operation Brightstar, 317–318
Operation Just Cause, 310–317
Operation New Life and Operation New Arrivals, 143–151
Operation Provide Hope, 321
Operation Urgent Fury, 305–310
Project Hope, 317
USNS *Mercy* mission, 319–320
Hummel, Lt. Pamela, 300 n11
Hundley, Maj. Linda, 516
Hunt, Col. Judith, 394
Hutcheson, Col. Rita, 430
Hutton, Col. John E., 306

# I

IMA. *See* Individual Mobilization Augmentee program
Immigration and Naturalization Service, Cuban Refugee Operation and, 290
Individual Mobilization Augmentee program
problems with, 272
Reserve Components Personnel and Administration Center assignment of ANC officers to positions they would occupy upon mobilization, 271–272
Infection control
infection rates as indicators of quality of care, 135 n69
nurse practitioners' role, 113
Innovative roles for nurses
advanced practice, 103–123
physician assistants, 118–119
research, 123–130
Inouye, Sen. Daniel
Army Nurse Corps officers' service in the office of, 175, 177, 179
bill on the baccalaureate degree requirement for nurses and, 209
financial support for TriService Nursing Research Group, 130
Graduate School of Nursing at USUHS and, 230
opening promotions for ANC officers beyond the one-star level and, 400–401, 404
photo, 178
rank parity for ANC officers, 400–401, 404, 410 n72
Institute of Surgical Research
burn team mission to Ufa, Russia, 320
nurses' contributions, 128
Iraq. *See* Operation Desert Shield/Operation Desert Storm; Operation Enduring Freedom; Operation Iraqi Freedom

ISR. *See* Institute of Surgical Research
Italy, closure of bases and hospitals, 344

## J

Jacques, Elliott, 365
JCCP. *See* Joint Casualty Collection Point
Jennings, Col. Bonnie M.
  Conceptual Model of Army Nursing Practice and, 203
  Coordinated Care Program and, 335
  photo, 336
  Task Force Aesculapius and, 365
  Workload Management System for Nurses and, 196
Jennings, Lt. Gen. Hal B.
  Dunlap's briefing on the implications of downsizing on the Army Nurse Corps, 81
  support for the baccalaureate degree requirement for nurses, 43
  views on assigning nurses to command positions, 389
Jensen, Col. Amelia, 135 n72
Jergens, Maj. Daniel, 320–321
Johnson, Capt. Jimmy, 505
Johnson, Col. Sandrah, 239
Johnson, Gen. Wally, 302 n36
Johnson, Maj. Grace, 309–310
Johnson-Bowles, Lt. Col. Joyce, 34
Johnson-Brown, Brig. Gen. Hazel W.
  biographical information, 14, 17
  Individual Mobilization Augmentee program and, 271
  integration movement and, 36
  National Council of State Boards of Nursing Licensure Examination and, 201
  Operation Desert Shield/Operation Desert Storm role, 416–417
  photos, 16, 554
  physical fitness views, 255
  research activities, 128–129
  review of ANC courses to identify deficiencies, 265
  ROTC summer camp for nurse cadets views, 68
  Standards of Nursing Practice and, 190–191
  task force recommendation for restoration of an educational program that would allow the Army to educate its own baccalaureate nurses and, 229–230
Joint Casualty Collection Point
  Operation Just Cause and, 312, 313, 327 n62
Joint Chiefs of Staff, Operation Just Cause and, 310
Joint Commission for the Accreditation of Healthcare Organizations, Workload Management System for Nurses and, 196
Joint Commission on the Accreditation of Hospitals
  function of, 21 n31
  Health Services Command audit, 8
  infection control standards, 113
  Madigan Army Medical Center accreditation and, 227
  paper form revisions and, 189–190
Joint Special Operations Task Force, Operation Just Cause, 312–317
Jones, Capt. Sheila, 370–371
Jones, Maj. Maudie, 476
Jordan
  Army Nurse Corps mission of 1984, 158–159
  Army Nurse Corps mission to the Jordanian Army Burn Treatment Centre, 157–158
  cultural issues, 156, 157
  Military Training Team mission, 154–157
Jorden, Capt. Michael, 451
Joseph, Assistant Secretary of Defense (Health Affairs) Stephen C., 377
Joss, Maj. Dave, 538 n77
Joy, Col. Robert J.T., 88, 125
Jump school. *See* Airborne training

## K

Kahn, 1st Lt. Nighat, 538 n83
Kamoureux, Col. Gloria K., 394
Kartley, Ann, photo, 319
Katial, Maj. Rene, 185 n25
Keenan, Maj. Jimmie
  Institute of Surgical Research burn team mission to Ufa, Russia, and, 320
  jump school participation, 71
  Task Force Falcon and, 524, 525, 526
Keller, Capt. Karen, 318
Kendrick, Capt. (P) David, 538 n83
Kennedy, Col. Terris
  budget cuts during the 1990s and, 337
  Conceptual Model of Army Nursing Practice and, 203
  nursing care requirements for mobilization study and, 263–264
  photo, 263
  service in Sen. Inouye's office, 185 n35
  Standards of Nursing Practice and, 211 n21
  views on the survival of nursing, 370
Kennedy, Marion K., 186 n46
Kennedy, Pres. John F., Presidential Commission on the Status of Women, 10
Keyser, Lt. Col. Collette, 264
Kimbrough Ambulatory Care Center, Fort Meade, Maryland, Ambulatory Procedure and Processing Center, 375
Kirby, Capt. Judith, 129

Kirghizstan, U.S. nation-building mission, 321
Kirkconnell, Lt. Ronald, 320, 329 n102
Klinker, Capt. Mary T., 151
Knight, Capt. Carolyn C., 117
Knox, Lt. Col. Edith, Career Activities Office role, 57 n42
Kobiela, 1st Lt., 537 n67
Koch, Capt. Johnnie, 321
Korea, closure of bases and hospitals, 344–345
Kosovo. *See* Former Republic of Yugoslavia
Krajnik, Capt. Sarah J., 530, 538 n77
Krapohl, Capt. Greta, 185 n25
Kulm, Capt. Margaret
    Guatemalan earthquake mission and, 152
    photo, 152
Kulvi, Lt. Col. Ruth, 104
Kuwait, Saddam Hussein's invasion of, 413

## L

Labbe, Lt. Col. Elizabeth A., 20 n23
Laine, Spec. Erick, 460 n9
Landstuhl Regional Medical Center, Germany
    assimilation of Air Force Nurse Corps officers into, 380
    Mother/Baby Early Discharge Program, 374
    Operation Restore Hope casualties and, 484, 495
    Preadmission Clinic, 374
LaNoue, Surgeon General, Lt. Gen. Alcide
    branch immaterial competitive category for promotion to AMEDD brigadier and major general and, 401
    Gateway to Care delivery approach and, 334
    Graduate School of Nursing and, 230
    Leader Development Decision Network process and, 394
    Task Force Aesculapius and, 364–366
    views on assigning nurses to command positions, 389–390, 394
Larabee, Maj. (P) James, 522
Larkin, Lt. Col. Jude
    photo, 197
    Workload Management System for Nurses and, 196
Lazarus, Capt. Russell L., 329 n102
Ledford, Surgeon General, Lt. Gen. Frank
    Adams-Ender's views on upgrading of position of director of personnel for the surgeon general and, 398
    Forward Surgical Teams and, 311
    views on assigning nurses to command positions, 389, 392
Lee, 1st Lt. Markus, 539 n92
Lescavage, Nancy, 185 n35
Letterman Army Medical Center, San Francisco, California
    closure of, 345–346
    Medicare Part B for patients and, 345–346, 362 n83
Liberia, Medical Mobile Training Team mission, 318
Llanes, Capt. Jenevie, 505
Long Term Civilian Training Program, 204
*Look* magazine, article on physician assistants, 119
Lussier, 2d Lt. Jessica, 539 n92
Lutz, Maj. Charles, photo, 517
Lynaugh, Joan E., 111

## M

MacDougall, Capt., 537 n67
Macedonia, Task Force Falcon and, 524, 527
MACH. *See* Moncrief Army Community Hospital, Fort Jackson, South Carolina
MACOM. *See* Medical Major Command
Madigan Army Medical Center, Tacoma, Washington
    Congestive Heart Failure Clinic, 375
    interdisciplinary approach, 375
Magnuson, 1st Lt. Sean, 538 n77
Major, Maj. Gen. John E., 198–199
Malcolm Grow Medical Center, Andrews Air Force Base, Alcohol and Drug Abuse Prevention and Control and, 378
Male nurses
    assigned to MTO&E units, 60–61
    discrimination against, 26–27
    health care administration specialty and, 25–26
    increase in the percentage of, 25
    jump school participation, 71
    in the post-Vietnam War era, 25–27
    white hospital duty uniforms and, 92–93
Mallot, Lt. Col. Susan, 430
Malone, Col. Eileen B., 408 n40
MAMC. *See* Madigan Army Medical Center, Tacoma, Washington
Mariel Boatlift. *See* Cuban Refugee Operation
Marital status. *See also* Pregnant servicemembers
    inequities in the prescribed length of overseas tours for bachelor and married officers, 28
    Operation Desert Shield/Operation Desert Storm and, 448–454, 464 n52, 464 n53
    preferential treatment in housing for married nurses, 27, 29
Marshall, Gen. George C., 10
Marshall, Lt. Col. Stephanie, 186 n42
Martin, Assistant Secretary of Defense (Health Affairs) Edward, 378
Martinkus, Capt. Nancy, 119–120

Martone, Capt. Dorothy, 135 n72
Marx, Maj. William, 226
MASHs. *See* Mobile Army Surgical Hospitals
Massenbury, Lt. Col. Toni, 548
Maternity leave
  debate over, 30–31
  hardship discharges and, 31
Mathewson-Chapman, Lt. Col. Marianne
  Operation Desert Shield/Operation Desert Storm and, 430
  photo, 431
Mathia, Lt. Col. William, photo, 439
Matos, Sgt. Myrna, 460 n9
Mayer, Assistant Secretary of Defense (Health Affairs) William E., 259
McCall, Col. Susan
  Graduate School of Nursing and, 232
  jump school participation, 71, 73
  Operation Just Cause and, 312, 313–314
  photo, 72
  Standards of Nursing Practice and, 194
  survey of Army nurses and non-commissioned officers, 342
McCarthy, Capt. Eileen, 135 n72
McCarthy, Col. Rosemary T.
  photo, 126
  Phyllis J. Verhonick Research Conference and, 129
  Pri-Team testing and, 100 n59
  Walter Reed Army Institute of Research role, 124–125
McCasland, Maj. Nickey J.
  HSC leadership, 20 n25
  relocation of the Career Activities Office and, 51
McClenney, Col. Lucretia, 34
McCloskey, Rep. Frank, 505
McClure, Lt. Col. Margaret, 272
McCommons, Lt. Col. Daisy, 135 n72
McDade, Maj. (P) Larry, 327 n67
McDaniel, Maj. Brenda C., 185 n25
McDannold, Lt. Scott, 512
McDermott, Capt. Diane, 147
McDevitt, Col., photo, 235
McKay, Capt. Bernadette A, 393
McKinney, SP4 Stephen, photo, 450
McLoughlin, Col. Audre
  mentorship program and, 206
  Officer Structure Study and, 251 n113
McMorris, Capt. Mark O., 268
McNeil, Maj. Jack L.
  Operation Urgent Fury and, 309, 325 n34
McQuail, Maj. Claire M., 20 n28
McRainey, Gerald, 498
Mechanic, Maj. Hedy, 128
MEDCOM. *See* U.S. Army Medical Command

MEDEL. *See* Medical Element of Joint Task Force Bravo, Honduras
MEDEX. *See* Medical Extension Program
Medic to RN Program, name change to AMEDD Enlisted Commissioning Program, 234
Medical Element of Joint Task Force Bravo, Honduras, 293–296
  weekly training exercises, 296
Medical Extension Program, description, 137 n92
Medical Field Service School, functions moved to the Academy of Health Sciences, 8
Medical Force 2000, Operation Desert Shield/Operation Desert Storm and, 414–415
Medical Major Command, headquarters, 363
Medical Major Command, replacement of the Health Services Command with, 363
Medical Training Center, functions moved to the Academy of Health Sciences, 8
Medical Treatment Facilities
  case management at, 376
  evaluation of MTF reorganization, 369–370
  interservice collaboration and, 377–379
  modernization efforts, 4
  nurse practitioners and, 106, 107, 109, 111
  nursing staff downsizing and, 368
  strategic focus, 364
  study of the utilization of registered nurses in the ambulatory setting, 370–371
Medical Unit, Self-contained, Transportable facilities
  concept description, 59
  conversion of EVACs and MASHs to, 59
  termination of, 59
Medina-Muniz, Lt. A., 300 n11
Mele, Capt. Robert J., 329 n102
Messerschmidt, Col. Mary
  automated information systems and, 199
  contract nurses and, 240
  Operation Desert Shield/Operation Desert Storm and, 476
  Pri-Team concept and, 87, 100 n59
Messing, Capt. Joel
  Cuban Refugee Operation and, 300 n11
  Operation Urgent Fury and, 325 n34
Metcalf, Lt. Col. Franklin
  photos, 319, 320
  Saudi Arabian National Guard advisor role, 318–319
Meyer, Gen. E.C., 255
Mezzano, Lt. Col. Joyce
  Operation Desert Shield/Operation Desert Storm and, 430
  photo, 431
Michael, Lt. Col. Marbeth, 153–154

*Index* xli

Middleton, Lt. Col. Chantal, photo, 439
Midwives
    education programs for, 105, 109
    nurse practitioner role, 105, 109
Milam, Capt., 537 n67
Milie, Capt. Teresa, 310, 325 n34
Military Occupational Specialties
    Direct Combat Probability Coding System, 168, 307
    Medical-Surgical Nurse, 161 n12
    restrictions applying to women, 168
Military Training Team mission to Jordan
    activities, 156–157
    cultural issues, 156
    description, 155–156
    goal of, 154–155
Miller, Col. Charles F., 504, 532 n6
Mission Oriented Protective Postures gear, 443, 454, 455, 458, 463 n34
Mittemeyer, Surgeon General, Lt. Gen. Bernhard T., 182
Mobile Army Surgical Hospitals. *See also specific units*
    Army Medical Department conversion of Evacuation Hospitals and Mobile Army Surgical Hospitals to Medical Unit, Self-contained, Transportable (MUST) facilities, 59
    mini-MASH units, 261
Mobilization Designee
    definition, 76 n33
    program expansion, 67
Modified Table of Organization & Equipment
    assignment of professional caregivers to, 60
    ceiling for Army Nurse Corps participation in, 60
    need to upgrade, 290
    problems in the utilization of nurses, 60–61
Mologne, Gen. Lewis
    military exercises in Honduras and, 302 n36
    Workload Management System for Nurses and, 196, 198
Molter, Lt. Col. Nancy
    photo, 208
    questionnaire development, 206–207
Moncrief Army Community Hospital, Fort Jackson, South Carolina
    deputy commander for patient services title, 385 n33
    nursing shortage and, 226, 245 n45
    organizational changes, 368–369
    pilot test to reorganize the Department of Nursing at, 368
    Same Day Surgery Unit, 368–369
Montague, Col. Mamie, 481 n30
Moore, Col. Constance J., photo, 231
MOPP gear. *See* Mission Oriented Protective Postures gear
Morris, Maj. Karen, 530, 538 n77
Moseley, Maj. Leonora M., photo, 126
MOSs. *See* Military Occupational Specialties
Mountcastle, Col. John W., photo, 497
MTFs. *See* Medical Treatment Facilities
MTO&E. *See* Modified Table of Organization & Equipment
MTT. *See* Military Training Team mission to Jordan
Mulhall, Maj. Debra, photo, 450
Murray, Lt. Judith A., 329 n102
MUST. *See* Medical Unit, Self-contained, Transportable facilities

# N

Nagra, 1st Lt. (P) Michael, 539 n92
Naleski, Maj. Gary, 317
National Capital Military Medical Education Consortium, 378
National Capital Region
    co-location of MACOM in, 363
    interservice collaboration in, 377, 380
    staff reduction, 382 n4
National Council of State Boards of Nursing, "advanced practice" definition, 19 n5
National Council of State Boards of Nursing Licensure Examination
    AMEDD Enlisted Commissioning Program and, 234–235
    commissioning of nurses and, 201–202
National Defense Act, ROTC and, 67
National Guard. *See* Army National Guard
National League for Nursing, support for the baccalaureate degree requirement for nurses, 43
National Naval Medical Center, interservice integration of programs, 378, 380
National Organization for Women, 10
NATO. *See* North Atlantic Treaty Organization
Navy Medical Department, Operation Desert Shield/Operation Desert Storm role, 417
Navy Nurse Corps. *See also* U.S. Navy
    Ambulatory Care Nurse Practitioner Program, 106
    baccalaureate degree requirement and, 209
    combat nursing course, 265
    Haitian refugees at Guantanamo Bay and, 543
    nurse practitioners and, 105–106
    nursing shortage and, 227
    Operation Desert Shield/Operation Desert Storm role, 417
    recruitment and retention challenges, 221, 339

recruitment goals, 240–241
Tri-Service Medical Information System and, 213 n46
NCLEX. *See* National Council of State Boards of Nursing Licensure Examination
NCR. *See* National Capital Region
Needham, 1st Lt. Bill, 538 n83
Neel, Surgeon General, Maj. Gen. Spurgeon H.
Health Services Command commander, 5
Physician-in-Charge Program and, 88
Newcomb, Lt. Col. Everett, 504
Newman, Capt. Peggy, photo, 155
Nicaraguan earthquake
Army Nurse Corps mission, 141–143
general purpose medium tents used, 160 n3
readiness issues, 143
setbacks during, 142–143
staff living conditions, 143
supply issues, 142–143
weather issues, 143
work shifts, 142
Nichols, Lt. Col. Glennadee, 125
Nickel, Lt. Col. Elsie Nickel, 21 n41
Nielsen-McArdle, Capt. Cynthia, 539 n92
Nieves, Capt. Wilfredo, 290–291
1980 Professional Development Workshop, Mobilization Designees, 283 n70
1970s: The Post-Vietnam War era
administrative questions, 79–95
educational concerns and career advancement, 41–53
evolution and reorganization, 3–23
gender and minority issues, 25–36
humanitarian relief and assistance missions, 141–159
innovative roles for nurses, 103–130
readiness challenges, 59–73
1980s: Decade of change
deployments during, 305–321
new leadership and expanding horizons, 167–183
nursing shortage, 219–241
physical fitness, 255–259
readiness issues, 259–276
refining quality of care strategies, 189–209
refugee and humanitarian operations, 287–298
1990s: Concluding decade of a century of service
ANC activities in Europe and CONUS during Operation Desert Shield/Operation Desert Storm, 467–478
Army and AMEDD role in Operation Desert Shield/Operation Desert Storm, 413–418
downsizing effects, 333–352
new frontiers for ANC officers, 389–404

Operation Restore Hope, 483–498
Operation Uphold Democracy in Haiti, 541–549
operations in the former Republic of Yugoslavia, 503–532
post-Cold War period, 333–352
revamping the AMEDD and the Army Nurse Corps, 363–381
94th General Hospital, Operation Desert Shield/Operation Desert Storm and, 468–469
Nixon, Patricia, request for women officers to serve as social aides at the White House, 173
Nixon, Pres. Richard, Selective Service System changes, 3
Nixon administration, formal tone of, 174
NMAs. *See* Nurse Methods Analysts
NNC. *See* Navy Nurse Corps
Nolfe, Lt. Col. Vera, 148
Nooney, Lt. Col. Nancy
military exercises in Honduras role, 293
photo, 155
Noriega, Manuel, 310, 312
North Atlantic Treaty Organization, cease-fire in Former Republic of Yugoslavia and, 512
Norton, Col. Dena
AMEDD Personnel Proponency Division role, 186 n42
mentorship program and, 206
Officer Structure Study and, 251 n113
Standards of Nursing Practice and, 211 n21
NPs. *See* Nurse practitioners
NRAB. *See* Nursing Research Advisory Board
Nunn, Sen. Sam, 57 n47, 57 n48
Nupen, Lt. Col. Judy, 458–459
Nurse Methods Analysts
food service centralization and, 116–117
health facility planning role, 114–117
patient categorization according to their nursing requirements, 116–117
Nurse Midwifery Program, Fort Knox, Kentucky, description, 109
Nurse practitioners. *See also* Army Nurse Corps Contemporary Practice Program; Pediatric Nurse Practitioners; Physician assistants
anesthesia nursing, 111–112
Automated Military Outpatient System Specialists, 117–118
educational concerns, 104–105, 118, 121, 123
health facilities planning and, 113–117
infection control and, 113
Intensive Care Units and, 111
nonmilitary model compared with the military model, 121
nurse educators' views, 121, 123
Operation New Life and Operation New

Arrivals and, 145
patient satisfaction with, 120
psychiatric nurses, 112–113
specialties, 104–105, 107, 111–113
views of the professional nursing community on, 103–104
Nurse Training Act, Pres. Carter's veto, 19 n8
"The Nursing Care Hour Standards Study" (Sherrod), 140 n139
Nursing Practice Model
expansion of to the Conceptual Model of Army Nursing Practice, 203
quality of care and, 202–203
Nursing Productivity Study, 371–372
Nursing Research Advisory Board, 129
Nursing Research Service
description of activities, 127
leadership of, 127
Nursing Reserve Officers' Training Corps, 86
Nursing shortage
Army consideration of the shortage as a "war stopper," 220
Army National Guard and U.S. Army Reserve and, 222, 238
Army Nurse Corps Accession Bonus Program and, 228
Army Nurse Corps Professional Development Funding Package and, 236
ceilings on promotions and, 81
Civil Service Registered Nurses and, 222–226
civilian health care organizations and, 85–86
civilianizing of military nursing slots, 81, 83
congressional recruitment and retention strategies, 228
contract nurses and, 226, 239–240
curtailing of new accessions and, 80–81
decline in authorizations and, 79–81, 83–84, 98 n31, 99 n46, 221, 246 n61, 338–342, 356 n22
decline in the number of college students considering a nursing career and, 220
disparity in pay between the military and civilians and, 219, 220, 338, 357 n25
DOPMA and, 237–238
educational issues, 222, 224, 228–234
improvement in the late 1970s, 85
local programs to relieve, 238–239
new technology and, 83
1980s issues, 219–241
post-Vietnam War era, 79–86
preferred retention rate, 243 n22
release of officers and, 81
transition from using the Health Services Command manpower survey to using the Workload Management System for Nurses, 221
Uniformed Services University of the Health Sciences nursing program and, 228–229
"zero-procurement objective" and, 80–81
Nuttall, Col. Edith M.
Army Nurse Corps Branch leadership, 21 n41
Army Nurse Corps leadership role, 14
Career Activities Office role, 57 n42
dispersal of 300 nursing slots, 81
photo, 82
views on maternity leave for pregnant officers, 31

# O

Occupational therapists, expanded responsibilities, 118
O'Dell, Lt. Col. Margaret, 125
ODS. See Operation Desert Shield/Operation Desert Storm
Office of Technology Assessment, workload and productivity of nurse practitioners, 120
Office of The Surgeon General. See also The Surgeon General
Army Nurse Corps recruiting responsibilities and, 84–85
Career Guidance and Planning Office, 48
DA Board of Inquiry on the Army Logistics System recommendations, 19 n11
Guatemalan earthquake and, 151
Individual Mobilization Augmentee program and, 271
internal directorates, 9
readiness issues, 65–66
relaxation of education standards to fill vacancies in the USAR and the ARNG, 64
relocation of, 8–9
reorganization of, 8–9
task force recommendation for restoration of an educational program that would allow the Army to educate its own baccalaureate nurses, 229
Oliver, Adm. Daniel T., photo, 176
Oliver, Lt. Col. Ronald, 318
Olson, Cadet Pam, photo, 69
1st Aeromedical Evacuation Squadron, 313–317
101st Airborne Division
married and co-located spouses and, 448–454
Operation Desert Shield/Operation Desert Storm and, 448–454
131st Field Hospital, Operation Uphold Democracy and, 544
1st Forward Surgical Team, Operation Just Cause and, 312–314, 327 n58
1st Infantry Division, Former Republic of Yugo-

slavia operations and, 523–524
115th Field Hospital, Former Republic of Yugoslavia operations and, 521–522
160th Forward Surgical Hospital, Task Force Falcon and, 526–527, 530
1208th U.S. Army Hospital, Operation Desert Shield/Operation Desert Storm and, 472, 474
Operation Babylift, Army Nurse Corps role, 151
Operation Backbone
  description, 344
  pilot test of, 361 n78
Operation Brightstar
  description, 317
  women's issues during, 318
Operation Continue Hope, description, 484
Operation Desert Shield/Operation Desert Storm
  AMEDD bed resources and, 417, 423 n25
  ANC activities in CONUS during, 470–478
  Army Medical Department role, 413–418
  Army Nurse Corps combat hospital activities, 435–459
  Army Nurse Corps leadership, 425–431
  Army Nurse Corps role, 173
  Army's stop-loss program and, 426
  children of deployed parents and, 448–454, 470, 477
  combat period, 413
  Combat Stress Control teams, 415
  Corps-level hospitals, 418
  countries participating in, 417
  cross-leveled staff at CONUS Table of Distribution and Allowances hospitals, 470, 480 n14
  Deployable Medical System and, 261
  Desert Shield Situation Group, 425–426
  echelons of care and, 415
  Enemy Prisoners of War and, 429–430
  family care plans and, 448
  family separations and, 458–459
  Forward Surgical Teams and, 312
  Gulf War Syndrome and, 477–478
  HUA shouts and, 451, 464 n59
  married and co-located spouses and, 448–454, 464 n52, 464 n53
  medical problems of soldiers, 447–448, 464 n47
  medical unit transportation challenges, 461 n19
  Patriot missile firings, 458
  precombat phase, 413
  SCUD missile attacks, 444, 454, 458, 463 n37
  "Shake 'n Bake" Officer Basic Course for USAR and ARNG officers, 415–416
  Soldier Readiness Processing and, 445, 463 n42
  truce and cease-fire, 413–414
  unified command organization of the U.S. military, 414
Operation Enduring Freedom, ANC involvement in, 556
Operation Iraqi Freedom, ANC involvement in, 556
Operation Joint Endeavor
  conclusion, 523
  Dayton Peace Accords monitoring and enforcing, 512
Operation Joint Guard, Support and Stability Operation, 523
Operation Just Cause
  Army/Air Force relations and, 314–316
  Army Nurse Corps role, 167, 173
  Gorgas Army Hospital and, 312, 326 n54
  joint (purple) teamwork during, 313, 327 n69
  objectives of, 310–311
  origins of, 310
  success of medical support for, 317
  "water buffalos" and, 313, 328 n73
Operation New Life and Operation New Arrivals
  Army Community Health Nurses and, 147–149
  cost of, 150
  fall of Vietnam and U.S. resettlement efforts, 143–151
  lessons learned from, 150–151
  personality clashes, 147
  rotation policy, 149–150
Operation Other Than War, name changed to Operation Restore Hope, 483
Operation Prayer Book/Blue Spoon. *See* Operation Just Cause
Operation Provide Hope, description, 321
Operation Provide Promise, units involved, 503–504
Operation Restore Hope
  AMEDD combat stress team and, 495
  Army medical units involved in, 484–498, 549
  Black Hawk helicopter attack, 484, 493–495
  celebrity visits, 498
  chalks of nursing personnel deployed, 488, 501 n15
  confusion over the deployment of Col. Elise Roy or Lt. Col. Carolyn Adams and, 487, 489, 500 n12
  cross-leveled active duty personnel and, 487
  media attention and, 499 n2
  Operation Other Than War changed to, 483
  personnel substitutions for extenuating circumstances, 487, 500 n10

phases of, 483–484
stress and, 495, 498
Operation Uphold Democracy
  Haitian facilities' usability and, 544, 551 n9
  hygiene facilities and, 547
  malaria and, 547
  Medical Rules of Engagement and, 544, 551 n12
  U.S Army units involved, 543–548
Operation Urgent Fury
  ANC officers receiving award for service during, 309
  Army Nurse Corps role, 167, 171, 305–310
  difficulties with, 305
  Gama Goat vehicles and, 308, 324 n25
  gender discrimination and, 308–309, 310
  lessons learned from, 310
  media criticism of, 306
  number of Army Nurse Corps officers participating in, 322 n3
  Professional Officer Filler System and, 305–310
  relationships between the Table of Organization and Equipment and PROFIS staff and, 309
  staff health problems during, 325 n38
Oral histories of Army Nurse Corps senior officers, 129, 171
Ostmann, Maj. Ronald, 327 n67
O'Sullivan, Capt. Joe, 538 n83
Owen, Lt. Col. Donna, 272

P
Pack, Lt. John T., 92
Pack, Lt. John T., photo, 94
Palmer, 1st Lt. M. Denise, 268–269
Panama
  closure of bases and hospitals, 345
  Operation Just Cause and, 310–317
Paper forms
  Clinical Nursing Records Study, 189
  overprints and, 189, 210 n4
  revisions of, 189
Paraoan, 1st Lt. Dianne, 539 n92
Parks, Brig. Gen. Madelyn N.
  anesthesia nursing views, 112
  biographical information, 14
  black beret views, 91
  Col. Florence A. Blanchfield Community Hospital naming and, 181–182
  Corcoran's command position and, 390
  criteria for promotion, 43
  decline in authorizations comments, 80
  letters from Barbieri and Spine, 164 n62
  photo, 15
  retirement of, 76 n41

ROTC summer camp for nurses views, 68
views on insignia placement changes, 95
views on male nurses in health care administration, 25–26
views on MTO&E unit problems, 60–61
views on preferential treatment for married nurses in housing, 27, 29
Parsons, Capt. Teresa
  jump school participation, 71
  Operation Desert Shield/Operation Desert Storm and, 446–448, 463 n46
  ROTC summer camp participation, 68
PAs. See Physician assistants
Pascarelli, 1st Lt. Frank, 460 n9
Patient classification system, 194–199, 211 n24
Paulson, Capt. Diane, Task Force Falcon and, 539 n92
Pawley, Lt. Col. John, photo, 485
Peake, Brig. Gen. James, 544, 551 n9
Pediatric nurse practitioners, 107–109
Penn, Col. Barbara, 409 n53
Perkins, Maj. Cory V., 234
Perry, Lt. Col. Lee, 186 n42
Persian Gulf War. See Operation Desert Shield/Operation Desert Storm
Phelps, Lt. Col. (P) Fredrick, 53
Philippines
  AMEDD team evaluation of health care facilities, 318
  eruption of Mount Pinatubo and, 320–321
  USNS Mercy humanitarian mission and, 319–320
Phillips, Capt. Jill, 279 n12
Phyllis J. Verhonick Research Conference, 129–130
Physical fitness. See Weight control and physical fitness
Physical therapists, expanded responsibilities, 118
Physician assistants
  civilian model adaptation, 118
  eventual acceptance of in AMEDD, 119
  resistance to, 118–119
Physician-in-Charge Program
  description, 88
  intent of, 88
  quality of care objective of, 88
  reaction of Army nurses to, 89
  six-month evaluation of, 88, 101 n70
Picariello, Capt. Jeanne
  photo, 258
  physical fitness research, 256, 259
Pierce, Col. Penny, 459
Pinski, Lt. Cynthia, 300 n11
Pixley, Surgeon General, Lt. Gen. Charles, 181
  Slewitzke's Command and General Staff

College leadership and, 48
views on assigning nurses to command positions, 389
PNPs. *See* Pediatric Nurse Practitioners
Pocklington, Brig. Gen. Dorothy B.
    career and achievements, 346–347, 392
    Individual Mobilization Augmentee program and, 271–272
    photo, 274
    women in command positions in USAR and ARNG and, 392–393
Policy Review Group on Women in the Army, 168
Pollock, Maj. Gen. Gale
    command position, 408 n39
    photo, 402
    promotion of, 404
Porisch, Maj. Lee, 327 n66
Porter-O'Grady, Dr. Tim, 370
Post-Cold War period
    Army Nurse Corps leaders during, 346–352
    Base Realignment and Closure Commission, 337, 342–347
    Coordinated Care Program, 335
    downsizing effects, 333–352, 354 n8
    Gateway to Care delivery approach, 334–335
    health maintenance organizations and, 337
    long-term effects of the downsizing, 346–347
    Registered Care Technician proposal, 336–337
    Selective Early Retirement Boards and, 339–340, 358 n39
    Special Separation Benefit, 340–341, 359 n49
    TRICARE, 335
    Voluntary Indefinite (VI) or Conditional Voluntary Indefinite (CVI) status, 338, 339, 341, 357 n33
    Voluntary Separation Incentives, 340–341, 359 n49
Postgraduate short courses
    Army's Long-Term Civilian Training program, 47
    chief, nursing education and staff development service and, 46–47
    civilian institutions of higher learning and, 47
Pregnant servicemembers
    hardship discharges and, 31
    improvement in the Army Nurse Corps numbers by retaining pregnant women, 85
    lost work-hours debate, 30–31
    maternity leave debate, 30–31
    misuse of pregnancy to evade service obligations, 31–32
    rights of pregnant servicewomen to remain on active duty, 11–12, 22 n55, 29–30
    survey of grassroots attitudes toward the Army's pregnancy policy, 31
    uniforms for pregnant nurses, 95
    waiver requests, 30
Presidential Commission on the Status of Women, 10
Pri-Team concept
    description, 87
    intent of, 86–87
    pilot tests of, 87
    quality of care investigation and, 86
Price, Lt. Col. Ida Graham
    concept of career planning for Army Nurse Corps officers and, 48
    photo, 50
Priest, Lt. Donna S., 329 n102
Primary Care Demonstration Project, 371
Primary Medical Care for the Uniformed Services Clinics
    locations of, 185 n20
    private contractors for, 169
Prior, Capt. Richard, photo, 490
Professional Officer Filler System
    change of command from the MSC commander in garrison to the PROFIS medical commander, 406 n19
    Operation Urgent Fury and, 305–310
    problems with, 394
PROFIS. *See* Professional Officer Filler System
Project AMEDD Vanguard, name change to Task Force Aesculapius, 383 n12
Project Hope, description, 317
Proud to Care survey, 232
    percent response to, 246 n57
Providence Hospital, Columbia, South Carolina, bonus to newly hired nurses, 220
Prucha, Lt. James, 112–113
Pryor, Capt. Sharon, 491–492
Psychiatric nursing, nurse practitioners' role, 112–113
Purdom, Lt. Col. Jean
    Operation Desert Shield/Operation Desert Storm and, 448, 450
    photos, 427, 450, 451, 452
Pyrogen Identifier, Rapid Response, 129

# Q

Quality of care
    Army Nurse Corps Fellows Program and, 206–208
    Army Nurse Corps Standards of Nursing Practice and, 88, 192–194
    automated information systems and, 199–201

baccalaureate degree requirement and, 201–202, 208–209
Conceptual Model of Army Nursing Practice and, 202–203
Department of Nursing Organizational Model and, 202
educational courses to improve officer professionalism, 203–205
infection rates as indicators of, 135 n69
National Council of State Boards of Nursing Licensure Examination and, 201–202
paper form improvements, 189–192
patient classification system and, 194–195
Physician-in-Charge Program and, 88
Preceptor Program and, 205–206
Pri-Team concept and, 86
Workload Management System for Nurses and, 195–199

## R

Racial and ethnic issues
contributions of African-American nurses, 33
discrimination, 33–36
increase in the percentage of African-Americans in the Army, 33
ROCKS volunteer program and, 33–34
Ramey, 1st Lt. Karen, 539 n92
RANCA. *See* Retired Army Nurse Corps Association
Randall, 1st Lt. Gayle, 538 n83
Ransom, Lt. Col. Victoria, 378, 380
Rausch, Maj. (P) Francis M., 20 n25
Rawlins, Sally H., 186 n46
Raymond, Capt. Susan M., 544–545
RCs. *See* Reserve components
*Reader's Digest*
negative view of U.S. medical readiness, 259
report on personnel shortages at Walter Reed Army Medical Center, 226–227
Readiness issues
AMEDD's "readiness" definition, 259
assignment of authorized officers to Forces Command units with a Memorandum of Understanding detailing the agreement, 269–271
Combat Casualty Care Course, 265
Deployable Medical System, 260–265
field exercise participation, 63, 276
field unit evolution, 59–61
grassroots efforts, 268
humanitarian relief and assistance missions, 159
negative media characterizations, 259–260
1970s, 59–73

1980s, 259–276
pre-positioning hospitals and, 285 n105
readiness elements, 259
Reserve and National Guard components and, 64–73, 273–276
retired ANC officers and, 271–273
weapons training for female soldiers, 61–62
weight control and physical fitness standards, 62–63, 255–259
Reagan, Pres. Ronald
military exercises in Honduras, 293
photo, 176
Reagan administration, "womanpause" movement, 168
Reddy, Col. Charles J.
Individual Mobilization Augmentee program and, 271–272
photo, 257
physical fitness of nurses, 256
Reed, Maj. Edwin D., 329 n102
Reeder, Lt. Col. Jean
Operation Desert Shield/Operation Desert Storm and, 472
photo, 474
Refugees. *See* Humanitarian relief and assistance missions
Regional Medical Commands
headquarters for, 364
Health Services Support Areas name change to, 364
operational focus, 364
subordinate commands, 364
Registered Care Technician proposal
description, 336
opposition to, 336–337, 355 n18
Registered Nurse Student Program, closure, 84
Reimer, Gen. Dennis, 401
Reineck, Col. Carol
AMEDD Personnel Proponency Division role, 186 n42
photo, 198
study of the utilization of registered nurses in the ambulatory setting, 370–371
views on the Workload Management System for Nurses, 198
views on weight control and physical fitness regulations, 62
Reis, 1st Lt. Joe, 460 n9
Republic of Georgia, U.S. nation-building mission, 321
Research activities. *See also* Institute of Surgical Research
Army Nurse Corps role, 123–130
Federal Nursing Research Interest Group, 130
Nursing Research Advisory Board, 129

nursing research committees, 129
Nursing Research Service and, 127
oral histories of Army Nurse Corps senior
   officers, 129
Phyllis J. Verhonick Research Conference,
   129–130
physical fitness research, 256, 259
research on activated reservists, 481 n30
U.S. Army Research and Development
   Command, 128–129
Walter Reed Army Institute of Research and,
   123–127
Workload Management System for Nurses,
   128
Research Analysis Corporation, 65–66
Reserve components. *See also* Army National
   Guard; U.S. Army Reserve
   Combat Casualty Care Course and, 266,
      268–269
Reserve Officers' Training Corps
   admission of women to, 5, 10, 67
   air assault training for nurses, 73
   airborne training for nurses, 71–73
   Alternative Advanced Summer Camp,
      67–68, 70
   Army Nurse Corps and, 67–73
   Cadet Troop Leadership Program, 67, 68
   financial advantages offered, 67
   four regions, 70, 76 n42
   Golden Gale scholarships, 233
   Green to Gold program, 233–234
   increase in the number of scholarships
      offered to collegiate nursing students,
      233–234
   nurse recruitment efforts, 70–71
   ROCKS volunteer program and, 33–34
   service obligations of pregnant graduates
      and, 31–32
   source for Army nurses, 5, 84
   specialized education programs, 67
   subsidization of nurses' education, 229–230
Retired ANC officers
   assignment to USAR or ARNG, 271–273
   15-year retirement, 340
   "hip pocket" orders, 271, 284 n82
   Operation Desert Shield/Operation Desert
      Storm role, 416–417, 418, 422 n17, 426
   readiness issues, 271–273
   Selective Early Retirement Boards for senior
      officers and, 338, 339–340
Retired Army Nurse Corps Association
   Army Nurse Corps Foundation and, 180
   Dunlap's leadership, 14
   election of first officers, 180
   formation of, 180
   goals, 181

name change to Army Nurse Corps Association, 180
original dues, 180
Return of Forces to Germany exercises, 63
Rexrode (Southby), Maj. Janet, 173–175
Rexrode (Southby), Maj. Janet, photo, 174
Reynolds, Capt. John, 460 n9
Ricciardi, Maj. Richard
   Former Republic of Yugoslavia operations
      and, 516
   photo, 517
Rice, Maj. Shelley A.
   Task Force Falcon and, 526, 539 n92
Richards, Lt. Col. Donn, 306
Richardson, Lt. Suzanne, photo, 493
Richie, Col. Sharon
   Congressional Fellowship Program participant, 175
   photo, 176
   recruiting and, 338
Ridenour, Rear Adm. Richard, 378
Rivera, Capt. Jose F., 73
Riviello, Lt. Col. Carmen F., 26
Rizzo, Capt. Michael
   Task Force Falcon and, 530
   Task Force Hawk and, 538 n77
RMCs. *See* Regional Medical Commands
Robertson, Maj. Kathryn
   educational mission to Jordan, 158–159
   nursing shortage at Fitzsimmons Army
      Medical Center and, 226
Robinson, Lt. Edythe, 542
ROCKS volunteer program, description, 33–34
Rockwell, Lt. Col. Kathy, 468–469
Roehr, Col. Kathleen, 407 n26
Rogers, Martha, 123
Roosevelt, Eleanor, 10
Rosado, Lt. Col. Adolfo, 300 n12
Rosasco, Col. Louise C.
   Army Nurse Corps leadership role, 14
   photos, 45, 116
   views on the baccalaureate degree requirement for nurses, 44
ROTC. *See* Reserve Officers' Training Corps
ROTC Nursing Advanced Camp
   description and participation, 68
   evolving problems with, 70
   name changed to Nurse Summer Training
      Program, 70
   objective of, 68
   prerequisites for attendance, 68
   visits by deans of university schools of
      nursing, 70
ROTCNAC. *See* ROTC Nursing Advanced
   Camp
Roy, Col. Elise Gates, 487

Rubbert, Capt. Mary P., 329 n102
Rumbaugh, Gen. James, 302 n36
Russia, Institute of Surgical Research burn team mission to Ufa, 320

## S

Saddam Hussein, invasion of Kuwait, 413
Sadler, Capt. Freida, 191–192
Samuels, Lt. Col. Gemryl, 542–543
Sandoval, Capt. Juan, 297
Sanford, Jay P., 229
Sarnecky, Lt. Col. Mary T., photo, 474
Saudi Arabia
  assistance missions to, 317
  nurse advisors to the Saudi Arabian National Guard, 318–319
Saulsbery, Col. Patricia A., 408 n39
Saulsbery, Lt. Col. Patricia, 177
Saye, Capt. Jackie, 300 n11
Scheffner, Col. Lawrence
  first male nurse to achieve the rank of colonel, 27
  photo, 28
Scheibmeir, 1st Lt. Monica, photo, 69
Schemp, Lt. Col. Catherine
  physical fitness program and, 279 n12
  TriService Nursing Research Group role, 130
Scherb, Col. Barbara J.
  AMEDD CSL and, 408 n40
  BI position, 409 n53
  photo, 178
  service in Sen. Inouye's office, 177
Schimmenti, Gen. Carmelita, 199
Schmidt, Maj. Linda, photo, 455
Schretenthaler, Capt. Patrick M., 317
Schulz, Capt. Jacqueline
  Former Republic of Yugoslavia operations and, 511
  photo, 511
Schwarzkopf, Gen. H. Norman, 414, 418
Scott, Lt. Col. Charlotte
  Former Republic of Yugoslavia operations and, 538 n83
  photo, 297
  weapons training recollections, 61
Scott, Lt. Col. Constance, 407 n30
Seeley, Lt. B. Eli, 522
Segler, Lt. Col. Esther, 288, 300 n11
Seitter, Maj. Gen. Girard, 365
Sekiguchi, Capt. June, 161 n10
Selective Early Retirement Boards
  downsizing and, 338, 358 n39
  negative effects, 340
  positive effects, 340
  process of, 339–340

Selective Service System, 3–4
Senior Service Schools, 394–395
September 11, 2001, terrorist attacks
  description, 555–556
SERBs. *See* Selective Early Retirement Boards
Serpe-Ingold, Col. Brooke
  Operation Desert Shield/Operation Desert Storm and, 476
  photo, 270
Seufert, Lt. Col. Helen J.
  infection control practices and, 113, 135 n66
7th Medical Command
  Former Republic of Yugoslavia operations and, 503
  Operation Desert Shield/Operation Desert Storm and, 467–468, 470
VII Corps
  Operation Desert Shield/Operation Desert Storm and, 418
Sexual harassment
  Army definition of, 32
  identification and management of, 32–33
  incidents at William Beaumont Army Medical Center, 32–33
Shackleford, Capt., 537 n67
Shank, Maj. John, 430
Shea, Rear Adm. Frances T., 393
Sheldon, Capt. Vicky, 185 n25
Shelton, Gen. Henry, 525
Shepard, Maj. Rosamond, 308–309, 325 n34
Sherrod, Lt. Col. Susie
  Nursing Care Hour Standards Study, 195, 262
  "The Nursing Care Hour Standards Study," 140 n139
  Phyllis J. Verhonick Research Conference and, 129
Short, Augusta L., 186 n46
Silver, Henry, 104, 120
Silvestre, Col. Patricia, 20 n28
Simmons, Brig. Gen. Bettye H.
  ANC philosophy relating to the BI concept and, 397
  career and achievements, 349, 352
  command position, 398
  downsizing and, 342
  Graduate School of Nursing and, 232
  photo, 350
  Standards of Nursing Practice and, 211 n21
  survey on the concerns and ideas of ANC officers, 392
  U.S. Army Medical Command and, 368
Simmons, Capt. Harriet A., 393
Simon, Lt. Patricia, 300 n11
Simpson, Maj. Kathleen
  Operation Desert Shield/Operation Desert

Storm and, 448, 450
  photos, 427, 449, 451, 452
Sinclair, Lt. Col. Janie A., 135 n66
Sine, Maj. Dina, 436
676th Medical Detachment
  Cuban Refugee Operation and, 289
62nd Medical Group
  Operation Restore Hope and, 484
61st Area Support Medical Battalion
  Operation Uphold Democracy and, 548
67th Combat Support Hospital
  Former Republic of Yugoslavia operations and, 512–515
  patient load, 514–515
67th Contingent Medical Force
  civilian assistance, 525–526
  exit strategy, 525
  redeployment to Germany, 526
  Task Force Falcon and, 524–526, 527, 530, 538 n79
  trauma victims and, 525
68th Medical Group
  Former Republic of Yugoslavia operations and, 504, 532 n7
Slewitzke, Brig. Gen. Connie L.
  Army Nurse Corps Fellows Program and, 206
  Army Nurse Corps leadership, 17, 169, 171
  assignment of authorized nurse officers to FORSCOM with a Memorandum of Understanding and, 269–271
  Command and General Staff College attendance and leadership, 47, 48, 120
  DEPMEDS role, 264
  Individual Mobilization Augmentee program and, 271–272, 284 n85
  Joint Services Nursing Advisory Group and, 262
  limitation of the tenure of retired ANC officers assigned to the reserve component, 271
  military exercises in Honduras role, 294
  nurse recruitment and retention efforts, 227–228, 246 n61, 246 n63
  Officer Structure Study and, 251 n113
  photos, 170, 207, 208, 554
  readiness issues for nurses and, 268
  Workload Management System for Nurses and, 196, 198, 199, 213 n41
SMART. *See* Systematic Modular Approach to Realistic Training program
Smith, Col. Barbara Jean
  Army Central leadership, 425–431
  career background, 433 n13
  Combat Casualty Care Course and, 266
  Operation Desert Shield/Operation Desert Storm and, 425–431, 477
  photos, 427, 428, 429, 431
Smith, Dr. Richard A., 137 n92
Smith, Lt. Col. Cassandra, 57 n42
Smith, Maj. Christie, 409 n53
Sokoloski, Lt. Col. Jim
  views on discrimination against male nurses, 26–27
A Solid Parenting Experience Through Community Teaching and Support program and description, 377
Somalia
  geographical location of, 483
  Operation Continue Hope, 484
  Operation Restore Hope, 483–498
Southby, Col. Janet R.
  nurse recruitment poster, 239
  Nursing Research Service role, 127
  photo, 379
  WRAMC and Malcolm Grow program integration and, 378
Southby, Richard, 334
Spane, Col. Jan, photo, 455
Spine, Lt. Col. Mary Lou
  Automated Military Outpatient System Specialist role, 117
  HSC leadership, 20 n23
  letters to Parks, 164 n62
  Military Training Team mission to Jordan and, 155–157
Squires, Capt. Grace, 61
Srsic-Stoehr, Lt. Col. Kathleen
  AMEDD Personnel Proponency Division role, 186 n42
  mentorship program and, 206
  photo, 207
Standards of Nursing Practice
  anesthesia nurse practice standards, 192, 194
  Army Pamphlet 40-5 and, 192, 194
  expansion of, 190, 192
  publication of, 88, 192
  Quality Assurance Plan for Nursing Service, 194
  word "diagnose" and, 190–191
Stanton, Lt. Col. Ann, 239
Stauffer, 2d Lt. Robert M., 71
Steffenson, Sgt. 1st Class David, 273–276
Stevens, Col. Greg, 532 n7
Stewart, Capt. Elizabeth, 329 n102
Stiner, Lt. Gen. Carl, 310
Stowe, Lt. Col. Harvey O., 439
Straley, Col. Rose V.
  Army Nurse Corps leadership role, 14
  Career Activities Office role, 57 n42
Strevey, Gen. Tracy, 302 n36
Strzelecki, Lt. Col. Stan, 327 n67

Sullivan, Col. Florence
    command position, 393
    photo, 393
Sullivan, Gen. Gordon
    branch immaterial competitive category for promotion to AMEDD brigadier and major general and, 401
    disapproval of Gen. Nancy Adams' command position assignment, 392
    seats for ANC officers at Command and General Staff College and Senior Service Schools and, 394–395
    testimony before Congress, 404
Sullivan, Lt. Col. Elenore F.
    Nursing Research Service role, 127
    photo, 126
The Surgeon General. *See also* Office of The Surgeon General; *specific surgeons general*
    MACOM and, 363
    Professional Education Review Board, 47
Sutterlin, Maj., Karalee, 538 n83
Sweden, Operation Restore Hope, 484, 491, 495
Sylvester, Donna, 100 n59
Synakowski, Capt. Ralph G., 112
Systematic Modular Approach to Realistic Training program
    criticism of, 276
    description, 273, 276
    formulation of, 273

# T

Table of Organization & Equipment. *See also* Modified Table of Organization & Equipment
    activities of hospitals during Operation Desert Shield/Operation Desert Storm, 468
    operational readiness and, 60
    relationships between the Table of Organization and Equipment and PROFIS staff during Operation Urgent Fury, 309
TAMC. *See* Tripler Army Medical Center, Honolulu, Hawaii
Task Force Aesculapius
    challenges of, 365
    elimination of the chief nurse consultant position, 365
    leaders of, 365–366
    objective of, 364–365
    Project AMEDD Vanguard name change to, 383 n12
Task Force Eagle
    description and activities, 512, 520, 522, 523, 537 n67
Task Force Falcon
    description and activities, 524–528, 530
    Maroon Forge training exercise and, 526–527
Task Force Hawk
    description and activities, 524
Task Force Ranger, attempt to capture Aidid in Somalia, 494–495
Taylor, Col. Russell, 524, 525, 526
Taylor, Lt. Gen. Richard, 43
Telenursing
    advantages of, 376–377
    description, 376
TFA. *See* Task Force Aesculapius
13th Evacuation Hospital
    Quality Assurance Plan for Nursing Service, 194
34th General Hospital
    Operation Desert Shield/Operation Desert Storm and, 469
396th Combat Support Hospital
    Former Republic of Yugoslavia operations and, 516, 520
307th Medical Battalion
    Operation Urgent Fury staging and, 305–310
Tierney, Marian A., 186 n46
Tito, Josip Broz, 503
TO&E. *See* Table of Organization & Equipment
Toven, Cadet Lisa A.
    photo, 235
    ROTC Green to Gold program and, 234
TPUs. *See* Troop Program Units
Tracy, Maj. Kathleen, 208
Tranel, Lt. Col. David, 314–315
Travis, Gen. Richard, 302 n36
Treleven, Capt. Ann, 185 n25
Tri-Service Medical Information System
    Army nurses as key players in, 213 n46
    Composite Health Care System and, 200–201
    origination of, 199
    purpose of, 200
TRICARE
    Coordinated Care Program transformation into, 335
    options for, 35
    regions, 335
TRIMIS. *See* Tri-Service Medical Information System
Tripler Army Medical Center, Honolulu, Hawaii
    Ambulatory Surgery Center, 372
    interservice collaboration and, 377
    Nursing Productivity Study, 371–372
    Pain Management Team, 387 n46
    Pre-Admission Unit (PAU), 372–373
    Same Day Admission Unit, 372–373
    A Solid Parenting Experience Through Community Teaching and Support program and, 377
    Specialized Nursing Care Center, 372

strategies to relieve the nursing shortage, 238–239
telenursing and, 377
TriService Nursing Research Group
description and activities, 130
Federal Nursing Research Interest Group name changed to, 130
Trivett, Lt. Col. Paula, 185 n25
Trobaugh, Maj. Gen. Eugene, 306–307, 323 n12
Troop Medical Clinics
Automated Military Outpatient System Specialists and, 118
physician assistants' role, 119
Troop Program Units
Army Nurse Corps reserve component and, 64–65
description, 64
Troumbley, Col. Patricia, 130
Truman, Pres. Harry S, Executive Order No. 9981 concerning racial discrimination, 33
TSG. *See* The Surgeon General
TSNR. *See* TriService Nursing Research Group
Tsoulous, Col. Demetrios G.
nursing staffing requirements estimation and, 264
Operation Desert Shield/Operation Desert Storm and, 426–427
Tutt, Capt. Karlo, 538 n83
21st Combat Support Hospital, 515–516, 521
21st Evacuation Hospital
Khobar Towers location and, 445, 463 n43
Nicaraguan earthquake of December 1972 relief mission, 141–143
Operation Desert Shield/Operation Desert Storm and, 445–448
replacement of the 85th EVAC with, 445
Soldier Readiness Processing and, 445, 463 n42
28th Air Transportable Hospital, Operation Uphold Democracy, 548
28th Combat Support Hospital
Operation Desert Shield/Operation Desert Storm and, 414
Operation Uphold Democracy and, 543, 545, 547–548
25th Infantry Division
eruption of Mount Pinatubo and, 320–321
250th Forward Surgical Team
Task Force Falcon and, 527
249th General Hospital
Former Republic of Yugoslavia operations and, 522–523
Individual Readiness Training, 522
Right Seat/Left Seat Ride policy for turnover, 523, 526, 527
212th Mobile Army Surgical Hospital

Blue Factory in Bosnia-Herzegovina and, 515
bonding with other U.N. forces and, 506–507
Contingency Medical Force support for Task Force Hawk, 524
Former Republic of Yugoslavia operations and, 504–508, 515, 528, 530–531, 536 n57
health fair sponsorship, 507
mission of, 505
number of patients cared for in Former Republic of Yugoslavia, 507
nursing staff, 505
redeployment to Germany, 506, 508, 533 n17
274th Surgical Detachment
Operation Uphold Democracy and, 543
2290th U.S. Army Hospital
Operation Desert Shield/Operation Desert Storm and, 472
Tyler, Lt. Col. Jackie, 430

## U

Ukraine, Operation Provide Hope, 321
Uniformed Services University of the Health Sciences
Combat Casualty Care Course, 118
Emergency Medicine Program, 118
Feasibility Study Group for a School of Nursing, 229
Graduate School of Nursing, 230–232
medical model and, 248 n82
nurse anesthesia program, 205
nursing program, 228–230
physician shortfalls and, 4
proposed closure of, 232
Uniformed Services Variable Incentive Pay Act for Physicians, physician shortfalls and, 4
Uniforms
Army green pantsuits, 92
black berets and, 91
caps, 93
changes in the 1970s, 90–95
durable press fatigues for women, 92
green sweaters and, 93, 102 n96
handbags and, 90–91
insignia placement and, 93, 95
for pregnant nurses, 95
umbrellas and, 90, 101 n80
white duty uniforms, 92–93
"Women's Summer Uniform, Warp Knit," 91–92
United Kingdom, contingency plans for hospitals designated for wartime activation, 318
United Nations

Former Republic of Yugoslavia operations and, 503, 512, 523–524
Operation Restore Hope and, 483–484, 493–494
Operation Uphold Democracy and, 548
resolution authorizing the formation of the Kosovo Force, 524
United Nations Security Council, Resolution 687 ending the Persian Gulf War, 413–414
U.S. Air Force. *See also* Air Force Nurse Corps
admission of women to ROTC, 19 n10
AMEDD's branch immaterial concept and, 394
baccalaureate degree as an entry-level requirement for nurses, 42
Contingency Hospital, Oman, role in Operation Desert Shield/Operation Desert Storm, 418
Former Republic of Yugoslavia operations and, 511–512
interservice collaboration efforts, 378
maximum age for initial appointment to the reserve, 251 n120
Operation Babylift and, 151
Operation Just Cause and, 313
Operation New Life and Operation New Arrivals and, 144
Operation Restore Hope and, 484
Operation Uphold Democracy and, 548
restrictions on women in combat positions, 168
USNS *Mercy* humanitarian mission and, 319–320
U.S. Army. *See also specific units*
Army of Excellence philosophy, 169, 189
continuing education programs for nurses, 44, 46
definition of "sexual harassment," 32
downsizing of the 1990s, 333–352
force modernization, 169
Force XXI doctrine, 334
Health Professional Loan Repayment Program, 238, 252 n125
Long-Term Civilian Training program, 47
New Specialized Training Assistance Program, 238
official policy on the Direct Combat Probability Coding System's application to women, 168
reductions in force after the Vietnam War, 79, 96 n1
restructuring of, 5–9
role in Operation Desert Shield/Operation Desert Storm, 413–418
stop-loss program, 426, 432 n6
U.S. Army Center for Health Promotion and Preventive Medicine, Adams-Ender's command, 367
U.S. Army Health Facility Planning Agency, nurse practitioners and, 113–114
U.S. Army Medical Command
headquarters location, 363
medical advisor for, 364
Nursing Division elimination, 368
strategic focus, 364
U.S. Army Medical Museum, Army Nurse Corps Association fundraising efforts, 180
U.S. Army Recruiting Command
Army Nurse Corps recruiting responsibilities, 84–85
interface with the ROTC for nurse recruitment efforts, 70
responsibilities, 65
U.S. Army Research and Development Command, nurses' role, 128–129
U.S. Army Reserve. *See also* Army National Guard; Reserve Officers' Training Corps
adequacy of numbers and, 9
Army Nurse Corps Accession Bonus Program and, 228
assignment of nurses with specialized skills to other areas, 268–269
assignment of retired Army Nurse Corps officers to, 271–273
challenges in the post-Vietnam War era, 64–67
direct mail campaign for nursing opportunities, 222, 238
extension of maximum age for initial appointment to the ARNG and USAR, 238
field exercise participation, 276
Former Republic of Yugoslavia operations and, 513–515, 516, 520, 531
Individual Mobilization Augmentee program and, 271–273
integration into regular Army units and, 469–470, 472, 474, 481 n28
more active and inclusive role for, 9
National AMEDD Augmentation Detachment, 238
New Specialized Training Assistance Program, 238
nursing shortage and, 222, 238
Operation Desert Shield/Operation Desert Storm and, 415–416, 418, 426, 468–470, 471–476, 481 n22
readiness issues, 65–67, 271
Ready Reserve elements, 64
recruiting problems, 64–65
"Shake 'n Bake" Officer Basic Course for Operation Desert Shield/Operation Desert Storm and, 415–416

Slewitzke's role, 171
source of nurses, 84
women in command positions and, 392
U.S. Army-University of Kentucky Nurse Midwifery Program
    Nurse Midwifery Program, Fort Knox, Kentucky and, 109
    origins of, 105
U.S. Central Command, 414, 418
U.S. Coast Guard, restrictions on women in combat positions and, 168
U.S. Code 10 USC 3579, 391
U.S. Congress. *See also specific members of Congress and legislation*
    amendment of USC 3579, 391
    Congressional Fellowship Program for Army Nurse Corps officers, 173, 175–179
    Congressional Liaison Office request for Army Nurse Corps to work with the House Armed Services Committee, 177
    Deployable Medical System funding, 260
    funding for nursing specialty retention incentives, 238
    Graduate School of Nursing funding, 230
    House Armed Services Committee, 177, 208–209
    incentive pay for Certified Registered Nurse Anesthetists, 232–233
    nurse recruitment and retention strategies and, 228
    passage of legislation authorizing the one-star rank for ANC chiefs and directors and the rank of colonel for the assistant chiefs, 401, 404
U.S. Department of Defense
    budget cuts, 333–334
    Civil Service Registered Nurses pay and, 224
    Coordinated Care Program, 335
    decline in authorizations for, 106
    Defense Medical Standardization Board and, 261
    Directive 6025.6 on licensing of nurses, 201
    interservice collaboration in health care facilities and, 377–379
    maternity leave regulations, 30
    National Disaster Medical System, 417
    1988 civilian nurse vacancies, 242 n6, 341
    Office of Reserve Medical Planning prediction of nursing shortages, 221–222
    Operation New Life and Operation New Arrivals and, 144
    opposition to the admission of women to the service academies, 10–11
    rights of pregnant servicewomen to remain on active duty, 11–12, 22 n55, 29–32

A Solid Parenting Experience Through Community Teaching and Support program, 377
    studies of a new health care system for domestic military bases, 18 n4
    Tri-Service Medical Information System and, 199
U.S. Department of Health and Human Services, study of the nursing shortage, 219–220
U.S. Department of State
    Guatemalan earthquake and, 151
    Institute of Surgical Research burn team mission to Ufa, Russia, and, 320
U.S. Department of Veterans Affairs. *See also* Veterans Administration
    TRICARE and, 335
U.S. European Command, ANC activities in during Operation Desert Shield/Operation Desert Storm, 467–470
U.S. Marine Corps
    Collecting and Clearing Company, 484, 495, 498
    Haitian intervention, 541
    Operation Restore Hope and, 483–484, 495, 498
    restrictions on women in combat positions, 168
U.S. Navy. *See also* Navy Nurse Corps
    AMEDD's branch immaterial concept and, 394
    baccalaureate degree as an entry-level requirement for nurses, 42
    curtailment of student subsidies for potential Navy nurses, 19 n7
    female nurses in command positions and, 393
    Former Republic of Yugoslavia operations and, 512
    interservice collaboration efforts, 378
    maximum age for initial appointment to the reserve, 251 n120
    Operation Just Cause and, 313
    Operation New Life and Operation New Arrivals and, 144
    Operation Restore Hope in Somalia and, 484, 495, 497
    Operation Urgent Fury and, 306
    restrictions on women in combat positions, 168
    USNS *Mercy* humanitarian mission and, 319–320
*U.S. News & World Report*, negative view of U.S. medical readiness, 260
U.S. Office of Personnel Management, Civil Service Registered Nurses pay and, 224
U.S. Public Health Service

Cuban Refugee Operation and, 287, 288, 289, 292
Graduate School of Nursing and, 230
USNS *Mercy* humanitarian mission and, 319–320
U.S. Southern Command, Nicaraguan earthquake of December 1972 relief mission, 141–143
USAR. *See* U.S. Army Reserve
USAREC. *See* U.S. Army Recruiting Command
Usher, Capt. Stacy, 185 n25
USNS *Mercy*, 319–320
USPHS. *See* U.S. Public Health Service
USS *Green Valley*, Operation Restore Hope and, 484
USS *Juneau*, Operation Restore Hope and, 484
USS *Mount Rushmore*, Operation Restore Hope and, 484
USS *Tripoli*, 484

## V

VA. *See* U.S. Department of Veterans Affairs; Veterans Administration
Vail, Lt. Col. James D.
anesthesia nurse practice standards and, 192, 194
photo, 193
Van Beest, 1st Lt. Lynette, 460 n9
Van Wagner, Col. Marcia M.
Operation Desert Shield/Operation Desert Storm and, 454–455
photo, 456
Vanatta, Col. JoEllen, 485, 487
Vanatta, Col. JoEllen, photo, 486
Vander Zyl, Brig. Gen. Sharon
Army National Guard role, 273
photo, 275
Velsmid, 1st Lt. Stephanie, 147
Verhonick, Maj. Phyllis
Phyllis J. Verhonick Research Conference and, 129
Walter Reed Army Institute of Research role, 123, 124
Verhonick, Maj. Phyllis, photo, 124
Veterans Administration. *See also* U.S. Department of Veterans Affairs
ambulatory care center, 377
beds for Operation Desert Shield/Operation Desert Storm casualties, 417
Civil Service Registered Nurses and, 224
Vietnam, Operation New Life and Operation New Arrivals, 143–151
Volunteer Army Student Nurse Program, description, 83

## W

Wadden, Lt. M., photo, 108
Walding, Capt. Audrey, 300 n11
Wallace, Col. Arthur P.
AMEDD CSL and, 408 n40
White House Medical Clinic service, 185 n25
Walter Reed Army Institute of Nursing
baccalaureate degree requirement and, 42
closure of, 4, 84, 85, 228
retention challenges, 228–229
selection of applicants, 83
Volunteer Army Student Nurse Program and, 83
Walter Reed Army Institute of Research
budget reductions and, 125
Department of Nursing role, 123–127
description and role, 123
founding of, 123
Military Nursing Practice and Research Course, 123
transfer of the Division of Nursing to WRAMC, 125, 127
Walter Reed Army Medical Center
case management at, 376
Department of Nursing activities during Operation Desert Shield/Operation Desert Storm, 472–476
designation as an Army Primary Casualty Receiving Center during Operation Desert Shield/Operation Desert Storm, 471–476
interservice integration of programs, 378, 380
joint Army/Navy staff for adult psychiatric patients, 378
Limb Preservation Clinic, 375
mission of, 471
nursing shortage and, 226–227
personnel authorizations for, 80
pilot test of the Pri-Team concept, 87
research project focusing on activated reservists, 472, 481 n30
transfer of the Division of Nursing from WRAIR to, 125, 127
USAR and ARNG personnel serving at during Operation Desert Shield/Operation Desert Storm, 471–476
Well Watch Clinic, 375
Walter Reed Health Care System
Ambulatory Procedure and Processing Center, 374–375
health care facilities included in, 387 n52
Washburn, Lt. Col. Theresa, 179–180, 186 n42

Washington, Capt. Lawrence, 27
*Washington Post,* negative view of U.S. medical readiness, 259–260
Weapons training, female soldiers and, 61–62, 307, 323 n15
Weathington, Capt. Elizabeth, 200
Weddington, Capt. Imelda, 436
Weight control and physical fitness
    Army Medical Specialist Corps dietitians and, 118
    Army Nurse Corps statistics, 256
    Army Physical Fitness Test, 255–256
    Army Regulation 600-9 and, 62
    A Healthy and Fit Force doctrine, 255
    promotion and, 62
    rapid mobilization and, 63
    readiness and, 62–63
Wells, Lt. Col. Lyndoll L.
    facilities planning role, 114
    photo, 116
Werley, Lt. Col. Harriet H.
    concept of career planning for Army Nurse Corps officers and, 48
    Nursing Research Service views, 127
    photo, 122, 126
    Phyllis J. Verhonick Research Conference and, 129
    Walter Reed Army Institute of Research and, 123, 124
West, Col. Iris J.
    Operation Restore Hope and, 498
    photo, 497
West, Secretary of the Army Togo, 394
Westmoreland, Gen. William, views of MEDCAP, 302 n40
Weston, Lt. Amy, photo, 528
Weydert, Lt. Col. Margaret E., 117
White House service
    Medical Clinic staffing by Army Nurse Corps nurses, 175
    women officers as social aides, 173–175
Whitelaw, Edith B., 186 n46
Wickham, Maj. Gen. James A.
    Corcoran's command position and, 390
Wickham, Maj. Gen. John A., 181–182
Wier, Lt. Col. Carolyn, photo, 439
Wiggall, Maj. Jennifer, 315
Wilford Hall Air Force Medical Center, 314–316
William Beaumont Army Medical Center, El Paso, TX, 32–33
Willow, Col. Garnet I.
    comments on reservists in regard to the Total Army Concept, 66–67
    photo, 66
Wilson, Sgt. 1st Class Mary, photo, 455

Wise, Col. Patricia B.
    command position, 408 n39
    service in Sen. Daniel Inouye's office, 176–177
Wise, Lt. Col. Mary J.
    Cuban Refugee Operation role, 290–291
    Pri-Team testing and, 100 n59
Witczak, Capt. Ann, 135 n72
WMSN. *See* Workload Management System for Nurses
Women in Military Service for American Memorial, Slewitzke's role, 171
Women's movement
    admission of women to ROTC and the service academies and, 10–11
    Defense Advisory Committee on Women in the Services and, 10
    legislation involving, 10
    military women's need for a waiver to provide care for minor children, 11
    pregnant service members, 11–12, 22 n55
    Presidential Commission on the Status of Women, 10
    spousal rights for military wives, 11
    "womanpause" backlash, 168, 184 n10
    women's suffrage movement effect on the Army Nurse Corps, 9
Women's Uniform Board, 91, 92
Woods, Nancy Fugate, photo, 336
Workload Management System for Nurses
    advantages of, 221
    Air Force Nurse Corps reluctance to use, 199
    Army Field Manual guidance for, 196
    background, 194–195
    Deployable Medical System and, 262–264
    description, 128
    "direct care" and "indirect care" definitions, 212 n28
    interface with Uniform Chart of Accounts for Personnel, 196
    need for, 195
    nurses' reservations about, 199
    patient outcomes and, 196, 211 n23
    rationale for, 214 n50
    requirement for use of, 195–196
    self-tutoring program for nurses on, 195–196
    Slewitzke's role, 171
    transition from using the Health Services Command manpower survey to, 221
Worldwide Organizational Structure for Army Medical Support Study Group, 5
WRAIN. *See* Walter Reed Army Institute of Nursing
WRAIR. *See* Walter Reed Army Institute of

Research
Wright, Col. Homer
  Former Republic of Yugoslavia operations and, 513
  photo, 513
Wright, Lt. Col. Donna
  Standards of Nursing Practice and, 211 n21
  study of the utilization of registered nurses in the ambulatory setting, 370–371
Wright, Maj. Ann, 308
Wright, Maj. Gen. Jim, photo, 513
Wygant, Lt. Col. MaryEllen, 539 n92

## X
Xenakis, Col. Stephen, 365

## Y
Yaney, Capt. Sandy, 279 n12
Yates, Capt. Robert
  Operation Just Cause and, 327 n66
Yip, Lt. Col. Gar
  fellowship participant, 206
  Tri-Service Medical Information System and, 200
Yoder, Col. Linda, 128
Yurek, Maj. Rebecca, 526–527

## Z
Zajchuk, Brig. Gen. Russ, 365–366
Zimmerman, Maj. Dan, photo, 515
Zuegner, Capt. Shawnda, photo, 521
Zunino, Lt. Col. Jeannette, photo, 439